Dr. Spock's Baby and Child Care

Benjamin Spock, M.D., practiced pediatrics in New York City from 1933 to 1947. He then became a medical teacher and researcher at the Mayo Clinic, the University of Pittsburgh, and Case Western Reserve University in Cleveland. The author of eleven books, he was a political activist for causes that vitally affect children: disarmament, day care, schooling, housing, and medical care for all. He had two sons, a stepdaughter, and four grandchildren. Dr. Spock, who died March 15, 1998, at age ninety-four, was married to Mary Morgan. *Dr. Spock's Baby and Child Care* has been translated into thirty-nine languages and has sold fifty million copies worldwide since its first publication in 1946.

Robert Needlman, M.D., is Associate Professor of Pediatrics at Case Western Reserve University, and co-founder of Reach Out and Read, a national organization that promotes reading aloud to young children. A practicing pediatrician for more than fifteen years, Dr. Needlman has contributed to numerous magazines, textbooks, and journals, and is a widely featured speaker on early learning, literacy, and child development. The Vice President of Developmental and Behavioral Pediatrics at The Dr. Spock Company and author of *Dr. Spock's Baby Basics* (also available from Pocket Books), Dr. Needlman lives in Cleveland, Ohio, with his wife and daughter.

BOOKS BY DR. BENJAMIN SPOCK

BABY AND CHILD CARE
(and Steven J. Parker, M.D.)

FEEDING YOUR BABY AND CHILD
(with Dr. Miriam E. Lowenberg)

RAISING CHILDREN IN A DIFFICULT TIME

A TEEN-AGER'S GUIDE TO LIFE AND LOVE

Published by POCKET BOOKS

Dr. Spock's Baby and Child Care

8TH EDITION

by **Benjamin Spock, M.D.**

REVISED AND UPDATED BY

Robert Needlman, M.D.

POCKET BOOKS

New York   London   Toronto   Sydney

The ideas, procedures, and suggestions in this book are intended to supplement, not replace, the medical advice of trained professionals. All matters regarding your child's health require medical supervision. Consult your physician before adopting the medical suggestions in this book, as well as about any condition that may require diagnosis or medical attention.

The authors and publishers disclaim any liability arising directly or indirectly from the use of this book.

 POCKET BOOKS, a division of Simon & Schuster, Inc.
1230 Avenue of the Americas, New York, NY 10020

Library of Congress Cataloging-in-Publication Data available

ISBN: 0-7434-7667-0

First Pocket Books trade paperback edition of this revised printing June 2004

10 9 8 7 6 5 4 3 2 1

POCKET and colophon are registered trademarks of
Simon & Schuster, Inc.

Illustrations on pages 68, 75, 98, 135, 138, 144, 153, 179, 187, 193, 235, 237, 278, 533, 704, 717, 752, 771, 792, 793, 794, 795, 796, 797, 798, 799, 802, 809 by Sharon Scotland, based on the work of Dorothea Fox, the original illustrator.

Manufactured in the United States of America

For information regarding special discounts for bulk purchases,
please contact Simon & Schuster Special Sales at
1-800-456-6798 or business@simonandschuster.com.

ACKNOWLEDGMENTS

Many people made this edition of *Dr. Spock's Baby and Child Care* possible. Chief among them, of course, is Dr. Spock himself, whose legacy lives on in these pages and in generations of people who were raised according to his kind and sensible advice. My mother owned a copy of the second edition, published in 1958. I was born in 1959.

I never met Ben Spock, but our lives crisscrossed at several points. We both majored in English at Yale, and both continued on at the same university for medical school (Ben eventually switched to Columbia). After medical school and a residency in pediatrics, I trained in developmental-behavioral pediatrics at Boston University, where one of my teachers was Dr. Steven Parker. Years later, Steve coauthored the seventh edition of *Baby and Child Care* with Ben. I eventually joined the faculty at Case Western Reserve University in Cleveland without knowing that I would be working in the same department, in the same clinic, and with several of the same colleagues as Ben. Among the residents I had the privilege of training was a particularly talented young doctor named Laura Jana. It turns out that Laura was also a personal friend of Ben Spock and his wife, Mary Morgan. After Ben's death, Laura and Mary—with Laura's twin sister—dreamed up the idea of translating Spock's work to the internet. Two years after she finished at Case, Laura enticed me to help her make the dream a reality.

All of this is to say that, in an odd way, I feel that I was destined to work on *Baby and Child Care*. But of course, destiny (or luck) is only part of the story. The project could never have been begun, let alone come to fruition, without a lot of people's faith and hard work. I owe thanks to Barry Zuckerman for talking me into trying out developmental-behavioral pediatrics "just for a year," then being a wonderful mentor for many years to follow; also to Steve Parker, Debbie Frank, Margot Kaplan-Sanoff, Howard Bauchner, Perri Klass, Kathleen Fitzgerald-Rice, Kathleen MacLean, Jean Nigro, Joel Alpert, Karen Olness, John Kennell, Howard Hall, Denny Drotar, and many other inspiring teachers and colleagues at Boston University and Case. To my many patients over the years, thank you for allowing me the privilege of caring for you and learning from you.

Thanks, also, to my medical colleagues at the Dr. Spock Company, Laura Jana, K. Lynn Cates, and Marjorie Greenfield for sharing their passion for parenting; to David Markus and Mona Behan for their superb editing; and to many others at DrSpock.com who threw their hearts into the venture. To Mary Morgan, Ben Spock's wife and collaborator of many years, I owe a special word of appreciation: Your steady trust in me has allowed me to believe that I might be able to do justice to Ben's voice and vision.

The eighth edition of *Baby and Child Care* has benefited from the insights and input of many experts: Tina Anderson-Schulin and Marjorie Greenfield for breast-feeding and Marjorie for everything related to pregnancy, labor, and delivery; Nathan Blum for toilet training; Laura Cummings for medications; Abdulla Gori and Andrea Mann for general pediatrics issues; Laura Harkness, Amy Lanou, and Neal Barnard for nutrition; Mary Lou Kumar for immunizations; James Kozik for dental issues; Bob Sege for child development, particularly school-age and adolescent; John Kennell for doulas and bonding; Sari Feldman for reading aloud; James Quilty for emotional development; Gloria Needlman for child development and education; and

Martha Wright for safety and first aid. Martin Stein, Ben's long-time colleague and friend and collaborator on the seventh edition, applied his sharp ear to multiple sections of the manuscript. Thank you, Marty, for being both critical and unwaveringly supportive. The generous contributions of these experts notwithstanding, the responsibility for the contents of this edition remains my own. Thanks, also, to Robert Lescher, Ben's agent for many years and now mine as well; and to Micki Nuding and Maggie Crawford, my editors at Simon and Schuster, for their painstaking attention to detail and ability to keep the big picture in sight.

Thanks to my parents, Allen and Gloria Needlman, for giving me life and a strong foundation. Finally, to Carol Farver, my love and my wife: Thank you for putting up with my atrocious work habits, for laughing at my jokes, and for inspiring me every single day. And to our daughter, Grace: You give me hope for the future, and a lot of joy in the meantime.

For Albert Farver

CONTENTS

SECTION II:
FEEDING AND NUTRITION

SECTION III:
RAISING MENTALLY HEALTHY CHILDREN

SECTION IV:
COMMON DEVELOPMENTAL AND BEHAVIORAL CHALLENGES

SECTION VI:
HEALTH AND SAFETY

PREFACE

About This Eighth Edition
Dr. Spock's Baby and Child Care

Since *Dr. Spock's Baby and Child Care* was first published in 1945, generations of parents have raised their children "by the book." The book gave parents sensible, expert advice. Beyond that, it gave them the voice of Dr. Benjamin Spock: warm, straightforward, and reassuring, a voice that made it seem as though the doctor were in the room talking to you. That voice talked to parents through seven editions of *Baby and Child Care*.

The challenge for this eighth edition—the first since Dr. Spock's death in 1998—is to keep that voice alive. And that means, as much as anything, allowing the words to change. Dr. Spock knew well that life means change. The seven-year-old is a very different child from the seven-month-old he was and from the seventeen-year-old he will become. Over the years, *Baby and Child Care* has always changed to reflect emerging issues in parenting, as well as medical advances. At the same time, like the baby growing up, the core identity of the work has stayed constant.

The changes in this new edition of *Baby and Child Care* are of two main kinds. I've continued Dr. Spock's practice of updating each section to ensure that the information is current. To help in this giant task, I've called upon a slew of experts to give their criticisms and suggestions, just as Dr. Spock always did. I've also chosen to emphasize a few new areas that are troubling many parents now, such as the risks and benefits of vaccines and children's responses to terrorism.

Other changes affect the book's organization and style. I've moved some sections to allow for a more clear-cut separation between the chapters that go age by age and those that focus on issues that cut across childhood, such as nutrition and discipline. Where Dr. Spock spoke directly about his own experience, I've either made the point a different way or put the quotation in a special box, labeled "Classic Spock." Throughout the rest of the book, the "I" who speaks from time to time is not Dr. Spock but his very respectful younger colleague.

Dr. Spock invented the modern parenting book and was a master pediatrician and writer. It would be foolish to imagine I could improve on his work. What I can do—and what I hope this new edition accomplishes—is to shine fresh light on an old treasure, so that another generation can find the information and encouragement they need as they go about life's most important task and most compelling adventure.

TRUST YOURSELF
AND YOUR CHILDREN

∸∸

TRUST YOURSELF

You know more than you think you do. Soon you're going to have a baby. Maybe you have one already. If you haven't had much experience, you may wonder whether you're going to know how to do a good job. If you feel good about how you've raised your baby, you may still have questions about the next challenge, whether that's a new sibling, toilet training, or the first day of preschool.

There may have been a time when parents knew exactly how to bring up their children or thought they did. But for most of us now there simply aren't clear-cut rules to follow. We have more options, but there are also more choices that have to be made. Is breast-feeding really necessary? Should you *always* pick up a crying baby, and what happens if you don't? Is it okay to return to work, and when? Is "educational television" really good for your toddler? And what about all those immunizations? Everywhere you turn, there are experts telling you what to do. The problem is, they often don't agree with each other!

Don't take too seriously all that the neighbors say. Don't be overawed by what the experts say. Don't be afraid to trust your own common sense. Bringing up your child won't be a complicated job if you take it easy, trust your instincts, and share concerns with your friends, family, and doctor or nurse practitioner. We know for a fact that the natural loving care that parents give their children is a hundred times more important than knowing how to make a diaper fit tight or just when to introduce solid foods. Every time you pick your baby up—even if you do it a little awkwardly at first—every time you change her, bathe her, feed her, smile at her, she's getting the feeling that she belongs to you and that you belong to her.

The more people have studied different methods of bringing up children, the more they have come to the conclusion that what good mothers and fathers instinctively feel like doing for their babies is usually best after all. All parents do their best job when they have a natural, easy confidence in themselves. Better to relax and make a few mistakes than to try too hard to be perfect.

Children learn from what their parents do right, but they also learn from what their parents do wrong. If you don't always respond instantly when your baby cries, your baby has the opportunity to learn self-soothing. When you lose your patience with your toddler (and every parent does, sometimes), your toddler learns that you have feelings, too, and has a chance to see how you get yourself back together. Children are driven from within themselves to grow, explore, experience, learn, and build relationships with other people. A lot of good parenting lies in simply allowing your child to go with these powerful drives. So while you are trusting yourself, remember also to trust your child.

How you learn to be a parent. Fathers and mothers don't really find out how to care for and manage children from books and lectures, though these may have value in answering specific questions and doubts. They learn the basics during their own childhoods, from the way they themselves were brought up. That's what they were always practicing when they "played house" and cared for their dolls. If a child is raised in an easygoing way, he is likely to be the same kind of parent. Likewise, a child who is raised by strict parents is likely to become a relatively strict parent himself. We all end up at least somewhat like our parents, especially in the way we deal with our children. Every parent has had the experience—and you will, too, if you haven't yet—of talking to your child and hearing your mother's or father's voice coming from your lips, with exactly the same tone and exactly the same words!

You might think about just how your parents raised you. What did they do that you now see as positive and constructive? You might also consider ways they raised you that you absolutely don't want to repeat. Having a child offers you the wonderful opportunity to think about what made you the kind of person you are today and what kind of parent you would like to be. It is just that sort of insight that will help you to understand and trust your own instincts and become a more confident parent.

You'll find that you will learn about how to be a parent gradually, through the experience of caring for your children. It's finding out that you can feed, change, bathe, and burp successfully and that your baby responds contentedly to your ministrations that will give you confidence and feelings of familiarity and love. These become the foundations of a solid, trusting relationship with your child. But don't expect to feel this way right off the bat.

All parents expect to influence their children, but many are surprised to find that it's a two-way street and that they learn an enormous amount about themselves and about the world from their parenting and from their children. You may find, as many others have, that being a parent becomes the most important step in your own growth and maturation as a person.

RAISING CHILDREN IN A CHANGING WORLD

We are all immigrants, in a way. Our nation has been enriched by wave after wave of immigrants. The experience of moving to a new country is one that many Americans share. It's stressful to leave behind everything familiar—family, language, culture, land. And it is doubly hard to raise children in a strange, new country. All of the rules are different. Values that held up for generations now may seem out of place. What was good parenting at home might even be considered child abuse here! No wonder parents who are new to this country often feel unsure of themselves, worried, or angry.

But it's not so different for parents who are born-and-bred Americans. Many of us long ago turned away from traditional worldviews that offered certainty and a clear-cut moral road map. We've moved away from our families of origin and no longer consider the experience of our parents to be a valid guide for us. In fact, our culture changes so quickly that we might question whether even our *own* childhood experiences are relevant to the experiences of our children today. Most parents of today grew up in a world where mothers were expected to stay home with their infants, where nobody walked around with a computer, and where the greatest threat to the United States was a country that no longer exists. We are all trying to make sense of a new and strange country and a rapidly changing world. In a way, we are all immigrants.

The key to success is flexibility. We have learned from immigrants that success depends on a family's ability to hold on to its core cultural values, while at the same time participating in mainstream society. This sort of flexibility isn't easy, but the alternatives are usually much worse. Families that cut off their ethnic and cultural roots altogether often find themselves adrift without any values to anchor them. Parents who try to build a wall around their families often find that the larger culture breaks in or that their children break out. Successful immigrant children learn to speak different languages at home and at school, and they also learn to switch back and forth between two sets of social rules. Successful immigrant parents find ways to support their children as they shuttle back and forth between worlds; they help them to embrace tradition and newness at the same time.

The same kind of flexible approach can help *all* parents cope with the challenges of raising children in a changing society. You need to be able to hold on to your core values but also stay open to what's new. You need to choose which changes to accept and which to reject. Books like this one can tell you about children and their needs at different stages of development, but they can't tell you what to do. In the end, you have to make your parenting choices according to your own sense of what is reasonable, important, and true.

WHAT ARE YOUR AIMS IN RAISING A CHILD?

Think about your goals. In an uncertain world, with more uncertainty to come, we do well to ask ourselves just what our goals are in raising our children. Is doing well in school our most important objective for them? Is the ability to sustain intimate human relationships more important? Do we want them to be individualistic with a competitive edge so they can succeed in a dog-eat-dog society? Or do we want them to learn to cooperate and sometimes to renounce their own desires for the good of others? What kind of adults do we want our children to become to be happy and productive members of society?

These questions cut to the heart of much of raising children. Parenting is about choices. To decide what's best for your child, you will always be well served by stepping back and thinking about these tough questions before making a decision. So many parents get totally caught up in the difficult day-to-day issues of *how* they are parenting that they lose perspective about *why* they are parenting in the first place. I hope that raising your children will help you to understand your own ideas about what's really important to you in life and that this insight will guide the choices you make about raising your child.

⟨⟩ CLASSIC SPOCK

We are disillusioned. In my sixty years as a pediatrician, I have witnessed marvelous changes in our society. Modern medicine can perform wonders, and children have never been healthier. Technology has provided all of us with comforts that, only a few decades ago, even the very rich couldn't have dreamed of. We are much more aware of what is happening around the world. The global village has become a reality. And there is the promise of much more to come.

At the same time I have witnessed an increasing tendency in literature, plays, and movies to belittle the kindly and spiritual aspects of humanity and to focus on its cruder side. Manners in social life have been coarsened and long-held religious beliefs eroded. The mass media cater to children's lowest tastes. And the gap between rich and poor between the haves and the have-nots in our society has widened.

In many ways we have lost our faith in the meaning of life and our confidence to understand our world and our society. My point here is that you are raising your children in the context of very confusing and rapidly changing times. Your goals and aspirations for your child are going to be greatly influenced by these times and the prevailing ideals and beliefs. A central core of values and beliefs—ones that remain unshaken by tumultuous social changes—will serve as your compass as you chart a course for your family. I hope that, at least once in a while, after yet another hectic day, you will sit back and reflect on where you are going and whether your day-to-day interactions with your children reflect your true values and dreams for their future.

PARENTS ARE HUMAN

Parents have needs, too. Books about child care, including this one, put so much emphasis on the child's needs—for love, for understanding, for patience, for consistency, for firmness, for protection, for comradeship—that parents sometimes feel physically and emotionally exhausted just from reading about what is expected of them. They get the impression that they are meant to have no needs or life of their own apart from their children. And they can't help feeling that any book that seems to be standing up for children all the time is going to be critical of parents when anything goes wrong.

To really be fair, this book should have an equal number of pages about the genuine needs of parents: their frustrations (both inside and outside the home), how tired they get, and their need to hear, at least once in a while, that they are doing a good job. There is an enormous amount of hard work that goes along with child care: preparing the proper diet, washing clothes, changing diapers, cleaning up messes, stopping fights and drying tears, listening to stories that are hard to understand, joining in games and reading books that aren't very exciting to an adult, trudging around zoos and museums, responding to pleas for help with homework, being slowed down in housework and yard work by eager helpers, going to parent-teacher association meetings on evenings when you are tired, and so on.

The fact is that child-rearing is a long, hard job, the rewards are not always immediately obvious, the work is often undervalued, and parents are just as human and almost as vulnerable as their children.

Of course, parents don't have children because they want to be martyrs. They have them because they love children and want to raise their very own, especially when they remember being loved so much by their own parents when they were little. Taking care of their children, seeing them grow and develop into fine people, gives most parents—despite the hard work—their greatest satisfaction in life. It is a creative and generative act on every level. Pride in worldly accomplishments usually pales in comparison.

Needless self-sacrifice and excessive preoccupation. Many conscientious people facing the new responsibility of parenthood feel that they are being called on to give up all their freedom and all their former pleasures, not as a matter of practicality but almost as a matter of principle. Others simply become obsessed with parenting, forgetting all their other interests. Even if they do occasionally sneak off to have some fun, they feel too guilty to get full enjoyment. They come to bore their friends and each other. In the long run, they chafe at the imprisonment and can't help unconsciously resenting their babies.

Total absorption in a new baby is normal for many parents. But after a while (usually by two to four months) your focus needs to broaden out again. In particular, pay attention to sustaining a loving, intimate relationship with your partner. Carve out some quality time with your husband, wife, or significant other. Remember to look at each other, smile at each other, and express the love you feel. Make an effort to find enough privacy and energy to continue your sexual relationship. Remember that a close, loving relationship between parents is the most powerful way children learn about how to be intimate with another person, a lesson that your child is likely to carry into his or her adult relationships. So one of the best things you can do for your child, as well as for yourself, is to let your child deepen, not inhibit, your relationship with your partner.

NATURE AND NURTURE

How much control do you have? It's easy to get the impression from many parenting books that how your child turns out is entirely up to you. Do a good job and you'll have a good child. Your neighbor, whose little boy is perfect in every possible way, feels terrific about herself. And if your child learns to talk later, or has more temper tantrums than he does, of course it's all your fault.

Except that it isn't. The truth is, some children are born with temperaments that make them more difficult to soothe, more fearful, more reckless, more intense, or in other ways more challenging for parents. If you are lucky, your baby will have an easy temperament, one that fits well with your own. If you are not so lucky—particularly if your child's temperament fits very poorly with your expectations and personal style—you may need to learn special skills to help your child grow in the healthiest possible direction and to get through parenthood without being driven crazy. For example, you may need to learn how to calm a colicky baby (although it's not something you'd ever *want* to have to know!) or how to help an extracautious child begin to take small risks.

But special skills are not enough. First, you'll need to accept that your child is who he is. As a parent, you have the most influence of anyone in shaping your child's developing personality, but you don't have anything near total control. Children need to feel accepted and to *be* accepted. Only after that can they work together with their parents to handle themselves in more and more effective ways.

Accepting the child you have. What happens if the child you've got differs from the kind of child you thought you wanted? This can be a major source of heartache between parent and child if you aren't aware of it. Of course, parents have well-formed personalities, too, which they can't change overnight. One gentle couple might be ideally suited to raise a boy with a sensitive nature but may not be nearly so ready for an energetic, assertive boy whom they find baffling and challenging, no matter how much they love him. Another couple may handle a spunky daughter with ease and joy but be quite disappointed with a quiet, thoughtful one.

It doesn't even matter that the parents are intelligent people who realize that they can't order the kind of child they wanted most. Being human, they have irrational expectations and can't help feeling let down.

Additionally, as children become a little older, they may remind us, consciously or unconsciously, of a brother, sister, father, or mother who made life hard for us at times. A daughter may have traits like her mother's younger sister, who used to be always in her hair, yet the mother may have no conscious realization that this is the cause of a lot of her irritation. A father may be excessively bothered by timidity in his young son yet never connect it with the fact that he himself had a terrible time overcoming his shyness as a child.

Some people call this *goodness of fit*—that is, how well your expectations, goals, hopes, dreams, and aspirations for your children fit with the talents and temperament they were born with. Goodness of fit plays a significant role in determining how well things go for you and your children as you go about the business of raising them.

Goodness-of-fit issues often cause great problems for families. If, for example, you are chronically disappointed that your child is not a math whiz or well coordinated and spend a significant amount of time trying to make him what he is not (and does not have the inborn talent to be), I can guarantee that trouble is brewing both for you and your child. If, on the other hand, you come to accept and love your child for who he really is (and not what you would like him to be), your life together is bound to be a lot smoother and happier.

Can you make your baby smarter? The short answer is yes . . . and no. Experts now agree that, on average, roughly half of a person's intelligence is determined by genes and half by other factors—such as nutrition, infections and other harmful events and of course experiences growing up. Here we're talking about the kind of intelligence that is measured by standard IQ tests (see "Learning and the Brain" in Section V). There are other kinds of intelligence, such as interpersonal intelligence (for example, the ability to understand others and be a good listener), athletic intelligence, and musical intelligence. These, too, almost certainly depend on both genes and experience.

A person's genes provide a rough blueprint for the brain; the details of the brains structure are filled in by experience. Genes direct nerve cells to move to the different areas of the brain and determine the main pathways that link different brain regions together. Experience and learning influence how the individual nerve cells connect with one another to form the minicircuits that underlie actual thinking. For example, when a child learns to speak English, certain brain connections in the language areas of the brain grow stronger. At the same time, connections that are unique to other languages (Chinese, say) disappear from want of use.

Genes influence how easily or quickly a person can pick up certain types of knowledge or skills. In this way, genes may point an individual's talents in a particular direction (being a "numbers person" or a "people person," for example). Genes also set limits on what a child can reasonably be expected to achieve. For example, in a full year of Little League, I never once managed to hit the ball. (Many of my patients have heard this story; I think it amuses them and also reassures them that you don't have to be good at everything to be successful in life.) Could I have learned to hit, with enough practice and coaching? Maybe, but it would have taken a huge effort to transform me into a fair hitter, and I doubt I'd ever have been really good.

The experiences a child has (batting practice, for instance) affect the brain's wiring, but the brain plays a large role in determining what experiences a child seeks and enjoys. Wise parents help their children discover and nurture their talents and also recognize that everyone has limitations that need to be respected, as well.

Superbabies? Learning brings about physical changes in the brain. But that does not mean that we can (or should) try to create superbabies by relentless stimulation and education. The best learning occurs when an infant is happy, relaxed, attentive, and actively involved, not when she is being oppressed with cold, unwanted, and unnatural facts. Flash cards really have no place at all in an infant's education.

The best experiences for infants are those that they inherently enjoy. To be beneficial, an experience has to make sense to your baby. You can tell that an experience is making sense when your baby smiles, laughs, coos, or gazes with bright, sparkly eyes. Little babies don't understand the words their parents are saying, but being talked to certainly makes sense to them!

Many products are marketed with the claim that they are "scientifically proven" to make babies smarter. These claims are all exaggerations, if not outright lies.

LOVE AND LIMITS

There's only one real trick to raising a mentally healthy child: a loving, nurturing, and mutually respectful relationship between you and your child. Take a moment to think about what it means to be loving, nurturing, and mutually respectful.

Loving means, first of all, accepting your child as an individual who is wonderful but not perfect. Every child has strengths and weaknesses, gifts and challenges. Some babies are naturally quiet and cuddly; others are loud and adventurous. Loving your baby means adjusting your expectations to fit your baby, not trying to adjust your baby to fit your expectations.

Another part of loving is finding ways to share happiness. That might mean playing a tickling game, looking at picture books together, going for a walk in the park, or just talking about different things. Children don't need to have these experiences all day long. But they *do* need *some* shared moments of happiness every day.

Of course, children have other needs, too. Understanding those needs and making the commitment to meet them is what nurturing is all about. Needs change. A newborn baby needs *everything*: feeding, changing, bathing, holding, and talking to. Over the first year of life, the repeated experience of being cared for creates a sense of basic trust in other people and optimism toward the world in general.

As their abilities grow, children need more and more chances to do things for themselves. They need challenges that are tough enough to stretch their skills but not so tough that they are overwhelming. Children need to be able to take risks while at the same time staying safe. Babies can't learn to feed themselves if they aren't first allowed to make a mess. Children learning to tie their own shoes have to try and fail, try and fail, and try again. A parent's job is to set the limits within which safe risk-taking can happen.

Mutual respect involves another kind of limit-setting. Children want what they want when they want it. They need to learn the difference between wanting and needing. Secure children know that they always get what they *need* but not always what they *want*. They also understand that other people have needs and wants, too. Children learn these lessons when parents treat them with kindness and respect and require respect, cooperation, and politeness in return. When it comes to raising children, love is *not* enough. Children need love *and* limits. (See chapters "What Children Need" and "Discipline" in Section III for more on emotional and moral development and effective discipline.)

THE DIVERSITY OF FAMILIES

There is no one right way to raise children; many different approaches can work. By the same token, there is no one best kind of family. Children can thrive with a mother and father, with a mother or father alone, with grandparents or foster parents, with two mothers or two fathers, or as part of large extended families. (I hope that this wonderful diversity is reflected throughout this book, although often, to save words, I use the familiar "mother and father" formula.)

Families that don't fit the typical mom-and-pop mode often face special challenges. They may have to battle prejudice, and it can be hard to find an accepting community. They may also have to consciously ensure that their children are exposed to a full range of people and experiences. For example, in families with gay or lesbian parents, it may take some planning to ensure that the children have a chance to develop close relationships with caring adults of both sexes. In families with children adopted from overseas, it may take planning to ensure that the children are exposed to their cultures of origin. In families with two busily employed parents, it may take planning to ensure that the children grow up with a sense of belonging to a community. Good parenting means planning for your children's needs; that's true in *all* families.

There are other challenges that are harder to overcome, like poverty, parental mental illness and addiction, and violence in the community and at home. Another set of special challenges are chronic illness or developmental problems in the children themselves. There are few families that are not touched, in some degree or another, by such forces. Still, most parents manage, through love and courage, to overcome these hurdles. And the children they raise often reflect those same wonderful qualities. As individuals and as a society, we need to recognize both the challenges *and* the strengths that parents, families, and children bring to the task of growing up healthy and whole.

Your Child, Age by Age

BEFORE YOUR CHILD IS BORN

⟡ ⟡

BABIES DEVELOP; PARENTS, TOO

Fetal development. When you think of all the incredible changes that go into turning a fertilized egg into a newborn baby, how can you not feel awe? By the time most women realize they're pregnant, about five weeks after their last menstrual period, the embryo is already pretty complex. Shaped like a disk, it has an inner layer of cells that will go on to become most of the internal organs, a middle layer of cells that will form muscles and bones, and an outer layer that will become the skin and the neurons of the brain and spinal cord. By eight weeks after conception (about ten weeks after the last menstrual period), all of the major organs have begun to form and the fetus is beginning to take on a human look. But it is still only two inches long and weighs about a third of an ounce.

Four or five months into the pregnancy—just about half way—marks a turning point. This is the time of quickening, when you first feel your baby moving. If an ultrasound hasn't been done, those little kicks and nudges may be the first palpable proof that there really is a baby in there—a thrilling moment!

Moving into the third trimester, after about twenty-seven weeks, the name of the game becomes growth, growth, and more growth. The baby's length doubles, the weight triples.

The brain grows even more quickly than that. At the same time, new behaviors appear. By twenty-nine weeks of gestation, a baby will startle in response to a sudden loud noise. But if the noise repeats every twenty seconds or so, the baby soon ignores it. This behavior, called habituation, is evidence of the emergence of memory.

If a pleasant sound is repeated—say the sound of your voice reading poetry—your unborn fetus is likely to remember this, too. After birth, babies choose to listen to their mother's voice over that of a stranger. If you have a favorite piece of music that you play over and over during the third trimester, chances are your baby will love it too, both before birth and after. Without a doubt, learning starts before birth. But that doesn't mean that you need to break out the flash cards along with the maternity clothes. Nobody has ever shown that special teaching adds anything to fetal learning. Instead, it's the natural stimuli—the sound of your voice, and the rhythms of your body—that are most nurturing to development.

⬿ CLASSIC SPOCK

There's nothing in the world more fascinating than watching a child grow and develop. At first you think of it as just a matter of growing bigger. Then, as the infant begins to do things, you may think of it as "learning tricks." But it's really more complicated and full of meaning than that.

In some ways, the development of each child retraces the whole history of the human race, physically and spiritually, step by step. Babies start off in the womb as a single tiny cell, just the way the first living thing appeared in the ocean. Weeks later, as they lie in the warm amniotic fluid, they have gills like fish and tails like amphibians. Toward the end of the first year of life, when they learn to clamber to their feet, they're celebrating that period millions of years ago when our ancestors got up off all fours and learned to use their fingers with skill and delicacy.

Mixed feelings about pregnancy. We have an ideal about motherhood that says that every woman is overjoyed when she finds that she is going to have a baby. She spends the pregnancy dreaming happy thoughts about the baby. When it arrives, she slips into the maternal role with ease and delight. Love is instantaneous, bonding like glue.

This is all true to a degree—more in one case, less in another. But it is also, of course, only one side of the picture. We now know what wise women have known all along—that there are normal negative feelings connected with a pregnancy, too, especially the first one.

To some degree, the first pregnancy spells the end of carefree, irresponsible youth. Clothes that were loose become tight, and clothes that were tight become unwearable. Athletic women find that their bodies don't move as they once did, a temporary effect but very real. A woman realizes that after the baby comes there will be new limitations on her social life and other outside pleasures. The family budget has to be spread thinner, and her partner's attention (and her own) will soon be focused in a new direction.

Feelings are different in every pregnancy. After you have had one or two, the changes due to the arrival of one more child do not look so drastic. But a mother's spirit may rebel at times during any pregnancy. There may be obvious reasons why one pregnancy is more strained: perhaps it came unexpectedly soon, one of the parents is having tensions at work, there is serious illness on either side of the family, or there is disharmony between mother and father. Or there may be no apparent explanation.

A mother who really wants another child may yet be disturbed by sudden doubts about whether she will have the time, the energy, and the unlimited reserves of love that will be called for in taking care of another child. Or the inner doubts may start with the father, who feels neglected as his wife becomes more and more preoccupied with the children. In either case, one spouse's disquiet soon has the other one feeling dispirited, also. Each parent may have less to give the other as the pregnancy progresses and concerns persist.

I don't want to make these reactions sound inevitable. I only want to reassure you that they do occur in the very best of parents, that they are usually part of the normal mixed feelings during pregnancy, and that in the great majority of cases they are temporary. In some ways, it may be easier to work through these feelings early, before the baby arrives. Parents who have had no negative feelings during pregnancy may have to face them for the first time after their babies are born, at a point when their emotional reserves are fully taken up by baby care.

Father's feelings during pregnancy. A man may react to his wife's pregnancy with various feelings: protectiveness of his wife, increased joy in the marriage, pride in his virility (one thing men always worry about to some degree), anticipatory enjoyment of the child. A certain amount of worry—"Will I be able to be a good father to this baby?"—is very common, especially in men who remember their own childhoods as having been difficult.

There can also be, way underneath, a feeling of being left out, just as small children may feel rejected when they find their mother is pregnant. This feeling may be expressed as crankiness toward his wife, wanting to spend more evenings with his men friends, or flirtatiousness with other women. These reactions are normal, but they are no help to his partner, who craves extra support at the start of this unfamiliar stage of her life. Fathers who can talk about their feelings often find that the negative emotions (fear, jealousy) shift aside, allowing the positive ones (excitement, connection) to come forward.

The supportive father in pregnancy and birth. The expectations for fathers have changed in recent decades. In the past, a father wouldn't have dreamed of reading a book on child care. Now, it almost goes without saying that fathers take some responsibility for child rearing (although in reality, women still do most of the work). Fathers also take a more active role before the baby is born. A father may go to prenatal doctor visits and attend childbirth classes with his wife. He may be an active participant in labor and the first parent to hold the baby. If the mother is unwell or the baby has special problems, the father may be the parent most actively involved with the baby in the early hours after birth. He no longer has to be the lonely, excluded onlooker.

Love for the baby may come only gradually. Many parents who are pleased and proud to be pregnant still find it hard to feel a personal love for a baby they've never held. Love is elusive and means different things to different people. Many parents begin to feel affection when they watch the first ultrasound that shows a beating heart. For others, it's feeling the baby move for the first time that makes them realize that there is a real baby developing, and affection begins to grow. For other parents, it's not really until they are well into the care of their baby. There is no "normal" time to fall in love with your baby. You shouldn't feel guilty if your feelings of love and attachment aren't as strong as you think they should be. Love may come early. It may come late. But 999 times out of a thousand, it comes when it needs to.

Even when feelings during pregnancy are primarily positive and the expectation is all that could be desired, there may be a letdown when the baby actually arrives, especially for first-time parents. They expect to recognize the baby immediately as their own flesh and blood, to respond to the infant with an overwhelming rush of maternal and paternal feelings, and to bond like epoxy, never to feel anything but love again. But in many cases this doesn't happen on the first day or even the first week. Completely normal negative feelings often pop up. A good and loving parent may suddenly think that having a baby was a terrible mistake—and feel instantly guilty for having felt that way! The bonding process is often a gradual one that isn't complete until parents have recovered somewhat from the physical and emotional strains of labor and delivery. How long that takes varies from parent to parent. There is no deadline.

Most of us have been taught that it's not fair to hope that the baby will be a girl or a boy, in case it turns out to be the opposite. I wouldn't take this seriously. It's hard to imagine and love a future baby without picturing it as one sex or the other; that's one of the early steps of the prenatal attachment process. Most expectant parents do have a preference for one or the other during pregnancy, even though they are quite ready to love a baby who turns out to be the opposite. So enjoy your imaginary baby, and don't feel guilty if you learn from a prenatal ultrasound or at birth that the baby is not the sex you had envisioned.

PRENATAL CARE

Get good prenatal care. Of all the things parents do to help their babies grow up healthy, going for prenatal checkups is one of the most important. As soon as pregnancy becomes a *possibility,* even before you know that you're pregnant, you should start taking a multivitamin containing folate to lower the risk of spinal cord malformations that can develop in the very first weeks of pregnancy, even before you miss your period. You may want to arrange a *pre*conception visit if you have questions: about fertility, the special health risks of pregnancy, or the risks of genetic disorders, for example.

Prenatal visits are a time for mothers and fathers to become partners in their baby's health and a time for you to think about the kind of delivery you want. Simple steps—taking prenatal vitamins, avoiding cigarettes and alcohol, and getting your blood pressure checked—can make a huge difference in your baby's health, and your own. Routine tests can uncover problems, such as infections, which can be treated before they affect your baby. Even if you're nearing the end of your pregnancy, if you haven't had a prenatal visit yet, it's not too late for your baby and you to benefit.

The usual schedule of prenatal visits is once a month for the first seven months, once every other week in the eighth month, and weekly after that. The visits are an opportunity for you to get advice about common issues, such as morning sickness, weight gain, and exercise. They also are the best way to be reassured that your pregnancy is going along well and that any infections or other serious conditions will be detected early and treated. Prenatal ultrasound is now routine in many places. Even a grainy, black-and-white ultrasound image can make the baby seem much more real, especially to fathers. And you'll have the option of finding out your baby's sex.

Choosing prenatal care. In many communities, women can choose from various providers of prenatal care, including obstetricians, family physicians, nurse midwives, certified midwives (who aren't nurses), and lay midwives. One consideration is the type of delivery you want. Obstetricians nearly always deliver in hospitals; lay midwives tend to specialize in home births. Another consideration is whether you like and trust your doctor or midwife. Does the professional listen to you and give you clear information? Is the person you see for prenatal visits the same person who will do your delivery? If not, do you trust that the other professionals in the group will also provide you with good medical care? Will the hospital and the obstetrics group accept your medical insurance?

DELIVERY

What kind of delivery do you want? Parenting is about choices, and one of the first you will be asked to make is the kind of childbirth you'd prefer. In the old days, there wasn't a lot of choice.

Mind-numbing anesthesia was common; you might get to see your baby for a few minutes when you awoke. Breast-feeding was out of the question for any self-respecting mother. And because doctors were so worried about the transmission of infection, the baby would spend the next week in the nursery, carefully ministered to by well-scrubbed nurses in antiseptic white gowns and hats while the mother lay flat on her back and recovered.

We've come a long way since those days, and now the choices are many. Natural childbirth or an epidural? Support during labor by a husband or partner, by a trained professional (a doula), or by a family member and a doula? Children in the delivery room? Lying down or squatting? Home or hospital? Doctor or midwife? Rooming in or having the newborn spend more time in the hospital nursery? Visiting nurse or lactation consultant at home or both?

No one approach suits every woman, and no method is clearly superior for the baby. As you make your choices, it's wise to consider what you *want*—your ideal delivery—while remaining flexible in case of unforeseen events. Childbirth is safer now than ever before, but it is still unpredictable. Plan to ask a lot of questions and do some more reading. *Dr. Spock's Pregnancy Guide,* by the obstetrician Marjorie Greenfield (Pocket Books, 2003), is a good source of reliable information that covers all the most important issues and is easy to read.

Doulas. "Doula" is a Greek word that means "woman's helper." Doulas are women who are trained to provide continuous support to women in labor. Some doulas also help out after the baby is born. During labor and delivery the doula guides the mother in positioning, movements, and other activities that can reduce discomfort and provides back rubs and other comforting physical contact. Perhaps most importantly, a doula who has been through many deliveries is often able to reassure a laboring woman when things really are okay, even though the woman may be feeling panicky or overwhelmed. It helps that doulas provide *continuous* support, staying alongside the laboring woman from start to finish.

A doula can be good for the mother *and* the father. It's the rare father who can soothe a laboring woman's pain and anxiety as well as a trained doula, especially when the father is anxious himself. By taking over these tasks, the doula frees up the father to be with his partner in a loving way, rather than as a coach. Most fathers feel supported by the doula, not replaced.

There has now been a good deal of research on the effects of doulas, and the results are powerful. In many studies, doulas reduce the need for cesarean sections and epidural spinal anesthesia. (Epidural anesthesia, although often a godsend, does have some risks: For example, it increases the risk that the baby may run a fever and therefore need to be given antibiotics for a couple of days after delivery.) You can get more information about doulas from Doulas of North America at www.dona.org.

Emotional responses to labor and delivery. Every woman responds differently to the stresses of labor and delivery. Some take pride in receiving no medications at all. Others are certain from the start that an epidural is for them. For some women, labor is a painful experience to be endured and, they hope, forgotten; others consider it a profoundly moving experience, a rite of passage. Some will push with each contraction for endless hours; others will become discouraged and wish for the doctor to pull out the baby with forceps or do a cesarean. Some exhausted women scream at their well-meaning husbands to get out of the delivery room and never come back. Some new mothers feel immediate love and affection for their infant; others, after hearing that their infant is fine, simply want to sleep for a little while. And most turn out to be wonderful, loving parents.

If your labor and delivery experience is not what you expected, it's normal to feel bad, even guilty. If you go in hoping for a natural birth and end up with a cesarean, it's natural that you might feel that somehow you were to blame (you weren't) or that your baby will be permanently harmed by the experience (almost never the case). Many parents fear that if they are apart from their baby for the first hours or days bonding will be permanently undermined. That also is not true. Bonding—the process of baby and parent falling in love with each other—develops over months, not hours.

❧ CLASSIC SPOCK

Parenthood is an ideal guilt-generating business, and labor often delivers the first volley. I think this situation has come about in part because of the fantasy that everything has to be perfect for the child to do well. Of course nothing could be further from the truth. First off, the "perfect" parent has yet to see the light of day. Secondly, there is no need to be "perfect" or to follow any one script. The process of human development is powerful. There is plenty of room for variation and even for making mistakes. Infants are incredibly resilient. As long as the infant is healthy, the type of childbirth is unlikely to have long-term consequences, unless there is so much guilt attached to the memory that it has a negative effect on parental self-confidence or starts the process with a strong but misguided sense of guilt. So my advice is to have your baby however seems right for you and your family. Then don't worry if what happens doesn't follow the script. Being a parent is tough enough without creating problems where there really aren't any.

CHOOSING YOUR BABY'S DOCTOR

Pediatrician, family doctor, or nurse practitioner? While you are pregnant, you can think about finding a physician or nurse practitioner for your baby if you don't already have one. Who should it be and how can you tell if the person will work out? You may already see a family doctor who is used to caring for babies, in which case the choice is simple. But if you deliver your baby with the help of an obstetrician, you'll need to find a doctor or nurse practitioner for your baby.

What qualities are you looking for? Some parents get along best with a doctor who is casual and laid back. Others parents want to be given directions down to the last detail. You might have more confidence in an older, more seasoned professional, or you might prefer one who is younger and more recently trained.

A nurse practitioner is a registered nurse who has received additional training and usually a master's degree so that he or she can function like a doctor in many ways. Nurse practitioners always work with doctor backup; how much the doctor is actually involved varies from practice to practice. Doctors often have more experience managing complex sickness; nurse practitioners may have more time scheduled for checkups and usually provide excellent preventive care. I wouldn't hesitate to use a nurse practitioner if he or she comes highly recommended.

A good first step in finding the right professional is to talk with other parents. Obstetricians and midwives often can give good recommendations, too.

The getting-to-know-you visit. If this is your first baby or you are moving to a new area, I'd strongly recommend that you schedule a visit to the doctor or nurse practitioner a few weeks *before* your due date. There is nothing like actually meeting someone to know if he or she has the type of personality that will make you feel comfortable enough to talk about whatever is on your mind. You can learn a great deal from such a prebirth visit and come away confident that your child's medical care is all set.

When you arrive for the visit, pay attention to the office staff and the office itself. Are the people pleasant and courteous? Are there things for children to do in the waiting room? Are there picture books? Does the space appear child-friendly?

There are a number of practical questions that the staff may be able to answer: How many physicians and nurse practitioners are there in the practice? How are phone calls handled? What happens if your baby becomes ill after office hours? What if you have an emergency during the day? What health insurance does the practice accept? What are its fees? Which hospital does it use? How much time is allotted for well-child checkups? (Fifteen minutes is about average nowadays, twenty to thirty is generous.)

A key issue is continuity of care. Will your child have one specific doctor or nurse practitioner, or do patients in the practice see whichever doctor happens to be available? Seeing whoever is available may involve less waiting, but many parents prefer for their child to have one identified professional who is "their" doctor. That way, the health professional gets to know you and your child well, and mutual trust can develop. Medical care for children requires a team effort—with the parent and the professional being the key team members. A parent may find it harder to feel that team spirit with a whole office of doctors.

When you talk with the doctor, choose a couple of issues to discuss that are important to you, such as the doctor's views on breast-feeding, allowing you to be present if your child needs to have a painful procedure, and how he or she handles issues that are not strictly medical, such as the question of cosleeping or toilet training. Pay attention to how you *feel* during the interview. If you feel comfortable, listened-to, and unrushed, you've probably found the right professional for you and your child; if not, you may want to visit some other practices.

Prenatal breast-feeding consultation. If you are unsure whether to breast-feed or bottle-feed, it's helpful to discuss the issue with the doctor or nurse practitioner you've chosen for your baby, or line up a prenatal consultation with a lactation

consultant. You may want to attend breast-feeding classes offered by many large practices or hospitals. Knowing more will
help you feel comfortable with your decision. If you decide to
breast-feed, a prenatal consultation can help you anticipate
any problems and deal with them ahead of time (see page 242
for more on breast-feeding).

PLANNING THE HOMECOMING

Arranging for extra help in the beginning. If you can figure out
a way to get someone to help you the first few weeks you are taking care of your baby, by all means do so. Having a supportive father around full time during the first couple of weeks can be
particularly helpful. Trying to do everything yourself can ex-
haust and depress you, and this can start you and the baby off on
the wrong foot. Most expectant parents feel a little scared at the
prospect of taking sole charge of a helpless baby for the first
time. If you have this feeling, it doesn't mean that you won't be
able to do a good job or that you have to have a nurse to show
you how. But if you feel really panicky, you will probably learn
more comfortably with an agreeable relative by your side. The
baby's father may not be a great support person, or he may be
feeling too anxious or overwhelmed himself.

Your mother may be the ideal helper if you get along with her
easily. If you feel she is bossy and still treats you like a child, it's
probably better if she doesn't stay when she visits. You want to
feel that the baby is your own and that you are doing a good job.
It will help to have a person who has taken care of babies before,
but it's most important of all to have someone you enjoy having
around.

You might consider hiring a housekeeper or doula for a few
weeks. Doulas are professionals who support women during
labor (see page 24). More and more doulas offer their services in
the weeks after birth as well. If your finances are limited, you
may still be able to afford someone to come in once or twice a

week to do the laundry, help you catch up on the housework, and watch the baby for a few hours while you take a rest or go out. It makes sense to keep your helper around for as long as you need the help (and can afford it).

Nurse home visits. Many hospitals and health plans offer nurse home visits one or two days after you take your baby home, particularly if the hospital stay has been short (less than a couple of days). Nurse visits are often very reassuring. They can be important, too, because some medical problems, such as jaundice, may not be apparent before the baby goes home. A visiting nurse can also be very helpful in dealing with breast-feeding problems or helping to arrange the services of a lactation consultant (see page 249).

Callers and visitors. The birth of a baby is an occasion that brings relatives and friends flocking. This is gratifying to the parents and fills them with pride. However, too much of it may be exhausting. How much is too much? It's different in different cases. Most mothers tire easily the first few weeks at home. They have just felt the effects of intense hormonal changes. Their usual sleep pattern has been disrupted. Perhaps more important still are the emotional shifts that are called for, especially with the first baby.

Visitors are pure pleasure to some people—relaxing, distracting, rejuvenating. To most of us, however, only a few old friends have such a good effect. Other visitors, to a greater or lesser degree, make us tense, even when we enjoy seeing them, and leave us fatigued, especially if we aren't feeling well. So you might want to limit visitors at the start, see how it goes, then increase the number very gradually if you find you have plenty of strength left over.

Most visitors get all excited when they see babies. They want to hold them, joggle them, tickle them, jounce them, waggle their heads at them, and keep up a blue streak of baby talk. Some babies can take a lot of this treatment, some can't take any. Most are in between. Pay attention to how your baby responds, and set a limit on handling if you think your baby may be feeling stressed or tired out by the attention. Relatives and friends who care about you and your baby won't be offended. Young children in particular often carry around viruses in their noses and on their hands that can make newborns ill. So it makes sense to keep young cousins and other relatives at a safe distance for the first three to four months; if they do touch your baby, make sure they wash their hands well first.

Preparing your home. If your home was built before 1980, there's a good chance that it contains lead paint. While it makes sense to remove any loose paint chips and perhaps paint over exposed, weathered patches, it isn't safe to try to remove the paint yourself using a heat gun or sander; the fine lead dust and vapors can raise your own lead level, which might affect your baby. Professional lead removal is safer, though expensive. For more on lead, see page 764.

If you are using well water, it's important to have it tested for bacteria and nitrates before the baby arrives. Nitrate salts in well water can cause blueness of the baby's lips and skin. Write or call your county or state health department. Well water won't have fluoride added, so you'll need to discuss fluoride supplements with your doctor.

HELPING SIBLINGS COPE

What to say while you're pregnant. It is good for a child to know ahead of time that he is going to have a baby brother or sister if he is old enough to understand such an idea at all (around a year and a half). That way he can get used to the idea gradually. Of course, you have to gear your explanations to your child's developmental level, and no amount of explanation can really prepare him for the experience of having a live demanding baby in the house. Your job is just to begin the dialogue about having a new brother or sister, where the baby will sleep, what the sibling's role will be in his care and to provide constant reassurance that you love him as much as ever. Don't overdo your enthusiasm or expect him to be enthusiastic about the baby. A good time to begin these discussions is once your body shape begins to change and you are past the very earliest stages of pregnancy when the risk of a miscarriage is highest.

The arrival of the baby should change an older child's life as little as possible, especially if he has been the only child. Emphasize the concrete things that will stay the same: "You'll still have your same favorite toys; we'll still go to the same park to play; we'll still have our special treats, we'll still have our special time together."

Make changes ahead of time. If your older child isn't weaned yet, it will be easier for her if you do it a few months *before* you deliver, not when she is feeling displaced by the new baby. If her room is to be given over to the baby, move her to her new room several months before, so that she feels that she is graduating because she is a big girl, not because the baby is pushing her out of her place. The same applies to advancing to a big bed. If she is to go to preschool, she should start a couple of months before the baby arrives, if possible. Nothing sets a child's mind against preschool so much as the feeling that she is being banished to it by an interloper. But if she is already well established in preschool, she has a social life outside the home, which will tend to lessen her feelings of rivalry at home.

During and after delivery. Some parents hope to strengthen family togetherness by including the older sibling in the delivery itself. But watching one's mother go through labor can be very upsetting for a young child, who might think that something awful is happening. Even older children can be disturbed by the stressful effort and the blood that are part of even the smoothest deliveries. From the mother's point of view, labor is tough enough by itself without having to worry about how a child is handling it. Other children can feel included by being nearby but not actually in the delivery room.

After the delivery, when everyone is nice and calm, is a good time to show the baby to an older sibling. He can be encouraged to touch the baby, talk to her, and help out in some simple task, like getting a diaper. He should have the feeling that he is an integral part of this family unit and that his presence is welcomed. He should visit as much as he wants but not be forced to if he doesn't.

Bringing the baby home. It's usually a hectic moment when the mother comes home after giving birth. She is tired and preoccupied. The father scurries about, being helpful. If the older child is there, he stands around feeling left out, thinking warily, "So this is the new baby."

It may be better for the older child to be away on an excursion, if this can be arranged. An hour later, when the baby and the luggage are in their place and the mother is at last relaxing on the bed, is time enough for the child to come in. His mother can hug him and talk to him and give him her undivided attention. Since children appreciate concrete rewards, it's nice to bring a present home for the sibling. A baby doll of his own or a wonderful new toy help him not feel abandoned. You don't have to keep asking him, "So how do you like your new sister?" Let him bring up the subject of the baby when he is ready to, and don't be surprised if his comments are unenthusiastic or even hostile.

Actually, most older siblings handle the first days of a new baby pretty well. It often takes several weeks before they realize that the competition is there to stay. And it will be months before the baby is old enough to start grabbing their toys and bugging them. The section on siblings (page 529) has more on how you can help siblings get along.

THINGS YOU'LL NEED

Buying things ahead of time. Some parents don't feel like buying anything until they have their baby. The idea that shopping for things ahead of time might cause the pregnancy to come to a bad end is common in many cultures. Parents may not want to tempt fate.

The advantage of getting and arranging things ahead of time is that it lightens your burden later. A certain number of mothers feel tired and easily discouraged when they begin taking care of the baby themselves. Even a little job like buying a bag of diapers looms as an ordeal.

What do you really need? Even if you don't have everything prepared ahead of time, it's wise to at least have some necessities on hand before you deliver. The sections that follow should help you decide what to buy ahead of time and what you might buy later (or never). For deciding which brand to purchase, I suggest you check the most recent copies of journals such as *Consumer Reports* for the latest information on safety, durability and practicality.

CHECKLIST

Things You'll Need Right from the Start:

✔ A safety-approved car seat (see page 35).

✔ A crib, cradle, bassinet, or cosleeper—even if the baby sleeps with you at night, he'll need a place for naps.

✔ Several snug-fitting cotton sheets, a plastic mattress cover, and two or three cloth mattress liners.

✔ Several small cotton blankets for swaddling and perhaps a heavier blanket for warmth.

✔ A few T-shirts or onesies; in cooler climates, two or three sleepers.

✔ Diapers, either disposable or cloth, or a diaper service (see page 67); wipes. (Cloth diapers have many uses, even if you choose disposables for the baby's bottom.)

✔ Nursing bras and (probably) a breast pump (page 278) if you plan to breast-feed.

✔ Two or three plastic bottles and nipples; more bottles and a supply of formula if you plan to bottle-feed.

✔ A cloth sling or front-pack baby carrier.

✔ A diaper bag with compartments for diapers, wipes, ointment, a folding plastic changing pad, and nursing supplies.

✔ A digital thermometer and a child's nose syringe with bulb suction.

Car seats. One of the biggest dangers your newborn faces is the ride home from the hospital—unless you use an infant car seat. Be sure the seat has a label showing that it meets government safety standards for use in cars. Always place your newborn in the back seat facing backward. Babies should *never* be placed in front of a working air bag; an exploding air bag can seriously injure or even kill a small child.

There are two basic kinds of car seats for babies. One kind always faces backwards and has a handle so that it can be used as a baby carrier. The other kind is a convertible seat that can be turned around to face forward once your baby is large enough (over twelve months old *and* over twenty pounds). Either kind is safe. If possible, get a new seat. If a seat has been in an accident in the past, it might not hold up in a second one, even if it looks okay. Over time the plastic weakens, so that a seat that has been in the family for years may not provide adequate protection. Choose a seat that uses a harness to hold the child rather than a shield or bar, which can injure a child in a crash.

Consumer Reports frequently updates its ratings of car seats. I also suggest you send for "The Family Shopping Guide to Car Seats" from the American Academy of Pediatrics (see Resource

Section for address) and call the Auto Safety Hot Line (800 424-9393) for information on car seat safety notices.

It's hard to put a car seat in correctly (I took a week-long course to learn how) so, if you can, have a certified child safety seat inspector show you how. Many hospitals and fire stations run free car seat installation programs. You can find one near you by calling the hospitals, or look online at www.nhtsa. dot.gov. You'll find more detailed information on car seats on page 735.

A place to sleep. You may want to get a beautiful, expensive bassinet, lined with silk. But your baby won't care. All she needs are sides to keep her from rolling out and something soft but firm in the bottom for a mattress. You might also decide to have your baby sleep in bed with you (see page 59 for the pros and cons).

Having a firm surface is important, because babies can more easily suffocate if they lie face down on a very soft mattress. (Even though babies *should* sleep on their backs to prevent crib death, sometimes they end up face down anyhow.) A simple bassinet on wheels is convenient at first. Sometimes there's a cradle that's been in the family for many years. A cardboard box or a drawer with a firm, tight-fitting pad also works well for the first couple of months.

A cosleeper is a three-sided box that sits alongside your bed with the opening facing you. It's wonderful to be able to reach your baby without getting up, especially if you are breast-feeding. For safety, it's important that the cosleeper attaches firmly to the bed, so that there isn't a gap a baby could be caught in.

Most parents start with a crib. For safety, a crib should have slats less than 2⅜ inches apart and any cut-out openings on the ends should also be less than 2⅜ inches across. It should have a snug-fitting mattress, childproof side locking mechanisms, and at least twenty-six inches from the top of the rail to the mattress set at its lowest level. Look out for sharp edges and for corner posts that stick up more than one-sixteenth of an inch; that's high enough to snag an article of clothing, which could trap or strangle a baby. It should be sturdy, with the mattress support firmly attached to the headboard and footboard. Cribs made before 1975 often have lead paint and are safe only if all the old paint has been stripped off. If you're buying a new crib, look on the box to see that it meets federal safety standards. For used cribs, hand-me-downs, and family heirlooms, *you* have to be the safety inspector.

Your baby doesn't need a pillow for her head, and you should not use one. Likewise, it's best to keep stuffed animals out of your baby's crib or cradle; little babies don't care much about them, and they may pose a suffocation risk. Cloth bumpers can look great, but they don't do much to protect small babies, and can also become a suffocation hazard if they come loose.

For more on sleep and sleep safety, see page 57.

Equipment for bathing and changing. Babies can be bathed in the kitchen sink, a plastic tub (get one with a wide edge to rest your arm on), a dishpan, or a washstand. A spraying faucet that works like a minishower is great for rinsing the baby's hair and keeping him warm and happy. Molded plastic bathing tubs with contoured pads or liners are useful and generally inexpensive.

A bath thermometer is not necessary but can be a comfort to the inexperienced parent. Always test the water temperature with your hand anyway. Water should never be hot, only lukewarm. Also, never run warm water into the tub or sink while the baby is in it unless you are sure that the temperature is constant. The temperature setting on water heaters should be set at a maximum of 120 degrees to prevent scalding.

You can change and dress your baby on a low table or bathroom counter, where water is handy, or on the top of a bureau that is at a comfortable height. Changing tables with a waterproof pad, safety straps, and storage shelves are convenient, though expensive, and may not be adaptable for other uses later. Some types fold; some have an attached bath. Wherever you change your baby (except on the floor) it's wise to keep one hand on your baby at all times: safety straps are nice backups, but don't trust them.

Diapers are discussed on page 67. For diaper wipes, you can use a washcloth with soap and water or you can use moist paper towels. If you want the convenience of premoistened diaper wipes, use the ones without chemicals and perfume, which can cause rashes.

Seats, swings, and walkers. An inclined plastic seat in which your baby can be strapped, carried short distances, and set down almost anywhere and from which she can watch the world go by is a useful accessory. (Some infant car seats can be used for this purpose, too.) The base should be larger than the seat; otherwise it will tip over when your baby becomes active. There are also cloth seats that move with the infant's movement. Be careful about placing your baby in any kind of seat on countertops and tables, as her movements might inch the seat off the edge.

Baby seats tend to be overused in that the baby is apt to be always in it and so is deprived of bodily contact with people (see page 48). A baby should be held for feedings, comforting, and at other times. Plastic baby seats are also not the best things for carrying babies: Your baby will be happier and more secure in a cloth sling or Snugli, and you get to have both arms free, with less strain on your shoulders.

Young babies usually love motion, and a swing can be wonderfully calming. A cloth baby sling does the same thing, of course, but a swing is useful to give you a break. I don't think that babies actually become addicted to swinging, but too many hours of the same hypnotizing motion probably isn't best for them.

Infant walkers are a major cause of injury (see page 117). Other than providing temporary amusement, their benefits are nonexistent and their dangers clearly proven. They should not be used. Manufacturers now make stationary walkers that bounce, swivel, or rock. They come with toys attached for entertainment and are much safer for children.

Strollers, carriages, and backpacks. A stroller is a handy way to take a young child when you shop or run other errands. Strollers are best for babies who can hold their heads up steadily. Newborns and little infants do better in a cloth front pack, from which they can look up into their parent's face and hear their heartbeats. A folding umbrella stroller can be easily carried on a bus or in a car, but be sure it's a sturdy one. Products that combine a car seat and stroller are attractive, and they make it easy to go from car to stroller without having to wake up a sleeping infant. On the other hand, they aren't as compact as the folding umbrella variety. Children should always be strapped into their strollers.

A carriage (pram) is like a bassinet on wheels; nice to have for the first few months if you plan on taking long strolls with your

baby but hardly necessary. An alternative, after your baby has outgrown the soft front pack, is to go to a backpack. These items can be very sophisticated, with metal frames and padded hip belts that let you carry a large baby or toddler without much strain. Your baby can look over your shoulder, chat with you, play with your hair, and fall asleep with her head nestled into your neck.

Play yards (playpens). Some parents and psychologists disapprove of the imprisonment of a baby in a pen, fearing that it may cramp the child's spirit and desire to explore, but I've known many babies who spent several hours a day in pens and who still ended up demon explorers with high spirits. A young infant can be left safely in her cradle or crib, but once your baby starts crawling, it's very helpful to have a confined place where she can play safely while you take care of other business. There are play yards designed to fold into compact travel-size cases, which are great for going on visits. They are recommended for children up to thirty pounds or thirty-four inches tall.

If you are going to use a play yard, you should start putting your baby in it each day from about three months. Babies differ—some tolerate play yards well, some poorly. If you wait until a baby starts to crawl (six to eight months), the play yard will surely seem like a prison and be met with persistent howls.

Bedding. Blankets made of acrylic or a polyester-cotton combination are easy to wash and nonallergenic. A knitted shawl is a particularly convenient form of blanket for babies because it wraps around them so easily when they are up and stays tucked in when it is over them in bed. Make sure there are no long threads for the baby to wrap around fingers or toes or large holes that a baby can get caught in. Blankets should be large enough to tuck well under a crib mattress. A baby wearing a fleece sleeper probably doesn't also need a blanket, unless the room is chilly. Babies should be comfortable, not overheated.

Cotton receiving blankets, which furnish little warmth, are useful for wrapping around the baby who would otherwise kick off the bed coverings or for tightly swaddling the young baby who is comfortable and secure and can sleep only when held immobile.

You'll probably want a plastic mattress cover. The plastic cover that comes on most new mattresses is not sufficient by itself; sooner or later urine gets into the air holes and makes it smell. A cloth mattress pad lets air circulate under the sheet; you'll need three to six pads, depending on how often you do laundry. Waterproof sheeting that has a flannelette covering serves the same purpose. A thin plastic bag such as one from the dry cleaner should *never* be used in a crib, because of the danger of suffocation if the baby's head gets tangled in it.

You will need three to six sheets. They should fit snugly so that they don't come undone and pose a suffocation risk. The best sheets are made of cotton knit. They are easy to wash, quick to dry, spread smoothly without ironing, and do not feel clammy when wet.

Clothing. Remember that your baby will be growing very rapidly during the first year, so be sure you buy her clothing to fit loosely. Except for diaper covers, it's generally better to begin with three- to six-month-size clothes instead of newborn or "layette-sized" clothing.

A baby or child doesn't need more in the way of clothing or covering than an adult; if anything, less. For example, nightgowns are entirely practical and can be worn night and day. The mittens on the ends of the sleeves, which are to keep babies from scratching themselves, can be worn open or closed. Long gowns make it harder for babies to kick off their coverings; short ones may be preferable for hot weather. Buy three or four; more if you can't do laundry every day.

Undershirts come in three styles: pullover, side-snap closing, and a one-piece type that slips over the head and snaps around the diaper. The type with side snaps is slightly easier to put on a small baby. Medium weight and short sleeves should be sufficient unless your home is unusually chilly. A one-piece shirt that snaps under the crotch (a onesie) stays in place easily. The most comfortable fabric for children is 100 percent cotton. Start with the one-year-old size or, if you are fussy about fit, the six-month size. Buy at least three or four. It will be convenient to have two or three more, especially if you don't have a washer and dryer. If you cut or pull off the tags, they won't irritate your baby's neck.

Stretch suits can work for day or night. Check the insides of the feet regularly. They can collect hair, which can wind around the baby's toes and be painful. Sweaters are useful to add extra warmth. Be sure that the neck opening has sufficient give or that there are shoulder snaps, well-secured buttons, or zippers up the back to adjust the fit.

Knitted acrylic or cotton caps are all right for going outdoors in the kind of weather that makes grown-ups put on caps or for sleeping in an equally cold room. Avoid using caps that are too large at night, because they can cover the baby's face as she moves around while sleeping. For milder weather caps are unnecessary; most babies don't like them anyway. You don't need booties and stockings, at least until your baby is sitting up and playing around in a cold house. Dresses make a baby look pretty but are otherwise unnecessary and are bothersome to the baby and the parent. A sun hat with a chin strap to keep it on is useful for the baby who will tolerate it. See page 115 about shoes.

Some parents find good used clothes or hand-me-downs a good choice for rapidly growing children. Watch out for scratchy lace close to the face and arms; it can make even an adult irritable. Headbands are cute, but if they're too tight or itchy (or if a ponytail is too tight), they can hurt the head. Most important, be on the lookout for any loose buttons or decorations that can pose a choking hazard and ribbons and cords that can get wrapped around a baby's arms or neck.

Toiletries and medical. Any mild soap will do for the bath. Avoid liquid baby soaps and deodorant soaps; they may cause rashes. For all but the most soiled areas, plain water works fine. There are "no-tears" shampoos that are gentle on babies' eyes. Cotton balls are useful at bath time for wiping the baby's eyes. Baby lotion is not really necessary unless your child's skin is dry, although it's pleasant to rub it on, and babies love massage. Many parents now prefer to use creams and lotions that don't have scent or color added. They often cost less than the usual baby products.

Baby oils, most made of mineral oil, have been used extensively for dry or normal skin or for diaper rash. But tests have shown that mineral oil itself may cause a very mild rash in some babies, so it is sensible not to use it routinely unless you find by testing that it has more advantage than disadvantage in your baby's case.

Baby talcum powder should be avoided because it is irritating to the lungs and can cause significant problems if inhaled. If you need powder, baby powder that is pure cornstarch is safer.

An ointment containing lanolin and petrolatum, in a tube or jar, protects the skin when there is diaper rash. Pure petrolatum jelly also works well, but it can be messy.

Infant nail scissors have blunted ends. Many parents find infant nail clippers easier to use and less likely to cut the baby. I prefer using a nail file: there's no chance of drawing blood, and files don't leave jagged edges that can cause scratches.

You'll need a thermometer to take your baby's temperature, in case of illness. Digital thermometers cost about $10, are fast, accurate, easy to use, and safe. High-tech ear thermometers are less accurate and much more expensive. Old-style thermometers that contain mercury aren't safe. If you have one already, don't just throw it in the garbage; call your local sanitation department for proper disposal.

If the mucus from a cold is interfering with feeding, a child's nose syringe with bulb suction is helpful to remove it. See page 799 for other items to keep in your medicine cabinet.

Feeding Equipment. If you're planning to breast-feed, you may not need any equipment other than yourself. Many nursing mothers find that it's also helpful to have a breast pump (see page 278). Hand-operated pumps are often slow and tiring to use; good motorized pumps are expensive but can be rented from medical supply stores, and many hospitals have programs that loan out pumps at low cost. If you pump, you'll need a few (at least three or four) plastic bottles to store the milk and the nipples to go with them. Breast pads, nursing bras, nipple shields, and other items are described in the breast-feeding section (page 242).

If you know ahead of time that your baby is going to bottle-feed, buy at least nine of the eight-ounce bottles. In the beginning you will use six to eight a day for the formula. Plastic bottles don't break when adults—or babies—drop them. You'll need to have a bottle brush, too. For water and juice (not needed in the first months), some parents prefer to use four-ounce bottles. Buy a few extra nipples, in case you are having trouble making the nipple holes the right size. There are all kinds of specially shaped nipples but no scientific proof for the claims made by their manufacturers. Some nipples withstand boiling and wear and tear better than others. Be sure to follow instructions on when to replace old nipples.

You don't need to sterilize baby bottles if your tap water is safe to drink (see page 288 on sterilization).

It is no longer considered necessary to warm a baby's bottle, although most babies prefer their formula at least room temperature. Hot water in a pot works well. An electric warmer is handy when the hot-water supply is undependable. There is a special warmer that plugs into an automobile cigarette lighter. *Never* warm a baby's bottle in a microwave oven: Hot spots in the milk can be scalding even when the bottle feels cool. Always test the milk temperature on the underside of your wrist.

Small round bibs are useful for keeping drool off clothes. For the mess that babies or children always make with their solid food, they need a large bib of plastic, nylon, or terry (or a combination), preferably with a pocket along the lower edge to catch the food that comes running down. A formed plastic bib with a food catcher on the bottom is easily rinsed. A terry bib can also be used for wiping the face—if you can find a dry corner. Bibs make wonderful gifts.

Pacifiers. If you decide to use them, three or four will do (see page 63). The practice of blocking up a baby bottle nipple with cotton or paper and using it as a pacifier is dangerous, because the contraption can easily fall apart, leaving little pieces that are a choking hazard.

YOUR NEWBORN, BIRTH TO ABOUT THREE MONTHS

⮔

ENJOY YOUR BABY

Challenges of the first three months. Once the awe, shock, relief, and exhaustion of delivery have worn off a bit, you'll probably find that caring for your new baby is a lot of work; wonderful, but still work. The main reason is that newborn babies rely on their parents to manage all of their basic life functions—eating, sleeping, eliminating, and keeping warm. Your baby can't tell you what she needs from moment to moment; it's up to you to figure out what to do.

Many parents find that all of their energy is focused on fine-tuning their babies: helping them eat when they're hungry and stop when they're full, stay awake more during the day and sleep more at night, and feel comfortable in a bright, buzzing world that is so much more stimulating than the womb. Some babies seem to take these challenges in stride. Others have a harder time adjusting. But by two or three months, most babies (and their parents) have the basics figured out, and it's time to start exploring.

Relax and enjoy your baby. From what some people—including some doctors—say about babies demanding attention, you'd think that they come into the world determined to get their parents under their thumbs by hook or by crook. This isn't true. Your baby is born to be a reasonable, friendly—though occasionally demanding—human being.

Don't be afraid to feed her when you think she's really hungry. If you are mistaken, she'll merely refuse to eat much. Don't be afraid to love her and enjoy her. Every baby needs to be smiled at, talked to, played with, and fondled gently and lovingly just as much as she needs vitamins and calories. That's what will make her a person who loves people and enjoys life. The baby who doesn't get any loving will grow up cold and unresponsive.

Don't be afraid to respond to her other desires as long as they seem sensible to you and you don't become a slave to her. When she cries in the early weeks, it's because she's uncomfortable for some reason: Maybe it's hunger or indigestion, fatigue, or tension. The uneasy feeling you have when you hear her cry, the feeling that you want to comfort her, is meant to be part of your nature, too. Being held, rocked, or walked may be what she needs.

Spoiling doesn't come from being good to a baby in a sensible way, and it doesn't happen all of a sudden. Spoiling comes on gradually when parents are afraid to use their common sense or when they really want to be slaves and encourage their babies to become slave drivers.

Parents want their children to turn out healthy in their habits and easy to live with. And children agree. They want to eat at sensible hours and eventually learn good table manners. Your baby will develop her own pattern of sleep according to her own needs. Her bowels will move according to their own healthy pattern, which may or may not be regular; and when she's a lot older and wiser, you can show her where to sit to move them. Sooner or later she will want to fit into the family's way of doing things with only a minimum of guidance from you.

Babies aren't frail. "I'm so afraid I'll hurt her if I don't handle her just right," a parent may say about her first baby. You don't have to worry; you have a pretty tough baby. There are many ways to hold her. If her head drops backward by mistake, it won't hurt her. The soft spot on her skull (the fontanel) is covered by a tough membrane—as tough as canvas—that isn't easily injured.

The system to control body temperature works well in most babies if they're covered halfway sensibly. They inherit good resistance to most germs. In a family cold epidemic, the baby is apt to have it the mildest of all. If a baby gets her head tangled in anything, she has a strong instinct to struggle and yell. If she's not getting enough to eat, she will probably cry for more. If the light is too strong for her eyes, she'll blink and fuss or just close them. She knows how much sleep she needs and takes it. She can care for herself pretty well for a person who can't say a word and knows nothing about the world.

TOUCH AND BONDING

Babies thrive on touch. Before birth, not only are babies enveloped, warmed and nourished by their mothers, they participate in every bodily movement their mothers make. After birth, in many parts of the world, babies are held against their mothers all day long in cloth carriers of one kind or another. They continue to share in all their mothers' movements as their mothers go about their regular jobs, whatever they may be—food gathering and preparing, tilling, weaving, house care—and they sleep in the same bed at night. These babies are breast-fed the instant they whimper. They not only hear but feel the vibrations of their mothers' words and songs. Often, as babies get a little older, they are carried about most of the day on the hips or backs of their older sisters. In these cultures, babies cry less, and spitting up and fretfulness are uncommon.

Our society has thought up a dozen ingenious ways to put distance between mothers and their babies. Babies are whisked away to a hospital nursery, where other people care for them, which makes parents feel incompetent. Babies are fed commercial formulas from bottles, so mothers and babies lose the opportunity for the most intimate bond in child-rearing. To us, it seems natural to put our babies on flat mattresses in immobile cribs, preferably in quiet rooms. We have infant seats in which babies can be strapped so that they don't have to be held when they're awake. There are even car seats that can be snapped right onto strollers, so parents never need to touch their babies at all. This is in contrast to the most successful treatment for the hurts, slights, and sadness of infants, children and adults—a good hug.

The urge for bodily contact is strong in both babies and parents. Physical touch releases hormones in the brain—both the baby's and the parent's—that heighten feelings of relaxation and happiness and reduce pain. When babies have their heels pricked for routine newborn screening tests, for example, they cry much less if they are being held skin to skin with their mothers. And premature infants grow better when they have skin-to-skin time every day.

Early contact and bonding. It's fascinating to watch what mothers in America naturally do when allowed to have their babies with them soon after birth. They don't just look at them. They spend a lot of time touching their limbs and bodies and faces with their fingers. As a group, mothers who have an opportunity to touch their babies in this way have easier relations with their babies even months later, and their babies are more responsive, too.

Observations like this led the pediatricians John Kennell and Marshall Klaus to use the term "bonding" to describe the process by which parents connect naturally with their newborn infants. One marvelous result of their research has been that hospitals all across the country encourage rooming-in for new mothers and their babies. In some enlightened hospitals, immediately after birth healthy newborns are dried and placed on their mothers' chests, where they snuggle in and often begin to nurse.

But bonding has also been widely misunderstood, leading to a lot of unnecessary worry. Parents, and even professionals, often seem to think that if bonding hasn't taken place in the first twenty-four to forty-eight hours, it never will. But this isn't true. Bonding occurs over time, and there is no deadline. Parents bond with children they adopt at any age. Bonding—the sense of connection and belonging between parents and children—is a very strong force. Bonding happens *despite* child-rearing practices that separate parents from their infants. Premature babies often spend the first months of life isolated in plastic incubators, but their parents still manage to reach in through the portholes.

✍ CLASSIC SPOCK

I think that parents in our society can get a better perspective on our methods by comparing them with what comes naturally in less technological societies. How to be natural? I'd draw the following conclusions:

- Natural childbirth and rooming-in should be available for all who want them.
- Mothers and fathers should have their baby to hold and fondle for an hour after the baby is born, especially if rooming-in is not available.
- Breast-feeding should be encouraged, especially by nurses, doctors, and families.
- Bottle-propping should be avoided except when there's no choice—as when a mother of twins has no help and has to prop for one baby, at least, at each feeding.
- Mothers and fathers should try to use a cloth carrier more than the infant seat, when they are at home or out and about. Cloth carriers that hold babies against their mother or father's chest are best.

Bonding and early return to a job. These days, most mothers return to their paid jobs very soon after having their babies. Financial necessity and demanding careers put huge pressure on women. Finding trustworthy child care can be very difficult (see "Work and Child Care" in Section III). Apart from that, mothers often grieve because they feel they are losing the precious first months of their babies' lives, and they worry about the effects of early separation on their babies.

Babies will form strong emotional bonds with mothers and fathers even when they are cared for by others during the day. Loving care provided in the mornings, evenings, weekends, and (of course) in the middle of the night is enough to cement the bond from the child's side (see "What Children Need" in Section III for children's feelings of attachment).

I've seen many mothers pull back emotionally in the first days of their baby's life because they are getting ready for the time, all too soon, when they will have to say good-bye. This is a natural self-protective response, but it can place great strain on a mother and on her relationship with her child. Fathers usually feel these strains less, because they are used to the idea of jumping right back into their jobs.

My advice to mothers (and fathers) who feel pressured to return to jobs earlier than they feel comfortable is, Listen to your heart. If there is any way you can stretch your maternity leave, even if it means a loss of income, you may end up glad you made that choice. By about four months most mothers feel much better about heading back to their jobs, having had a chance to really connect with their babies and eager for the adult companionship of work.

EARLY FEELINGS

The blue feeling. It's possible that you will find yourself feeling discouraged for a while when you begin taking care of your baby. It's a fairly common feeling, especially with the first one. You may not be able to put your finger on anything that is definitely wrong. You just weep easily, or you may feel bad about certain things.

A feeling of depression may come on a few days after the baby is born or not until several weeks later. The commonest time is when a mother comes home from the hospital. It isn't just the work that gets her down; it's the feeling of being responsible for the household plus the entirely new responsibility of the baby's care and safety. A woman who was used to going to work every day is bound to miss the companionship of colleagues. Then there are the physical and hormonal changes at the time of birth, which will probably alter the mother's mood to some degree.

If you begin to feel blue or discouraged, try to get some relief from the constant care of the baby in the first month or two, especially if your child cries a great deal. Go for a walk or work out. Work on some new or unfinished project—writing, painting, sewing, building; something creative and satisfying. Visit a good friend, or get your friends to come and see you. Activities like these can help lift your mood. At first you may not feel like doing anything. But if you make yourself take action, you will feel better. And that's important for your baby and your family, as well as for yourself.

Also talk with your partner about how you are feeling, and be prepared to listen, too. It's pretty common for a new father to feel rejected because the baby gets all the attention. A natural response—although not a helpful one—is for the father to withdraw emotionally or become whiney and critical just when the mother needs support the most. Feeling unsupported, a mother may become angry, sad, or depressed; this of course just makes the situation worse. Talking together is critical if couples are going to avoid this kind of vicious cycle.

If your mood does not lift in a few days or if it is getting worse, you may be suffering from what is referred to as postpartum depression. "Baby blues" almost always goes away by two months; postpartum depression can go on and on. Real postpartum depression may happen in as many as 10 to 20 percent of pregnancies. Rarely, it is so severe that there is even a risk of suicide. If you or your partner has a severe mood change at any time, especially after pregnancy, get medical help right away. No one knows exactly what causes postpartum depression, but women who suffered from depression before are more vulnerable.

This is not the sort of problem you can simply talk yourself out of; you need professional help. You can start by talking with your doctor, who may refer you to a mental health professional. The good news about postpartum depression is that it is *treatable*. Both talk therapy and antidepressant medication can be very helpful. No new mother should have to suffer with this problem alone.

The father's feelings in the early weeks at home. A father shouldn't be surprised if he has mixed feelings at times toward his wife and his baby. These feelings can arise during the pregnancy, during the commotion of the labor and delivery stage, or after they are home again. He can remind himself that his feelings are probably not nearly so churned up as his wife's, especially immediately after the homecoming. She has been through an intense hormonal change. If it's her first baby, she can't help feeling anxious. All babies will make great demands on a mother's strength and spirits at the beginning.

What this adds up to is that most women need a great deal of support from their partners at this time. They need help with care of the baby and any other children and with housework. Even more, they need patience, understanding, appreciation, and affection. The father's job may be complicated by the fact that if his wife is tired and upset, she might not thank him for his efforts. Indeed, she may be critical or complaining. Even so, when fathers understand how much they are needed, they can put their negative responses aside, choosing instead to play their crucial supporting role.

⬿ **CLASSIC SPOCK**
The first few weeks at home, most new parents find that they are more anxious than usual and just plain exhausted. They worry about the baby's crying and fretful spells, sus-

pecting that something is seriously wrong. They worry about every sneeze and every spot of rash. They tiptoe into the baby's room to see whether she is still breathing. It's probably instinctive for parents to be overly protective at this period. I suppose it's nature's way of being sure that the millions of new parents throughout the world, some of whom may be immature, take their new responsibility seriously. A little concern might be a good thing. Fortunately, the anxiety wears off.

PARENTS' SEXUAL RELATIONS AFTER DELIVERY

The process of pregnancy, labor, and delivery may interfere (for a time) with many parents' sexual relations. Near the end of pregnancy, intercourse may become uncomfortable or at least physically challenging. Following delivery, there is a normal period of discomfort, readjustment of the body to its prepregnancy state, hormonal shifts, and the hard work, sleep deprivation, and fatigue of caring for a newborn. Sex may be crowded out for days, weeks, even months.

This can also be a difficult time for a man's libido. He may simply be tired. For some men, the shift in perspective of their partner from lover to mother is difficult to reconcile with sexual feelings. All manner of deep emotional contradictions may arise. Some men, for example, have been raised with the Madonna or whore complex. It's hard for them to understand how a woman can be both a mother and a lover; the feelings may seem mutually incompatible (just as some of us can't even begin to picture our parents as sexual beings, even though we are the proof incarnate of that sexuality).

If you recognize that sexual intercourse can be slow in returning, you won't be so alarmed at its temporary absence. And just because you have put sexual intercourse on hold, that does not mean that all sexual relations must cease. Take time for cuddling, hugging, kissing, a romantic word, an appreciative glance, an unexpected gift of flowers.

Balancing parenthood with the other aspects of your life is one of the skills of successful parenting and successful marriage. Almost all parents get back on track sexually after a while. What makes the biggest difference is that, in the tumult of caring for a new baby, they don't lose sight of how much they love and care for each other and that they make a conscious effort to express that love by word and by touch. Try reading poetry to each other, going for a walk together (without the baby), exchanging warm oil massages, meditating together, having a quiet meal together, and sharing lots of hugs and kisses.

CARING FOR YOUR BABY

Being companionable with your baby. Be quietly friendly with your baby whenever you are with him. He's getting a sense of how much you mean to each other all the time you're feeding him, burping him, bathing him, dressing him, changing his diapers, holding him, or just sitting in the room with him. When you hug him or make noises at him, when you show him that you think he's the most wonderful baby in the world, it makes his spirit grow, just the way milk makes his bones grow. That must be why we grown-ups instinctively talk baby talk and waggle our heads when we greet a baby, even grown-ups who are otherwise dignified or unsociable.

One trouble with being an inexperienced parent is that part of the time you take the job so seriously that you forget to enjoy it. Then you and the baby are both missing something. Naturally, I don't mean that you should be talking a blue streak at him all the time he's awake or constantly joggling or tickling him. That would tire him out and in the long run might make him tense. You can be quiet much of the time you are with him. It's the gentle, easygoing kind of companionship that's good for him and good for you. It's the comfortable feeling that goes into your arms when you hold him, the fond, peaceful expression on your face when you look at him, and the gentle tone in your voice.

Your newborn's senses. All of your baby's senses work at birth (and indeed, were working *before* birth), to different degrees. Touch and motion are already well developed, which may explain why holding, swaddling, and rocking have such a calming effect. Smell is also well developed. Babies detect odors in the amniotic fluid before birth, and very early on, they come to prefer the smell of their mothers.

Newborns can hear, but their brains process the nerve signals that represent sound slowly. If you whisper in a baby's ears, it may take several seconds before the baby responds, trying to find the source of the sound. Because of the way the inner ear develops, babies hear higher-pitched sounds better and prefer speech that is slow and musical—the way parents seem naturally to talk to them.

Babies can also see, but they are very nearsighted. Their eyes focus best at nine to twelve inches, about the distance to the mother's face when nursing at the breast. You can tell when a baby catches you with his eyes, and if you slowly move your face from side to side, his eyes may follow you. Babies prefer looking at faces. We are social creatures from the start. Babies' eyes are very sensitive to light. They tend to keep them closed in a normally lit room, opening up when the lights go down.

Your baby is an individual. Parents who have more than one child know that newborn babies have their own personalities. Some are very calm, others more excitable. Some are regular in their eating, sleeping, and bowel habits, others are irregular. Some can handle lots of stimulation, others need a quieter, darker, less busy environment. When babies are alert, with eyes open and a look of concentration on their faces, they are taking in information about the world around them. One baby stays in this alert, receptive mode for many minutes at a time; another baby shifts in and out, alternating alertness with periods of drowsiness or fussing. As you take care of your baby, you'll begin to figure out how to help keep the alert state going by providing enough talking, touching, and playing but not too much. Your baby will also become more skillful in letting you know when he wants more and when he has had enough. You begin to work as a team. This process takes place over weeks and months.

FEEDING AND SLEEPING

Feeding. There is so much to say about feeding that breast-feeding and formula feeding each have their own chapter in Section II (starting on page 242). Babies can do well with either breast milk or formula, but there are enough advantages to breast-feeding, for both baby and mother, that it's worth thinking carefully before choosing. When you feed your baby, hold her, smile at her, and talk with her, you are nurturing her body, mind, and spirit. When it's working well, feeding feels good for your baby and you. Some babies feed well right from the start; others take several days before they begin to catch on. If feeding problems last longer than a week, even with help from family members and experienced friends, it's wise to get professional help (see page 620).

Sorting out day and night. The first sleep problem many new parents face is a baby who has mixed up day and night. He seems to like to sleep more during the day; his wakeful hours tend to be at night. This shouldn't be surprising. After all, he couldn't care less whether it's night or day, so long as he's fed, cuddled, and kept warm and dry. In the womb, it was pretty dark anyway, and he never had the chance to accommodate to the day-night cycle.

For this reason, I give all parents the same advice. Play with your baby a lot during the daytime. Wake him up to feed him if the usual amount of time has elapsed since the last feeding. If you're going to play with him, do it when it's light outside. Nighttime is a different story. When you feed him after dark, do it efficiently and with less fanfare. Don't wake him to feed him when it's dark out unless there is a medical reason to do so. Let him learn very early on that daytime is fun time and nighttime is kind of low-key and boring. By two to four months, most babies have learned to be more awake during the day and to sleep for longer periods at night.

How much should a baby sleep? Parents often ask this question. Of course the baby is the only one who can answer it. One baby seems to need a lot, another surprisingly little. As long as babies are satisfied with their feedings, are comfortable, get plenty of fresh air, and sleep in a cool place, you can leave it to them to get the amount of sleep they need.

Most babies in the early months sleep from feeding to feeding if they are getting enough to eat and not having indigestion. There are a few babies, though, who are unusually wakeful right from the beginning and not because anything is wrong. If you have this kind of baby, there's nothing you need to do about it.

As babies get older they gradually stay awake for longer periods and take fewer naps during the day. You're apt to notice it first in the late afternoon. In time they become wakeful at other periods of the day. Each baby develops a personal pattern of wakefulness, tending to be awake at the same times every day.

Sleep habits. Many babies easily get used to the idea that they always go to bed and sleep right after a meal. Many other babies are very sociable after meals. You can choose which routine fits best with the schedule of the whole family.

Newborns sleep wherever they are. By about three or four months, it's a good idea for babies to get used to falling asleep in their own beds, without company (unless you plan to have your baby sleep with you for a long time). This is one way to prevent later sleep problems. A baby who expects to be held and rocked before she goes to sleep may want such comfort for months, even years. Then when she awakens in the night, she may want these pleasures again.

Babies can get accustomed to either a silent home or an average noisy one. So there is no point in tiptoeing and whispering around the house in the early days. The infant and child who, awake or asleep, is used to ordinary household noises and human voices usually sleeps right through a visit of talking and laughing friends, a radio or television tuned to a reasonable volume, even somebody's coming into the room. There are, however, certain infants who appear to be hypersensitive to sounds. They are startled easily by the least noise and appear to be happiest when it's quiet. If you have such a baby you'll probably need to keep the house quiet while she sleeps, or she will constantly wake and fuss.

Sleeping with your baby. Experts often have strong opinions about this, pro and con. I think it is a matter of personal choice. Parents and babies sleep together in many cultures around the world. A parent who is an unusually deep sleeper or is under the influence of medications, drugs, or alcohol, might roll over and smother her baby. But for most parents, I think the risk of this happening is extremely small. A much bigger risk is that the parent might not get a good night's sleep because of always being aware of the baby next to her. There is no evidence that sleeping together—or *not* sleeping together—affects a baby's physical or emotional health. So it makes sense to do what feels right and comfortable for you. If you do sleep with your baby, it's important to follow the safety precautions below.

Children can sleep in a room by themselves from the time they are born as long as the parents are near enough to hear them when they cry. An inexpensive intercom can help. If your child starts out sleeping in your room, two to three months is a good age to move her out: when she's sleeping through the night and doesn't need so much care. By six months, a child who regularly sleeps in her parents' room may become dependent on this arrangement and be unwilling to sleep anywhere else. It then often becomes harder to make the change to sleeping in a separate room, although it's never impossible.

On back or stomach? This used to be a hotly debated question. Not any more. Today's slogan is "Back to Sleep." All infants should be put to sleep on their backs (faceup) unless there is a medical reason not to do so. This simple change in sleep position from front to back has reduced the number of sudden infant death syndrome (SIDS) deaths by 50 percent. (Find out from your doctor or nurse practitioner if there is any reason for your baby to sleep on her stomach or side.)

Why the change? Many studies have now shown that the risk of SIDS is lessened when infants sleep on their backs. And sleeping faceup seems to have no adverse effects on healthy infants. Most babies easily take to sleeping on their backs if they've never gotten used to sleeping the other way. Sleeping on the side isn't as safe as sleeping on the back since side-sleeping babies often roll facedown. So from the beginning, put your baby to sleep on her back. Babies who spend all of their time lying faceup sometimes develop flat spots on the backs of their heads, so it's a good idea to give your baby time lying on her stomach *when she is awake and you are watching her.*

CHECKLIST

Sleep Safety Tips:

✔ Always put babies to sleep on their backs (faceup), unless advised otherwise by a doctor.

✔ Remove soft, fluffy blankets, pillows, crib bumpers, and other cloth items—they increase the risk of suffocation.

✔ Use a safety-approved cradle, cosleeper, or crib (see page 36). If in doubt, look for a label from a well-known testing service, such as *Consumer Reports,* or check with the U.S. Consumer Product Safety Commission (www.uspsc. gov).

✔ Avoid overdressing or overbundling your baby; overheating increases the risk of SIDS.

✔ Protect your baby from second-hand cigarette smoke, which increases the risk of SIDS, and has other harmful effects as well.

CRYING AND COMFORTING

What does all that crying mean? This is usually an important question, especially with a first baby. Crying in an infant does not have the same meaning as it does in an older child. It is the baby's main form of communication and has many meanings, not just pain or sadness. As babies grow older, crying is much less a problem because older babies cry less and parents know what to expect and worry less.

But in the first weeks, baffling questions pop into your mind: Is she hungry? Is she wet? Is she uncomfortable? Is she sick? Does she have indigestion? Is she lonely? Parents are not apt to think of fatigue, but it's one of the commonest causes.

It is fairly easy to answer some of these questions, but a lot of fretting and crying can't be so readily explained. In fact, by the time they are a couple of weeks old, almost all babies—especially first babies—get into fretful periods that we can give names to but can't explain exactly. When the crying is regularly limited to one period in the evening or afternoon, we can call it colic. Colic sometimes goes along with distension of the abdomen and the passing of gas. If the baby is fussing off and on any old time of the day or night, we can sigh and say that at this stage she is just a fretful baby. If she's unusually tense and jumpy, some use the term hypertonic baby (different from the "hyperactive" label that is often used for older children).

Fussy or inconsolable crying occurs in otherwise healthy babies all over the world during the first three months. It usually increases over the first six weeks or so, then gradually decreases. Compared with babies in the United States, babies from less-industrialized countries typically have shorter fussing bouts, but they still fuss. The period between birth and about three months is one of adjustment of the baby's immature nervous and digestive systems to life in the outside world. A smooth adjustment is harder for some babies to achieve than others.

Few things are more upsetting to a parent than a little baby who cries and cannot be comforted. So it's important to remember that excessive crying in the early weeks is usually temporary, not a sign of anything serious. If you're concerned (and who wouldn't be?), have the doctor carefully examine your baby, more than once if need be, and reassure you. The other key thing to remember—and it bears repeating—is that it is *never* safe to shake a baby to make the fussing stop. For much more on babies who cry and can't be comforted (colic), see page 98.

Sorting out the causes. It used to be thought that a good mother would learn to recognize her baby's different cries and know just how to respond. In reality, even excellent parents generally can't tell cries apart by their sounds. Instead, they figure out the cause by recognizing patterns and trying different things. Here are some possibilities to consider (and see the checklist on page 66, too):

- Is it hunger? Whether you're feeding your baby on a fairly regular schedule or according to her desire, you may get an idea of what her pattern is—at what times of day she wants more to eat, at what times is she apt to wake early. Some babies never develop a regular pattern, which makes it harder to figure out what they need at any given moment. For example, if your baby took less than half her usual amount at her last feeding, that may be the reason she's awake and crying an hour later, instead of at the usual three hours. Of course, sometimes a baby who has taken much less than her usual amount may sleep contentedly until her next regular feeding time. If she cries less than two hours after a full feeding, however, it's unlikely that it's because she's hungry.

- Does she crave sucking? The act of sucking is calming for babies, even without getting any milk or formula in return. If your baby is fussy but you think she's well fed, it's perfectly fine to offer a pacifier or encourage her to find her own fingers. Most babies suck for pleasure in the early months, then stop on their own sometime in the first or second year of life. Early sucking does not cause long-term pacifier addiction (for more on pacifiers, see 45).

- Can she have outgrown her formula or the breast-milk supply, or is the supply decreasing? A baby doesn't outgrow the milk supply all of a sudden. She will have been breast-feeding for a longer time or have been polishing off every bottle for several days, then looking around for more. She begins to wake and cry a little earlier than usual but not a lot. In most cases, it's only after she has been waking early because of hunger for a number of days that she begins to cry after a feeding.

- Does she need to be held? Young babies especially may need the physical sensations of being held and rocked in order to calm down. Some are comforted by being swaddled, wrapped up snugly in a blanket so that their arms can't move about. It may be that swaddling and rocking are comforting because they re-create the familiar sensations of being in the womb. White noise—the sound of a vacuum cleaner, a radio turned to static, or a parent saying "Shhhh"—can have a similar calming effect.

- Is she crying because she's wet or has had a bowel movement? Most babies don't seem to care, especially when they are young infants, but some act more fastidious than others. Check the diaper and try changing her. If she wears cloth diapers, check the safety pins; one may be sticking into her. This doesn't happen once in a hundred years, but you can look to be sure. Also check for hair or threads wrapped around her fingers or toes.

• Is it indigestion? The occasional baby who has a hard time digesting her milk may cry an hour or two after a feeding, when the milk is most actively being digested. If you are breast-feeding, consider changing your own diet—cutting down on milk or caffeine, for example. If you are bottle-feeding, ask your doctor or nurse practitioner if a formula change is worth a try. Some researchers find that switching to a hypoallergenic formula reduces crying in many babies; other experts disagree with this tactic unless there are other signs of allergy, such as rash and a family history of food allergies.

• Is it heartburn? Most babies spit up, some more than others. For a few, it hurts when the milk comes up, because the stomach acid irritates the esophagus (the tube from the mouth to the stomach). Babies who cry from heartburn usually do so soon after feeding, when the milk is still in the stomach. You can try burping the baby again, even if you got a burp before. If this kind of crying happens often, you should discuss it with your doctor or nurse practitioner. (The medical term for this problem is gastro-esophageal reflux disease, or GERD; see page 120.)

• Is the baby ill? Sometimes babies cry because they just aren't feeling well. Often a baby who is becoming sick first becomes very irritable, only later becoming obviously ill. Usually there will be other symptoms aside from crying—a running noise, cough or loose bowels—to tip you off that she's ill. If your baby is not only crying inconsolably but has symptoms of illness or looks different in her general appearance, behavior, or color, take her temperature and call your doctor or nurse practitioner.

- Is she spoiled? Though older babies can be spoiled, you can be sure that in the first months, your baby is not crying merely because she's spoiled. Something is bothering her.

- Is it fatigue? Some young babies seem to be made in such a way that they can never drift peacefully into sleep. Their fatigue at the end of every period of being awake produces a tension that is a sort of hump they must get over before falling asleep. They have to cry. Some of them cry frantically and loudly. Then gradually or suddenly, the crying stops, and they are asleep. Young babies may react by becoming tense and irritable when they have been awake an unusually long while, or when they have been stimulated more than usual by being with strangers, by being in a strange place, or even by being played with by their parents. Instead of it being easier for them to fall asleep, it may be harder. If the parents or strangers try to comfort them with more play, more talk, more jouncing, it only makes matters worse.

So if your baby is crying at the end of a wakeful period and after she has been fed and had her diaper changed, try assuming first that she's just tired and put her to bed. If she continues to cry, you can try leaving her on her own for a few minutes to give her a chance to settle down by herself.

Another baby who has become overfatigued may relax sooner if kept in gentle motion—by being pushed back and forth in a rocking bassinet, rocked in the carriage, or held in your arms or a carrier and walked quietly, preferably in a darkened room. It's reasonable to try walking or rocking a baby occasionally during an unusually tense spell. A baby swing is sometimes very helpful for this purpose. Some parents put their babies in a baby seat on top of the dryer and run it; the sound and vibration can be comforting. I suggest that you make sure your baby is securely belted in, and use duct tape to make sure the seat cannot vibrate off the dryer onto the floor. But you may not always want to put your baby to sleep this active way. She might become more and more dependent on it and continue to demand it. Then you're stuck. (The section on colic, beginning on page 98, has more on hard-to-comfort infants.)

CHECKLIST

Tips for Comforting a Crying Baby:

✔ Offer a feeding, or a pacifier.

✔ Change the diaper.

✔ Hold, swaddle and rock or vibrate (*never* shake).

✔ Play white noise (vacuum cleaner, radio static, or shushing).

✔ Darken the room and reduce stimulation.

✔ Reassure yourself that your baby is fine and you've done all you can. Take a break and give your baby time to calm down on her own.

DIAPERING

Cleaning your baby. It isn't necessary to wash your baby when changing a wet diaper. In cleaning your baby after a bowel movement, you can use plain water on cotton balls or a washcloth, baby lotion and tissues, or diaper wipes. Store-bought premoistened wipes are handy, but they often contain perfumes and other chemicals that can cause rashes. With girls, always wipe from front to back. For boys, put a spare diaper loosely over the penis until you're ready to fasten the diaper; this will keep you from getting sprayed if he urinates before you're done. It's nice to let the skin air dry. It's important to wash your hands with soap and water after changing the diaper to prevent the spread of harmful germs.

When to change. Most parents change the diapers when they pick their baby up for feeding and again before they put him back to bed. Parents who are very busy have found they can save time and laundry by changing only once at each feeding—usually after it, because babies frequently have a bowel movement while eating. Most babies are not bothered by being wet, but a few are extrasensitive and have to be changed more often. If children have sufficient covers over them, the wet diaper does not feel cold. It is when wet clothing is exposed to the air that evaporation makes it cold.

Disposable diapers. Most parents today choose to use disposable diapers for convenience and because they absorb more fluid. Disposables can seem dry because they absorb moisture well, but they still need changing about as often as cloth. The costs of cloth and disposable diapers are similar when a diaper service is used. Cloth diapers washed at home cost less but take a lot more work. Some families choose to use cloth diapers to reduce the consumption of wood pulp and the clogging of landfills. Not surprisingly, the manufacturers of disposables have promoted the idea that disposables aren't any worse for the environment than cloth, but their arguments have never made sense to me. Occasionally a new superabsorbent diaper splits open, releasing some of its gelling material (the stuff that soaks up the fluid). Some parents mistake this material for insects or even a rash, but it's not at all harmful.

Cloth diapers. If you use a diaper service, you'll get a bag of clean diapers delivered each week. If you wash your own, you'll need at least a couple dozen, but although you save money (the cost is less than half of a diaper service), you spend a lot of time and energy doing it. Many parents choose prefolded cloth diapers which close with Velcro. If you prefer the old-fashioned type, there are two things to remember when putting them on: Position the most cloth where there will be the most urine, and don't allow so much diaper to bunch between the legs that it keeps them widely separated.

With a full-size newborn baby, you can fold the usual large square or rectangular diapers to fit. First fold lengthwise in thirds so that there are three thicknesses. Then fold about one-third of the end over. As a result, half of the folded diaper has six layers; the other half has three. A boy needs the double thickness in front. A girl needs the thickness in front when she's lying on her belly (not to sleep, of course, but to play) and in back when she lies on her back to sleep. When you put in the pins, slip two fingers of the other hand between the baby and the diaper to

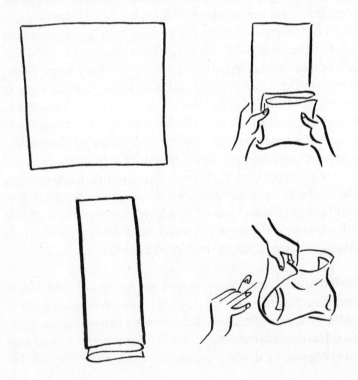

prevent sticking the child. The pins slide through the cloth more easily if you've kept them stuck into a bar of soap.

In the past, parents put their babies in waterproof plastic pants to protect the sheets (and themselves). Modern diaper wraps made out of high-tech, breathable materials allow more air to circulate around the baby's bottom (a real help in reducing moisture and the resulting rashes). But they are not 100 percent waterproof, so they tend to leak a bit. An alternative is to use two diapers. The second one can be pinned around the waist like an apron or folded into a narrow strip down the middle.

Washing diapers. You want a covered pail partially filled with water to put used diapers into as soon as they are removed. If it contains one-half cup of borax or bleach per gallon of water, this will help in removing stains. When you remove a soiled diaper, scrape the movement off into the toilet with a knife or rinse it by flushing while you hold it in the toilet (hold tight). Clean the diaper pail each time you do a diaper wash. (If you use a diaper service, of course, you just toss the diaper and its contents into the plastic pail supplied by the diaper company; the company picks up the pail and leaves you a big bag of nice clean diapers.)

Wash the diapers with mild soap or mild detergent in a washing machine or washtub (dissolve the soap well first), and rinse two or three times. The number of rinsings depends on how soon the water stays clear and on how delicate the baby's skin is. If your baby's skin isn't sensitive, two rinsings may be enough. If your baby has a tendency to develop diaper rash, you may need to take additional precautions—at least at the times the rash appears and perhaps regularly (see page 122).

If the diapers (and other clothes) are becoming hard, unabsorbent, and gray with soap deposit (the same as the ring in the bathtub) you can soften and clean them by using a water conditioner. Don't use a fabric softener—these leave a coating that reduces the cloth's absorbency.

BOWEL MOVEMENTS

Meconium. For the first day or so after birth, the baby's movements are composed of material called meconium, which is greenish-black in color and of a smooth, sticky consistency. Then they change to brown and yellow. If a baby hasn't had a movement by the end of the second day, the doctor should be notified.

The gastrocolic reflex. The bowels are apt to move soon after a meal in most babies because the filling of the stomach tends to stimulate the intestinal tract all the way down. This hookup is called the gastrocolic reflex (gastro = stomach, colic = intestines). The movement is more apt to occur after breakfast because of the resumption of stomach and intestinal activity after the long night's quiet.

Sometimes this reflex works very actively in the early months of life, especially in a breast-fed baby, who may have a movement after every nursing. More inconvenient still is the pattern of the occasional babies who strain soon after the start of each breast or bottle feeding, producing nothing but continuing to strain so hard, as long as the nipple is in their mouths, that they can't nurse. You have to let their intestines quiet down for fifteen minutes, then try again.

Breast-fed babies. A breast-fed baby may have many or few movements daily. Most have several movements a day in the early weeks. Some have a movement after every nursing. The movements are usually of a light yellow color and may be watery, pasty, or seedy, or they may have the consistency of thick cream soup. They are almost never too hard.

Many breast-fed babies change from frequent to infrequent movements by the time they are one, two, or three months old. (This occurs because breast milk is so well digested that there is little residue to make up bulk in the movements.) Some then have one movement a day, others a movement only every other day or even less often. This is apt to alarm a parent who has been brought up to believe that everyone should have a movement every day. But there is nothing to worry about so long as the baby is comfortable. The breast-fed baby's movement stays just as soft when it is passed every two or three days or even less frequently.

Bottle-fed babies. The baby who is fed commercially prepared formula usually has from one to four movements a day at first. (An occasional baby has as many as six.) As he grows older, the number tends to decrease to one or two a day. Movements in babies fed formula are most often pasty and of a pale yellow or tan color. However, some young babies always have stools that are more like soft scrambled eggs (curdy lumps with looser material in between). The number and color of the stools is not important if their consistency is good (soft but not watery) and the baby is comfortable and gaining well.

The commonest disturbance of the bowel movements of a baby on cow's milk is a tendency to hardness. See page 844 for constipation. A very few bottle-fed babies tend to have loose, green, curdy movements in the early months. If the movements are always just a little loose this can be ignored, provided the baby is comfortable, gaining well, and the doctor or nurse practitioner finds nothing wrong.

Straining with stools. Some babies who have infrequent movements begin to push and strain a lot when two or three days have gone by, yet the movement is soft when it does come out. This isn't constipation: The stools aren't hard. I think the problems arises from poor coordination. The baby is pushing out with one set of muscles and holding back with another set, so nothing happens except a lot of effort. As the baby's nervous system improves, the problem goes away.

Sometimes adding two to four teaspoons of puréed, strained

prunes to the daily diet helps make the baby's bowels more regular, even though the baby doesn't otherwise need solid food yet. There is no call for medicine and it is better not to use suppositories or enemas, lest the baby's intestines come to depend on them. Try to solve the problem with prunes or prune juice.

Changes in the movements. You can see that it doesn't matter if one baby's movements are always a little different from another baby's movements, as long as each is doing well. It's more apt to mean something and should be discussed with the doctor or nurse practitioner when the movements undergo a real change. For example, green movements can occur with both breast-fed and bottle-fed babies. If the movements are always green and the baby is doing fine, there is nothing to be concerned about. If they were previously pasty then turn lumpy, slightly looser and slightly more frequent, it may be a spell of indigestion or a mild intestinal infection. If they become definitely loose, frequent, and greenish and the smell changes, this is almost certainly due to an intestinal infection, whether mild or severe.

Generally speaking, changes in the number and consistency of the movements are more important than changes in color. A bowel movement exposed to the air may turn brown or green. This is of no importance.

Mucus in the bowel movements is common when a baby has diarrhea. It just means that the intestines are irritated. Similarly, it may occur in indigestion. It can also come from higher up—from the throat and bronchial tubes of a baby with a cold or of a healthy newborn baby—some babies form a great deal of mucus in the early weeks.

When a new vegetable is added to the diet (less frequently in the case of other foods), some of it may come through looking just the same as when it went in. If the food also causes signs of irritation, such as looseness and mucus, give much less of it the next time. If there is no irritation, you can continue the smaller amount or increase slowly until the baby's intestines learn to digest it better. Beets can turn the whole movement red.

Small streaks of blood on the outside of a bowel movement usually come from a crack, or fissure, in the anus, caused by hard bowel movements. The bleeding is not serious in itself, but the doctor should be notified so that the constipation can be treated promptly.

Larger amounts of blood in the movement are rare and may come from malformation of the intestines, severe diarrhea, or intussusception (see page 840). The doctor should be called or the child promptly taken to a hospital.

THE BATH

When to bathe. Most babies, after a few weeks' experience, have a wonderful time in the bath. So don't rush it; enjoy it with your baby. It's usually most convenient in the early months to give the bath before the midmorning feeding, but before any feeding is all right—not after, because you then want the child to go to sleep. By the time your baby is on three meals a day, you may want to change to before lunch or before supper. As the child becomes older still and stays up for a while after supper, it may be better to give the bath after supper, especially if she needs her supper early. Bathe her in a reasonably warm room, the kitchen, if necessary.

Sponge baths. Though it's the custom in the United States to give a complete tub or sponge bath every day, it certainly isn't necessary more than once or twice a week as long as the baby is kept clean in the diaper area and around the mouth. On the days when you don't give a full bath, give a sponge bath in the diaper area. A tub bath is apt to be frightening to the inexperienced parent—the baby seems so helpless, limp, and slippery, especially after having been soaped. Babies may feel uneasy in the tub at first because they can't be well supported there. You can give a sponge bath for a few weeks until you and your baby feel more secure or even longer—if you prefer. Most doctors advise avoiding tub baths until the navel is dried up. This makes sense, but nothing awful will happen if the navel gets wet.

You can give a sponge bath on a table or in your lap. You'll want waterproof material under the baby. If you are using a hard surface like a table, there should be some padding on it (a large pillow, folded blanket, or quilt) so that the baby won't roll easily. Rolling frightens young babies. Wash the face and scalp with a washcloth and clear warm water. The scalp may be soaped once or twice a week. Lightly soap the rest of the body when and where needed with the washcloth or your hand. Then wipe off the soap by going over the whole body at least twice with the rinsed washcloth, paying special attention to creases.

Getting ready for a tub bath. Before starting the bath, be sure you have everything you need close at hand. If you forget the towel, you'll have to go after it holding a dripping baby in your arms. Take off your wristwatch. An apron protects your clothes. Have at hand:

- soap
- washcloth
- towel
- absorbent cotton for nose and ears if necessary
- lotion
- shirt, diapers, pins, nightie

The bath can be given in a washbowl, dishpan, kitchen sink, or plastic tub. Some tubs have sponge cutouts to support and position the baby properly. The regular bathtub is hard on a parent's back and legs. For your own comfort, you can put a dishpan or tub on a table or on something higher, like a dresser. You can sit on a stool at the kitchen sink.

The water should be about body temperature (90 to 100 degrees). A bath thermometer is a comfort to the inexperienced parent but isn't necessary. Always test the temperature with your elbow or wrist. It should feel comfortably warm, not hot. Use only a small amount of water at first, an inch or two deep, until you get the knack of holding the baby securely. A tub is less slippery if you line it with a towel or diaper.

Giving the tub bath. Hold the baby so that her head is supported on your wrist and the fingers of that hand hold her securely in the armpit. Wash your baby's face first with a soft washcloth without soap, then wash the scalp. The scalp needs to be soaped only once or twice a week. Wipe soap suds off the scalp with a damp washcloth, going over it twice. If the washcloth is too wet, the soapy water may get into the eyes and

sting. (There are shampoos for babies that do not sting the eyes like ordinary shampoos.) Then you can use the washcloth or your hand to wash the rest of the body, arms, and legs. Wash lightly between the outer lips of the vagina. (See page 80 about washing a circumcised or uncircumcised penis.) When you use soap, it's easier to soap with your hand than a washcloth. If the skin gets dry, try omitting soap except once or twice a week.

If you feel nervous at first for fear you'll drop the baby in the water, you may soap her while she is on your lap or a table. Then rinse her off in the tub, holding her securely with both hands. Use a soft bath towel for drying, and blot rather than rub. If you begin giving tub baths before the navel is completely healed, dry it thoroughly after the bath with cotton balls.

Lotion. It's fun to apply lotion to a baby after a bath, and the baby likes it, too, but it is really not necessary in most cases. Baby lotion may be helpful when the skin is dry or there is a mild diaper rash. Baby oils and mineral oil are less often used since they sometimes cause a mild rash. Baby powder containing talcum should be avoided because it is harmful to the lungs if inhaled. Baby powder that is pure cornstarch works almost as well and is safer.

BODY PARTS

Skin. Newborn babies develop all sorts of spots and rashes, most of which go away on their own or fade enough that they become hard to see. Yet some rashes do signal a serious medical condition, so, it's sensible to ask the doctor or nurse practitioner to look at any unfamiliar rash. For more on rashes (including diaper rashes) and birthmarks, see page 84.

Ears, eyes, mouth, nose. You need to wash only the outer ear and the entrance to the canal, not inside. Use only a washcloth, not a cotton swab (which just pushes the wax further in). Wax is formed in the canal to protect and clean it. The eyes are bathed constantly by tears (not just when the baby is crying). This is why it is unnecessary to put drops in healthy eyes. The mouth ordinarily needs no extra care.

The nose has a beautiful system for keeping itself clear. Tiny invisible hairs on the cells lining the nose keep moving the mucus down toward the front of the nose, where it collects on the larger hairs near the opening. This tickles the nose and makes the baby sneeze or rub the stuff away. When you are drying the baby after the bath, moisten, then gently wipe out any ball of dried mucus with the corner of the washcloth. Don't fuss at this if it makes the baby angry.

Sometimes, especially when the house is heated, enough dried mucus collects in the noses of small infants to partially obstruct their breathing. Each time they breathe in, the lower edges of the chest are pulled inward or retracted. An older child or adult would breathe through the mouth, but most babies can't keep their mouths open. See page 782 for ways to clear a plugged-up nose.

Nails. The nails can be cut easily while the baby sleeps. Clippers may be easier than nail scissors. If you file the nails smooth, there are no sharp edges to scratch your baby's face when she waves her hands around and there is no risk of pinching or clipping her fingertips. If you sing a song while you file, nail care can become a pleasant part of your routine.

The soft spot (fontanel). The soft spot on the top of a baby's head is where the bones of the skull have not yet grown together. The size of the fontanel at birth is different in different babies. A large one is nothing to worry about, although it's bound to close more slowly than a small one. Some fontanels close as early as nine months; some slow ones not till two years. The average is twelve to eighteen months.

Parents worry unnecessarily about touching the soft spot. It is covered by a membrane as tough as canvas, and there is no risk of hurting a baby there with ordinary handling. When the light is right, you can see that the fontanel pulsates at a rate between the breathing rate and the beat of the heart.

The navel. In the womb, the baby is nourished through the blood vessels of the umbilical cord. Just after birth, the doctor ties the cord and cuts it off close to the baby's body. The stump that's left dries up and eventually drops off, usually in about two to three weeks, though it may take longer.

When the cord falls off, it leaves a raw spot, which takes a number of days or weeks to heal over. The raw spot should merely be kept clean and dry so that it doesn't get infected. If it is kept dry, a scab covers it until it is healed. It doesn't need a dressing and will stay drier without one. Once the cord falls off, the baby can have tub baths. Just dry the navel afterward with a corner of the towel, or cotton balls if you like, until it is all healed. There may be a little bleeding or drainage a few days before the cord falls off and until the healing is complete. If the scab on the unhealed navel gets pulled by clothing, there may be a drop or two of blood. This amount is of no importance.

It is wise to keep the diaper below the level of the unhealed navel so that it doesn't keep the navel wet. If the unhealed navel becomes moist and produces a discharge, it should be protected more carefully from constant wetting by the diaper, and the skin fold around the cord should be cleaned each day with a cotton swab dampened with alcohol. If healing is slow, the raw spot may become lumpy with what's called granulation tissue, but this is of no importance. The doctor may apply a chemical that will hasten drying and healing.

If the navel and the surrounding skin become red, there is a smelly discharge, or both, infection may be present. You should get in touch with your doctor or nurse practitioner right away, because these infections can be serious.

The penis. The foreskin is a sleeve of skin that covers the head (glans) of the penis when the baby is born. The open end of the foreskin is large enough to let the baby's urine out but small enough to protect the tip of the penis from diaper rash. (See page 847 about sores on the end of the penis.) As the baby grows, the foreskin normally begins to separate from the glans and becomes retractable. It usually takes about three years for this separation and retractability to become complete. It may take longer for some boys, even until adolescence, to have a fully retractable foreskin, but this is no cause for concern. Routine washing, even without retracting the foreskin, will keep the penis clean and healthy.

At the end of the baby's foreskin you may see a white, waxy material (smegma). This is perfectly normal. Smegma is secreted by the cells on the inside of the foreskin as a natural lubricant between the foreskin and the glans.

Circumcision. When a penis is circumcised, the foreskin is cut off, leaving the head of the penis exposed. Circumcisions are usually done within the first week of life. The exact origins of circumcision are unknown, but it has been practiced for at least four thousand years, in many parts of the world and for many reasons. To Jews and Muslims, it has religious significance. In some cultures, circumcision is a puberty rite, marking a boy's passage to adulthood.

In the United States, circumcision has commonly been performed for other reasons. Some parents worry that it will upset their uncircumcised son to look different from his circumcised father or older brothers. Many doctors believe that the normal accumulation of smegma under the foreskin may cause occasional mild inflammation or infection, although routine washing seems to be just as effective as circumcision in preventing these problems. Scientists used to think that the wives of uncircumcised men were more likely to get cervical cancer, but modern research has disproved this. Uncircumcised boys tend to get slightly more bladder or kidney infections in childhood than circumcised boys. Most doctors now agree that there is no medical justification for routine circumcision, and the number of circumcisions has dropped over the past decade.

If you are considering circumcision, you should know that it's a safe operation. There are some risks from the procedure, such as bleeding or infection, which usually can be easily treated. Circumcision is clearly painful, so many doctors now use local anesthesia (numbing shots) or other methods of pain relief. In general, babies recover from the stress of the operation in about twenty-four hours. If your baby seems to be uncomfortable for longer than this or if there is persistent oozing of blood or swelling of his penis, report it to your doctor promptly. A spot of blood or several spots on successive diaper changes merely means that a small scab has been pulled off.

Penis care. Good genital hygiene is important from birth on, whether the penis is circumcised or not. It's part of children's learning general habits of personal cleanliness. If the baby isn't circumcised, the penis should be washed whenever the baby is given a bath. You don't have to do anything special to the foreskin; just a gentle washing around the outside of it will remove any excess accumulation of smegma. Some parents may want to be extra sure that the foreskin and glans are as clean as possible. In this case, you can clean beneath the foreskin by pushing it back very gently, just until you meet resistance. Never forcibly retract the foreskin. This hurts and may lead to infections or other complications. The foreskin will become more retractable by itself over time.

If the baby is circumcised, change his diaper often while the wound is healing. This will lessen the chance of irritation from his urine and bowel movements. During this healing time, about a week, follow your doctor's advice on taking care of the baby's penis: what to do about the bandage, bathing and drying, and using an ointment or lotion. After the wound has healed, wash the penis just as you do the rest of the baby.

It is common for boy babies to have erections of the penis, especially when the bladder is full or during urination or for no apparent reason. This has no importance.

TEMPERATURE, FRESH AIR, AND SUNSHINE

Room temperature. A room temperature of 65 to 68 degrees for eating and playing is right for babies weighing over five pounds, just as it is for older children and adults. Smaller babies have a harder time controlling their body temperature and may therefore need to be kept warmer and dressed in extra layers. Very small babies control their body temperature best when they are held in contact with a parent. Avoid the cold or hot drafts from an air conditioner or heat vent.

In cold weather, the air outside contains very little moisture. When this air is heated in a house it acts like a dry sponge, sucking up moisture from the skin and nose. Dried mucus makes it hard for babies to breathe and may lower their resistance to infections. Any source of moisture can help: house plants, pans of water on the radiators, or humidifiers (see page 819). The warmer the room temperature, the more drying the air becomes.

The problem of providing sufficiently cool air for a baby is further complicated by the inexperienced parents' natural anxiety and protectiveness. They tend to keep their baby too well covered in a room that is too hot. Under these conditions some babies develop heat rash even in winter. Overheating also increases the risk of crib death.

How much clothing. A normal baby has as good an internal thermostat as an adult as long as he isn't put into so many layers of clothing and covering that his thermostat doesn't work properly. Babies and children who are reasonably plump need less covering than adults. More babies are overdressed than underdressed. This isn't good for them. If a person is always too warmly dressed, the body loses its ability to adjust to changes and is more likely to become chilled. So in general, put on too little rather than too much, then watch the baby. Don't put on enough to keep the hands warm; most babies' hands stay cool when they are comfortably dressed. Feel the legs or arms or neck. The best guide is the color of the face. Babies who are getting cold lose the color from their cheeks, and they may begin to fuss, too.

In cold weather a warm cap is essential, because babies lose lots of their body heat from their heads. A cap in which to sleep in very cold weather should be of knitted acrylic, so that if it slips over the face the baby can breathe through it.

When putting on sweaters and shirts with small openings, re-member that a baby's head is more egg-shaped than ball-shaped. Gather the sweater into a loop, slip it first over the back of the baby's head, then forward, stretching it forward as you bring it down past the forehead and nose. Then put the baby's arms into the sleeves. When taking it off, pull the baby's arms out of the sleeves first. Gather the sweater into a loop as it lies around the neck. Raise the front part of the loop up past the nose and forehead while the back of the loop is still at the back of the neck, then slip it off toward the back of the head.

Practical coverings. It is better to use all-acrylic blankets or bags when a baby is sleeping in a cool room (60 to 65 degrees). They have the best combination of warmth and washability. Knitted shawls tuck and wrap more easily than woven blan-kets, especially when the baby is up, and because they are thin-ner you can adjust the amount of covering to the temperature more exactly than you can with thick blankets. Avoid coverings that are heavy, such as solid-feeling quilts. In a warm room (over 72 degrees) or in warm weather, a baby really needs only cotton covering. All blankets, quilts, and sheets should be large enough to tuck securely under the mattress, so that they will not work loose and pose a suffocation hazard.

Fresh air. Changes of air temperature help tone up the body's system for adapting to cold or heat. A bank clerk is much more likely to become chilled staying outdoors in winter than a lumberjack, who is used to such weather. A baby living continuously in a warm room usually has a pasty complexion and may have a sluggish appetite. An eight-pounder can certainly go out when it's 60 degrees Fahrenheit or above. The temperature of the air is not the only factor. Moist, cold air is more chilling than dry air of the same temperature, and wind is the greatest chiller. Even when the temperature is cooler, a twelve-pound baby may be comfortable in a sunny, sheltered spot if dressed appropriately.

If you live in a city and have no yard to park your baby in, you can push the child in a carriage. If you get in the habit of carrying the baby in a carrier on your chest or back, you will be wonderfully conditioned as the baby gets bigger. Your baby will love riding in close contact with you and be able to look around or sleep. If you enjoy being out and can afford the time, the more the better.

✍ CLASSIC SPOCK

It's good for a baby (as for anyone else) to get outdoors for two to three hours a day, particularly during the season when the house is heated. I grew up and practiced pediatrics in the northeastern part of the United States, where most conscientious parents took it for granted that babies and children should be outdoors two to three hours a day. Children love to be outdoors, and it gives them pink cheeks and good appetites. So I can't help but believe in the tradition.

Sunshine and sunbathing. The body needs sunlight to make active vitamin D. But even if babies can't spend time in a sunny room or outside, they can still get all the vitamin D they need from their formula or from vitamin drops (see page 239). Unfortunately, sunlight also exposes children to ultraviolet (UV) rays, which can result in skin cancer years later. Infants are especially vulnerable, because their skin is thin and contains relatively little melanin, the pigment that protects against UV damage. Babies with dark skin are safer; those with pale skin and blond or red hair are most at risk. Beaches, pools, and boats are especially hazardous, because the UV rays are reflected up from the water as well as coming down from above.

Dermatologists recommend that children and adults use sunscreen, either cream or lotion, with a sun protection factor of at least 15; higher for those with more sun-sensitive skin. Sunscreens are safe for infants, but a baby who will be in the sun for more than a few minutes should be covered up: a hat with a wide brim, made from a material that will block the sun's rays, and long-sleeved pants and top. Even with those precautions, a fair-skinned baby should not sit poolside for a long time, since the reflected rays are also damaging. (See page 750 for more on sun protection.) Sunbathing—exposure to UV light to get a tan—is unhealthy at any age.

COMMON NEWBORN CONCERNS

Birthmarks. It's the rare newborn who does not have one or more birthmarks. Doctors, who see these all the time, may not remember to reassure parents about spots that have no medical significance and are destined to fade in time. So if you have questions, be sure to ask them.

Stork bites and angel's kisses. Many babies have a collection of red, irregularly shaped spots on the nape of the neck (stork bites), upper eyelids (angel's kiss), or between the eyebrows when they are born. These birthmarks are nests of little blood vessels that have grown because of exposure to the mother's hormones in the womb. Most disappear gradually (stork bites may persist), and nothing needs to be done for them.

Port-wine stains. Areas of skin that are flat with a deep purplish-red coloring may occur on the temples and cheeks or other parts of the body. Some of these stains do fade, particularly the lighter ones; others are permanent. Laser treatments are now used for some of the larger permanent port-wine stains. Occasionally this rash is associated with other problems.

Hyperpigmented spots. These slate-blue patches used to be called Mongolian spots, but they occur in babies of all nationalities, especially those with darker skin. They often occur around the buttocks but may be scattered anywhere. They are simply areas of increased pigment in the top layer of the skin and almost always disappear completely in the first two years.

Moles. Moles can be of all sizes and be smooth or hairy. All moles should be checked by your doctor or nurse practitioner, especially if the mole starts to grow or change color. Most are entirely benign, though a few have the potential for cancerous transformation later in life. They can be removed surgically if they are potentially dangerous, disfiguring, or irritated by clothing.

Strawberry marks and cavernous hemangiomas. Strawberry marks are fairly common though they usually show up later in the first year of life. They start as pale areas, then over time change into raised marks of an intense, deep-crimson color that look very much like the outside of a shiny strawberry. These marks usually grow for a year or so, then stop and shrink until they disappear. Generally, half are completely gone by age five, 70 percent by age seven, and 90 percent by nine years. Medical treatment with lasers or surgery is occasionally necessary, but it's best if you can just let nature take its course. Ask your doctor. Cavernous hemangiomas are fairly large blue-and-red marks caused by a collection of distended veins deep in the skin. They may disappear completely on their own. They can be removed if necessary.

Sucking blisters. Some babies are born with blisters on their lips, hands or wrists. They are caused by finger-sucking in the womb. Other babies develop white dry blisters in the middle part of their lips from sucking. Sometimes the blisters peel. Sucking blisters clear up in time with no special treatment.

Blue fingers and toes. The hands and feet of many newborns look blue, especially if they are at all cool. Some babies with pale skin also show a bluish mottling all over their bodies when undressed. These color changes are caused by slow blood circulation in the skin and are not a sign of illness. Babies often have bluish lips. Blueness of the gums or the skin around the mouth sometimes signals low blood oxygen, especially if there is also difficulty breathing or feeding. If you see this, call your doctor or nurse practitioner.

Jaundice. Many newborn babies develop jaundice, a yellow tinge of their skin and eyes. The yellow color is from a substance called bilirubin, which is produced when red blood cells are broken down. Usually the bilirubin is taken up by the liver and passed in the stools (giving them their brownish-yellowish color). The liver of newborn babies, however, is still immature, and the intestines may not be very active for the first few days, so the bilirubin remains in the blood and makes the skin yellow.

A little jaundice is very common. It goes away over the first few days and causes no problems whatsoever. In rare cases, when the production of bilirubin is especially rapid or the liver is especially slow to respond, the bilirubin level can climb to dangerous levels. It's easy to measure bilirubin levels in a drop of blood, and treatment with special lights (that cause the bilirubin to break down) keeps the bilirubin in the safe range. If your baby seems yellow in the first week of life, have the doctor or nurse practitioner take a look.

Sometimes jaundice persists beyond the first week or two.

This usually occurs in a baby who is breast-feeding. Some doctors recommend stopping breast-feeding altogether for a day or two. Others recommend continuing or even increasing breast-feeding. In either case, the baby invariably does well. Very rarely, persistent jaundice signifies a chronic problem of the liver, a condition that needs to be diagnosed through special tests.

Breathing problems. New parents usually worry some about a new baby's breathing because it is often irregular and at times so shallow that they can't hear it or see it. They may worry, too, the first time they hear their baby snoring faintly. Both of these conditions are normal. If anything concerns you about your baby's breathing, however, it's always right to ask the doctor or nurse practitioner.

Umbilical hernia. After the skin of the navel heals over, there is often still an opening in the deeper, muscular layer of the abdomen where the umbilical vessels passed through. When the baby cries, a small part of the intestine is pushed through this hole (umbilical ring), making the navel puff out somewhat. This is called an umbilical hernia. When the ring is small, the protrusion of the hernia is never much larger than a pea and the ring closes over in a few weeks or months. When the ring is large, the protrusion may be larger than a cherry and it may take months or even years to close.

It used to be thought that the closing of the umbilical ring could be hastened by putting a tight strap of adhesive and a coin across the navel to keep it from poking out. Actually, that doesn't make any difference. Keeping the baby from crying is impossible and also doesn't help. Umbilical hernias almost never cause any trouble, as other hernias sometimes do, and time almost always does the trick. If an umbilical hernia is still large at six to eight years and shows no decrease, surgical repair may be recommended. Very rarely, a hard and tender swelling develops at the site of an umbilical hernia. This condition needs prompt medical attention (but it is very, very rare).

Swollen breasts. Many babies, both boys and girls, have swollen breasts for some time after birth. In some cases a little milk runs out (this used to be called witches' milk, although I can't imagine why). The breast swelling and milk are the result of hormones that passed in the womb from the mother to the baby. Nothing needs to be done for this condition, as the swelling will surely disappear in time. The breasts should not be massaged or squeezed, since this is likely to irritate them and may lead to infection.

Vaginal discharge. At birth, girl babies often have a vaginal discharge of white, thick, sticky mucus. This condition is caused by the mother's hormones (the same ones that can cause a baby to have swollen breasts) and goes away on its own without treatment. At a few days of age, many girl babies have a little bit of bloody discharge. This is similar to a period and is caused by the withdrawal of maternal hormones after delivery. It usually lasts only a day or so. If a bloody discharge persists after the first week, have it checked out by your doctor or nurse practitioner.

Undescended testicles. In a certain number of newborn boys, one or both testicles are not in the scrotum (the pouch in which the testicles are normally contained) but are farther up in the groin or even inside the abdomen. Many of these undescended testicles come down into the scrotum soon after birth.

It's easy to be fooled into thinking a testicle is undescended. The testicles are originally formed inside the abdomen and move down into the scrotum only shortly before birth. There are muscles attached to the testicles that can jerk them back up into the groin or even back into the abdomen. This is to protect the testicles from injury when this region of the body is struck or scratched. There are lots of boys whose testicles withdraw on slight provocation. Even chilling of the skin when undressed may be enough to make them disappear into the abdomen. Handling the scrotum in an examination frequently makes them disappear. Therefore, a parent shouldn't decide that the testicles are undescended just because they are not usually in sight. A good time to look for them is when the boy is in a warm bath. Testicles that have been seen at any time in the scrotum, even if only rarely, need no treatment; they will surely settle down in the scrotum by the time puberty is under way.

If one or both testicles has never been seen in the scrotum by the time a boy is nine to twelve months old, he should be examined by a competent pediatric surgeon. If one or both are found to be truly undescended, surgery can often correct the problem, saving the testicles' function.

Startles and jittery movements. Newborn babies are startled by loud noises and sudden changes in position. Some are much more sensitive than others. When you put these babies on a hard surface and they jerk their arms and legs, it's likely to rock their bodies a little. This unexpected motion is enough to make sensitive babies nearly jump out of their skins and cry with fright. They may hate the bath because they are held so loosely. They need to be washed in their parent's lap then rinsed in the tub while held securely in both hands. They should be held firmly and moved slowly at all times. They gradually get over this uneasiness as they grow older.

The trembles. Some babies have trembly or jittery moments in the early months. The chin may quiver or the arms and legs may tremble, especially when the baby is excited or is cool just after being undressed. This trembling is usually nothing to be disturbed by. It is just one of the signs that the baby's nervous system is still young. The tendency passes away in time.

Twitching. Some babies twitch occasionally in their sleep; once in a while there is one who twitches frequently. This, too, usually disappears as the baby grows older. Mention it to the doctor or nurse practitioner as something to check.

THE FIRST YEAR,
FOUR TO TWELVE MONTHS

A TIME OF FIRSTS

Discoveries in the first year. If the first three months of life are about getting basic systems working smoothly, months four through twelve are about discovery. Infants discover their own bodies and gain control of muscles large and small. They explore the world of things and begin to figure out the fundamentals of cause and effect. And they learn to read other people's feelings and predict how their own actions will affect those feelings. These momentous discoveries take infants to the very threshold of language. Some cross that threshold before their first birthday, others cross it some time later.

The meaning of milestones. Doctors tend to focus on easy-to-see milestones: rolling over, sitting up, standing, walking. It's true that a baby who is very late starting these may have developmental problems. But many healthy children are early, many are late, and the timing turns out not to be very important. More meaningful are the milestones that mark the child's connection with other people: smiling in response to being smiled at, listening when talked to, paying close attention to a parent's face to see if a new situation is safe, and noticing whether a parent is pleased or displeased. Parents are usually tuned into these social milestones, even though they may not keep track of them as they do the sitting-standing-walking ones.

Along with timing, pay attention to the *quality* of your baby's behavior. One child prefers to sit and watch, taking everything in but doing relatively little; another is constantly active, impatient to move, and quick to lose interest. One seems constantly alert to every small change; another is blissfully unaware. One is serious, another is bubbly. These are all perfectly fine ways for a baby to be, but they call for different input from parents. (See "What Children Need" in Section III for more on temperament.)

✍ CLASSIC SPOCK

There are developmental timetables you can consult to see if your child is doing exactly what she is "supposed" to be doing and when she is supposed to be doing it. For fifty years I have resisted putting such developmental timetables in this book. First off, every baby and child's pattern of development is different from every other child's. One may be very advanced in her general body strength and coordination—a sort of infant athlete. And yet she may be slow in doing skillful things with her fingers or in talking. Children who turn out later to be smart in schoolwork may have been very slow to talk in the beginning. Likewise, children of average talent may have shown advanced early development.

I think it's a big mistake to obsessively note exactly when every developmental milestone is achieved compared with the "average" baby. What is most important is that the child's general pattern is a progressively forward one. Besides, development tends to go in forward spurts and backward slides. There is often a backward slide just before a forward move. Parents should not become alarmed when there are small regressions, any more than they should try to speed up those developmental attainments. There is no evidence that making a concerted effort to teach a child to walk or talk or read early has any real long-term benefit, and it could cause some problems as well as frustrate parents. Children need an environment that allows for the next developmental achievement but doesn't push the child into it.

CARING FOR YOUR BABY

Companionship without spoiling. It's good for a baby in his play periods to be somewhere near his parents (and brothers and sisters, if any) so that he can see them, make noises at them, hear them speak to him, occasionally have them show him a way to play with something. But it isn't necessary or sensible for him to be in a parent's lap or arms or to have his mother or father amusing him for the majority of the time. He can be enjoying their company, profiting from it, and still be learning how to occupy himself. When new parents are so delighted with their baby that they are holding him or making games for him most of his waking hours, he may become dependent on these attentions and demand more and more of them.

Things to watch and things to play with. As they grow older, young babies increasingly spend more time awake. At such times they want something to do, and they want some companionship. At two, three, and four months, they enjoy looking at bright-colored things and things that move, but mostly they enjoy looking at people and their faces. Outdoors, they are delighted to watch leaves and shadows. Indoors, they study their hands and pictures on the wall. There are bright-colored crib toys that you can suspend between the top rails of the crib. Place them just within arm's reach—not right on top of a baby's nose—for the time when they begin reaching. You can make mobiles yourself—cardboard shapes covered with colored paper that hang from the ceiling or a lighting fixture and rotate in slight drafts (they aren't strong enough for playing with or healthful for chewing)—or you can hang suitable household objects within reach—spoons or plastic cups, for instance. (Be careful to keep any strings short so they can't become strangulation hazards if your baby pulls them down.) All of these toys are nice, but never forget that it is human companionship, above all else, that babies love and that particularly fosters their development.

Remember that everything eventually goes into the mouth. As babies get toward the middle of their first year, their greatest joy is handling and mouthing objects: collections of plastic objects linked together (made for this age), rattles, teething rings, animals and dolls of cloth, household objects (make sure they are safe in the mouth). Don't let a baby or small child have objects or furniture that have been repainted with paint containing lead, thin plastic toys that can be chewed into small, sharp pieces, or small glass beads and other small objects that can be choked on.

FEEDING AND GROWTH

Feeding decisions. Feeding in the first year is a big enough topic that it has its own chapter (starting on page 219). Here it's enough to mention some of the main themes. The American Academy of Pediatrics urges mothers to breast-feed for the first twelve months at least. Still, six months is probably long enough to give your baby most of the biological benefits of breast milk, and *any* amount of time is better than none.

Infant formulas can be made from either cow's milk or soy beans. Neither has a clear-cut advantage over the other, although experts disagree on this point. Homemade formulas and low-iron formulas generally don't provide adequate nutrition. Cow's milk isn't recommended for babies under twelve months, and there is debate about the value of cow's milk altogether (see page 285 for formulas and page 285 for dairy foods).

Most parents introduce solid foods around four months of age, starting with iron-fortified cereals and gradually adding vegetables, fruits, and meats. It's reasonable to wait a week or so before adding a new food to see whether your baby has tolerated the last item without stomach upset or a rash. There's no rush, but babies are more likely to accept new foods that are introduced during the first year or so of life than later.

Mealtime behavior. This can be difficult for many parents because babies love to play with food. Slinging squash and poking peas is an important way babies find out about the physical world; teasing and provoking parents is an important way they learn about the world of relationships. Parents need to share in the fun but also set appropriate limits ("You can pick up your mashed potatoes, but if you throw them, dinner is over"). You know that feeding is going well if both you and your baby come away feeling happy. If mealtimes regularly leave you tense, worried, or angry, it's time to make a change. A good place to start is by talking with your baby's doctor.

Around nine months, a baby may start showing signs of independence in feeding. He wants to hold the spoon himself, and he turns his head to the side if you try to do it for him. This behavior is often the first sign that the baby is developing a will of his own, a development that will continue full force in the coming years. (A good way to handle the spoon issue, by the way, is to give your baby one spoon to hold and use as best he can while you use a second spoon to actually get some oatmeal in his mouth.)

Growth. Babies roughly double their birth weight by about four months and triple it by a year. Doctors usually plot children's weight, length, and head size on growth charts that give the average and normal range for each age. These charts can be reassuring: A healthy growth pattern is a good sign that your baby is getting enough food (but not too much) and that other body systems are working well. Occasionally I feel I have to discourage a parent from focusing too much on the numbers. Bigger is not necessarily better, and while a growth curve at the 95th percentile means that a child is likely to be one of the largest in his preschool class, it doesn't mean much more than that.

SLEEPING

Bedtime rituals. Many adults have comforting bedtime routines: We like our pillow just right and the covers to fit a certain way. Babies are just the same. If they learn to sleep only while being held, that may become the only way they can get to sleep.

If, on the other hand, they learn to put themselves to sleep, they can also do so in the middle of the night and save their parents a lot of sleepless nights. So I recommend that once your baby is three or four months old, you try to put her to bed while she's awake and let her learn to go to sleep on her own. You'll be glad when she begins to gets herself back to sleep after awakening at night. (For more on babies who refuse to go to sleep, see page 98.)

Early waking. Some parents like to get up with the sun and enjoy early mornings with their babies. But if you prefer to sleep, you probably can train your baby to sleep later or at least be happy in bed in the morning. In the middle part of the first year, most babies become willing to sleep later than the uncivilized hour of 5 or 6 A.M. However, most parents have developed such a habit of listening for their babies in their sleep and jumping out of bed at the first murmur that they never give the children a chance to go back to sleep. As a result, parents may find themselves still getting up before 7 A.M. when the child is two or three years old. And a child who has been used to company so early for so long will demand it.

Sleep bags and sleepers. By six months, when babies can move about in their cribs, most parents find it more practical to put them to bed in sleep bags or sleepers than to try to keep blankets over them. (They simply crawl out from under the covers.) The bags are shaped like long nighties that cover the feet and have sleeves. Many can be let out in the length and shoulders as the child grows. The sleepers are shaped like coveralls or snowsuits and enclose each leg separately, including the foot. (The sole of the foot may be of tough, nonskid material.) It is most convenient when the zipper goes from neck to foot. Check the insides of the feet regularly. They can collect hair, which can wind around the baby's toes and be painful.

If a baby or child is going to sleep in a room warm enough that *you* would be comfortable wearing a cotton shirt or sleeping under a cotton blanket, the baby's bag or sleeper shouldn't be warmer than cotton blanketing. If the room is cold enough that an adult would require a good wool or acrylic blanket for covering, the baby will need a heavier bag or sleeper and a blanket.

Changes in sleep. By about four months, most babies do most of their sleeping at night, perhaps waking up once or twice, and nap two or three times a day. Toward the end of the first year, most babies are down to two naps a day. The total amount of sleep varies from baby to baby. Some sleep as little as ten to eleven hours total, others as much as fifteen to sixteen. Total sleep time gradually decreases over the first year.

Around nine months of age, many babies who have been good sleepers start waking up and demanding attention. This change occurs at about the same time that babies discover that a toy or other object that disappears under a cloth actually still exists. Psychologists call this intellectual breakthrough "object permanence." From the baby's point of view, it means that out of sight is no longer out of mind. (You know your baby is developing object permanence when you can't just take things away anymore: If you hide them behind your back, your baby keeps reaching for them.)

The same thing happens in the middle of the night: When your baby wakes up and finds herself alone, she now knows that you are nearby even if out of sight, so she cries for company.

Sometimes a simple "Go to sleep" will be enough to resettle a baby; at other times you might need to pick your baby up to re-

assure her that you really are there. If you put her back down before she is completely asleep, she has the chance to practice getting back to sleep on her own.

Sleep problems. Many babies develop problems falling or staying asleep. These problems often start with a minor illness, such as a cold or ear infection, and may last long after the infection has cleared up. Parents who are away at work all day sometimes find it hard to say good night in the evening. I often hear "When I get home at seven and she goes to sleep at eight, we don't have any time together." It strikes me that here the baby's sleeplessness is not so much a problem as a solution. Still, a baby who fights going to sleep or wakes up time after time puts a terrible strain on parents and is pretty miserable herself. A long section on sleep problems and what you can do about them starts on page 145.

CRYING AND COLIC

Normal crying versus colic. All babies cry and fret sometimes, and it's usually not too hard to figure out why. The section **Cry-**

ing and Comforting (starting on page 61) also applies to babies through the first year of life. Crying tends to increase until about six to eight weeks old; then, mercifully, it begins to diminish. By three to four months, most babies fuss for a total of about an hour a day.

For some babies, however, the crying just goes on and on, hour after hour, week after week, no matter what the well-meaning, frantic parents do. A standard definition of colic is inconsolable crying for more than three hours a day for more than three days a week and for more than three weeks. In reality, any crying, screaming, or fussing that lasts much longer than expected in an otherwise healthy baby who has no apparent reason to cry qualifies as colic. Colic means pain from the intestines, but it's not at all clear that this is the cause of crying in these infants.

There seem to be two distinct patterns of crying by infants with colic. For some, the crying is generally limited to one period in the evening—typically five to eight. The infant is contented and easy to soothe for most of the day; then when evening rolls around, the trouble begins. He cries, sometimes inconsolably, for the next few hours. This raises a question: What happens in the early evening that makes him so fretful? If it were indigestion, for example, he would have it any time of day, not just in the evening. Other infants cry at any and all times of day or night. Some of these infants also seem to be generally tense and jumpy. Their bodies don't relax well. They are easily startled or cry at slight noises or on any quick change of position. If, for instance, a baby is laid on his back on a firm surface and rolls to one side, is held too loosely in the arms, or the person carrying him moves him suddenly, he may almost jump out of his skin. He may hate a tub bath for the first couple of months for this reason.

Responding to colic. It's hard on the parents of a fretful, hypertonic, colicky, or irritable baby. If your baby is colicky or irritable, she may be soothed when you first pick her up. But after a few minutes she's apt to be screaming harder than ever. She thrashes with her arms and kicks with her legs. She not only refuses to be comforted; she acts as if she is angry at you for trying. These reactions are painful for you. You feel sorry for her, at least in the beginning. Then you feel increasingly inadequate because you're not able to do anything to relieve her. As the minutes go by and she acts angrier and angrier, you feel that she is spurning you as a parent and underneath you can't help feeling mad at her. But being angry at a tiny baby makes you ashamed of yourself, and you try hard to suppress the feeling. This makes you tenser than ever.

There are various things you can try to help the situation, but I think you first have to come to terms with your feelings. All parents feel anxious, upset, fearful, and incompetent if they can't calm their infant. Most feel guilty, especially if it is their first baby, as if the baby is crying because they have done something wrong (not true). And most parents also get angry at the baby. This is normal. There is no doubt that this squalling creature is turning your life upside down, and it's natural to feel some resentment and anger even if you know that it's not really your baby's fault, that he's not crying on purpose, that he's not really mad at you. Some parents then feel guilty about their angry feelings, as if somehow they are even worse parents because they have these negative feelings. So the first step in dealing with a colicky infant is to come to terms with your feelings about it. You may still experience the same feelings, but at least you will have some awareness that you are feeling them, and you'll know that all parents go through the same thing.

Never shake a baby. Feelings of desperation and anger drive some parents to shake their babies in a last-ditch effort to get them to stop crying. But the result—a real tragedy—is often severe, permanent brain damage, even death. Before you get to the point where shaking feels like a solution, get help. Your baby's doctor is a good place to start. Most cities and towns also have parent-support hotlines that you can call at any hour of the day or night (call 411 or look in the community services listings in the phone book). It's also important to make sure that any other adults who take care of your child know that shaking a baby is never safe.

Medical evaluation. If you have a baby with colic, the first thing to do is have her checked by the doctor or nurse practitioner to make sure there is no obvious medical cause for the crying. It can be very reassuring if a baby is growing and developing normally and has had a careful physical examination; sometimes repeated doctor visits are necessary. (A colicky baby who is *not* growing normally deserves a very thorough medical evaluation.)

Once you know that your baby has "just" colic, you can rest assured that colicky babies don't grow up to be any less happy, smart, or emotionally healthy than other babies. The trick for you is to get through the next few months with your confidence and good spirits intact.

Help for your baby. In consultation with your doctor or nurse practitioner, here are some other things to try with colicky infants (also see page 61, Crying and Comforting, and pages 269 and 270). All of these approaches work some of the time; none works all of the time. Offering a pacifier between feedings (in the immortal words of one pediatrician, "if only to obstruct the orifice from which the cacophonous sound emanates"); swaddling the baby snugly in a receiving blanket; rocking her in a cradle or carriage; using a front carrier for long walks; taking her for a ride in the car; a swing (although most infants get bored and resume crying after a few minutes); giving her a belly massage (with lubricating lotion); placing a hot-water bottle on her belly; herbal tea, a formula change, or, if you're breast-feeding, a change in your diet (for example, no milk or caffeine); or playing music. You can also try laying her across your knees or a hot-water bottle and massaging her the back. The bottle should not be so hot that you cannot rest the inside of your wrist against it without discomfort. Then, as an extra precaution, wrap the bottle in a diaper or towel before laying the baby against or on it.

Hypertonic babies often do best on a quiet regime: a quiet room, few visitors, low voices, slow movements in handling them, a firm hold in carrying them, a big pillow (with a waterproof cover) to lie on while being changed and sponge-bathed so that they won't roll, or swaddling in a receiving blanket most of the time.

If none of these methods work and the baby is not hungry, wet, or sick, then what? I think it's perfectly acceptable to put the baby down in his crib, let him cry for a while, and see if he will calm himself. It's hard to listen to a crying infant without trying to do something, but, realistically, what else is there for you to do except maybe acquire hearing loss from his crying into your ear? Some parents will go out for a little walk and let the baby cry; others can't bear to leave the room. Do whatever feels right for you; there is simply no right or wrong way to handle this situation. After a period of time, if your baby is still crying, pick her up again and try everything all over again.

Help for yourself. You should also ask what you can do for yourself. You may be the kind of parent who isn't bothered too much after you have found out that there is nothing seriously wrong with your baby and after you have done all that you can to make her happy. That's fine, if you are made that way. But many parents get worn out and frantic listening to a baby cry, especially when it's the first. It may be especially difficult if you are constantly with your baby. It can really help to get away from home and the baby for a few hours at least twice a week, more often if it can be arranged. It's best if the parents can go out together. Hire a sitter or ask a friend or neighbor to come to relieve you.

If you're like many other parents, you may hesitate to do this. "Why should we inflict the baby on somebody else? Besides, we'd be nervous being away for so long." But you shouldn't think of time off like this as just a treat for you. It's very important for you, for the baby, and for your spouse that you not get exhausted and depressed. If you can't get anyone to come in, perhaps you can take turns one or two evenings a week to go out to visit friends or see a movie. Your baby doesn't need two worried parents at a time to listen to her. Try also to get friends to come visit you. Remember that everything that helps you keep a sense of balance, everything that keeps you from getting too preoccupied with the baby, also helps the baby and the rest of the family in the long run. Also, even though it may seem awkward, remember to make sure that whoever watches your baby knows never to shake a baby.

SPOILING

Can you spoil a baby? This question comes up naturally in the first few weeks at home if a baby is fussing a lot between feedings instead of sleeping peacefully. You pick him up and walk him around and he stops crying, at least for the time being. Lay him down, and he starts all over again. But you don't need to worry much about spoiling in the first six months. The chances are great that such a young baby is feeling miserable. If he stops fussing when picked up, it's probably because the motion and distraction and perhaps the warm pressure on his abdomen from being held make him forget his pain or tension at least temporarily.

The answer to the spoiling question really depends on what lessons you think babies are learning in the first months of life. It is unlikely that they are capable of learning to expect their every whim to be attended to twenty-four hours a day. That's what being spoiled would mean. But we know that young infants can't anticipate the future; they live entirely in the here and now. They also can't formulate this thought: "Well, I'm going to make life miserable for these people until they give me everything I want"—another key component of the spoiled child.

What infants are learning during this period is a sense of

basic trust (or mistrust) in the world. If their needs are met promptly and lovingly, they come to feel that the world is a benign place, a place where good things generally happen and bad experiences are soon rectified. The famous psychiatrist Erik Erikson felt that this sense of basic trust becomes a core of the baby's character. So the answer to the question "Can a young baby be spoiled?" is no, not until he's old enough to understand why his needs aren't immediately being met (maybe at nine months of age). A better question is: "How can you instill a sense of basic trust in babies?"

Spoiling after six months. You can be more suspicious by six months. By the time babies are six months old, colic and other causes of physical discomfort are usually behind them. Naturally, some of these babies who were held and walked a great deal during their colicky period have become accustomed to constant attention. They want their walking and the company to continue.

Take the example of a mother who can't stand to hear her baby fret, even for a minute, and who carries him most of the time he's awake: By the age of six months the baby cries immediately and holds out his arms to be picked up as soon as his mother puts him down. Housework has become impossible. The mother can't help resenting her enslavement, but she can't tolerate the indignant crying, either. The baby is likely to sense the parent's anxiety and resentment and may respond by becoming even more demanding. This situation is different from that of a mother who willingly picks up her baby at the slightest whimper or carries him in a sling all day even if he doesn't fret.

Reasons for spoiling. Why does a parent get involved in these ordinary types of spoiling? In the first place, it usually happens with the first baby. For most people, a first baby is the most fascinating plaything in the world. When an adult can be obsessed for a while with a new car, it's easy to see why a baby is all-absorbing for months.

But delight is not the only factor. Parents are apt to project all the hopes and fears they've had about themselves onto their firstborn. There's the anxiety, too, and the unfamiliar sense of being entirely responsible for the safety and happiness of a helpless human being. The baby's crying makes a powerful demand on you to do *something*, but you are not always sure *what*. With your second baby you have more assurance and a sense of proportion; you know that children have to be denied some things for their own good, and you don't feel guilty about being hardhearted when you know for sure you're doing the right thing.

Some parents are more easily drawn into spoiling than others. Some feel guilty for working long hours or for having felt angry at their baby. Some have had to wait a long time for a baby and suspect that they may not be able to have another. Some have too little confidence in their own worthiness, so become willing slaves to a child. Some have adopted a baby and feel that they have to do a superhuman job to justify themselves. Some have studied child psychology in college or worked professionally in the field and feel doubly obligated to prove their capability. Some feel angry or guilty when they hear a baby crying and find the tension unbearable.

Whatever the underlying factor, all these parents are a little too willing to sacrifice their own comforts and rights by giving their babies anything they ask for. This might not be too bad if babies knew what was sensible to ask for. But they *don't* know what's good for them. It's their nature to expect guidance from the parents. This comforts them. When the parents are hesitant, it makes babies uneasy. If parents always anxiously pick babies up whenever they fuss—as if it would be terrible to leave them there for a few moments—the babies, too, get the feeling that this would be terrible. And the more parents submit to babies' orders, the more demanding the children become. Parents then feel resentful. Later they feel guilty and again give in.

How do you unspoil? The earlier you detect the problem (after six to nine months of age), the easier it is to cure. But it takes a lot of willpower and a little hardening of the heart to say no to your baby and in one way or another set limits. To get yourself in the right mood you have to remember that, in the long run, unreasonable demandingness and excessive dependence are worse for babies than for you and get them out of kilter with themselves and the world. So you are reforming them for their own good.

Make out a schedule for yourself, on paper if necessary, that requires you to be busy with housework or anything else for much of the time your baby is awake. Go at it with a great bustle—to impress your baby and yourself. Say you are the mother of a baby boy who has become accustomed to being carried all the time. When he frets and raises his arms, explain to him in a friendly but very firm tone that this job and that job must get done this afternoon. Though he doesn't understand the words, he will understand the tone of voice. Stick to your busywork. The first hour of the first day is the hardest.

One baby will accept the change better if his mother stays out of sight a good part of the time at first and talks little. This helps him to become absorbed in something else. Another will adjust more quickly if he can at least see his mother and hear her talking to him, even though she won't pick him up. When you bring him a plaything or show him how to use it or when you decide it's time to play with him a bit at the end of the afternoon, sit down on the floor beside him. Let him climb into your arms if he wants, but don't get back into the habit of walking him around. If you're on the floor with him, he can crawl away when he eventually realizes you won't walk. If you pick him up and walk him, he'll surely object noisily just as soon as you start to put him down again. If he keeps on fretting indefinitely when you sit with him on the floor, remember another job and get busy again.

What you are trying to do is to help your baby begin to build frustration tolerance—a little at a time. If she does not learn this gradually from early infancy (roughly six to twelve months), it will be a much harder lesson to learn later on.

PHYSICAL DEVELOPMENT

A baby starts by using his head. In a gradual process, a baby learns to control his body. It starts with the head then works down to the trunk, hands, and legs. A lot of early movements are programmed into the tracks of the brain. Before he's born, a baby already knows how to suck. And if something touches his cheek—the nipple or your finger, for example—he tries to reach it with his mouth. After a few days he's more than ready to do his part in nursing. If you try to hold his head still, he becomes angry right away and twists to free it. (Probably he has this instinct to keep from being smothered.) On his own, he follows objects with his eyes, usually by about one month, if not before, and begins to reach for things.

Using their hands. As soon as they are born, some babies can put their thumbs or fingers in their mouths any time they want to. Ultrasound examinations during pregnancy show they were probably doing it before delivery. But most can't get their hands to their mouths with any regularity until they are two to three months old. And because their fists are still clenched tight, it usually takes them longer still to separately get hold of a thumb.

At about two to three months, many babies will spend hours just looking at their hands, bringing them up until, surprised, they bang themselves in the nose—only to stretch their arms out and start all over again. This is the beginning of eye-hand coordination.

The main business of hands is to grab and handle things. A baby seems to know ahead of time what he's going to be learning next. Weeks before he can actually grab an object, he looks as if he wants to and tries to grab it. At this stage, if you put a rattle into his hand, he holds on to it and waves it.

Around the middle of the first year, he learns how to reach

something that's brought within arm's reach. At about this time, he'll learn how to transfer an object from one hand to the other. Gradually, he handles things more expertly. Starting around nine months, he loves to pick up tiny objects, especially those you don't want him to (like specks of dirt), carefully and deliberately.

Right-handedness and left-handedness. The subject of handedness in children is a confusing one. Most babies use either hand equally well for the first year or two, then gradually become right- or left-handed. It is unusual for a baby to have a preference for one hand in the first six to nine months. Right- or left-handedness is an inborn trait, with approximately 10 percent of people being left-handed. Handedness tends to run in families; some families will have several lefties, others may have none. Trying to force a left-handed child to become right-handed is confusing to the brain, which has been set up to work by a different scheme. Incidentally, handedness also applies to a preference for one leg or eye over the other.

Rolling over and falling off. The age when babies roll over, sit up, creep, stand up, or walk is more variable than the age when they get control of their head or arms. A lot depends on temperament and weight. A wiry, energetic baby is in a great rush to get moving. A plump, placid one may be willing to wait until later.

A baby, by the time she first tries to roll over, shouldn't be left unguarded on a table for even as long as it takes you to turn your back. Since you can't really be sure when that first roll will happen, it's safest simply to always keep a hand on your baby when she's up high. By the time she can actually roll over, anywhere from two to six months, it is not safe to leave her even in the middle of an adult's bed. It is amazing how fast such a baby can reach the edge, and many do fall from an adult bed to the floor, which makes a parent feel very guilty.

If, after falling from a bed, a baby cries immediately, then stops crying and regains his normal color and activities within a few minutes, he probably has not been injured. If you notice any change in behavior in the next hours or days (fussier, sleepier, not eating, for example), call your doctor or nurse practitioner and describe the event; in most cases, you will be assured that your baby is well. If you child has lost consciousness, even for a short time, it's best to call the doctor promptly.

Sitting up. Most babies learn to sit steadily without support at seven to nine months. But even before babies have the coordination to succeed, they want to try. When you take hold of their hands, they attempt to pull themselves up. This eagerness often raises the question in a parent's mind: how soon can I prop my baby up in the carriage or high chair? In general, it's better not to prop babies straight up until they can sit steadily by themselves for many minutes. This doesn't mean that you can't pull them up to a sitting position for fun, sit them in your lap, or prop them on a slanted pillow in the carriage as long as the neck and back are straight. It's a curled-over position that's not good for long periods.

A high chair is of greatest advantage when babies are eating meals with the rest of the family. On the other hand, falling out of a high chair is worrisome and not uncommon. If you are going to use a high chair, get one with a broad base, so that it doesn't tip over easily, and always use the strap to buckle your baby in. Don't *ever* leave a baby alone in a chair, high or low.

Squirming while being changed. One of the things babies never learn is that they ought to lie still while being changed or dressed. It goes completely against their nature. From the time they learn to roll over until about one year, when they can be dressed standing up, they may cry indignantly or struggle against lying down as if they have never heard of such an outrage.

There are a few things that help a little. One baby may be distracted by a parent who makes funny noises, another by a small bit of cracker or cookie. You can have an especially fascinating toy, like a music box or a special mobile that you offer only at dressing time. Distract your baby just before you lay her down; don't wait until she starts yelling.

Creeping and crawling. Creeping—when your baby begins to drag himself across the floor—can begin any time between six months and one year. Crawling—when your baby gets up on his hands and knees and moves about—usually starts a few months after creeping. Occasionally, some perfectly normal babies never creep or crawl at all; they just sit around until they learn to stand up.

There are a dozen different ways of creeping and crawling, and babies may change their style as they become more expert. One first learns to creep backward, another sideways, like a crab. One wants to crawl on her hands and toes with her legs straight, another on his hands and knees, still another on one knee and one foot. The baby who learns to be a speedy creeper may be late in walking; the one who is a clumsy creeper or never learns to creep at all has a good reason for learning to walk early.

Standing. Standing usually comes in the last quarter of the first year, though a very ambitious and motorically advanced baby may stand as early as seven months. Occasionally you see one who doesn't stand until after one year though seeming to be bright and healthy in all other respects. Some of these are plump, easygoing babies. Others just seem to be slow getting coordination in their legs. I wouldn't worry about such children as long as your doctor or nurse practitioner finds that they are healthy and they seem fine in other ways.

Quite a number of babies get themselves into a jam when they first learn to stand up but don't yet know how to sit down again. The poor things stand until they are frantic with exhaustion. The parents take pity on their boy and unhitch him from the railing of his playpen and sit him down. He instantly forgets all about his fatigue and pulls himself to his feet again. This time he cries within a few minutes. The best a parent can do is to give him especially interesting things to play with while he's sitting, wheel him in the carriage longer than usual, and take comfort in the fact that he'll probably learn how to sit down within a week. One day he tries it. Very carefully he lets his behind down as far as his arms reach and, after a long moment of hesitation, plops down. He finds that it wasn't such a long drop and that his seat is well padded.

As the weeks go by, he learns to move around while hanging on, first with two hands, then with one. This is called cruising. Eventually he has enough balance to let go altogether for a few seconds when he is absorbed and doesn't realize what a daring thing he's doing. He is getting ready for walking.

Walking. Lots of factors determine the age at which a baby walks alone: inheritance probably plays the largest role, fol-

lowed by ambition, heaviness, how well she can get places by creeping, illnesses, and bad experiences. A baby who is just beginning to walk when an illness lays her up for two weeks may not try again for a month or more. One who is just learning and has a fall may refuse to let go with her hands again for many weeks.

Most babies learn to walk between twelve and fifteen months. A few muscular, ambitious ones start as early as nine months. A fair number of bright children do not begin until eighteen months or even later. You don't have to do anything to teach your child to walk. When her muscles, her nerves, and her spirit are ready, you won't be able to stop her. (The devices called walkers don't help babies learn to walk sooner and are unsafe; see page 117.)

ᐁ CLASSIC SPOCK

I remember a mother who got herself into a jam by walking her baby around a great deal before he was able to do it by himself. He was so delighted with this suspended walking that he demanded it all day long. Needless to say, she was tired and bored long before he was.

Bowlegs, toeing in, toeing out. A parent of an early walker may worry that it's bad for the baby's legs. As far as we know, children's physiques are able to stand whatever they're ready to do by themselves. Babies sometimes become bowlegged or knock-kneed in the early months of walking but this happens with both late walkers and early walkers. Most babies toe out to some degree when they start to walk then gradually bring the front part of the feet in as they progress. Some start with the feet sticking right out to the sides, like Charlie Chaplin, then end up toeing out only moderately. The average baby starts toeing out moderately and ends up with the feet almost parallel. The baby who starts out with feet almost parallel is more apt to end up toeing in. Toeing in and bowlegs often go together.

How straight the legs, ankles, and feet grow depends on several factors, including the pattern of development babies are born with. Some babies seem to have a tendency to knock-knees and ankles that sag inward. The heavy child is more apt to develop these conditions. Other babies seem to be born with a tendency to bowlegs and toeing in. I think this is especially true of the very active, athletic ones. Another factor may be the position babies keep their feet and legs in. For instance, you occasionally see a foot that becomes turned in at the ankle because the baby always sits with that foot tucked under him in that position. It's possible that some babies develop toeing in by always lying on their stomachs with their feet pointed toward each other. Now that we know that sleeping on the stomach increases the risk of SIDS (see page 882), this problem is less common.

Your doctor or nurse practitioner, during the regular examinations, will watch the ankles and legs from the time the baby begins to stand up. This is one reason why regular visits are important during the second year. If weak ankles, knock-knees, bowlegs, or toeing in develop, corrective measures may be recommended, but most of these conditions resolve themselves over time.

LEARNING ABOUT PEOPLE

Changing reactions to strangers. You can get an idea of how your baby goes from phase to phase in development by watching his reaction to strangers at different ages. This is how it goes in a doctor's office for a typical baby until he's about a year old: At two months he pays little attention to the doctor. As he lies on the examining table, he keeps looking over his shoulder at his mother. The four-month-old is the doctor's delight. He breaks into a body-wiggling smile just as often as the doctor smiles and makes noises at him. By five or six months, the baby may have begun to change his mind; by nine months he is certain: The doctor is a stranger and therefore to be feared. When the doctor approaches, he stops his kicking and cooing. His body freezes, and he eyes the doctor intently, even suspiciously, for maybe twenty seconds. Finally his chin puckers, and he begins to shriek. He may get so worked up that he cries long after the exam is over.

Stranger anxiety. The nine-month-old baby is suspicious not only of the doctor; anything new and unfamiliar makes him anxious, even a new hat on his mother or his father's clean-shaven face if he is used to seeing his father with a beard. This behavior is called stranger anxiety, and it's very interesting to think about what has changed to make your baby go from loving everyone to being a suspicious worrywart.

Before about six months of age, babies can recognize when they have seen something before (we know, because they tend to stare longer at such things), but they don't seem to really *think* about things as being either strange or familiar. This is probably because in a four-month-old, the thinking part of the brain— the outer layer or *cortex*—is not yet fully online. By six months, the cortex is much more functional. One result is that babies now have much better memory skills. They clearly recognize the difference between what is familiar and what is strange, and they seem to have the ability to understand that strange things may be dangerous. You can almost watch this thought process take place, as your baby first stares at the stranger, then back at you, then back to the stranger, and finally, several seconds, later bursts into tears.

At six to nine months babies are much smarter, but they still aren't good at predicting, based on past experience, what is likely to happen next. A six-month-old lives pretty much in the present. So when there is a stranger right in front of him, he can't understand why it's not a familiar person, and he can't figure out how any good will come of this situation. He also can't do much about the situation except protest and cry. By twelve to fifteen months, when stranger anxiety is generally on the way out, the infant is better at learning from the past and anticipating the future: "Maybe I don't know who this person is, but nothing awful has happened in the past, so I can handle this stranger without panicking."

Some babies (about one in seven) become particularly anxious in response to strange things and people. Even as small infants, their hearts beat faster when they see something unexpected, and all through childhood they tend to be extracautious. As toddlers, for example, they often hang back for a long time in a new situation before joining in. This temperament trait is sometimes called slow-to-warm-up, a very appropriate name. It is inborn, a result of the way the child's brain works, not early parenting practices. Most importantly, it is not an illness, and it is not something that needs to be fixed.

If your baby seems especially sensitive about new people and new places in the middle of the first year, it's sensible to protect him from fright by making strangers stay at a distance until he gets used to them. Don't keep him from seeing strangers, though. In time, through repeated exposure, things that were strange become more familiar, and even slow-to-warm-up children become more comfortable.

CLOTHES AND EQUIPMENT

Shoes: when and what kind? In most cases, there's no need to put anything on your baby's feet until he walks outdoors. Indoors, babies' feet stay cool just the way their hands do, so they aren't uncomfortable barefoot. In other words, there's no necessity for knitted booties or soft shoes in the first year unless the floor is unusually cold.

After a baby is standing and walking, there's a real value in leaving the child barefoot most of the time when conditions are suitable. The arches are relatively flat at first. The baby gradually builds the arches up and strengthens the ankles by using them vigorously in standing and walking. Walking on an uneven or rough surface also fosters the use of the foot and leg muscles.

Of course, a child who is walking needs shoes outdoors in cold weather and when walking on pavements and other surfaces that are hazardous. But it's good for a child to continue to go barefoot (or with socks) indoors till the age of two to three and outdoors, too, in warm weather at the beach, in the sandbox, and other safe places.

Semisoft-soled shoes are best at first, so that your child's feet have a better chance to move. Shoes with fancy supports are pretty much a waste of money. The important thing is to have the shoes big enough so that the toes aren't cramped but not so big that they almost slip off.

Small children outgrow their shoes at a discouragingly fast rate, sometimes in two months, and parents should form the habit of feeling the shoes every few weeks to make sure they are still large enough. There must be more than just enough space for the toes because as the child walks, the toes are squeezed forward into the front of the shoe with each step. There should be enough empty space in the toe of the shoe as the child stands that you can get about half your thumbnail (about one-quarter inch) onto the tip of the shoe before running into the child's toe. You can't judge while the child is sitting down, since the feet fill more of the shoe when a person is standing. Naturally, the shoes should be comfortably wide, too. There are soft, adjustable shoes that can be let out a full size. It's helpful to have a nonskid sole so that your child learns to walk before he learns to skate. You can rough up a smooth sole with coarse sandpaper.

Choose inexpensive shoes as long as they fit well. Sneakers are just fine as long as they don't cause excessive sweating. The feet are pudgy the first couple of years; as a result, low shoes sometimes do not stay on as well as high-top shoes. There isn't any other reason for ankle-high shoes; the ankles don't need extra support.

Playpens. A playpen can be a great help, especially for the busy parent, from about three months on. A playpen in the family room, kitchen, or home office lets a baby be near the action without the danger of being stepped on or spilled on. When babies are old enough to stand up, the playpen gives them a railing to hold onto and a firm foundation under their feet. In good weather, they can sit safely in the playpen on the porch and watch the world go by.

If you are going to use a playpen, it's best if your baby gets accustomed to it at three to four months, before he has learned to sit and crawl and before he has had the freedom of the floor. Otherwise he might consider it a prison from the start. By the time he can sit and crawl, he has fun going after things that are a few feet away and handling larger objects, like cooking spoons, saucepans, and strainers. When he becomes bored with the playpen, he can sit in a bouncing chair or a chair-table arrangement. It's good for him to have some free creeping time, too.

Even if they are willing, babies should not be kept in playpens all the time. They need time for explorative crawling—with an adult watching. Every hour or so they should be played with, hugged, and perhaps carried around in a chest carrier for a spell. Between twelve and eighteen months, the period of time for which most babies will tolerate the playpen grows increasingly shorter.

Swings. Swings are useful after babies have learned to sit and before they learn to walk. Some swings have motors, some are for use in doorways, others have springs so the baby can bounce. The springs should have covers to prevent finger injury, or the coils should not be more than one-eighth inch apart. One baby is happy swinging for a long time, another grows bored fairly soon. Swings keep babies from getting into as much trouble as they might creeping, but babies shouldn't spend their whole days in swings. They need lots of opportunities to creep, explore, stand, and walk.

Walkers. Walkers used to be very popular, because it looks as if they should help babies learn to walk earlier. Actually, walkers get in the way of learning to walk since all the infant has to do is thrash her legs without worrying about balance. Various skills are needed to walk, and the baby may be less motivated to learn all of them. After all, she gets around fine under her own steam. Why learn something new—walking—that is more difficult?

Walkers are also dangerous and have been responsible for many injuries. They raise the baby's height, so she can reach objects that may hurt her; they raise her center of gravity, so it's easier for her to tip over; and they allow her to move forward at an amazingly fast rate. Terrible injuries have come from babies falling down flights of stairs in their walkers. The manufacture of baby walkers should be discontinued. If you already own one, the safest course is to take the wheels off so it can't roll or throw it out.

COMMON PHYSICAL ISSUES IN THE FIRST YEAR

It's best to consult your doctor or nurse practitioner promptly about any change in your baby's health. Don't try to diagnose it yourself—there is too much chance of error. There are many other causes of the problems mentioned here. This discussion is primarily to help parents to adjust to a few common types of mild physical concerns of early infancy after the doctor or nurse practitioner has made a diagnosis.

Hiccups. Most babies hiccup pretty regularly after meals in the early months. In fact, many babies can be seen hiccuping on the prenatal ultrasound and felt doing it toward the end of pregnancy. It doesn't seem to mean anything; and there is nothing that you need to do, aside from seeing if they have to burp. If you want to try something, a drink of warm water occasionally stops them.

Spitting up and vomiting. The term spitting up is popularly used when the stomach contents spill gently out of the baby's mouth, usually in small amounts. The muscle that is supposed to close off the entrance to the stomach just doesn't hold the contents down well the way it does in an older child or adult. Any movement may cause the spitting up: joggling, squeezing too tightly, laying the baby down, or the digestive motions of the stomach itself. Most babies do a lot of spitting up during the early months. This is usually of no significance. Some spit up several times after every feeding. Others do it only occasionally. (Milk stains can be more easily removed from sheets, diapers, and clothing if they are first soaked in cold water.)

In most babies the tendency to spit up is greatest in the early weeks and months. It decreases as they get older. Most have stopped altogether by the time they can sit up. Occasionally it goes on until the child is walking. Once in a while, babies start spitting up only when they are several months old. Sometimes teething seems to make it worse for a while. Spitting up is messy and inconvenient, but it's not important if the baby is gaining weight well, isn't bothered by coughing or gagging, and is happy.

The word vomiting is used when the stomach contents are ejected with enough force to propel them at least a few inches away from the mouth. It alarms new parents when their baby first vomits a large amount of milk. But this is not serious as long as it doesn't happen often and the baby seems otherwise happy and healthy. There are a few babies who vomit a large amount as often as once a day, especially in the early weeks. Naturally, if your baby spits up or vomits regularly, you should discuss it with the doctor or nurse practitioner, particularly if there are other signs of indigestion. It is worthwhile taking extra care to burp the baby; but in most cases the spitting up or vomiting goes right on, no matter how you change the formula or reduce the quantity or burp him.

If babies have vomited what seems to be their whole feeding, should they be fed again right away? If they seem happy enough, don't feed them, at least until they act very hungry. The stomach may be a little upset, so it is better to give it a chance to quiet down. Remember that the amount vomited usually looks larger than it actually is. There are babies who you would swear are vomiting most of every feeding but still go on gaining satisfactorily.

Whether the spit-up milk is sour and curdled is not important. The first step in digestion in the stomach is the secretion of acid. Any food that has been in the stomach for a while is acidified. The effect of acid on milk is to curdle it.

Gentle spitting up or occasional vomiting after feeds is nothing to worry about. When should you call the doctor?

- Spitting up along with irritability, crying, gagging, arching of the back, coughing or poor weight gain. These can be signs of gastroesophageal reflux (see page 64).
- New onset of vomiting more than once or twice, especially if the vomiting is forceful, or if what comes up looks yellowish or greenish, a sign that there is bile in it.
- Vomiting accompanied by fever, a change in activity (sleepier, less playful, irritable), or other signs of illness.
- Vomiting or spitting up that causes you concern for any reason. Even if it turns out to be plain old spitting up, it's never wrong to seek reassurance from your baby's doctor.

Changes in the color of the stool. Nothing seems to upset some parents as much as a change in the color of bowel movements. Brown, yellow or green—it simply doesn't matter. Like designer fashions, bowel movements come in many colors. None is healthier than the next. You should be concerned if the bowel movement turns black (this may indicate lots of blood, which turns black and tarry-looking as it goes through the intestines), or red (possibly blood), or chalk white, which can indicate a problem with the bile.

Constipation. Constipation refers to hard, dry stools that are difficult to pass. It's not the number of bowel movements each day that determines whether a baby (or older child or adult) has constipation. Occasionally, passing hard stools can cause small streaks of red blood on the stool. While not uncommon, any blood in the stool should be discussed with your doctor or nurse practitioner.

One baby always has a bowel movement at the same time of day, another at a different time each day. Some babies have more than one bowel movement a day; others go days without having a bowel movement. One is just as healthy as the other. There is no advantage to be gained by trying to make the irregular baby regular. In the first place, it usually can't be done. In the second place, trying to get a movement from a baby who isn't ready is likely to lead to a frustrating, fruitless power struggle.

Breast-fed babies, more than formula-fed babies, commonly have infrequent movements after the first few months. By three or four months, it isn't constipation when a breast-fed baby has a movement only every other day, or even every several days, as long as the movement is still very soft. There is no need for a baby to have a movement every day.

Constipation sometimes starts when the older breast-fed baby is begun on solid foods. Apparently his intestine has had such an easy time with breast milk that it doesn't know what to do with different foods. The baby develops firm, infrequent stools and seems uncomfortable. You can offer a little sugar water (one teaspoon of granulated sugar to two ounces of water); prune, apple, or pear juice (start with two ounces and work your way up); or stewed prunes (start with two teaspoons a day and work your way up). Some babies get cramps from prunes, but most take it well. Usually constipation is a temporary problem; if it lasts longer than a week, check with the doctor or nurse practitioner.

Formula-fed babies can also become constipated. You can try the same remedies suggested above. If they don't solve the problem, consult your baby's doctor or nurse practitioner.

Diarrhea. Mild diarrhea is common in babies. A baby's intestine is sensitive for the first year or two and may be upset not only by bacteria and viruses but also by a new food or too much fruit juice. Fortunately, this kind of upset is usually mild and of no great consequence. There may be a couple of extra stools that are looser than usual. Commonly, they are greenish and the odor may be different. The most important characteristic of this kind of mild diarrhea is that the baby acts well or almost well. He is playful, active, urinating as often as usual, and doesn't have more in the way of illness than perhaps a slightly stuffy nose or a mild reduction in appetite. In a couple of days, without any special treatment, the symptoms usually disappear. You can offer some extra water or a rehydration solution such as Pedialyte or remove a food that has been added recently.

It used to be that a baby with mild diarrhea would be taken off solids and formula and given instead a lot of liquids that are high in sugar (such as Jell-O water, soda, or apple juice). Research has shown that this traditional diarrhea diet actually increases and prolongs diarrhea. So for mild, brief infant diarrhea, offer breast milk or formula and the baby's regular diet, and let him eat as much as he seems hungry for. This is what works best. If the diarrhea lasts more than two to three days, you should consult your doctor or nurse practitioner, even if your baby continues to act healthy. For more on diarrhea and dehydration, see page 838.

Rashes, in general. It's always reasonable to show an unidentified rash to your baby's doctor or nurse practitioner. Rashes are often hard to describe in words, and though most rashes aren't too serious, some are signs of illnesses that need prompt medical attention.

Common diaper rash. Most babies have sensitive skin in the early months. The diaper region is particularly apt to suffer because diapers retain water next to the tender skin and don't allow the area to breathe. In fact, any of us would get a rash in the groin if we had to wear a diaper twenty-four hours a day. That's why the best treatment for almost any diaper rash is usually to have the baby go diaperless for as long as possible—a few hours a day is ideal. Right after a bowel movement, for example, is a good time to let your baby hang in the breeze, since there is less likelihood of action in that area in the near future. Fold a diaper underneath your baby or put him on a large waterproof pad, and try to keep the diaper under him (even so, boys are apt to spray—so keep some paper towels handy). The warm air and lack of contact with material usually does the trick. Almost all babies develop a few spots of diaper rash from time to time. If it is slight and goes away as fast as it came, no special treatment is necessary, except air-drying.

Don't wash the diaper area with soap while there is a rash, because soap can be irritating. Use plain water instead of diaper wipes. You can give the skin a protective coating by slathering on petroleum jelly or any of the diaper ointments. Some diaper services use special rinses in the case of diaper rash. If you wash the diapers at home, you can add a half cup of clear white vinegar to the last rinse.

In older babies, diaper rashes are often caused by the skin's being in prolonged contact with the warm, acidic urine. Air-drying and frequent diaper changes usually do the trick. A diaper rash caused by yeast (also called candida) will have bright red spots that often come together to form a solid, red area bordered by spots. The folds in the diaper area are usually bright red with bright red spots on the prominences. Treatment is with a prescription antiyeast cream. A rash with blisters or pus (especially with fever, but even without) is likely to be caused by bacteria and should be treated by a doctor.

Rash from diarrhea. Irritating bowel movements during an attack of diarrhea sometimes cause a very sore rash around the anus or a smooth, bright red rash on the buttocks. The treatment is to change the diaper just as soon as it becomes soiled—

no small task. Then clean the area with oil or, if the area is too sore to wipe, hold the baby's bottom under warm water from a running faucet, pat him dry, and apply a thick covering of a protective ointment (one brand is as good as another). If this doesn't work, the diaper should be left off and the diaper area exposed to the air. Sometimes it seems that while the baby has diarrhea, nothing helps very much. Fortunately, this rash cures itself soon after the diarrhea is over.

Rashes on the face. There are several mild face rashes that babies have in the first few months that aren't definite enough to have names but are very common. Milia are minute shiny white pimples without any redness around them. They look like tiny pearls in the skin. In this case, the oil glands in the skin are producing oil, but since they haven't opened up to the skin yet, the oil packets just sit there. Over the next weeks or months, the oil ducts open up and the oil is expressed.

Some babies have collections of a few small red spots or smooth pimples on the cheeks and forehead. They look like acne, and that's exactly what they are. They are caused by exposure to the mother's hormones in the womb. These may last a long time and get a parent quite upset. At times they fade then get red again. Different ointments don't seem to do much good. These spots always go away eventually.

Erythema toxicum consists of splotchy red patches that are a quarter to a half inch in diameter, some with a tiny white pimple head. In darker-skinned infants, the splotches can be purplish in color. They come and go on different parts of the face and body. We don't know what causes this common rash, but once it goes away, it doesn't come back. Larger, pus-filled blisters or pimples may be infections and should be reported promptly to the doctor or nurse practitioner.

Rashes on body and scalp. *Prickly heat* is very common in the shoulder and neck region of babies when hot weather begins.

It is made up of clusters of very small pink pimples surrounded by blotches that are pink in light-skinned babies and may be dark red or purplish in dark-skinned ones. Tiny blisters form on some of the pimples. When they dry up they can give the rash a slightly tan look. Prickly heat usually starts around the neck. If it is bad, it can spread down onto the chest and back and up around the ears and face, but it seldom bothers a baby. You can pat this rash several times a day with absorbent cotton dipped in a solution of bicarbonate of soda (one teaspoon bicarbonate of soda to one cup water). Another treatment is dusting with cornstarch baby powder (we don't recommend talcum powder anymore because it can irritate the lungs). Most prickly heat goes away on its own without any special treatment. It is more important to try to keep the baby cool. Don't be afraid to take off the baby's clothes in hot weather. After all, there's no evidence that early experience of nakedness leads to children's growing up to be nudists.

Cradle cap (seborrhea) is a usually mild disorder that appears as patches on the scalp that look like greasy yellow or reddish crusts. Seborrhea can also occur on the face, in the diaper area, and elsewhere on the body. You can oil the patches to soften them then wash with a mild dandruff shampoo, brushing out the scales that come from the patches. Don't leave the oil on long before shampooing it out. Medicated shampoos and prescription medication can also help. Cradle cap rarely persists beyond the first six months.

Impetigo is a bacterial infection of the skin. It's generally not serious, but it is contagious and should be treated promptly by your doctor or nurse practitioner. It starts with a very delicate small blister that contains yellowish fluid or white pus and is surrounded by reddened skin. The blister is easily broken, leaving a small raw spot. It does not develop a thick crust in infants as it does in older children. It's apt to start in a moist place, such as the edge of the diaper or in the groin or armpit. New spots may develop. Over-the-counter antibacterial ointments and air-drying can help. Arrange clothing and bedclothes so that they do not cover the spot or spots, and keep the room warmer than usual to compensate, if necessary. Prescription antibiotic ointment usually solves the problem quickly. During impetigo, disinfect the diapers, sheets, underclothing, nighties, towels, and washcloths, using ordinary sodium hypochlorite bleach in the wash according to the directions on the bottle.

Mouth troubles. *Thrush* is a very common mild yeast infection of the mouth. It looks as if patches of milk scum were stuck to the cheeks, tongue, or the roof of the mouth. But, unlike milk, it does not wipe off easily. If you do rub it off, the underlying skin may bleed slightly and look inflamed. Thrush can make babies' mouths sore, and they may appear uncomfortable when they nurse. Thrush can occur in all babies and has nothing to do with poor hygiene on your part. A prescription medication painted onto the thrush with the tip of your small finger several times a day usually cures it, although it may come back later. If there will be a delay in getting medical advice, it is helpful to have the baby drink half an ounce of water after the milk. This washes the milk out of the mouth and gives the thrush fewer nutrients to live on. Don't be fooled by the color of the inner sides of the gums where the upper molar teeth will be. The normal pale color is sometimes mistaken for thrush by parents on the lookout for it.

Cysts on the gums and the roof of the mouth. Some babies have one or two little pearly white cysts on the sharp edge of their gums. They may remind you of teeth, but they are too round and don't make a click on a spoon. Similar cysts can often be seen on the roof of the mouth along the ridge that runs from front to back. They have no importance and eventually disappear.

Teething is discussed on page 803.

Eye troubles. Many babies develop a mild redness of the eyes a few days after birth. This is probably caused by an immature tear duct that may be partially obstructed. It doesn't require any treatment, as it usually clears up by itself.

Blocked tear duct. Another kind of very mild but chronic infection of the eyelids occurs in the early months in quite a number of babies, most commonly in only one eye. The eye waters and tears excessively, particularly in windy weather. White matter collects in the corner of the eye and along the edges of the lids. This discharge may keep the lids stuck together when the baby wakes up. This condition is caused by an obstructed tear duct. The tear duct leads from a small opening at the inner corner of the eyelid, first toward the nose, then down the side of the eye socket and into the nose cavity. When this duct is partly plugged, the tears can't drain off as fast as they form. They well up in the eye and run down the cheek. The lids keep getting mildly infected because the eye is not being cleansed well by the tears. The usual treatment is a combination of prescription eye ointment or drops and gentle massage of the tear ducts to open them up. Your doctor or nurse practitioner will show you how to do this.

Blocked tear ducts are fairly common and not serious, and they do not injure the eye. The condition may last for many months. The tendency is outgrown in most cases, even if nothing is done. If after year it is still bothersome, an eye doctor can clear the duct with a simple procedure. When the lids are stuck together, you can soften the crust and open them by gently applying water with your clean fingers or a clean washcloth and warm water (not hot, because the eyelid skin is very sensitive to temperature). A plugged tear duct does not cause redness of the white of the eye.

Conjunctivitis. This bacterial or viral infection of the lining of the white of the eye causes the whites of the eyes to look bloodshot or pink. Usually there is a discharge of yellow or white pus from the eye. The doctor or nurse practitioner should be called promptly.

Crossed eyes. It is common for a baby's eyes to turn in or out too much at moments in the early months. In most cases they become steady and straight as the child grows older, usually by three months. If, however, the eyes turn in or out all the time or much of the time, even in the first month, or if they are not steady by three months, an eye doctor should be consulted. Many times parents think their baby's eyes are crossed when they are really straight. This is because the skin between the eyes (over the bridge of the nose) is relatively wider in a baby than in an older person. This extra skin covers a little of the white of the eye (toward the nose), causing it to appear to be much smaller than the white on the outer side (toward the ear). It's also not uncommon in a newborn baby for the lid of one eye to droop a little lower than the other or for one eye to look smaller. In most cases, these differences become less and less noticeable as the baby grows older. The baby's eyes should be examined, though, to be sure that they are straight.

Another reason babies' eyes sometimes appear crossed is that when they are looking at something in their hands, they have to converge (cross) the eyes a lot to focus on it since babies' arms are so short. They are only converging their eyes normally, as adults do to a lesser extent. Their eyes won't get stuck in that position. Parents often ask whether it is safe to hang toys over the crib, since the baby sometimes becomes cross-eyed when looking at them. Don't hang a toy right on top of a baby's nose, but it's perfectly all right to hang it a foot away or more. (See page 756 for safety considerations.)

It is important that infants' eyes be examined promptly if there is a question about whether they are straight, because an eye that is always crossed will gradually become nonseeing if efforts are not begun early to make the child use it. When the two eyes do not coordinate and converge on an object, each eye will see a somewhat different scene; the child sees double. This is so confusing and uncomfortable that the brain automatically learns to ignore and suppress the vision of one eye. Over the first couple of years, the brain loses the capacity to process visual information from that suppressed eye, and the eye will for all intents and purposes be blind. If this goes on too long, it becomes impossible to bring back the vision in that eye. This condition is known as lazy eye.

The eye doctor's job is to promptly put the lazy eye back to work, usually by having the child wear a patch over the good eye for long periods of time. The eye doctor may also prescribe glasses to further encourage the coordinated use of both eyes. Then comes the decision as to whether there should be an operation. Occasionally, several operations have to be performed before the result is satisfactory.

Breathing troubles. Babies sneeze frequently. Sneezing is not a sign of a cold unless the nose runs, too. Most often sneezing is caused by dust and dried mucus that have collected in the front of the nose, tickling it.

Chronic noisy breathing occurs in some young babies. Although it's usually without significance, every baby with noisy breathing should be examined by a doctor or nurse practitioner. Many babies make a soft snoring noise in the back of the nose. It's just like a grown-up snoring, except that babies do it while they are awake. It seems to be caused by the fact that they haven't yet learned to control their soft palates. They'll outgrow it.

A common type of chronic noisy breathing is caused by underdevelopment of the cartilage around the larynx (voice box). As the baby inhales, the cartilage flops together and rattles, causing the noise that doctors call stridor. It sounds as if the babies are choking, but they can breathe that way indefinitely. In most cases stridor occurs only when the babies are breathing hard, as when they have a cold. It usually goes away when they are quiet or asleep. It may be better when they lie face down. If your baby has stridor, by all means talk with your doctor or nurse practitioner, but usually no treatment is needed; mild stridor goes away as the baby grows older.

Noisy breathing that comes on suddenly, particularly in

an older infant or child, has an entirely different significance from that of the chronic variety. It may be due to croup, asthma, or other infection and requires prompt medical attention (see page 698).

Breath-holding spells. Some babies get so furiously angry when they are frustrated that they cry then hold their breath and turn blue. When this first happens, it's bound to scare the wits out of their parents. (These are often babies who are quite happy at other times.) You should be reassured that no one can hold her breath to death. In the worst-case scenario, the baby holds her breath for so long that she blacks out, and her body automatically assumes control and starts breathing again. The occasional baby holds her breath so long she not only blacks out but also has seizure-like movements. Again, this is terrifying to watch but not actually dangerous.

Other babies, when startled or suddenly in pain, will pass out after just a single cry. This is a different form of breath-holding spell.

Talk with your doctor or nurse practitioner about any breath-holding episodes so he or she can make sure that everything is all right physically. Once that's settled, there isn't much that can be done. Occasionally, breath-holding spells occur in children because they are anemic. Iron drops can help. You can try to divert your baby's attention when she starts to fuss by encouraging another activity, but this won't work all the time. It helps to remember that breath-holding spells are not dangerous and usually stop by the time the child starts kindergarten.

YOUR TODDLER, TWELVE TO TWENTY-FOUR MONTHS

⌒⌒

WHAT MAKES THEM TICK?

Feeling their oats. One year is an exciting age. Babies are changing in lots of ways: in their eating, how they get around, how they understand the world, what they want to do, and how they feel about themselves and other people. When they were little and helpless, you could put them where you wanted them, give them the playthings you thought suitable, feed them the foods you knew were best. Most of the time they were willing to let you be the boss and took it all in good spirit. It's more complicated now that they are around a year old. They seem to realize that they're not meant to be baby dolls the rest of their lives; that they're human beings with ideas and wills of their own.

At fifteen to eighteen months, your child's behavior makes it clear that she's heading for what is often called the terrible twos, a slanderous term, because two years is a marvelous and exciting— if challenging—age. When you suggest something that doesn't appeal to her, she feels she must assert herself. Her nature tells her to. It's the beginning of the process called individuation, when she begins to become a person in her own right. The honeymoon with you is over, at least partly, because to become her own person she needs to push back against your control.

So she may begin to say no in words or actions, even about

things that she likes to do. Some call this negativism, but stop and think what would happen if she never felt like saying no. She'd become a compliant robot if she never disagreed with you, and she'd never learn anything through trial and error, which is the best way to learn. She's getting smarter all the time and more and more able to make some of her own decisions (even if they are wrong).

The process of separating from you begins at this stage. While it can be painful—you may feel rejected, and it's hard to give up control—this separation is absolutely necessary for your child's growth as a human being. So say good-bye to that special bond of unquestioning, unconditional love that your infant once gave you and say hello to a more complicated relationship with this newly emerging person.

Independence and outgoingness. A baby gets more dependent and more independent at the same time. This sounds contradictory, and of course it is. But so are babies! A parent complains of a year-old boy, "He's begun to cry every time I go out of the room." This doesn't mean that he is developing a bad habit; it means that he's growing up and realizing how much he depends on his parents. It's inconvenient, but it's a good sign. Yet at this same age he is also becoming more independent; he is developing the urge to be on his own, discover new places, befriend unfamiliar people.

Watch a baby at the crawling stage when his parent is washing the dishes. He plays contentedly with some pots and pans for a while. Then he becomes bored and decides to explore in the dining room. He creeps around under the furniture there, picking up little pieces of dust and tasting them, carefully climbing to his feet to reach the handle of a drawer. After a while he seems to feel the need of company again, for he suddenly scrambles back into the kitchen. At one moment you see his urge for independence getting the upper hand; at another, his need for security. He satisfies each in turn.

As the months go by, he becomes bolder and more daring in his experiments and explorations. He still needs his parents but not so often. He is building his own independence, but part of his courage comes from knowing he has security when he needs it.

Independence comes from security as well as from freedom. A few people get it twisted around. They try to train independence into children by leaving them in a room by themselves for long periods, even though they are crying for company. But when parents force the issue this hard, a child learns that the world is a mean place, which makes him even more dependent in the long run.

So your baby at around a year old is at a fork in the road. Given a chance, he will gradually become more independent: more sociable with outsiders (both grown-ups and children), more self-reliant, and more outgoing. Stranger anxiety, so intense at nine months, begins to wane. If he's confined a great deal, kept away from others, and used to having only his parents around, it may take longer for him to become sociable outside of the home. The most important thing is for a one-year-old to have a strong attachment to his consistent caregivers. If he has a solid foundation of emotional security, outgoingness will eventually come.

The passion to explore. One-year-olds are determined explorers. They poke into every nook and cranny, finger the carving in the furniture, shake a table or anything else that isn't nailed down, want to take every single book out of the bookcase, climb onto anything they can reach, fit little things into big things then try to fit big things into little things. In short, they are into everything.

Like many things, their curiousity is a two-edged sword. On one hand, it's the way your child learns. He has to find out about the size, shape and movableness of everything in his world and test his skill before he can advance to the next stage, just the way he'll have to go through the grades before he can go to high school. His incessant explorations are a sign that he's bright in mind and spirit.

On the other hand, this can be a physically exhausting and trying time for you, requiring your constant attention to allow him to explore but at the same time making sure that he is safe and that his experiences are beneficial to his growth and development.

HELP YOUR TODDLER EXPLORE SAFELY

Exploration and risk. When a baby has learned to walk, it's time to let her out of her carriage or stroller on her daily outings. Never mind if she gets dirty; she should. Try to find a place where you don't have to be after her every minute and where she can get used to other children. If she picks up cigarette butts, you have to jump up and take them away, then show her something else that's fun. You can't let her eat handfuls of sand or earth because they will irritate her intestines and may give her worms. If she puts everything in her mouth, give her a hard cracker or some clean object to chew on to keep her mouth busy.

Such are the ordinary risks of independence at this age. Keeping an able-bodied walking baby tucked in her stroller all the time will keep her out of trouble, but it will also cramp her style, hinder her development, and dampen her spirit.

Avoiding injuries. One year is a dangerous age. Parents cannot prevent all injuries. If they were careful enough or worried enough to try, they would only make a child timid and dependent. All children will get some cuts and bruises as a natural part of their active, healthy play. If you keep your guard up and take a few simple precautionary measures, you can protect your children from serious injury. See "Preventing Injuries" in Section VI.

Let them out of the playpen. One child is willing to stay in the playpen, at least for short periods, as late as a year and a half. Another, by the time she's nine months, thinks it's a prison. Most accept it well enough until they learn to walk, around the age of fifteen months. Let your baby out of the playpen when she feels unhappy there but not necessarily at the first whimper. If you give her something new to play with, she may be happy there for another hour. Outgrowing the pen is a gradual process. At first she becomes sick of it only after a long spell. Gradually she becomes impatient earlier. It may be months before she objects to being put in at all. In any case, let her out each time she's sure she's had enough.

Harness or wrist leads? Many toddlers naturally stay close to a parent when in a supermarket or mall, but some very active and adventurous ones are apt to wander off, giving their parents heart attacks. For these children, a harness that ties around the upper body or a wrist lead can be very practical.

Will some people give you disapproving stares for leashing your child? Possibly. Should that worry you? Probably not. Safety is the main objective, and anything that helps your child to feel safe while exploring and at the same time allows you to relax and enjoy your child is a good thing. (Naturally, a harness or lead should never be used to tie the toddler to something while the parent goes off in another direction.)

✑ CLASSIC SPOCK

When I tell parents that their toddler has outgrown the playpen or the crib and that they ought to let her on the floor, they are apt to look unhappy and say, "But I'm afraid she'll hurt herself. At the least, she'll wreck the house." Sooner or later she must be let out to roam around, if not at ten months, at least by fifteen months, when she's walking. And she's not going to be any more reasonable or easier to control then. At whatever age you give her the freedom of the house, you will have to make adjustments, so it's better to do it when she is ready.

Arranging the house for a wandering baby. How do you keep a year-old baby from hurting herself or the household furnishings, anyway? First of all, you can arrange the rooms she'll be in so that she's allowed to play with most of the things she can reach. Then you'll rarely have to tell her she can't play with something. (If you forbid her to touch most of the reachable objects, you will drive her and yourself mad.) If there are plenty of things she can do, she's not going to bother so much about the things she can't do.

Practically speaking, this means taking breakable vases and ornaments from low tables and shelves and putting them out of reach. It means taking the valuable books off the lower shelves of the bookcases (put the old magazines there instead). Jam the good books in tight so that she can't pull them out. In the kitchen, put the pots and pans and wooden spoons on the shelves near the floor and put the china and packages of food out of reach. Fill a lower bureau drawer with old clothes, toys, and other interesting objects and let your baby explore it, empty it, and fill it to her heart's content.

Setting limits: no is not enough. Even when you baby-proof completely, there will always be a few things that your toddler will have to leave alone. After all, there have to be lamps on tables. She mustn't pull them off by their cords or push the tables over. She mustn't touch the hot stove or turn on the gas or crawl out a window.

No isn't enough at first. You can't stop a toddler just by saying no, at least not in the beginning. Even later, it will depend on your tone of voice, how often you say it, and whether you really mean it. It's not a method to rely on heavily until she has learned from experience what it means—and that you mean it. Don't say no in a challenging voice from across the room. This gives her a choice. She says to herself, "Shall I be a wimp and do as she says, or shall I be mature and grab this lamp cord?" Remember that her natural instinct is egging her on to try things and to balk at directions. Chances are she'll keep on approaching the lamp cord with an eye on you to see how angry you get. It's much wiser the first few times she goes for the lamp to go over promptly and whisk her to another part of the room. You can say no at the same time to begin teaching her what it means. Then quickly give her a magazine or an empty box, anything that is interesting—and safe.

Suppose she goes back to the lamp a few minutes later? Remove her and distract her again, promptly, definitely, cheerfully. Say, "No, no," at the same time that you remove her, adding it to your action for good measure. Sit down with her for a minute to show her what she can do with the new plaything. If necessary, put the lamp out of reach this time or even take her out of the room. You are cheerfully but firmly showing her that you are absolutely sure in your own mind that the lamp is not a thing to

play with. You are keeping away from choices, arguments, cross looks, scoldings—which may not do the job and are likely to make her irritable.

You might say, "But she won't learn unless I teach her it's naughty." Oh, yes, she will. In fact, she can accept the lesson more easily if it's done in this matter-of-fact way. When you disapprovingly waggle a finger from across the room at babies who haven't yet learned that no really means no, your crossness rubs them the wrong way. It makes them want to take a chance on disobeying. And it's no better if you grab them, hold them face to face, and give them a talking-to. You're not giving them a chance to give in gracefully or forget. Their only choice is to surrender meekly or defy you.

Take the example of a baby who is getting close to a hot stove. A parent doesn't sit still and say "No-o-o" in a disapproving voice; she jumps up and gets the baby out of the way. This is the method that comes naturally if the parent is really trying to keep the child from doing something, not just engaging in a battle of wills.

❧ CLASSIC SPOCK

I think of a Mrs. T., who complained bitterly that her sixteen-month-old daughter was "naughty." Just then Suzy toddled into the room—a nice girl with a normal amount of spunk. Instantly Mrs. T. looked disapproving and said, "Now, remember, don't go near the radio." Suzy hadn't been thinking of the radio at all, but now she had to. She turned and moved slowly toward it.

Mrs. T. gets panicky just as soon as each of her children in turn shows signs of developing into an independent person. She dreads the time when she won't be able to control them. In her uneasiness, she makes an issue when there doesn't need to be any. It's like the boy learning to ride a bicycle who sees a rock in the road ahead. He is so nervous about it that he keeps steering right for it.

FEARS AROUND ONE YEAR

Fear of separation. Many healthy children develop a fear of being separated from their parents beginning around the age of a year. This is probably the same instinct that makes the young of other species, such as sheep and goats, follow closely after their mothers and bleat when separated. Without this instinct, a newborn lamb might wander away and become lost.

In humans, separation anxiety also kicks in at about the time that children develop the ability to wander away, around one year. Some bold, busy children show very little separation anxiety; others show a lot. This difference is not so much a matter of parenting as it is a reflection of inborn temperament. You can't change a timid child into a bold one, but you can help such a child to feel gradually more and more confident by giving patient acceptance and gentle encouragement.

Around eighteen months or so, many children who have been happy explorers develop a new, heightened clinginess. They can imagine being apart from their parents, and the image is frightening. This period of anxious clinging usually fades away some-time around age two to two and a half, as children learn that sep-arations are always followed by reunions.

Frightening sounds and sights. Your baby at a year may be fascinated by one thing for several weeks on end—the tele-phone, for instance, planes overhead, or electric lights. Re-member that he learns best by touching, smelling, and tasting things and that as a little scientist he needs to conduct his ex-periments over and over again. Let him touch and become fa-miliar with objects that are not dangerous or disturbing.

But the hardy explorer also begins to develop fears of certain things at this time. He may be frightened by strange objects that move suddenly or make a loud noise, such as folded pictures that pop up from a book, the opening of an umbrella, a vacuum cleaner, a siren, a barking dog, a train, even a vase of rustling branches.

All children have fears; this is a normal element of the devel-opmental process. It's not hard to understand why. Fears occur when the child's understanding of an object or event is too poorly developed to explain why this object has suddenly come into his life and why this startling event has occurred and to know whether the situation is really safe. We all fear that which we do not understand. In the second year of life, that covers a lot of territory. I'd suggest simply avoiding these startling things as much as possible until he figures them out. If the vacuum cleaner bothers him, tell him when you're about to turn it on and let him see how you do it and do it himself a few times while you hold him. If he's still scared, don't use the vacuum for a time while he's nearby. Always be comforting and sympathetic. Don't try to convince him that it's a ridiculous fear; his terror makes perfect sense to him at his level of understanding.

Fear of the bath. Between the one and two years, your child may become frightened of the bath. She may fret about slipping underwater, getting soap in her eyes, or even seeing and hearing the water go down the drain. She needs to have a bath, so you need to figure out how to make it a less traumatic experience and allow her to come to terms with it. To avoid getting soap in her eyes, soap her face with a washcloth that is not too wet, and rinse several times with a damp but not dripping washcloth. Use baby shampoo that won't sting her eyes. Babies who are afraid to get into the bathtub shouldn't be forced to. You can try using a dishpan, but if she is afraid of that too, give her sponge baths for several months until her courage returns. Then start with just an inch of water, and remove the baby before you pull the stopper.

Leeriness of strangers. At this age, a baby's nature tells her to be leery and suspicious of strangers till she has had a chance to look them over. Then she wants to get closer and eventually make friends—in one-year-old fashion, of course. She may just stand close and gaze or solemnly hand something to the newcomer, then take it back, or bring everything movable in the room and pile it in the person's lap.

Many adults don't have the sense to let a small child alone while she sizes them up. They rush up to her, full of talk and enthusiasm. So she beats a hasty retreat to her parent for protection from this uninvited invader. As a result, it takes longer for her to work up her courage to be friendly. I think it helps for a parent to remind a visitor in the beginning, "It makes her shy when you pay attention to her right away. If you ignore her for a while, she'll try to make friends sooner."

When your baby is old enough to walk, give her plenty of chances to get used to seeing strangers. Take her to the grocery store a couple of times a week. As often as you can, take her someplace where other small children play. She won't be very interested in playing with the others yet, but at times she will want to watch. As she gets used to seeing others play, she will be more ready for cooperative play when the time comes, between two and three.

CHALLENGING BEHAVIORS

Dawdling. A mother of an eighteen-month-old boy walks with him every day to the grocery store. She complains that instead of walking right along, he wanders across the sidewalk and climbs the front steps of every house they pass on the way. The more she calls to him, the more he lingers. When she scolds him, he runs in the opposite direction. She is afraid that he is developing a behavior problem.

This baby doesn't have a behavior problem, though he may be made to have one. He's not at an age when he can keep the grocery store in mind. His natural instincts say to him, "Look at that sidewalk to explore! Look at those stairs!" Every time his mother calls to him, it reminds him of his newly felt urge to assert himself.

What can the mother do? If she has to get to the store promptly, she can take him in his stroller. But if she's going to use this time for his outing, she should allow four times longer than if she were going alone and let him make his side trips. If she keeps moving—slowly—he'll want to catch up to her every once in a while.

Trouble stopping fun activities. It's time to go in for lunch, but your small daughter is digging happily in the dirt. If you say, "Now it's time to go in," in a tone of voice that means, "Now you can't have any more fun," you will get resistance. But if you say cheerfully, "Let's go climb the stairs," you may give her a desire to go.

But suppose she's tired and cranky that day and that nothing that's indoors has any appeal. She just becomes disagreeably resistant right away. I'd pick her up casually and carry her indoors, even if she squeals and kicks. Do this in a self-confident way, as if you were saying to her, "I know you're tired and cross, but when we have to go in, we have to." Don't scold her; that won't make her see the error of her ways. Don't argue with her, because that won't change her mind; you will only become frustrated. A small child who is feeling miserable and making a scene is comforted underneath by sensing that the parent knows what to do without getting angry.

Young children are very distractible, and that's a big help. Year-old babies are so eager to find out about the whole world that they aren't particular where they begin or stop. Even if they're absorbed by a ring of keys, you can make them drop it by giving them an empty plastic cup. If toward the end of the first year your baby fights against having the food washed off his face and hands with a cloth after meals, set a pan of water on the tray and let him dabble his hands in it while you wash his face with your wet hand. Distractibility is one of the handles by which wise parents guide their children.

Dropping and throwing things. Around the age of one year, babies learn to drop things on purpose. They solemnly lean over the side of the high chair and drop food on the floor or toss toys, one after the other, out of the crib. Then they cry because they haven't got them. Are these babies deliberately trying to annoy their parents? No. They aren't even thinking about their parents. They are fascinated by a new skill and want to practice it all day long, the way an older child wants to ride a new two-wheeler. If you pick up the dropped object, they realize it's a game that two can play and are delighted.

Unless you want to play this game a lot, it's better not to get in the habit of picking up dropped toys right away. Instead, simply put your baby on the floor when he gets in this dropping mood. If you don't want him throwing food from the high chair, promptly take the food away when he starts dropping and put him down to play. You can firmly say, "Food is for eating, toys are for playing," but there's no need to raise your voice. Trying to scold a baby out of dropping things leads to nothing but frustration for the parent.

Temper tantrums. Almost all children have temper tantrums between one and three years. Some temperamentally intense

infants start as early as nine months. They've gained a sense of their desires and individuality. When they're thwarted, they know it and feel angry. A temper tantrum once in a while doesn't mean anything; a child is bound to be frustrated sometimes.

A surprising number of tantrums are a result of fatigue or hunger or of putting a child into a situation that is too stimulating. (Most shopping mall tantrums fall into this category.) If the tantrum is of this sort, a parent can ignore the apparent cause and deal with the underlying problem: "You're tired and hungry, aren't you? Let's get you home and fed and to bed, and you'll feel a lot better."

Some tantrums arise out of fear. This happens all the time at the doctor's office. The best thing to do in these situations is to be calm and reassuring. No good comes from scolding a scared child.

Tantrums happen more frequently in children who tend to be easily upset by changes or who are especially sensitive to sensory input (noises, motion, or the feel of clothing against the skin, for instance). Tantrums often last longer in persistent children. Once they get started, it's hard for them to stop, whether they're playing, practicing walking, or screaming at the top of their lungs. Excessive tantrums—for example, more than three a day, lasting more than ten to fifteen minutes each—are sometimes a sign of illness or stress, so it's reasonable to consult your child's doctor. See page 542 for more on tantrums and other acting-out behaviors.

SLEEP ISSUES

Nap hours are changing. Nap times are shifting in most babies around the age of a year. Some who were taking a nap at about 9 A.M. may refuse it altogether or show that they want it later in the morning. If they take it late, they are unready for their next nap until the middle of the afternoon. This probably throws off their bedtime after supper. Or they may refuse the afternoon nap altogether. A baby may vary a lot from day to day at this period, even going back to a 9 A.M. nap after two weeks of refusing it. So don't come to a final conclusion too soon. Put up with these inconveniences as best you can, realizing that they are temporary. With some babies who are not ready to sleep in the first part of the morning, you can remove the need for the before-lunch nap by putting them in their beds anyway, around nine in the morning, if they are willing to sit or lie quietly for a while. Of course, another kind of baby only gets in a rage if put to bed when she's not sleepy, so nothing is accomplished.

If a baby becomes sleepy just before noon, it's the parent's cue to move lunch up to 11:30 or even eleven for a few days. The long nap will then come after lunch, but for a while, cutting down to one nap a day, whether morning or afternoon, may make the baby frantically tired before suppertime.

Don't get the idea from this section that all babies give up their morning nap in the same way or at the same age. One is through with it at nine months; another craves it and benefits from it as late as two years. There is often a stage in a baby's life when two naps are too many and one is not enough! You can help babies through this period by giving them supper and putting them to bed for the night a little earlier for the time being.

Bedtime routines. Though you need to be a little flexible about sleep issues, it's also very helpful to have a bedtime routine. When things happen in the same way every day, it gives a young child a comforting sense of control. Bedtime routines can include stories, songs, prayers, hugs, and kisses. What's important is that the same things happen in roughly the same order. Television or videos and roughhouse play tend to keep children excited and awake, so these activities are best left out of the bedtime routine. For more on sleep issues, see pages 96 and 97.

EATING AND NUTRITION

Changes around one year. Around twelve to fifteen months, growth normally slows down and a toddler's appetite is likewise apt to level off. Some actually eat *less* than they did a few months before, causing their parents to worry. But if a child's growth plots out okay on the standard growth curve at the doctor's office, you can be assured that he is getting enough. If you make the mistake of showing your toddler that you want him to eat more, chances are he'll reward you by eating less, just to show you who's in charge. A better strategy is to give your baby small helpings, so he can enjoy demanding more, and not to pay much attention to how much goes in. Instead, watch your baby to see whether he is happy and full of energy and pay attention to the growth chart.

Early in the second year, many parents wean their babies from the breast or the bottle (see pages 280 and 303). Unless you are giving your toddler a nondairy diet (page 337), the drink of choice should be whole cow's milk. Toddlers need the high fat content of whole milk (or full-fat soymilk) to build their brains. After age two, it's sensible to switch to 1 percent or skim milk to lower the risk of heart disease as an adult. See page 239 for more on vitamins, vegetables, and other nutritional issues. For picky eating, food fads, and other worrisome eating aspects, see page 357.

Eating is a learning experience. For children to approach eating in a reasonable and healthy manner, they need to learn to pay attention to the body signals that tell them when they are hungry and when they've had enough. They need confidence that food will be there when they're hungry and that they won't be forced to eat when they're not hungry. You help your toddler learn these important lessons by making good food available and leaving it up to your child to decide how much to eat.

Table manners are also important. Every toddler experiments with mixing and smearing, testing the limits of what is acceptable. When your toddler crosses the line—throwing mashed potatoes, for instance—all you need to do is tell her firmly but calmly that food is for eating. Then remove her from the table and find her a ball or a cloth toy to throw. When eating turns to playing and it's clear that your child isn't hungry any more, it's time for the meal to end. Twenty minutes or so is usually long enough.

TOILET TRAINING AND LEARNING

Readiness to train. At twelve to eighteen months, most toddlers aren't ready for toilet training. They don't have the body awareness yet to recognize when they have to go, nor the control to hold everything in then let it out at the right time. Mostly, they don't really understand why they should sit on the potty instead of just filling up their diapers. Toddlers typically find their bodily productions interesting, not disgusting. They don't see what all the fuss is about if the contents of their diapers get smeared around a bit.

Of course, there are some toddlers who train early, making all the *other* parents think that their children are behind. But for most children, training much before age eighteen months is bound to be difficult and unsatisfying, and many aren't ready until two or two and a half. The psychologists Nathan Azrin and Richard Foxx describe an approach using powerful behavior modification techniques in their book, *Toilet Training in Less Than a Day*. But the instructions are fairly complicated; if you don't follow them to the letter or your child doesn't cooperate, you're both likely to end up frustrated.

So my advice to most parents is to wait with training until a child is two to two and a half. At that age, most can master the potty without a fuss. If you do start earlier and things don't go well, I don't think you have to worry that you've caused long-term psychological damage (as long as you didn't use harsh punishment or abuse), but the training process may involve more upset and take longer in the end. See page 575 for more on toilet training.

Toilet learning. While most one-year-olds aren't ready for *training*, they can certainly *learn* about the potty. If you let your child into the bathroom with you and there is a child-sized potty, your toddler may sit on it or even pretend to use it, just as she mimics vacuuming and other adult activities. This early interest is a sign that your child is learning about toileting, but it doesn't mean she's ready to take the next step. If you pressure her or even overdo the praise, there's a good chance she'll balk.

Part of using the toilet is washing the hands afterward, and many toddlers are happy to have an excuse to get their hands wet and soapy. It's helpful to talk about what you're doing in the bathroom as you do it so that your child learns the words. I favor simple terms like pee and poop rather than cutesy baby talk or euphemisms (wee-wee or number two, for example). By talking in a straightforward way, you let your child know that toileting is simply a fact of life, not something secret, shameful, exciting, or mysterious.

YOUR TWO-YEAR-OLD

BEING TWO

A tumultuous time. Some refer to this period as the "terrible twos." It's not really a terrible time, though; it's a terrific time, although few call it the "terrific twos." It's a time when your child is beginning to come into her own and learn what it's like to be an independent person. It's a time when her language skills and imagination are increasing at a breathtaking pace. But it's also a time when her understanding of the world is still so limited that many things can be scary.

Two-year-olds live in contradictions. They are both independent and dependent, loving and hateful, generous and selfish, mature and infantile. They stand with one foot in the warm, cozy, dependent past and the other in an exciting future full of autonomy and discovery. With so much excitement going on, it's no wonder that two is a challenging age for parents and children alike. But terrible, it isn't. It's really pretty amazing.

Two-year olds learn by imitation. In a doctor's office, a two-year-old girl solemnly places the stethoscope bell on different spots on her chest. Then she pokes the otoscope in her ear and looks puzzled because she can't see anything. At home she follows her parents around, sweeping with a broom when they sweep, dusting with a cloth when they dust, brushing her teeth when they do. It's all done with great seriousness. She is making giant strides forward in skill and understanding by constant imitation.

Young children also imitate their parents' behavior patterns. For example, when you treat others politely, your two-year-old learns to be polite. It's okay to tell a two-year-old to say please and thank you, but it's much more effective to let him hear *you* use those words in appropriate circumstances. (Don't expect to see politeness right away, but by four or five, your early investment in politeness is bound to begin to pay off.) In the same way, young children who see parents using hurtful language or threats often develop similar troublesome behaviors. That doesn't mean that parents can't ever argue or disagree. But a steady diet of angry conflict is harmful to children, even if they are just bystanders.

Communication and imagination. At two, one child speaks in three- and four-word sentences while another is just beginning to link two words together. A two-year-old who only says a few isolated words probably should have a hearing test and developmental evaluation, even though the chances are good that the child will simply be a late talker.

Imagination and language grow together. It's wonderful to watch a young child's imagination unfold over the year from twenty-four to thirty-six months. What starts out as simple imitation and experimentation becomes rich make-believe play. As a spur to imagination, let your child experience blocks, dolls, musical instruments, old shoes, cookie dough, water for splashing and pouring, and as many other interesting objects you can think of. Expose your child to nature, even if just the neighborhood park. Look at picture books together (see page 640), and let your child use paper and crayons. Scribbling is the first step on the path to writing.

One thing I strongly recommend *against* is television. Even high-quality children's television can limit a child's imagination, simply because it does all the work, demanding so little effort from the child. Even at two, television teaches children to become passive consumers of entertainment, rather than learning how to amuse themselves. (For more on television, see page 466.)

Parallel play and sharing. Two-year-olds don't play cooperatively with each other very much. Although they may love to watch each other's occupations, they mostly enjoy playing alongside each other in what is called parallel play. There is no point in trying to teach a two-year-old to share; he simply isn't ready. To share, a child has to understand that something *belongs* to him—that he can give it away and expect to get it back. That a two-year-old won't share has nothing to do with how generous a person he will become when he is older. But this doesn't mean you have to accept bad manners, even if he hasn't a clue why you consider his grabbing a toy away from a companion to be bad form. You can firmly but cheerfully take the toy away from him, return it to its rightful owner, and quickly try to distract him with another object of interest. Long harangues about why he should share things are wasted breath. He will start to share when he understands the concept of sharing (usually around three to four) and not before.

WORRIES AROUND TWO

Separation fears. By age two, some children have gotten over their toddler clinginess, others haven't. A two-year-old seems to realize clearly who it is that gives her a sense of security, and she shows it in different ways. A mother complains, "My two-year-old seems to be turning into a mama's girl. She hangs on to my skirts when we're out of the house. When someone speaks to us, she hides behind me." Two is a great age for whining, which can be a kind of clinging (see page 560). She may be timid about

being left anywhere by her parents. She's apt to be upset if a parent or other member of the household goes away for a number of days or if the family moves to a new house. It's wise to take her sensitivity into account when changes in the household are being considered.

Here's what can happen when a sensitive, dependent child of two years, particularly an only child, is abruptly separated from the parent who has spent the most time with him. Perhaps it is the mother, and she has to go out of town unexpectedly for a couple of weeks. Or she decides that she has to go to work and arranges for a stranger to come in and take care of the child. Usually the child makes no fuss while the mother is away, but when she returns, he hangs on to her like Velcro and refuses to let the other person come near. He panics whenever he thinks his mother may be leaving again.

Bedtime separations. Separation anxiety is worst at bedtime. The terrified child fights against being put to bed. If his mother tears herself away, he may cry in fear for hours. If she sits by his crib, he remains lying for only as long as she sits still. Her slightest move toward the door brings him instantly to his feet.

If your two-year-old child has become terrified about going to bed, the surest advice, though the hardest to carry out, is to sit by her crib in a relaxed way until she goes to sleep. Don't sneak away before she is asleep. That will alarm her again and makes her more wakeful. This campaign may take weeks but should work in the end. Making the child more tired by keeping her up later or omitting her nap may help a little but usually won't do the whole job. Even if she's exhausted, a panicky child can keep herself awake for hours. You have to take away her worry, too.

If your child was frightened because one of you left town, try to avoid going away again for many weeks. If you have taken a job for the first time since your child was born, say good-bye each day affectionately, cheerfully, and confidently. If you have an anguished, unsure-whether-you're-doing-the-right-thing expression, it will add to your child's uneasiness.

Concern about wetting the bed. Sometimes when a two-year-old has bedtime anxieties, there is also worry about urinating. The child keeps saying "Wee-wee" or whatever word he uses. His mother takes him to the bathroom, and he does a few drops, then cries "Wee-wee" again as soon as he is back in bed. You might say that he is just using this as an excuse to keep her there. This is true, but there is more to it. Children like this one are really worried that they may wet the bed.

They sometimes wake every two hours during the night thinking about it. This is the age when the parents are apt to show disapproval when there is an accident. Maybe the child figures that if he wets, his parents won't love him so much and will therefore be more likely to go away. If so, he has two reasons to fear going to sleep. If your child is worried about wetting, keep reassuring her that it doesn't matter if she does wee-wee in bed—that you'll love her just the same.

⬅ CLASSIC SPOCK

A child who is frightened by separation—or anything else—is very sensitive to whether her parents feel the same way about it. If they act hesitant or guilty every time they leave her side, if they hurry into her room at night, their anxiety reinforces her fear that there really is great danger in being apart from them.

This may sound contradictory after I've said that a parent must reassure a frightened two-year-old by sitting by her bed as she goes to sleep and by not going away on any more trips for a number of weeks. I mean that parents must give her this special care the way they give special consideration to a sick child. But they should try to be cheerful, confident, unafraid. They should be looking for signs of the child's readiness to give up her dependence, step by step, and encourage her and compliment her. This attitude of theirs is the most powerful factor in getting her over her fear. That and the maturational forces which, with time and maturity, will allow the child to better understand and master her fears.

Children may use separation anxiety to control. A child clings to his mother because he has developed a genuine fear of being separated from her. Then if he finds that she is so concerned about his fear that she will always do anything he wants for reassurance, he may begin to use this as coercion. There are three-year-olds, for instance, who are anxious about being left at preschool whose parents to reassure them not only stay at school for days but stay close to the children and do what they ask. After a while, you begin to see that such children are exaggerating their uneasiness because they have learned to use it to boss their parents around. A parent should say, "I think you are grown up now and aren't afraid to be in school. You just like to make me do what you want. Tomorrow I won't need to stay here anymore."

How to help a fearful two-year-old. When it comes to the management of children's fear, a lot depends on how important it is from a practical point of view for them to get over it in a hurry. There's no great necessity for anxious children to be hurried into making friends with dogs or going into deep water in the lake. They'll want to do these things as soon as they dare.

On the other hand, children should not be allowed to come into the parents' bed every single night (unless you've decided that cosleeping is for you; see page 59). They should be comforted and soothed in their own beds so that sleeping with the parents doesn't become a pleasant habit for which there is no motivation for the child to stop.

Once children have started preschool, it's better for them to go regularly unless they're deeply terrified. A skillful teacher can help a child become engaged in play so that the separation becomes easier. A child with a school-refusal problem must go back to school sooner or later; the longer it is put off, the harder it is. Parents are wise to consider whether overprotectiveness is playing a part in these various separation fears. This is a tough task, and parents are certainly entitled to help from a doctor or other professional.

Some causes of overprotectiveness. Overprotective feelings occur mostly in devoted parents who are inclined to feel guilty when there is no need to.

Often, the hidden cause is anger. The parent and child who are afraid to recognize that there are naturally moments when they resent each other, when each wishes that something bad would happen to the other, have to imagine instead that all the dangers in the world come from somewhere else and grossly exaggerate them. The child who denies the resentment in her parents and herself places it in monsters or robbers or dogs or lightning, depending on her age and experience. She clings tightly to her parents for protection and to reassure herself that nothing is really happening to them. A mother, for instance, may suppress her occasional resentful thoughts and exaggerate the dangers of kidnappers or home accidents or inadequate diet. She has to stay close to the child to make sure the dangers don't strike, and her anxious expression convinces the child that her own fears are well founded.

Of course, the answer is not for parents to take out all their angriest feelings on the child or to let her be abusive toward them. But it is certainly helpful for parents to recognize the inevitability of their occasional feelings of resentment toward their child and to admit them to each other. It helps to clear the air if parents occasionally admit to a child how angry they felt—especially if the anger was not quite fair. And it's good to say to a child once in a while, "I know how angry you feel toward me when I have to make rules like this for you."

CHALLENGING BEHAVIORS

Negativism. In the period between age two and age three, children are apt to show signs of negativism and other inner tensions. Your baby probably began to be balky and negativistic way back when she was fifteen months old, so this is nothing new. But it reaches new heights and takes new forms after two. One-year-old Petunia contradicts her parents. Two-and-a-half-year-old Petunia even contradicts herself! She has a hard time making up her mind, then wants to change it. She acts like a person who feels she is being bossed too much, even when no one is bothering her or when she tries to boss others. She insists on doing things just so, doing them her own way, doing them exactly as she has always done them. It makes her furious to have anyone interfere in one of her jobs or rearrange her possessions.

The child's nature between two and three seems to be urging her to decide things for herself and to resist pressure from other people. Trying to fight these two battles without much worldly experience seems to make her tight inside. For that reason, it's often hard to get along with a child between two and three.

The parents' job is to keep from interfering too much, and,

when possible, let their children work at their own pace. Let your child help to dress and undress himself when he has the urge. Start his bath early enough so that he has time to dawdle and scrub the tub. At meals, let him feed himself without urging. When he is stalled in his eating, let him leave the table. When it's time for bed, going outdoors, or coming in, steer him while conversing about pleasant things. Get things done without raising issues. Your goal is keep him from being a little tyrant but not to sweat the small stuff.

Two-year-olds behave best when parents set firm, consistent, and reasonable limits. The key is to choose those limits carefully. If you find yourself saying no a lot more than yes, you're probably setting too many arbitrary limits. A battle of wills with a two-year-old is exhausting, so save it for issues that are truly important. Safety issues, such as sitting in the car seat, are clearly important. Wearing mittens on a cold day may not be so very important. (After all, you can always stuff the mittens in your coat pocket and whip them out when your two-year-old's hands become cold.)

Temper Tantrums. Nearly every two-year-old has a tantrum from time to time; some healthy children have lots of them. Tantrums usually start around age one (see page 542) and peak around age two to three. There are many causes: frustration, fatigue, hunger, anger, and fear. Children who are temperamentally intense, persistent, and sensitive to change tend to have more of them. Sometimes a parent can see a tantrum brewing and head it off by distracting a child, offering a well-timed snack, or leaving a situation that is just too stimulating. At other times, the tantrum blows up in an instant. All you can do is wait for the storm to blow over.

During a tantrum, it's helpful to stay nearby so that your child doesn't feel alone. At the same time, it's best not to get angry at your child, threaten punishment, plead for calm, or try too hard to make everything better. Any of these responses just tend to make tantrums occur more often and last longer. Afterward, it's best to move on to a positive activity and put the upset in the past. A quick word of praise along the lines of "Nice job pulling yourself together" can let your child salvage some self-esteem and learn to recover faster the next time. Remind to praise yourself, too, for staying calm and rational—not easily done when your two-year-old is having a melt-down.

Whining. Young mammals of many species whine for attention and nurturance (think of puppies.) So whining is natural and universal, but it's still annoying. Early on you have no choice but to try to figure out what your child needs. Once your child can use words, however, it's reasonable to insist that *she* do that. A firm, unemotional, "Use your words, I don't listen to whining," is all it usually takes, although you may have to repeat this message over many months before it fully sinks in. Be aware that if you sometimes give in to whining—the temptation to do so is strong—it may become much harder to put a stop to it. See page 560 for more on whining and what to do.

Favoritism toward one parent. Sometimes a child around thirty- to thirty-six months can get along with either parent alone, but when the other one comes on the scene she flies into a rage. It may be partly jealousy, but at an age when she's sensitive about being bossed around and trying to do a little bossing herself, she may just feel outnumbered when she has to take on two important people at once.

It's more often the father who is particularly unpopular at this period; he sometimes has the feeling he's pure poison. He shouldn't take the child's reaction too seriously or feel hurt and turn away from her. It will help if he regularly cares for her by himself, doing things that are fun, as well as everyday chores, such as feeding and bathing. That way she gets to know him as an enjoyable, loving, and important person, not just an intruder. If a child objects at first when her father takes over, he should cheerfully but firmly carry on, and the mother should have the same firm and cheerful attitude as she leaves.

Taking turns this way will give each parent one-on-one time with their child and also time alone. But there is also value in time spent all together, even if the two-year-old acts cranky. It's good for a child (particularly a first child) to learn that her parents love each other, want to be with each other, and will not be bullied by her.

DIET AND NUTRITION

Changes in the diet. A two-year-old can eat pretty much what the family does. You still need to be aware of choking hazards—small or hard foods such as peanuts, grapes, carrots, and hard candies—and keep these out of your child's diet. If you've been giving your toddler whole milk, you can switch to 1 percent or skim. Brain growth slows down after age two, so a high-fat diet isn't needed. Also, getting used to a lower-fat diet early in childhood probably lowers the risk of heart disease years later.

Young children usually can't wait five to six hours between meals. Three meals and three snacks is a reasonable schedule. Snacks should be healthy and substantial, not junk food.

Food choices. Most two-year-olds handle cups and spoons with ease but may still need help with forks and knives. Since many two-year-olds resent getting help, even if they need it, you may want to focus on foods that can be eaten with a spoon or fingers.

Young children need practice making food choices. Peas or squash? Burger on the bun or off? One or two small choices is enough; more and bigger choices are likely to be overwhelming and may lead to tantrums. Wise parents offer a small selection of attractive foods at each meal, so that whatever the child chooses is healthy.

Food choices start with what you bring home from the store.

Choose fresh vegetables instead of chips and other high-fat snacks, fruits instead of cookies and cakes, and juice or water instead of soda. If you want your child to eat healthy, the best strategy is to keep the house stocked with healthy foods and keep the junk food out. See page 325 for more on nutrition and health.

Food fads and fights. One two-year-old wants only grilled cheese every meal; another demands noodle soup. Usually such fads last only a few days, then fade away only to be replaced by other food obsessions. In the interest of peace and harmony, you may want to give in to some extent. Five days in a row of peanut butter and jelly for lunch isn't harmful, and if there's milk, fruit, or some green vegetable at other meals, chances are your child is getting a reasonably balanced diet. If you think about what your child eats not in just one day but over the course of a week or so, you may see that the diet is pretty well balanced after all.

Many two-year-olds get locked into power struggles with their parents about food. On the child's side, worrisome behaviors include food refusal, extreme pickiness, demands for special foods, gagging, or tantrums; on the parent's side, nagging, cajoling, threatening, or outright force-feeding. See page 357 for ways to deal with these common problems.

TOILET TRAINING

One step toward independence. By twenty-four to thirty-six months, when most children have learned how to use the toilet, most parents can't wait to see their last dirty diaper. But in their hurry to have the process over with, many parents push, prod, or pester, with the result that training takes longer and is more stressful than it needs to be. Toilet training is part of a learning process that begins in the first year (see page 147) and ends several years later with a child who handles toileting, including wiping and hand-washing, who feels comfortable about bodily processes, and has adopted her parents' views on privacy and modesty. If you take this long view, you may feel more comfortable allowing toilet training to move forward at its own pace. For more on toilet training, including specific suggestions on how and when to start and what to do, see page 575.

YOUR PRESCHOOLER, THREE TO FIVE YEARS

————— ∽∾ ∾∽ —————

DEVOTION TO THE PARENTS

A less-rebellious age. Boys and girls around three have reached a stage in their emotional development when they feel that their fathers and mothers are wonderful people and they want to be like them. The automatic resistance and hostility that were just below the surface in the two-year-old seem to lessen after three in most children.

The feelings toward the parents aren't just friendly now; they are warm and tender. However, children are not so devoted to their parents that they always obey them and behave well. They are still real people with ideas of their own. They want to assert themselves, even if it means going against their parents' wishes at times.

While I emphasize how agreeable children usually are between three and five, I ought to make a partial exception for four-year-olds. A lot of assertiveness, cockiness, loud talk, and provoking comes out around four years in many children, when they come to the realization that they know everything—a misconception that mercifully soon fades.

Striving to be like the parents. At two years of age, children eagerly imitate their parents' activities. If they are playing at mopping the floor or hammering a pretend nail, their focus is on the use of the mop or the hammer. By three years of age, the quality of their imitation changes. Now they want to be like their parents as people. They play at going to work, tending house (cooking, cleaning, laundering), and caring for children (a doll or a younger child). They pretend to go for a drive in the family car or to step out for the evening. They dress up in their parents' clothes, mimic their conversation, manners, and mannerisms. Psychologists call this process identification.

Identification is a lot more important than just playing. It's how character is built. It depends more on what children perceive in their parents and model themselves after than on what the parents try to teach them in words. This is how children's basic ideals and attitudes are laid down—toward work, toward people, toward themselves—though these will be modified later as they become more mature and knowing. This is how they learn to be the kind of parents they're going to turn out to be twenty years later, as you can tell from listening to the affectionate or scolding way they care for their dolls.

Gender awareness. It's at this age that a girl becomes more aware that she's female and will grow up to be a woman. So she watches her mother with special attentiveness and tends to mold herself in her mother's image: how her mother feels about her husband (lord and master—or beloved partner) and the male sex in general, about women (confidantes or competitors), about girl and boy children (if the child of one sex is favored over the other or each individual is appreciated for herself or himself), toward work and housework (chore or challenge). The little girl will not become an exact copy of her mother, but she will surely be influenced by her in many respects.

A boy at this age realizes that he is on the way to becoming a man, and he therefore attempts to pattern himself predominantly after his father: how his father feels toward his wife and the female sex generally, toward other men, toward his boy and girl children, toward outside work and housework.

In addition to the predominant identification with the parent of the same sex, there's a degree of identification with the parent of the opposite sex. This is how the two sexes come to understand each other well enough to be able to live together.

Fascination with babies. Boys and girls now become fascinated with all aspects of babies. They want to know where babies come from. When they find out that babies grow inside their mothers, they are eager to carry out this amazing act of creation themselves—boys as well as girls. They want to take care of babies and love them, the way they realize they were cared for and loved. They will press a younger child into the role of a baby, spending hours acting as father and mother to him, or they'll use a doll.

It's not generally recognized that little boys are as eager as girls to grow babies inside themselves. When their parents tell them that this is impossible, they are apt to refuse to believe it for a long time. "I will *too* grow a baby," they say, really believing that if they wish something hard enough, they can make it come true. In a similar way, a preschool girl may announce that she is going to grow a penis. Ideas of this kind are not signs of dissatisfaction with being one sex or the other. Instead, I think, they come from the young child's belief that he or she can do everything, be everything, and have everything.

ROMANTIC AND COMPETITIVE FEELINGS

Wishes and worries. Boys become romantic toward their mothers, girls toward their fathers. Up to this age, a boy's love for his mother has been predominantly of a dependent kind, like that of a baby. Now it also becomes increasingly romantic, like his father's. By the time he's four, he's apt to insist that he's going to marry his mother when he grows up. He isn't clear on just what marriage consists of, but he's absolutely sure who is the most important and appealing woman in the world. The little girl who is growing in her mother's pattern develops the same kind of love for her father.

These strong romantic attachments help children to grow spiritually and to acquire wholesome feelings toward the opposite sex that will later guide them into good marriages. But there is another side of the picture that creates unconscious tension in most children at this age. When people, old or young, love someone very much, they can't help wanting that person all to themselves. So as a little boy of three or four or five becomes more aware of his possessive devotion to his mother, he also becomes aware of how much she already belongs to his father. This irritates him, no matter how much he loves and admires his father. At times he secretly wishes his father would get lost, then feels guilty about having such disloyal feelings. Reasoning as a child does, he imagines that his father has the same jealous and resentful feelings toward him.

The little girl develops the same possessive love for her father. She wishes at times that something would happen to her mother (whom she loves so much in other respects) so that she can have her father for herself. She may even say to her mother, "You can go away for a long trip, and I'll take good care of Daddy." But then she imagines that her mother is jealous of her, too—a frightening thought. If you think about classic fairy tales like "Snow White," you can see these fantasies and worries brought to life in the figure of the wicked stepmother.

Children try to push these scary thoughts out of their minds, since the parent, after all, is so much bigger and stronger, but they are apt to come to the surface in their play and dreams. These mixed feelings—of love, jealousy, and fear—toward the parent of the same sex can come out in the bad dreams that little children of this age are so apt to have: dreams of being chased by giants, robbers, witches, and other frightening figures.

Moving past possessiveness. This romantic attachment to the parent of the opposite sex in the preschool years is what you might call nature's way of molding children's feelings in preparation for their eventual life as spouse or parent. But it wouldn't do for the attachment to go so far or become so strong that it lasts throughout life or even throughout childhood.

Nature expects that children by six or seven will become discouraged about the possibility of having the parent all to themselves. The unconscious fears of the parent's supposed anger will turn their pleasure in dreaming about romance into an aversion. From now on children will shy away from kisses by the parent of the opposite sex. Their interests turn with relief to impersonal matters, such as schoolwork and sports. They try now to be just like other children of their own sex, rather than like their parents.

A father who realizes that his young son sometimes has unconscious feelings of resentment and fear toward him does not help the boy by trying to be too gentle and permissive with him. It's no help, either, for the father to try to avoid making his son jealous by pretending that he (the father) doesn't really love his wife very much. In fact, if a boy becomes convinced that his father is afraid to be a firm father and a normally possessive husband, the boy will sense that he has his mother too much to himself and will feel guilty and frightened. He will miss the inspiration of a confident father, which he must have in order to develop his own self-assurance.

In the same way, a mother best helps her daughter to grow up by being a self-confident mother who doesn't let herself be pushed around, who knows how and when to be firm, and who isn't afraid to show her affection for and devotion to her husband.

It complicates life for a boy if his mother is a great deal more permissive and affectionate toward him than his father is. The same is true if she seems to be closer and more sympathetic to her son than she is to her husband. Such attitudes have a tendency to alienate a boy from his father and make him fearful of him.

In a corresponding manner, the father who is putty in his daughter's hands and is always undoing the mother's discipline or the father who acts as if he enjoys his daughter's companionship more than his wife's is being unhelpful not only to his wife but to his daughter as well. This interferes with the good relationship that a daughter should have with her mother to grow up to be a happy woman.

Incidentally, it is entirely normal for a father to be a bit more lenient toward his daughter and a mother toward her son and for a son to feel a little more comfortable with his mother and a daughter with her father, since there is naturally less rivalry between male and female than between two males or two females.

In the average family there is a healthy balance among the feelings of father, mother, sons, and daughters that guides them through these stages of development without any special effort.

How parents can help. Parents can help children through this romantic, jealous stage by gently making it clear that they belong to each other, that a boy can't ever have his mother to himself and a girl can't have her father to herself, and that the parents aren't shocked to realize that their children are sometimes mad at them on this account.

When a girl declares that she is going to marry her father, he can act pleased with the compliment, but he should also explain that he's already married and that when she grows up she'll find a man her own age to marry.

When parents are being companionable together, they needn't and shouldn't let a child break up their conversation. They can cheerfully but firmly remind her that they have things to talk over and suggest that she get busy, too. Their tactfulness will keep them from prolonged displays of affection in front of her, just as it would if other people were present, but they don't need to spring apart guiltily if she comes into the room unexpectedly when they're hugging or kissing.

When a boy is rude to his father because he's jealous or to his mother because she's the cause of his jealousy, the parent should insist on politeness. And the converse is equally true if a girl is rude. But at the same time, the parents can ease the child's feelings of anger and guilt by saying that they know the child is sometimes cross at them.

CURIOSITY AND IMAGINATION

Intense curiosity. At this age, children want to know the meaning of everything they encounter. Their imagination is rich. They put two and two together and draw their own conclusions. They connect everything with themselves. When they hear about trains, they want to know right away, "Will I go on a train someday?" When they hear about an illness, it makes them think, "Will I have that?"

A gift for imagination. Preschool children are virtuosos of imagination. When children of three or four tell a made-up story, they aren't lying in our grown-up sense. Their imagination is vivid to them. They're not sure where the real ends and the unreal begins. That is why they love having stories told or read to them. That is why they are scared of violent television programs and movies and shouldn't see them.

You don't need to scold your child or make him feel guilty for occasionally making up stories. You can simply point out that what he said isn't actually so, although he may *wish* it were so. In this way, you're helping your child learn the difference between reality and make-believe.

An imaginary friend who shows up now and then, perhaps to help with a particular adventure—daring to go into the basement alone, for example—is a sign of a normal, healthy imagination. But sometimes a child who feels lonely will spend hours each day telling about imaginary friends or adventures, not as a game but as if he believes in them. When you help such a child to make friends with real children, the need for fantasy playmates often lessens.

✑ CLASSIC SPOCK

Children need hugging and piggyback rides. They need to share in parents' jokes and friendly conversations. If the adults around them are undemonstrative, children dream of comfy, understanding playmates as the hungry man dreams of chocolate bars. If the parents are always disapproving, the children invent a wicked companion whom they blame for the naughty things they have done or would like to do.

SLEEP ISSUES

Most children give up taking naps sometime before age four but may still need a period of quiet rest in the afternoon. If they sleep much less than ten hours a night, they're bound to be over-tired (although there is a wide range of normal sleep needs at this age, from about eight hours to as many as twelve or thirteen). Sleep problems that began earlier in life, such as excessive bedtime stalling or frequent waking, often continue through the preschool years (see page 96). But new sleep problems also often arise during the preschool years, even for children who have been good sleepers. Nightmares and night-terrors are common at this age (see next page).

Sleep problems can also develop out of the normal feelings of possessiveness and jealousy described above. The child wanders into the parents' room in the middle of the night and wants to get into their bed because (without putting these thoughts into words) he doesn't want them to be alone together. If he is allowed to stay, he might end up literally kicking his father out of the bed. It's much better for him, as well as for his parents, if they promptly and firmly, but not angrily, take him back to his own bed.

FEARS AROUND THREE, FOUR, AND FIVE

Imaginary worries. New types of fear crop up fairly often around the age of three and four—fear of the dark, of dogs, fire engines, death, crippled people. Children's imaginations have by then developed to the stage where they can put themselves in other people's shoes and picture dangers that they haven't actually experienced. Their curiosity is pushing out in all directions. They want to know not only the cause of everything but what these things have to do with them. They overhear something about dying. They want to know what dying is. As soon as they get a dim idea, they ask, "Do I have to die?"

These fears are more common in children who were made tense by battles over such matters as feeding and toilet training, children whose imaginations have been overstimulated by scary stories or too many warnings, children who haven't had enough chance to develop their independence and outgoingness, children whose parents are too protective. The uneasiness accumulated before now seems to be crystallized by the child's new imagination into definite dread.

That is not to say that any child who develops a fear has been handled mistakenly in the past. The world is full of things young children do not understand, and no matter how lovingly they have been raised, they recognize their own weakness and vulnerability. Some children—about one in seven—have brains that are biologically programmed to respond to changes with anxiety. And all children, no matter how carefully they are brought up, are frightened by something.

Fear of the dark. If your child develops a fear of the dark, try to reassure her. This is more a matter of your manner than your words. Don't make fun of her, be impatient with her, or try to argue her out of her fear. If she wants to talk about it, as a few children do, let her. Give her the feeling that you want to understand but are absolutely certain that nothing bad will happen to her. Naturally, you should never threaten her with monsters, policemen or the devil.

Avoid scary movies and television programs and cruel fairy tales. The child is enough afraid of her own mental creations. Call off any battle you're engaged in about eating or staying dry at night. Keep her behaving well by firm guidance, rather than by letting her misbehave then making her feel guilty about it afterward. Arrange to give her a full, outgoing life with other children every day. The more she is absorbed in games and plans, the less she will worry about her inner fears. Leave her door open at night if that is what she wants, or leave a dim light on in her room. It's a small price to pay to keep the goblins out of sight. Neither the light nor the conversation from the living room will keep her awake as much as her fears will. When her fear subsides, she will be able to tolerate the dark again.

Fear of animals. Preschool children often develop a fear of one or more animals, even if they have never had a bad experience with them. It doesn't help to drag a scared child to a dog to prove that nothing bad will happen. The more you pull, the more the child will feel he has to pull in the opposite direction. As the months go by, the child will try to get over his fear and approach a dog. He'll do it faster by himself than you can ever persuade him to.

Fear of the water. It's almost always a mistake to pull a child, screaming, into the ocean or a pool. It is true that occasionally a child who is forced in finds that it is fun and abruptly loses the fear, but in more cases, it works the opposite way. Remember that despite the dread she feels, the child is longing to go in.

Questions about death. Questions about death are apt to come up at this age. Try to make the first explanation casual, not scary. You might say, "Everybody has to die someday. Most people die when they get very old and sick, and their body just stops working."

You have to tailor your answer to your child's developmental level. For example, "We lost Uncle Archibald," can strike terror into the heart of any child who has himself gotten lost. Since this is the age when children take everything literally, it's especially important not to refer to death as going to sleep. Many children will then become terrified of going to sleep and dying themselves, or else they'll say: "Well, wake him up."

It's much better to explain as simply as possible—without sugarcoating the facts—that death is a state where the body stops working completely. You can then use the opportunity to discuss your family's beliefs about death. Most adults have some degree of fear and resentment of death; there is no way to present the matter to children that will get around this basic human attitude. But if you think of death as something eventually to be met with dignity and fortitude, you'll be somewhat able to give that same feeling to your child. Also remember to invite questions and to answer them simply and truthfully. Remember to hug her and remind her that you're going to be together for a very long time. (See page 511 for more on helping children cope with death.)

Helping your child cope with fears. It is not your job as a parent to banish all fears from your child's imagination. Your job is to help your child learn constructive ways to cope with and conquer those fears. In the eloquent words of Selma Fraiberg in *The Magic Years:* "The future mental health of the child does not depend on the presence or absence of ogres in his fantasy life. It depends on the child's solution to the ogre problem."

When a child has fears of dogs and fire engines and policemen and other concrete things, she may try to get used to the worry and overcome it by making up games about it. This playing-out of a fear is a great help if the child is able to do it. A fear is meant to make us act. Our bodies are flooded with adrenaline, which makes the heart beat faster and supplies sugar for quick energy. We are ready to run like the wind or to fight like wild animals (flight or fight). The running and fighting burn up the anxiety. Sitting still does nothing to relieve it. If children with a fear of dogs play games in which they become the masters of a toy dog, it partly relieves them. If your child develops an intense fear or a number of fears that cross over into other parts of his daily life, you ought to get the help of a children's mental health professional. For more on fears, see page 139.

WORRIES ABOUT INJURY AND BODY DIFFERENCES

Why these worries arise. Children at this age want to know the reason for everything, worry easily, and apply dangers to themselves. If they see a crippled or deformed person, they first want to know what happened to that person, then they put themselves in the person's place and wonder if that injury might happen to them.

This is also the age in which there is naturally a great interest in physical mastery of all kinds (hopping, running, climbing), which makes body intactness very important and its being broken very upsetting. This explains why a child at the age of two and a half or three can get so upset about a broken cookie, refusing one that's in two pieces and demanding a whole one.

Body and sexual differences. Children develop these fears not only about real injuries. They even get mixed up and worried about the natural differences between boys and girls. If a boy around the age of three sees a girl undressed, it may strike him as odd that she hasn't got a penis as he does. He's apt to say, "Where is her wee-wee?" If he doesn't receive a satisfactory answer right away, he may jump to the conclusion that some accident has happened to her. Next comes the anxious thought,

"That might happen to me, too." The same misunderstanding may worry the little girl when she realizes that boys are made differently. First she asks, "What's that?" Then she anxiously wants to know, "Why don't I have one? What happened to it?" That's the way a three-year-old's mind works. Children may be so upset that they're afraid to question their parents.

✺ CLASSIC SPOCK

This worry about why boys are different from girls shows up in different ways. I remember a boy just under three who, with an anxious expression, kept watching his baby sister being bathed and telling his mother, "Baby is boo-boo." That was his word for hurt. His mother couldn't make out what he was talking about until he got bold enough to point. At about the same time he began to hold on to his own penis in a worried way. His mother was unhappy about this and assumed it was the beginning of a bad habit. It never occurred to her that there was a connection between these two developments.

I also remember a little girl who became worried after she found out about boys and kept trying to undress different children to see how they were made, too. She didn't do this in a sly way; you could see she was fearful. Later she began to handle her genitals. A boy three and a half first became upset about his younger sister's body and then began to worry about everything in the house that was broken. He would ask his parents nervously, "Why is this tin soldier broken?" There was no sense to this question, because he had broken it himself the day before. Everything that was damaged seemed to remind him of his fears about himself.

It's wise to realize ahead of time that normal children between two and a half and three and a half are likely to wonder about things like bodily differences, and if they aren't given a comforting explanation when they become curious, they're apt to come to worrisome conclusions. It's no use waiting for them to say, "I want to know why a boy isn't made like a girl," because they won't be that specific. They may ask some kind of question, or they may hint around, or they may just wait and become worried. Don't think of this as an unwholesome interest in sex. To them it's just like any other important question, at first. You can see why it would work the wrong way to shush them, scold them, or blush and refuse to answer. That would give them the idea they are on dangerous ground, which you want to avoid.

On the other hand, you don't need to be solemn, as if you were giving a lecture. It's easier than that. It helps, first of all, to bring the child's fear out into the open by saying that he probably thinks a girl had a penis but something happened to it. Then you try to make it clear, in a matter-of-fact, cheerful tone, that girls and women are made differently from boys and men; they are meant to be that way. A small child understands an idea more easily from examples. You can explain that Johnny is made just like Daddy, Uncle Harry, David, and so on and that Mary is made like Mommy, Mrs. Jenkins, and Helen (listing individuals the child knows best).

A little girl needs extra reassurance because it's natural for her to want to have something she can see. (One little girl complained to her mother, "But he's so fancy and I'm so plain.") It will help her to know that her mother likes being made the way she is, that her parents love her just the way she is. This may also be a good time to explain that girls when they are older can grow babies of their own inside them and have breasts with which to nurse them. That's a thrilling idea at three or four.

SCHOOL AGE:
SIX THROUGH ELEVEN YEARS

FITTING INTO THE OUTSIDE WORLD

After about five or six, children turn into kids. Relationships with parents, while still critically important, shift to the background. Kids are more concerned with what the other kids say and do. In little ways at first, then increasingly over time, they become independent of their parents, even impatient with them. They develop a stronger sense of responsibility about matters they think are important. They are interested in impersonal subjects like arithmetic and engines. In short, they're beginning the job of emancipating themselves from the family and taking their places as citizens of the outside world.

Self-control. Children after six become strict about some things. Think of the games children enjoy at this age. They're no longer so interested in make-believe without a plan. They want games that have rules and require skill. In hopscotch, jacks, and jump rope (not to mention video games), you have to do things in a certain order, which becomes harder as you progress. If you miss, you must penalize yourself, go back to the beginning, and start over. It's the very strictness of the rules that appeals to children.

This is the age for starting collections, whether it's stamps, cards or stones. The pleasure of collecting is in achieving order-liness and completeness. At this age, children have the desire to put their belongings in order. Suddenly they neaten their desk, put labels on the drawers, or arrange their piles of comic books. They don't keep their things neat for long, but you can see that the urge must be strong just to get them started.

Independence from parents. Children after six go on loving their parents deeply underneath, but they usually don't show it as much on the surface. They're often cooler toward other adults, too. They no longer want to be loved merely as an appealing child. They're gaining a sense of dignity as individuals and want to be treated as such.

From their need to be less dependent on their parents, they turn more to trusted adults outside the family for ideas and knowledge. If they mistakenly get the idea from an admired science teacher that red blood cells are larger than white blood cells, there's nothing their parents can say that will change their minds. The ideas of right and wrong that their parents taught them have not been forgotten. In fact, they have sunk in so deep that they now think of them as their own creations. Children are impatient when their parents keep reminding them of what they ought to do because they know already and want to be considered responsible.

Bad manners. Children drop some of the words their parents use out of their vocabulary and pick up a little tough talk. They want the style of clothes and haircut that the other kids have. They may leave their shoelaces untied with the same conviction with which people wear party buttons during a political campaign. They may lose some of their table manners, come to meals with dirty hands, slump over the dish, and stuff too much food into their mouths. Perhaps they absentmindedly kick the leg of the table. They drop their coats on the floor. They slam doors or leave them open.

Without realizing it, they are really accomplishing three things at once. First, they're looking to children of their own age as models of behavior. Second, they're declaring their right to be more independent of parents. Third, they're keeping square with their conscience since they're not doing anything that's morally wrong.

These bad manners and bad habits are apt to make their parents unhappy. They imagine that the child has forgotten all that they so carefully taught. Actually, these changes are proof that their child has learned what good behavior is—otherwise he wouldn't bother to rebel against it. When he feels he has established his independence, he will probably resume following his family's standards of behavior.

Not that every child is a hellion at this age. One who gets along happily with easygoing parents may show no open rebelliousness at all, but if you look carefully, you will see signs of a change of attitude.

What do you do? After all, children must take a bath once in a while, and get neatened up on holidays. You may be able to overlook some of the minor irritating ways, but you should be firm in matters that are important to you. When you have to ask them to wash their hands, try to be matter of fact. A lighthearted, humorous approach can help, too. It's the nagging tone, the bossiness, that they find irritating and that unconsciously spurs them or to further balkiness.

SOCIAL LIVES

Importance of peers. For kids, being accepted by peers is a matter of greatest importance. Ask the children in any classroom and they all can tell you who is popular and who is "weird." Kids with negative reputations often have a hard time making friends, so their days at school are lonely and demoralizing. It's no wonder, then, that school-age children often seem to go to great lengths to fit in, even if it means opposing some family rules.

How happily people get along as adults in their jobs and in family and social life depends a great deal on how they got along with other children when they were young. If parents give children high standards and high ideals at home, they form part of their character and show up in the long run, even if they go through a period of bad English and rough manners in the middle period of childhood. But if parents are unhappy about the neighborhood they live in and the companions their children have, give their children a feeling that they are different from the others, or discourage them from making friends, they may grow up unable to get along comfortably with anyone. Then the high standards won't be of much use to the world or themselves.

Helping children to be sociable and popular. These are some of the early steps in bringing up children to be sociable and popular: not fussing over them in their first years; letting them be around other children their size from the age of a year; allowing them freedom to develop independence; making as few changes as possible in where the family lives and where the children go to school; letting them, as far as possible, associate with, dress like, talk like, play like, and have the same allowance and other privileges as the other average children in the neighborhood. Of course, that doesn't mean letting them take after the town's worst scoundrel. And you don't have to take your child's word about what the other children are allowed to do.

If a boy is having trouble making friends, it helps most if he can be in a school and class with a flexible program. Then the teacher can arrange things so that he has chances to use his abilities to contribute to class projects. This is how the other children will learn to appreciate his good qualities and to like him. A good teacher who is respected by the class can also raise a child's popularity in the group by showing that she appreciates that child. It even helps to put him in a seat next to a very popular child or to let him be partners with that child in activities.

There are things that the parents can do at home, too. Be friendly and hospitable when your child brings others home to play. Encourage him to invite friends to meals and serve the dishes that they consider super. When you plan weekend trips, picnics, excursions, movies, and other activities, invite another child with whom your child wants to be friends—not necessarily the one you would like him to be friendly with. Children, like adults, have a mercenary side, and they are more apt to see the good points in a child who provides treats for them.

Naturally, you don't want your child to have only bought popularity; that kind won't last anyway. What you are after is to prime the pump, to give him a chance to break into a group that may be shutting him out because of the natural clannishness of this age. Then, he can take over from that start and build real friendships of his own.

Clubs and cliques. This is the age for the blossoming of clubs. A number of kids who are already friends decide to form a secret club. They work like beavers making membership buttons, fixing up a meeting place (preferably hidden), drawing up a list of rules. They may never figure out what the secret is. But the secrecy idea probably represents the need to prove they can govern themselves, undisturbed by grown-ups and unhampered by other, more dependent children.

It seems to help children, when they're trying to be grown up, to get together with others who feel the same way. Then the group tries to bring outsiders into line by making them feel left out or picking on them. This sounds conceited and cruel to grown-ups, but that's because we are accustomed to using more refined methods of disapproving of each other. The children are only feeling the instinct to organize community life. This is one of the forces that makes our civilization click. However, the natural tendency to form groups can become destructive, leading to cruel teasing or even physical attacks. Then parents and teachers need to step in.

As children enter middle school age, at age ten or eleven, the pressure to belong can be intense. Tight-knit groups, or cliques, make their own rules for who's in and who's out. Physical attractiveness, athletic or academic ability, money, the right clothes, the right talk: All are tickets in. A child who has none of these desirable traits may find herself left out altogether—a lonely and often miserable predicament. A sympathetic and skillful teacher or guidance counselor can sometimes help turn things around; at other times, a psychologist or other professional can help a child acquire the social skills she needs.

Bullies. Bullying is another common way that normal social forces can get out of hand. A bully is a leader who has learned to gain power and status by victimizing vulnerable children. Bullying is bad for everyone. The victims often suffer anxiety, physical aches, or depression, and the outlook is even worse for the bullies. Having learned that they can succeed through intimidation, they have a hard time finding other ways to get along. As a result, as adults they often have difficulties staying employed and tend to run afoul of the law. It's not reasonable to expect a child who is a victim to stand up and defeat a bully. But when parents, teachers, and children all work together, they can make their schools bully free. A good resource is *Bullying at School* by Dan Olweus, and you can also search the internet.

Organized activities. By the time they're seven years old, many children are involved in organized after-school activities every day. This is particularly true in single-parent families and those in which both parents work outside the home. Sports, gymnastics, music, and dance can all enrich children's lives if they're done in moderation and without excessive competitiveness. But children also need some time to just hang out, alone or with friends, using their creative imaginations to decide what to do. If a child's life is very full during the week, parents may need to make a conscious decision to keep some weekend time unscheduled and free.

AT HOME

Work and chores. In many societies, school-age children work in family farms or businesses or in workshops or factories. In years past, most children in the United States also worked alongside adults. It's only in the past fifty years that school has been the main or only occupation expected of children. By the time children are eight or nine, it's very good for them to feel that they can contribute meaningfully to their family's well-being. If there's no family business that a child can work in, it's good for him to have chores that allow him to feel that he is truly helping out. A six-year-old can help set and clear the table; an eight-year-old can help with cleaning or pulling up weeds; a ten-year-old can do simple cooking.

Chores are one of the ways children learn about doing their

share in the household, the same way they will later participate in the larger society. Chores often conform to stereotyped sex roles—cooking for girls, lawn work for boys—but they don't have to. Chores are an opportunity to help children take a broader view of their capabilities.

If you are consistent and matter-of-fact about their responsibilities, the children will be, too. It's best not to make lots of exceptions or let children get away with not finishing their tasks. There are always some extra chores—washing the car, perhaps, or painting a fence—and these may be a way for children to earn money at home.

Allowance. An allowance is a way for children to learn about handling money and about saving or spending. Most children can begin to understand these ideas at age six or seven, so that's a good time to start giving an allowance. The amount will depend on your family custom and finances and the pattern in your community. Children should make their own choices about how to spend their allowance, as long as it isn't for something the parents have ruled out, like excessive sweets. An allowance shouldn't be used as payment for routine chores, however. Chores are a way that family members contribute to the work of the family. The reason to do chores is "Because everyone in the family helps out."

Homework. Early on, homework can help a child learn to work independently. Later on, homework allows children to practice what they've learned during the school day. Children who do more homework generally do better academically. But homework should take no more than about twenty minutes a night in first through third grade, forty minutes in fifth and sixth grade, and two hours in seventh through ninth. Sometimes a school simply assigns too much. In other cases, a child who has learning problems manages to get the work done only by putting in much more time than her classmates. When homework is tougher than it should be, teachers and parents can work together to find out why and provide the right help. See page 668 for more on homework.

COMMON BEHAVIOR CONCERNS

Lying. Younger children often lie simply to escape the consequences of their misdeeds. Did they take those cookies? Well, they didn't really *mean* to, they just sort of did it, so in a way, perhaps the answer is no—or so the child may think.

Children need to learn that *saying* something is so does not *make* it so. They also learn that it's better to own up early rather than make things worse by lying. They learn through moral stories told by parents and teachers and through experience.

Why does an older child lie? Everyone, grown-up or child, gets in a jam occasionally when the only tactful way out is a small lie. This is no cause for alarm. But if a child tells a lie to deceive, the first question to ask yourself is: Why does the child feel she has to lie?

A child isn't naturally deceitful. When a girl lies regularly, it means that she is under too much pressure of some kind. If she is failing in her schoolwork and lies about it, it isn't because she doesn't care. Her lying shows that she does care. Is the work too hard for her? Is her mind confused by other worries so that she can't concentrate? Are her parents setting too high standards?

Your job is to find out what is wrong, with the help of the teacher, a guidance counselor, a school psychologist, or a psychiatrist. You don't have to pretend that she has pulled the wool over your eyes. You might say gently, "You don't have to lie to me. Tell me what the trouble is and we'll see what we can do."

But she won't be able to tell you the answer right away, because she probably doesn't know it herself. Even if she knows some of her worries, she can't break down all at once. Helping her to express her feelings or worries takes time and understanding.

For stealing, an issue that often goes along with lying, see "How Children Think" in Section V.

Cheating. Young children cheat because they don't like losing. A six-year-old thinks that the point of playing is to win. He's gleeful as long as he's on top, then miserable if he falls behind. Learning to lose gracefully takes years. Eventually, kids figure out that everyone has more fun when everyone plays fair. They don't learn this from grown-ups as much as from each other. A group of eight-year-olds is likely to spend more time arguing about *how* to play a game than they do actually playing it. A tremendous amount of learning takes place during these debates.

At first, children see the rules as something fixed and unchangeable. Later, as their concept of right and wrong becomes more mature and flexible, they realize that rules can be changed, as long as all the players agree.

Of course, children can also enjoy games where no one loses and everyone wins. More of these noncompetitive games are available, in stores or over the internet (see the resource section, page 922, for noncompetitive games). Playing noncompetitive games may help a child realize that the object of playing a game is to have fun, not to beat your opponent.

Compulsions. The tendency toward strictness becomes so strong in many children around eight, nine, and ten that they develop nervous habits. You probably remember them from your own childhood. The commonest is stepping over cracks in the sidewalk. There's no sense to it; you just have a superstitious feeling that you ought to. Other examples are touching every third picket in a fence, making numbers come out even in some way, saying certain words before going through a door. If you think you have made a mistake, you must go back to where you were absolutely sure that you were right, then start over.

We now know that a very strong tendency to compulsiveness is often the result of brain characteristics that are inherited. Rarely, a child suddenly develops severe compulsions as a complication of an infection with strep (see page 828). From a psychological perspective, compulsions may be a way for children to deal with anxious feelings. One source of anxiety may be hostile feelings toward parents that the child cannot acknowledge. Think about the childhood saying, "Step on a crack, break your mother's back." Everyone has hostile feelings at times toward the people who are close to him, but his conscience would be shocked at the idea of really harming them and warns him to keep such thoughts out of his mind. And if a person's conscience becomes excessively stern, it keeps nagging about such bad thoughts even after he has succeeded in hiding them away in his subconscious mind. He still feels guilty, though he doesn't know what for. It eases his conscience to be extra careful and proper

about such a senseless thing as how to navigate a crack in the sidewalk.

The reason a child is apt to show compulsions around the age of nine is not that his thoughts are more wicked but that his conscience just naturally becomes stricter at this stage of development.

Mild compulsions are so common around the ages of eight, nine, and ten years that for the most part they can be considered normal. Mild compulsions, like stepping over cracks, shouldn't be a concern, in a child who is happy, outgoing, and doing well in school. On the other hand, I'd call on a mental health professional for help if a child has compulsions that occupy a lot of his time: for instance, excessive hand-washing or if he is tense, worried, or unsociable.

Tics. Tics are nervous habits, such as eye-blinking, shoulder-shrugging, grimacing, neck-twisting, throat-clearing, sniffing, and dry coughing. Like compulsions, tics occur most commonly around the age of nine, but they can begin at any age after two. The motion is usually quick, regularly repeated, and always in the same form. It is more frequent when the child is under tension. A tic may last on and off for a number of weeks or months then go away for good or be replaced by a new one. Blinking, sniffing, throat-clearing, and dry coughing often start with a cold but continue after the cold is gone. Shoulder-shrugging may begin when a child has a new loose-fitting garment that feels as if it were falling off. Children may copy a mannerism from another child with a tic, especially from a child they look up to, but these mannerisms don't last long.

The main cause of tics seems to lie in the development of the brain. But psychology also plays a role. Tics are more common in tense children with fairly strict parents. There may be too much pressure at home. Sometimes the mother or father is going at the child too hard, directing him, correcting him whenever he is in sight. Or the parents may be showing constant disapproval in a quieter way, setting standards that are too high, or providing too many activities, such as dancing, music, and athletic lessons. If the child were bold enough to fight back, he would probably be less tight inside. But being, in most cases, too well brought up for that, he bottles up his irritation, and it keeps backfiring in the form of a tic.

No child should be scolded or corrected on account of his tics. They are out of his control. The parents' whole effort should go into making his home life relaxed and agreeable, with the least possible nagging, and making his school and social life satisfying. About one child in ten has mild tics like this; they almost always go away with benign neglect. Maybe one in a hundred children will continue to have multiple tics that persist for over a year. This one child may have Tourette's Syndrome (see Glossary of Medical Terms) and should be checked by the doctor or nurse practitioner.

Posture. Good or bad posture results from a number of factors. One—perhaps the most important factor—is the skeleton the child is born with. You see individuals who have been round-shouldered from babyhood, like their mother or father before them. Some children seem to be born with a relaxed set of muscles and ligaments. Other children look tightly knit, in action or at rest. It's hard for them to slump.

There are also rare diseases that affect posture, and chronic illness and chronic fatigue (from any cause) can cause children to slump and sag. Overweight sometimes exaggerates swayback, knock-knees, and flat feet. Unusual tallness makes the self-conscious adolescent duck the head. A child with poor posture needs regular examinations to make sure that there is no physical reason.

Many children slouch because of a lack of self-confidence. This may result from too much criticism at home, difficulties in school, or an unsatisfactory social life. People who are buoyant and sure of themselves show it in the way they sit and stand and walk. When parents realize how much the child's feelings have to do with his posture, they can handle the problem more wisely.

The natural impulse of a parent, eager to have a child look good, is to keep after posture: "Remember the shoulders," or "For goodness' sake, stand up straight." But the posture of children who are stooped over because their parents have always kept after them too much won't be improved by more nagging. Generally speaking, the best results come when the child receives posture work through dance or other body-movement classes or from a physical therapist. In these places, the atmosphere is more businesslike than at home. The parents may be able to greatly help a boy in carrying out his exercises at home if he wants help and they can give it in a friendly way. But their main job is to help the child's spirit by aiding his school adjustment, fostering a happy social life, and making him feel adequate and self-respecting at home.

ADOLESCENCE: TWELVE TO EIGHTEEN YEARS

A TWO-WAY STREET

Teenagers and their parents both have to find a way to let go of each other gradually and as gracefully as possible. In some families, this happens smoothly. In many others, there are struggles, often caused by the parents' not being aware of the normal developmental issues in adolescence. The process can be much more comfortable when parents remember that their teenagers aren't really out to get them but are in fact just trying to establish their own adult identities.

Adolescents have a lot to cope with. Puberty reshapes their bodies in ways that change how they feel about themselves and how the rest of the world responds to them. Sexual urges can be exhilarating and terrifying at the same time. Our culture adds to the turmoil by sending mixed messages about adolescent sexuality, on the one hand idolizing it (just think of all the ads featuring young, sexy bodies), and on the other hand treating it as a dangerous force that needs to be quelled and controlled. School, a welcome haven for many teens, feels like a prison to others. The ability to think abstractly leads many teens to question the society they are preparing to join as adults. Idealism can be a powerful force for good, but it is often upsetting, too.

It helps for parents to remind themselves that the fundamental values they taught their children are likely to still be there, underneath the swirl of conflicting urges and ideas. Most teens, after all, hold to their family's core beliefs, even if they dye their hair a color never seen in nature.

And yet there are real dangers, too. Risky sexual behavior, alcohol use, and drugs can all have long-term, even permanent consequences, and many mental health problems make their first appearance in the teen years. So parents have to be aware of the pitfalls even while trusting their teens to get through. A focus on the long-term goal—a healthy, well-functioning young adult—may help parents sort out behaviors that are truly a concern from those that are merely annoying.

Being a wise parent to adolescents has always been a difficult job at best. Some unknown parent once said, "Oh, to be only half as wonderful as my child thought I was and only half as stupid as my teenager thinks I am."

PUBERTY

Puberty marks the beginning of adolescence. It consists of two to four years of rapid growth and development leading up to physical maturity and the ability to reproduce.

Timing. The first thing to realize is that there is a wide age range at which puberty begins. The largest number of girls begin their development at around the age of ten and have their first period at about twelve and a half. It's not abnormal for girls to start at nine; some may start even earlier. Breast development may not begin until as late as twelve or thirteen, in which case the first menstrual period may not come until fourteen or fifteen. The average boy starts puberty two years later than the average girl, at around twelve; some healthy boys start as late as fourteen or fifteen. Assessment of pubertal development should be a part of the annual checkup for teens. If puberty starts either very early or very late, the doctor or nurse practitioner needs to make sure that there is no medical condition causing the unusual timing.

The earliest changes of puberty occur deep inside the brain. Hormones flow from the brain through the bloodstream to the gonads (testicles or ovaries), switching them into high gear. The gonads in turn produce the main sex hormones, testosterone and estrogen, that trigger the rest of puberty. What exactly sets the brain into action in the first place, no one knows for sure. Heredity, nutrition, and general health all influence the timing of puberty. In the United States, improved (or, at least, increased) nutrition during childhood has lowered the age of puberty by several years, and there is controversy about whether other factors, such as pesticides or hormones in foods, may also play a role.

Puberty development in girls. Let's trace what happens to the average girl who starts puberty at age ten. When she was seven years old, she was growing two to two and a half inches a year. When she was eight, her rate of growth slowed down to perhaps one and three-quarter inches a year. Nature seemed to be putting on the brakes. Suddenly, at about ten, the brakes let go, and she begins to shoot up at the rate of three to three and a half inches a year for the next two years. Instead of putting on five to eight pounds a year, as she used to, she now gains from ten to twenty pounds a year. Her appetite increases significantly to make this gain possible.

Other things are happening, too. At the beginning of this time, her breasts begin to develop. The first thing noticed is a hard lump under the nipple. This may be frightening to parents because of the fear of breast cancer, but it is the normal onset of breast development. For the first year and a half the breast has a conical shape, but as her first menstrual period nears, it rounds out into more nearly a hemisphere. Occasionally, one breast begins to develop months before the other. This is fairly common and nothing to worry about. The earlier developing breast tends to stay larger through puberty and may on occasion remain so permanently.

Soon after the breasts begin to develop, pubic hair starts to grow. Later, hair appears in the armpits. The hips widen. The skin texture changes. At twelve and a half, the average girl has her first menstrual period. This event is called menarche. By now her body has begun to look more like a woman's. From this time on, her growing slows down rapidly. In the year after her first period she will grow perhaps one and a half inches; in the year after that, perhaps three-quarters of an inch. In many girls menstrual periods are irregular and infrequent for the first year or two. This is not a sign that something is wrong; it only shows that full maturity was not reached at the time of the first period.

There is no one age at which puberty begins; each girl has an individual maturational rate and timetable. That a girl starts puberty much earlier or later than average usually doesn't mean that her glands aren't working right. It means only that she is on a faster or slower timetable. This individual timetable seems to be an inborn trait: parents who were early developers are more apt to have children who are early developers, and the same holds for late developers. The thirteen-year-old who has shown no signs of pubertal development can be assured that she will develop, even though it may take her longer to do so.

There are other variations besides the age at which puberty development begins. In some girls, pubic hair appears months before the breasts start to develop. And once in a while, hair in the armpits is the earliest sign of change instead of a late one. The length of time between the first signs of puberty development and the coming of the first period is usually about two and a half years. If a girl has been fully mature for over two years or is over sixteen and has not had her first period, she should be evaluated by her physician.

It can be upsetting if the onset of puberty is later or earlier than average. The girl who begins puberty at eight may feel awkward and self-conscious when she finds herself the only girl in her class who's shooting upward and acquiring the shape of a woman. The responses of teachers, parents, and peers can also be confusing. Also bothered is the girl who's on a slow timetable. The thirteen-year-old who has shown no signs of puberty development may think she's abnormal. Reassurance from her doctor may be helpful.

Puberty development in boys. The average boy begins two years later than the average girl, at twelve in contrast to her ten. The earlier developers among boys begin as early as ten, a few younger still. Plenty of slow developers start as late as fourteen, and there are a few who wait longer.

Pubic hair begins to grow first, then the testicles grow, and finally the penis begins to increase, first in length, then in diameter. All these events begin before the growth spurt, and may be known only to the boy himself (in contrast to a girl's development, where the first sign of puberty, breast development, is obvious to others).

During puberty, a boy may grow in height at double the rate as before. Height often increases first, along with arm length and shoe size, giving the early adolescent boy a gangly, uncoordinated look. The muscles fill in later, creating more of a manly shape. At about the same time, the hair in the armpits and on the face grows thicker and longer. Then the voice cracks and deepens. In some boys, a small area under the breast nipples enlarges and may become tender; this is normal. In a few, the breasts enlarge enough to cause embarrassment and worry. This occurs more often in boys who are overweight. Medical reassurance can be helpful.

After about two years, the boy's body has pretty much completed its transition. In the following few years he will continue to grow more slowly, finally stopping at around eighteen. Some later-developing boys will continue to grow even into their early twenties. Early pubertal development in boys is seldom upsetting; for a couple of years, an early-developing boy may be the tallest and strongest in the class (though very early development, before about age ten, should be evaluated medically).

Late development, on the other hand, can be very upsetting. The boy who is on a slow timetable of development, who is still a "shrimp" at fourteen when most of his friends have turned almost into grown men, usually needs reassurance, and sometimes counseling, to help him cope. Size, physique, and athletic ability count for a lot at this age. Some parents, instead of reassuring their son that he will develop in time and grow eight or nine inches in the process, take him on a hunt for a doctor who will give him growth hormone treatment. This only convinces him that something is really wrong with him. True, there are hormone preparations that bring on the signs of puberty at whatever age they are given. However, there is no evidence that long-term psychological benefits will follow, and these treatments may cause a boy to end up shorter than he normally would be by prematurely stopping his bone growth. For the rare occasion when there may be too little or too much growth hormone production, a pediatric endocrinologist (hormone specialist) should be consulted before any decision is made about giving hormones.

OTHER HEALTH ISSUES

Body odor. One of the earliest changes of adolescence is more profuse and stronger-smelling perspiration in the armpits. Some children (and parents, too) are not aware of the odor, which can cause unpopularity with schoolmates. Hygiene now becomes especially important. Daily washing with soap and perhaps the regular use of a suitable deodorant will control the odor.

Acne. Our understanding of the cause and treatment of pimples (acne) has changed a lot in recent years. The texture of the skin becomes coarser at puberty. The pores enlarge and secrete up to ten times more oil than previously. Some of the pores may become clogged with a combination of oil (sebum) and dead skin cells. (The skin cells that line the pores naturally die and peel off at regular intervals, to be replaced by new ones.) When this plug of cells and oil comes into contact with the air, it oxidizes and turns black. This is how blackheads form. Bacteria that normally live on the skin may get into these enlarged, plugged pores and cause a pimple, which is a small infection. The same basic process that causes the usual acne pimples can also cause a deeper, scarring type of acne, which tends to run in families.

Two misconceptions about acne have been cleared up by recent research. We now know that the pimples of acne are not caused by dirt, and we have also learned that certain foods, such as chocolate and fried foods, do not affect this skin condition. Pimples occur as a natural part of puberty in nearly all teenagers, whether they have dry or oily skin. Since squeezing a pimple can make the infection worse, teenagers should be encouraged to avoid doing it.

Some adolescents, worried about sex, imagine that their pimples are caused by sexual fantasies or masturbation. They can be assured that this isn't true.

Children are entitled to all the help they can get with pimples, from their regular doctor, nurse practitioner, or a skin specialist, for the sake of improving their present appearance and spirits and to prevent the permanent scars that sometimes develop. With modern methods of treatment, great improvement can be made in most cases, and even the deeper, scarring type of acne can be kept under control. In some cases, a physician or nurse practitioner may prescribe an antibiotic, a topical benzoyl peroxide cream, or a medicine related to vitamin A. Prescription treatments are often much more effective than over-the-counter ones.

Whatever the specific methods prescribed, there are also general measures that are believed to be helpful. Vigorous daily exercise, fresh air, and direct sunshine (wearing a suitable sunscreen to avoid sunburn) seem to improve many complexions. And it's generally a good idea to wash the face with a mild soap or soap substitute and warm water in the morning and again at bedtime. There are soaps and topical medications that contain 5 to 10 percent benzoyl peroxide that can be purchased without a prescription. And there are many water-based cosmetic preparations (oil-based ones should be avoided) available for covering pimples and blemishes while nature takes its course. After the hormonal surges of puberty die down, acne normally fades away.

Diet in adolescence. After the age of ten to twelve, it may become increasingly difficult to get children to accept a diet that is different from that of their friends and age-mates. Up to then they usually go along with their parents' ideas, especially if the parents are in agreement. In fact, they don't think of such meals as a diet; they are just foods that appear regularly at mealtime. But after they have eaten with friends or at school for a few months, they may want to eat more hamburgers, potato chips, french fries, cheese, and ice cream and other sweet and creamy desserts. Other teens restrict their intakes excessively (see page 373). It's helpful to remember that teens who are active and growing quickly can eat huge portions and need every calorie.

◌ CLASSIC SPOCK

If you are strongly in favor of a plant-based diet, as I am, what can you do? There's often no easy answer. My own inclination is to continue to serve the plant-based foods at home, without comment or argument. (I'm generally in favor of enjoyable, polite meals, without scoldings. Save the correction of table manners for brief private sessions, after meals.) If your children ask why you don't serve animal-based foods, including dairy products, explain matter-of-factly and cheerfully, not defensively, that a plant-based diet has been shown to be helpful for athletic success, long life, and low level of disease; you naturally want your children to have these advantages. Don't get into a long argument. If they demand to know why other parents don't follow similar rules, you can say truthfully that you don't know. [For more on plant-based diets, see page 337.]

If your children wonder what would happen if they broke your dietary rules at school, other children's homes or restaurants, you can point out that they will be increasingly out of your sight and must decide more things for themselves. And you don't want to snoop or punish them; you only want to serve them the best possible foods. Certainly the most powerful influence is for both parents to eat, politely, the thoughtful meals that have been prepared. Don't hold back on the children's favorite dishes until they have eaten what you consider the most healthful items—that's always counterproductive.

There is an important reason why it's sensible to avoid food arguments during adolescence. This is when rebellion against the parents' diet is apt to be strongest and when the desire to eat the same foods as classmates and friends is strongest. Parents and nutritionists who have gone through this phase with adolescent children testify that there is a better chance that the children will revert to their parents' diet in time if no issue is made of the rebellion. When a long, bitter conflict occurs over diet in adolescence, its pattern is more likely to persist—for years.

Sleep. Along with the adolescent growth spurt comes an increased need for sleep. The average ten-year-old can get by with eight or nine hours a night; the average teen may need nine or ten. Teens also naturally go to bed later and later and want to get up later and later in the morning. But of course school interferes, forcing them to get up early, even though they stayed up late. A teen who becomes sleepier (or crankier) through the week then tries to catch up by sleeping fourteen hours straight on Saturday is not getting enough sleep. In this way, teens are very much like many adults in our too busy society. The consequences of too little sleep can include poor school performance, irritability with parents and siblings, even symptoms of depression. It can be very difficult to help a busy teen get enough sleep. But one of the main culprits, late night television, is fairly easy to deal with. Just say no. My own feeling is that television has no place in anyone's bedroom.

Exercise. With adolescents being as busy as they often are, it may not seem necessary to advise that they get enough exercise. But schools often drop physical education requirements in high school, leading to a decline in physical fitness. Regular exercise, through competitive sports, dance, martial arts, or other pursuits, helps teens maintain energy, avoid obesity, and perhaps prevent depression. More is not necessarily better, however. Excessive exercise can be a sign of anorexia nervosa (see page 373).

PSYCHOLOGICAL TASKS

The physical changes of puberty have a distinct onset and end point. The psychological changes are more difficult to categorize. One way to look at adolescent emotional development is to think of the psychological tasks that adolescents face on their way to adulthood. It's useful, too, to think of adolescence as occurring in three stages: early, middle, and late. The main psychological tasks change from stage to stage, as described in the sections below.

Psychological Tasks of Adolescence
- ✔ Coming to terms with their new physical selves
- ✔ Developing a new male or female emotional identity
- ✔ Resolving the differences between the norms and values of their peers and those of their parents
- ✔ Establishing and expressing their own moral convictions
- ✔ Developing a sense of self-responsibility
- ✔ Demonstrating the potential for financial self-sufficiency

A central problem for adolescents and young adults is to find out what kind of people they will be, what work they will do, what principles they will live by. This is partly a conscious, partly an unconscious process. In groping to find this identity, adolescents may try out a variety of roles: dreamer, cosmopolitan, cynic, leader of lost causes, ascetic, and so on. Some adolescents seem to find themselves early and directly; others take a long time and many side roads before they find their paths.

Adolescents have to separate themselves emotionally from their parents in order to find out who they are and what they want to be. Yet they are largely made from their parents—not only because they have inherited their genes from them but also because they have been patterning themselves after them all their lives. They must now pry themselves apart. The eventual outcome will be influenced by the extent of their dependency, the intensity of their rebelliousness and rivalry, and the kind of outside world they live in and what it asks of them.

Taking risks. One way adolescents move toward independence is by taking risks. It's easy for teens to underestimate risks, because they tend to see themselves as invulnerable. They *have* always been fine and therefore expect they always *will* be. Appeals to logic often fall on deaf ears; teens live in the real present, not the hypothetical future.

Not all risks are bad. A teen who bicycles across country or spends hour after hour practicing skateboard jumps is gaining skills, building self-esteem, and learning to exercise judgment. As adults, we are able to calculate risks and weigh benefits because as adolescents we learned, through trial and error, how much risk we were willing to take and what the cost of those risks can be.

Risk-taking, however, also has a dark side. The child who experiments with cigarettes just to be cool is likely to end up addicted to nicotine. Alcohol is an accepted part of adult culture, and it is all too easy for teens to drink. Getting drunk is a form of risk-taking—How much can you hold? Can you keep control?—that can easily end in tragedy when an intoxicated teen gets behind the wheel of a car. Illegal drug use can progress to abuse and addiction in both troubled teens and in adolescents from good homes. Sexual activity is another way teens tempt fate. Nationally, the number of teen pregnancies is dropping, but the number of unwed teen parents in the United States is still higher than in many other wealthy nations.

The challenge for parents is to help teens take risks sensibly. Education on the dangers of cigarettes, alcohol, drugs, and irresponsible sex needs to start *before* the teen years. It's good that many elementary and middle schools teach these subjects, but parents need to be involved, too. You need to be very clear about your values, and teach by example as well as by word. It's also wise to avoid putting your child in situations where the temptations are too great. Allowing a sixteen-year-old to stay late working on the school newspaper conveys trust and encourages responsibility. Leaving a fourteen-year-old home alone for a weekend invites unwise risk-taking.

EARLY ADOLESCENCE

Changing bodies and minds. From twelve to about fourteen, the main psychological challenge is to come to terms with rapidly changing bodies—one's own and one's peers'. These years also see the widest variations in physical development. The average girl is nearly two years ahead of the average boy in development—towering over him in height and more sophisticated in her interests. She may be interested in going to dances and being treated as if she were glamorous while he is still an uncivilized little boy who thinks it shameful to pay attention to her. During this whole period it may be better for social functions to include different age groups for a better fit.

Early adolescents are acutely self-conscious about their bodies. They may exaggerate and worry about defects and they often believe that everyone else is focused on their bodies, too. If a girl has freckles, she may think they make her look horrible. A slight peculiarity in the body or how it functions can easily convince an adolescent that he is abnormal.

Early adolescents may not be able to manage their new bodies with as much coordination as previously, and the same is true of their new feelings. They are apt to be touchy and easily hurt when criticized. At one moment, they feel like grown-ups and want to be treated as such. The next moment, they feel like children again and expect to be cared for.

Friendships. Adolescents often feel ashamed of their parents for a few years, particularly when their friends are present. This is partly related to their anxious search for their own identities, and it partly reflects the extreme self-consciousness of the age period. They have an intense need to be just like their friends and to be totally accepted by them. They fear that they might face ridicule and rejection by their friends if their parents deviate in any way from the neighborhood pattern.

In trying to establish their identity, early adolescents often turn away from their parents, a move that threatens to leave them feeling alone. To counter this they often make intimate ties with friends of the same age, more often at first ties to those of the same sex. Close friendships support the early adolescent during a period when she gives up her identity as her parents' child and before she finds her own.

Sometimes a teen finds himself through finding something similar in his friend. He mentions that he loves a certain song, hates a certain teacher, or craves a certain article of clothing. His friend exclaims with amazement that he has always felt the very same way. Both are delighted and reassured. Each has lost a degree of his feeling of aloneness and peculiarity and gained a pleasurable sense of belonging.

As another example, two girls may talk constantly all the way home from school, talk for another half hour in front of the home of one of them, then finally reluctantly separate. As soon as the other reaches her home, she telephones her friend, and they resume the mutual confidences.

The importance of appearance. Many adolescents help to overcome their feelings of aloneness by slavishly conforming to the styles of their classmates—in clothes, hairdos, language, reading matter, songs, entertainers. These styles have to be different from those of their parents' generation. And if they irritate or shock their parents, so much the better. It is revealing, though, that even those youths who adopt an extreme style to differentiate themselves from their parents will still conform to the style of at least a few of their friends or perhaps of some idolized figure, such as a rock star.

Parents can be most helpful to teenagers by trying to understand their behavior then helping them to understand themselves. If you explain why you object to certain styles, you may be able to persuade your children to change without your having to issue an "or else" order. Or, the teenager who feels free to discuss and argue with her parents may end up persuading them to accept her point of view. Adults tend to be slower than youths in accepting new styles. What may horrify or disgust us one day may later become as acceptable to us as to our children. This was true with the long-hair styles and dungarees introduced by youths in the 1960s, the pants for girls that so upset school authorities at one time, and even fluorescent hair colors.

Early teen sexuality. Most early teens fantasize about sex, and many experiment with kissing and petting. A minority experience actual intercourse. Masturbation is nearly universal, and depending on family religious teachings, it may bring with it varying degrees of guilt or shame. Erections, either spontaneous or in response to sexual fantasies, make many boys who are already quite self-conscious even more uncomfortable. Most boys also experience ejaculation of semen during sleep (wet dreams). One boy takes these in stride; another worries there might be something wrong with him.

Sexual feelings and experimentation are not always directed towards the opposite sex. The issue of homosexuality is often confusing and frightening to both teens and parents. Early teens tend to be intolerant of anything that suggests homosexuality. The intensity of this homophobia probably has to do with secret fears in some teens that they might themselves be homosexual. It's not unusual for early teens to engage in same-sex genital touching, then worry that they are gay. Some will indeed go on to develop a primarily homosexual orientation; others will not.

Given the strong antigay bias in mainstream American culture, it's difficult for teens to show affection for same-sex friends, let alone talk about sexual feelings that might hint at homosexuality. A sensitive doctor or nurse practitioner can sometimes provide information and reassurance. One reason why every teen should have a chance to talk confidentially with their doctor without a parent present is so such sensitive conversations can take place. Homosexual adolescents face special stresses and need special support, as described in the section starting on page 459.

MIDDLE ADOLESCENCE

Freedom and its limits. At fifteen to seventeen, middle adolescents have two important tasks. First, they must come to terms with their sexuality and the conflicting emotions aroused as they begin romantic encounters. Second, they must separate emotionally from their parents and find that they can function independently. As a part of this process, the dependence-independence struggles often intensify.

Adolescents often complain that their parents don't allow them enough freedom. It's natural for children approaching adulthood to insist on their rights, and their parents may need to be reminded that their children are changing. But parents don't have to take every complaint at face value. Adolescents are eager to grow up. At the same time, they are afraid of growing up. They are unsure of their capacity to be as knowledgeable, masterful, sophisticated, and charming as they would like to be, but their pride won't allow them to recognize this doubt. When they unconsciously doubt their ability to carry off some challenge or adventure, they're quick to find evidence that it is their parents who are blocking their way, not their own fears. They reproach their parents indignantly or blame them when talking with friends.

You should suspect this unconscious maneuver when your teen suddenly announces a plan for some escapade that is way beyond anything he's done before. For example, he and some friends—boys and girls—plan to go camping for a weekend without parents. Teens who come up with such schemes may be looking for clear rules and consistency; indeed, they may be asking to be stopped. They are also on the lookout for evidence of hypocrisy in their parents. To the extent that their parents are obviously sincere about their rules and ideals, their children feel obligated to continue to adhere to them. But if they can uncover hypocrisy in their parents, this relieves them of the moral duty to conform and offers a welcome opportunity to reproach their parents. At the same time, it may undermine their sense of safety.

Jobs and work. Middle adolescence is when many teens first take on serious jobs, beside the occasional babysitting or yard work. In moderation, paid work can build self-esteem, responsibility, and independence. Work also allows teens to widen their social contacts and explore fields that may eventually lead to careers. Many teens, however, spend so much time on the job that they don't have time to socialize or do homework and are chronically overtired and cranky. It's also important to be aware that many jobs carry significant health and safety risks. Parents may need to step in to keep work from getting out of hand.

Sexual experimentation. Middle adolescence is when many teens experiment with sex of various sorts. Kissing and petting are almost universal; oral-genital sex happens frequently (many teens don't think of this as real sex); and many experience sexual intercourse. In a large survey from 1983, 55 to 75 percent of nineteen-year-olds reported that they were nonvirgins. Middle teens often date in groups, though some also date one on one. Romances are often brief, with relationships taking a back seat to attraction and experimentation. This is not to say that all middle-adolescent romances are superficial or of no consequence. The emotions—both joy and misery, elation and dejection—often have an intensity rarely rivaled in later, more settled periods of life.

Realistically, parents are limited in their ability to control their middle adolescents' sexual behavior. Educational programs stressing abstinence as the only choice have obvious appeal but have not been shown to reduce teen pregnancy. If teens are intent on sexual experimentation, the rules laid down by parents may not stop them; they may even make the sex seem more exciting and attractive, because it is off limits.

A more effective strategy may be for parents to keep communication open, let their children know how they feel about premarital sex, limit opportunities for inappropriate sexual behavior (for example, no unchaperoned sleepovers), and trust their teens to act responsibly. Many parents have a hard time talking with their teens about sex. Fortunately, doctors and nurse practitioners are often well trained in having these discussions and can help parents communicate their feelings and concerns in a positive, effective manner. For more on talking about sex, see page 452.

Homosexuality. Adolescence is a complex time for any youngster. The pressure of school activities, and dating can create a powerful sense of exclusion or differentness in gay and lesbian teens, which may trouble them or make them unhappy. If you think your child is struggling with issues of sexual identity, it's very important to let him or her feel that there is a place to turn to for help. Sadly, statistics show that a high percentage of teenage suicides and attempted suicides are related to issues of sexual identity.

Heterosexual parents may not know how to begin talking to a teenager about sexual orientation. Remember, it's likely that your child is as afraid of the subject as you are and may feel threatened if abruptly confronted. To start with, try to make the subject of sexual orientation something that the family can casually discuss. Introduce books, videos, and music into the family collections that are created by openly gay, lesbian, or bisexual artists or that deal with those themes. (Actually, it's wise to talk openly about these issues starting from the elementary or middle school years; see page 446 on raising sexually healthy children.) It's also important to be aware of and critical of homophobia. It's no help to a gay or lesbian teenager to hear his or her family members tell insulting jokes or tolerate prejudiced comments made by friends or relatives.

For some adolescents, their sexual orientation becomes clear to them quickly, and they embrace it as a strong identity. Other teenagers may go through a phase of experimentation before settling on an identity they feel most comfortable with. Teenagers shouldn't be pressured into assuming a gay or lesbian identity before they are ready. If a teenager expresses a sense of alienation, isolation, or deep confusion about his or her sexual orientation, parents should arrange for professional counseling—not to change their teen's orientation but to help the boy or girl deal with any shame or anxiety that might undermine his or her self-esteem. The greatest gift a parent can give a child is a sense of pride and dignity. For a gay or lesbian teen, having access to positive role models and the ability to deal with sexual diversity frankly and honestly will go a long way toward building self-esteem.

If you're raising a gay or lesbian adolescent, you may want to seek support for yourself as well. Organizations such as Parents and Friends of Lesbians and Gays, which has chapters across the country, provide information and advice and hold events. Most cities and large towns have gay and lesbian switchboards or hot lines that can provide useful information, and gay and lesbian community centers have outreach programs for gay and lesbian youths and their parents. These facilities are listed in the classified telephone directory under "Gay and Lesbian" or "Social and Human Services."

LATE ADOLESCENCE

Tasks of the age. By age eighteen to twenty-one, conflicts between adolescents and their parents are beginning to subside. The major tasks during this period of late adolescence are choosing a career direction and developing more meaningful and lasting emotional relationships.

A few years ago, the general expectation was that older teens would be preparing to go off to college or take a job that would allow them to live independently. Adolescents who chose college then graduate school might stretch their late adolescent years well into their late twenties or early thirties. More recently, many older teens have either chosen or felt compelled to continue living in their parents' homes. As society and the economy continue to change, the challenges of late adolescence will change, too.

Idealism and innovation. With increased knowledge and independence comes the desire to improve the world, find new methods that will supersede the old, make discoveries, create new art forms, displace tyrants, and right wrongs. A surprising number of scientific advances have been made and masterpieces of art created by individuals on the threshold of adulthood. They were no smarter than the older people in their fields, and they were certainly less experienced. But they were critical of traditional ways, biased in favor of the new and untried, and willing to take risks. That was enough to do the trick. This is often how the world makes progress.

Finding their way. It sometimes takes youths five to ten years to find their own positive identity. Meanwhile, they may be stalled at a halfway stage, characterized by passive resistance to and withdrawal from mainstream society (which they equate with their parents) or by excessively rebellious radicalism.

They may decline to take an ordinary job as their parents may have done; instead, they adopt unconventional dress, grooming, acquaintances, and residence. To them, these decisions seem like evidence of vigorous independence. But by themselves, these things don't yet add up to a positive stand on life or a constructive contribution to the world. They are essentially a negative protest against their parents' conventions. Even when the striving to be independent shows up only in the form of eccentricities of appearance, it should be recognized as an attempted step in the right direction, one that may later lead to a constructive, creative stage. As a matter-of-fact, the young people who strain so visibly to be free are apt to come from families with unusually strong ties and high ideals.

Other youths, idealistic and altruistic in character, often take a sternly radical or purist view of things for a number of years—in politics, the arts, or other fields. Various tendencies of this age period operate together to draw them into these extreme positions: heightened criticalness, cynicism about hypocrisy, intolerance of compromise, courage, and a willingness to sacrifice in response to their first awareness of the shocking injustices of the society they live in.

A few years later, having achieved a satisfactory degree of emotional independence from their parents and having found out how to be useful in their chosen field, they are more tolerant of the frailties of their fellow human beings and readier to make constructive compromises. It's not that they become complacent conservatives. Many remain progressive, some remain radical. But most become easier to live and work with.

ADVICE FOR PARENTS

Don't be afraid to make rules. Most adolescents are bound to feel rivalrous and rebellious at least some of the time, whether or not the parent is reasonable. The first and most important point by far is that adolescents need and want guidance—even consistent rules—from their parents, no matter how much they argue against them. Their pride won't let them openly admit the need, but in their hearts they often think, "I wish my parents would make definite rules for me, as my friends' parents do." They sense that it is one aspect of parents' love to want to protect their children from misunderstandings and embarrassing situations out in the world, from giving the wrong impression and gaining an unfortunate reputation, from getting into trouble through inexperience.

Show respect, and expect it in return. This doesn't mean that parents can be arbitrary, inconsistent, or overbearing. Adolescents have too much dignity and indignation for that. They want to discuss the issues on what they feel is an adult-to-adult basis. If the argument ends in a draw, though, the parents shouldn't be so scrupulously democratic that they assume the child is as likely to be right as they are. The parents' experience should be presumed to count for a lot. In the end, the parents should confidently express their judgment and, if appropriate, their explicit request. They owe their child this clarity and certitude. Parents should indicate, without necessarily saying so in words, that they realize the youth will be out of their sight most of the time and will therefore comply because of her conscience and respect for her parents, not because the parents can make her obey or can watch her at all times.

Parents need to discuss with their young adolescent children the hour at which they are expected to come home from parties and dates, where they are going and with whom, and who is to drive. If the child asks why they want to know, they can answer that good parents feel responsible for their children. "Suppose there is an accident," parents can say, "We ought to know where to inquire or to search." Or the parents can say, "If there is a family emergency we will want to be able to reach you." For the same reasons, parents should tell their children where they're going and when they expect to be home. And if there is a delay or a change in plan, adolescents (and parents) should call home before they are overdue. With the agreement of their children, the parents can set a certain hour and be waiting for them. This reminds children that the parents are genuinely concerned with their conduct and safety. When children have a party at home, the parents should be there.

Parents shouldn't dictate to their adolescent children or talk down to them. They should have mutually respectful, adult-to-adult discussions. Young people have never been willing to be guided beyond a certain point by their parents, but that doesn't mean that they haven't benefited from discussions.

Many parents, aware of their adolescent children's impatience with their parents' views and respectful of their drive for independence, carefully conceal their own opinions and refrain from criticizing adolescent tastes and manners for fear of seeming old-fashioned or oppressive. However, it's more helpful for parents to talk freely about their views and about how things were in their youth, doing so as if they are talking to a respected adult friend, not as if laying down the law or thinking their opinions are right simply because they are older.

Dealing with defiance. But, parents ask, what if the child openly defies or quietly disobeys a request? In the early years of adolescence, if the child-parent relationship is sound and the rules or limits are reasonable, few children defy or disobey in serious matters, although they may protest loudly. Parents who feel a lack of control on key issues of safety or behavior should seek help from a doctor or other professional so they can take control appropriately.

In the later years, the parents may choose to back their teen's decision, even if it goes against their best judgment. For example, a seventeen-year-old has her heart set on going to art school, but her parents think premed is a better choice. In such cases, the teen needs to be encouraged to make her own decision, even if it turns out to be a mistake. Parents need to help their children find and follow their dreams and aspirations, even if they are very different from those of the parents.

Even when an older adolescent defies or disobeys a parental direction, this does not mean that the direction did no good. It certainly helps inexperienced persons to hear all sides. Even if they decide not to take their parents' advice, they may still be making a reasonably sound decision, perhaps having knowledge or insights the parents lack. Certainly, as they progress into adulthood, they must be prepared to reject advice on occasion and take responsibility for their decisions. If young people reject their parents' advice and get into trouble, the experience will increase their respect for their parents' judgment, though they probably won't admit it.

Take the stance of a concerned parent (which you are). If your teen is doing something that seems dangerous or unwise, it's more effective to let your teen know that you are concerned than simply to criticize or lay down the law. "You always seem unhappy after you go on a date with Jim" is likely to be more effective than "Jim's a stinker!"

Contract for safety. Let your teen know that you'll pick him up anytime, anywhere, no questions asked. As unpleasant as this sounds, it is far better than having to deal with the injuries or legal problems that may result from driving intoxicated, for example. Teens also need access to confidential medical care so that they are free to discuss any questions that they may not feel comfortable sharing with their parents. Good medical care doesn't make teens promiscuous; just the opposite.

Take reasonable antisuicide precautions. These include, most important, not keeping guns at home. Also, if your teen seems sad, down, or distant; if he loses interest in things that he used to love; or if his grades suddenly drop off, keep the possibility of depression in mind and seek help.

Use your best judgment. Suppose parents don't know what to say or think about some issue. They can discuss it with not only their child but other parents. But individual parents should not feel bound to adhere to other people's codes, even if they are the only parents who disagree. In the long run, parents can do a good job only if they are convinced they are doing the right thing. And what is right for them is what, after hearing the arguments, they *feel* is right.

Some questions to ask yourself when deciding whether to allow a specific behavior: Is it safe? Is it legal? Does it undermine a core moral principle? Has your child considered the consequences? Is your child acting freely or is someone else (a teacher or a peer) exercising undue influence? By focusing on such questions, you may be able to decide on your own best course of action and may also be able to help your teen make a wise decision.

Expect civil behavior and participation. Individually and in groups, adolescents should be expected to behave civilly to people and be cordial to their parents, family friends, teachers, and the people who work with them. At times it is natural for youths to have a mildly hostile attitude toward adults—with whom they are inevitably rivalrous—whether they are aware of it. But it does them no harm—and much good—to have to control this hostility and be polite anyway. Their politeness certainly makes a great difference to the adults concerned.

Adolescents should also have serious obligations to help their families by doing regular chores and special additional jobs. This benefits them by giving them a sense of dignity, participation, responsibility, and happiness as well as helping the parents.

You can't *enforce* these rules, but you are entitled to express them in discussions with your children. It helps adolescents to hear their parents' principles, even if they don't always conform to them.

Feeding and Nutrition

FEEDING IN THE FIRST YEAR

WHAT FEEDING MEANS TO THE BABY

A baby knows a lot about diet. She is the one who knows how many calories her body needs and what her digestion can handle. If she regularly doesn't get enough, she'll probably cry for more. If there's more in the bottle than she feels like eating, let her stop when she wants to. Take her word for it.

Think of the baby's first year this way: She wakes up because she's hungry, cries because she wants to be fed. She is so eager when the nipple goes into her mouth that she may shudder. When she nurses, you can see that it is an intense experience. Perhaps she starts to perspire. If you stop her in the middle of a nursing, she may cry furiously. When she has had as much as she wants, she is usually groggy with satisfaction and falls asleep. Even when she is asleep, she sometimes looks as if she were dreaming of nursing: Her mouth makes sucking motions, and her expression is blissful.

This all adds up to the fact that feeding is her great joy. She gets her early ideas about life from the way feeding goes. She gets her first ideas about the world from the person who feeds her.

When parents constantly urge their baby to take more than she wants, she is apt to steadily become less interested. She may try to escape from the experience by going to sleep increasingly earlier in the feeding, or she may rebel and become balky. She's apt to lose some of her active, positive feeling about life. It's as though she has gotten the idea that life is a struggle, that those people are always after her, that she has to fight to protect herself.

So don't urge babies to take more than they are eager for. Let them go on enjoying their meals and feeling that you are their friend. This is one of the principal ways in which their self-confidence, their joy in life, and their love of people will be firmly established during the first year.

The important sucking instinct. Babies nurse eagerly for two separate reasons: They're hungry, and they love to suck. If you feed them a lot without giving them enough chance to suck, their craving for sucking will go unsatisfied and they will try to suck something else—their fists, thumbs, or clothes. (It is true that the sucking need varies greatly from baby to baby.)

SCHEDULES

Strict schedules. In the first half of the twentieth century, babies were usually kept on very strict, regular schedules. Doctors did not know the cause of the serious intestinal infections that afflicted tens of thousands of babies with severe diarrhea yearly. It was believed that these infections were caused not only by the contamination of milk but also by wrong proportions in the formula and irregularity in feeding.

Strict regularity worked well enough with a majority of babies. When they had an ample feeding at breast or bottle, it lasted them for two to four hours, because that is the way a young baby's digestive system usually works.

But there were always a few babies who had trouble adjusting to regularity in the first month or two: babies whose stomachs couldn't seem to hold four hours' worth of milk, babies who went to sleep halfway through feedings, restless babies, colicky babies. They would cry miserably every day, but their mothers and doctors dared not feed them—even pick them up—off schedule. This was hard enough on the babies. It was probably harder still on the parents.

With pasteurization of milk in the commercial dairy and the availability of clean, safe water, severe diarrhea became much less of a problem for babies. But it took many more years before doctors dared to experiment with flexible schedules.

Self-demand feeding. The first experiments in self-demand feeding were carried out by Dr. Preston McLendon, a psychologist, and Frances P. Simsarian, a new mother, on Ms. Simsarian's new baby. They wanted to find out what kind of schedule babies would establish if they were breast-fed whenever they seemed hungry. The baby awoke infrequently the first few days. Then, from just about the time the milk began to come in, he awoke surprisingly often—about ten times a day—in the second half of the first week. Then by the age of two weeks he had settled down to six or seven feedings a day, at irregular intervals. By ten weeks he had arrived at a schedule of being fed at two- to four-hour intervals.

They called this an experiment in self-demand feeding. Since that experiment in 1942 there has been a general relaxation in infant feeding schedules, which has had a wholesome effect on babies and parents. It's now recognized that the average number of hours between feedings for a breast-fed baby in the first two weeks of life is two. But some babies will nurse every three hours and some as often as every hour and a half.

What regularity and scheduling are all about. Most babies have a natural tendency to establish a regular pattern of feeding and sleeping. Though the intervals between feedings may vary within each twenty-four-hour period, they'll tend to be consistent from one day to the next. The pattern will change as the baby grows, and periods of wakefulness will become more prolonged and filled with activity. Through the parents' guidance, this pattern is shaped into a schedule, which helps both baby and parents move into a comfortable and predictable rhythm.

Scheduling doesn't necessarily mean feeding every four hours or every three hours, though some babies and families do arrive at that kind of strict schedule. Some newborns seem to come out of the hospital already set at a two- to four-hour feeding interval. Others seem to fashion a schedule of their own, though it may take a few weeks for them to become consistent about it. At some times in the day, babies seem hungrier than at others and want to eat more frequently. For much of the time, they awaken to eat every hour and a half to four hours. They may have a five-hour sleep period, which may come as easily during the day as at night. They may have a stretch of fretfulness lasting several hours, which usually occurs in the early evening. During these hours the breast-fed baby is happy if she is almost continuously at the breast and will cry if she is put down. A bottle-fed baby may act hungry but if offered a bottle not eat much. She may suck avidly at the pacifier. Some unhappy parents say that their newborns "have their days and nights switched." These babies will sleep like a log during the day and are almost impossible to arouse. During the night, they are up to feed and fret every hour and a half (see page 227 on preventing this problem).

In the early weeks the period of longer sleep tends to shift to nighttime. The evening fussiness gradually improves over the first few months, though it may seem to take forever. During the first few months, times for feeding, playing, and even fussing alternate predictably with daytime sleeping.

By comparison, a baby approaching her first birthday usually sleeps through the night, though she may awaken early for a breast- or bottle-feeding, then return to sleep for an hour or two. She eats three meals and a couple of snacks, has a nap or two, and goes to sleep at a reasonable hour, often after a last breast- or bottle-feeding.

How do all these changes happen in a year? It isn't only what the parents do. It's the baby herself, gradually lengthening the time between feedings and shortening the sleep periods. With her own maturation, she just naturally tends to fit into the family's schedule.

Establishing a schedule. The main consideration for babies is that they not have to cry with hunger for long periods or feel uncared for. All babies have a tendency to develop a regular schedule of becoming hungry. This will come much more rapidly if the parents guide them a bit. Babies don't mind at all being awakened for a feeding after an interval of three or four hours.

Smaller babies tend to eat more frequently than bigger babies. They all tend to gradually lengthen the interval between feedings as they grow bigger and older. Breast-fed babies on average eat more often than bottle-fed babies, because breast milk is digested more easily and quickly than cow's milk or soy formulas. By one, two, or three months of age, babies come to realize they don't need the middle-of-the-night feeding and give it up. Somewhere between the fourth and twelfth month, they will be able to sleep through the feeding at the parents' bedtime, too.

In these tendencies—to more regular and fewer feedings— the baby can be greatly influenced by the parents' management. If during the day a mother wakes her baby boy whenever he's still asleep four hours after the last feeding, she is helping him to establish regular daytime eating habits. If when he stirs and whimpers a couple of hours after the last feeding she holds back for a few minutes and gives him a chance to go back to sleep or offers a pacifier if he really wakens and cries, she is helping his stomach adjust to a longer interval. If, on the other hand, she always picks him up and feeds him promptly when he stirs, even when only shortly after the last feeding, she keeps him accustomed to short intervals and small feedings.

Individual babies differ widely in how soon they comfortably settle down to regular schedules. A great majority of the ones who are good feeders, who aren't too fussy, and who are getting plenty to drink from breast or bottle can be eased into a reasonably consistent schedule and will give up the middle-of-the-night feeding a couple of months after birth.

On the other hand, if a baby is a listless, sleepy feeder at first or a restless, fretful waker (pages 96), or if the breast-milk supply is not yet well established, it will be more comfortable for all concerned to go more slowly. But even in these cases, there will be less perplexity on the part of the parents every day—about whether to give a feeding right away or wait—and an earlier settling-down on the part of the baby if the parents are always working gently toward more regular feedings, with an average interval of two to three hours for breast-fed babies and three to four hours for bottle-fed ones.

⋙ CLASSIC SPOCK

There has been some misunderstanding about the relationship between self-demand feeding and schedules. The main purpose of any schedule is to do right by the baby. But another purpose is to enable the parents to care for their child in a way that will conserve their strength and spirits. This usually means getting down to a reasonable number of feedings at predictable hours and giving up the night feeding as soon as the baby is ready.

Some young parents, eager to be progressive, assume that if they want to get away from the rigid scheduling of the past they must go all the way in the opposite direction, feeding their baby any time she wakes and never waking her for a feeding. This may work out well enough if the baby is a peaceful one with a good digestion, if the parents don't have to worry about their own schedules, and if they don't mind being awakened between midnight and 6 A.M. (Of course, very young babies will certainly need to be fed during these hours.) But if the baby happens to be a restless, fretful one, this approach can lead to a great many feedings and very little rest for the parents for several months. And in a few cases it encourages the baby to be still waking for a couple of night feedings even at the end of the first year.

If parents prefer to feed their baby on an irregular, self-demand schedule for many months, there will be no harm done to the baby's nutrition. It does no harm to the parents, either, if they're people who just hate to do anything by the clock. But if they're fairly regular about the rest of their lives and have other things to get done, I only worry that they have gotten the idea that the more they give up for the baby the better it is for the child or that they have to prove that they are good parents by ignoring their own convenience.

These attitudes tend to create difficulties in the long run.

How to work toward a regular schedule. The easiest way to begin scheduling a baby is to wake her during the day if she is still asleep four hours after her last feeding. You won't have to urge her to eat; she will probably act starvingly hungry in a few minutes.

But suppose she wakes an hour after her last feeding. You don't have to feed her the minute she whimpers. She herself is not sure whether she's hungry. But if instead of settling back to sleep she fully wakens and starts crying hard, it does no good to wait any longer.

What if she starts a pattern of waking soon after each feeding? Perhaps she needs more to eat. If she is breast-fed, nursing her more frequently will increase the milk supply in a few days, so she'll be able to take more at each feeding and again lengthen the time between feedings. (It's important for the mother to take care of herself so that she can produce more milk as the baby needs it; see page 247.) If the baby is bottle-fed, increase each feeding by an ounce or more to see if that helps lengthen the intervals.

Just how soon should you give another feeding? If the baby

who generally can go three to four hours awakens after two to two and a half hours and seems really hungry, it is all right to feed her then. But suppose she wakes an hour or so after her last feeding? If she finished her usual bottle at her last feeding, the chances are against her being hungry again so soon. It is more likely that she has been awakened by indigestion. You might try burping her again or see whether she will be comforted by a couple of ounces of water or a pacifier. There is no rush to feed her again, though you may decide to try it in a little while if nothing else works.

You can't be sure it's hunger just because a baby tries to eat her hand or takes the bottle eagerly. Often a baby who is having colic will do both these things. It seems the baby herself can't distinguish between colic pains and hunger pains.

In other words, you don't always have to feed a baby every time she cries. If she is crying at the wrong times, you have to study the situation. She may be wet or too warm or cold; she may need to burp or be comforted, or she may just need to let out a few cries to release tension. If this keeps happening and you can't figure it out, discuss the problem with your doctor or nurse practitioner. (For more on crying, see page 61.)

Middle-of-the-night feedings. The easiest rule for night feedings is not to waken your baby but to let him wake you if he wants to. A baby who still needs that feeding usually wakes surprisingly close to the hour of 2 A.M. Then some night, probably when he's between two and six weeks old, he will sleep through until 3 or 3:30. Feed him then. The next night he may wake still later. Or he may wake, cry in a drowsy way, and go back to sleep if he is not fed right away.

When babies are ready to give up the middle-of-the-night feeding, somewhere between six and twelve weeks, they usually do it in a hurry, in two or three nights. A breast-fed baby may nurse longer at his other feedings. For a bottle-fed baby, you may want to increase the amount in his other bottles to make up for the bottle he's given up, if he wants the extra amount. Night feedings should be given quietly in a darkened room, in contrast to daytime feedings, which can be accompanied by more stimulation.

Giving up the middle-of-the-night feeding. If a baby reaches the age of two to three months and weighs twelve pounds but still wakes for a middle-of-the-night feeding, it's sensible to try to influence him to give it up. Instead of hurrying to him as soon as he stirs, you can let him fuss for a little while. If he doesn't quiet down but is instead soon crying furiously, apologize and feed him promptly. Then try again in another week or two. From a nutritional point of view, a twelve-pound baby who eats well during the day doesn't really need this feeding.

The feeding at the parents' bedtime is the one that you can probably time to your own convenience. Most babies, by the time they are a few weeks old, are perfectly willing to wait until 11 P.M. or even midnight for it. If you want to get to bed early, wake the baby at ten or even a little before. If a later feeding is more convenient, suit yourself, as long as the baby is willing to stay asleep.

For those babies who are still waking for middle-of-the-night feedings, it's best not to let them sleep through the ten or eleven o'clock feedings, even if they're quite willing to do so. When they're ready to give up one of them, you'll want them to give up the middle-of-the-night feeding first, so that your sleep won't be interrupted.

For those babies who are already off the middle-of-the-night feeding but are still irregular about their daytime feeding hours, I'd continue to wake them at 10 or 11 P.M., provided they're willing to be fed. This at least ends the day on schedule, helps very much to avoid a feeding between midnight and four and tends to encourage them to sleep until five or six the next morning.

GETTING ENOUGH AND GAINING WEIGHT

Average weight gain. The average baby's weight is a little over seven pounds at birth and fourteen pounds between three and five months. That is to say, the average baby has doubled its birth weight by three to five months. In actual practice, babies who are small at birth are apt to grow faster, as if trying to catch up, and babies who are born big are less apt to double their birth weight by three to five months.

The average baby gains close to two pounds a month (six to eight ounces a week) for the first three months. (Of course, some healthy ones gain less, and others more.) Then the baby slows down. By six months, the average gain is down to a pound a month (four ounces a week). That's quite a drop in a three-month period. In the last quarter of the first year, the average gain is down to two-thirds of a pound a month (two to three ounces each week) and, during the second year, to about a half pound a month (two ounces a week).

As babies grow older, as you see, they gain more slowly. They also gain more irregularly. Teething or illness may take their appetite away for several weeks, and they may hardly gain at all. When they feel better, their appetite revives, and their weight catches up with a rush.

You can't decide much from how babies' weights change from week to week. What they weigh each time will depend on how recently they have urinated, how recently they have moved their bowels, how recently they have eaten. If you find, one morning, that your baby boy has gained only four ounces in the past week when before he had always gained seven, don't jump to the conclusion that he is starving or that something else is wrong. If he seems perfectly happy and satisfied, wait another week to see what happens. He may make an extra large gain to make up for the small one.

For the breast-fed baby, wetting the diapers at least six to eight times a day, being alert and happy when awake, sleeping well, and having a weight gain from week to week are good indications that he's getting enough to eat. Always remember, though, that the older he gets, the slower he will gain.

ᘒ CLASSIC SPOCK

How much weight should babies gain? The best I can say about weight gain is that babies should gain at the rate they seem to want to gain at. Most babies know. If they are offered more food than they need, they refuse it. If they are given less, they show their hunger by waking earlier before feedings and eating their fists.

We can talk about average babies if you remember clearly that no baby is average. One baby is meant to be a slow gainer; another is meant to be a fast gainer. When doctors talk about an average baby, they mean only that they have added together the fast gainers, the slow gainers, and the medium gainers.

How often to weigh. Most parents don't have scales, so most babies get weighed only when they go to see their doctor, which is often enough. When a baby is happy and doing well, weighing more frequently than once a month serves no purpose but to satisfy curiosity. If you have scales, don't weigh more often than once a month. On the other hand, if your baby is crying a lot, having indigestion, or vomiting a great deal, more frequent weighing at the doctor's office may help you and your doctor or nurse practitioner to decide what the matter is. For instance, excessive crying in a child who is gaining weight rapidly usually points toward colic (see page 98), not hunger.

Slow weight gain. Many healthy babies gain weight slowly, compared with the average. That babies are gaining slowly doesn't mean for sure that they are meant to. If they are hungry all the time, that is a pretty good sign that they are meant to be gaining faster. Once in a while, slow gaining means that a baby is sick. Slow gainers need to be seen regularly by a doctor to make sure that they are healthy.

Occasionally you see exceptionally polite babies who are gaining slowly and who don't seem hungry. But if you give them more to eat, they take it willingly and gain more rapidly. In other words, not all babies yell when they are being fed too little.

Fat babies. It's hard for some people to change their belief that fatness in babies is attractive and desirable. Relatives and friends may compliment the parents on it as if it were proof of superior care. Some parents think of baby fat as a reserve—like money in the bank—against some possible future adversity or illness. Of course this isn't so. Babies who carry around a lot of fat are no happier or healthier than leaner ones, and they tend to develop rashes where their fat folds rub together. Fatness in infancy does not necessarily mean that the baby will be fat for life, but it's not a kindness to babies to fatten them up.

Refusal to nurse in later months. Once in a while, a baby between four and seven months old acts queerly at feeding time. The mother will say that her baby boy nurses hungrily at breast or bottle for a few minutes, then becomes frantic, lets go of the nipple, and cries as if in pain. He still seems very hungry, but each time he goes back to nursing, he becomes uncomfortable sooner. He takes his solid food eagerly.

This distress may be caused by teething. As the baby nurses, the suction engorges his painful gums and makes them tingle unbearably. You can break each nursing period into several parts and give solid food in the intervals, since the distress comes on only after a period of sucking. If he is on a bottle, you can experiment with enlarging the hole in the nipple so that he finishes the bottle in a shorter time with less strenuous sucking. If the baby's discomfort is excessive and comes on promptly, you might give up the bottle altogether for a few days. Give him his milk from the cup if he is skillful enough, from a spoon, or mix a large amount of it with his cereal and other foods. Don't worry if he doesn't get his usual amount.

An ear infection, complicating a cold, may cause enough pain in the jaw joint so that babies will refuse to nurse even though they may be able to eat solids pretty well. Occasionally a baby will decline to take the breast during the mother's menstrual periods. Offering the breast more often at that time may help the baby take at least a little. Pumping or manually expressing the breast milk may help to relieve the fullness and keep the supply going. Once the period is over, both the baby and mother can return to business as usual.

Drinking water for a baby. If your drinking water is not fluoridated, your doctor will prescribe fluoride either in the baby's vitamin drops or separately. See pages 805 for why fluoride is important.

Some babies want water; others don't. It is sometimes recommended that a baby be offered a few ounces of water between meals once or twice a day. It isn't really necessary, because the amount of fluid in breast milk or formula will satisfy the baby's ordinary needs. It is more important to offer water if the baby has a fever, or during excessively hot weather, especially if his urine turns dark yellow, or he appears extra thirsty. Babies who ordinarily refuse water often take it at these times. Some mothers have found that adding small amounts of apple juice to the water gets the baby interested. If you are giving extra water, it's important to continue giving the regular amount of formula or breast milk as well. Babies given *only* water can become ill.

A lot of babies don't want *any* water from the time they are a week or two old until they are about a year. During this time they fairly worship anything with nourishment in it but are insulted by plain water. If your baby likes it, by all means give it to him once or several times a day when he is awake between meals but not just before a meal. You can give him as much as he wants as long as he is taking his usual amount of formula or breast milk as well. He probably won't want more than two ounces. But don't urge him to take water if he doesn't want it. There's no point in getting him mad. He knows what he needs.

You may particularly want your baby to drink water if he is taking little milk because of an illness or if the weather is hot. If he won't take his water plain, you might try giving him sugar water. Add one level tablespoonful of granulated sugar to a pint of water, stirring until it's dissolved.

CHANGES AND CHALLENGES

Slowing down after six months. A baby may take solids eagerly for the first few months, then suddenly lose much of his appetite. One reason may be that a baby's rate of weight gain naturally slows down over the course of the first twelve to fifteen months. In the first three months, a typical baby gains close to two pounds a month. By six months she is apt to be down to a pound a month; otherwise, she would become too fat. Also, she may be bothered by teething. One baby wants to leave behind a lot of her solid food; another turns against her formula or breast milk. After six months, some babies refuse to be fed. If you let them have finger food while you offer food in a spoon, it often will solve this problem.

When your baby's appetite falls off after six months, it may be time to go to a schedule of three meals a day in the daytime, whether she is still on breast or bottle at bedtime. If a baby's appetite still doesn't revive with these measures, it's important to get her to the doctor to be sure that she's otherwise healthy.

Refusing vegetables. If your one-year-old daughter suddenly rejects the vegetable she loved last week, let her do it. If you don't make a fuss today, she will probably come back to it next week or next month. But if you insist on her taking it when she seems to dislike it, you only make her decide that that particular food is her enemy. You turn a temporary dislike into a permanent hate. If she turns down the same vegetable twice in succession, don't serve it for a couple of weeks.

It is naturally irritating to a parent to buy a food, prepare it, then have it turned down by an opinionated wretch who loved the same thing a few days before. It is hard not to be cross and bossy at such a time, but it is worse for the child's feeling about food to try to force or urge her to eat it. If she turns down half her vegetables for a while, as is common in the second year, serve her the ones that she does like. This is the wise and pleasant way to take advantage of the great variety of fresh, frozen, and canned vegetables that we have. If she turns against all vegetables for a while but loves her fruit, let her have extra fruit. If she takes enough fruit, milk (soy or cow's), and good quality grains, she won't miss the nutrients in vegetables.

Eating less and choosier at a year. Somewhere around a year old, babies are apt to change their feelings about food. They become choosier and less hungry. This is not surprising. If they kept on eating and gaining the way they did when they were little babies, they'd turn into mountains. Now they seem to look the meal over and ask themselves, "What looks good today and what doesn't?" What a contrast to their behavior at eight months. In those days they felt starved when mealtime came around. They'd whimper pathetically while their parent tied the bib and lean forward for every bite. It wouldn't matter much what was served. They were too hungry to care.

There are other reasons, aside from not being as hungry, that now make them choosy. They've begun to realize, "I'm a separate person with ideas of my own," so they become definite in their dislikes of a food they were doubtful about before. Their memory is getting better, too. They probably realize that "The meals here are served up pretty regularly, and they stay around long enough for me to get what I want." Also, teething often takes away a child's appetite, especially when the first molars are on their way. He may eat only half his usual amount for days, or he may occasionally refuse an entire meal.

Finally and perhaps most important is the fact that appetite naturally varies from day to day and week to week. We grown-ups know that one day we grab a big glass of tomato juice; another day split-pea soup looks better. It is the same way with children and babies. But the reason you don't see this variation more often in infants under a year is that most of the time they are too hungry to turn anything down.

Fed up with cereal. Many babies get tired of cereal sometime in the second year, especially for supper. Don't try to push it in. There are many substitutes you can offer, such as bread or pasta (see page 315 for more). Moreover, even if they give up starches for a few weeks, it won't hurt them.

Tastes change. Expect your baby's tastes to change from month to month. The chances are great that if you don't make a battle of it, your child will eat a reasonably balanced diet from week to week, though it may be lopsided from meal to meal or day to day. If it stays unbalanced for weeks, however, you should discuss the problem with your doctor or nurse practitioner.

⟨⟨ CLASSIC SPOCK
Standing and playing at meals. This may be quite a problem even before the age of a year. It comes about because the baby is less ravenous for food and more interested in all kinds of new activities, like climbing, handling the spoon, messing in the food, tipping the cup upside down, dropping things on the floor. I've seen a one-year-old being fed a whole meal standing up backward in the chair and even while being followed around the house by a long-suffering parent with a spoon and dish in her hands.

Fooling around at meals is only a sign that children are growing up and that parents are sometimes more keen about children eating than the children are. This behavior is inconvenient and irritating and can lead to feeding problems, too. I wouldn't let it go on. You'll notice that children climb and play when they're partly or completely satisfied, not when they're really hungry. So whenever they lose interest in food, assume they've had enough, let them down from the chair, and take the food away.

It's right to be firm, but you don't need to get mad. If they immediately whimper for the meal, as if to say they didn't mean they weren't hungry, give them one more chance. But if they show no regret, don't try to give them the meal a little later. If they get extra hungry between meals, give them a little more than usual for their snack, or give them the next regular meal early. If you always stop the meal casually when they lose interest, they will do their part by paying attention when they are hungry.

Now I want to state a reservation. Babies around a year old have a powerful urge to dip their fingers into the vegetable, to squeeze a little cereal in their hands, and to stir a drop of milk around on the tray. This isn't fooling. They may be opening their mouths eagerly for food at the same time. I wouldn't try to stop them from experimenting just a little bit with the feel of food. But if they try to turn the dish over, hold it down firmly. If they insist, keep it out of reach for a while or end the meal.

SELF-FEEDING

Early practice. The age at which babies feed themselves depends largely on the adults' attitude. Some infants are efficiently spoon-feeding themselves before the age of a year. At the other extreme, overprotective parents swear that their two-year-olds can't possibly feed themselves at all. It all depends on when you give them a chance. Most babies show an ambition to manage the spoon by nine to twelve months, and if they have opportunity to practice, a lot of them can do a good job without help by fifteen months. Babies get some preparation for spoon-feeding way back at six months when they hold their own bread crusts and other finger foods. Then at around nine months, when they get chopped foods, they want to pick up each piece and put it in their mouths. Babies who have never been allowed to feed themselves with their fingers are apt to be delayed in taking to spoon-feeding.

A polite baby of ten to twelve months may just want to rest a hand on his mother's or father's hand when being fed. But most babies, when the urge comes, try to yank the spoon out of the parent's hand. Don't think this has to be a tug-of-war; give the baby that spoon and get another one to use yourself. The baby will soon discover that feeding himself is more complicated than just getting possession of the spoon. It may take weeks for him to learn how to get a speck of food on the spoon and weeks more to

learn not to turn it upside down between the dish and his mouth.

Making messes. When babies become bored with trying to eat and stir or slop the food instead, it's time to move the dish out of reach, perhaps leaving a few crumbs of meat or bread on the tray for them to experiment with. Even when they're trying very hard to feed themselves correctly, they make plenty of accidental messes. This you've got to put up with. If you're worried about the rug, put a big plastic tablecloth under the high chair. Children's spoons with wide, shallow bowls and short, curved handles work well. Or use a regular teaspoon.

Giving up control. When your one-year-old can feed herself, let her take over completely. It isn't enough to let the baby have a spoon and a chance to use it; you've got to gradually give her more reason to use it. At first she tries because she wants to do things for herself. But after she sees how complicated it is, she's apt to give up the whole business if you keep on rapidly feeding her anyway. When she begins to be able to get a speck to her mouth, you ought to let her have a few minutes alone with the food at the beginning of the meal, when she's hungriest. Then her appetite urges her on. The better she becomes at feeding herself, the longer at each meal she should have to do it.

By the time she can polish off her favorite dish in ten minutes, it's time for you to get out of the picture. This is where parents often go wrong. They say, "She can eat her own cereal and fruit all right now, but I still have to feed her her vegetable and potato." This attitude is risky. If she's able to manage one food, she has skill enough to manage the others. If you go on feeding her the ones she doesn't bother with, you build up a sharper and sharper distinction between the foods she wants and the foods you want her to take. In the long run, this takes away her appetite for your foods. But if you put thought into serving a well-balanced diet from among the foods she presently enjoys and let her feed herself entirely, the chances are great that she will strike a good balance from week to week, even though she may slight this or that food from time to time.

✑ CLASSIC SPOCK
Don't worry about table manners. Babies want to eat more expertly, more neatly, all by themselves. They want to graduate from fingers to spoon and from spoon to fork as soon as they feel equal to the challenge, just as they want to try all the other difficult things that they see others doing. Dr. Clara Davis noticed this in the babies she was observing, and they weren't coached at all. She pointed out that puppies show the same urge to learn eating manners without being taught. In the beginning, the puppies stand in a pan of milk and dip their faces. First, they learn to keep their feet out; next, to lap the milk without dipping their faces; finally, to lick their whiskers politely at the end.

I have been making quite a point about letting children learn to feed themselves somewhere between the ages of twelve and fifteen months, because that is the age when they want to try. Suppose a parent keeps a baby from doing it at this age and then at twenty-one months declares, "You big lummox, it's time for you to feed yourself." Then the child is apt to take the attitude, "Oh, no! It's my custom and my privilege to be fed." At this more advanced stage, trying to manage a spoon is no longer exciting. In fact, the child's whole sense of what's proper rebels against it, and the parents have lost the golden opportunity.

Don't take all this so seriously that you think there is only one right age, don't worry because your baby is not making sufficient progress, and don't try to force the issue; that would only create other problems. I'm only making the point that babies want to learn this skill and can do so more easily than many parents realize. It is important for parents gradually to give up feeding the child when he is able to take over.

VITAMINS, SUPPLEMENTS, AND SPECIAL DIETS

Vitamin D. Breast milk provides most of the vitamins a baby needs, but it contains very little vitamin D. Normally, babies make their own vitamin D through exposure to sunlight. But in our modern world, many babies spend all day indoors, especially in winter. So experts recommend that all breast-fed babies get an extra 200 units (IU) of vitamin D, just to be on the safe side. The usual baby vitamins that you can buy in the drug store contain 400 IU of vitamin D per dose, along with vitamins A and C. (This is actually twice the vitamin D your baby really needs but is still a safe dose; check the label to be sure you're giving the right amount.) You simply fill the dropper up to the line and squirt the vitamins into your baby's mouth at the beginning of one of the feedings of the day, once a day, every day, starting at about one month. Be aware, though, that more is not better. Too much vitamin D is harmful, so stick to the standard dose.

Vitamin B$_{12}$. Vitamin supplements should be given to breast-fed infants of mothers on plant-based diets and weaned infants who are being raised on plant-based diets. Such diets have many health advantages (see page 337), and adding vitamin B$_{12}$ is a simple way to ensure complete nutrition. For infants between six months and a year of age, 0.5 microgram of vitamin B$_{12}$ is recommended. For children from one to three years, 0.7 microgram is recommended.

Other vitamins. Most baby formulas are fortified with enough vitamins that additional ones aren't necessary. Breast milk also contains enough vitamins for the first six months, except vitamin D and vitamin B$_{12}$ when mothers are eating plant-based diets (see above). Multivitamin drops usually contain vitamins A, D and C and also many B vitamins. Cereals and other foods that babies eat usually provide sufficient B vitamins, and fruits and vegetables provide A and C. So while there is certainly no harm in taking multivitamins, they usually are not worth the expense. Your child's doctor or nurse practitioner will tell you if you should be giving extra vitamins.

Iron. Iron-fortified formulas provide enough iron. Breast-milk has less iron but it is much more easily absorbed. Store-bought infant cereals are usually iron-fortified, and cereal two or three times a day along with formula or breast milk usually provides enough iron. If you're giving your baby mostly home-made foods and breast milk, you may need to add iron drops. One dropperful a day of a baby's multivitamin with iron preparation usually takes care of any iron needs.

Fluoride. Fluoride is recommended for infants if the water supply is not fluoridated. If your child drinks fluoridated water, there is no need for extra fluoride. For infants between six months and three years, 0.2 to 0.5 milligram is recommended.

Low-fat diets. A low-fat diet is not wise for infants and children under two years of age. Some fat is needed for proper growth and brain development, and children under two years need the concentrated calories provided by fats, peanut butter, and other nut butters. Children who eat meat and full-fat dairy products usually get plenty of fat. *Essential* fats (see page 329) are found in vegetable oils. The typical North-American diet is very high in fat; most children over the age of two (and most of us grown-ups) would be better off taking in far less fat. But babies are different. Low-fat diets under age two can cause serious growth problems and may result in long-standing learning problems. Of course, if your baby has a special medical condition, you should follow the doctor's advice.

BREAST-FEEDING

BENEFITS OF BREAST-FEEDING

Health benefits. When commercial infant formulas were developed, they were advertised as being the "scientific" way to feed a baby. But in the last twenty years, science has found just the opposite: For most babies, breast milk is healthier than formula. Breast milk contains antibodies and other substances that help babies fight off infections. The iron in breast milk comes in a form that is very easy for babies to absorb. Formula manufacturers have to add much *more* iron for the same amount to get into the baby. Certain chemicals in breast milk may be important for optimal brain development. Newer (and very expensive) formulas now include some of these chemicals, but breast milk contains so many different substances that no formula manufacturer can completely reproduce it.

A number of scientific studies have even shown that on the whole, breast-fed babies are a little smarter than formula-fed ones. It may be that breast milk itself improves brain development, or it may be that the women who choose to breast-feed are smarter on average, so their babies are, too.

Practical and personal benefits. From a purely practical point of view, breast-feeding can save hours of time every week, because there are no bottles to wash; no formulas to buy, carry home, and mix; no refrigeration to worry about; and no bottles to warm. You will particularly appreciate the convenience if you ever have to travel. And breast-feeding costs less.

Breast-feeding can help mothers lose weight after pregnancy (it takes a lot of calories to make milk). The baby's sucking releases oxytocin, a hormone that helps the uterus shrink back to its prepregnancy size. Oxytocin also causes feelings of contentment and happiness. The most convincing evidence of the value of breast-feeding comes from mothers who have done it. They speak of the tremendous satisfaction they experience from knowing that they are providing their babies with something no one else can give them and the feelings of closeness they get from breast-feeding.

⬅ CLASSIC SPOCK

Parents don't get to feel like parents, come to enjoy being parents, or feel the full parental love for their child just because a baby has been born to them. Particularly with their first infant, they become real parents only when they take care of their child. The more success they have in the beginning in doing their part and the more visibly their baby is satisfied by their care, the sooner and more enjoyably they slip into the role. In this sense, breast-feeding does wonders for a young mother and her relationship with her baby. She and her baby are happy in themselves and feel more loving toward each other.

How long to breast-feed? The American Academy of Pediatrics recommends breast-feeding for at least the first twelve months of life. Most experts agree that six months of breast-feeding confer most of the medical benefits and that *any* amount is better than none at all.

The need for vitamin D. One substance breast milk does *not* supply is vitamin D. Babies are able to make vitamin D themselves if they are exposed to sunlight on a regular basis. Babies who stay indoors much of the time may be low on vitamin D, resulting in serious problems with bone development. So the American Academy of Pediatrics now recommends that breast-fed babies be given vitamin D drops, 200 units per day (one standard dropperful), beginning no later than age 2 months and continuing as long as they are taking mostly breast milk.

FEELINGS ABOUT BREAST-FEEDING

Mixed feelings. A few women, usually because of the way they themselves were brought up, are deeply uncomfortable at the prospect of breast-feeding; it may seem immodest or animal-like. Likewise, quite a few fathers, including some very good ones, object to breast-feeding; they can't help feeling jealous. Others, however, feel great pride in their wives' nursing their babies.

Sexual feelings. It is too seldom mentioned that after a couple of weeks, breast-feeding becomes definitely pleasurable for the mother. Most nursing mothers describe a powerful feeling of love and connection. Some nursing mothers say that the plea-surable sensations which they feel in their breasts and in their genital region while they are nursing are similar to the sensa-tions they experience during sexual excitement. A woman may feel confused and guilty about the similarity in these sensa-tions unless she understands that they are entirely normal.

Some mothers and fathers are embarrassed by milk's leaking during lovemaking (others find this arousing). So you can see that it's really important for the parents to openly discuss their feelings about nursing. Sometimes having this discussion with the doctor, nurse practitioner, or lactation consultant present can help the parents realize that there's nothing wrong with feel-ing the way they do.

Leaking. Many nursing mothers have the experience of having milk leak from their breasts when another woman's baby cries hungrily nearby. This is embarrassing to mothers who don't understand that this, too, is entirely normal.

HOW TO GIVE BREAST-FEEDING A FAIR TRIAL

Tips for success. You hear of women who want to nurse their babies but don't succeed. Sometimes medical conditions make breast-feeding difficult or ill-advised. But by far, most women who choose to breast feed can succeed if they give breast-feeding a fair trial.

Three factors can make a big difference: keeping away from formula; not getting discouraged too soon; and sufficient stimulation of the breasts. I'd add that it helps greatly to have a supportive coach, either a trained lactation consultant or a woman with a lot of experience of breast-feeding. While books can give you encouragement and ideas, there's no substitute for experienced assistance if you are having difficulty. Most postpartum nurses, midwives, and obstetricians know who the best breast-feeding coaches are. If you're new at breast-feeding, it makes sense to find your coach early, so your breast-feeding can get off to a good start. See below for more on community resources for breast-feeding mothers.

Other tips: Have your baby with you as much as possible in the first hours and days after birth. Continuous rooming-in from birth on is best. Allow your baby to start breast-feeding in the first hour if she is ready. A newborn baby who has been dried and laid naked on her mother's abdomen will often wriggle up to the breast and begin to nurse before she is even an hour old. Let your baby feed as often as she wants at the beginning, until nursing and your milk supply are well established. With practice, babies become more skilled at latching on and sucking; and the more your baby nurses, the more milk you'll make.

Signs of success. It can be difficult to know whether your baby is getting enough breast milk, especially at first. Signs that breast-feeding is working include:

- Your baby nurses every two to three hours (or more) for ten minutes or longer.
- During nursing, you hear slurping or swallowing sounds and feel your breast emptying.
- Your baby has at least three or four thin or seedy bowel movements a day, usually mustard-colored.
- Your baby has at least six wet diapers a day.
- Your baby seems happy and energetic when awake.

    If you're not sure you're succeeding, it's important to get expert assistance. An experienced lactation consultant can work wonders, but breast-feeding problems are always much easier to fix if they're caught early. So again, if you are in doubt, ask for help.

Avoid early formula. If a baby is given formula from a bottle for the first three or four days of life, the chance of successful breast-feeding is diminished. It's much easier to express milk from a bottle than from a breast, and babies, being as lazy as the rest of us, will usually choose the easiest way. The baby who is satisfied by plenty of formula will not try hard at the breast. Inexperienced mothers then believe that the baby prefers the bottle to the breast, but this is not really true. The best policy is to avoid formula for as long as possible, certainly until breast-feeding is well established and the baby's preferences are set.

Listen to your supporters. The attitudes of the doctor who delivered the baby, the hospital nurses, and the doctor or nurse practitioner who's looking after the baby will have a powerful effect in encouraging or discouraging breast-feeding. So will the attitudes of relatives and friends. A supportive father can make the difference between a positive experience and an early end to breast-feeding.

Seek out and listen to friends and family members who have successfully breast-fed. Don't let your other friends discourage you. Perhaps this is as good a time as any to mention that a mother who is attempting to breast-feed may occasionally be subjected to a surprising amount of skepticism on the part of friends and relatives who are otherwise sympathetic. There are remarks like: "You aren't going to breast-feed, are you?" "Why in the world are you trying to do that?" "With breasts like yours, you'll never succeed." "Your poor baby is hungry. Are you trying to starve the child to prove a point?" The milder remarks can perhaps be blamed on surprise; the meaner ones strongly suggest envy. Even later, if there is any question about continuing to nurse, you'll find several friends who'll urge you to stop. If you choose to breast-feed, find people who support your decision and listen to them. Your mother or mother-in-law may be a key ally, or you may want to connect with community resources that support breast-feeding (see page 249).

Milk supply concerns. Sometimes a mother becomes discouraged just as her milk is coming in or perhaps a day or two later because she isn't producing very much. This is no time for her to quit. She hasn't given herself half a chance.

The mother is best off if she makes sure that she is getting enough to eat and drink and as much rest as possible. Then she needs to put the baby to the breast more often. Increased breast stimulation causes milk production to go up. Middle-of-the-night nursings are especially important at first in giving the breasts regular stimulation. Young babies are often more awake—and, therefore more effective nursers—in the middle of the night. So in the early weeks it's better to encourage nighttime feeding if that's when your baby most wants to feed, because that is the best way for your milk supply and your baby to grow. Plan to sleep more during the day so that you can be up more at night. Often, when breast-feeding a new baby, you need to get used to working the night shift.

If a baby isn't taking much to begin with, so that milk production continues to increase, it helps to empty the breasts after the feeding. Some mothers can express milk by hand (page 277), but the easiest way is with a high-quality electric breast pump (see page 278).

What if the baby seems to be losing weight? Newborns normally lose about one-tenth of their body weight in the first week; after that they should gain steadily. Of course, babies cannot be kept off formula indefinitely if they remain miserably hungry and continue to lose weight. If a mother keeps in frequent touch with the doctor or nurse practitioner, he or she will help her decide at each step such questions as how many days the baby can go before resorting to formula, how much nursing the mother's nipples can stand, and how frequently to nurse. Note, though, that the doctor or nurse practitioner is influenced in many of these decisions by the mother's attitude toward nursing. If she makes it clear that she is eager to succeed, she encourages the doctor to give the help that will make it possible.

It's useful to know about supplemental lactation systems. These devices consist of a piece of narrow tubing taped to the breast and attached on the other end to a plastic bottle. When the baby sucks on the nipple, formula flows through the tubing into the baby. After nursing in this way, the mother must then use an efficient breast pump to empty her breasts as much as possible to stimulate milk production. These systems, used under the guidance of a lactation consultant, give babies the nourishment they need and increase the mother's breast-milk supply.

Why some mothers give up. Many mothers start breast-feeding in the hospital and continue for a short time afterward, but then get discouraged and give up. They say, "I didn't have enough milk," "My milk didn't seem to agree with the baby," or "As the baby grew bigger my milk was no longer sufficient."

Why is it that it's only in bottle-feeding countries like ours that the breast milk supply so often seems to fail? The mother here who tries to breast-feed, instead of feeling that she is doing the most natural thing in the world and assuming that she'll succeed like everyone else, feels that she's attempting to do the unusual, the difficult thing. Unless she has great self-confidence, she keeps wondering whether she will fail. In a sense, she's looking for signs of failure. If her baby cries one day a bit more than usual, her first thought may be that her milk has decreased. If the baby develops indigestion or colic or a rash, she is quick to suspect her milk.

Her anxiety makes her feel that the bottle is the answer. And the trouble is that the bottle is always available. She was probably given formula directions or packs of prepared formula when she left the hospital ("just in case"). Babies on the breast who are given ample amounts of formula several times a day practically always nurse less eagerly at the breast. And milk left in the breast is nature's method of signaling to the glands to make less.

In other words, the combination of a mother lacking confidence in her ability to breast-feed and the availability of bottles of formula is a most efficient method of discouraging breast-feeding. To put it positively: The way to make breast-feeding a success is to go on breast-feeding and keep away from formula, at least until the breast-milk supply is well established.

Of course, employment outside of the home can be a major barrier to breast-feeding. Even the knowledge that they will eventually have to go back to work is enough to discourage many women from starting or sticking with breast-feeding. However, with planning, determination, and a good breast pump, it's often possible to continue nursing. Many women are able to continue breast-feeding in the evenings and mornings, and the child-care provider (or father) gives bottles during the day. If the mother is able to pump at work, the daytime bottles can be of stored breast milk.

Community resources for nursing mothers. Many hospitals now have lactation consultants who counsel breast-feeding mothers. Most physicians and nurse practitioners are also well versed in supporting breast-feeding. The La Leche League is composed of mothers who have succeeded at breast-feeding and are eager to give advice and support to inexperienced mothers. Consult your phone book or ask a nurse at the local health department. The International Childbirth Education Association instructors in your community can provide support and can usually refer you to a lactation consultant. These experienced, knowledgeable consultants, certified by the International Board of Lactation Consultants, have a remarkably high rate of success with mothers who are having breast-feeding problems (a certified lactation consultant may choose to have the initials IBCLC after her name). Breast-feeding support groups can be very beneficial. The Nursing Mothers' Council can also help.

THE NURSING MOTHER'S PHYSICAL CONDITION

General health. Nursing mothers need to take good care of themselves. During this period, it's healthy to unplug the phone, nap when the baby naps, let the housework go, forget outside worries and obligations, limit visitors to one or two comfortable friends, and eat and drink wisely.

Most women can breast-feed safely and successfully. If you take medication for a chronic medical condition, it's wise to check with your obstetrician or your baby's doctor before starting. If you are determined, there are often ways to proceed. For example, even women who have had mastectomies for breast cancer can still nurse their babies, using special equipment. Lactation consultants are very resourceful people.

Breast size. Some women with small breasts assume that they will be less able to produce milk in sufficient quantity. There is no basis for this belief. When a woman is not pregnant and not nursing, the milk-producing glands are inactive and make up only a minor part of the breast. The rest is mainly fat. Large breasts have more fat tissue, small breasts have less. As a woman's pregnancy progresses, hormones stimulate the milk glands to develop and enlarge. The arteries and veins that serve the glands enlarge, too, so that the veins become prominent on the surface of the breasts. The milk, when it comes a few days after delivery, causes further enlargement of the breasts. A woman with very large breasts may want to consult a lactation consultant for advice about special techniques to make breast-feeding easier.

Flat or inverted nipples. The areola is the ring of darker skin surrounding the nipple. Normally, gently compressing the areola between a finger and thumb will cause the nipple to stick out more. Nipples that go back in are called inverted. Women with inverted nipples should consult a lactation consultant *before the baby is born* so that breast-feeding can get off to a good start.

Exercise. Regular exercise helps to tone the body, lift the spirits, and lose weight if need be. A brisk, thirty-minute walk several times a week, with the baby in a carrier, can be very helpful. In addition to aerobic exercise, weight training can build strength and increase your metabolic rate so that you burn calories faster. This weight training doesn't require elaborate equipment. A lot can be accomplished with cheap hand weights, an exercise book from the library, and just a few minutes each day. There is no evidence that it will harm the baby if a nursing mother plays sports.

Changes in breast shape. Some mothers shy away from breast-feeding because they are concerned about the effect of nursing on the shape and size of their breasts. The breasts enlarge during pregnancy and even more in the first days after birth, whether or not the baby is nursed. They become much less prominent and firm by the time a baby is a week old, even if the mother continues to nurse successfully, so much so that she may wonder whether her milk has gone.

An important factor—whether nursing is never started or is ended at one, three, six, or twelve months—is the character of the supporting tissue of the breasts. There are women whose breasts have flattened without their ever having nursed a child. Many women breast-feed several babies with no deleterious effect on their figures, and others end up liking their bodies more.

Two precautions that are probably important. The mother should wear a well-fitting bra that supports the breasts not only when she is nursing but also during the later part of pregnancy, when the breasts have become enlarged. This is to prevent stretching of the skin and the supporting tissues during the time the breasts are heavier. It is well worthwhile to buy nursing bras, whose fronts can be opened for nursing (get the kind that can be opened easily with one hand).

The mother's diet during nursing. Some mothers hesitate to nurse their babies because they have heard that they will have to give up too many foods. Generally speaking, this is not so.

Occasionally a baby becomes upset every time the mother eats a certain food. For example, when a mother drinks cow's milk, some of the dairy proteins pass into the breast milk and may irritate the baby's stomach (some very sensitive children even develop an allergic rash from this secondhand cow's milk). Caffeine, chocolate, and some spicy foods will sometimes do the same thing. Naturally, if this happens several times in succession with a particular food, the mother should give that one up.

Some medications get into the milk though not usually in large enough quantities to affect the baby. Check with your doctor about which drugs are safe or unsafe to take while breast-feeding. Of course, smoking is unhealthy for mothers and children, both during pregnancy and after.

A nursing mother who drinks a glass or two of wine or beer a day will not harm her baby. But the first months of having a new baby are stressful, and a new mother might easily decide to have one drink to relax, then another, and another. So if there is alcoholism in your family—as there is in many—or if you think you could possibly develop that problem, you may want to avoid alcoholic beverages while breast-feeding.

A nursing mother does need to be sure that her diet contains plenty of the elements that the baby withdraws through her milk. A large amount of calcium is excreted in the milk; it enables the baby's bones to grow rapidly. If the mother takes in too little, calcium for the baby will be withdrawn from the mother's bones. She also should take in as much fluid as the baby is getting from her plus a little extra for her own needs. If you normally drink little milk or have chosen a nondairy diet, you can get plenty of calcium from calcium-supplemented juices, or soy milk or from calcium supplement tablets. High-calcium nondairy foods are listed on page 355.

The nursing mother's daily diet should include plenty of vegetables, especially leafy green vegetables like broccoli and kale; fresh fruit; beans, peas, and lentils, which have vitamins, plenty of calcium; and traces of healthful fats; and whole grains. These foods are rich in vitamins and minerals and also in fiber, which helps keep the bowels running smoothly. Small servings of meat are fine, but some people feel a vegetarian diet may be healthier yet (see page 338).

A benefit of increasing vegetables and reducing meats is that animals tend to concentrate pesticides and other harmful chemicals in their meat and milk. This is especially true of fish. Breast-feeding mothers should probably limit their intake of tuna, for example, and avoid altogether other fish that have a high mercury content (see page 766). Traces of toxic chemicals can easily end up in a mother's breast milk if she eats lots of meat products. Plant foods are much less contaminated, even if they are not organically grown.

A multivitamin preparation prescribed by the doctor is also a good idea. You should avoid taking any vitamin in a daily dose larger than the one recommended by the manufacturer, unless your doctor has advised it. Many obstetricians suggest that mothers simply continue taking their prenatal vitamins.

There are two sides to the matter of fluids. There is no good to be gained from drinking more fluid than feels comfortable, because the body promptly gets rid of excess water in the urine. On the other hand, a new, excited, busy mother may forget to drink as much as she needs and go thirsty through absentmindedness. A good time to drink something is ten to fifteen minutes before you expect to nurse.

Does nursing tire the mother? You occasionally hear it said that breast-feeding takes a lot out of a woman. Many women do feel fatigued in the early weeks of nursing, but so do many who feed by the bottle. They have not yet gotten all their strength back after the delivery and hospitalization. The nervous tension of caring for a new baby is tiring. But it's also true that the breasts are providing a good number of calories each day for the baby, so a mother must eat more than usual just to keep her weight and strength up. If a nursing mother is healthy and happy, her appetite will naturally take care of the need for extra calories for the baby's milk. Needless to say, a nursing mother who is not feeling well or is losing weight should promptly consult her doctor.

A mother who is nursing is forced to spend several hours each day sitting down. Sometimes bottle-feeding mothers become more tired out because they feel compelled to do household chores, while a nursing mother has an excellent excuse to let someone else worry about the laundry. Nursing is certainly tiring for the mother who has to wake up three times a night. An eager father can't take over that chore entirely, of course, but he can bring the baby in to the mother, change the diaper if need be, and return the baby to the crib. Once the nursing is well established, if the father wants to offer a bottle of breast milk in a nighttime feeding, there's no harm in that. If mother nurses at nine and goes to sleep, father can give a bottle around midnight. The mother will be reasonably well rested in time for the 3 A.M. feeding. With luck, both parents can look forward to stopping the nighttime feeds in four to six months.

Menstruation and pregnancy. Some women don't menstruate as long as they continue to nurse. Others menstruate regularly or irregularly. Once in a while, a nursing baby will be mildly upset during the mother's menstruation or temporarily refuse to nurse.

The likelihood of becoming pregnant goes down while breast-feeding. If a mother is not supplementing, the baby is less than six months old, and the mother is not having a period, there is only a very small chance (about 2 percent) that she will become pregnant, even with no contraception. It's important to consult your doctor about when to resume the family-planning method of your choice.

GETTING STARTED AT BREAST-FEEDING

Relaxation and letdown. You'll probably notice that the state of your feelings has a lot to do with how easily your milk comes. Worries and tension can hold the milk back. So try to get troubles off your mind before beginning. Take deep breaths and relax your shoulders. If possible, lie down for fifteen minutes before you expect your baby to wake and do what is most relaxing, whether it's shutting your eyes, reading, or perhaps listening to music.

After you have been nursing for a few weeks, you may notice a distinct sensation of the milk being "let down" or "coming in" at nursing time. It may start leaking from the breasts when you hear your baby begin to cry in the next room. This shows how much feelings have to do with the formation and release of the

milk. Not all mothers experience the feeling of letdown, however.

Positioning. Find a comfortable position and take care that
your baby is properly positioned on your breast, so that he can
latch on effectively. Latching on to the breast occurs when part
of the areola (the dark area around the nipple) is inside your
baby's mouth. A mother can assist her baby to find a comfortable and effective nursing position by controlling the baby's
head with one hand and moving the nipple and areola into his
mouth with the other.

For women with large breasts, it's very helpful to have a supportive nursing bra to hold the breast up; it's simply too difficult
to hold up a heavy breast *and* a heavy baby with one arm.

Sitting position. Some mothers prefer to nurse sitting up. The
cradle hold works well in a sitting position. Hold your baby with
his head in the crook of your elbow, facing your breast, with his
back supported by your forearm. You can hold his bottom or
thigh with your hand. His face, chest, stomach, and knees should
all be facing you. A pillow under him and another under your
elbow will provide good support. With your opposite hand, support your breast by placing your four fingers under it and your
thumb on top, well above the areola.

Gently tickle your baby's lower lip with your nipple until he
opens his mouth very wide. (Be patient; this sometimes takes a
few minutes.) When your baby's mouth is wide open, pull him
in close so his mouth is on the nipple and his gums are well

around the nipple, with most or all of the areola in his mouth. His nose will be touching your breast, but there's usually no need to make an airspace, unless you hear him snuffling as he tries to nurse. If his breathing seems at all obstructed, pull his bottom closer to you or lift up your breast gently with your lower fingers. This will make the extra space he needs to nurse without his nose being plugged.

Lying on your side: If you prefer to nurse lying on your side, or if you're more comfortable that way because you've had stitches, have someone help you position pillows behind your back and between your legs. Your baby should lie on his side facing you. You may need to experiment with pillows under your baby and under your head and shoulder to bring the nipple to the right height for your baby. Let's say you're on your left side: Curl your left arm around your baby in the cradle hold then get him latched on as described above.

The football hold is one you can use if you had a cesarean section, to nurse a small baby, or just for a different position. Sit in a comfortable chair (most prefer a

rocking chair) or in bed with lots of pillows keeping you upright. Rest your arm on a pillow and tuck your baby's trunk and
legs under your elbow, with his head resting in your hand and
his legs pointing straight up the back of the chair or the pillows
behind you. Help your baby latch on to the breast as described
for the cradle hold.

Latching on and sucking. In order to suck effectively, babies
have to latch on, by taking the whole nipple and much of the
areola into their mouths. The nipple should be pointing toward the roof of the baby's mouth. A baby latching on does the
same thing you do when you eat a really fat sandwich. You need
to hold the breast a little bit like that overstuffed sandwich,
squeezed between your thumb and forefinger, with one hand
on either side.

Babies do not get the milk simply by taking the nipple into
their mouths and sucking. The milk is formed in glands
throughout the breast. It passes through small ducts toward the
center of the breast, where it collects in a number of storage

spaces, or sinuses, located in a circle right behind the areola. A short duct leads from each sinus through the nipple to the outside (there are a number of openings in each nipple). When babies are nursing properly, most or all of the areola is in their mouths, and the main action is the squeezing of the sinuses (behind the areola) by the babies' gums. This forces the milk through the nipple and into the mouth. The sucking action of the baby's tongue is not so much to draw the milk through the nipple as to keep the areola drawn into the mouth and to get the milk from the front of the mouth into the throat.

If babies take only the nipple into their mouths, they get almost no milk. If they clamp down on the nipple, it is likely to become sore. But if they take most or all of the areola into their mouths, their gums squeeze the areola and cannot hurt the nipple. If babies start to mouth and clamp down on the nipple alone, they should be promptly stopped. Slip your finger into the corner of the mouth or between the gums if necessary to break the suction. Always break the suction before pulling the breast out, otherwise the nipple is apt to become bruised and sore. Then help your baby latch on again, with the areola well into the mouth. If your baby persists in clamping onto the nipple, stop that feeding.

It's common for the breasts to become engorged when the milk first comes in. This may pull the nipple flat, which in combination with a firm breast may make it difficult for a newborn to latch on. Your baby may become frustrated. Warm compresses and expressing some milk for a few minutes before nursing will pull the nipple out enough to help your baby get the areola into her mouth. Some women find that cold compresses work better for them.

✎ CLASSIC SPOCK

There are two things to avoid when putting babies to the breast. The first is holding the head with both hands when trying to direct it toward the breast. Babies hate to have their heads held; they fight to get free. The other is squeezing the cheeks to get the mouth open. Babies have an instinct to turn toward anything that touches their cheeks. This reflex helps them find the nipple. When you squeeze them on both cheeks at the same time, you baffle and annoy them. When a baby is refusing to take the breast and carrying on, a mother can't help feeling spurned, frustrated, and irritated. She shouldn't let her feelings be hurt by this inexperienced but apparently opinionated newcomer. If she can keep trying for a few more feedings, the chances are that the baby will figure out what it's all about.

Care of the nipples. Some doctors recommend regular massage of the nipples to toughen them during the last month of pregnancy. But it's not clear that this helps, and a lot of rubbing may actually cause cracking or soreness. Excessive washing with soap can also cause the nipples to become dry and sore. The best rule is, if it hurts, don't do it. Also, if you notice that nipple massage causes your uterus to contract, it's wise not to do it.

After the baby begins to nurse, glands in the areola secrete a lubricating substance. No other special care of the nipples, no wiping or ointment, should ordinarily be necessary. If it is, a purified lanolin made especially for breast-feeding, such as Purelan or Lansinoh, can be very soothing.

Some experienced mothers are convinced that the most helpful step for keeping nipples healthy is to allow a small amount of breast milk to dry on them after a feeding. Nipples will also be healthier in a bra without a waterproof lining, so that the nipple is not constantly damp. Any preparation that causes drying and cracking of the nipples should be avoided, such as harsh soaps or solutions that contain rubbing alcohol.

There's no reason for a nursing mother to develop cracked nipples if the infant is nursing correctly. Cracked, sore nipples are a sign to get assistance with nursing technique. With good technique, nursing should be a comfortable experience, not an ordeal.

Nipple soreness. If soreness starts to develop, the first things to check are the way the baby is latching onto the breast and the nursing position. The frequency of nursing should be increased to promote the emptying of the breasts and to prevent the baby from becoming too hungry. Changing the nursing position so that the pressure of the baby's gums is on different areas of the areola is also helpful. (For more on sore and cracked nipples, see page 273.) Sometimes when nipples are very sore, the only thing to do is pump and give the baby a bottle, giving the nipples a rest. This is a situation where help from an experienced lactation consultant can be the key to continued nursing success.

Inverted nipples. If a mother's nipples are flat or retracted (drawn back into the breast by the supporting tissue), it may further complicate getting a baby started at the breast, especially if the baby is excitable. If she searches around and can't find the nipple, she may cry angrily and pull her head back. There are several tactful things you can try. If possible, put her to breast when she wakes up, before she gets cross. If she cries at the first attempt, stop right away and comfort her before trying again. Take your time. It sometimes makes a nipple stand out better to massage it lightly with the fingers. A few women have truly inverted nipples that never become erect, but this doesn't prevent nursing. They sometimes benefit from the use of breast shells or milk cups (see following page). Your doctor, nurse, or lactation consultant will explain how to use them. An efficient breast pump can also help draw the nipples out.

Actually, the nipple's importance in nursing is in guiding the baby to draw the areola into her mouth. The supporting tissues that retract the nipple also make it more difficult for the baby to draw the areola forward and shape it to her mouth. Probably the most valuable procedure is for the mother (or nurse) to squeeze some of the milk from the sinuses by manual expression (see page 277) so that the areolar region will be softer and more compressible. Then press the areola between thumb and finger into a more protruding shape when putting it into the baby's mouth.

A breast shell or milk cup. Many women have found these valuable in making retracted or inverted nipples stand erect, lessening engorgement by pressing on the areolar region, and keeping the nipple dry. The shell is worn under the bra except when nursing. An inner dome with a hole in it fits over the nipple. A more prominent dome, attached to it, protects the nipple from the bra and creates a space for milk that leaks from the nipple. (Milk leaking directly into a bra keeps the nipple wet.) The pressure of the inner dome and the rim on the sinuses is believed to lessen engorgement; also, the pressure makes the nipple protrude. The protrusion continues for a while after the cup is removed. These cups should be worn in the last weeks of pregnancy if the nipples are flat or inverted.

HOW THE NURSING PATTERN GETS ESTABLISHED

The early natural feeding pattern. Even though the milk doesn't usually come in for a few days, nursing early and often encourages the milk supply and helps to prevent engorgement. Rooming-in is therefore of enormous help to a mother getting started in breast-feeding. Some babies may be agreeable in adapting to a schedule set by the nursery; others are very irregular at first in their wakefulness and hunger. If they wake and cry at a time when they can't be brought from the nursery to their mothers, they may cry themselves into a deep sleep by the time the schedule calls for a feeding. With rooming-in, a mother has only to reach over and put her baby to breast whenever she thinks her child is hungry. So the baby never has to cry for long or get overtired.

Hospitals that favor rooming-in and breast-feeding often let babies be put to breast soon after birth. Ideally (and in more hospitals), this could even be done in the delivery room, right after the baby is dried off. Babies are often wide awake right after delivery; if they are laid on their mother's abdomen or chest, they will often find the nipple on their own with no help at all.

After their initial alert period, many babies are sleepy and not very hungry for the first two or three days, waking only at long intervals. This is particularly likely to be so when their mothers have had sedation or anesthesia. After that, babies are likely to shift to a pattern of frequent waking—as often as every hour or two—for a few days.

Other babies are wakeful and hungry from the start. They may want to be fed ten to a dozen times in twenty-four hours for the first week or two, before settling down to something like eight to ten feedings in the second, third, or fourth week. The key is not to limit feeding; let the baby nurse when he wants to.

When the milk comes in. At first the breast doesn't produce milk at all; rather, a liquid called colostrum. Although there's not much of it, and it looks thin, colostrum is high in nutrients and infection-fighting substances.

There is considerable variation in the time and manner in which the milk comes in. It most often starts to come in on the third or fourth day of the baby's life. It tends to come in earlier in mothers who have had a child before or who room-in with their babies and are able to feed them on demand in the hospital. Sometimes it comes so suddenly that the mother can name the hour. With others, progress is much more gradual. It's on about the third or fourth day that many babies become distinctly more wakeful and hungry. This is one of the many examples of how smoothly nature works things out.

Studies of babies who have been breast-fed whenever they ap-

peared hungry have shown that a majority of them want to
nurse up to ten or twelve times a day between the third and sixth
days. (The stools may become frequent on these days, too.)
Mothers who are particularly anxious to make a success of
breast-feeding are apt to feel disappointed by this frequency on
the assumption that it means the breast-milk supply is inadequate. This is incorrect. The baby has now settled down to the
serious business of eating and growing and is providing the
breasts with the stimulation they must have if they are to meet
the increasing demands. It is during this latter half of the first
week, too, that the breasts receive the strongest stimulation from
the hormones. It is no wonder that in the first few days, the
breasts sometimes become too full or that there sometimes isn't
enough to satisfy the newly hungry baby. Still, the system works
remarkably well.

Hormone production slows down at the end of the first week.
After that, it is how much the baby demands that determines
how much milk the breasts produce. In the changeover period
(usually the second week), there may not be quite enough milk
until the breasts adjust to the demand. The baby's hunger
teaches the breast how much to produce, not just in the second
or third week but through the succeeding months. In other
words, when the baby is several months old, if she wants more,
the supply may still be increasing.

How long to nurse at each feeding. It used to be assumed that
it was better to limit the nursing time at first, then gradually
increase it as the nipples adjusted. The idea was to prevent
nipple soreness. But experience has shown that it's better to let
the babies decide from the beginning. If they are always allowed to nurse when hungry and for as long as they wish, they
take the time to latch on properly, thus avoiding nipple soreness. Longer nursing from the start allows the letdown reflex,
which at first is slower to respond, to come into play. This
means that a new mother who wants to breast feed needs to

prepare herself for doing that and not very much else. Other adults in the family need to take up the slack, allowing the nursing mother to focus on meeting the needs of the newborn.

How often can you nurse? In one sense the answer is "As often as your baby appears hungry and as often as you feel able to accommodate her." Mothers in nonindustrialized societies occasionally nurse again as soon as a half hour after the last feeding, though the baby will probably nurse only briefly at one or the other of these feedings. The mother in our society who has successfully nursed a previous baby and has plenty of self-assurance might not hesitate to nurse occasionally after an hour if she thought there was a special reason for hunger.

But it wouldn't be helpful to tell you to nurse whenever your baby cries. Babies cry for reasons other than hunger—colic, other forms of indigestion, spells of irritability that we don't understand, fatigue that for some reason doesn't bring sleep (see page 61). An anxious, inexperienced mother can get to a point of frantic fatigue if she's worrying and nursing all day and half the night. This worrying can cut down on the milk supply and interfere with the letdown reflex, too.

So in one way, the answer is to nurse as often as you wish. But in another way, it may help the inexperienced mother to protect herself a bit. It's okay to let a baby fuss a bit in the hope that she'll go back to sleep; sometimes if the father takes the baby and holds her against his bare chest, the warmth and smell—different from the mothers—will be soothing; sometimes swaddling or rocking can help. But if none of these things work, you have to go back to feeding.

A baby who sucks and sucks and never seems content may not be getting much milk. Make sure you hear gulping sounds; check that the baby is having several loose stools a day and wetting frequently; have the doctor check that her weight gain is good. Get a lactation consultant's help early, before the problem becomes severe.

One or both breasts? In many parts of the world, where nursing is the main way babies are fed and mothers carry their babies around with them in slings while they work, babies wake and are frequently put to breast. They nurse relatively briefly at one breast, then fall asleep again. In our society, which runs pretty much according to the clock and in which many babies are put in a crib in a quiet room after a feeding, the tendency is toward fewer, larger feedings. If a mother produces ample amounts of milk, her baby may be satisfied with one breast at each feeding. Each breast receives the stimulation of very complete nursing, even though this occurs only once in four to eight hours.

In many cases, however, the amount of milk in one breast does not satisfy the baby, so both breasts are given at each feeding, the left being offered first at one feeding, the right first at the next. Some mothers and doctors advocate both breasts anyway. A simple, reliable method is to let the baby finish one breast first, then offer the other. You'll know when the baby is finished when he lets go. He might take a little from the second breast or a lot; the choice is his. Letting the baby decide guarantees that he ends the feeding full but not too full.

Patterns of early nursing behavior. A physician with a sense of humor who has studied the behavior of hundreds of babies when first put to breast points out the different types. *Eager beavers* avidly draw the areola in and suck vigorously until satisfied. The only problem is that they may be too hard on the nipple if they are allowed to clamp down on it. *Excitable babies* may become so agitated and active that they keep losing the breast, and then, instead of trying again, they scream. They may have to be picked up and comforted for several minutes before they are calm enough to try again. After a few days they usually settle down. *Procrastinators* can't be bothered to nurse the first few days; they are waiting until the milk comes in. Prodding them only makes them balky. They do well when the time comes. *Tasters* must, for a little while, mouth the nipple and smack their lips over the drop of milk they taste before they settle down to business. Efforts to hurry them only make them angry. *Resters* want to nurse for a few minutes, then rest a few minutes before starting again. They can't be rushed. They usually do a good job in their own way, but it takes them longer.

There are other patterns of behavior in the early weeks of nursing that make the mother's job much more difficult and may drive her nearly mad. Fortunately, most babies outgrow these inconvenient patterns in a few weeks.

Short nursers who fall asleep. These babies never seem to nurse vigorously, and they fall asleep five minutes or so after starting. You don't know whether they have taken a reasonable amount. It wouldn't be so bad if they'd sleep for two or three hours, but they may wake and cry again a few minutes after they're put back to bed. We don't really know what causes this behavior. One possibility is that the baby's nervous and digestive systems are not yet working well enough together. Perhaps the comfort of their mothers' arms and the breast in the mouth is enough to put them back to sleep, then when they're put back into the harder, cooler bed, their hunger wakes them up again. When they're a little older and know what it's all about, their hunger will keep them awake until they're satisfied. If your baby becomes sleepy or restless after a few minutes at one breast, try shifting right away to the other breast to see if the easier flow of milk will help. Of course, you'd like her to work at least fifteen minutes on one breast to be sure that it is well stimulated, but if she won't, she won't.

Irritable nursers. Other babies, hungrier, more wide awake, or more assertive, react with irritation when they find they can't get enough milk. They jerk their heads away from the breast and yell, try again, become mad again. The fact that the baby doesn't nurse well only increases the mother's uneasiness, and a vicious cycle sets in. If a mother understands how tension can interfere with let down, she can use her ingenuity to find her own best way to relax before and during nursing. Music, a magazine, television: Whatever works best is what she should adopt.

IS YOUR BABY GETTING ENOUGH?

Weight gain and satisfaction. It's good to remember that in those parts of the world where there are no scales and no doctors, the mother simply assumes that her baby is receiving plenty if the child acts contented and looks well and that this works well in at least nine out of ten cases.

Generally speaking, you and the doctor will decide based on your baby's behavior over a number of weeks and her weight gain. Neither alone is conclusive. A baby who is happy and gaining fast is obviously getting enough. A baby who is gaining weight at the average rate but who cries hard every afternoon or evening probably has colic. A baby who gains slowly but is quite contented is, in most cases, a baby who is meant to be a slow gainer. However, there are a few babies who don't protest even when they are not gaining at all. It's the baby who is gaining very slowly and acting hungry most of the time who's probably not getting enough. The baby who is not getting enough to eat may act either unusually upset or lethargic. He'll wet fewer than six diapers a day, his urine will be dark or smell strong, and he'll have infrequent bowel movements.

Any baby who is not gaining weight well by the end of the second week of life should be awakened every two or three hours and encouraged to feed more frequently. Babies who are sleepy at the breast can be encouraged to feed by being burped and switched to the other breast. If this routine is repeated four or five times during a feeding, most babies will be gaining weight and nursing more vigorously after five to seven days.

Breast-fed babies should have a weight check roughly one week after birth and be seen by their doctor or nurse within two weeks after they leave the hospital, sooner if breast-feeding did not go smoothly in the hospital or if there are any concerns about weight gain or milk flow. In the long run it's best to assume that your baby is getting enough unless your baby and the doctor or nurse practitioner definitely tell you differently. Certainly, at any one feeding, you should be satisfied if your baby seems to be.

Hard to tell how much. This question of whether the baby's getting enough is likely to baffle the new mother. You can't tell from the length of nursing time or the appearance of the breasts or milk. A good rule of thumb is that by the fifth day of life, babies will usually wet six to eight diapers and have four to ten bowel movements a day and will be nursing eight to twelve times each twenty-four hours.

You certainly can't tell from the length of time the baby nurses. She continues to nurse after she's already obtained most of the milk—sometimes for ten more minutes, sometimes for thirty—because she's still getting a trickle of milk, because she enjoys sucking, or because she's having a good time. Careful observation and weighing of slightly older babies have shown that the same baby will appear to be entirely satisfied with three ounces at one feeding and ten at another.

Most experienced mothers have decided that they can't tell from the apparent fullness of the breasts before feeding how much milk is there. In the first week or two, the breasts are noticeably full and firm from hormonal changes; after a while they normally become softer and less prominent, even though the milk supply is increasing. A baby can get six or more ounces from a breast that to the mother does not seem at all full. You can't tell anything from the color and appearance of the milk, either. Breast milk always looks thin and bluish compared with cow's milk.

Crying and hunger. Hunger is not the most common reason for crying. Mothers often worry when their babies begin to fret right after feedings or between them. Their first thought is that their milk supply is failing. This assumption is not usually correct. The fact is that almost all babies, especially first babies, have fretful spells, usually in the afternoon or evening. Bottle-fed babies fuss as much as breast-fed ones. Babies who are getting all the milk they can possibly hold have crying spells just the same as babies who are receiving less (see pages 61 and 98 for more on crying and colic). If a mother understands that most of the fussing in the early weeks is not caused by hunger, she won't be so quick to lose confidence in her breast-milk supply.

Though much less likely, it is of course possible that a baby frets because she's hungry. However, hunger is much more apt to wake a baby a little earlier for the next feeding than to bother her in the first hour or two after the last. If she is hungry, it may be because her appetite has taken a sudden spurt, or it may mean that her mother's milk has decreased slightly from fatigue or tension. In either case, the answer is the same: Take it for granted that she'll wake and want to nurse more frequently and vigorously for a day or a few days until your breasts have adjusted to the demand; she will probably then go back to her previous schedule.

For a fretful baby, the key is to give breast-feeding a good chance to work. Any thought of giving a bottle of formula should be postponed for at least a couple of weeks. The baby should be allowed to nurse as often as she wants for as long as she wants. If she makes a reasonable weight gain in that week or two, consideration of formula should again be put off, for at least two more weeks.

It can happen, however, that a mother begins to feel frantic about nursing a fussy or colicky baby. In these cases, it's best to give the nursing a break. Try a bottle, or let someone else (father, friend, grandparent) take over the comforting. If the mother feels she can take care of herself for a short while, she can return to the nursing with renewed energy. As always, if you are concerned that your baby may not be getting enough, it's always right to consult your baby's doctor.

THE WORKING MOTHER

Nursing and working. What about the woman who hesitates to nurse because she plans to go back to work? (Not that raising a child is not work; it is. But I am using "work" to mean a job away from home.) If you're determined, chances are that you can make breast-feeding succeed. Mothers who successfully combine work and breast-feeding often give frequent feedings after work and don't try to keep their babies on a schedule. Many employers now allow nursing mothers breaks during which they can pump their breasts to keep the flow up. (See page 276 for more on pumping.)

Mothers who work can breast-feed their babies all day long on their days off. This helps to maintain a good milk supply. Even if you decide not to nurse after you resume work, it will be good for the baby's health to breast-feed the baby your first few weeks after coming home. Before you have your baby, you may find it helpful to talk to mothers who have nursed after going back to work.

Combining breast-feeding and bottle-feeding. Here are some suggestions offered by experienced mothers who have nursed after going back to work (also, see page 278).

Wait until your baby is three to four weeks old, if possible, to introduce the bottle. By this time your baby should be used to nursing on something of a schedule, and your milk flow should be well established.

One fast way to express and store milk is to nurse your baby on one breast while using the breast pump on the other (it may take some practice to do this). This really helps because the let-down reflex from nursing seems to allow the milk to be pumped more easily. Another strategy is to pump one hour after a feeding. Doing this will increase your milk supply (just as if you were feeding another baby).

Breast milk keeps eight days in the refrigerator and four to six months in the freezer. Smell and taste it, to be sure it's not sour, before giving it to your baby. Once you start a bottle of stored breast milk, discard any unused portion after two hours. Most good breast pumps allow you to pump directly into small bottles with good sealer caps. These can be labeled and stored in the freezer. Or you can use ice cube trays to make individual cubes. Wrap the cubes with plastic wrap, giving you portions of one and one-half ounces for the child-care provider to put in a bottle. Never add warm milk to a bottle of cold or frozen milk; doing so encourages spoiling.

Begin by giving a bottle of breast milk three times a week. Many babies won't take the bottles from their mothers—they know the difference—so the father, an older brother or sister, or the sitter may need to take over. Warm milk works best; breast-fed babies aren't used to cold temperatures yet. Some babies will have no difficulty accepting a bottle; with others it's a struggle and requires patience.

If your baby is reluctant to take the bottle, try leaving the room or even the house. (Some babies will refuse the bottle if they can even hear their mothers talking.) You can also try holding your baby in a nonnursing position. For example, she can be lying in your lap with her feet toward you and her head toward your knees as you offer her the bottle. Sometimes babies who really seem to like a sweet taste will accept apple juice, diluted half and half with water, from the bottle better than they will milk. It's best to avoid juice altogether up to three or four months; after that, about four ounces of juice a day is the most a nursing baby should get, since juice has very low nutritional value compared with human milk.

Ideally, before you return to work, your baby should be taking at least one bottle a day well. It helps to express or pump your milk while you're at work to keep your supply up and prevent engorgement. Try to nurse right before and right after work and to express your milk twice if you're working longer than six hours.

PROBLEMS DURING BREAST-FEEDING

Biting the nipple. Biting may make the nipples so sore that nursing has to be stopped. You can't blame a baby for trying a few bites when her gums are tingling during teething or after a couple of teeth have come in. She doesn't realize it hurts her mother.

Most babies can be quickly taught not to bite. Instantly slip your finger between her gums and gently say no. If she does it again, put your finger in again, say no, and end the feeding. It's usually late in the feeding anyway when a baby bites.

Fussing at the breast. Occasionally a baby who has been nursing well for four to five months will cry or fuss a few minutes after starting to nurse. Teething pain might be the cause. For more on this, see page 803.

Pains during nursing. You may be bothered the first week or so by cramps in your lower abdomen as soon as the baby starts nursing. Nursing releases hormones that cause the uterus to contract, returning it to its nonpregnant size. The cramps disappear after a while. For the first few days or weeks, sharp pains in the nipple that last a few seconds after the baby begins to nurse are very common, mean nothing, and soon go away.

Sore or cracked nipples. Pain that persists throughout the nursing may point to a cracked nipple, and a careful examination should be made. (A very few mothers are unusually sensitive and continue to feel pain even when their nipples remain healthy.) If a nipple is cracked (often because a baby has not latched on properly), a combination of more frequent nursing, frequent changes of the baby's nursing position, and applications of ice packs can prevent engorgement and make it easier for the baby to latch on to the areola, rather than the nipple.

The physician or nurse practitioner may prescribe an ointment or dressing, such as hydrogel.

Breast engorgement. When the breast is overfull with milk, the entire breast becomes firm and uncomfortable. Most cases are mild, but in the infrequent severe one, the breast is enlarged, surprisingly hard, and very painful. Left untreated, engorgement can also result in decreased milk supply.

The usual mild case can be promptly relieved by having the baby nurse. It may be necessary to soften the areolar region first by manual expression if it is too firm for the baby to get it into her mouth; a breast shell (page 262) can also help.

A severe case may require several kinds of treatment. Try massaging the entire breast, starting at the outer edges and working toward the areola. Try this in a warm shower; the water is relaxing, the water makes it easy to massage the breasts, and there's no mess if milk squirts all over. You can use an ointment containing purified lanolin or a vegetable oil to avoid irritating the skin, but keep the ointment off the areola: it makes it too slippery for areolar expression. Breast massage may be performed once or several times a day, either by the mother or a helper. The application of cloths wet with comfortably hot water seems to help prepare the breasts for massage. An electric breast pump can also help relieve the engorgement, in combination with massage or alone (see page 278).

Between nursings or treatments, firm support should be given to the breasts from all sides by a large, firm brassiere. Acetaminophen or ibuprofen can help with the pain. You can apply an ice bag or hot-water bottle for short periods, or try cool cabbage leaves. This total engorgement nearly always occurs, if at all, in the latter half of the first week and usually lasts only a couple of days. It is rare after that.

Engorgement behind the areola. The most frequent cause of engorgement is the overfilling of the sinuses, the storage spaces located behind the areola. This is not uncomfortable for the mother, but it may make the areolar region so firm and flat that the baby cannot take it into her mouth to compress it with her gums. The only thing she can get hold of is the nipple, and she is likely to clamp down on it and perhaps make it sore.

The answer is for the mother to express some milk from the sinuses so that the areolar region will become soft and compressible enough for the baby to take it into her mouth (for a technique of milk expression by hand, see page 277). A breast shell (page 262) can also help.

You don't need to express much milk to soften the areolar region; two to five minutes from each breast should be enough. Then you can compress the areolar region from above and below as you put the breast into your baby's mouth to help her get started. This type of engorgement is most likely to occur in the latter half of the first week. It usually lasts two to three days and does not return as long as nursing continues normally.

Engorgement from plugged ducts. A third type of engorgement is similar to total engorgement in that it is outside the areolar region and is painful. But it is confined to only one segment of the breast and results from plugged ducts. It is more likely to occur after the hospital period. Treatment is similar to that for total engorgement.

- hot applications followed by massage of the engorged area
- support by an efficient nursing bra
- use of an ice bag or hot-water bottle between treatments
- increased frequency of nursing
- nursing with the baby's nose pointing toward the blocked segment, because the suction is strongest in the middle, under the baby's nose

- frequent changes of the baby's nursing position
- adequate rest for the mother

Breast infection or abscess (mastitis). If a sore spot develops inside the breast, there may be an infection, which occasionally leads to a breast abscess. The skin may become red over the sore spot, and fever and chills may develop. Headache, achiness, and other flulike symptoms are often the first signs of breast infection. You should take your temperature and get in touch with your doctor or nurse practitioner. With modern methods of treating infections, it's best for the baby to continue to nurse through the infection. Emptying the breast *completely,* at least once a day, helps.

When the mother is ill. In ordinary illnesses, during which the mother stays home, it is customary to allow the baby to continue to nurse as usual. To be sure, there is a chance of the baby's catching the ailment, but this would be true even if the infant weren't being nursed. Besides, most infections are contagious before symptoms are noticed. You can protect your baby by washing your hands more often. Babies on the average have milder colds than older members of the family because they received many antibodies from their mothers before birth. Some mothers notice a decrease in milk supply when they're sick, but it comes right back with increased nursing.

MANUAL EXPRESSION AND BREAST PUMPS

Nursing mothers need a way to empty their breasts that doesn't rely on baby-power. Engorged breasts need emptying but may be too hard for infants to handle. A small number of babies cannot nurse, either from prematurity, a cleft palate, or other medical condition. Mothers employed outside the home often prefer to collect their milk to give later by bottle to using formula. Manual expression—using the fingers or perhaps a cup to squeeze the milk out of the breast—is a useful skill to acquire. But for any kind of regular milk collection, there's no substitute for a high-quality electric breast pump.

Manual expression. The best way to learn manual expression is from an experienced person while you are in the hospital. It's a good idea to get some instruction even if you don't anticipate using it. A visiting nurse or a lactation consultant can teach you at home later, if necessary. A mother can learn by herself, but it takes longer. In any case, it is an awkward business at first, and several practice sessions may be necessary before you become efficient. Don't be discouraged.

Milk produced throughout the breast flows through tiny tubes and collects in sinuses, or sacs, located behind the areola. In manual expression, the breast is massaged first, then the milk is squeezed out of the sinuses, each of which has a small tube leading through the nipple to the outside. If you are going to express only a small amount of milk—for instance, to relieve engorgement under the areola—you can use any handy cup or baby bottle to catch it. If you are going to express as much as you can to give to the baby right afterward, you can collect it in a clean cup and pour it into a regular baby bottle (see page 296 for bottle-feeding tips). Unused milk needs to be refrigerated or frozen (page 295). It's a good idea to wash your hands well before expressing milk manually.

The finger-and-thumb method. Massage the breast to bring the milk to the sinuses. To apply the pressure where the sinuses lie, deep behind the areola, place the tips of thumb and finger on opposite sides of the areola, just at the edge of the darker skin Then press thumb and finger in deeply until they meet the ribs. In this position, squeeze them rhythmically together while sliding the fingers forward slightly to push the milk along. Use one hand to express the breast on the opposite side and the other hand to hold the cup to catch the milk. The important thing is to press in deeply enough and at the edge of the areola. Don't squeeze the nipple itself. You may be able to get more milk with each squeeze if you not only press thumb and finger toward each other but pull slightly outward with them (toward the nipple) at the same time, to complete the milking motion. After a bit, shift the thumb and finger partway "around the clock," to be sure that all the sinuses are being pressed. If the finger and thumb become tired—they will at first—you can shift back and forth from side to side.

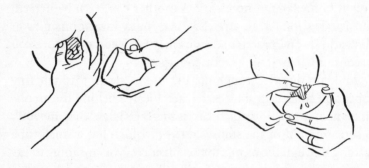

Breast pumps. Mothers who have to express their milk regularly—especially working mothers who may do it for many weeks or months—usually prefer to use a breast pump. Modern pumps are both high-powered and portable. It's worth buying or renting a high-quality one. A good pump is likely to cost from $250 to $300. Inexpensive hand-operated ones work so slowly that they aren't really practical. Many hospitals have low-cost rental programs. WIC, the federally funded women, infant and children nutrition program, provides high-quality breast pumps to low-income women for free. Medicaid sometimes has grant programs to supply high-quality pumps as well.

BREAST AND BOTTLE COMBINATIONS

An occasional bottle is all right. Must a mother who wants to continue breast-feeding never give a bottle under any circumstances? No, it isn't that critical. Most of the mothers who want to give a bottle regularly once a day find that they can do so without discouraging the breast-milk supply, provided the supply has been well established for a few weeks and it's only one bottle a day. And certainly a mother who has not been giving a bottle regularly can give one occasionally. Perhaps she will have to miss a feeding. Or perhaps she is extremely tired or upset, and the baby has acted entirely dissatisfied with one feeding. One bottle doesn't stop breast-feeding. But it's harder to continue with breast-feeding after you've given a bottle two or three times a day.

Introducing a bottle. A bottle containing breast milk or formula can be given once or twice a week starting at three to four weeks. If you plan to wean your baby from breast to bottle sometime between two and nine months, it's a good idea to offer a bottle at least once a week, though you could nurse just as well. The reason is that some babies become so set in their ways during this age period that they will refuse to take a bottle of milk if they are not used to it. This can cause quite a struggle. A baby rarely gets this opinionated before the age of two months, and after nine months she can be weaned directly to the cup if you prefer and she readily accepts it.

Breast and bottle both. Combining breast and bottle is useful if you are planning to return to a job, want your partner to be able to take a more active role in feeding, or can't produce enough milk to completely satisfy your baby. The concern is that the breast-milk supply may gradually decrease or that your baby may come to prefer the bottle, rejecting breast altogether.

If you are producing a reasonable amount of milk—say half or more of what your baby needs—you may want to make a real effort not to use formula at all. Chances are good that your milk supply will increase in response to the increased demand. If not, you can continue a combination of breast- and bottle-feeding or wean your baby completely to the bottle.

WEANING FROM THE BREAST

The meaning of weaning. Weaning is important not only for the baby but for the mother as well, not only physically but emotionally. A mother who has set great store by nursing may feel mildly let down and depressed after she stops, as if she has lost some of her closeness to the baby or has become a less worthwhile person. It may help to make weaning a gradual process. Weaning doesn't have to be an all-or-nothing phenomenon. A woman can nurse one or two times a day until her baby is two years old or can discontinue nursing entirely.

The ordinary weaning process begins with the introduction of solid foods, around four to six months, and is gradually completed in the next six to eighteen months, depending on the baby and the mother.

Weaning from breast to bottle. Many women choose to nurse for a few months but not for most of the year. How long is it important to nurse? There's no hard-and-fast answer to this, of course. The physical advantages of breast milk are most valuable to the baby at first, but there is no age at which they suddenly become of no benefit. The emotional advantages of breast-feeding will not cease at any definite period, either (see also page 242).

One sensible time to wean to the bottle is at three to four months. By this age, the baby's digestive system will have settled down. She will be nearly over any tendency to colic. She will be pretty husky and still gaining weight rapidly. But if a mother would like to stop breast-feeding at one to two months, those are satisfactory times to wean, too. If you plan to wean to the bottle at some age beyond one month, it is wise to get the baby accustomed to the bottle from the age of one month on by giving one bottle regularly two or three times a week or, if you prefer, every day.

If the breasts have been producing a good amount of milk, the weaning should preferably be gradual from the beginning. Begin at least two weeks before you want weaning to be complete. First, omit one breast-feeding a day, the one when your breasts are the least full; give a bottle instead. Let the baby take as much or as little as she wants. Wait two or three days until your breasts become adjusted to the change, then omit another breast-feeding and substitute a second daily bottle. Again wait two or three days, then omit another breast-feeding. Now the baby gets the breast at only two feedings and a bottle at each of the other three. You will probably need to wait three or even four days each time before omitting these last two nursings. Any time your breasts become uncomfortable, you can use a breast pump for a few minutes or express some milk in a warm shower, just enough to relieve the pressure.

If the baby won't take the bottle. A baby four months old or more who has not regularly had a bottle may balk completely. For a week, try offering a bottle once or twice a day, before the breast or solid food. Don't force it; don't get her angry. Take the bottle away if she refuses and give her the rest of her meal, including the breast. In a few days' time she may change her mind.

If she's still adamant, omit an afternoon breast-feeding altogether and see if this makes her so thirsty that she will try the bottle in the early evening. If she still holds out, you will probably have to give her the breast, because it will be uncomfortably full. But continue to omit an afternoon nursing for several days. It may work on a subsequent day even though it didn't on the first.

The next step is to omit every other breast-feeding throughout the twenty-four hours and reduce the amount of solid foods, so that she's pretty hungry; or omit solids altogether. You can use a breast pump or manual expression (pages 278 and 277) just enough to relieve the pressure and discomfort.

If you need to wean quickly. Occasionally a mother's milk supply may become insufficient, or there may be other reasons to wean quickly. The simplest method to wean a baby rapidly is to make up a twenty-four-hour supply of formula and divide it into as many bottles as the baby takes breast feedings. Give her a bottle at each feeding after the breast, letting her take as much or as little as she wants. Omit first the breast-feeding when your breasts are the least full. Two days later also omit the breast-feeding when your breasts are the least full. Discontinue the remaining breast-feedings, one every two or three days. If your milk is decreasing only gradually and the baby is only slightly dissatisfied, it will work better to introduce the bottles one feeding at a time.

Rarely, a woman has to suddenly stop breast-feeding. In this case, manual expression should be avoided. It may give temporary relief but will stimulate the breasts to produce more milk. One method is to apply pressure and ice bags to the breasts. This is a pretty uncomfortable business, and your doctor can prescribe appropriate medication to relieve the pain. "Dry-up" pills don't help and shouldn't be used. They're expensive, have side effects, and often produce a rebound effect, which increases the pressure in the breasts. If you do choose to express a small amount of milk, you'll probably be much more comfortable during the process, but it will also take longer for your milk supply to dry up.

Weaning from breast to cup. After nine to twelve months, it may be easiest to wean from breast to cup, omitting the bottle altogether. About that time most babies show signs that they need to nurse less. They stop nursing several times during a feeding and want to play. They may have to be nudged back onto the breast. With encouragement, they will learn how to take more milk from the cup and will switch over completely in a few weeks with no sign of deprivation or regret.

On the other hand, there are many breast-feeding mothers who definitely want to go to at least one year of age or even to two years, and that's fine, too.

Either way, it's a good idea to begin offering a sip of formula or other liquid from the cup from the age of six months so that your baby gets used to it before she is too opinionated. By nine months, encourage her to hold the cup herself. If by nine months she is nursing for shorter periods, she may be ready for gradual weaning. Now offer her the cup at all her meals and increase the amount as she shows her willingness to take more, but continue to breast-feed her at the end of the meal. Next, leave out one of her daily breast-feedings, the one she seems the least interested in, and give her only the cup. This is usually at breakfast or lunch. In a week, omit another breast-feeding if she seems willing; in another week, the last one. Her willingness to be weaned may not progress steadily. If she gets into a period when she is miserable from teething or illness, she may want to retreat a little. This is natural enough, and there is no harm in accommodating her.

When weaning is carried out this gradually, there is usually no problem with the mother's breasts. If, however, they become uncomfortably full at any time, the mother needs only to use manual expression for fifteen to thirty seconds to relieve the pressure.

Most mothers are surprised to find they are reluctant to end this emotional tie; some will put off weaning week after week. Sometimes a mother will be afraid to give up nursing altogether, because the baby is not taking as much from the cup as she used to take from the breast. This may postpone the weaning indefinitely. It's safe to stop the nursing once the baby is taking an average of four ounces from the cup at each meal or a total of twelve to sixteen ounces a day. After the nursing is stopped, she will probably increase the amount she takes from the cup up to a total of sixteen ounces or more. This is usually enough, with all the other things she is eating.

∾ CLASSIC SPOCK

Fewer babies have been breast-fed in the twentieth century—all over the world. But in recent years, breast-feeding has increased in America, particularly among women who have attended college. This is partly due to the new knowledge about the physical and emotional advantages, partly to the general respect among the young for nature and the desire to do things the natural way. We are beginning to see more babies from lower-income and minority families being breast-fed. I hope this trend will continue.

FORMULA FEEDING

―――――――― ❧ ❧ ――――――――

CHOOSING AND PREPARING FORMULA

Not so long ago, babies were raised on infant formula as a matter of routine. Today we know that there are real health benefits to mother's milk. Still, it's possible to raise healthy babies on formula, and many women use it either alone or in combination with breast milk. If you've decided on formula, your next decision is which one?

The standard infant formulas are made from cow's milk in which the butterfat has been replaced by vegetable oils. Carbohydrates, vitamins, and minerals have been added, and the protein content has been reduced. Iron is added to most formulas. Babies given low-iron formulas are very likely to become iron-deficient.

Cow's milk formulas. In a way, it's surprising that most infants can thrive on formula, given how different baby cows are from baby humans. Indeed, cow's milk itself—as opposed to cow's milk *formula*—is *not* safe for infants. The protein and sugar mix is wrong, and infants fed straight cow's milk are likely to become seriously ill. In the past, some mothers made up their own formulas using evaporated milk. These home-made mixtures aren't as safe as commercially manufactured formula.

Formulas made from nuts and grains likewise aren't nutritionally sound.

The federal WIC (women, infants, and children) program is
available to all low-income mothers, so that nearly all American
families should be able to purchase formula if they need to.

Soy formulas. Infant formulas made from soy beans are available in all hospital nurseries and grocery stores. While they
were once reserved for children who can't drink cow's milk formulas, due to allergy or digestion problems, most doctors now
consider soy formula appropriate for any full-term infant who
is not breast-feeding. Premature infants weighing less than
about four pounds at birth shouldn't use soy formulas.

Be sure to use a soy-based *formula,* not regular soy milk. Soy-
based baby formulas have added nutrients to meet the needs of a
rapidly growing child; the soy milk for older children and adults
does not. Soy formula is available fortified with iron. Iron-
fortified formula should be used from four months on, if not
from birth. WIC will supply soy formula on request.

Health benefits and risks. Soy milk formulas offer some
health advantages over those made from cow's milk. Some infants develop allergies to proteins in cow's milk formula, and
such formula may be a cause of excessive crying. Other research points to proteins in cow's milk as a possible contribu-
tor to childhood-onset diabetes.

Soy formulas don't have these problematic proteins, and they
are also free of lactose, which some infants find hard to digest.
Although the research does not show that soy formulas cure
colic, some parents report that their infants clearly feel better on
soy formula.

On the other hand, there may be health risks to soy formulas,
too. They tend to have much higher concentrations of aluminum. It's clear that aluminum does no good in the body, and
in preterm infants (at least) it can cause serious harm. Research

has not shown that the aluminum in soy formulas is harmful to full-term infants. Still, ingested aluminum has been linked to the development of Alzheimer's disease in older people (there are other contributors as well). Some scientists have also speculated that certain chemicals in soy formulas (phytoestrogens) may in rare cases interfere with the healthy development of the sexual organs. Again, scientists are undecided about this point, but there is enough evidence to at least raise the question.

On balance, then, neither kind of formula is clearly ideal, which again points to the value of breast-feeding if at all possible. For some babies and parents, one benefit or risk may outweigh the others. For example, if you've decided to raise your child on a low-dairy diet—a reasonable approach that is discussed in detail beginning on page 325—it makes sense to choose a soy-based formula.

Allergy. Many parents are concerned about allergy to cow's milk protein. Severe forms of this allergy are hard to miss. The symptoms include diarrhea, poor weight gain, and a dry, irritated rash. Milder forms may be more difficult to detect, because so many babies are fussy or develop a little rash now and then.

A family history of milk allergy can be an important clue. However, most adults who can't digest cow's milk are not actually allergic; they simply make too little of the enzyme (lactase) needed to break down the main sugar in milk (lactose). Most infants make enough lactase, even if their parents don't. To further complicate matters, many children who are truly allergic to cow's milk protein are *also* allergic to soy protein. For these children, there are specialized formulas that contain neither cow nor soy protein. It's best to use these formulas under a doctor's guidance.

Liquid, concentrate, or powder. Formulas come in three forms: ready-to-use liquid, concentrated liquid, and powder.

There is no nutritional difference. Powder costs least, ready-to-use the most. It's fine to use some of each—powder for every day, ready-to-use in the expensive, prepoured bottles for trips. It's important, though, when you do use powder or concentrate, to carefully follow the mixing instructions (see page 292 for details).

Iron-fortified or low iron. Iron is important for building red blood cells and for brain development. Iron deficiency in infancy can cause learning problems later in childhood. So it's very important for babies to have enough iron in their diets. Mothers often believe that the iron in iron-fortified formula causes constipation. Research hasn't found this to be the case. But even if it were, I'd still argue for iron-fortified formula. There are ways to handle constipation (see page 844), but the ill effects of iron deficiency can be permanent.

WASHING AND STERILIZATION

Do you need to sterilize? Sterilization of formula and bottles is no longer routinely recommended in the United States for people using reliable city or country water supplies, which is most people. If you are not sterilizing, it's best to prepare one bottle at a time, immediately before feeding. However, if you use well water or for any other reason have any question about your water supply, check with your doctor, public health nurse, or health department to see whether you have to sterilize.

Those who have to sterilize will find directions on page 290. Sterilization techniques and equipment may vary according to your doctor or county health department. If you are uncertain of your water quality, consult your county health department for their recommendations on the exact procedures. Also, they can advise you on when it's safe to stop sterilizing. A general rule is to sterilize as long as you make a twenty-four-hour supply of formula with unreliable water.

Washing. Careful washing of the bottles, nipples, screw rings, disks, and jars is particularly important if you are not sterilizing. You can do a quicker and more efficient job of washing the bottle equipment if you rinse the bottle, nipple, and ring soon after your baby has finished each bottle, before the remaining formula residue has dried. Then use dish detergent and a brush later, when it's convenient. You can also just rinse the bottles and rings and put them in the dishwasher. (Nipples likely deteriorate in the dishwater, so it's best to wash them by hand.) Clean a quart storage jar and its lid the way you clean the nursing bottles.

A bottle brush is helpful for washing the insides of the bottles. To get the inside of the nipples clean, you can use a nipple brush, then use a needle or toothpick to clear each nipple hole and squirt water through the holes.

Bottles with disposable plastic liners. This kind of bottle appeals to parents who are willing to pay a little more to save time washing or sterilizing. If your doctor or nurse practitioner advises you to sterilize, you'll still have to boil the nipples and caps for five minutes.

The holder is a cylinder of hard plastic, open at both ends. It has slits on two sides, with ounce markings at the edges, so that you can look through to see how much formula you have put in the inner liner or how much the baby has drunk. You can't use these ounce markings for diluting formula; they're not accurate enough.

To use these bottles, you tear a clear plastic liner off the roll and slip it into the holder, slightly folding it lengthwise so that it will go in easily. Then use the end tabs to stretch it open and fold it back over the upper end of the holder. Avoid touching the inside of the nipple and the part that goes into the baby's mouth. In other words, handle the nipple by the outside edges. Be sure to discard the end tabs after assembling each bottle. Even a small baby can pull one off and swallow it. There are large plastic caps that fit over the nipples while the containers are in the refrigerator or during trips.

Equipment for sterilization. You can buy a stove-top sterilizer, which is essentially the same thing as a kettle, or an electric sterilizer that turns itself off at the right time. Sterilizers usually come with all the racks, bottles, disks, nipples, and rings you'll need to get started, along with bottle and nipple brushes and tongs. Or you can get a kettle large enough to hold, in a wire rack, enough bottles for twenty-four hours—usually six, seven, or eight bottles in the early weeks—along with all the separate bottle equipment.

A pair of tongs sterilized with the rest of the equipment is helpful to lift the bottles out of the rack if they are still hot. Handle the nipples by the edges, not by the tip that may touch the formula and will later go into the baby's mouth.

Sterilization techniques. *Terminal sterilization.* With this approach, you put formula made with unsterilized water into unsterilized bottles, then sterilize them together. This method is used only when you will be filling all your nursing bottles at once. Terminal sterilization is not suitable if you plan to use disposable bottles or store the entire formula in a quart container, filling only one bottle at feeding time.

Follow the directions for making whichever kind of formula you're using. You don't need to use boiled water or sterilized bottle equipment (because everything will be sterilized all at once), but the bottles and nipples should be thoroughly cleaned in the regular way. Fill all the nursing bottles, insert the nipples upside down, cover them with the disks, then screw the rings on loosely. Leave the screw rings loose so that there will be a space for the hot air to escape as the bottles heat up and for the air to reenter as the bottles cool again.

Follow the directions for using your stove-top or electric sterilizing kit. Or put one to two inches of water in a kettle, place the bottles in a rack, lower the rack into the kettle, and cover it. Bring the water to a boil, and boil for twenty-five minutes. Use a timer to be sure. Turn off the heat and let the kettle cool (with the top still on) until the bottles are lukewarm, about an hour or two. Tighten the screw rings and refrigerate all the bottles.

There will be less clogging of the nipple holes if the formula is allowed to cool slowly, for an hour or two, without being shaken. This will allow any scum to form into one large, firm piece, which will then stick to the inside of the bottle.

Aseptic sterilization. With this approach, you sterilize the bottle equipment by itself, then make a sterile formula with boiled water and put the sterile formula into the prepared bottles. With aseptic sterilization it's fine to fill all your nursing bottles or disposable bottles at once, or you can fill a quart container.

Follow the directions that come with your stove-top or electric sterilizer. If you're using a regular kettle, put the bottles in the rack upside down so that the steam can more easily get into them and the water can run out. The same goes for the container holding the nipples and other equipment. Put a couple of inches of hot water in the bottom of the kettle, add the racks, put the top on, bring the water to a boil, and boil hard for five minutes. Use a timer. Let the kettle cool.

The bottles are now ready for the formula. Store them in a clean place if you won't be filling them right away. If you want a sterile place to lay nipples, screw rings, and disks while you are bottling the formula, put them on the inverted top of the kettle or sterilizer.

To sterilize a quart jar. You can use any glass quart jar for storing formula. (Most plastic containers become misshapen when boiled.) Choose a pan large enough to hold the jar lying on its side and the lid, and fill with water. Bring to a boil and boil five minutes. When the jar is cool enough to handle, drain it well and pour the entire amount of sterilized formula into it. Seal loosely so that air can enter as the formula cools, and refrigerate.

When feeding time comes around, pour the required number

of ounces into a sterilized nursing bottle or a disposable bottle. Then put the quart jar back in the refrigerator.

What to sterilize. You don't have to boil everything. Even if you have to sterilize the formula and boil the drinking water, you don't have to be as fussy with the other things that your baby will eat and drink. You don't have to boil dishes and cups and feeding spoons, because germs don't get a chance to grow on clean, dry utensils.

When you first buy teething rings, pacifiers, and toys that babies put in their mouths, you can wash them with soap. But there is no need to keep on washing them afterward, unless they fall on the floor, because the only germs on them will be the babies' own germs, which they're used to.

When to stop sterilizing. When can you stop sterilizing the formula and bottles? Ask your doctor, public health nurse, or county health department when it's safe to stop sterilizing. If you can't consult anyone, you can go by the general rule that as long as you are making a twenty-four-hour supply of formula that contains water, you have to sterilize the formula and bottles.

MIXING THE FORMULA

If you are using powdered formula or concentrate, always follow the mixing instructions on the package. A formula that's too strong or too weak isn't well tolerated by or satisfying to the baby.

Mixing powdered formula. Powdered formula comes in sixteen-ounce cans, with measuring scoops and reclosable plastic lids. It's the cheapest of the prepared formulas, and it's very convenient for an occasional bottle for a breast-fed baby, eliminating waste. It's also very useful for travel. Take along measured amounts of powder and boiled or distilled water; you can mix the formula at feeding time and avoid the need for refrigeration. The powder and water must be mixed together in the right order to avoid lumps; follow the instructions on the can.

If you're mixing a batch to last twenty-four hours, measure the amount of water needed and mix the formula in a clean pitcher or mixing bowl. A whisk or eggbeater is helpful. Pour all the formula into clean nursing bottles, disposable bottles, or a clean quart jar that you use to fill one bottle at feeding time. Cover and refrigerate.

If you need to make only one bottle, add formula to water, following the instructions on the label. Refrigerate the mixture if you won't be feeding the baby immediately. Formula can keep twenty-four to forty-eight hours in the refrigerator; after that, it's safest to throw it away.

Concentrate. Concentrated liquid formula comes in cans and must be diluted with an equal amount of water before it can be used. Less convenient than the ready-to-use formula, this concentrated formula costs only about two-thirds as much, and the cans are less bulky to store or travel with.

Before you open the can, wash and rinse the top, and also wash the can opener. To measure the correct amount of water, add one can of liquid concentrate to one can of water, or pour four ounces of concentrate into a bottle, and add four ounces of water. Be sure to refrigerate whatever you don't feed the baby.

Ready-to-use formula in cans and bottles. It's already sterilized and no water needs to be added, so it's very convenient. Before you open the can, wash and rinse the top and also wash the can opener. Pour the formula directly from the can into clean bottles. Cap the bottles, and refrigerate until you're ready to use them. Or fill one clean bottle at a time, keeping it capped and refrigerated until you feed the baby. The unused portion should be kept refrigerated in the covered can. Plastic snap-on covers are available where formulas are sold.

You can also buy formula already in bottles, ready to feed. It costs more but saves a little time and may be easier if you give a bottle only now and then.

BOTTLING THE FORMULA

How many bottles? Most babies want to be fed more frequently at first, especially if they are small (under seven pounds). Bottle-fed babies may want to be fed six to ten times every twenty-four hours the first week. If you had rooming-in, you may have discovered your baby's needs in the hospital. On the other hand, most babies start off slow and then become more wakeful and hungry after three or four days, so don't be surprised.

Generally, from one week to one month, babies want seven to eight feedings in twenty-four hours, decreasing to five to seven feedings at one to three months, four to five feedings at three to six months, and three to four feedings at six months to one year. Keep in mind that it takes up to three hours for a feeding to leave the stomach.

How much in each bottle? Start with four ounces. Your baby will let you know when that is no longer enough and you need to go up to eight. In the first month of life, most seven-pound babies will want less than twenty-one ounces of formula in twenty-four hours; eight-pound babies, less than twenty-four ounces. This amount may vary from week to week. Babies grow in fits and starts, a lot one week, less the next. Their appetites vary from week to week with their growth. It's best to listen to your baby: Let her tell you when she's hungry and when she's full. When her sucking slows down, if she's had what seems like a reasonable amount, stop. If she fusses, give her more.

FORMULA REFRIGERATION

Saving formula. If you use less than a full can of concentrated liquid formula or ready-to-use formula, save what is left for the next day. Leave it in the can, cover the top, and put it in the refrigerator. If you don't use it up the next day, discard what's left. Never keep an opened can longer than the time specified on the label.

The same rule applies if you make a quart jar of formula or fill all the nursing bottles from one batch of formula: keep it in the refrigerator, and what you don't use the next day, discard. Never keep bottled formula more than twenty-four hours to forty-eight hours, as specified on the label.

How long after a bottle has been taken out of the refrigerator can you still use it? During the time when a bottle is at drinking temperature, room temperature, or pleasant outdoor temperature, bacteria that got into the formula will multiply rapidly. To be on the safe side, don't give your baby a bottle that has been out of the refrigerator for more than two hours, whether it's a full one or one that has been partly consumed. (An unopened bottle that was filled and sealed in the factory can sit at room temperature for months, of course.)

If you will need to feed the baby two or three hours after leaving home, put the bottle as soon as you take it out of the refrigerator in an insulated bag with a small ice pack or some ice cubes. Do not use formula that is no longer cold to the touch. Another option is to carry powdered formula and bottled water, mixing whatever you need when you need it.

If you have a young baby who sometimes goes to sleep after taking a few ounces, then wakes up within an hour for the rest, promptly put the half-finished bottle back into the refrigerator. Discard any half-drunk bottles after one hour.

If you cannot keep the formula cold. If you ever get into a situation where you can't keep the baby's bottles cold until feeding time—for instance, if your refrigerator stops working or your electricity goes off—use single-serving, ready-to-feed bottles (keep some on hand), discarding anything that remains after feeding. If you often find this happening to you, the easiest solution is to use commercial powdered formula, mixing it with water before each use, one bottle at a time. If you have to sterilize, keep a bottle of distilled water and some disposable bottles on hand along with the powdered formula.

Contrary to popular belief, a bottle from the refrigerator doesn't have to be warmed before feeding. It can be given to the baby straight from the refrigerator.

GIVING THE BOTTLE

The first few days. Usually the first bottle is offered four to six hours after the baby is born, though it can be started earlier if he seems hungry. Babies are likely to want little the first few feedings. It's often three or four days before they want the amounts you expect them to need; indeed, it may be a week or more. Don't worry; it may be better for their digestion to start gradually. They'll find out what they need in a few days, when they become more active.

Warming the bottle. Babies enjoy just as much and do just as well on formula that is warmed, at room temperature, or right out of the refrigerator, as long as it comes at the same temperature at each feeding. Many parents still warm the bottles because they have always thought of bottles as being warmed and because breast milk is warm, so it seems unkind to give a baby cold milk. It isn't.

If you do warm the bottle, do it in a saucepan, a pitcher of hot water, or a washbasin. If there is no hot-water faucet near the baby's room, it's more convenient to use an electric bottle warmer. Body temperature is the right temperature to aim for.

The best way to test this is to shake a few drops on the inside of your wrist. If it feels hot, it is too hot.

Microwave warning: The best advice is *never* heat a baby's bottle in a microwave oven. The contents may be hot enough to burn the baby even when the bottle feels cool to your touch. Microwave ovens aren't suitable for sterilizing bottle equipment or formula, either. If you *do* resort to the microwave sometimes (and I know that many parents do, regardless of what the experts say), it is *very important* that you *stir the formula well* with a spoon so that there are no hot spots in the formula. Then feel the temperature of the formula with your finger or drop a few drops on your wrist before offering it to your baby. If the formula feels hot, it's hot enough to burn your baby's mouth.

Getting into position. Sit in a comfortable chair and hold the baby cradled in your arm. Most parents want a chair with arms and perhaps a pillow under the elbow. Some find that a rocking chair is perfect. Keep the bottle tilted up so that the nipple is always full. Jiggling the bottle does no good. Most babies want to work steadily until they have taken all the formula they need. Angle the bottle so that the air pocket is well above the nipple, so the baby doesn't swallow a lot of air. Nevertheless, there are some babies who swallow a lot of air while nursing and if the air bubble in the stomach gets too big, they feel uncomfortably full and stop nursing in the middle of the bottle. If this happens, burp the baby, then go on with the feeding. A few babies need to be burped two or even three times in the course of a bottle; others, not at all. You will soon find out what works for your baby.

As soon as your baby stops drinking and seems satisfied, let that be the end of the feeding. Babies know better than anyone else how much they need.

Bottle propping. It's good for the parent to hold the baby during bottle-feedings. This is the position that nature intended.

The baby and parent are as close as can be, and they can watch each other's faces. Feeding is a baby's greatest joy by far, and it's good for the baby to link this with the parent's presence and face. Babies who take their bottles lying flat on their backs sometimes develop ear infections if the formula runs down the eustachian tubes into the middle ear.

Overfeeding and spitting up. Altogether, the most a baby should need in a twenty-four-hour day (with rare exceptions) is about thirty-two ounces; most babies do well with closer to twenty-four ounces. A baby who takes much more than thirty-two ounces may be using the bottle more as a comfort object than a source of nutrition. Sucking on a pacifier may serve the same needs. Or it may be the parent who resorts to feeding the baby whenever it fusses or cries. There are other comforting measures that may work better (see page 61).

When babies overfeed, they tend to vomit a lot, to relieve the uncomfortable stomach pressure. See page 118 for more on spitting up and vomiting.

Making the nipple holes the right size. If the nipple holes are too small, the baby will get too little and fuss or become tired and go to sleep long before finishing the bottle. If babies have to suck too hard, they also tend to swallow lots of air, causing gassiness. If the holes are too large, the baby may choke or get indigestion; in the long run, it may get too little sucking satisfaction and thus do more thumb-sucking. Gulping formula too quickly also increases swallowed air and gassiness.

For most babies, the right speed is when the bottle takes about twenty minutes of straight sucking time. The holes are generally right for a young baby if when you turn the bottle upside down, the milk comes out in a fine spray for a second or two, then changes to drops. If it keeps coming in a spray, the holes are probably too large; if it comes in slow drops from the beginning, the holes are probably too small.

Most bottles are designed with small holes in the rubber shoulders of the nipples or some other channel for letting air into the bottle as the baby withdraws milk. If you screw the nipple ring down tighter, the passage is reduced in size (or closed altogether), resulting in a partial vacuum so that the baby has to suck harder and takes longer to finish the bottle. A looser ring allows faster drinking. (Bottles that use disposable liners don't need air holes: The liner collapses as the baby sucks.)

The holes in many new nipples are too small for a young baby but are right for an older, stronger one. If they are too small for your baby, enlarge them carefully as follows: Stick the blunt end of a fine (No. 10) needle into a cork. Then, holding the cork, heat the needle point in a flame until it's red-hot. Stick it a short distance into the top of the nipple. You don't have to poke it into the old hole. Don't use too large a needle or poke it in too far, until you test your results; if you make the holes too large, you'll have to throw the nipple away. You can make one, two, or three enlarged holes. If you have no cork, wrap a piece of cloth around the blunt end of the needle or hold it with a pair of pliers.

Nipple holes clogged with scum. If you have trouble with clogged nipple holes, you can buy nipples that are crosscut. The milk does not pour out, as you might expect, because the edges of the cut stay together until the baby sucks. You can make small crosscuts in your regular nipples with a sterilized razor blade. First pinch the nipple tip to make a narrow ridge, then cut across it. Then pinch at a right angle to the first pinch and make another cut. Crosscut nipples should not be used for feeding pureed foods from a bottle.

∽ CLASSIC SPOCK

Don't urge babies to take more than they want. The main trouble with bottle-feeding, to my mind, is that the caretaker can see how much formula is left. Some babies always want the same quantity at every feeding of the day, but there are others whose appetites are much more variable. You mustn't get the idea that your baby has to have a certain amount at each feeding. It may help you acquire a more relaxed feeling about this if you realize that breast-fed babies may get as much as ten ounces at the morning nursing and as little as four ounces at the evening feeding and be perfectly happy with each. If you can trust breast-fed babies to take what they need, you can trust your bottle-fed baby.

It is necessary to make this point because quite a number of children develop feeding problems. They lose the natural appetite that they were born with and balk at all or many of their foods. In nine out of ten cases, these problems develop because the parents have been trying, sometimes since infancy, to get their child to eat more than she wants. When you succeed in getting a baby or child to take a few more mouthfuls than she is eager for, it looks to you as if you have gained something. But this isn't so. She will only cut down at her next feeding. Babies know how much they want, and they even know the different kinds of foods that their bodies are calling for. Urging children isn't necessary, and it doesn't get you anywhere. It is harmful because it begins, after a while, to take away the child's appetite and makes her want to eat less than her system really needs.

In the long run, urging does more than destroy appetite and make thin children. It robs them of some of their positive feeling for life. Babies are meant to spend their first year getting hungry, demanding food, enjoying it, and reaching satisfaction. This lusty success story is repeated at least three times a day, week after week. It builds into them self-confidence, an outgoing nature, and trust in their parents. But if mealtime becomes a struggle, if feeding becomes something that is done to them, they go on the defensive and build up a balky, suspicious attitude toward meals and toward people.

I don't mean that you have to snatch the bottle away for

good the first time your baby pauses. Some babies like to rest a bit several times during a feeding. But if she seems indifferent when you put the nipple back in her mouth (and doesn't need to be burped), then she's satisfied, and you should be too.

Babies who wake in a few minutes. What about the babies who go to sleep after they've taken four of their five ounces then wake up and cry a few minutes later? Waking like this is more apt to be due to an air bubble, colic, or periodic irritable crying than to hunger. Babies won't notice a difference of an ounce, especially if they've gone to sleep. In fact, babies will often sleep just as well when they've taken only half their usual amount, though they may wake a little early.

It's perfectly all right occasionally to give the rest of the formula a little later if you feel sure that your baby's hungry for it. But it's better to assume first that she's not really hungry and give her a good chance to go back to sleep, with or without a pacifier. In other words, try to postpone the next feeding for two to three hours. But if your baby is truly hungry, feed her.

The young baby who only half finishes. A mother may bring a baby home from the hospital and find that he stops taking his bottle, falling asleep when it's still half full. Yet they said in the hospital that he was taking it all. The mother keeps trying to rouse him to wedge another quarter of an ounce in, but it's slow, hard, frustrating work. What's the trouble? He may be a baby who hasn't quite come to yet. (An occasional baby stays sluggish like that for the first two or three weeks, then comes to life with a bang.)

The constructive thing to do is to let the baby stop when he wants to, even if he's taken only an ounce or two. Won't he get hungry long before it's time for the next feeding? He may or he may not. If he does, feed him. "But," you say, "I'll be feeding him all day and all night." It probably won't be that bad. The point is that if you let a baby stop feeding when he feels like it, let him come to feel his own hunger, he will gradually become more eager for his feedings and take larger amounts. He will then be able to sleep for longer periods. You can help him to learn to wait longer and be hungrier by trying to stretch out the interval between feedings to two, two and a half, then three hours. Don't pick him up just as soon as he starts fussing. Wait a while. He may go back to sleep. If he cries hard, though, you'll have to feed him.

Sluggishness and refusing to eat can also be signs of illness in a young baby. If you are concerned, have your baby seen by the doctor. It is never wrong to ask for professional advice, especially with a new infant.

Fussing or falling asleep. The baby who fusses soon after starting a bottle or promptly goes to sleep may be frustrated by a clogged or too small nipple hole. See if the milk comes out in a fine spray when the bottle is inverted. Even if it doesn't, enlarge the nipple hole a little anyway, as an experiment.

Bottles in crib or bed. Once babies' teeth come in, it's important that they do not fall asleep with a bottle of formula. Formula left on the teeth promotes the growth of bacteria, which cause tooth decay. It's not uncommon to see babies whose top front teeth are completely eaten away, a serious health problem. Falling asleep with milk in the mouth can also lead to ear infections. Some milk can run down the eustachian tube, which connects the back of the throat to the middle ear (the part of the ear behind the eardrum.) Then bacteria can grow in the milk behind the eardrum and start an infection.

After six months, many babies want to sit up, take the bottle away from the parent, and hold it themselves. Practical parents, seeing that they're not needed, may put such babies in their cribs, where they drink their bottles and put themselves to sleep all in one operation. This may seem like a handy way to put babies to sleep, but in addition to causing tooth and ear problems, it makes it impossible for some of them to go to sleep without a bottle (see below). When the parent tries to withhold a bedtime bottle at nine, fifteen, or twenty-one months, the baby will cry frantically and be unable for a long time to fall asleep. So if you want to prevent bedtime problems later, when you let your baby hold her own bottle, keep her in your lap or the high chair.

WEANING FROM BOTTLE TO CUP

Readiness for weaning. Some parents are eager to get their babies weaned to the cup by a year. Others feel strongly that babies are entitled to the breast or bottle for two years. The decision depends partly on the parents' wishes and partly on the baby's readiness.

Some babies show less interest in sucking by five or six months. Instead of nursing eagerly for twenty minutes, as they used to, they stop after five minutes to flirt with their parents, play with their bottles or hands. These are the early signs of readiness for weaning. These babies will go on being casual toward the breast or bottle at eight, ten, or twelve months, though they'll usually take it as long as it's offered. They like to take formula from the cup, and they continue to do so.

Attachment to the bottle. Some babies become *more* attached to the bottle at six to ten months. The parent of one of these babies will say, "Oh, how she loves her bottle! She watches it all the time she's taking her solid food. When it's time, she snatches it eagerly. She strokes it lovingly all the time she's drinking it and murmurs to it. She's very suspicious about formula from the cup, though she took it willingly before six months." Many of these babies continue to be very dependent on the bedtime bottle until they are a year and a half to two years old. They are unable to settle down or go to sleep without it and are still firmly opposed to formula in the cup or glass. (It's interesting that they are willing to take water or juice from the cup.)

Babies who are allowed to take their bottles to bed by themselves are more likely to become attached to their bottles in the second half of the first year. The bottle becomes a precious comforter at bedtime, reminding children of their early months when their greatest pleasure and security came from their intensely close relationship with their parents. The bottle becomes a parent substitute. Children who are still taking their bottle in the parent's lap at five to seven months don't tend to develop the same attachment to the bottle, because their real parent is right there.

So to keep your baby from forming a lasting dependence on the bottle, which may delay final weaning until eighteen to twenty-four months, always give him his bottles while you hold him, and don't let him take his bottles to bed.

If your baby already has a bedtime bottle attachment after about six months (or when the first tooth emerges), it's important to at least change what's in the bottle, from formula to water. That way, bottle mouth cavities won't be such a problem. If you make this change gradually, watering down the nighttime bottles bit by bit, you should be able to get your baby to accept straight water at night without much of a fuss. From there it may be easier for your baby to give up the nighttime bottle altogether.

Sips from the cup by five months. It's a good idea to offer babies a sip of formula from the cup each day when they're five months old. You aren't going to try to wean them to the cup right away. You only want to accustom them, at an age when they're not too opinionated, to the idea that formula comes in cups, too.

Pour half an ounce of formula into a small cup or glass once a day. Your baby won't want more than one sip at a time, and she won't get much at first, but she'll probably think it is fun. Once the baby is comfortable taking formula from the cup, offer her water and diluted juice from the cup, too. This way she'll learn that all liquids can come in a cup.

Helping a baby get used to the cup. Once the cup has been introduced, offer it matter-of-factly once or twice at each solid meal, holding it to your baby's lips. Keep the cup in sight so he can indicate if he'd like more. (If you usually give him a bottle at the end of his meal, keep it out of sight until then.) He'll also be interested in anything you're drinking, and you can hold your glass to his lips and let him have a taste, if the contents are suitable.

You can let him try his own skills, too. Suppose he's six months old and wants to grab everything and put it in his mouth. Give him a small, narrow, empty plastic glass or cup that he can hold easily by himself or a two-handled baby's mug. When he does it fairly well, put a few drops of formula into the cup. Increase the amount as he gains in skill. If he becomes balky or loses interest in trying it himself, don't urge him. Drop the matter for a meal or two, then offer the cup again. Remember that in the early months of cup drinking, he'll probably want only one swallow at a time. Many babies don't learn to take several gulps in succession until they are a year to a year and a half old. One good place to practice is in the bathtub.

Children between one and two who are suspicious of the old cup they have always been offered may be delighted with a new cup or glass of a different shape or color. Offering them cold milk sometimes changes their minds. Some parents have found that adding a little cereal to the cup of milk makes it different enough to be acceptable for drinking. Adding the cereal can gradually be stopped a few weeks later.

There are special cups designed for weaning that have a lid with a flat spout. The lid keeps the milk from spilling; the spout goes into the baby's mouth. Later, the baby can use it without the lid and spout. Some parents like them because they prevent spilling for the first few months of cup drinking, until the baby gains skill. Other parents object that a baby may balk at the transition from bottle to weaning cup, then object again as he changes to a cup or glass without a spout. There are weaning cups with two handles, which are easier for a baby to hold, and others with a weighted base.

Why wean at about one year. The main reason for weaning babies from the bottle by one year is that this is the age when they'll accept the change most easily. By this age, most babies will be holding their bottles at feeding time, and it's best to let them take over. But you can help them be more grown up by getting them started with a cup. (If the parents have gotten into the habit of letting the baby feed herself and then drop off to sleep with a bottle in bed, this may lead to bedtime problems. See page 303 for more about avoiding the bottle in bed.)

Other reasons to wean: Some parents are bothered by the sight of a toddler wandering around or playing with a bottle in her hand, taking a swig now and then. They think it looks babyish or dopey. Also, toddlers who sip on milk or formula on and off during the day are prone to develop tooth decay: The sugary fluid coats the teeth, promoting the growth of bacteria. Toddlers who take frequent sips of formula may eat poorly as well, because the steady trickle of milk takes the edge off their appetite, and their growth may suffer.

Wean the baby gradually. Take it easy and follow your baby's lead. Perhaps your baby is nine to twelve months old, is becoming a little bored with her bottle, and likes formula from the cup. Gradually increase the amount in the cup. Give her the cup at every meal. This leaves increasingly less in the bottle. Then omit the bottle that she takes least interest in, probably the lunch or breakfast one. In a week, give up the second bottle; a week later, the third. Most babies love their supper bottle most and are the most reluctant to give it up. Others feel that way about the breakfast bottle.

Willingness to be weaned doesn't always steadily increase. Misery from teething or a cold often makes babies want more of the bottle for the time being. Follow your baby's needs. The trend that made him start to give up the bottle before will set in again when he feels better.

The reluctant weaner. Babies who are reluctant to give up the bottle at nine to twelve months may take one sip from the cup and impatiently push it away. Or they may pretend they don't know what it's for; they let the formula run out at the sides of their mouths and smile innocently. They may relent a little at twelve months, but it is more likely that they'll remain suspicious until fifteen months or even later. Put an ounce of formula in a small glass that they can handle and set it on the tray every day or so, in hopes that they'll drink it. If one sip is all they take, don't even try to give them two. Act as if it doesn't make any difference to you.

When a suspicious baby does start to take a little formula from the cup, you must still be patient, because it will probably take several more months before he is ready to give up the bottle altogether. This applies particularly to the supper and bedtime bottle. Many late weaners insist on a bedtime bottle till about two years of age, particularly if they have been in the habit of going to bed with one.

Parents' weaning worries. Sometimes it's the parent who is worried about weaning. Sometimes a baby is kept on the bottle because her parents worry that she isn't taking as much from the cup as she used to take from the bottle. Let's say that at nine to twelve months she's drinking six ounces from the cup at breakfast, six ounces at lunch, and four ounces at supper and that she's not especially eager for the bottle, but if her mother gives it to her at the end of the meal, she is willing to take a few

ounces more that way. A baby of nine to twelve months who is
taking as much as sixteen ounces a day from the cup and not
acting as if she misses the bottle can be taken off the bottle altogether if the parents wish.

Another problem may develop for the parent who uses the
bottle as a pacifier in the second year. Whenever the child has a
crying spell in the daytime or wakes at night, the mother or father kindheartedly makes another bottle. The child may get as
many as eight bottles in the twenty-four hours, a total of two
quarts of formula. This naturally takes away most of the baby's
appetite for meals. It's important nutritionally that children not
take more than a quart (thirty-two ounces) of formula or milk
a day.

STARTING SOLID FOODS

HEALTHY DIETS START YOUNG

Food preferences. As your baby begins to eat solid food, he or she is passing a milestone toward independence. In the process, you have a once-in-a-lifetime opportunity to introduce eating habits that will promote good health in the years to come. Children tend to adopt the eating patterns that are presented early. When healthful foods are the order of the day, children follow this pattern as a matter of course. This is important, because it is easy for children to learn habits that carry them in the wrong direction.

Food tastes are formed early in life and tend to persist. For example, an individual's preference for how much table salt she or he wants is set in infancy and early childhood. High salt consumption can lead to the development of high blood pressure. So when parents add salt to their baby's foods (because the parents like added salt, not because the baby asks for it), they may increase the risk of high blood pressure down the road.

Preferences for fatty foods also seem to start early. Some, though not all, cases of lifelong obesity probably start in infancy with diets that are too rich in sugar and fat. The saturated fats and cholesterol that are such a large part of the typical child's diet in the United States play a part in the development of artery blockages and heart attacks in later life, especially in those with a family history of these problems (see "Nutrition and Health" in Section II).

Surgeons concerned with cancer of the large intestine in older adults now believe that a major cause of this disease of civilization is the very slow passage of the intestinal contents in people whose diet all their lives has lacked sufficient roughage because they have eaten so little whole-grain cereal and bread and so few vegetables and fruits. Helping children to prefer these naturally healthful foods will pay many dividends in the years to come.

Healthier diets. Our understanding of nutrition has grown enormously over the past several years. We used to advocate including generous amounts of meat and dairy products in children's diets. We have learned that children are better off getting more of their nutrients from plant sources. Vegetables, fruits, grains, and beans are rich in vitamins, minerals, and fiber at the same time they are low in fat, with no cholesterol at all. We have only recently come to appreciate how valuable these seemingly humble plant foods can be and to recognize the range of health problems that can be prevented when they are put front and center in the diet.

It is easiest if the parents join their children in healthful eating practices. Though most of us were raised with eating habits that were different from those we now understand to be ideal, many of us are rethinking the way we eat and are trying to make healthier choices. As we do so, we help our children make healthier choices, too.

☜ CLASSIC SPOCK
Many families are using smaller servings of meat, trimming the fat, and switching to low-fat dairy products. These are steps in the right direction. I would suggest, however, that you go a step further, drawing your family's nutrition from plant foods rather than ones from animal products or fried,

oily foods. Let me encourage you to explore plant-based foods and to have as many meatless meals as you can.

WHEN AND HOW TO START

When to start solid food. There's no set age by which it's important to start solid food. At the start of the twentieth century, solid food was introduced when a baby was a year old. As the years passed, doctors experimented with giving it earlier and earlier, even at one to two months. Nowadays doctors customarily recommend offering the first solid food sometime between four and six months.

There are two definite advantages in starting in the first half year: babies take to the idea more easily than when they are older and more opinionated, and a variety of solid foods adds to the diet nutritious substances, particularly iron. There is no great advantage starting much before three or four months. Breast milk or formula supplies all the calories most babies need for the first six months. The immature digestive system doesn't make much use of starch for several months; much of it just comes out in the bowel movement.

If you have a family history of food allergies, the doctor may advise you to wait past six months or even longer before introducing certain solid foods, since the older a baby is when he receives a new food, the less likely he is to develop an allergy to it.

A big factor in giving solids earlier has been the eagerness of parents who don't want their baby to be even one day later than the baby up the street. They put pressure on doctors and on their babies. But with eating, like many aspects of development, earlier does not mean better. If you pay attention to your baby's signs, you can pick up cues to tell you when starting solids is developmentally right for him. Look to see that he can hold his head up well. He may be interested in table foods and may try to grab your food. See how he responds when you put a small amount of food on his tongue.

Young infants have a reflex that causes them to thrust out their tongues in response to solid foods. It's awfully frustrating to try to feed solids to a baby who still has an active tongue-thrust reflex. If your baby sticks out his tongue as soon as any little bit of food touches it, don't force the issue. Instead, wait a few days and try again.

There's no rush. Give your baby time to learn to like solid foods. A doctor or nurse practitioner usually recommends starting with a teaspoonful or less of a new food, working up gradually to two to three tablespoonfuls if the baby wants it. This gradual progression is to make sure the baby learns to like the food and isn't upset. Just give a taste for several days, until the baby shows signs of enjoying it.

Solids before or after the milk? Most babies who are not used to solids expect their milk, and they want their milk first when it's feeding time. They are indignant if offered a spoonful of something solid instead. So start with the formula or breast-feeding. A month or two later, when your baby has learned that solid foods can ward off starvation just as well as milk, you can experiment with moving the solids up to the middle or beginning of the meal. Eventually, almost all babies are happy to take their solid food first, then top it off with the beverage, the way so many adults do.

What kind of spoon? A teaspoon is pretty wide for a small baby's mouth, and most spoons have a bowl so deep that the baby can't scoop all the contents out. A spoon made especially for babies is better, or use a small demitasse spoon, preferably one with a shallow bowl. Some parents like to use a flat butter spreader or wooden tongue depressor—the kind that doctors use—which can be bought in bulk at the drugstore. There are spoons with rubber-coated bowls for teething babies who want to bite on the spoon. For one-year-old self-feeders, there are spoons with bowls that swivel to stay level, and there are also wide-bowled, short-handled spoons that work well.

How to introduce solid foods. The child should be sitting upright in a sturdy high chair and wearing a bib. The process will be easier when the child is hungry but not ravenous or overtired. A baby girl taking her first teaspoonful of solid food is quite funny. She looks puzzled and disgusted. She wrinkles her nose and forehead. You can't blame her. After all, the taste is new, the consistency is new, the spoon may be new. When she sucks on a nipple, the milk gets to the right place automatically. She's had no training in catching hold of a lump of food with the front of her tongue and moving it back into her throat. She just clacks her tongue against the roof of her mouth, so most of the cereal gets squeezed back out onto her chin. You will have to scoop it off her chin and back into her mouth. Again, a lot will ooze out, but don't be discouraged; some goes inside, too. Be patient until she is more experienced.

It doesn't much matter at which meals you start the solid foods. Just don't give it at the feeding when she's least hungry. It often works well to offer solids an hour or so after a regular breast- or bottle-feeding. The baby should be wide awake, in a good mood, and ready for an adventure, and so should you. Begin with only one meal of solids a day until you're both used to it. It's probably best to limit solid meals to no more that two a day until the baby is six months old, because breast milk or formula is so important for the baby's nutrition in the early months.

Cereal. The order in which solids are introduced is not important. Cereal is commonly given first. Unfortunately, its taste doesn't always have great appeal for a baby. Different babies prefer different ones. There is some advantage in getting a baby used to variety, but it's wise to introduce only one new food at a time. It often helps to mix cereal with a familiar beverage, either expressed breast milk or formula, whichever the baby is used to.

If you are starting with cereal, it's a good idea to mix it a little thinner than the directions on the box say. It will then seem more familiar to the baby and be easier to swallow. Also, many babies and small children dislike food with a sticky consistency.

Which cereals? At first, most parents give the precooked cereals made especially for babies, of which there is a wide variety. They are ready to eat as soon as they're mixed, which is a great convenience. Most of them are fortified with iron, which may otherwise be lacking in a baby's diet. It's wise to start with one cereal at a time and offer it for four or five days. Sometimes, if a baby belongs to a family with many allergies, the doctor may suggest starting cereals at a later age than usual, beginning with rice, oats, corn, or barley and omitting wheat for several more months since wheat causes allergic reactions more often than other cereals. Also, the doctor may delay mixed-grain cereals until the baby has shown a capacity to take each of the separate kinds without trouble.

You can also give your baby the same cooked cereals you serve the other members of the family. But these grown-up cereals shouldn't be the mainstay of your baby's diet, because they do not have enough iron in them to meet a growing baby's needs.

The baby who balks at cereal. You will know within a few days after starting how your baby is going to take to cereal. Some babies seem to decide "It's odd, but it's nourishment, so I'll eat it." As the days go by, they grow more and more enthusiastic. They open their mouths for it like baby birds in the nest.

But there are others who decide on the second day of cereal that they don't like it at all. And on the third day, they dislike it more than on the second. If your baby feels this way, take it easy. If you try to push the cereal into your baby against his will, he will become increasingly rebellious. You will become exasperated, too. In a week or two he may become so suspicious that he will balk at the bottle also. Offer the cereal just once a day. Give only enough to cover the tip of the teaspoon until he is used to it. Add a little fruit to see if he likes it better that way. If in two or three days he is becoming more set against it in spite of all these precautions, stop altogether for a couple of weeks. If he still balks when you try again, report the problem to your doctor.

It's a great mistake to get into an argument with babies about their first solid food. Sometimes a long-lasting feeding problem starts this way. Even if it doesn't last, it's bad for parents and babies to have an unnecessary fight.

If your baby balks at cereal, you might start with fruit instead. Babies are puzzled by fruit, too, the first time they have it. But within a day or two, practically all decide they love it. By the end of two weeks they are ready to assume that anything that comes on a spoon is wonderful. Then you can add cereal, too.

Fruits. Fruits are often the second or third solid foods added to the diet, a few weeks after babies have become used to cereal and perhaps vegetables. Some doctors prefer fruit as the first solid food because babies usually take to it so enthusiastically; other doctors don't want to encourage a preference for sweet foods.

Apple juice, diluted at first, is often given around the time a baby starts solid foods. Your doctor will help you decide when to offer it. (Orange juice and other citrus juices often cause rashes, so it's best to start these later, at about a year of age.)

Apples, peaches, pears, apricots, and prunes are the usual fruits. For the first six to eight months of a baby's life, the fruit is stewed, except for raw, ripe banana. You can use fresh or frozen fruit that you have stewed for the rest of the family; strain or sieve it for the baby. You can also use canned fruit that you serve to other members of the family. It's best to buy canned fruit packed in water or its own juice instead of syrup, or you can buy the small jars of strained baby fruits. Look at the label to make sure it is all fruit. (Fruits packed in syrup can be useful if your baby's bowel movements are hard.) A banana should be very ripe. It should have black spots on the skin and be tan inside. Mash it smooth with a fork. Add a little formula or breast milk if it seems too thick for your baby.

You can give fruit at any one of the feedings, even twice a day, depending on your baby's appetite and digestion. Increase each fruit gradually as your baby learns to like it. Most babies are satisfied with half a baby jar. You can give the other half the next day. Fruit can be kept three days if it is well refrigerated. But don't feed your baby out of the jar unless you plan to use it up at one meal; saliva introduced into the container can spoil food rapidly.

Fruit has the reputation of being laxative, but most individuals, including infants, show no definite looseness or cramps from any of the fruits mentioned above, except for prunes, prune juice, and sometimes apricots. Prunes are mildly laxative for almost all babies; this makes them a doubly valuable food for those who tend to have hard stools or constipation. For the baby who needs a laxative and likes fruit, puréed prunes or prune juice can be given at one feeding and some other fruit at another feeding each day.

If your baby's bowels become loose, you will probably want to omit prunes and apricots for a couple of months and give other fruits only once a day.

After age six months or so, you can add or substitute other raw fruits besides bananas: scraped apple, pear, avocado. (Berries and grapes are commonly postponed until the baby is two years of age, for fear of choking. Even then, you should mash them until the baby is at least three years old.)

Vegetables. Strained cooked vegetables are commonly added to the diet after a baby has gotten used to cereal, fruit, or both. A possible advantage of adding vegetables before fruits is that the baby will not expect a sweet taste. The vegetables usually offered first are string beans, peas, squash, carrots, beets, and sweet potatoes.

There are other vegetables—such as broccoli, cauliflower, cabbage, turnips, kale, and onions—that, as usually cooked, are so strong-tasting that some babies don't like them. If your family likes these foods, try straining and serving them to your baby, perhaps mixed with a little apple juice to counteract their strong taste. Corn is not given initially because of the large skins on the kernels, which can cause choking.

You can serve your baby fresh or frozen vegetables, cooked or strained, and pureed in a food processor, blender, or grinder. Store-bought baby vegetables in jars are fine, too. Buy straight vegetables rather than mixtures. Feed your baby out of the jar only if you plan to use the whole jar, because saliva can spoil foods. Work up to several tablespoonfuls or half a baby jar, as desired. The rest, if refrigerated, can be given the next day. Cooked vegetables spoil fairly rapidly.

Babies are more likely to be choosy about vegetables than cereals or fruits. You will probably find that there are one or two vegetables your baby doesn't like. Don't urge them; but try them again every month or so. There's no point in fussing over a few foods when we have so many to choose from.

Changes in bowel movements and skin. It's common for undigested vegetables to appear in the bowel movements when the baby starts them. This is not a bad sign so long as there is no looseness or mucus, but increase the amount of each vegetable only slowly until the baby's digestion learns to handle it. If a vegetable causes looseness or much mucus, omit it for the time being, trying a very small amount after another month.

Beets may color the urine or show up red in the bowel movement. This is nothing to worry about if you remember that it is caused by beets, not blood. Green vegetables often turn the bowel movement green. Spinach causes chapping of the lips and irritation around the anus in some babies. If this occurs, omit spinach for several months, then try again. Babies who eat a lot of orange or yellow vegetables, such as carrots or squash, often develop an orange or yellow tinge to their skin. This condition is not dangerous, and it goes away once the baby cuts back on the yellow and orange vegetables.

Higher-protein foods. Once your baby is familiar with cereals, vegetables, and fruits, you can introduce other foods. Try very well cooked beans or legumes, like lentils, chickpeas, and kidney beans. If you use canned beans, put them in a strainer and rinse them well to remove some of the sodium. Start with a small amount of cooked beans. If you notice that your baby develops an irritated bottom and you see bits of undigested bean in his bowel movement, wait a few weeks before reintroducing them, and make sure they are very well cooked. Tofu is also a good choice. Many babies happily eat it in small cubes or mixed with applesauce, other pureed fruits, or vegetables.

Most people rely on meats, fish, poultry, eggs, or dairy products as protein sources. However, these products are now seen by many nutritionists in a much less favorable light (see page 337 for more on this point). Children who become used to them in their early years may pay a price in adulthood for the fat, cholesterol, and animal protein these foods contain. Whether you decide to raise your child on an exclusively vegetarian diet, it makes good sense to explore vegetarian foods early so that your children can enjoy the advantages these foods offer.

There is a special concern about meats for very small children. Poultry, beef, pork, and other meats often contain bacteria that can cause serious infections. Such illnesses have become alarmingly common in recent years. Infants are much more sensitive to them than adults. Meats must always be thoroughly cooked so that there is no pinkness at all, and any surfaces or utensils touched by raw meat must be carefully cleaned with soap and water. (See page 839, **Food poisoning,** for more on food safety.)

Eggs. For a very long time, egg yolk was thought to be an important source of iron. Recent research has shown, however, that the iron in egg yolk is poorly absorbed by babies' intestines. It has also been found that egg yolk may interfere with iron absorption from other sources unless it is taken with a source of vitamin C. Also, egg yolk contains a large amount of cholesterol, which can play a part in hardening of the arteries and heart attacks later in life, especially in those with a family history of these ailments. It was known long ago that egg white can cause allergic reactions in some babies, especially those with a family history of allergies.

Dinners. There are a variety of "dinners" in jars for babies. They usually consist of small amounts of a meat and vegetable with a larger amount of potato, rice, or barley. When there is a tendency to allergy, these mixtures may be confusing unless the baby has already eaten each of the foods included in the mixture without reaction. If you buy vegetables, grains, beans, and fruits in separate jars, it's easier to know how much of each your baby is getting.

MEALS AT SIX MONTHS

Two meals a day or three? By six months of age, your baby will probably be eating cereal and a variety of fruits, vegetables, and beans. He may be taking one, two, or three meals of solids a day. A common arrangement for a moderately hungry baby is cereal for breakfast, vegetable and tofu or well-cooked beans for lunch, cereal and fruit for supper. But there are no hard-and-fast rules. It all depends on your convenience and your baby's appetite.

For instance, a not very hungry baby might be given fruit at breakfast, a vegetable and tofu or beans at lunch, and cereal alone at supper. A baby who tends to be constipated can be given prunes every night along with the cereal and another fruit at breakfast or lunch. You may want the baby to have beans and vegetables at supper with the rest of the family, and cereal and fruit at lunch.

Many breast-fed and some bottle-fed babies are just beginning solids at six months. Their digestion and eating interests are more mature than when they were four months old. You can introduce new foods to these babies more rapidly, and quickly move them up to three meals a day.

Finger foods. By the time babies are six to seven months old, they want to and can pick foods up in their hands and suck and munch on them. This is good preparation for spoon-feeding themselves at about a year. If babies are never allowed to feed themselves with their fingers, they're less likely to have the ambition to try a spoon.

The traditional first finger food is a crust of stale whole-wheat bread or toast. A small dry bagel is also great. Babies can suck it and chew it with their bare gums. Their gums may be tingling with teething, in which case they'll enjoy the biting. As their saliva gradually softens the bread or toast, some of it rubs off or dissolves in their mouths, enough to make them feel they're getting somewhere. Most of it, of course, ends up on their hands, faces, hair, and the furniture. Teething biscuits often contain extra sugar, which tends to makes babies crave sweets. It's better to have your baby get used to enjoying things that aren't so sweet.

By eight to nine months, most babies have developed enough hand coordination to pick up small objects. At this point, you can start putting pieces of fruit or cooked vegetable and tofu chunks on your baby's high chair tray for her to pick up with her fingers. (This is also the age when you have to make sure your floors are free of possible choking hazards. A good rule of thumb is that if it can fit inside a toilet paper tube, it's a choking hazard.)

Babies love being offered pieces of food from their parents' plates. Some babies refuse finger foods if the parents offer them but will happily feed themselves those same foods. Many babies like to cram everything into their mouths all at once. A good strategy is to offer such a baby only one piece of food at a time in the beginning.

Typically, the first tooth emerges at about seven months. By one year, many babies have four to six sharp biting teeth. (But the timetable for the appearance of teeth varies a great deal from baby to baby. Many perfectly healthy babies don't have their first tooth till after a year of age.) Most babies won't get their first molars for grinding until around fifteen months. But with or without teeth, somehow they manage most table foods so successfully that by their first birthday almost all babies can be taken off prepared baby foods and allowed to finger-feed themselves from the family's foods, as long as the pieces are cut up small enough and hard foods that are choking hazards are avoided.

Mashed and lumpy foods. Sometime after six months, you'll want your baby to get used to lumpy or chopped foods. If a baby goes much beyond then eating nothing but pureed things, it will get harder and harder to accept lumpy textures. People have the idea that babies can't handle lumps until they get a fair set of teeth. This isn't true. They can mash lumps of cooked vegetables or fruit and pieces of whole-wheat bread or toast with their gums and tongue.

Some babies seem to be born more squeamish about lumps than others. Other babies and older children who gag on particles of food have become that way either because the parents introduced chopped foods too abruptly or too late or because they have been forcing food when the child didn't want it.

There are two important points to remember when shifting to chopped foods. First, make the change a gradual one. When you first serve chopped vegetables, mash them up thoroughly with a fork. Don't put too much in your baby's mouth at a time. When your baby is used to this consistency, gradually mash less. Second, allow your baby to pick small lumps or cubes up in his fingers and put it in his mouth himself. Babies can't stand to have a whole spoonful of lumps dumped into their mouths when they're not used to it.

So start the change at about six months by offering finger foods. You can mash and chop the cooked vegetables and fresh and stewed fruits that you prepare for the rest of the family, or you can buy the chopped (junior) foods in jars prepared for babies. You don't have to make all the foods lumpy, but it's good for your baby to get used to eating some lumps each day.

Meats, if they are used, should generally continue to be served ground or minced fine. Most small children dislike chunks of meat that they can't chew easily. They often chew on such a piece for a long time without getting anywhere. They don't dare try to swallow too big a piece, as adults may do when they are desperate. This may lead to gagging. There are good reasons to avoid or delay the use of meats in any case (see page 339).

Potatoes, pasta, and rice are popular with most children and can be introduced along with other table foods. Whole-grain pasta and brown rice contain more fiber and vitamins than more refined products. Also, try other grains, like bulgur and quinoa, for variety.

Making your own baby food. Many parents choose to prepare their own infant foods some or all of the time. This can be safely done. Making your own baby food gives you control over the ingredients and the preparation method. You can use fresh, organically grown foods. And homemade foods cost less than store-bought.

There are fine books available on this subject. You'll need a food mill, blender, or food processor. You can reheat individual portions in the small compartments of an egg-poaching pan or in a double-boiler or microwave oven. Be sure to stir the food well and test the temperature—especially if it's been heated in a microwave—before feeding it to the baby. Microwaves create hot spots in food, so one spoonful can be cool, the next one scalding. Foods can be cooked in quantity and pureed to a consistency that your baby likes. If necessary, they can be moistened with water, expressed breast milk, or formula. They can be frozen in serving portions in ice cube trays or on cookie sheets and stored in plastic freezer bags until they're used. Foods for children under a year should not be seasoned.

If your child is to eat table foods, your seasoning habits may have to be modified to avoid excess salt or sugar. A small, hand-held food grinder comes in handy for sharing grown-up food with a baby.

Commercial baby foods. When baby foods in jars were first produced, they consisted of single vegetables, single fruits, or single meats. Now, many companies offer mixtures of vegetables and starches, fruits and starches, and "dinners," consisting of starches, vegetables, and meats. Most often, the starches are refined rice, refined corn, and refined wheat. The refining of any grain reduces its vitamins, proteins, and roughage.

When you buy baby food in jars, read the fine print on the label. When the large print says "creamed beans," the fine print may say "beans with cornstarch." Choose plain fruits or plain vegetables to be sure that your baby is getting enough of these valuable foods and is not being overloaded with refined starches. Avoid jars that contain added sugar or salt.

Don't get started on cornstarch puddings and gelatin desserts. They don't have the right food values, and both contain a lot of sugar. Instead, give your baby plain strained fruits. A baby who has never been exposed to refined sugar will find these to be delightfully sweet.

Choking on solid foods. All babies choke a little as they get used to eating lumpy foods, just as they all fall when they're learning to walk. The ten most common foods associated with choking in children under the age of five are:

- hot dogs
- round candy
- peanuts
- grapes
- cookies

- meat chunks or slices
- raw carrot slices
- peanut butter
- apple chunks
- popcorn

Nine times out of ten, choking babies easily bring the food up or swallow it by themselves and don't need any help at all. If they can't bring it up or swallow it right away, pull the food out with your fingers if you can see it. If you can't see it, put the baby over your lap, with her head down and bottom up. Hit her firmly between the shoulder blades a couple of times with the palm of your hand. This virtually always solves the problem, and she's ready to go back to her meal. See page 790 for emergency treatment of choking.

Some parents worry so much about what to do if their baby chokes that they delay giving finger and lumpy foods until long after the baby is old enough for them.

The problem is not caused by young children's inability to chew and swallow. It's the result of the sudden deep inhalation that a child takes when he laughs, giggles, cries, or is surprised. The inhalation can send food from the mouth directly into a lung, blocking it off or causing it to collapse.

This doesn't mean that children under five should never have these foods. (Although hot dogs and hard, round candies are best avoided at any age.) The child should eat sitting at a table under careful adult supervision. Encourage him to chew well, and cut burgers, veggie hot dogs, grapes, and similar foods into smaller pieces.

NUTRITION AND HEALTH

WHAT IS GOOD NUTRITION?

It's natural for parents to give their children the foods they remember from their own childhoods. Food traditions are as much a part of culture as language; they bind families together and link the present to the past. On the other hand, we've learned that some diets are healthier than others. For many of us, the more we know about nutrition and health, the more determined we are to change our own diets and what we give our children.

One problem, though, is that nutritional knowledge itself keeps changing. If you read the newspaper regularly, paying attention to each new scientific study, you're almost sure to come away confused. If you were actually to follow each new recommendation, you'd never know what was going to show up on your plate. A lot of nutritional advice is geared to adults, but what works for a body that is fully grown may not always be best—or even safe—for one that is rapidly growing.

Amid the controversies, however, most experts now agree that diets that revolve around fatty meats, large portions of cheese, fried foods, and highly processed foods are unhealthy. Diets built mainly on fruits, vegetables, grains, and legumes provide the best disease-fighting nutrition. Many professional recommendations add low-fat dairy foods, such as skim milk, and relatively small portions of meat; others feel that diets with no meat and dairy are even more beneficial.

For you as a parent, then, the challenge is to incorporate healthy eating patterns into your lives in a way that fits for your family. Perhaps you will simply cut down on fried foods, red meat, and whole milk. Perhaps you will feel comfortable and motivated to make more substantial changes in what you and your family eat. The chapter that follows lays out a range of options to help you make changes that make sense to you.

AS A SOCIETY, WE NEED TO CHANGE

The evidence couldn't be more compelling: The large amount of animal fat and calories in the typical North American diet contribute to a host of ills in adults, including heart disease, strokes, high blood pressure, diabetes, and some cancers, not to mention obesity. What's more, many of these diseases have their roots in childhood. As early as age three, many American children already have fatty deposits in their arteries—the first steps on the road to heart attacks and strokes. Seventy percent of children at age twelve have these early signs of blood-vessel disease; and virtually all twenty-one-year-olds have them. Before long, high blood pressure and other problems start taking their toll. Obesity is spreading across the United States like an epidemic among children, bringing both physical and psychological problems. Severely overweight children are much more likely to develop diabetes and joint problems, for example. They often suffer socially, as well.

But there is hope for our children. Food preferences are learned early. Children who are cheerfully and regularly offered a variety of healthy foods (vegetables, fruits, whole grains, and beans) learn to eat and even prefer these foods. The trick is to make these foods a regular part of the family diet without putting too much emphasis on their being "good for you" (with the clear implication that "nobody really likes to eat this stuff"). Telling a child "If you eat your broccoli, I'll give you some dessert" just makes them hate broccoli. If healthful foods are part of the family routine, children accept most of them naturally.

Guiding our children toward healthy eating habits is sometimes a challenge. Children are not particularly concerned about the problems that come from unhealthful diets. The foods served at school may not be what you would offer at home. And television often gives children the wrong message. Just think about the kinds of foods that are the subjects of flashy advertisements for children: There are plenty of ads for potato chips but none for baked potatoes. Children are bombarded with commercials for sugarcoated cereals and high-fat junk foods. They know these commercial jingles even before they can read. It's no wonder they grow up with the message firmly implanted that high-fat foods are best.

The link between television viewing and obesity is very strong. The more television a child watches, the greater the risk of obesity. Better health is just one of the many good reasons to limit television viewing (see page 466 for more on television).

As a general rule, children pay more attention to what their parents do than to what they say. So if we want our children to get a healthy start in life and to maintain their health by continuing to eat nutritious foods, there needs to be a shift in the whole family's diet, starting with the parents.

BUILDING BLOCKS OF NUTRITION

Before we talk about the everyday foods that children eat, we ought to discuss the more important chemical substances that foods are composed of and what the body uses them for. You can compare a child's body to a building under construction. A lot of different materials are needed to build it and keep it in repair.

But a human being is also a working machine. It requires fuel for energy and other substances to make it work properly.

Proteins. The main building material of the body is protein. The muscles, heart, brain, and kidneys, for instance, are made largely of protein (aside from water). Bones consist of a protein matrix that's filled in with minerals. Children need protein to continually increase the size of every part of their bodies and to repair wear and tear. Proteins also provide energy. Meat, fish, eggs, and dairy products are sources of concentrated protein, but they also have cholesterol and fat. Vegetables, beans, and grains can supply all the protein a growing child needs, without the saturated fat and cholesterol contained in animal foods.

Complex and simple carbohydrates. These are the starches and sugars that supply much of your child's energy requirements. Complex carbohydrates contain fiber, and because they have to be broken down before they can be absorbed and used as fuel, they provide a fairly constant supply of energy. Vegetables, fruits, whole grains, and legumes are good sources of complex carbohydrates.

Simple carbohydrates, such as sugar and honey, provide quick energy, but since they are easily absorbed they don't stave off hunger for very long. As a result, they can lead to overeating and overweight. Sugary or highly processed foods like candy, doughnuts, and white bread provide "empty calories"—that is, calories with no other nutrients; they also increase tooth decay. Despite lots of research, however, there is no evidence that sugar causes hyperactivity, except perhaps in a very small number of children.

Fats. Fats and oils (liquid fat) supply energy and building materials for the body. Ounce for ounce, fats contain twice as many calories as either carbohydrates or proteins. There are two main kinds of fats that appear naturally in foods. *Saturated* fats are solid fats found mainly in meat and dairy products. *Unsaturated* or *polyunsaturated* fats are liquid fats, found primarily in plant-based foods, especially nuts, seeds, and oils. A third type of fat is produced during food processing: *Trans* fats are made when unsaturated fats are hydrogenated, or made solid. Trans fats appear in margarines, shortening, most processed baked goods, and all foods that have hydrogenated vegetable oil as an ingredient. Saturated and trans fats—the solid fats—contribute to heart disease and strokes; unsaturated fats do not appear to have this effect.

A few varieties of fat are essential, meaning that they must be part of the diet since the body can't make them itself. The two main essential fatty acids for humans are linoleic and linolenic acid, which are found mainly in soy products, nuts and seeds, and many leafy green vegetables. Human milk is rich in essential fatty acids; cow's milk contains very little. Omega-3 fatty acids, the group that includes linolenic acid, are particularly concentrated in fish and in flax seed. (You can find ground flax seed in most natural food stores; it tastes especially good in smoothies, salads, and breakfast cereals.)

Fiber or roughage. Vegetables, fruits, whole grains, and legumes contain a lot of material that our intestines can't digest and absorb but is important nonetheless. Nutritionists make a distinction between soluble fiber, such as is found in pectin and oats, and insoluble fiber, which is the roughage in celery for example.

Fiber—roughage—plays a key role in promoting normal bowel movements by providing part of the bulk that helps to stimulate the intestines to function. A person on a low-fiber diet—let's say milk, meat, and eggs—is likely to become constipated because there is simply too little substance left in the lower intestines to form healthy bowel movements. Fiber also appears to be helpful in maintaining the health of the intestines and colon. It now appears that a major factor in cancer of the large intestine is the slow passage of food caused by the lack of roughage in our overrefined diet. Fiber also helps lower cholesterol levels. Granulated sugar and refined grains, such as white flour, contain little if any fiber; meat, dairy products, fish, and poultry contain none at all.

Calories. The fuel energy value of food is measured in calories. Water, minerals, and vitamins have no calories, that is, they have no fuel or energy in them. Fat is rich in calories; an ounce of fat contains twice as many calories as an ounce of carbohydrate (including sugar; see page 346) or protein. Butter, margarine, and vegetable oil, which are almost pure fat, and cream and salad dressings, which are very high in fat, are therefore very high in calories. Many meats, poultry, fish, and eggs are high in calories because of fat content, as are a few vegetables (avocado, for example). Most cheese is high in fat, and therefore high in calories. Ounce for ounce, sugar, honey, and syrups are also high in calories, because they have no water or roughage to dilute the calories. High-fructose corn syrup, a major ingredient in soft drinks and many juice products, is basically concentrated sugar and therefore high in calories.

Most vegetables are low in calories because they are made up of water, complex carbohydrate, protein, and fiber, with very little fat. Whole grains, which have a high proportion of fiber, contain fewer calories ounce for ounce than simple carbohydrates, such as sugar. Nuts tend to be high in fat and in calories.

Many people get into the habit of thinking of calories as bad. Of course, that's nonsense. Without calories (energy), life would stop. What's bad is an excess of calories beyond what the body needs for normal growth and activity. When it comes to calories, balance is everything.

Water. Although it provides no calories or vitamins, water is vital to the makeup and working of the body. (A child's body is

60 to 70 percent water, depending on age and build.) Breast milk and infant formula generally provide enough water to meet a baby's needs. For toddlers and children, water is the most important beverage, especially in hot weather or during exercise, when the body loses a lot of water through sweating and evaporation. Most foods are composed largely of water; that is how children receive some of their daily needs.

Minerals. Many different minerals play vital roles in the structure and functioning of the body; they include calcium, iron, zinc, copper, magnesium, and phosphorous. The minerals are taken in from food, then are gradually lost when skin cells die and flake off and in bowel movements and urine. In adulthood, the intake and loss of minerals need to balance. Growing children need to take in more than they lose so that they can build new bones, muscles, skin, and other tissues.

All natural, unrefined foods contain a variety of valuable minerals. The refining of grains removes some of the mineral content. Boiling vegetables doesn't change their mineral content but can reduce certain vitamins. Nearly all foods are rich in phosphorous and magnesium, so there's no need to worry about children getting enough, except under very unusual circumstances. Calcium, iron, and zinc are another story, however.

Calcium. Bones and teeth are made up mostly of calcium and phosphorus. Over the years, doctors have counseled children and teens to consume plenty of calcium in order to prevent weakening of the bones in old age (osteoporosis). According to the National Academy of Sciences, children from age one to three need 500 milligrams of calcium a day; age four to eight, 800; age nine through eighteen, 1300. A convenient way to take in this much calcium is through dairy products, hence the national advertising campaign urging everyone to drink more milk.

Recently, however, experts have begun to question whether

children and adolescents really need this much calcium. In one study of girls aged twelve to twenty, for example, calcium intakes above 500 milligrams (about 40 percent of the standard recommend amount) did not seem to increase bone density. What *did* matter was a girl's level of physical activity: more active girls had higher bone densities.

Other research suggests that dairy products also tend to increase the amount of calcium that is *lost* each day in the urine, whereas other sources of calcium do not. (Clearly, the point of taking in lots of calcium is to *keep* it; calcium that is excreted in the urine might as well not have been taken in at all.) The health benefits of getting calcium from nondairy sources are discussed in detail in the following pages (see pages 340–43).

While milk and other dairy products are the main source of calcium in North American diets, calcium can also come from a variety of vegetables, beans, and calcium-supplemented foods (see the table on page 355). For example, calcium-enriched orange juice, which is widely available, contains as much calcium as milk, as do most soy and rice milks. Calcium supplements are inexpensive and usually accepted well by children. Of course, calcium in pill form doesn't provide any of the other nutrients found in calcium-rich vegetables or milk.

Milk also provides vitamin D, of course (see page 340). Children on dairy-free diets need a good source of vitamin D— either plenty of sun exposure or a vitamin supplement—so that they can absorb all the calcium they need.

(Fluoride, another mineral that promotes bone and especially tooth health, is discussed on page 805; most city water contains enough fluoride, but well water generally does not.)

Iron. Iron is a crucial ingredient of hemoglobin, the substance in red blood cells that carries the oxygen used by every cell in the body. Iron also plays a role in the development and functioning of the brain. Even a mild iron deficiency in early childhood can result in long-standing learning problems. Breast milk contains a highly absorbable form of iron, assuring that exclusively breast-fed babies get enough iron for healthy brain development, at least for the first six months. Infant formulas have extra iron added for the same reason. For brain development, low-iron formulas are *not* adequate.

Cow's milk is actually quite low in iron, and infants fed straight cow's milk are at high risk of developing iron deficiency. Moreover, cow's milk can interfere with iron absorption. In some infants, cow's milk also causes bleeding in the intestines, which increases the loss of iron. For these reasons, *infants should not be given cow's milk before one year of age.* They should drink breast milk or infant formula. Iron-fortified cereals and other iron-rich foods become important after about age six months. Meats contain iron, but children can also meet their iron needs by eating iron-rich vegetables and iron-fortified foods without getting the saturated fat and cholesterol found in meat. Most children's multivitamins contain iron.

Zinc. This mineral is an important component of many enzymes in the body. Zinc is needed for cell growth. Zinc deficiency shows up first as a problem with cells that normally grow quickly, such as the cells that line the intestines, cells in wounds that are healing, and the immune cells that fight off infection. Breast milk contains a form of zinc that is well absorbed by babies. Zinc is found in meat, fish, and cheese and also whole-grain cereals, peas, beans, and nuts. While zinc from plant sources is free of cholesterol and animal fat, zinc from plant sources tends to be less easily absorbed, so that young children on vegan diets (see page 338) need to eat plenty of zinc-rich foods and perhaps take a daily multivitamin with zinc for extra insurance.

Iodine is necessary for functioning of the thyroid gland. Iodine deficiency is one of the most important causes of mental retardation worldwide. The addition of iodine to table salt makes iodine deficiency very rare in the United States.

Sodium is present in table salt and most prepared foods. Sodium is one of the main blood chemicals. The kidneys keep sodium levels under tight control. For example, if your child lunches on canned soup—which most likely contains a great deal of sodium (check the label)—his kidneys will have to work to get rid of all the extra sodium. In the process, some other minerals, including calcium, will also be lost in the urine. In fact, high sodium intake appears to contribute to bone weakness in later life and to high blood pressure in some people.

Vitamins. These are special substances that the body needs in small amounts. All vitamins can be obtained from a diet of lean meat, low-fat dairy, vegetables, whole grains, fruits, beans and peas, nuts and seeds. Diets that avoid meats and dairy products can also provide all of the necessary vitamins and may actually be richer in certain vitamins, such as folate and vitamin C. One important exception is vitamin B_{12}, which is found only in animal sources, supplemented cereals, and a few other fortified products. A child who consumes no meat or dairy products should therefore probably take a multivitamin supplement. A daily multivitamin also makes sense for a child who is a very picky eater or who just doesn't appear to be growing well. Some experts recommend a daily multivitamin for *every* child. One vitamin pill a day is far preferable to fighting with your child to finish his vegetables or eat more raw fruit.

Vitamin A. The body makes vitamin A from beta-carotene, the chemical that makes carrots and butternut squash orange. Body systems that rely on vitamin A include the lungs, intestines, urinary systems, and especially the eyes. Vegetables and fruit, especially yellow and orange ones, supply all of the vitamin A children need. Probably the only children with vitamin A deficiency are those with a chronic intestinal illness or chronic malnutrition. Taking in excessive amounts of vitamin A from supplements can be harmful to children and adults; this will not happen by eating a lot of vegetables.

Vitamin B complex. Scientists used to think that there was just one vitamin B, which had several actions in the body. But when they studied it, "it" turned out to be a dozen different vitamins, mostly occurring in the same foods. Since the B vitamins are not yet all known or understood, it is better for people to eat plenty of the natural foods they mostly occur in than to take them separately in pill form. The four known to be most important for human beings are now called by their chemical names: thiamine, riboflavin, niacin, and pyridoxine. Every tissue in the body needs these four vitamins.

Thiamine (B_1), riboflavin (B_2), and niacin (B_3 or nicotinic acid) occur in fair amounts in milk, eggs, liver, and meat and in brown rice, whole grains, peas, beans, peanuts, fortified breads, pasta, and cereals. Deficiencies of these vitamins in children are unlikely unless the diet consists mainly of refined starches and sugar. Pyridoxine (B_6) is found in bananas, cabbage, corn, oats, split peas, wheat bran, cantaloupe, and blackstrap molasses. These, along with most grains, supply the child's daily needs.

Cobalamin (B_{12}) is widely distributed in animal foods, including milk, but absent in most foods from the vegetable kingdom. Children who don't eat animal products can get B_{12} from cereals and soy milk products fortified with it (often listed as cobalamin or cyanocobalamin on the label). For added safety, these children should also take a daily children's multivitamin to ensure getting adequate vitamin B_{12}.

Folic acid or folate. Important in the manufacturing of DNA and red blood cells, folic acid is found in spinach, broccoli, turnip greens, whole grains, and fruits, such as cantaloupe and strawberries. It's hard to overestimate the role of folic acid in preventing serious birth defects involving the development of the spinal cord (spina bifida). This isn't an issue for children, but as soon as a young woman is the age when she can become pregnant, it's wise to take a folic acid supplement to insure that there's plenty of this key vitamin on hand.

Vitamin C (ascorbic acid). The development of bones, teeth, blood vessels, and other tissues depends on vitamin C, as do many other body functions. Vitamin C is most abundant in oranges, lemons, grapefruit, raw or properly canned tomatoes and tomato juice, and raw cabbage and in lesser amounts in many other fruits and vegetables. Vitamin C is easily destroyed in cooking, however. People whose diets contain lots of vegetables and fruits rich in vitamin C tend to have lower cancer rates, although some of the credit for this may go to other nutrients in these foods. Deficiency of vitamin C is rare in North America. The main symptoms are bruising, rash, painful bleeding of the gums, and joint pain.

Vitamin D. This vitamin increases absorption of calcium and phosphorous from the intestine and aids their incorporation into bones. Unlike other vitamins, vitamin D is one that the body makes for itself. Sunlight stimulates the manufacture of vitamin D in the skin, so people naturally produce this vitamin when they regularly spend time outdoors. In cold weather, of course, people tend to cover up and stay indoors, and children with dark skin need more sun exposure because the pigment in their skin blocks some of the rays.

Mothers need extra vitamin D during pregnancy and breast-feeding. Dark-skinned babies who are exclusively breast-fed need a vitamin D supplement. To be on the safe side, the American Academy of Pediatrics now recommends a daily vitamin D supplement of 200 units for *every* breast-fed child, starting at six months (see page 239).

Vitamin E. This vitamin is found in nuts, seeds, whole-grain cereals, many vegetable oils, and such vegetables as corn, spinach, broccoli, and cucumbers. One of the roles of vitamin E may be to help the body deal with harmful chemicals that may contribute to aging or cancer. A vegetarian diet is bound to be naturally rich in vitamin E. It's not clear that taking a lot of additional vitamin E does any good, and it is possible to overdose. On the other hand, a child whose diet is very poor in vegetables may benefit from a daily multivitamin that contains vitamin E.

Vitamin toxicity. Megavitamins—vitamins in doses ten or more times higher than the minimum daily allowance recommended by the Food and Drug Administration—can be dangerous to children. Vitamins A, D, and K are the ones most likely to be toxic in high doses and can cause serious problems; other vitamins such as pyridoxine (B_6) and niacin can also have severe negative effects. Before you give your child vitamins in higher than usual doses, check with your child's doctor or nurse practitioner.

A HEALTHIER DIET

There's no question that the typical American diet is too rich in fat, sugar, and salt. Pretty much everybody agrees that children should eat more vegetables and whole grains and less meat, cheese, and sweets. Dr. Spock's nutritional philosophy went several steps farther. He believed that the healthiest diet was plant-based, with no meat, eggs, or dairy products at all. This approach is not as far out as it may seem, and in fact his conclusions were based on solid research studies. Even though official government health agencies and large expert groups, like the American Academy of Pediatrics, support milk and small amounts of meat for children, respected scientists disagree about what is nutritionally best, and many side with Dr. Spock.

⊗ CLASSIC SPOCK

I have personally been on a nondairy, low-fat meatless diet since 1991, when I was eighty-eight years old. Within two weeks of beginning this diet, my chronic bronchitis went away after years of unsuccessful antibiotic treatments. I have several middle-aged and older friends who have halted heart disease by eliminating dairy products, meats, and other high-saturated-fat foods from their diet. To achieve this kind of success, it's important to substitute whole grains and a variety of vegetables and fruits and to become more active. . . . I no longer recommend dairy products after the age of two years. Of course, there was a time when cow's milk was considered very desirable. But research, along with clinical experience, has forced doctors and nutritionists to rethink this recommendation.

Where does that leave you as a parent? In nutrition, as in many other areas of child-rearing, there is no one right answer that's best for everyone. A diet based on the U.S. Department of Agriculture's Food Guide Pyramid, including small portions of meat, low-fat milk, and a variety of plant-based foods, is a common choice for many children. On the other hand, a diet that's mostly or completely free of milk and meat, though it requires some thought to set up, can be equally delicious and may offer even more long-term health benefits to you and your children.

Are vegetarian and vegan diets safe? A meat-free diet is called vegetarian; a diet without meat, eggs, milk, or anything made from milk (such as butter and cheese) is called vegan. Nutritionists agree that children can thrive on vegetarian and vegan diets. With a lacto-ovo vegetarian diet (one that includes dairy and eggs) there is very low risk of nutritional deficiencies. In fact, on this diet a child's nutrition is likely to be much better than his friends', with more fiber and more vitamins. With a vegan diet (no milk products or eggs), parents need to take special care that their children are getting enough calcium, zinc, and vitamin B_{12}. This is easily done: A multivitamin and mineral supplement can offer the needed insurance.

Young children need plenty of calories, but their stomachs don't have much volume. For that reason, their diets need to contain concentrated sources of calories (for example, nuts, oils, or higher-protein foods). Low-calorie diets are not appropriate for young children; balanced, nutrient-rich diets are.

Of course, children on vegetarian or vegan diets are not the only ones who can develop nutritional deficiencies. Children who eat meat and drink milk may become deficient in folate, fiber, or vitamin E if they avoid vegetables.

Nutritional deficiencies are most likely to appear in the toddler years, after children have been weaned from breast milk or formula, while their brains and bodies are still growing very rapidly and before they are able to open the refrigerator on their own. More subtle nutritional problems often occur during adolescence, another time of rapid growth. When parents are aware of these issues, they can make sure that their children get the nutrition they need.

If you decide on a vegan diet, the pages that follow can get you started. But, as with any diet change, you'll probably want to read more to avoid pitfalls and get ideas for increasing convenience and pleasure. You may also want to consult with a professional nutritionist, who can give you personalized information and support. Books and pamphlets can be helpful, but they are no substitute for working with someone you trust.

The benefits of eating less meat. Most families have become more conscious about the fat content of meats, and many are choosing the lower-fat cuts. There is no question that it's better to eat smaller portions of meats than larger ones (the recommended portion of steak, for example, is the size of a pack of playing cards).

It may be healthier yet to cut way down on meats or eliminate meat and poultry from the diet altogether. Children can get plenty of protein from beans, grains, and vegetables; by doing so, they can avoid the animal fat and cholesterol found in meats. Unfortunately, switching from red meat to chicken does not help very much. Chicken can have just as much cholesterol as beef (about 100 milligrams of cholesterol in a four-ounce serving) and almost as much fat. Researchers have also learned that the cancer-causing chemicals that form in beef as it cooks also form in chicken.

Children who grow up getting their nutrition primarily from plant foods rather than meats have a health advantage. They are less likely to develop weight problems, diabetes, high blood pressure, and some forms of cancer. Meatless meals may also help your child to keep stronger bones, since the proteins found in meats result in increased loss of calcium in the urine (see page 342 for details).

Another reason why some families look more favorably at plant-based choices is food safety. In recent years, the frequency of disease-causing bacteria in meat, poultry, and eggs has risen sharply, which is why health authorities insist that these products be carefully handled and thoroughly cooked.

Many families gradually change their diets as they come to learn of the advantages to doing so. If you still serve meats regularly, you may want to try as many meatless meals as possible, explore new cookbooks, and experiment with new products that take the place of meats. Some of these, such as meatless burgers and hot dogs, are in the freezer case of your grocery or health food store. If you decide to adopt a vegetarian diet for your family, it's important to know enough about nutrition to be sure that the diet is complete. In particular, a daily multivitamin, particularly one with vitamin B_{12} (see page 335) is important for those on completely plant-based diets.

Concerns about cow's milk. Milk and other dairy foods are the main sources of calcium and vitamin D for North American children, and they provide much of the protein and fat as well. Most of us grew up being told that milk was good for you, so it's hard for us to imagine that milk may actually pose health risks or that alternative sources of nutrition might be better. While some of the concerns about dairy products are widely agreed on, others—which I'll point out—are more controversial.

Dairy products are often high in saturated fats, which promote artery blockage and weight problems as children grow. In fact, according to the National Institute of Child Health and Human Development, milk is the leading source of fat in children's diets in the United States—higher than burgers, fries, cheese, and chips. While milk and yogurt are available in low-fat versions, most cheeses, ice cream, and other dairy products are very high in fat—and it is the wrong kind of fat. The essential fats needed for brain development are found in vegetable oils. Milk, whether skim or whole, is very low in these healthy fats.

There are other concerns about dairy products, too, even the low-fat ones. Dairy foods can impair a child's ability to absorb iron and cause blood loss from the digestive tract in small children and in those older children who have true allergies to cow's milk. (Straight cow's milk is *not* safe for infants under twelve months. Formulas made from cow's milk should have added iron, to assure that enough iron is absorbed; low iron formulas should be given for only short periods, if at all.) These problems, combined with the fact that cow's milk has little iron of its own, can lead to iron deficiency (see page 332 for the connection between iron and brain development).

Other health problems may be aggravated or even caused by milk products. These include asthma and other respiratory problems, chronic ear infections, eczema (a chronic skin condition with itching and flaking), and constipation. Exactly why these problems occur is not known, but allergy to proteins in cow's milk plays a role in some cases. If asthma or eczema run in the family, there's a good chance that milk may be a contributing cause. Removing dairy products from the diet sometimes eliminates these problems; avoiding cow's milk altogether may prevent them.

There is good evidence that in children who are genetically vulnerable, milk drinking can increase the risk of developing juvenile onset diabetes. Part of cow's milk protein chemically resembles a protein found in the human pancreas that has to do with the production of insulin. In a few children, an allergic reaction to the cow's milk protein may lead to the destruction of the pancreas's insulin-making ability, resulting in diabetes.

There is also evidence—fairly convincing, I think—that a diet high in cow's milk predisposes older men to prostate cancer. Prostate cancer is the second most common cancer in men (after skin cancer).

Finally, as children grow up, many will have stomachaches, bloating, diarrhea, and gas caused by the milk sugar, lactose. These symptoms result from the fact that the ability to digest milk sugar disappears for many people in late childhood. In nature, animals do not drink milk after infancy, and that is probably the normal pattern for humans, too.

Cow's milk, calcium, and bones. Childhood and adolescence are key times for building bone. The standard dietary advice is that children need approximately 900 milligrams of calcium a day, the equivalent of three eight-ounce glasses of milk.

Thanks in part to clever and persuasive advertising, everyone "knows" that milk is an important source of calcium. But among themselves, scientists debate the pluses and minuses of cow's milk when it comes to bone health. In several well-done studies, *no* connection was found between the amount of cow's milk children drink and the amount of calcium they store in their bones. That is a really remarkable finding. If drinking cow's milk is important for bone growth, you'd expect that people who drink more milk would have stronger bones. But they don't. In fact, the United States has both very high per capita milk consumption and very high rates of osteoporosis.

There are many possible explanations for this. One is that calcium intake is just one of many factors that influence bone density. Exercise is also very important. It matters not just how much calcium gets taken in but also how much leaves the body. Diets that are high in milk and dairy are often also high in sodium in the form of salt and salty processed foods. Many softdrinks are also high in sodium. In some people, high sodium intake results in the loss of calcium through the urine. The proteins in milk and meat also tend to be high in certain amino acids that cause the kidneys to lose calcium. So as far as building bones is concerned, it may be just as good, if not better, to take in less calcium as well as less sodium and animal protein.

Healthful, calcium-rich foods. Other calcium sources offer many advantages that dairy products do not have. Most leafy green vegetables and beans have a form of calcium that is absorbed as well as or even a bit better than that in milk. With this calcium come vitamins, iron, complex carbohydrates, and fiber, generally lacking in cow's milk. Vegetables and legumes are a healthy source of calcium and have many other nutritional advantages. Refer to the list of calcium-rich foods on page 355.

It's very unlikely, however, that any child can take in enough calcium from leafy vegetables alone; he'd have to eat an unreasonably large volume of kale, for example. But other foods provide calcium, too, such as beans (see page 345). Calcium-enriched soy or rice drinks are just as tasty on cereal as cow's milk (once you get used to them), and they are free of animal proteins and fats. These beverages, as well as calcium-enriched orange and grapefruit juices provide as much calcium, ounce per ounce, as cow's milk.

SENSIBLE FOOD CHOICES

In the past few decades, we have learned a lot about how to use nutrition to help children stay healthy. We used to think of vegetables, grains, and beans as side dishes. We kept meat and dairy products as our favored foods and were not particularly concerned about fat and cholesterol in children's diets. We now know better. Research shows very clearly that vegetables, grains, beans, and fruits should take center stage. They provide the nutrition children need to grow and avoid the cholesterol and animal fat that can cause so many problems.

Unfortunately, few of us were raised on diets that emphasized vegetables, grains, and beans, so we are not always sure how to plan complete meals. Here are some steps to simplify things. Some will sound like basic common sense; others may be new to you. But each step is important.

Leafy green vegetables. Broccoli, kale, spinach, collards, watercress, Swiss chard, napa and chinese cabbage, bok choy, and other green vegetables are loaded with the absorbable calcium, iron, and many vitamins that your child needs. Include two or three servings of a leafy green vegetable every day. Leafy greens should always be cooked very quickly, some just one or two minutes, so that they come out bright green. They can be seasoned with a little sea salt when your child is older, but it's best to avoid added salt for young children lest they develop a taste for salty foods.

Other vegetables. Vegetables should make up 25 to 30 percent of the diet. It's best to select fresh organic vegetables at a farmers' market or a local garden or, best of all, grow your own. Vegetables from an organic farm, the organic foods section of the supermarket, or the local farmers' market carry the advantage of being free of pesticides. Growing some of your own produce with the help of your children is an excellent way to have fresh, healthy food and to share a great experience.

Freshness is always the key to good nutrition in vegetables. Frozen and canned vegetables often retain many of the nutrients, too, and may be less expensive. Vegetables won't be boring if you emphasize variety in both your choice of vegetables and their preparation. Cooking vegetables correctly will enhance your child's appetite and make the meal more appealing.

It helps to offer more than one vegetable at a meal, selecting those your child likes. Your child may prefer vegetables prepared a certain way: fresh watercress leaves in a salad, for example, rather than cooked watercress. Pushing children to eat vegetables they do not care for doesn't work in the long run. It's better to keep the selection of vegetables new and interesting so that your child will be tempted to explore.

Beans and bean products. Beans are rich in protein, calcium, and many other nutrients and should be a regular part of the diet. Tofu and tempeh, both made from soybeans, can be used in many main dishes and soups. A meal of beans and brown rice—or any bean and grain combination—will give your child plenty of protein and fiber with very little fat.

Fruits, seeds, and nuts. These foods can be delicious treats and additions to the diet. Fruits are better digested when cooked. Apples, pears, and other fruits in season and grown locally are best, and organic produce is healthier than pesticide-treated brands. (Organic produce is more expensive, but overall, a vegetable-rich diet may be *less* costly than a diet rich in meats.) Seeds and nuts can be dry-roasted and ground to make digestion easier. Almond butter and organic peanut butter make delicious treats for children and are a healthy substitute for candy or ice cream. (To avoid allergies, it is wise to introduce peanuts into the diet after a year of age; the same goes for almonds and other tree nuts.)

Whole grains. A generous part of a child's diet should be composed of whole grains. Short-grain brown rice, barley, oats, millet, whole-wheat noodles and pasta, and whole-grain bread contain complex carbohydrates, which are filling, nutritious, and a great energy source for growing children. They also provide protein, fiber, and important vitamins.

Fats and oils. The healthiest oils are sesame oil, olive oil, corn oil, flaxseed oil, and polyunsaturated vegetable oils. Use only a small amount to brush the bottom of the skillet, or use a vegetable oil spray. Vegetable fats are much healthier than animal-derived fats; nevertheless, use only a modest amount of whatever oil you choose. Margarine may be just as harmful as butter because the processing creates a type of fat (trans fats: see page 328) that may be as bad for our arteries as saturated fats. Instead of using margarine or butter on a baked potato, try Dijon mustard, salsa, or steamed vegetables. Jam and cinnamon work well on toast without the layer of butter in between, and whole-grain bread is delicious with no topping at all.

Meat and fish and fowl. Lean meats, fish, and poultry can provide high-quality protein and energy. The U.S. Department of Agriculture lumps these foods together with dry beans, nuts, and eggs. Adults should have three servings a day from this group, children two. Each serving, however, is small: only about two to three ounces, or roughly the size of a deck of playing cards. It is possible to savor a piece of meat of these modest dimensions, but not if you are accustomed to sitting down to a ten-ounce steak (more than three portions worth).

It's simple to incorporate meat into a healthy diet. Start by trimming away the visible fat from beef and pork, and removing the skin from poultry. Small amounts of meat can add flavor to large dishes of rice or vegetables. A small portion of top-notch meat or fish can make a meal fancy, without excessive cost or cholesterol. Meat may be the star of your culinary creations, but it performs best with a strong supporting cast of vegetables; it shouldn't be on stage all alone.

Sugar. Refined sugar is a simple carbohydrate, full of calories that have little nutritional value. Instead, a child's diet—and an adult's—should be rich in complex carbohydrates, which are found in grains, beans, and vegetables. For a sweet treat, the healthiest choices are fresh fruits and fruit juices. Use apple juice when cooking fruits instead of water and sugar. Or you may want to boil some raisins and use the juice, which is very sweet. You can also substitute rice syrup or barley malt for sweetness. When you use sweet vegetables, such as pumpkin, corn, squash, and carrots, you don't need to add sugar. At first these foods don't taste sweet in the sense that they don't taste like sugar. But after you take sugar out of your cooking, you will notice the real taste of sweet vegetables and fruits.

Salt. Cook grains with a pinch of sea salt, and don't use salt at the table. The only advantage of typical table salt is that it is fortified with iodine, an essential nutrient. Plants vary in their iodine content; sea vegetables are very rich in it. Substitutes for sea salt are soy sauce, miso, or ground-up sesame seeds mixed with a pinch of sea salt. Excess salt intake can make it harder to stay in calcium balance because excess salt may cause calcium to pass through the kidneys into the urine.

Beverages. The beverage children really need is pure, clean water. For variety, they can have "teas" made from grains, herbs, or fruit juices, and they can also enjoy sweet vegetable drinks made from squash, onion, carrots, or cabbage. Be aware of caffeine in coffee, of course, and also in black and green tea and in many popular soft drinks marketed to children. (Chocolate also contains a fair amount of caffeine.) You can substitute herbal teas with no caffeine or a grain "coffee" made from roasted barley.

Sweets. Cookies, cakes, rich crackers, and pastries quickly satisfy a child's appetite for a short time but give him practically no minerals, vitamins, fiber, or protein. These sweets and snacks are also the greatest source of invisible fat. They cheat children by making them feel well fed when they are being partly starved and by spoiling their appetite for better foods.

You don't have to be so suspicious of rich, refined foods that you stop your children from eating cake at a birthday party or on other special occasions. It's the steady diet of such foods that deprives them of nutrition. There's no sense starting them at home when there is no need, and there is no reason to train your child to expect a rich dessert after every dinner.

Highly sweetened foods, such as jams, jellies, and candy, contain excessive sugar. They quickly satisfy the appetite, spoiling it for better foods, and they promote obesity and tooth decay. Give children their cereal and fruits without extra sugar. If it is occasionally convenient to serve canned fruit, pour off the syrup or buy canned fruit packed in fruit juice without added sugar.

Candy, sodas, and ice cream are usually eaten between meals while children are away from home with their friends. If your child has not been trained to love these foods at home, he is less likely to eat a lot of them when away from home.

SIMPLE MEALS

The business of diet sounds complicated, but it needn't be. Actually, it's probably much simpler than we used to think. The ideal diet is based on fruits, vegetables, whole grains, peas, and beans. Meat, poultry, and fish can be cut back to small portions or eliminated entirely. If you're giving your child milk and other dairy foods, you may want to add or substitute some of the other sources of calcium we've talked about. If you're giving your child a completely vegan diet, be sure to include a daily multivitamin and read up on vegan diets (see "Nutrition and Prevention Medicine" in the Resource Guide, page 932). However you are choosing to feed your child, you may want to consult with an experienced dietitian or trusted friend who can guide you along. Roughly speaking, the following foods are required every day:

- Vegetables, green or yellow, three to five servings. Ideally, some should be raw.
- Fruit, two or three servings, at least half of them raw. Fruit and vegetables may be interchanged.

- Legumes (beans, peas, and lentils), two or three servings.
- Whole-grain bread, crackers, cereals, or pasta, two or more servings.

Suggested meals. These are only guidelines. You can vary the meals according to your child's preferences and your family's routines. Fruit or tomato juice can be given between meals if needed. Whole-grain sourdough bread can be given with meals if desired. Once you've decided on the kind of diet you want for your child, check with your child's day-care provider or school; you may have to supply your child's food.

Breakfast
- Fruit or fruit juice or leafy green vegetables
- Whole-grain cereal, bread, toast, or pancakes
- Scrambled tofu with greens
- Soy milk
- Vegetable soup

Lunch
- A filling dish, such as baked beans; soup with crackers, toast, or barley; whole-wheat or oat cereal; millet or barley soup with vegetables; whole-grain bread or sandwiches with tofu spread or nut butter; a potato; steamed, boiled, or stir-fried leafy greens
- Vegetable or fruit, raw or cooked
- Dry-roasted sunflower seeds
- Soy milk, noncaffeine tea, or apple juice

Dinner
- Leafy green vegetables, fast-cooked in a little water
- Beans or a bean product, such as tofu or tempeh
- Rice, bread, pasta, or other grain

- Raw fruit or applesauce
- Juice or water

Variations. Many parents complain that they don't know how to vary lunch. A good rough rule is to serve three items.

1. A filling dish with plenty of calories
2. A fruit or a vegetable
3. A leafy green vegetable (kale, broccoli, collards, leeks) cooked in one of a variety of ways

Breads and sandwiches of several kinds can be the filling dish as children approach the age of two. You can use rye, whole-wheat, oatmeal, sourdough, or multi-grain bread to start with. In general, avoid butter, margarine, and mayonnaise, which are full of fat and low on nutrition. Nut butters, used sparingly, are preferable. Mustard is a fat-free, well-accepted spread for sandwiches and potatoes. Ketchup is loaded with sugar; salsa can be delicious and is much healthier.

Sandwiches can be made with a wide variety of other foods, plain or in combination: raw vegetables (lettuce, tomato, grated carrot, cabbage), stewed fruit, chopped dried fruit, peanut butter, tofu mashed with an eggless, low-fat mayonnaise.

A fairly substantial dish is a broth or soup containing lots of barley or brown rice or a vegetable soup, plain or creamed, with a couple of handfuls of whole-wheat toast cut into small cubes to toss in. Also lentil, split-pea, and bean soups are a good balance with a grain dish and a green vegetable.

Simple unsalted whole-grain crackers can be served plain or with one of the spreads mentioned above.

Potato is a good, filling, low-fat dish. A baked potato can be topped with vegetables, baked beans, mustard, black pepper, or salsa. A small amount of ketchup or salsa will entice many a child to eat a greater variety of vegetables.

Cooked, precooked, or dry cereal can be made more exciting by adding sliced raw fruit, stewed fruit, or chopped dried fruit. I recommend that you avoid adding sugar.

Instead of a filling first course followed by stewed or raw fruit, you might serve a cooked green or yellow vegetable or a vegetable or fruit salad. A banana makes an excellent, filling dessert.

Pasta, hot or cold, is an excellent source of complex carbohydrates and fiber. It may be mixed with steamed vegetables or tomato sauce. Some children don't like grains and pasta. They will do just fine nutritionally on a variety of fruits, vegetables, and beans. Their taste for grains will develop later if it's not forced on them early on. Noodles made without eggs are available in many grocery stores. Noodles made with whole grains are best. You can add noodles to a stir-fry or have them in broth with added greens.

A world of vegetables. Vegetables are so important that they deserve featured status on a child's plate. During the first year, the baby has probably had most of the following cooked vegetables: spinach, peas, onions, carrots, asparagus, chard, squash, tomatoes, beets, celery, potatoes. By six months of age, most table vegetables eaten by the rest of the family can be fed to your infant after pureeing them in the blender. These same vegetables can be bought in a jar of baby food. Read the nutritional information on the label, choosing the one that appears to be the least adulterated. Beware of baby foods that are diluted with water or contain starch or tapioca. This makes them nutritionally inferior to what you make at home in your blender.

By the end of the first year, the vegetables can be offered in a more coarsely pureed, lumpy consistency. Peas should be mashed slightly to avoid their being swallowed whole. Steamed vegetables, such as carrots, potatoes, and green beans, cut into pieces make good finger foods.

Sweet potatoes or yams can be used at times instead of white potatoes. If you have stuck to the easily digested vegetables up to the age of a year, you can gradually try the less popular, sometimes less digestible ones, such as lima beans (mashed), broccoli, cabbage, cauliflower, turnips, and parsnips. If you persist in offering them without forcing them on your child, over time he may develop a taste for them.

Wait until two years to serve corn kernels. Children younger than that don't chew them; they pass through unchanged. Use only tender corn. When cutting it off the cob, don't cut too close, so each kernel will be cut open. At three to four, when you start corn on the cob, slice down the center of each row of kernels, so that they are all open.

The more easily digested raw vegetables are usually started between one and two years. The best are peeled tomatoes, sliced string beans, shredded carrots, and scraped chopped celery. They should be well washed. Go slowly at first, seeing how they are digested. You can use orange juice or sweetened lemon juice as a dressing. (Be careful to avoid raw carrot sticks and other hard vegetables that children can choke on.)

Vegetable and fruit juices may be started at the same time. These are not as healthful as the whole food, because the juice lacks the fiber contained in the fruit or vegetable. Juicers that keep the fiber in the juice are preferable, if you have one. One advantage of juice over cooked vegetables is that no vitamins are destroyed in cooking. If a child has temporarily turned against plain vegetables, consider vegetable soups: pea, tomato, celery, onion, spinach, beet, corn, and soups with large amounts of mixed vegetables. Some commercially prepared vegetable soups are very high in salt, however, so you need to read the label carefully. Many commercially prepared soups need to be diluted with equal amounts of water. If they're given to children undiluted right from the can, they can be harmful because the salt is too highly concentrated.

Vegetables are among the most nutritious foods you can feed your child, but if your child refuses to eat many, there are ways around that problem; see the following page.

TIPS FOR HAPPY EATING

Have fun with food. A wide variety of food ingredients is crucial to the success of any cook; it makes meals more appealing. Let your child enjoy different colors, textures, and tastes.

Keep mealtime free of the distractions of television and telephone. Some families say grace or meditate for a few minutes, which can establish a spirit of thankfulness and togetherness. Scoldings should not be part of the dining experience, even for the spills and lapses of manners that will inevitably occur.

Don't judge foods on calories, vitamins, or minerals alone. Other important considerations are fat, protein, carbohydrates, fiber, sugar, and sodium. Remember that not all essential foods need to be eaten at any one meal. What's important is what is taken in over a day or two.

Everybody in the long run needs a balance of low- and high-calorie foods as well as a balanced diet in other respects. If a person takes one aspect of diet too seriously and forgets the others, it's likely to lead to trouble. An adolescent girl, for example, acquires a fanatical zeal to reduce. She leaves out all the foods that she has heard have more than a few calories and tries to live on salad, juice, fruit, and coffee. She is bound to be sick if she continues. Serious-minded parents who have the mistaken idea that vitamins are the whole show and starches are inferior may serve their child carrot salad and grapefruit for supper. There aren't enough calories in that to satisfy a rabbit. A plump mother from a plump family, ashamed of her son's scrawniness, may serve him only rich foods, crowding out the vegetables, beans, and grains. In the process, he is likely to be deprived of minerals and vitamins.

Temporary substitutes for vegetables. Suppose a child has refused vegetables in any form for weeks. Will her nutrition suffer? Vegetables are especially valuable sources of minerals, vitamins, and fiber. But various fruits supply many of those same minerals, vitamins, and fiber. Whole grains also offer some proteins and many of the vitamins and minerals found in vegetables. So if your child refuses to eat vegetables for a period of time, don't make a big issue out of it. Continue to keep mealtime relaxed and fun. If you are really concerned, give your child a daily multivitamin. Her taste for vegetables will return unless you turn eating them into a power struggle, in which case she may refuse to eat them just to show you who is the boss.

Taming a sweet tooth. Craving for sweets and fatty foods often starts at home, where a rich dessert follows every meal, candy is always on hand, and the highest reward is a junk-food splurge. When parents say, "You can't have your ice cream until you finish your vegetables," they give the wrong message, using junk food as a bribe. Teach your young child, instead, that a banana or a peach is the greatest treat of all.

Children tend to eat whatever their parents eat. If you drink a lot of soda, eat a lot of ice cream or candy, or have chips around all the time, your children will want these things, too. (I think that sweets brought by a grandparent who visits occasionally can be regarded as a special treat.)

Feeding between meals. Use common sense between meals. Many young children, and some older ones, too, want a snack between meals (others never snack). If it's the right kind of food given at a sensible hour and presented in the right way, a snack shouldn't interfere with meals or lead to diet problems. When the regular meals contain plenty of carbohydrates in the grains and vegetables, children are much less likely to feel ravenous between meals.

Milk isn't a good snack food, since it is more likely to take away the child's appetite for the next meal. Fruits or vegetables are the best bet. Occasionally, though, you see children who never eat very much at one meal and who become excessively hungry and tired before the next; they may thrive when given more caloric and rich snacks between meals.

For most children, the snack is best given midway between meals, no closer than an hour and a half before the next one. Even here, there are exceptions. There are children who, though they receive juice in the middle of the morning, still get so hungry and cranky before lunch that they pick fights and refuse to eat. Having a glass of orange or tomato juice twenty minutes before lunch, may improve their disposition and appetite. What and when to feed a child between meals is a matter of common sense and doing what suits the individual child.

Parents may complain that their child eats badly at meals then always begs for food between meals. This problem doesn't arise because the parents have been lenient about offering snacks between meals. Quite the contrary. In every case I have seen, the parents have been urging or forcing the child to eat at mealtimes and holding back on food at other times. It's the pushing that takes away the appetite at meals. After months of it, the very sight of the dining room is enough to make the child's stomach revolt. But when the meal is safely over (though little has been eaten), the stomach feels natural again. Soon it's acting the way a healthy, empty stomach is meant to act: It's asking for food. The solution, then, is not to deny children food between meals but to let mealtime be so enjoyable that their mouths water then, too. After all, what is a meal? It's food specially prepared to be appetizing. When a child finds meals less appealing than snacks, something is wrong.

CALCIUM SOURCES
(approximate milligrams per serving)

100
1 cup of cooked kale
1 cup of baked, refried, or navy beans
3½ ounces of tofu

1 cup of cottage cheese
1 tablespoon of blackstrap molasses
1 English muffin
1½ cups of boiled sweet potato

150
1 cup of cooked broccoli
1 ounce of mozzarella or feta cheese
½ cup cooked collards
1 cup soft-serve ice cream
5 medium figs, dried

200
1 cup of beet or turnip greens
1 ounce of cheddar or jack cheese
3 ounces of canned sardines, with bones, or salmon

250
1 ounce of Swiss cheese
½ cup of firm tofu
1 cup of stewed rhubarb

300
1 cup of cow's milk
1 cup of yogurt
½ cup of ricotta cheese
1 cup of enriched soy or rice milk*
1 cup of calcium-fortified orange or apple juice

Sources: Jean A. T. Pennington, *Bowes and Church's Food Values of Portions Commonly Used* (New York: Harper & Row, 1989).

---

* Check the label; some brands contain 200 milligrams per cup, rather than 300.

FEEDING PROBLEMS AND EATING DISORDERS

―――――― ⋘ ⋙ ――――――

HOW FEEDING PROBLEMS START

Why do so many children eat poorly? Most commonly because so many parents are conscientious about trying to make them eat well! You don't see many feeding problems in puppies or in young humans in places where mothers don't know enough about diet to worry. Some children are born with a wolf's appetite that stays big even when they're unhappy or sick. Others have more moderate appetites that are more easily affected by their health and spirits. Almost without exception, babies are born with enough appetite to keep them healthy and gaining weight at the proper rate.

The trouble is that children are also born with an instinct to balk if pushed too hard and one to be disgusted by food with which they've had an unpleasant experience. There's a further complication: children's appetites change, almost by the minute. For a while, a child may feel like eating a lot of squash or a new breakfast cereal; the next month the same foods disgust her.

If you understand this, you will see that feeding problems can begin at different stages in a child's development. Some babies balk in their early months if their parents try to make them finish more of their bottle than they want, or if when the first solid food is introduced, they aren't given a chance to become gradually used to it, or they are pressured to eat when they are not in the mood. Many become pickier and choosier after the age of eighteen months because they aren't meant to be gaining so fast then, are more opinionated, or perhaps because of teething. Urging them to eat reduces the appetite further and more permanently. A very common time for eating problems to begin is at the end of an illness. If an anxious parent begins pushing food before the appetite returns, the pressure may quickly increase the child's disgust.

Not all eating problems start from mere urging. A child may stop eating because of jealousy of a new baby or worries of many kinds. Whatever the original cause, the parents' anxiety and urging usually make the problem worse and prevent the child's appetite from returning.

◁ CLASSIC SPOCK

A cure takes time and patience. Once an eating problem is established, it takes time and understanding to undo. The parents have become anxious. They find it hard to relax again as long as the child is eating poorly, yet their concern and insistence are the main things that are keeping the child's appetite down. Even when they reform, by a supreme effort, it may take weeks for the child's timid appetite to come back. She needs a chance to slowly forget all the unpleasant associations with mealtime.

Her appetite is like a mouse, and the parents' anxious urging is the cat that has been scaring it back into its hole. You can't persuade the mouse to be bold just because the cat looks the other way. The cat must leave the mouse alone for a long while.

Parents have feelings, too. And they are strong feelings if they have a chronic feeding problem on their hands. The most obvious one is anxiety: that the child will develop a nutritional deficiency or lose resistance to ordinary infections. The doctor tries again and again to reassure them that children with eating problems are no more susceptible to diseases than other children, but this is hard for them to believe (and, indeed, when poor eating continues long enough, it *does* weaken the immune system). The parents are likely to feel guilty, imagining that their relatives, in-laws, neighbors, and doctor consider them neglectful parents. They probably don't, of course. It's more likely that they understand, since they probably have had at least one child in the family who's a poor eater, too.

Then there's the parents' inevitable feeling of frustration and anger at a whippersnapper who completely foils their efforts to do right by her. This is the most uncomfortable feeling of all, because it makes conscientious parents feel ashamed of themselves.

It's an interesting fact that many parents whose children have eating problems recall having had an eating problem themselves in their own childhood. They remember only too well that urging and forcing did not work, but they find themselves powerless to do otherwise. The strong feelings of anxiety, guilt, and irritation are partly leftovers from the same feelings implanted in their own childhood.

There's rarely danger for the child. It's important to remember that children have a remarkable inborn mechanism that lets them know how much and which types of food they need for normal growth and development. It is rare to see serious malnutrition, vitamin deficiency, or infectious disease result from a child's picky eating habits. The child's eating pattern should be discussed with the doctor at the time of checkups, of course. Working together with a supportive physician can relieve some of the pressure and worry that comes with caring for a picky eater. A daily multiple vitamin tablet can assure that a child is getting the vitamins and minerals he needs.

WHAT TO DO

Make mealtime pleasant. The aim is not to *make* the child eat but to let her natural appetite come to the surface so that she *wants* to eat. Try hard not to talk about her eating, either threateningly or encouragingly. Don't praise her for taking an unusually large amount or look disappointed if she eats little. With practice, you should be able to stop thinking about it. That's real progress! When your child feels no more pressure, she can pay attention to her own appetite.

You sometimes hear the advice, "Put the food in front of the child; say nothing; take it away in thirty minutes, no matter how much or how little has been eaten; and give nothing else until the next meal." It is true that usually when children are hungry, they will eat. So this advice is all right if it is done not in anger or as a punishment and if it's carried out in the right spirit; that is to say, if the parent does not fuss or worry about the child's eating and remains agreeable. But angry parents sometimes apply the advice by slapping the lunch plate in front of the child and saying grimly, "Now, if you don't eat this in thirty minutes, I'm going to take it away, and you won't get a thing to eat until supper!" Then they glare at her, waiting. Such threatening hardens her heart and takes away any trace of appetite. The balky child who is challenged to an eating battle can always outlast a parent.

You want your child to eat not because she has been beaten in a fight, whether you have been forcing her or taking her food away; you want her to eat because she feels like eating.

Start by offering the foods she likes best. You want her mouth to water when she comes to meals so that she can hardly wait to begin. The first step in building up that attitude is to serve for two or three months the wholesome foods she likes best, omitting the foods she actively dislikes and offering as balanced a diet as possible.

If your child dislikes only one group of foods, eating most other kinds fairly well, you can substitute one food for another—

fruits for vegetables, for example—until her appetite swings around or her suspiciousness and tension at meals abate (see page 366).

Accept your child's food choices. A parent might say, "Those children who dislike just one type of food aren't real problems. Why, my child likes only peanut butter, bananas, oranges, and soda pop. Once in a while he'll take a slice of white bread or a couple of teaspoons of peas, but he refuses to touch anything else."

This is a more difficult feeding problem, but the principle is the same. You might serve him a sliced banana and a slice of enriched bread for breakfast; a bit of peanut butter, two teaspoons of peas, and an orange for lunch; a slice of enriched bread and more banana for supper. Let him have seconds or thirds of any of the foods if he asks for them. Give him a multivitamin as nutritional insurance. Serve different combinations of this diet for days. Firmly hold down the soft drinks and other junk foods. If his stomach is awash with syrup, it takes away what little appetite he has for more valuable foods.

If at the end of a couple of months he is looking forward to his meals, add a couple of teaspoons (no more) of some food that he sometimes used to eat (not one he hated). Don't mention the new addition. Don't comment, whether he eats it or leaves it. Offer this food again in a couple of weeks. Meanwhile, try another. How fast you go on adding new foods will depend on whether his appetite improves and how he takes to the new foods.

Make no distinctions between foods. Let him eat four helpings of one food and none of another, if that's what he prefers, as long as the food is wholesome. If he wants none of the main course but does want dessert, let him have dessert in a perfectly matter-of-fact way. If you say, "No dessert until you've finished your vegetables," you further take away his appetite for the vegetable or the main course and increase his desire for desserts.

The result is the opposite of what you want. The best way to handle the dessert problem is not to serve any dessert except fruit more than a night or two a week. If a nonfruit dessert is served, it should be given to all family members.

It's not that you want children to go on eating lopsided meals forever. But if they have a feeding problem and are already suspicious of some foods, your best chance of having them come back to a reasonable balance is to let them feel that you do not care one way or the other about what they eat.

It's a great mistake for parents to insist that children who have feeding problems eat "just a taste" of a food they are suspicious of as a matter of duty. If they have to eat anything that disgusts them, even slightly, it lessens the chance that they will ever change their minds and like it. And it lowers their enjoyment of mealtimes and their general appetite for all foods. Certainly, never make them eat at the next meal food they refused at the last. That's looking for trouble!

Serve less than they will eat, not more. To any child who eats poorly, serve small portions. If you heap her plate high, you will remind her of how much she is going to refuse and you'll depress her appetite. But if you give her a first helping that is less than she is going to eat, you will encourage her to think "That isn't enough." You want her to have that attitude. You want her to think of food as something she is eager for. If she has a really small appetite, serve her miniature portions: a teaspoon of beans, a teaspoon of vegetables, a teaspoon of rice or potatoes. When she finishes, don't say eagerly, "Do you want some more?" Let her ask, even if it takes several days of miniature portions to give her the idea. It's a good idea to serve the miniature portions on a very small plate so that the child doesn't feel humiliated by sitting in front of tiny portions of food on a huge plate.

Stay in the room . . . or leave. Should the parents stay in the room while the child is eating? This depends on what the child is used to and wants and how well the parents can control their worry. If they have always sat there with him, they can't suddenly disappear without upsetting him. If they can be sociable and relaxed and get their minds off the food, it's fine for them to stay, whether or not they are eating their own meal. If they find that even with practice they can't get their minds off the child's eating or stop urging him, it may be better for them to retire from the picture at the child's mealtime—not crossly, not suddenly, but tactfully and gradually, a little more each day, so that he doesn't notice the change.

No acts, bribes, or threats. Certainly the parents shouldn't put on an act to bribe the child to eat: a little story for every mouthful or a promise to stand on their heads if he finishes the spinach. Although this kind of persuasion may at the moment seem to make the child eat a few more mouthfuls, in the long run it dampens his appetite. The parents have to keep upping the ante to get the same result, and end up putting on an exhausting vaudeville act for five mouthfuls.

Don't ask a child to eat to earn his dessert, a piece of candy, a gold star, or other prize. Don't ask him to eat for Aunt Minnie, to make his mother or father happy, to grow big and strong, to keep from getting sick, or to clean his plate. Children should not be threatened with physical punishment or loss of privileges in an attempt to get them to eat.

Let's state the rule one more time: Don't ask, bribe, or force a child to eat. There is no harm in a parent's telling a story at suppertime or playing music, if that has been the custom, so long as it is not connected with whether the child is eating.

✑ CLASSIC SPOCK

It isn't necessary to be a doormat. I have said so much about letting a child eat because he wants to that I may have given the wrong impression to some parents. I remember a mother who had been embroiled in a feeding problem with her seven-year-old daughter—urging, arguing, forcing. When the mother understood that the child probably had, underneath, a normal appetite and a desire to eat a well-balanced diet and that the best way to revive it was to stop battling over meals, she swung to the opposite extreme and became apologetic. The daughter by this age had a lot of resentment in her from the long struggle. As soon as she realized that her mother was all meekness, she took advantage of her. She would pour the whole sugar bowl on her cereal, watching out of the corner of her eye to see her mother's silent horror. The mother would ask her before each meal what she wanted. If the child said, "Hamburger," she obediently bought and served it. Then the child, as like as not, would say, "I don't want hamburger. I want frankfurters," and the mother would run to the store to buy some.

There is a middle ground. It's reasonable for a child to be expected to come to meals on time, to be pleasant to other diners, to refrain from making unpleasant remarks about the food or declaring what she doesn't like, to eat with the table manners that are reasonable for her age. It's fine for the parents to take her preferences into account as much as is possible (considering the rest of the family) in planning meals or to ask her occasionally what she would like as a treat. But it's bad for her to get the idea that she's the only one to be considered. It's sensible and right for the parents to put a limit on sugar, candy, soda, cake, and the other less wholesome foods. All this can be done without argument as long as the parents act as if they know what they are doing.

SPECIAL PROBLEMS

Needing to be fed. Should the parents feed a poor eater? A child who is given proper encouragement will take over his own feeding somewhere between twelve and eighteen months. But if worried parents have continued to feed him until age two or three or four, probably with a lot of urging, it won't solve the problem simply to tell him, "Now feed yourself."

The child now has no desire to feed himself; he takes being fed for granted. To him, being fed is an important sign of his parents' love and concern. If they stop suddenly, it hurts his feelings and makes him resentful. He is liable to stop eating altogether for two or three days, longer than any parents can sit by doing nothing. When they feed him again, he has a new grudge against them. And when they try another time to give up feeding him, he knows his strength and their weakness.

A child of two or more should be feeding himself as soon as possible. But getting him to do it is a delicate matter that may take several weeks. You mustn't give him the impression that you are taking a privilege away. You want him to take over because he wants to.

Serve him his favorite foods, meal after meal, day after day. When you set the dish in front of him, go into the kitchen or the next room for a minute or two, as if you had forgotten something. Stay away a little longer each day. Come back and feed him cheerfully with no comments, whether or not he has eaten anything in your absence. If he becomes impatient while you are in the next room and calls you to come and feed him, go right away, with a friendly apology. He probably won't progress steadily. In a week or two, he may get to the point of self-feeding at one meal and insisting that you feed him at others. Don't argue at all during this process. If he eats only one food, don't urge him to try another. If he seems pleased with himself for doing a good job of self-feeding, compliment him on being a big boy, but don't be so enthusiastic that he gets suspicious.

Suppose that for a week or so you have left him alone with good food for as long as ten to fifteen minutes and he's eaten nothing. Then you ought to make him hungrier. Gradually, over three or four days, cut down to half of what you customarily feed him. This should make him so eager that he can't help starting to feed himself, provided you are tactful and friendly.

By the time the child is regularly feeding himself as much as half a meal, I think it's time to encourage him to leave the table rather than be fed the rest of the meal. Never mind if he has left out some of his foods. His hunger will build up and soon make him eat more. If you go on feeding him the last half of the meal, he may never take over the whole job. Just say, "I guess you've had enough." If he asks you to feed him some more, give him two or three more mouthfuls to be agreeable then casually suggest that he's through.

After he has taken over completely for a couple of weeks, don't slip back into the habit of feeding him again. If some day he's very tired and says, "Feed me," absentmindedly give him a few spoonfuls then say something about his not being very hungry. I make this point because I know that a parent who has worried for months or years about a child's eating, spoon-fed him much too long, and finally let him feed himself is greatly tempted to go back to feeding him again the first time he loses his appetite or is sick. Then the job has to be done all over again.

Gagging. The child beyond the age of a year who can't tolerate anything but pureed food has usually been fed forcibly or at least urged vigorously. It isn't so much that she can't stand lumps. What makes her gag is having them pushed into her. The parents of gagging children usually say, "It's a funny thing. She can swallow lumps all right if it's something she likes very much. She can even swallow big chunks of meat that she bites off the bone."

There are three steps in curing a child of gagging. The first is to encourage her to feed herself completely (see the section above). The second is to get her over her suspicion of foods in general (see page 360). The third is to go unusually slowly in giving her food with a coarser consistency. Let her go for weeks or even months, if necessary, on pureed foods, until she has lost all fear of eating and really enjoys it. Don't even serve her meats during this time if she does not enjoy them finely ground.

In other words, go only as fast as the child can comfortably take it. A few babies have such sensitive throats that they gag even on pureed foods. In some of these cases, the cause seems to be the pasty consistency of the food. Try diluting it a little with milk or water. Or try chopping vegetables and fruits fine instead of mashing them.

In most hospitals, there are speech and language pathologists or occupational therapists who specialize in problems of gagging and swallowing. Working with one can be very helpful.

Thin children. Thinness has various causes. Some children are thin by heredity. They come from thin stock on one or both sides of the family. From the time they were babies, they have been offered plenty to eat. They aren't sickly, and they aren't nervous. They just never want to eat a great deal, especially of rich foods.

Other children are thin because their appetites have been taken away by too much parental urging (see page 357). Other children can't eat for other nervous reasons. Children who worry about monsters, death, or a parent's going away and leaving them, for example, may lose a lot of their appetite. Angry arguments or physical fighting between parents can be terribly upsetting to children and take away their appetites. The jealous younger sister who drives herself all day long to keep up with her older sister burns up a lot of energy and gives herself no peace at mealtime, either. As you can see, the tense child is thinned by a twofold process: the appetite is kept down, and the restlessness uses up extra energy.

Many children throughout the world are malnourished because their parents can't find or afford the proper food. Even in the wealthy United States, a large number of children—perhaps as many as one in four—experience times when they cannot count on having enough to eat. This food insecurity not only interferes with children's growth; it also wreaks havoc on their ability to learn in school. Hunger is truly a national scandal.

Some chronic physical diseases cause malnutrition. Children who become thin during an acute illness usually recover their weight promptly if, during convalescence, they are not urged to eat until their appetite recovers.

A sudden loss of weight is serious. If a child abruptly or slowly loses a lot of weight, he should have a careful checkup—promptly. The most common causes of weight loss are diabetes (which also produces excessive hunger, thirst, and frequent urination), worry about serious family tensions, tumors, and the obsession in adolescents with the need to diet. (See page 373 on anorexia nervosa.)

Care of a thin child. A thin child should, of course, have regular medical checkups. This is more important if the child acts tired or has lost weight or failed to gain a reasonable amount. Thinness, failure to gain weight, and fatigue can be signs of either emotional troubles or physical illness, often both. If your child is nervous or depressed, consult a child guidance clinic or a family social agency. Talk his situation over with his teacher. It's wise to think about his relations with parents, brothers, sisters, friends, and schoolmates. If you have gotten into a power struggle with your child over feeding, try to relax and take the pressure off your child and yourself.

Eating between meals is helpful for those thin children whose stomachs never seem to want to take much at a time but who are willing to eat often. It doesn't help to allow constant snacking. Instead, offer one nutritious snack after breakfast, another after lunch, and a third at bedtime. It's tempting to give a thin child high-calorie, low-nutrition junk foods for snacks, either as a bribe or for the comfort of seeing him eat something. But it's better to offer foods with more nutritional values.

A healthy child may stay thin despite a large appetite. This is probably the way she or he was meant to be. Many such children prefer relatively low-calorie foods, like vegetables and fruit, and shy away from rich desserts. If your child has been slender since infancy but doesn't seem to have any kind of problem and gains a reasonable amount of weight every year, relax. She or he is meant to be that way.

Fat children. In the fifty years since this book was first published, children's genes have not changed, but obesity has become a true epidemic. All over the United States, more children are seriously overweight than ever before. At the same time, more children are developing the form of diabetes that normally affects only obese adults. Fat babies often become lean children and grow up to be lean adults. But by school age—six or seven—a child who is very overweight is likely to grow into an obese adult, with all the risks that obesity brings, including high blood pressure, heart attacks, and cancer.

Among the many causes of fatness are cutbacks in school physical education programs, neighborhoods that don't provide safe play areas and recreation programs, and increased television viewing and playing of computer games. Many people think the cause of obesity is thyroid or other hormonal trouble, but this is rarely the case, especially if the child is at least average in height. Several factors can increase a child's chances of becoming overweight; they include heredity, temperament, appetite, and unhappiness. If both parents are overweight, the child's chance of becoming obese is as high as 80 percent. This has led many to think of genes as the principal cause of obesity. It's clear that lifestyle patterns, such as excessive fat intake and inactivity, play an equally important role.

Another key factor is appetite. The child who has a tremendous appetite that runs to rich foods like potato chips, meats, cheese, cake, cookies, and pastry is naturally going to be heavier than the child whose taste runs principally to vegetables, fruit, and grains. But this only raises the question of why some children crave large amounts of rich foods. We don't understand all the causes of this, but we recognize the children who seem to have been born to be big eaters. They start with a huge appetite at birth and never lose it, whether they're well or sick, calm or worried, whether the food they're offered is appetizing or not. Perhaps they learn to appreciate fatty foods because those are the sort that are offered as treats and rewards for good behavior or to express their parents' love for them. They're fat by the time they're two to three months old and often stay that way at least through childhood.

Unhappiness is sometimes a factor. For example, a child who is unhappy in first or second grade may turn to food. This is the period when children draw away from their close emotional dependence on their parents. If they don't have the knack of making friends with other children, they feel left out in the cold. Eating sweet and rich foods serves as a partial substitute. Worries about schoolwork or other matters sometimes make children seek comfort in overeating, too.

Obesity in adolescence. Overweight often develops during puberty. Appetites normally increase as adolescents begin their growth spurts. Loneliness can also play a part. During adolescence, many children become self-conscious from the changes they are experiencing, which may lessen their ability to get along enjoyably with their fellows.

No matter what caused it in the beginning, obesity may become a vicious circle. The fatter the child, the harder it is for her to enjoy exercise and games; the less active she is, the more energy her body has to store as fat. It's a vicious circle in another way, too: the fat child who can't comfortably enter into games may come to feel even more like an outsider and is liable to be teased and excluded.

Preventing and treating obesity. Obesity is a most serious problem for any child. Since it's likely to be associated with physical and mental problems, it should be combated as soon as it appears. If a baby becomes unusually plump during his first year, this shouldn't be considered cute. It should be treated with dietary shifts right away. Often it's possible to satisfy such a child fairly well with a lot of vegetables, fruits, whole grains, and beans and to cut way down on sugars, fats, and foods made from highly processed (white) flour. If you do decide to make diet changes of this sort, be sure to work closely with your child's doctor to be sure that you aren't overdoing it.

Not every child who becomes plump is unhappy. There seems to be a normal tendency for many children, including the cheerful and successful ones, to put on extra weight in the seven- to twelve-year-old period. Very few of these children become excessively obese; they are just slightly overpadded. Most of them stay plump during the two years of very rapid puberty development, then slim down as they get further into adolescence. Many girls, for instance, become slimmer around fifteen years of age without great effort. Once you know that this mild school-age plumpness is common and that it often goes away later, you can avoid making an issue of it.

Dieting. What can you do about fat children? Right away you might say, "Put them on a diet." It sounds easy, but it isn't. Think of the grown-ups you know who are unhappy with their weight yet aren't able to stick to a diet. If the parents serve the child lower-fat foods, the whole family must go without the richer dishes or the overweight child is kept from eating the very things his heart craves most while the rest of the family enjoys them. Children can see that this is clearly unfair, and the feeling of being treated unfairly may further increase the craving for sweets. Whatever is accomplished in the dining room may be undone at the refrigerator or fast-food counter between meals.

The prospect of slimming down is not as dismal as I have made it out to be. Tactful parents can do a good deal to keep temptation away from their overweight family members without making an issue of it. They can eliminate rich, fatty desserts. They can stop keeping cake and cookies in the kitchen and can provide fresh fruit for between-meals nibbling. They can serve low-fat foods to the whole family, with plenty of vegetables, fruits, grains, beans, and peas. When families adopt a vegetarian diet and keep vegetable oils to a minimum, weight problems generally improve, as do other health conditions. This is not a diet in the usual "lose weight fast" sense. It is meant to be a permanent change in the way the entire family eats, a new way of eating that is more nutritious and that the child will accept in time. Any weight loss is simply a bonus of healthier eating habits.

A child should be encouraged to learn about various nutritious foods: where they come from, how they are prepared, and their ethnic origins. She should also participate in choosing and purchasing food. The supermarket provides a wonderful opportunity to teach children about various foods and good nutrition.

A child who shows any willingness to cooperate in making healthy lifestyle changes should certainly be encouraged to talk with the doctor, preferably alone. Having this kind of discussion with a professional may give the child the feeling of running her own life like a grown-up. Anyone takes dietary advice better from an outsider. Children do not need medicine to reduce. The treatment is a change in eating patterns, from fatty foods to healthy ones.

Since overeating is often a symptom of loneliness or maladjustment, the most constructive thing is to make sure that the child's home life, schoolwork, and social life are as happy and satisfying as possible. If despite your efforts to help, the extra weight is more than a little or the child is gaining weight too rapidly, you should seek medical assistance.

Self-dieting sometimes becomes a problem and a danger in adolescence. A group of girls excitedly work themselves up to going on some wild diet they've heard about. Within a few days, hunger makes most of them break their resolutions, but one or two may persist with fanatical zeal. Occasionally a girl loses alarming amounts of weight and can't resume a normal diet even when she wants to (see next section below on anorexia nervosa). The group hysteria about dieting has awakened in her a deep revulsion against food. Another girl in the early stages of puberty declares, "I'm getting much too fat," even though she is so slender that her ribs are showing. The child who becomes obsessed with dieting needs the help of a children's psychiatrist or psychologist.

Therefore, if dieting is being considered, the first step, for a number of reasons, is to consult a doctor. The doctor's first task is to determine whether dieting is necessary or wise. Adolescents are more likely to accept the doctor's advice than that of their parents. If it is agreed that dieting is wise, it should certainly be prescribed by the doctor or dietitian, who will take into account the child's food tastes and the family's usual menus to work out a diet that is not only nutritionally sound, but practical for that home. Finally, since weight loss puts strain on the dieter's health, anyone who is planning to reduce should be examined at regular intervals to make sure that the rate is not too fast (a pound a week is usually safe) and that the dieter remains strong and healthy.

Weight-loss diets should be based mainly on changing the *type* of food children eat (and on increasing regular exercise), rather than focusing on the *amount* of food. When the family serves low-fat plant-based foods—pasta, beans, vegetables, rice dishes—in place of oily fried foods, meats, and dairy products, weight loss typically occurs with no one going hungry and without anorexia, which can result from a severe low-calorie diet.

EATING DISORDERS

Our culture places tremendous pressure on women to be slender. Television and women's magazines, in particular, bombard us with images of unnaturally thin women. Many people come to believe that there is something wrong with them if they don't look this way. Even girls in elementary school feel this pressure strongly. As many as 60 percent of girls as young as ten or eleven believe that they are too fat and should diet. A large number of adolescents develop true eating disorders. If you have a basic understanding of anorexia and bulimia, you'll be able to reduce the risk for your children and get help early if they need it.

Definitions and causes. The term eating disorder usually refers to anorexia nervosa and bulimia nervosa. The main feature of anorexia is compulsive dieting with severe weight loss. The main feature of bulimia is out-of-control eating (bingeing) followed by self-induced vomiting, laxative abuse, or other extreme means to limit weight gain.

Eating disorders are common. Anorexia and bulimia strike somewhere from 2 percent to 9 percent of females (the actual numbers are hard to know, since people with eating disorders often hide them). While most eating disorders occur in teenage girls and young women, about 5 to 10 percent of people with eating disorders are male.

Scientists don't know exactly why some people develop these disorders while others do not, though new research suggests that there may be an inherited, genetic vulnerability. People who develop anorexia are often outwardly successful (earning good grades, for example) but inwardly feel inadequate. They may have trouble expressing emotions, particularly anger. Their self-destructive dieting behavior becomes a way to do that. They may feel that they are not in control of their lives and that weight loss is something that is in their control.

Addicted to thinness. One way to look at eating disorders is as a form of addiction, not to a drug but to the act of dieting or bingeing on food. Like alcohol or drug addiction, eating disorders often start out as something that seems positive (losing a little weight is good; relaxing with a drink feels good, too, at first). In some people, bingeing and dieting are attempts to self-treat depression or psychological trauma. Initially, this approach seems to work. Then the addiction takes over, controlling every aspect of the person's life. Just as the alcoholic is always thinking about how to get his next drink, the anorexic is always thinking about how to get rid of the next few ounces of body weight, and the bulimic is always thinking about how to lose a few pounds or feeling ashamed of a recent binge.

A person with an eating disorder cannot simply decide to stop having the disorder, any more than a person with drug addiction can decide to simply stop using. While some women say that they have overcome eating disorders on their own, my sense is that this is rare. Eating disorders almost always require professional treatment, often by a team of professionals that includes physicians, psychologists, nutritionists, and others. Recovery is rarely quick or easy. However, with therapy and hard work, people with eating disorders *can* recover.

Psychological changes. Anorexia nervosa is about more than just dieting too much. A person with anorexia nervosa—most patients are teenage girls or young women—believes that she is overweight, even when she is obviously way too thin. This delusion persists even if her parents, friends, and doctors tell her she is underweight and even though she is (or is becoming) weak and ill. This extreme fear of gaining weight dominates her thoughts. Being fat is the worst possible fate she can imagine; nothing else is nearly as important.

In medical terms, anorexia means a loss of appetite, but many people with anorexia nervosa are actually hungry all the time. They wage a constant fight against the hunger they feel in order to attain the abnormal, waiflike body shape they have come to see as normal. They may be obsessed with food, cooking elaborate meals that they do not eat. Some may exercise compulsively, two or three time a day; and if they slip up and eat something fattening, they exercise even more to burn away the calories. Anorexia nervosa often accompanies other psychiatric disorders, such as clinical depression. People with the disorder may alienate their friends and family, who see the person's self-destructive behavior but cannot talk her out of it.

Physical changes. Along with the changes in behavior and thinking, there are physical changes in people who have anorexia nervosa. A diagnosis of anorexia nervosa requires that a person have lost a significant amount of weight to the point that they are well below the normal lower limit for their age and height. With the loss of body fat, hormone levels fall and young women's menstrual periods cease (or do not start). Males with anorexia also have abnormal sex-hormone levels. As the state of undernourishment worsens, the bones lose calcium and weaken. There is damage to muscles throughout the body, including the heart and other organs. About one of ten people with anorexia nervosa die prematurely as a result of the disease.

Treatment. Because anorexia is a complex disorder with physical, psychological, and nutritional components, it's best treated by an experienced doctor or team, which can include a psychologist or psychiatrist, family therapist, and nutritionist. Try to find a program that specializes in the comprehensive treatment of eating disorders.

The first priority is weight gain. People who are severely underweight typically need to be hospitalized to ensure that they put on pounds safely. Different types of psychotherapy can be helpful. These commonly focus on helping the person change how she thinks about her body and what it means to be attractive and successful. She needs to learn to take satisfaction in other activities (friends, art, or simply having fun) and to express her feelings in nondestructive ways. Medication can help treat depression or other psychiatric problems that accompany the eating disorder.

Prevent eating disorders. Eating disorders rarely spring up out of the blue. Like many problems, they start out small, then grow. Preventing them is almost always easier than treating them. The principles below apply equally to boys and girls, both in grade school and high school.

From the beginning, focus on healthy eating and regular exercise rather than on thinness. An excessive focus on thinness can lead to bulimia and anorexia. Not only that: In many children, pressure from parents to slim down has just the opposite effect, leading to overeating and weight gain.

Respect your child's natural body type. If your child has a medium build (neither very thin nor very chunky), let her know that you think she is perfect. If people in your family tend to have a rounder physique, there is little to be gained from trying to reshape your child. Instead, focus on healthy activities and sensible eating.

Avoid teasing your child about being chunky or pudgy. You don't mean harm, of course, but children are extremely sensitive to this sort of joking. They take the message to heart, and the idea develops that they really do need to diet. As parents, we absorb the same thin-is-beautiful message that is everywhere in our culture (of course we want our children to be beautiful and successful). It's very important that we keep these attitudes to ourselves, however.

If your child is naturally slender, that's great, but don't go on and on about how wonderful it is to be thin. Naturally thin children may be at increased risk of developing anorexia nervosa, because it is easier for their bodies to burn calories. If they receive a lot of praise or admiration for being thin, the temptation to embrace thinness as an end in itself can be strong.

Talk with your children about how television, movies, and print advertisements glorify thinness. "Look at that actress," you might say while watching television together. "She's really thin! Most real people who are healthy aren't that skinny." It's up to you to counteract the attempt by businesses to sell their products by promoting one particular ideal of beauty that focuses on thinness.

Even children's cartoons tend to glorify one particular body shape (tiny waist, large breasts in female characters; in males, huge shoulders and chest, and again a very small waist). Children absorb this beauty ideal from hour after hour of viewing. This is yet another good argument for limiting (or eliminating) television for young children.

Pay attention to hints that your child is thinking a lot about weight. If she seems fascinated by fashion models or rail-thin celebrities, try to encourage other interests—for example, art or music—that don't focus so much on body type. If she begins talking about dieting, change the focus if you can to being healthy rather than becoming thin. Even for children who are chunky, dieting is rarely the best answer. It's better to eat sensibly and to make sure that each day has a time for physical activity.

Pay special attention if your child is involved in ballet or in sports that focus on the body, such as gymnastics or wrestling (because of the importance of weight limits). For children and teenagers, coaches should see it as their first duty to ensure that their young athletes and artists are healthy. They should not suggest weight-loss diets and should work with parents to watch for signs of unhealthy dieting.

Some studies have shown that children who develop eating disorders are often perfectionists. Children like this tend to be more successful than their classmates but less happy. With such a child, it's important to try to lessen the pressure to succeed as much as possible. It might help to steer your child toward team sports instead of individual ones, which often bring greater pressures.

If your child takes dance or music lessons, look for a teacher who emphasizes joyful self-expression over perfect technique. Appreciate your child's good grades, but be sure to openly recognize other things about her as well—good sense or loyalty to friends, for example—so she learns that high grades are not the most important thing about her.

Examine your own behavior. If you are constantly dieting, you're teaching that weight is something to be fought and controlled. If you do need to lose weight, it's probably best to think of and talk about your diet as part of a whole plan to lead a healthier life, not just something you're doing to look good. Focusing on good health is a better message for your child and will probably be more effective in the long run for you, too.

Raising Mentally Healthy Children

WHAT CHILDREN NEED

———— ✤ ✤ ————

EARLY RELATIONSHIPS

Relationships and the wider world. What stimulates normal, well-rounded development—emotional, social, and intellectual? Babies and children, by their nature, keep reaching out to people and things. Loving parents, watching and coaxing, respond enthusiastically to their baby's first smiles with smiles of their own; similar interactions are repeated every waking hour for months. Parents give food at times of hunger, comfort at times of misery. All of these things reinforce the child's feelings of being well cared for and connected to others.

These first feelings form the foundation of a sense of basic trust that will color the child's future relationships. Even her interest in things and her later capacity to deal with ideas in school and at work rest on this foundation of love and trust.

A child needs to know that there is a least one loving, reliable adult to whom she belongs. Starting from such a secure base, the child can more readily face the challenges of growing up: going to school, trying difficult things, and coping with obstacles and disappointments. Positive traits in children emerge naturally when a child is given much love and nurturing. Then when she is exposed to a variety of experiences, she has the confidence and motivation to attempt to master those skills that match her in-born talents.

As children grow, they reach out to embrace the world. Through the ages, the natural interplay between this outward reaching and the parents' sensitive loving responses has been sufficient to produce bright, capable, sociable, loving young people. There's only one real trick to raising a mentally healthy child: a loving, nurturing, and mutually respectful relationship between you and your child.

ᗯ CLASSIC SPOCK

Enjoy children as they are—that's how they'll grow up best. Every baby's face is different from every other's. In the same way, every baby's pattern of development is different. One may be very advanced in her general bodily strength and co-ordination—an early sitter, stander, walker—a sort of infant athlete. And yet she may be slow in doing careful, skillful things with her fingers or in talking. Even babies who are ath-letes in rolling over, standing, and creeping may turn out to be slow to learn to walk. Babies who are advanced in their physical activities may be very slow in teething and vice versa. Children who turn out later to be smart in schoolwork may have been so slow in beginning to talk that their parents were afraid for a while that they were slow; and children who have just an ordinary amount of intelligence are sometimes very early talkers.

I am purposely picking out examples of children with mixed rates of development to give you an idea of what a jumble of different qualities and patterns of growth each in-dividual person is composed.

One baby is born to be big-boned and square and chunky, while another will always be small-boned and delicate. Some individuals really seem to be born to be fat. If they lose weight during an illness, they promptly gain it back after-ward. The troubles that they have in the world never take away their appetites. The opposite kind of individuals stay on the thin side, even when they have the most nourishing food to eat, even though life is running smoothly for them.

Love and enjoy your children for what they are, for what they look like, for what they do, and forget about the qualities that they don't have. I don't give you this advice just for sentimental reasons. There's a very important practical point here. The children who are appreciated for what they are, even if they are homely, or clumsy, or slow, will grow up with confidence in themselves and happy. They will have a spirit that will make the best of all the capacities that they do have and of all the opportunities that come their way. But the children who have never been quite accepted by their parents, who have always felt that they were not quite right, will grow up lacking confidence. They'll never be able to make full use of what brains, what skills, what physical attractiveness they have. If they start life with a handicap, physical or mental, it will be multiplied tenfold by the time they are grown up.

EMOTIONAL NEEDS

Early care. It's in the first two to three years of life that children's personalities are most actively molded by the attitudes of their parents or those who provide most of their care. Babies who are cared for mainly by loving, enthusiastic parents, perhaps with the help of others, surge ahead. By contrast, babies who are raised in understaffed orphanages, spending their days lying neglected in their cribs, wither in body, intellect, and emotions, and may never fully recover. (We learned this from detailed studies of orphanages in the United States in the 1950s; tragically, we've recently relearned the same lessons through studies of children adopted from orphanages in other parts of the world.)

Parents give their children their love, their pride and joy in their tiny accomplishments, thoughtful playthings, answers to their questions, and a willingness to let them play freely as long as they do no damage. Parents read to their children and talk with them about everything around them. These are the attitudes and activities that foster emotional depth and keen intelligence.

Whether children will grow up to be lifelong optimists or pessimists, warmly loving or distant, trustful or suspicious will depend to a considerable extent—although not entirely—on the attitudes of the individuals who had the responsibility for a major portion of their care in their first two years. The personalities of parents and caregivers are therefore of great importance.

One person acts toward children as if they are basically bad, always doubting them, always scolding them. Children raised in this way may grow up doubting themselves and full of guilt. A person with more than average hostility finds a dozen excuses every hour for venting it on a child, and the child acquires a corresponding hostility. Other people have the itch to dominate children; unfortunately, they can easily succeed.

In the first year, a baby has to depend mainly on the attentiveness, intuition, and helpfulness of adults to get her the things she needs and craves. If the adults are insensitive or indifferent to her, she may become apathetic or depressed.

Continuity of caregiving. A special need of young children is continuity in their caregivers. From the age of a few months, babies come to love, count on, and derive their security from the one parent, or at most a very few people, who provides the major part of their care. Even at six months, babies become seriously depressed, losing their smile, appetite, and interest in things and people if the parent who has cared for them disappears for more than a brief time. There will be depression, less in degree, if a person who regularly assists the parent leaves. Small children who have been moved from one foster home to another several times may lose some of their capacity to love or trust deeply, as if it's too painful to be disappointed repeatedly.

For this reason, it's important that the parent or other person who has given the major part of a child's care not give it up in the first two to three years, at least not until a successor has very gradually taken over. The sucessor, in turn, needs to be committed to sticking with the job. In the group care of young children, if there are several staff people assigned to a group of children, each child should be paired up with one or two of them, so that the relationship will be more like that of child and parent.

Emotional needs after three years. Children know that they are inexperienced and dependent. They count on their parents for leadership, love, and security. They watch their parents instinctively and pattern themselves after them. This is how they get their own personalities, their strength of character, their assurance, their ability to cope. They learn in childhood how to be adult citizens, workers, spouses, and parents by identifying with their own parents.

The greatest gift from parents is love, which they express in countless ways: a fond facial expression, spontaneous demonstrations of physical affection, pleasure in their children's accomplishments, comforting them when they are hurt or frightened, controlling them to keep them safe, and, to help them become responsible people, giving them high ideals.

Children gain trust in themselves from being respected as human beings by their parents or caregivers. This self-assurance helps them to be comfortable with themselves and all kinds of people for the rest of their lives. Respect from parents is what teaches children to give respect to their parents in turn.

Learning to be a man or woman. Boys and girls by three years focus on their parents' roles. A boy senses that his destiny is to be a man, so he particularly watches his father—his interests, manner, speech, pleasures; his attitude toward work; his relationships with his wife and with his sons and daughters; how he gets along and copes with other men. A girl's need of a father at this time is not as obvious on the surface but is just as great under-neath. Some of her relationships throughout life will be with males. She gets her ideas about what males are supposed to be primarily by watching her father. The kind of man she eventu-ally falls in love with and marries will probably reflect in one way or another the personality and attitudes of her father: for example, whether he's dominating or gentle, loyal or straying, pompous or humorous.

A mother's personality will be copied in many respects by her admiring daughter. How the mother feels about being a woman, a wife, a mother, a worker will make a strong impression on her daughter. How she gets along specifically with her husband will influence her daughter's future relationship with her own hus-band. A mother is her son's first great love. In obvious or subtle ways, this will determine his romantic ideal. It will influence not only his eventual choice of a wife but also how he gets along with her.

Two parents are preferable. Other things being equal, it is preferable for children to live with two parents (one may be a stepparent) if they love and respect each other. Two parents can emotionally support each other. They can balance or counteract each other's unjustified worries and obsessions about the chil-dren. The children will have a pattern of marital relations to guide them when they are adults. If the parents are of opposite sex, the children will know both sexes both realistically and ide-alistically. If not, special efforts can be made to give children this helpful breadth of experience.

This is not to say that children can't grow up to be healthy with only one parent; many do. If they lack a father, they create one—in their imagination—from what they remember, what their mother has told them, and the appealing characteristics of friendly men they see from time to time. This synthetic father can supply fairly well the masculine image they need. Similarly, a child without a mother creates one from memory, family stories, and relationships with other women. Certainly it would be a great mistake for a parent to make a hasty, unsuitable marriage just to provide a child with a second parent.

PARENTS AS COMPANIONS

Friendly, accepting parents. Boys and girls need the chance to be around their parents, to be enjoyed by them, to do things with them. Unfortunately, working parents are likely to come home wanting most of all to relax after a long day. If they understand how valuable their friendliness is, they will feel more like making a reasonable effort to at least greet the children, answer questions, and show an interest in anything they want to share. This is not to say that the conscientious father or mother should force himself or herself beyond his or her endurance. Better to chat for fifteen minutes enjoyably and say, "Now I'm going to read my paper," than to spend an hour grumpily playing.

A boy needs a friendly father. Sometimes a father is so eager to have his son turn out perfect that it gets in the way of their having a good time together. The man who is eager for his son to become an athlete may take him out at an early age to play catch. Naturally, every throw, every catch, will have its faults. If the father constantly criticizes, even in a friendly tone, the boy becomes uncomfortable inside. It isn't any fun. Also, it gives him the feeling of being no good, in his father's eyes and in his own. A boy comes around to an interest in sports in good time if he's naturally self-confident and outgoing. Sensing the approval of his father helps the boy more than being coached by him does. A game of catch is fine if it's the son's idea and if it's for fun.

A boy doesn't grow spiritually to be a man just because he's born with a male body. The thing that makes him feel and act like a man is being able to pattern himself after men and older boys with whom he is friendly. He can't pattern himself after a person unless he feels that this person likes him and approves of him. If a father is always impatient or irritated with him, the boy is likely to feel uncomfortable not only when he's around his father but also when he's around other men.

So a father who wants to help his son grow up comfortable about being a man shouldn't jump on him when he cries, scorn him when he's playing games with girls, or force him to practice athletics. He should enjoy him when he's around, give him the feeling he's a chip off the old block, share a secret with him, sometimes take him along on excursions.

A girl needs a friendly father, too. A friendly father plays a different but equally important part in the development of a girl. She patterns herself after him only to a limited degree, but she gains confidence in herself as a girl and a woman from feeling his approval. In order not to feel inferior to boys, she should believe that her father would welcome her in backyard sports, on fishing and camping trips, in attendance at ball games, whether or not she wants to accept the invitation. She gains confidence in herself from feeling his interest in her activities, achievements, opinions, and aspirations.

By learning to enjoy the qualities in her father that are particularly masculine, a girl gets ready for her adult life in a world that is half made up of men. The way she makes friendships with boys and men later, the kind of man she eventually falls in love with, the kind of married life she has are all influenced strongly by the kind of relationship she had with her father in her childhood and by the relationship her parents enjoy with one another.

Mothers as companions. Boys and girls need their mother's companionship in more ways than just the time they spend together in their daily routines. They need opportunities for special activities with her, the same way they need them with their father. These might be trips to museums, movies or sporting events or going hiking, shooting baskets, or riding bikes. The point is that it shouldn't be an obligation for the mother; it should be something both she and the children really enjoy.

What about single parents? Children benefit from positive relationships with both their mothers and their fathers. But what if, as is commonly the case, there is only one parent available or the parents are of the same sex? Must the child's psychological well-being inevitably suffer?

The answer to this question is a resounding no. While it is true that children need both male and female role models, they need not live in the same home. What children need most of all is nurturing and love, a consistent presence in their lives of someone who provides emotional support and teaches them the ways of the world. A child growing up with a single parent who can provide these necessities will be far better off than a child whose mother and father neglect his needs because of their own unhappiness. Most children from single-parent families find role models outside the home—a special uncle or aunt, perhaps, or a close friend of the family.

We have learned that children are resilient: Give them what they need and they will blossom. It is the necessities of love, consistency, and care that come first in a child's life. With those in hand, a child can do well in all sorts of different family constellations (see pages 480).

THE FATHER AS PARENT

Shared responsibility. Men have been participating increasingly in all aspects of home and child care, even though as a society we still think of parenting as women's work. There is no reason fathers shouldn't be able to care for their children as well as mothers do and contribute equally to their children's security and development. Everyone in the family benefits when parenting responsibility is shared, even if the division of labor isn't strictly 50-50. But much of the benefit is lost if this work is done as a favor to the wife, since that implies that raising the child is not really the father's responsibility; that he's merely being extraordinarily generous. At its best, parenting occurs in the spirit of equal partnership.

A father with a full-time job, even if the mother is staying at home, will do best by his children, his wife, and himself if he takes on half or more of the management of the children (and also participates in housework) when he is home from work and on weekends. The mother's leadership and patience will probably have worn thin by the end of the day (as would the father's if he were alone with the children all day). Children profit from experiencing a variety of styles of leadership and control by both parents, styles that neither exclude nor demean but enrich and complement the other.

When a father does his share of the work at home as a matter of course, he does much more than simply lighten his wife's work load and give her companionship. It shows that he believes this work is crucial to the welfare of the family, that it calls for judgment and skill, and that it's his responsibility as much as it is hers when he is home. This is what sons and daughters need to see in action if they are to grow up with equal respect for the abilities and roles of men and women.

What fathers can do. In child care, fathers can give bottles, feed solid foods, change diapers (for too long, fathers have gotten away with the clever ruse that they lacked the intelligence, manual dexterity, and visual-motor skills to be capable of changing a smelly diaper), select clothes, wipe away tears, blow noses, bathe, put to bed, read stories, fix toys, break up quarrels, help with questions about homework, explain rules, and assign duties. Fathers can participate in the whole gamut of domestic work: shopping, food preparation, cooking and serving, dishwashing, bed-making, housecleaning, and laundry. Dr. Spock's mother began teaching him these jobs when he was around age seven.

There are increasing numbers of at-home fathers married to

women with full-time jobs, and these men assume the major share of care for the children and home while their children are small. Studies show that as a rule, children raised by such "Mister Moms" grow up as emotionally and mentally healthy as children reared in more traditional families. Fears that boys will somehow grow up as sissies or that girls will grow up unfeminine have no basis in fact.

❦ CLASSIC SPOCK

Pay and prestige have traditionally been men's prime values in twentieth-century America. From my point of view, this emphasis has played a major role in misleading many men into excessive competitiveness, excessive materialism, frequent neglect of relationships with wives and children, neglect of friendships, neglect of community relationships and cultural interests, and stress-related health problems. I don't mean to deny that a sufficient income is absolutely essential for the two-parent family and even more important for the single-parent family. What I am concerned about is that our obsession with getting ahead at work often puts an intolerable strain on family life and makes many women as well as men view the outside job as their central responsibility in life.

I believe that both boys and girls should be raised with a deep conviction that the family is the richest and most enduring source of satisfaction in life. Then women could feel less pressure to accept men's traditional values, and men, freed from their narrow obsession with work and status, could begin to practice women's many skills and try to adopt their values. It will be a great day when fathers and mothers consider the care of their children as important to them as their jobs and careers and when all career decisions are balanced with careful consideration of their effect on family life.

You know, I've talked to a lot of parents. As their children became adults and moved out of the home, not one mother or father has ever said to me that they regretted spending too much time with their families. But I can't tell you how many have regretted that they didn't carve out more time to spend with their families when they had the chance.

SELF-ESTEEM

Self-esteem, not self-satisfaction. Everybody, beginning in childhood, is entitled to a comfortable assumption that she is likable, that she is loved, and that doing her best is good enough. But children don't need to feel satisfied with themselves and appreciated by those around them *all the time*. Parents sometimes feel that they have to constantly compliment their children, whether they deserve it or not, in order to be sure that their children are not deprived of self-esteem. They don't.

Part of self-esteem is self-confidence. Praising a child can build self-confidence, but if the praise isn't genuine, the child will see straight through it. One way of helping your child build self-esteem is to help him cope with a range of emotions and be assured his parents can also deal with a range of emotions. The child who is showered with compliments, only to be insulted when a parent is angry, will not develop self-esteem. Rather, he will be anxious and insecure. Consistency and firm limits do more to build self-esteem than do hollow compliments.

⤖ CLASSIC SPOCK
I find it easier to emphasize and clarify aspects of low self-esteem and its causes, perhaps because my mother was particularly eager to ward off conceit in her children, which she thought of as obnoxious in itself and likely to lead to more serious faults. I still recall today how, when one of her friends complimented me on my looks in adolescence, she hastened to say, after the friend left, "Benny, you are not good-looking. You just have a pleasant smile." All six of her children grew up feeling somewhat unattractive and underachieving.

As a child I was so often reprimanded for "naughty" acts that every time I came home from playing or from school I felt a cloud of guilt around my shoulders. "What have I done wrong?" I would wonder, when actually I had rarely done anything wrong; I was a goody-goody. This was because my mother was so critical, so much on the lookout for misdemeanors, that my five siblings and I felt chronically guilty. When I had occasionally done something slightly wrong, my mother would immediately detect it from my hangdog manner and demand to know what it was. I never tried to deny it; I thought there was no use. I believed she had a magical ability to detect wrongdoing and that the sooner I confessed the sooner the trial, sentencing, and punishment would be over!

I am describing how it worked in our family only to make the point that in the matter of self-esteem the first and most important step, I feel, is not so much to build it up with a succession of compliments as to avoid tearing down the natural self-assurance with which children are born. Then you don't have to run the risks of conceit and excessive self-satisfaction that can result from too much praise.

Most children, even during my childhood, were not given the sense of unworthiness that my stern mother instilled in my siblings and me; and many fewer children today are given even a moderate sense of guilt. Nevertheless, I believe, from noticing what goes on in many families, that the parents still depend for their discipline on scolding or at least on a tone of voice that says, "I expect you to do the wrong thing."

The positive promotion of self-esteem. Children don't need compliments for every act of good behavior or small achievement. Take the example of the child whose parents encourage him to learn to swim by praising him to the skies every time he merely ducks his head underwater. After an hour of this he still demands "Watch me swim" every minute, though he has made no real progress; he has only developed a greater appetite for praise and attention. Excessive compliments don't nurture independence (although they are much less destructive than the opposite, belittling and constant scolding).

Next to avoiding chronic scolding and belittling, the soundest way to foster self-esteem in your child is to show her an *enjoying love*. This means not just a devoted love that proves your readiness to make sacrifices for her but an enjoyment of being with her, of hearing some of her stories and jokes; a spontaneous appreciation of some of her artwork or some of her athletic feats. You also show an enjoying love by occasionally suggesting an unexpected treat, an excursion, or a walk together. It also means showing an attitude of parental respect for the child, such as one might show to a valued friend. This means not being rude, not being disagreeable, not being indifferent to her but instead being polite and gracious. There is no reason for us to feel free to be rude, gruff, or indifferent to our children just because they are younger.

The one mistake most often made by parents who do show respect for their children is a failure to expect respect from them in return. Children, like adults, feel more comfortable and happier when dealing with people who are self-respecting and who naturally as a result show they expect respect from others. You don't have to be disagreeable to convey this expectation. When a child belches loudly at the dinner table, it's more effective to remind him to cover his mouth than to yell at him. Ideally, respect is a two-way street.

The press for achievement. Even though it has been discovered that if you try hard enough, you can teach a two-year-old to read or a one-year-old to recognize flash cards, this is not a wise thing to do. Some parents, armed with the hope that all it takes is the right playthings from infancy and the right mental stimulation at home and in school, try to fashion a precocious, brilliant child. But this kind of parental ambition, though understandable in a country where intelligence is so highly prized, is mistaken and likely to backfire. Mental capacity is only one aspect of a person, and it may well fail to make him or her a success in life unless it is balanced with warmth, common sense, and a respect for others. There are always costs of pushing a child too early to succeed: the relationship between parent and child can become strained and overfocused on intellectual success rather than emotional closeness, and the child may neglect some areas of her development in an attempt to achieve mastery in one targeted area.

Trying to create a superkid is a big, if understandable, mistake that many parents make. Of course we all want our children to make the best use of their talents and to learn as much as they can. But early attempts to artificially inflate those talents are misguided and sometimes detrimental. There is no real evidence that pushing a child early confers any later advantage. Being the first kid on the block to do almost everything doesn't mean that a child will end up any more competent than later bloomers. And artificial precocity always comes with a cost. Attempts to jump ahead in one area—learning to read early, for example—almost always come at the expense of another important area of functioning, such as getting along with other children. Children develop best when their inborn talents and nature are allowed to blossom at their own pace.

BEYOND PARENTING

So far, everything I've said in this chapter has perhaps given the impression that parents are in control of their children's mental health. That's only partially true, of course. There are many other forces that push a child toward greater, or less, mental health. Some of these forces are internal, such as inherited mental and physical illnesses and temperament. Other forces arise within families: Siblings are powerful shapers of a child's emotional landscape, and birth order plays an important role. Still other forces play out in neighborhoods and schools and in society at large, areas where a parent's influence is often very limited. If this book focuses on parents, it's not because all these other forces aren't important—sometimes they're the most important—but because parenting is where you have the most control. Still, it's helpful to think about the other forces that affect your child's mental health, because how you respond to these forces *can* make a difference.

Heredity. We know that many mental and emotional disorders are influenced by a person's genes: that is, by heredity. Depending on the illness, the strength of this influence can be modest or very great. For example, if both parents have manic-depressive (also called bipolar) disorder, the chances are better than 50-50 that the child will, too. Anxiety, obsessive-compulsive disorder, and schizophrenia are all heavily influenced by heredity, as is attention deficit hyperactivity disorder (ADHD), and many others.

In fact, it is likely that genes play a role in *every* mental health problem, either increasing or decreasing a child's susceptibility to life's challenges (what psychologists sometimes call the "environment"). Differences in susceptibility explain in part why two children raised by the same parents in the same household often follow very different mental health paths. The other part, of course, is that even in the same family, the challenges (environment) can be quite different for different children.

Heredity also works in more subtle ways, by affecting a child's temperament, or style of behaving. One child is bubbly and outgoing; another is quiet and observant. One child seems to respond to small changes in temperature, noise, or light level; another barely seems to notice. One child always approaches situations with a positive outlook; another starts with a negative attitude and has be won over to the positive.

Children who are often negative, intense, and persistent have been said to have a difficult temperament or, worse, to be difficult children. But it's clear that temperamental patterns are either difficult or easy in relation to what is expected of a child. The temperaments of most six-year-old boys, with their high need for physical activity, for example, are difficult in the context of most first-grade classrooms, which demand a lot of sitting still. You can't choose your child's temperament, but by understanding and accepting it, you can choose to respond in ways that help your child learn to function well with you and with peers, and other adults.

Siblings. Parenting books often ignore the crucial role that siblings play in a child's growing up. But if you think about your own childhood, you'll probably agree that siblings—or the lack of them, if you are an only child—had a tremendous effect on your personality. Perhaps you modeled yourself after an older brother or sister who seemed to be able to do everything right, or maybe you chose to do very different things to stake out your own territory. If you were lucky, your siblings supported you; but if you had siblings who didn't (or don't) mesh well with your personality, you know how very difficult that can be.

There are ways for parents to take some of the edge off sibling jealousy (see page 529), but whether siblings really like each other or just tolerate each other depends a lot on chance. Siblings who are close in age and compatible in temperament may be lifelong best friends. Siblings whose temperaments clash may never feel truly comfortable and relaxed together.

Parents often reproach themselves because they feel differently about each of their children. But they are expecting the impossible of themselves. Good parents love their children equally in the sense that they are devoted to each, want the best for all, and will make any necessary sacrifices to achieve it. But since children are all different, no parent can feel the same about any two of them. It's human, normal, and inevitable that we feel differently about each of our children, that we should be impatient with characteristics in some and proud of others. It is the acceptance and understanding of these different feelings, rather than feeling guilty about them, that allows us to treat each of our children with the love and special attention he or she needs.

Birth order and spacing. It's fascinating how birth order seems to influence a person's personality. For example, oldest children tend to be task-oriented leaders and organizers. Youngest children are often spontaneous, self-involved, and a bit irresponsible. Middle children have less clear-cut roles and often end up defining themselves outside their families of origin. Only children tend to combine the characteristics of an oldest child (high-achieving, for example) and a youngest one (attention seeking, for example).

These are only generalizations, of course. The dynamics of each family are unique. For example, if more than five years have passed between children, a youngest child might respond in some ways like an only child; if there is only about a year between children, they may act like twins. If the oldest child refuses to take over leadership of the siblings, a younger child may take on that role. A parent who is herself an oldest child may get along well with her own oldest but find her youngest child to be annoying (like her youngest sibling). As a parent, you may be able to understand these forces, but you really can't control them.

Peers and school. After age six to seven, the peer group becomes increasingly important. A child's manner of speaking and dress and what he likes to speak about, are all likely to be colored, if not controlled, by kids in the neighborhood, at school, and on television. If baggy pants and untied laces are in, there's nothing any parent can do to make shorts and loafers cool.

Sometimes, neighborhood and peer forces may actively threaten a child's mental health. For example, children who are bullied (or who are themselves bullies) may be at greater risk of developing long-term behavior disturbances. The child who doesn't fit in at school and has no friends is at high risk for depression. As a parent, you often have to step back and let your child deal with the challenges of peer relationships. At other times though, you may have to step in (more on page 665).

RAISING CHILDREN IN A TROUBLED SOCIETY

American society is extraordinarily stressful. Normal family tensions are heightened in many ways: our society is excessively competitive and materialistic, many working parents find less satisfaction and pleasure at their jobs while finding the good day care they depend on more difficult. There is less spiritual and moral direction than in the past, the traditional supports of the extended family and community are breaking up, and a growing number of people are concerned that the environment and international relations are deteriorating.

ᕦ CLASSIC SPOCK
I believe that there are two changes needed to relieve these tensions and move toward a more stable society. The first is to raise our children with different, more positive ideals. Children raised with strong values beyond their own needs—cooperation, kindness, honesty, tolerance of diversity—will grow up to help others, strengthen human relations, and bring about world security. Living by these values will bring far greater pride and fulfillment than the superficial success of a high-paying position or a new luxury car. The second change is for us to reclaim our government from the influence of giant corporate interests that care little for human individuals, the environment, or world peace, and whose only aim is maximal profit. We must become much more politically active, so that our government will serve the needs of all citizens.

To find out more about the local, state, and national groups that are working on the problems that concern you the most, you can write to the Children's Defense Fund, 25 East Street, NW, Washington DC 20001 (or go to www.childrensdefense.org). The fund has worked with Congress for over twenty years on the programs most needed by children and families.

WORK AND CHILD CARE

———— ⚬⚬ ————

FAMILY AND CAREER

We've gone from the idea that a woman's work is in the home to the idea that a woman is working only if she has a paying job. Neither idea makes sense. Raising children is challenging and creative work. On the other hand, if a mother knows that she needs a career or a certain kind of job for fulfillment, she should not give it up simply for the sake of her child. Children do not benefit in the long term from such sacrifices; they need happy parents. For that matter, fathers who find fulfillment in taking care of children ought to be encouraged to make that choice. A growing number are doing just that.

Nonparent infant care. The majority of American children under one year of age now spend at least part of their day in the care of someone other than their parents. But even though nonparent infant child care has been the norm for more than a decade, it's still controversial. Studies periodically come out showing that it is, or isn't, harmful in one way or another to the average child. These studies are interesting to social scientists but not particularly helpful for parents who have to make choices. You are not the average parent, and your child is not the average child. The bottom line in these studies is that if you choose child care, find *high-quality* care (more on this below).

Parents often have mixed feelings about returning to work when their infants are young. They may feel eager to get back on the job, if only to have adults to talk with during the day. But they often also feel sad about leaving their babies, anxious that something will go wrong while they are away or that their babies will forget them, jealous of mothers who are staying home, or guilty. They feel they have to choose between their jobs and their babies. It is a terribly tough decision. Then again, many mothers feel that they have no choice. They need the money. One working mother of a two-week-old who planned to return to her job in another month told me, "I've already begun to miss him." If you can find a way to take more time off with your new baby, even if it results in financial sacrifice, you may be happier in the long run.

The Family and Medical Leave Act. This 1993 federal law is a fine example of a progressive, family-centered policy that came about as a result of pressure from many child advocate groups. It requires employers with more than fifty employees to allow up to twelve weeks of unpaid leave to a mother or father after the birth or adoption of a child. Twelve weeks is really a minimum, I think. In other technologically advanced countries, new mothers are allowed far longer with their babies before they have to return to their jobs. Even so, many American mothers feel that they cannot realistically stay out the full twelve weeks.

How long a leave should you take? As a general rule, the longer, the better. Taking three to six months off is great if you can manage it. This gives your baby time to settle in to pretty regular feeding and sleeping routines and to become used to the rhythm of her family. It also gives you time to adjust to your own physiological and psychological changes, establish nursing, and add a bottle or two during work hours. By about four months, most babies are showing more interest in the world around them, so the process of separating for several hours a day is more acceptable to most parents.

Remember, fathers can also provide child care. If the mother can take the first six weeks and the father can take over for the next six, that gives you twelve weeks before starting child care.

☜ CLASSIC SPOCK

Should you send your child to day care? I think this is a very personal decision that must be based on your family's needs. If you want to send your infant to day care, I wouldn't feel at all guilty about it. He'll do just fine, so long as the quality of the care is high. In the long run, children do best when their parents are happy and fulfilled. It's much better for a child to attend a good day-care center than to be at home with a parent who is lonely and miserable and who resents staying at home all day with the baby. On the other hand, if you do choose to stay home full time with your baby for as long as possible, that's a wonderful choice also. I think the advocates on both sides do a disservice to parents when they imply that there is only one way to handle the situation. The best situation is the one that works best for your family.

TIME WITH YOUR CHILD

Quality time. When both parents or a single parent have outside jobs, they usually try to arrange work schedules that will give them maximum time with their young children. In two-parent families, the attention of one parent at a time can be quite satisfying to children. Preschool children may be allowed to stay up late in the evenings if it is possible for them to sleep late in the mornings or nap at day care. The number of hours of companionship is less important than the quality or spirit of the time spent together. This is what's behind the expression "quality time."

From a practical point of view, quality time implies interactions that are close, nurturing, and lovingly responsive. Quality time can occur while driving, at mealtimes, or at any time together. Trips to the supermarket or department store can always be enhanced with time for talking and listening and teaching. So quality time does not imply doing anything out of the ordinary. It is the accumulated day-to-day interactions, not trips to the circus, that have the most profound effect on a child's development.

The idea of quality time itself is fine. But conscientious, hardworking parents may think they have an obligation to talk, play, or read with their children long after the parents' patience and enjoyment have run out. Parents who regularly ignore their own needs and wishes to provide quality time for their children may come to resent the sacrifice; then the spirit of friendliness and responsiveness dissipates. And a child who senses that he can make his parent give him more time than the parent feels like giving, may become pesky and demanding.

Another concern about the expression quality time: Some parents misinterpret the phrase to mean that it really doesn't matter how much time they spend with their children, as long as the time they *do* spend is jam-packed with quality. But *quantity* of time is also important: time spent together in unexciting tasks with mundane interactions. Children need to simply be around their parents, watching them in action, learning from their day-to-day example, and knowing they are an important part of their lives. The trick is to find the right balance: to spend as much time as possible with your children but not at the expense of fulfilling some of your own personal needs.

Special time. "Special time" is a pleasant way to make sure there is at least some quality time every day. Special time is a brief period—five to fifteen minutes is usually plenty—that you set aside every day to spend with each child individually. What's special about special time is not what you actually do with your child; what's special is that it is your personal, exclusive time together, when your child gets your undivided attention. Taking away special time should never be done as a punishment. Your child deserves a little special time each day simply by virtue of being your child and being loved. Special time is a powerful way to connect with your child.

The temptation to spoil. Working parents may find that because they are starved for their child's company and perhaps feel guilty about seeing her so little, they are inclined to shower her with presents and treats, bow to all her wishes regardless of their own, and generally let her get away with murder. Appeasing a child doesn't satisfy her and is likely to make her greedy.

It's fine for working parents to show their child as much agreeableness and affection as comes naturally, but they should also feel free to stop when they're tired, consider their own desires, avoid giving daily presents, spend only what money is sensible, and expect reasonable politeness and consideration from their children. In other words, they should act like self-confident, all-day parents. Not only will the children turn out better; they will enjoy their company more.

CHILD CARE ALTERNATIVES

Some parents are able to arrange their work schedules to allow one or the other to be at home most of the time; a sitter can fill in the rest. If this solution is not possible, there are four types of day care to choose from: care by relatives, in-home care, family day care, and group care. Each has its advantages and disadvantages.

Altered work schedules. Often the best situation is one in which the parents' work schedules can be altered, so that both can work full time yet one can be at home for most of the day. Industrial workers can sometimes arrange to work different shifts, or an employer may offer flexibility in working hours. Of course, parents need to be together at sleeping times as well as for some of the child's waking hours. A nonparent caregiver can fill in any uncovered hours. A relative with whom the parents see eye to eye may be an ideal fill-in caregiver.

Another solution is for one or both parents to cut down to a part-time job for two to three years, until the child is old enough to attend preschool or a day-care center. This solution is of course out of reach for those families that require two full-time breadwinners to meet their expenses.

In-home caregivers (sitters). Some working parents engage a housekeeper or caregiver ("caregiver" is a more meaningful word than "sitter") to come to their home. If the caregiver works several hours a day, this person may well become the second most formative influence on the young child's developing personality, after the parents. So parents should find a person who shows much the same kind of love, interest, responsiveness, and control as they do.

The most important trait is the person's disposition. She should be affectionate, understanding, comfortable, sensible, and self-confident. (Of course, a paid caregiver may be male.) She should love and enjoy children without smothering them with attention. She should be able to control them without nagging or severity. In other words, she should happily get along with them. It is a help when interviewing a prospective caregiver to have your child with you. You can better tell how she responds to a child by her actions than by what she says. Avoid one who is cross, reproving, fussy, humorless, or full of theories about raising children.

A common mistake that parents make is to look primarily for a person with a lot of experience. It's natural that they should feel more comfortable leaving a child with someone who knows what to do for colic or croup. But illnesses and injuries are a very small part of a child's life. It's the minutes and hours of every day that count. Experience is fine when it's combined with the right personality. With the wrong personality, it's worth very little.

Cleanliness and carefulness are more important than experience. You can't let someone make the baby's formula who refuses to do it correctly. Still, there are many untidy people who are careful when it's important to be so. Better a person who is too casual than one who is too fussy.

Some parents focus on the education of a caregiver. But education is less important than a caregiver's personal qualities, especially with young children. Others are concerned that the caregiver may speak little English. But most children are not confused by the different languages of the caregiver and parents. If the caregiver stays with the child for a long time, the child may reap the benefits of having learned two languages in his early years.

Sometimes inexperienced young parents settle for a caregiver about whom they don't really feel right, because they've decided they can't do any better or the person talks a good line. The parents should keep looking until they find someone they really like.

Concerns about caregivers. A common problem is that a caregiver may favor the youngest child in the family, especially one born after she joined the household. She may call that one "Granny's baby," for example. If she can't understand the harm in doing this, she should not stay. Favoritism of this sort is destructive to both the child who is favored and the ones who are not.

There's also the very common—and human—concern as to whose child it is. Some caregivers have a great need to take over the child, push the parents aside, and show that they always know best. They may be quite unconscious of this need and can rarely be reformed. It's natural for parents to be unconsciously jealous when they see that their child has become dependent upon and affectionate toward a caregiver. This may make them excessively critical—even disrespectful—of the caregiver. If a caregiver is any good, a child will certainly become attached to her, and the parents may have twinges of jealousy. But if they are conscious of this and face it honestly, they can adjust to it. Children who come to love their sitters don't love their parents any less.

In a sense, then, the most important questions for caregivers and parents are whether they can be honest with themselves, listen to each other's ideas and criticisms, keep the lines of communication open, respect each other's good points and good intentions, and cooperate for the benefit of the children.

Care by relatives. It's great if there's a relative—a grandparent, for example—who can take care of your child. But all of the issues that apply to un-related caregivers, as discussed above, also apply to family. It's very important that any family member who helps care for your child understands that you are still the parent, that what you say goes. As long as you have this understanding, care by a relative can be a wonderful alternative.

Day-care centers. Day-care center is a term used to specify out-of-home group care of children during their parents' working hours, often 8 A.M. to 6 P.M. Some day-care centers are subsidized by government agencies or employers. At its best, day care offers the advantages of the preschool: an educational philosophy, trained teachers, and full educational equipment.

Day-care centers in the United States originated during World War II, when the federal government wanted to encourage mothers with young children to work in war industries. At the beginning primarily for the care of children from age two to five, they now frequently provide care for younger children, including infants, and after-school care for kindergartners and first and second graders.

Day-care centers are usually open year-round. They offer a stable, structured setting with an explicit child-care philosophy that you can evaluate. However, this type of care is often expensive. Also, the staff turnover is typically high, so it's likely that your child won't consistently be cared for by the same person. The level of training of the staff and the child-to-staff ratio are variable. There are great differences in the quality of day-care centers, as there are with the other types of child care. Day-care centers are often licensed and may be accredited as well (see page 413).

Family day care. Family day cares, where a provider and one or two assistants look after a small number of children in the provider's home, are a popular choice. In fact, many more children attend family day cares than larger day-care centers. Family day care may be more convenient and affordable than large day-care centers and more flexible in its hours. A smaller, familylike atmosphere may be more comfortable for a young child. Staff turnover is usually less of a problem, so children have the opportunity to develop trusting relationships with one or two care providers—a very good thing.

On the other hand, many family day cares are unlicensed and unaccredited (see page 414). Therefore, it's harder to be sure that basic health and safety measures are in place. Also, because there are fewer adults involved, the potential for abuse or neglect of children is higher. So if you choose a family day care, it's very important that you feel completely comfortable with the providers and are welcome to drop in any time and stay as long as you want. Your child should be glad to go to the day care. When you pick your child up, you should hear from the staff what your child did during the day.

Is day care good for young children? There is a raging debate in the United States whether day care is good or bad for very young children. Some claim that group experiences are inappropriate for children in the first few years of life. The opponents of day care worry that children raised at an early age by multiple caregivers will have difficulty with subsequent interpersonal relationships. They contend that there is no better teacher for a child than an intensely involved parent.

Advocates of day care tell a different story. They assert that there are many proper ways to raise a young child. They point to cultures in which infants are raised by siblings and extended family without apparent ill effects. They remind us that there are no studies demonstrating that high-quality day care is harmful to the emotional development of children. They worry that parents who work and send their infants to day care will feel needlessly guilty that they are somehow hurting their child. Infants are resilient creatures up to a certain point, and there is no reason why high-quality day care should harm their development. Children need adults who are devoted to them, whether it's a single parent or a team of day-care teachers. They need consistency in their relationships, but this can be provided both at home and in many day-care centers.

In fact, carefully done studies show that high-quality day care—of small groups of children by carefully selected, well-trained teachers—is not harmful for most children. Exposure to caring adults and other children in a safe, stimulating environment can promote curiosity and learning. On the other hand, if large groups of children are cared for by poorly trained teachers, the experience has the opposite effect. One finding is especially interesting. Children who go to group day care for an extended period tend to be more oriented toward and responsive to their peers than to adults, and some boys show more aggressive behavior. Children who do not attend group care tend to be more oriented toward adults and less responsive to their peers. Will this difference affect a child's later functioning in school or persist into adulthood? Nobody knows.

Everyone agrees that the quality of day care is a critical factor for children's well-being. Responsive, nurturing, stimulating, consistent care is vital; the kind of care provided by a stable, well-trained staff in a well-funded day-care setting. Unfortunately, there are nowhere near enough day-care centers with such high standards. And what few there are are too expensive for the average family. The only solution is unending political pressure for local and federal support for high-quality child-care programs.

Child care as partnership. All the adults who take part in caring for a child should see themselves as partners. Parents and nonparent caregivers need to share information and insights and support each other. If your child has worked very hard at a particular challenge in day care—say, using a crayon—you ought to hear about it when you pick her up in the evening. In the same way, if your child was often up during the night because of a thunderstorm, the child-care provider needs to hear about that in the morning.

When I was a young doctor studying child development, some of my most important lessons came from the teachers at my daughter's day-care center. I would make a point of spending fifteen to twenty minutes at the end of the day or sometimes in the morning, sitting on the floor with the teachers and children. I learned a lot about parenting by watching those very skillful professionals at work. If you can develop a relationship of cooperation and mutual respect with your child's caregiver, your child will benefit and you as a parent will benefit too.

CHOOSING DAY CARE

Finding programs. First you need to compile a list of the available day cares or preschools in your community. Start with friends who can give you personal recommendations. Go online (public libraries offer free internet access) to the website for Child Care Aware (www.childcareaware.org), and follow the instructions to locate the child care resource and referral organization for your area. These nonprofit organizations help parents find appropriate child care. They provide lists of programs, information about licensing and accreditation, group size, and other important aspects.

Calls and visits. Call the programs on your list to find out if they offer the kind of care you want. Ask for the names and phone numbers of families willing to serve as references. Call them and ask about the details of the care, including the use of physical punishment and other disciplinary techniques. Visit sites and watch for warm, nurturing interactions between the caregivers and children, appropriate supervision and safety measures, and activities appropriate to the children's development. Are the children relaxed? Do they trust the teachers and turn to them for help? Do they cooperate with other children and have few fights? A friendly relationship between teachers and children will show in the relationships among the children.

Visit the day-care center regularly. Unannounced visits during the day can reassure you that all is well. Parents should feel welcome at the school, and their visits should be allowed at any time.

Licensing and accreditation. If a child-care center or home day care is licensed, it provides the level of safety required by the state. For example, licensed programs have to meet specific standards for fire safety and infection control. Accreditation is different. To be accredited, a program has to meet higher standards for quality of care, including the training of providers, group size, space, equipment, and educational activities. A well-trained provider is more likely to understand what your child needs and to respond in a way that supports your child's development. Accreditation is provided by national organizations, such as the National Association for the Education of Young Children (NAEYC). For much more about licensing and accreditation and child care in general, you can go to www.naeyc.org and www.childcareaware.org.

Group size. One of the most important features of high-quality child care programs is that each child receives individual attention. For that to happen, groups or classrooms must not be too large, and no single adult can be responsible for too many children. The younger the child, the more individual attention he needs. The National Association for the Education of Young Children recommends the following maximum group sizes:

Child's age	Maximum number of children per adult	Maximum number of children in a group
Infants (birth to 12 months)	4	8
Toddlers (12 to 24 months)	4 or 5	12 (with 3 teachers) or 10 (with 2 teachers)
2-year-olds (24 to 30 months)	6	12
2½-year-olds (30 to 36 months)	7	14
3, 4, and 5 year olds	10	20
Kindergartners	12	24
6- to 12-year-olds	15	30

AFTER-SCHOOL CARE

After age six, and even more so after age eight, children seek and enjoy independence. They turn for their ideals and companionship to adults who are not their parents, especially to good teachers, and to other children. Although they can get along comfortably for hours at a time without needing an adult's support, they still benefit from knowing that they belong somewhere, particularly after school. A motherly or fatherly neighbor may be able to substitute until one of the working parents comes home. After-school play centers are valuable to all children, particularly to those whose parents work.

Latchkey children. Because of the lack of affordable, good-quality after-school play centers or groups, there are millions of latchkey children in our country. After school, they let themselves into their apartments or houses with their own keys and fend for themselves until a parent comes home from work.

A responsible, self-reliant child can do well caring for herself, provided she feels secure and has enough to do. Careful planning can help both the parent and child to feel confident. It's important that latchkey children know how to reach their parents if they need to and have a nearby adult to turn to in an emergency. They need careful safety instructions: what to say when answering the phone or when a stranger knocks at the door, for example. They need to know what they can do—for example, how much television is okay—and what is off-limits.

Although you may think that older children would do better than younger ones in self-care, that's not always true. Teens who have a lot of unsupervised time are more likely to engage in risky behaviors, such as smoking, using drugs and alcohol, and having sex. Teens (like toddlers) often feel more comfortable with firm limits on their behavior, even though they protest.

BABYSITTERS

Babysitters are a boon to parents and can help a child to develop independence. It's important that you and your child know your sitter well. Let's assume that it's a woman (though there is no reason why it should not be a man). For night-sitting with a baby who doesn't waken, it may be necessary only for the sitter to be sensible and dependable. But for babies who waken, the sitter should be a person the child knows and likes. It is frightening to most children to waken and find a stranger.

You can learn about capable sitters or a reliable agency

through friends whose judgment you trust. Watch the sitter in action with your children to make sure that she understands and loves children and can manage them with kindness and firmness. Engage the sitter a few times when you will be there with her for a while. The young children can get used to her before she herself has to do much for them. As the children gradually accept her, she can do more for them. It is important that you stick to one or two sitters as much as possible.

To keep things straight, it's sensible to have a permanent notebook for the sitter, listing the child's routine, some of the things she may ask for (in her words), the telephone numbers of the doctor and a neighbor to call in an emergency if you can't be reached, bedtime hours, what in the kitchen the sitter may help herself to, the whereabouts of linen, nightclothes, and other things that may be needed, and how to turn the furnace up or down. Most of all, you should know your sitter and know that your child trusts her.

Young or old? It's a matter of maturity and spirit rather than years. There are children as young as fourteen who are extremely capable and dependable, though it's unfair to expect such qualities in most people that age. Some adults may prove unreliable or harsh or ineffectual. One older person has a knack with children; another is too inflexible or too anxious to adapt to a new child. Many communities have babysitter training courses, offered through the Red Cross or local hospitals, that cover safety and first aid procedures. It makes sense to select a sitter who has had this sort of training. With a young sitter—a junior high or high school student, for example—it's reassuring to know that the sitter's parents are at home and available if a true emergency arises.

DISCIPLINE

WHAT DISCIPLINE IS

Discipline does not mean punishment. When most people use the word discipline, what they really mean is punishment. While punishment is a part of discipline (hopefully, only a small part), it is by no means the whole story. Discipline comes from the word disciple. It really means to teach.

That is the true goal of discipline: to teach children the rules of behavior, what behavior society and other people expect from them, so that they grow up to be socially productive, as well as personally fulfilled, individuals.

Of course you can create a harsh system of rewards and punishments so that, like good little robots, your children will behave perfectly most of the time. But what would be the effect on the child's spirit, on his sense of self-worth, on his personal happiness, on his feelings toward others?

On the other hand, imagine a child whose every whim is indulged, whose every action, good or bad, is lavishly praised. Such a child might have a certain measure of happiness, but most people wouldn't want to be within ten feet of him.

Your delicate task is to teach your child the how and the why of acceptable behavior but never at the expense of his sense of self-worth and optimism.

Strict or casual discipline? This looms as a big question for many new parents. Most find their own balance in a little while, but for a few parents it remains a worrisome question, no matter how much experience they've had.

Another word used for a casual approach to discipline is permissiveness. This word means different things to different people. To some it implies merely an easygoing, casual style of management; to others it means foolishly overindulging a child, letting him do or have anything he wants.

The choice between strictness or casualness is not the most important issue. Good-hearted parents who aren't afraid to be firm when it is necessary may get good results with either moderate strictness or moderate casualness. On the other hand, a strictness that comes from harsh feelings or an excessive permissiveness that is timid or vacillating may have poor results. The real issue is what spirit the parent puts into managing the child and what attitude is instilled in the child as a result.

Stick to your convictions. Parents who naturally lean toward strictness should probably raise their children that way. Moderate strictness—requiring good manners, prompt obedience, and orderliness—is not harmful to children so long as the parents are basically kind and the children are growing up happy and friendly. But strictness is harmful when parents are overbearing, harsh, and chronically disapproving or when they make no allowances for a child's age and individuality. This kind of severity produces children who are either meek and colorless or mean-spirited.

Parents who incline to an easygoing style of management, are satisfied with casual manners as long as the child's attitude is friendly, or happen not to be particularly strict—for instance, about promptness or neatness—can also raise children who are considerate and cooperative, as long as the parents are not afraid to be firm about those matters that are important to them.

When parents get unhappy results from too much permissiveness, it is not so much that they demand too little, as it is that they are timid or guilty about what they ask or are unconsciously encouraging the child to rule the roost.

If parents are hesitant in asking for reasonable behavior—because they have misunderstood theories of self-expression, are self-sacrificing by nature, or afraid of having their children dislike them—they can't help resenting the bad behavior that comes instead. They keep getting angry underneath without really knowing what to do about it. This bothers their children, too. It is apt to make them feel guilty and scared, and it also makes them meaner and all the more demanding. If, for example, babies acquire a taste for staying up in the evening and their parents are afraid to deny them this pleasure, they may turn into disagreeable tyrants who keep their mothers and fathers awake for hours. Parents are bound to dislike them for their tyranny. If parents can learn to be firm and consistent in their expectations, it's amazing how fast the children will sweeten up, and the parents will, too.

In other words, parents can't feel right toward their children in the long run unless they can get them to behave reasonably, and children can't be happy unless they behave reasonably.

ᢁ CLASSIC SPOCK

The question of permissiveness. Though I've been accused of permissiveness, I don't consider myself permissive at all, and all the people who've used this book and spoken to me about it feel the same way. The people who call me permissive all admit that they haven't read the book and wouldn't use it. The accusation came for the first time in 1968, twenty-two years after the book came out, from a prominent clergyman who objected strongly to my opposition to the war in Vietnam. He said that my advice to parents to give "instant gratification" to their babies and children was what made these babies grow up to be irresponsible, undisciplined, unpatriotic young adults who opposed their country's war in Vietnam.

There is no instant gratification in this book. I've always advised parents to respect their children but to remember to ask for respect for themselves, to give firm, clear leadership, and to ask for cooperation and politeness.

The parent who shies away from discipline. Quite a few parents shy away from guiding and controlling their children (though they may often play with them), leaving most of this work to their spouse. Mothers who aren't sure of themselves may get into the habit of saying, "Just wait until your father gets home!" Fathers may hide behind the newspaper or remain glued to the television set when a crisis occurs. Some of the nonparticipating fathers explain, when their wives reproach them, that they don't want their children to resent them. Instead they want to be pals with their children. It's good for children to have friendly parents who will play with them, but children need parents to act like parents. They will have many friends in their lifetime but only one set of parents.

When a parent is timid or reluctant to give leadership, the children feel let down, like vines without a pole to grow on. When parents are afraid to be definite and firm, their children keep testing the limits, making life difficult for both them and themselves, until the parents are finally provoked into cracking down. The parents are then likely to feel ashamed and back off again.

The father who avoids the disciplinary role simply forces his wife to discipline for two. Moreover, he doesn't end up with the friendly relationship he seeks. Children know that misbehavior irritates adults. When they are dealing with a father who pretends not to notice, they are uneasy. The children may imagine that he is concealing an anger much more dangerous than it really is. Some children may fear this kind of father more than the one who participates freely in their management and expresses his irritation. With an expressive father, children have opportunities to learn what his displeasure means and how to deal with it. They find out that they can survive it. This gives them a kind of self-assurance, just as they gain confidence when they overcome their fears and learn to swim or ride a bike.

Confusion about discipline. In traditional societies, where ideas about children stay the same generation after generation, most parents have no doubt about the best way to raise and discipline their children. By contrast, in the United States, ideas about children have changed so rapidly that many parents are confused. Many of these changes have been driven by science. In the past century, psychologists, psychiatrists, and other scientists have made many important discoveries about children and child-rearing. For example, they have discovered that children need the love of good parents more than anything else; that they work hard, by themselves, to be more grown up and responsible; that many of those who get into the most trouble suffer more from a lack of affection than a lack of punishment; that children are eager to learn if they are instructed in ways that are right for their age and are taught by understanding teachers; that some jealous feelings toward brothers and sisters and occasional angry feelings toward parents are natural; that a childish interest in the facts of life and some aspects of sex is normal; that harsh repression of aggressive feelings and sexual interest may lead to an anxious child; that unconscious thoughts are as influential as conscious ones; that each child is an individual and should be allowed to be one.

All these ideas sound commonplace today, but when first expressed they were very startling. Many of them ran counter to beliefs that had been held for centuries. It is not possible to change so many ideas about the nature and needs of children without mixing up a lot of parents. Parents who had a comfortable childhood were least confused. They may have been interested in hearing about these new ideas but when it came to actually managing their children, they did it in much the same way they were brought up themselves. This is the natural way to learn child care: from having been a child in a happy family.

The parents who have trouble with the new ideas are usually those who aren't happy about their own upbringing. Many of them feel both resentful and guilty about the strained relations that existed between themselves and their parents. They don't want their own children to feel that way about them, so they welcome new theories. But they often read meanings into them that are not what the scientists intended. They may assume, for instance, that *all* that children need is love; that they shouldn't be made to conform; that they should be allowed to express their aggressive feelings toward parents and others; that whenever anything goes wrong, it's the parents' fault; that when children misbehave, the parents shouldn't get angry or punish them but should try to show them more love.

All of these misconceptions are unworkable if carried too far. They encourage children to become demanding and disagreeable. They make children feel guilty about their excessive misbehavior. They make parents strive to be superhuman. When children behave badly, the parents try to suppress their anger for a while, but eventually they have to explode. Then they feel guilty and bewildered. This leads to more misbehavior on the child's part.

Some parents—who may themselves be very polite people—allow their children to be surprisingly obnoxious, not only to themselves but also to outsiders. They don't seem to see what is going on. When studied carefully, some of these situations reveal that the parents were always compelled to be much too good as children and to suppress all their natural resentment. Now they get a subtle pleasure from letting their own flesh and blood act out all the disagreeableness they themselves had to bottle up, pretending all the time that this is in accord with the best modern theories of child-rearing.

Guilt gets in the way. There are many situations in which parents may always feel a bit guilty toward one child or another. There are obvious cases: the mother who goes to work without first settling in her own mind whether she is neglecting her child; parents who have a child with a physical or mental handicap; parents who have adopted a baby and can't get over the feeling that they have to do a superhuman job; parents who have been brought up with so much disapproval that they always feel guilty until they are proved innocent; parents who studied child psychology in college and therefore know all the pitfalls and feel they have to do a superior job.

Whatever the cause of the guilt, it tends to get in the way of easy management of a child. The parents are inclined to expect too little from the child and too much from themselves. They often try to be patient and sweet-tempered even after their overworked patience is really exhausted and the child has gotten out of hand and needs definite correction. Or they vacillate when the child needs firmness.

A child, like an adult, knows when she is getting away with too much naughtiness or rudeness, even when her parents close their eyes to it. She feels guilty inside. She would like to be stopped. But if she isn't corrected, she's likely to behave increasingly worse. It's as if she is saying, "How bad do I have to be before somebody stops me?"

Eventually her behavior becomes so provoking that her parents' patience snaps. They scold or punish her. Peace is restored. But the trouble with parents who feel guilty is that they are ashamed of having lost their temper. So instead of letting well enough alone, they try to undo the correction, or they let the child punish them in return. Perhaps they permit the child to be rude to them in the middle of the punishment, take back the penalty before it has been half paid, or pretend not to notice when the child misbehaves again. In some situations, if the child does not retaliate at all, a parent begins to subtly provoke her to do so—without realizing, of course, what she or he is up to. This may sound complicated or unnatural to you. If you can't imagine a parent's letting a child get away with murder or, worse still, encouraging it, it shows only that you yourself don't have a problem with guilt feelings. Guilt isn't a rare problem, though.

Many conscientious parents occasionally let a child get out of hand when they feel they have been unfair or neglectful, but most soon recover their balance. However, when a parent says, "Everything this child does or says rubs me the wrong way," it's a pretty good sign that the parent feels overguilty and is chronically submissive and permissive and that the child reacts to this with constant provocation. No child can be that irritating by accident.

If parents can determine in which respects they may be too permissive and can firm up their discipline, they may be delighted to find that their child becomes not only better behaved but much happier. Then they can really love their child better, and the child in turn will respond to this.

PUNISHMENT

Is punishment necessary? Many good parents feel that they have to punish their children once in a while. Others find that they can successfully manage without ever having to. A lot depends on how the parents were brought up. If they were occasionally punished for good reason, they naturally expect to have to punish in similar situations. If they were kept in line by positive guidance alone, they are likely to find that they can do the same with their children.

On the other hand, there are a fair number of poorly behaved children. The parents of some of them punish a lot; the parents of others never do. So we can't say either that punishment always works or that the lack of it always works. It depends on the general nature of the parents' discipline.

Before we go further with the subject of punishment, we ought to realize that it is never the main element in discipline, only a vigorous reminder that the parents feel strongly about what they say. We have all seen children who were punished plenty and yet remained ill-behaved.

The main source of good discipline is growing up in a loving family, being loved and learning to love in return. We want to be kind and cooperative (most of the time) because we like people and want them to like us. (Many habitual criminals are people who in childhood were never loved enough to make much difference to them. Many of them were also abused or were witnesses to significant violence and turmoil.) Children gradually reduce their grabbing and begin to share somewhere around the age of three, not primarily because they are reminded by their parents—though that may help—but because their feelings of enjoyment and affection toward other children have sufficiently developed.

Another vital element is children's intense desire to be as much like their parents as possible. They work particularly hard at being polite, civilized, and responsible in the period from three to six. They play very seriously at taking care of their dolls, keeping house, and going out to work, as they see their parents do.

Firmness and consistency. The everyday job of the parent is to keep the child on the right track using firmness and consistency. Though children do the major share of civilizing themselves, through love and imitation, there is still plenty of work left for parents to do. In automobile terms, the child supplies the power; the parents do the steering. Some children are more challenging than others—they may be more active, impulsive, and stubborn—and it takes more energy to keep them on the road.

Children's motives are good most of the time, but they need guidance. The parents need to say, "We hold hands when we cross the street," "You can't play with that; it may hurt someone," "Say thank you to Mrs. Griffin," "Let's go in now, because there is a surprise for lunch," "We have to leave the wagon here because it belongs to Harry, and he wants it," "It's time to go to bed so you'll grow big and strong," and so on.

How well this guidance works depends on whether the parents are reasonably consistent (nobody can be completely consistent), mean what they say (not just sounding off), and direct or prohibit the child for a good reason (not just because they feel like being bossy).

When it makes sense to punish. You don't sit by and watch a small child destroy something then punish him afterward. You resort to punishment, if you use it at all, once in a while, when your system of firmness breaks down.

The best test of a punishment is whether it accomplishes what you are after without having harmful effects. If it makes a child furious, defiant, and worse-behaved than before, it certainly isn't working. If it seems to break the child's heart, it's probably too strong for him. Every child reacts somewhat differently.

There are times when a child breaks a plate or rips his clothes by accident or carelessness. If he gets along well with his parents, he feels just as unhappy as they do, and no punishment is needed. Indeed, you may have to comfort him. Jumping on a child who already feels sorry can banish his remorse and cause him to argue.

If you're dealing with an older child who is always fooling with the dishes and breaking them, it may be fair to make him buy replacements from his allowance. A child beyond the age of six is developing a sense of justice and will see the fairness of a reasonable penalty. However, it's best to go light on the legalistic, take-the-consequences kind of punishment before six and not to use it at all before three. You don't want a small child to develop a heavy sense of guilt. The job of a parent is to keep the child from getting into trouble, rather than to act as a severe judge after it's happened.

Avoid threats as much as possible. Threats tend to weaken discipline. It may sound reasonable to say, "If you don't keep out of the street with your bicycle, I'll take it away." But in a sense, a threat is a dare: It admits that the child may disobey. It will impress him more to be firmly told he must keep out of the street, if he knows from experience that his parents mean what they say. On the other hand, if you see that you may have to impose a drastic penalty, like taking away his beloved bike for a few days, it's better to give fair warning. It is silly and quickly destroys all a parent's authority to make threats that are never carried out. Scary threats, such as monsters and cops, are never really helpful and can often lead to serious behavior problems. You don't want your child walking around afraid all the time.

Physical punishments (spanking). Hurting children to "teach them a lesson" is traditional in many parts of the world, and most American parents say that they believe in spanking. Most experts disagree. There are several reasons to avoid physical punishment. For one thing, it teaches children that the larger, stronger person has the power to get his way, whether or not he is in the right. Some spanked children then feel quite justified in beating up smaller ones. The American tradition of spanking may be one reason there is much more violence in our country than in any other comparable nation.

When a good executive in an office or foreman in a shop is dissatisfied with the work of an employee, he doesn't rush in shouting and whack the worker on the seat of his pants. He explains in a respectful manner what he would like; in most cases this is enough. Children are not that different in their wish to be responsible and to please. They react well to praise and high expectations.

In the olden days most children were spanked, on the assumption that this was necessary to make them behave. In the twentieth century, as professionals studied children here and in other countries, they came to realize that children can be well behaved, cooperative, and polite without ever having been punished physically. I have known hundreds of such children myself. There are countries where physical punishment is unknown.

Parents often justify spanking on the grounds that they were spanked themselves and "It didn't do me any harm." On the other hand, nearly all of these parents can remember having strong feelings of shame, anger, and resentment in response to spankings. I suspect that these parents were able to grow up psychologically healthy *in spite of* the spankings, not *because of* them.

Nonphysical punishments. There is a logic to many nonphysical punishments. If a baby grabs his mother's nose and yanks, he is put on the floor. The punishment is to be separated from mother (although he's right at her feet). Parents who use this mild form of time-out quickly teach their infants to control the urge to take hold of everything, if that thing is somebody's face. Another young child hits at her parent's face, just to get attention. This behavior often gives rise to an ironic scene: The parent slaps the child's hand while saying, "No hitting." A more effective response is to say, "Ow! That hurts," put the child down, and find something else to be interested in for a couple of minutes. Instead of attention, the child's unpleasant behavior has earned her the opposite.

Another form of nonphysical punishment, effective with older toddlers, is a time-out in a playpen for a few minutes. Consider the toddler who insists on trying to pull the plastic safety plugs out of the electrical outlets, a definite no-no. This persistent child ignores your spoken limit; when you direct her to another activity, she gleefully runs back to the outlet. She thinks she is playing a great game. Instead of unwillingly joining the game, you put the toddler in her playpen, saying simply, "Time out," and leave her there for a couple of minutes. Most toddlers hate being taken away from whatever it is they are interested in, so you can expect wails of protest. But this mild form of punishment is an effective way of teaching your toddler that you mean business.

A more formal time-out procedure works well for preschool and young elementary school children. A time-out means time away from attention and entertainment. At home, you might choose a time-out chair that is fairly isolated from the flow of activity; not so far away that you aren't aware of what your child is doing but not right in the middle of things, either. When you announce a time-out, your child needs to sit in the time-out chair until you tell him it's time to get up. You can use an egg timer, set for one minute per year of age. (Much longer than that and a young child is likely to forget why he was put in time-out and feel sad or resentful.) If the child gets up before the timer dings, it is reset, and he has to serve his sentence from the beginning again.

Some parents find that putting a child in his room and telling him that he can come out when he is ready to cooperate works well. A theoretical disadvantage of this is that it may make the bedroom seem like a prison. On the other hand, it teaches the child that being around other people is a privilege that can be lost, and that a good thing to do when one is mad is to find a way to be alone for a bit to calm down.

For older children, it often works well if the punishment flows directly from the crime. If a child leaves toys all over the living room after you've asked him firmly to pick them up, the toys might be stored, put where he can't get at them for a few days. If a teenager refuses to throw her laundry in the hamper, she may find herself without a clean shirt for school (a severe punishment for many though not all teens). An older teen who stays out late without calling may lose for a while the privilege of going out at night until he can show that he can handle himself responsibly. Effective punishments have a logic that even the child being punished has to acknowledge. They teach the crucial life lesson that actions have consequences.

Overpunishing parents need help. When I meet a parent who says she has to punish her child "all the time," I know that this is a parent who needs help. A few parents have extreme difficulty controlling their children. They say their child won't obey or that he's just bad. The first thing you see when you watch such a parent—let's say it's a mother—is that she doesn't appear to be really trying, even though she wants to and thinks she is. She threatens, scolds, or punishes frequently. But one such mother almost never carries out a threat. Another, though she punishes, never in the end succeeds in making the child do what she said he had to do. And another makes him obey once, then five minutes later and again ten minutes later, she lets him get away with it. Another laughs while scolding or punishing. Another just keeps shouting at the child that he's bad or asks a neighbor, in front of the child, whether she has ever seen a worse one.

Parents like these unconsciously expect the child's bad behavior to continue and believe they can do nothing effective to stop it. They invite misbehavior, without realizing it. Their scolding and punishing are only an expression of frustration. When they complain to neighbors, they only hope to get comforting agreement that the child is truly impossible. Frustrated parents like these have often had an unsatisfactory childhood, during which they never received sufficient assurance that they were basically good and well behaved. As a result, they don't have enough confidence in themselves or their children. These parents need help from an understanding professional.

TIPS FOR LIMIT-SETTING

You can be both firm and friendly. A child needs to feel that her mother and father, however agreeable, have their own rights, know how to be firm, and won't let her be unreasonable or rude. She likes them better that way. Their firmness trains her from the beginning to get along reasonably with other people.

Spoiled children are not happy creatures, even in their own homes. When they go out into the world, whether it's at age two, four, or six, they are in for a rude shock. They find that nobody is willing to kowtow to them; indeed, they learn that everybody dislikes them for their selfishness. Either they go through life being unpopular or learn the hard way how to be agreeable.

Conscientious parents often let a child take advantage of them for a while—until their patience is exhausted—and then turn on the child crossly. But neither of these stages is really necessary. If parents have a healthy self-respect, they can stand up for themselves while still being friendly. For instance, if your daughter insists that you continue to play a game after you are exhausted, don't be afraid to say cheerfully but definitely, "I'm all tired out. I'm going to read a book now, and you can read yours, too."

Or maybe she balks at getting out of the wagon of another child who has to take it home. Try to interest her in something else, but don't feel that you must go on being sweetly reasonable forever. Lift her out of the wagon and keep her out, even if she yells for a minute.

Angry feelings are normal. When a child is rude to her parent—perhaps because she has had to be corrected or is jealous of her brother or sister—the parent should promptly stop her and insist on politeness. At the same time, the parent might say that he knows she is cross at him sometimes (all children get mad at their parents sometimes). This may sound contradictory to you; it sounds like undoing the correction. Acknowledging a child's feelings does not excuse the child's misbehavior. It helps a child to realize that her parents know she has angry feelings but are not enraged at her or alienated from her on account of them. This realization helps her get over her anger and keeps her from feeling guilty or frightened because of it. Making this distinction between hostile feelings and hostile actions works out well in practice. In fact, a cornerstone of mental health is to be able to recognize one's own feelings and make reasonable decisions about whether to act on them. By helping your child find the words to describe her emotions, you support the development of her emotional intelligence, a crucial ingredient in life success.

Don't say, "Do you want to . . ." Just do what's necessary. It's easy to fall into the habit of saying to a small child, "Do you want to sit down and have your lunch?" "Shall we get dressed now?"

"Do you want to do wee-wee?" Another common approach is "It's time to go out now, okay?" The trouble is that the natural response of the child, particularly between one and three, is "no." Then the poor parent has to persuade the child to give in to something that was necessary anyway.

These arguments use up thousands of words. It is better not to offer a choice. When it's time for lunch, lead or carry him to the table, still chatting with him about the thing that was on his mind before. When you see that he needs to go to the bathroom, lead him there or bring the potty chair to him. Undo his clothes without even mentioning what you're up to.

Every time you take a child away from something he's absorbed in, it helps to be tactful. If your fifteen-month-old is busy fitting one hollow block inside another at suppertime, you can carry him to the table still holding his blocks, taking them away when you hand him his spoon. If your two-year-old is playing with a toy dog at bedtime, you can say, "Let's put doggie to bed now." If your three-year-old is chugging a toy automobile along the floor when it's time for the bath, you can suggest that the car make a long, long trip—to the bathroom. When you show interest in what he's doing, it puts him in a cooperative mood.

As your child grows older, he becomes less distractible and develops more concentration. Now it works better to give him a friendly warning. If a four-year-old has spent half an hour building a garage of blocks, you can say, "Put the cars in now; I want to see them inside before you go to bed." This works better than pouncing on him without warning when the most exciting part of the play is still to come or giving him a cross warning.

All this takes patience, though, and naturally you won't always have it. No parent ever has.

Don't give the small child too many reasons. You sometimes see a child between the ages of one and three who becomes worried by too many warnings. The mother of a certain two-year-old boy always tries to control him with ideas: "Jackie, you mustn't touch the doctor's lamp, because you will break it, and then the doctor won't be able to see." Jackie regards the lamp with a worried expression and mutters, "Doctor can't see." A minute later he tries to open the door to the street. His mother warns him, "Don't go out the door. Jackie might get lost, and Mommy won't be able to find him." Poor Jackie turns this new danger over in his mind and repeats, "Mommy can't find him." It's bad for him to hear about so many bad endings. It fosters a morbid imagination. A two-year-old baby shouldn't worry much about the consequences of his actions. This is the period when he is meant to learn by doing and having things happen. It's not that you should never warn your child in words; only that you shouldn't always lead him with ideas out beyond his depth.

Then there is the overconscientious father who feels he should give his three-year-old daughter a reasonable explanation of everything. When it's time to get ready to go outdoors, it never occurs to him to merely put the child's coat on in a matter-of-fact way and go out. He begins with "Shall we put your coat on now?" "No," says the child. "Oh, but we want to go out and get some nice fresh air." She is used to her father's feeling obliged to give a reason for everything. This encourages her to make him argue for every point. So she says, "Why?" but not because she really wants to know. "Fresh air makes you strong and healthy so that you won't get sick." "Why?" she says. And so on and so forth, all day long. This kind of meaningless argument and explanation will not make her a more cooperative child or give her respect for her father as a reasonable person. She would be happier and get more security from him if he had an air of self-confidence and steered her in a friendly, automatic way through the routines of the day.

When your child is young, rely most heavily on physically removing her from dangerous or forbidden situations by distracting her with something interesting and harmless or simply by picking her up. As she grows older and learns the lesson, remind her with a matter-of-fact "No, no," then offer another distraction. If she wants an explanation or reason, give it to her in simple terms. Don't assume that she wants an explanation for every direction you give. She knows that she is inexperienced and counts on you to keep her out of danger. It makes her feel safe to have you guiding her, provided you do it tactfully and not too much.

PARENTS' FEELINGS MATTER

⊜ CLASSIC SPOCK

I think that idealistic young people approaching parenthood assume that if they are the right sort, they will have unlimited patience and love for their innocent baby. But this is not humanly possible.

Parents are bound to become cross. When your baby has been crying angrily for hours despite all your patient efforts to comfort her, you can't go on feeling sympathetic. She seems like a disagreeable, obstinate, unappreciative creature, and you can't help feeling angry, really angry. Or perhaps your older son has done something he knows very well he shouldn't have done. Maybe he was so fascinated with a breakable object of yours or so eager to join some children on the other side of the street that he couldn't resist the temptation to disobey. Or maybe he was cross at you for having denied him something or angry at the baby for receiving so much attention. So he misbehaved from simple spite.

When a child disobeys a well-understood and reasonable rule, you can't simply be a cool statue of justice. Any good parent feels strongly about right and wrong. You were taught to feel that way in your own childhood. It's your rule that has been broken. It's probably your possession that has been damaged. It's your child, about whose character you care a great deal, who has done wrong. It's inevitable that you become indignant. The child naturally expects this and is not hurt by it if your reaction is fair.

Sometimes it takes you a long time to realize that you are on the way to losing your temper. The boy may have done a series of irritating acts from the time he appeared at breakfast: making disagreeable remarks about the food, half deliberately knocking over a glass of milk, playing with something forbidden and breaking it, picking on a younger child, which you tried to ignore in a supreme effort to be patient. Then at the final act, which perhaps wasn't so bad, your resentment suddenly boils over, shocking you with its vehemence. Often when you look back over such a series of exasperating actions, you can see that the child was really asking for firmness all morning, and that it was your well-intentioned effort at patience that made him go from one provocation to another, looking for a check.

We also become cross with our children as a result of the pressures and frustrations we feel from other directions. For example, a father comes home on edge from troubles that he has at work. He criticizes his wife, who then snaps at the older boy for something that ordinarily brings no disapproval; he in turn picks on his younger sister.

Better to admit anger. We have been discussing the inevitability from time to time of parental impatience and resentment. It's just as important to consider a related question: Can parents comfortably accept their angry feelings? Parents who aren't excessively strict with themselves are usually able to admit their irritation. A naturally outspoken good mother whose little boy has been bedeviling her is able to say to a friend, half jokingly, "I don't think I can stand being in the house with him for another minute," or "I'd enjoy giving him a thorough walloping." Though she may not act on these thoughts, she isn't ashamed to admit them to a sympathetic friend or herself. It relieves her feelings to recognize them clearly and blow them off in talk. It also helps her to see what she has been putting up with and be firmer in putting a stop to it.

It's the parents who set impossibly high standards for them-

selves, who have angry feelings at times which they can't believe
that good parents should, who really suffer. When they detect
such emotions stirring in themselves, they either feel unbearably
guilty or strenuously deny them. But when a person tries to bury
such feelings, they only pop up somewhere else: as, for example,
tension, tiredness, or a headache.

Another indirect expression of anger is overprotectiveness. A
mother who can't admit that she feels antagonism toward her
children may imagine instead all the awful things that might
beset them from other directions; she worries excessively about
germs or traffic. She tries to ward off these dangers by hovering
over her children, which tends to make them overdependent.

Admitting your angry feelings helps you feel more comfortable, and it helps your child, too. In general, what makes a parent
miserable makes the child miserable, too. When a parent believes that antagonistic feelings are too horrible to admit, the
child develops the same dread of them. In child guidance clinics,
we see children who develop fears of imaginary dangers—fear
of insects, of going to school, of being separated from their
parents—that prove on investigation to be a disguise for ordinary anger toward their parents, which these children dare not
recognize.

To put it the other way around, children are happier around
parents who aren't afraid to admit their anger; they can then be
more comfortable about their own angry feelings. Justified
anger that's expressed clears the air and leaves everyone feeling
better. Of course, not all the antagonism expressed toward children is justified. Here and there you see a harsh, unloving parent
who verbally or physically abuses a child at all hours of the day
with little reason and no shame. This constant flow of uncalled-
for anger is very different from the irritation of parents whose
conscientiousness and devotion to their children is plain to see.

A loving parent who feels angry most of the time, whether expressed openly or not, is suffering from real emotional strain
and should seek help from a mental health professional. The

anger may be coming from some entirely different direction. An ongoing state of anger or irritation is often a sign of depression. Depression, which affects a great many parents—especially mothers of young children—is a terribly painful condition. Thankfully, it is also very treatable (see page 51).

Impatience and approval are part of child-rearing. The very human tendency to react intensely to our children's behavior works positively for us, as we strongly foster in our children the good traits that our parents fostered in us. We do this automatically, without having to think about it, because we learned our ideals so thoroughly in childhood. Otherwise, rearing our children would be ten times as hard as it is.

It's the feeling of irritation particularly toward one child that makes parents feel most guilty, especially if there is no clear reason for it. A mother says, "This one always rubs me the wrong way. Yet I'm constantly trying to be sweeter to her and to overlook her bad behavior."

But feeling guilty about our chronic impatience with one child or another may produce increasing complications in our relations with her. Our guilt is then harder on her than our irritations.

MANNERS

⌬ CLASSIC SPOCK

Some call ours an uncivil society, and if you look around you, you may agree. It seems to be increasingly acceptable for adults and children to use swearwords, to yell at each other for the slightest reason, to cut in front of others in line. The rule seems to be: "Every man for himself. Get ahead while you can."

I remember when people were more courteous, when the pace was slower, and when getting ahead was not the prime ambition. There are many reasons for this breakdown in civility, and now many parents seem to feel that it's old-fashioned to care about manners and that children should be allowed to develop naturally. Some people have even accused me of being responsible for such "overpermissive" practices—an accusation I find ironic because I think I'm just the opposite. I think that teaching good manners should be part and parcel of all child rearing. Good manners give the right message to children; that there are certain acceptable ways to do things in our society, that showing courtesy toward others makes everyone happier and more loving.

Good manners come naturally. Teaching children to say please or thank you is not really the first step. The most important thing is to have them like people and feel good about their own worth as a person. If they don't, it will be hard to teach them even surface manners.

It is also important to avoid making them self-conscious with strangers. We're prone, especially with our first child, to introduce him right away to a new grown-up and have him say something. But when you do that to a two-year-old, you embarrass him. He will feel uncomfortable as soon as he sees you greet somebody, because he knows he's about to be put on the spot. It's much better in the first three to four years, when a child needs time to size up a stranger, to draw the newcomer's conversation away from him, not toward him. A child of three or four is likely to watch a stranger talk to his parent for a few minutes then suddenly break into the conversation with a remark like "The water came out of the toilet all over the floor." This isn't Lord Chesterfield's kind of manners, but it's real manners: He feels like sharing a fascinating experience. If he maintains this spirit with strangers, he'll learn soon enough how to be friendly in a more conventional way.

It is also important for children to grow up in a family whose members are always considerate of each other. Then they absorb kindness. They want to say thank you because the rest of the family says it and means it. They enjoy shaking hands and saying please. The example of parents' politeness toward each other and the children is crucial.

It's important to teach children how to be polite and considerate, even though it doesn't always come easily, especially with younger children. It's a useful exercise to think about what is important in your family. What kind of courtesy and manners would you like to see in your children? Be sure to set the right example. If it is done in a friendly spirit, they will be proud to learn. More important, everybody likes children with sensibly good manners and resents those who are rude or thoughtless. So parents owe it to their children to make them likable. The appreciation the children receive will then make them friendlier in turn.

GRANDPARENTS

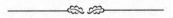

Grandparents have the freedom to see their grandchildren uncritically. Parents, who must take responsibility for improving their children, may need to be reminded from time to time of just how wonderful their children really are. With the perspective that comes of age and distance, grandparents can often assure parents that any difficult behaviors the child may be showing are really just bumps in the road, not mountain ranges to cross. At times, too, grandparents may be called on to step in for parents who are away at work or ill. Grandparents who take on more permanent parenting responsibilities face special challenges.

A resource for parents. Grandparents can be a great help to young parents in all kinds of ways. They can also derive great pleasure from their grandchildren. They often ask wistfully, "Why couldn't I have enjoyed my own children the way I enjoy my grandchild? I suppose I was trying too hard and feeling only the responsibility."

In many parts of the world grandmothers are considered experts, and a young mother takes it for granted that when she has a question about her baby or needs a little help, she'll ask her mother. When a mother has this kind of confidence in the grandmother, she can get not only advice but comfort. In our country, though, a new mother is often more inclined to turn to her doctor first, and some women never think of consulting their mothers. This is partly because we are so used to consulting professional people—doctors, guidance counselors, marriage counselors, social workers, psychologists, clergy—about our personal problems. Also, we take it for granted that knowledge advances rapidly, so we often think that even if someone knew how to do a job twenty years ago, he will be behind the times today.

A more basic reason is that many young parents still feel too close to adolescence. They want to prove to the world and to themselves that they can manage their own lives. They may be afraid that the grandparents will want to tell them what to do, as if they were still dependent. They don't want to put themselves back in that position.

Tensions are normal. In some families, all is harmony between parents and grandparents. In a few, disagreements are fierce. In others there is a little tension, most commonly concerning the care of the first child, but it wears off with time and adjustment.

The fortunate young woman who has lots of natural self-confidence can turn easily to her mother for help when she needs it. And when the grandmother makes a suggestion on her own, the mother finds that she can accept it if it seems good or tactfully let it pass and go her own way. But most young parents don't have that amount of assurance at first. Like almost everybody else in a new job, they are sensitive about possible inadequacies and touchy about criticism.

Most grandparents remember this well from their earlier days and try hard not to interfere. On the other hand, they have the experience, they feel they've developed good judgment, they love their grandchildren dearly, and they can't help having opinions. They see surprising changes from the time when they cared for babies—for example, out-of-home child-care for infants or later toilet training. Even when they accept new methods, they may be bothered by what to them seems to be excessive zeal in carrying them out.

I think that if young parents have the courage, they can keep relations most comfortable by permitting or even inviting the grandparents to speak up about their opinions. Frank discussions are usually, in the long run, more comfortable than hints or uneasy silences. A mother who is pretty sure she is managing the baby properly can say, "I realize that this method doesn't seem quite right to you, so I'm going to discuss it again with the doctor to be sure that I've understood his directions." The mother isn't giving in; she reserves the right to make her own decision in the end. She is only recognizing the grandmother's good intentions and evident concern. The young mother who shows reasonableness will reassure the grandmother not only in regard to the present problem but also in regard to the future in general.

A grandmother can help the mother do a good job by showing confidence in her and accepting her methods as far as possible. This puts the mother in a mood to ask advice when she is in doubt.

Grandparents as caregivers. When children are left in the care of their grandparents, whether for half a day or for two weeks, there should be frank understanding and reasonable compromising. The parents must have confidence that in important matters the children will be cared for according to their beliefs. On the other hand, it's unfair to expect the grandparents to carry out every step of management and discipline as if they were exact copies of the parents. It won't hurt children to be a little more respectful to the grandparents, if that's what they want, have their meals on a different schedule, or be kept cleaner or allowed to be dirtier. If the parents don't feel right about the way the grandparents care for the children, they of course shouldn't ask them to take care of them.

Some parents are sensitive about advice. Higher than average tension may arise if the young mother received a lot of parental

criticism in childhood. This inevitably leaves her inwardly unsure of herself, outwardly impatient with disapproval, and
grimly determined to demonstrate her independence. She may
take to new philosophies of child-rearing with unusual enthusiasm and push them hard. They seem like a wholesome change
from what she remembers. They are also a way to show the
grandparents how old-fashioned they are. Parents who find that
they constantly upset the grandparents should at least ask themselves whether they are doing it on purpose, without realizing it.

The managerial grandparent. Occasionally a grandmother is
so constituted that she was always too managerial with her own
child and can't stop now that her child is herself a parent. That
parent may have a tough time keeping a perspective at first. For
instance, the daughter dreads advice. When it comes, it makes
her angry, but she does not dare express her feelings. If she accepts the advice, she feels dominated. If she turns it down, she
feels guilty. How, then, can the beginning mother in this situation protect herself?

In the first place, she can remind herself that she is now the
mother and that the baby is hers to take care of as she thinks
best. She should be able to get support from the doctor if she has
been made to doubt her own method. She is surely entitled to
the support of her husband, especially if it's his mother who is
interfering. If he thinks that in a certain situation his mother
is right, he should say so privately to his wife; at the same time he
should show his mother that he stands with his wife and against
interference.

The young mother will come out better if she can gradually
learn not to run away from the grandmother nor to be afraid to
hear her out. Either reaction reveals, in a way, that she is too weak
to stand up to her. Harder still, she can learn how not to get boiling mad inside or how not to explode in a temper. She's entitled to
get angry, it's true. But pent-up anger and explosions are signs
that out of fear of making the grandmother mad she has been

submissive for too long. A dominating grandmother usually senses these indirect signs of timidity and takes advantage of them. A mother shouldn't feel guilty about making her mother angry, if it must come to that. And it shouldn't be necessary to blow up at the grandmother—or, at least, not more than once or twice. The mother can learn to speak up for herself right away, in a matter-of-fact, confident tone, before she gets angry: "The doctor told me to feed her this way," "You see, I like to keep him as cool as possible," or "I don't want her to cry for long." A calm, assured tone is usually the most effective way to convince the grandmother that the mother has the courage of her convictions.

In these occasional situations with a lot of continual tension, it is often helpful for the parents, perhaps the grandparents also, to consult a professional person—a wise family doctor, psychiatrist, social worker, or sensible minister—in separate interviews, so that each can present the picture as she or he sees it. Eventually they can come together for a final discussion. Regardless, it should be understood that in the end the right and responsibility to make decisions belong to the parents.

Grandparents as parents. Many children are raised by their grandparents while their parents are incapacitated by mental illness or addiction. Grandparents often take on this responsibility with mixed feelings: love for their grandchildren, anger at their own children, and perhaps guilt and regret as well. The task can be wonderfully gratifying but is often exhausting. Grandparents in this situation may yearn for the normal relationship, that is, to spoil their grandkids, then go home to a quiet house.

Custodial grandparents also often worry about what will happen if their health gives out. Government agencies that provide support for children in foster care often do not extend the same level of support to grandparents acting as foster parents. A supportive family and community can make a huge difference. Many cities have grandparent groups that provide parenting tips and camaraderie (see Resources Guide, page 917).

SEXUALITY

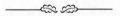

THE FACTS OF LIFE

Sex education starts early, whether you plan it or not. It is common to think that sex education means a lecture at school or a solemn talk by a parent at home. This is taking too narrow a view of the subject. A child is learning about the facts of life all through childhood, if not in a good way, then an unwholesome way. The subject of sex is a lot broader than just how babies are made. It includes how men and women get along with each other and what their respective places in the world are.

Here are a couple of bad examples: Suppose a boy has a father who is abusive of the boy's mother. You can't educate the boy with a lecture at school telling him that marriage is a relationship of mutual love and respect. His experience tells him differently. When he learns about the physical side of sex, whether from a teacher or other children, he will fit that information into the picture he has of a man's being disagreeable to a woman.

Or take the example of a girl who grows up feeling unwanted because she thinks her parents prefer her younger brother. She will resent men because she believes that they get all the breaks and that women are always the victims and that this situation cannot be changed. It won't matter how many books or talks you give her about sex and marriage. Whatever she hears or experiences she will fit into the pattern she has fixed in her mind: The man takes advantage of the woman, who is helpless to alter the pattern.

So children begin their sex education as soon as they can sense how their mother and father get along with each other, how their parents feel about their sons and daughters, and the differences between their bodies and those of their parent, siblings, and playmates of the opposite sex.

෬ CLASSIC SPOCK

I believe that sex is as much spiritual as it is physical and that children need to know that their parents feel this way. This is what makes falling in love such an intense emotional experience. The lovers want to care for each other, please each other, comfort each other. They eventually want to have fine children together. If they are religious people, they want God to be part of their marriage. These aspirations are part of what makes for a firm and idealistic marriage.

This can't be explained to a one-year-old, of course, though the intense, dependent love between him and his parents is laying the groundwork. But by the age of three, four, and five, when a child's generous love goes out to the parents, it is good for children to hear and see that their parents not only want to hug and kiss each other but that they also yearn to be kind, helpful, and respectful to each other.

When parents answer children's questions at this age period and older, about where babies come from and what is the father's role, it's important for children to hear the parents speak feelingly about the part played by their devotion to each other, how they want to do things for each other, give things to each other, have children together, take care of them together, and how this goes along with the physical affection and wanting to put the seed from the penis into the vagina. In other words, parents shouldn't ever let the anatomical and physiological explanation of sex stand alone but should always connect it with the idealistic, spiritual aspects.

Sex education for babies. Sex education can start even before children can talk or ask questions. During bathing and changing, parents can get into the habit of talking comfortably about parts of the body, including their babies' genitals. "Now we'll wipe your vulva" or "Let's get your penis cleaned up!" Using the right words—penis or vulva, rather than "wee-wee" or "thing," for example—takes away some of the aura of taboo from the genitals. In time, too, parents become more comfortable talking about sexual body parts without squirming—good preparation for the years ahead.

Children ask questions around age three. Children begin to get more exact ideas about the things that are connected with sex around the ages of two and a half to three and a half. This is the "why" stage, when their curiosity branches out in all directions. They probably want to know why boys are made differently from girls. They don't think of it as a sex question; it's just another in a series of important questions. But if they gain the wrong impression, that will become mixed up with sex later and give them distorted ideas.

Where do babies come from? This question is also pretty sure to come up in the period around three. It's easier and better to begin with the truth than tell a fairy story and have to change it later. Try to answer the question as simply as they ask it. Young children are easily confused by too much information at one time. They understand better when information is given in small, simple explanations. For instance, you can say, "A baby grows in a special place inside the mother, called the uterus." You don't have to tell them more than that for the time being.

But maybe in a few minutes, maybe in a few months, they will want to know a couple of other things: How does the baby get inside the mother? How does it get out? The first question is apt to be embarrassing to the parent, who may jump to the conclusion that the child is now demanding to know about conception and sex relations. They are of course making no such demand. They think of things getting into the stomach by being eaten and perhaps wonder if the baby gets in that way, too. A simple answer is that the baby grows from a tiny seed that was in the mother all the time. It will be months before they will want to know or be able to understand what part the father plays.

Some people feel that children should be told at the time of their first questions that the father contributes by putting his seed into the mother. Perhaps this is right, especially in the case of the little boy who feels that the man is being left out of the picture. But most experts agree that it is not necessary to try to give a three- or four-year-old an exact picture of the physical and emotional sides of intercourse. It's more than children bargain for, you might say, when they ask their question. All that's necessary is to satisfy their curiosity at the level of their understanding and, more important, to give them the feeling that it is all right to ask anything.

To the question of how babies get out, a good answer is something to the effect that when they are big enough they come out through a special opening that's just for that purpose, the vagina. It's important to make it clear that it is not the opening for bowel movements or urine.

A young child is very apt to stumble on evidence of menstruation and interpret it as a sign of injury. A mother should explain that all women have this discharge every month and that it doesn't come from a hurt. Something about the purpose of menstruation can be explained to a child of three or older.

Why not the stork? You may say, "Isn't it easier and less embarrassing to tell them about the stork?" But even a child as young as three whose mother or aunt is pregnant may suspect where the baby is growing from observing the woman's figure and overheard bits of conversation. To have his parent nervously telling him something different from what he suspects is the truth is likely to mystify and worry him. Even if he doesn't suspect anything at three, he is surely going to find out the truth or half-truth when he's five or seven or nine. It's better not to start him off wrong then have him decide that you're something of a liar. And if he finds that for some reason you didn't dare tell him the truth, it puts a barrier between you and makes him uneasy. He's less likely to ask you other questions later. Another reason for telling the truth when he's three is that children at this age are satisfied with simple answers. You get practice and build a foundation for the harder questions that come later.

Sometimes small children who have been told where the baby is growing confuse parents by talking as if they also believe the stork theory. Or they may mix up two or three theories at the same time. This is natural. Having vivid imaginations, small children believe part of everything they hear. They don't try, as grown-ups do, to find the one right answer and discard the wrong ones. You must also remember that children can't learn anything from one telling. They learn a little at a time, coming back with the same question until they feel sure they've got it straight. Then at each new stage of development, they're ready for a new slant.

Be prepared to be surprised. Realize ahead of time that your child's questions will never come in exactly the form or at the moment you expect. A parent is apt to visualize a scene at bedtime when the child is in a confidential mood. Actually, the question is more likely to be popped in the aisle of a supermarket or while you are talking on the street with a pregnant neighbor. If it does, curb the impulse to shush the child. Answer on the spot if you can. If that is impossible, say casually, "I'll tell you later. These are things we like to talk about when other people aren't around."

Don't make too solemn an occasion of it. When children ask

you why the grass is green or dogs have tails, you answer in an offhand way that gives them the feeling that it is the most natural thing in the world. Try to get the same spirit of naturalness into your answers about the facts of life. Remember that even if for you this subject is charged with feeling and embarrassment, for them it is a matter of simple curiosity. Even if you are embarrassed, chances are the child will not be upset if your response is straightforward.

Other questions—"Why don't babies come until you are married?" or "What does the father do about it?"—may not come until children are four or five or older, unless they observe animals or have friends with baby brothers or sisters. Then you can explain that the seed comes out of the father's penis and goes into the uterus, a special place different from the stomach, where the baby will grow. It may be some time before they try to visualize this situation. When they are ready for that, you can say something in your own words about loving and embracing.

The child who hasn't asked. What about the child who has reached the age of four or five or more without asking any questions at all? Parents sometimes assume that this means the child is very innocent and has never thought of these questions. But most people who have worked closely with children are inclined to doubt this. It is more likely that the child has the impression, whether the parents mean to give it or not, that these matters are embarrassing. You can be on the lookout for indirect questions, hints, and little jokes that a child uses to test parents' reactions.

For example, a child of seven who supposedly doesn't know anything about pregnancy may call attention to his pregnant mother's large abdomen in a half-embarrassed, half-joking way. Here is a good chance—better late than never—for the parents to explain. A little girl at the stage of wondering why she isn't like a boy sometimes makes valiant efforts to urinate standing up. There are occasions almost every day in a child's conversation about humans, animals, and birds when parents on the lookout for indirect questions can help the child ask what she wants to know. The parents then have an opportunity to give her a reassuring explanation, even though she hasn't asked a direct question.

How schools can help. If the mother and father have answered earlier sexual questions with a minimum of discomfort, their children will keep turning to them as they grow older and want more exact knowledge. The school has a chance to help out, too. Many schools have children in kindergarten or first grade take care of animals, such as rabbits, guinea pigs, or white mice. This gives them an opportunity to become familiar with all sides of animal life—feeding, fighting, mating, birth, and suckling the young. It is easier in some ways to learn these facts in an impersonal situation, and it supplements what children have learned from their parents. What they find out in school, they will probably want to discuss and clear up further at home.

By the fifth grade, it is good to have biology, including a discussion of reproduction, taught in a simple way. Some of the girls in the class are entering puberty and need accurate knowledge of what is happening to them. The discussion from a scientific point of view in school should help the child to bring it up more personally at home.

Sex education, including its spiritual aspects, should be part of a broad health and moral education from kindergarten through grade twelve, ideally carried out harmoniously by parents and teachers.

TALKING WITH TEENS ABOUT SEX

Does sex education encourage sex? Many parents are afraid that talking about sex with their teenagers will be taken as permission for the teen to have sex. Nothing could be further from the truth. If anything, the more children learn about sexuality from talking with their parents and teachers and reading accurate books, the less they feel compelled to find out for themselves. Taking the mystery from sex makes it less appealing to a teen, not more. Learning about abstinence—why and how to say "No, thank you"—is also helpful. But there is good evidence from many studies that abstinence education alone does not lead to a reduction in irresponsible and unsafe sexual activity. To be effective, education about sex and sexuality has to cover everything, including the biology of reproduction and contraception, the way sex is sold in the media, emotional and spiritual aspects of sex, religious and other values, and abstinence.

Talk; don't just have "The Talk." With adolescents, as with younger children, it's best for talk about sex to come up easily from time to time rather than as a big solemn lecture. It's easiest to talk with a teenager about sex if sex has been an open topic of conversation all along (see page 446). One way to make sex a routine part of conversation is to comment on the sexual images that are everywhere: on television and in newspapers and magazines. If your seventh grader knows that you are comfortable talking about sex, he won't be freaked out when you talk with him about sex when he's a freshman or sophomore in high school. A good time to talk about sex is when you're in the car together, perhaps driving your child to some fun activity. Having scenery to look at can help you both feel less self-conscious, and being in the car of course makes it hard for your teen to get up and walk away.

Keep the tone wholesome. One mistake that is easy to make, especially if the parents themselves were brought up to fear sex, is to concentrate on its dangerous aspects. A nervous mother may make her daughter so scared of becoming pregnant that the poor girl will have a terror of boys under all circumstances. Or the father may overfill his son with dread of venereal disease. The child who is moving into adolescence should of course know how pregnancy takes place and that in being promiscuous there is an increased danger of disease, but these disturbing aspects of sex shouldn't come first. The adolescent should think of sex as primarily wholesome, natural, and beautiful.

These discussions should include talking about contraception, with specifics about the responsibilities of both boys and girls. If you just aren't comfortable enough to talk about sex with your teenager, it's important to find another adult that you both trust who can do it.

Trust your child. Worried parents find it hard to believe something that people who study young people know well: Happy, sensible, successful adolescents rarely get into trouble with sex. All the common sense, self-respect, and kindly feeling toward people they have built up through the years keep them on an even keel even when they are sailing through an entirely new phase of development. To turn it around, the adolescents who get into trouble with the wrong kind of companions are usually children who for years have been mixed up within themselves and with others.

Girls and puberty. The subject of puberty should come up before the first changes appear. In girls this is usually around age ten and can be as early as eight. Girls starting puberty need to know that during the next two years their breasts will develop, hair will grow in the genital region and under the arms, they will grow rapidly in height and weight, and their skin will change its texture, perhaps becoming prone to pimples. In about two years they will probably have their first menstrual period. (For more on puberty, see page 192.)

How you tell them about their menstrual periods makes a difference. Some mothers emphasize what a curse they can be, but it is a mistake to stress that part to a child who is still immature and impressionable. Other mothers emphasize how delicate a girl becomes at such times and how careful she must be. This kind of talk also makes a bad impression, particularly on those girls who feel that their brothers have had all the advantages or who worry about their health. Girls and women can live perfectly healthy, normal, vigorous lives right through their menstrual periods. It is only the occasional girl who has cramps severe enough to keep her out of activities, and there are good treatments for them.

The thing to emphasize about menstruation is that the uterus is being prepared for growing a baby. It helps put the child in the right mood as she awaits her first period to give her a box of sanitary pads. This helps make her feel more grown up and ready to deal with life rather than waiting for life to do something to her.

Boys and puberty. Boys need to be told about sex before they begin puberty, usually around age twelve but sometimes as early as ten. You should explain about the naturalness of erections and nocturnal emissions. Nocturnal emissions, often called wet dreams, are an ejaculation of semen (the fluid stored in the prostate gland) during sleep, often in the course of a dream of a sexual nature. Parents who know that nocturnal emissions are certain to occur and also that boys will at times feel a strong urge to masturbate sometimes tell the boy that these things are not harmful as long as they don't happen often. But it's probably a mistake for a parent to set a limit. The trouble is that adolescents easily become worried about their sexuality, imagining that they are different or abnormal. Being told "This much is normal, that much is abnormal," is likely to make them more preoccupied with sex. Boys need to be told that it's equally normal to have many or few nocturnal emissions and that some perfectly normal boys have none at all.

HOW SEXUALITY DEVELOPS

✎ CLASSIC SPOCK

We are sexual beings to our very core from the day we're born until the day we die. Sexuality is inborn, part of our nature, but exactly how that nature is expressed depends largely on familial, cultural, and social values. Some cultures embrace human sexuality as a fundamental and natural part of day-to-day life. Our culture, on the other hand, has been strongly influenced by our puritanical forebears, leaving us disquieted about our sexuality and how to express it. If you look around at how sexuality is used in our culture—for advertisements, for titillation, to make a profit—it may seem as if we are getting less puritanical. But I think this is an illusion. In fact, our society's obsession with sex is based on its very repression. It is the denial of our human sexuality that fuels its exploitation in all areas of life.

Sensuality and sexuality. Sensuality refers to taking pleasure in all the physical senses. Sexuality narrows the field to the reproductive organs. Babies are sensual creatures. They take great, uninhibited pleasure in their whole bodies, especially in certain areas like the mouth and genitals. They eat with gusto, smacking their lips when full, raising a ruckus when hungry. They delight in the pleasures of their body: being held, stroked, kissed, tickled, and massaged. The pleasure principle reigns supreme.

Over time, depending on how the world responds to their sensuality, infants begin to connect certain emotions and ideas with pleasurable sensations. If an infant who is rubbing her genitals is told "No! Don't do that! That's nasty!" she'll associate that sensation with disapproval. Though she may stop that behavior, the desire for pleasure of course does not vanish, nor does the infant understand why this pleasurable activity is prohibited.

As children grow, they need to bring their enjoyment of sensual pleasures into line with what society accepts. They learn, for example, that it's okay to pick your nose or to scratch certain parts of the body but not when other people are watching. An understanding of the idea of privacy develops gradually. A young child will say that she wants her privacy in the bathroom yet will think nothing of romping through the house with nothing on. By the time they enter first grade, children usually understand privacy much as adults do.

Masturbation. Between four and eight months of age, infants discover their genitals the way they discovered their fingers and toes: by randomly exploring their body parts. They feel pleasure when they stroke their genitals; as they become older, they remember these pleasurable sensations. So from time to time, they will intentionally stroke their genitals.

By eighteen to thirty months, children have become aware of gender differences, focusing specifically on the boy's penis and the girl's lack of one. (This is how children see it until they learn that girls have a vagina and a uterus in which to grow babies, which boys lack.) This natural interest in the genitals at this time leads to an increase in masturbation.

By age three, children who haven't been forbidden to masturbate will do it from time to time. In addition to stroking their genitals with their hands, they may rub their thighs together, rhythmically rock back and forth, or make thrusting pelvic motions while sitting on the arm of a couch or chair or lying on a stuffed animal. Children at this age will also stroke their genitals to comfort themselves when they're tense or frightened or fear that something bad will happen to the genitals.

Most school age children continue to masturbate, less openly and less frequently. Some masturbate a lot, some only a little. Children masturbate for pleasure, and they continue to use the calming, comforting effects of masturbation to deal with anxieties of all kinds.

Early sexual curiosity. Preschool-age boys and girls are often openly interested in each other's bodies and, if permitted, will spontaneously engage in show-and-touch to satisfy sexual curiosity. In school-age children, comparing penis size in boys and the appearance and size of the clitoris in girls is normal, part of the general process of seeing how you measure up to your peers. Some children engage in this sort of investigation; others do not.

How much modesty in the home? In less than a century, Americans have made a full swing from the excessive modesty of the Victorian period to the partial nudity of bathing suits and the complete nudity in quite a few homes of today. It's common for young children of both sexes to see each other undressed at times, in the home, at the beach, and in the bathroom of a preschool; and there is no reason to think that this exposure has any ill effects. Children are interested in each other's bodies just as they are curious about many things in the world around them.

When young children regularly see their parents naked, however, there may be more cause for concern. The main reason is that young children's feelings for their parents are so intense. A boy loves his mother much more than he loves any little girl. He feels much more rivalrous with his father and more in awe of him than any boy. So the sight of his mother naked may be overstimulating, and the chance to compare himself unfavorably with his father every day may make him feel inadequate. This sense of inadequacy may stay with him long after he, too, has mature genitals. Sometimes a boy can be so envious that he may feel like doing something violent to his dad. For example, nudist fathers sometimes relate how their three- or four-year-old sons make snatching gestures at the father's penis during the morning shave. Then the boy feels guilty and fearful. A little girl who regularly sees her father nude also may be overstimulated.

This isn't to say that all children are upset by parental nudity. Many are not, especially if the parents do it out of a wholesome naturalness, not in a lascivious or showy way. Since we don't always know the effect on the child, I think it's wise for parents to keep reasonably covered once their children turn two and a half or three. Before that, it's helpful if children accompany their parents into the bathroom so they can see what the toilet is for. Occasionally a parent is caught off guard when a curious child comes into the bathroom. The parent shouldn't act shocked or angry. It's necessary to say only, "Will you wait outside until I get dressed?"

When should you start insisting on your privacy? Here you are wise to pay attention to your own comfort level. The point when you feel uncomfortable about your child's seeing you naked is a good time to start. If you are uncomfortable, your children will sense it. This will increase the emotional charge of the situation.

Starting at the age of six or seven, most children want more privacy for themselves, at least at times. Since at this point they are also much more capable of managing toileting and hygiene on their own, it makes sense to respect their requests for privacy.

GENDER DIFFERENCES AND HOMOSEXUALITY

By age two, boys know that they're boys, and girls know that they're girls, and they usually accept whichever sex they happen to be. Early on it's common for boys to think they can have babies and girls to think that they ought to have penises. Such wishes are not a sign of deep psychological disturbance. They are a sign of the young child's belief that anything is possible. If you want a penis, well, you can have a penis!

Gender identity develops as a result of both biological and social factors. Testosterone and estrogen, the main hormones that determine whether the body develops as male or female, also affect the developing brain. Male brains are different from female brains, but the differences between the sexes in such things as aggressiveness or skillful use of language are actually much *smaller* than the differences between individuals. In other words, there are plenty of sensitive, peace-loving boys, and plenty of assertive and competitive girls.

How gender differences are learned. People are likely to show admiration for the accomplishments of little boys and the cuteness of little girls. Girlish clothes are designed to make an adult say, "How pretty you look!" This is complimentary in one sense, but it also gives girls a sense that they are primarily appreciated for their appearance rather than their achievements. Often children's books show boys building things or going on adventures while girls watch the boys or play with dolls. Girls are commonly warned not to climb trees or onto garage roofs, being told they are not strong enough or will get hurt more easily. Boys are given toy cars, construction sets, sporting equipment, and doctor kits. Girls are given dolls, sewing sets, nurse kits, and articles of adornment. There's nothing wrong with any of these gifts in themselves, especially if the child asks for them. The harm comes when adults consistently impose these distinctions, implying that females (or males) are good only at specific occupations.

Boys are assigned chores in the garage, in the basement, or on the lawn; girls work inside the house. Of course housework is important to the welfare of the whole family, so it should be accorded dignity, but when it is done only by females in a society that accords so much prestige to males, it will be looked down on by both sexes.

Boys often cover up their feelings of inadequacy or inferiority by taunting girls, saying that they are unable to run fast or throw a ball and so can't be on the team. Unfortunately, some parents and teachers tell girls that because of their nature they won't be able to succeed at advanced mathematics or physics or function as engineers. By adolescence many girls have become convinced that they are inferior to men in such areas as abstract reasoning, complex planning skills, and emotional control. The acceptance of these aspersions in itself destroys self-confidence and may bring about the very impairment of abilities that are alleged (by many men and some women) to be lacking in females.

Homosexuality and homophobia. In our society, from 5 percent to 10 percent of adult men and women are gay or lesbian.

Because there is still considerable stigma attached to homosexuality, many gays and lesbians conceal their sexual orientation; as a result, it is difficult to calculate the exact percentage.

Gays and lesbians are now more visible in our popular culture—in films, magazines, and television—and public figures like musicians, fashion designers, athletes, and even politicians are increasingly willing to declare that they are gay or lesbian. Despite this, or perhaps because of it, many people still have an unreasonable fear of homosexuality. This fear is called homophobia. In its most common form, it is the fear heterosexuals have that they themselves may be gay or that gays and lesbians are abnormal. These fears may lead to treating homosexuals as scapegoats, saying they brought the AIDS plague on themselves or that parents should not allow their children close contact with gay and lesbian adults. In its most violent form, homophobia leads to hate crimes (gay-bashing) and to laws that limit the freedoms of gays and lesbians.

Some parents think that if their children have contact with gay or lesbian adults, that they may become gay, but there is no evidence that the sexual orientation of either gay or heterosexual children can be changed or influenced through example. There is increasing evidence that at birth people are predisposed to a heterosexual or homosexual orientation. It is clear that a person's primary sexual orientation is set in the earliest years of development. Whatever lifestyles a child is exposed to or protected from will not change his or her primary adult sexual orientation.

If your child asks about gays and lesbians or if you're talking generally to a child of six or older about sex, I think you should explain quite simply that some men and women fall in love with and live with people of the same sex. If homosexuality is considered a sin in your family's religion you will need to be especially sensitive in how you handle the issue, since a child of yours may indeed grow up to be homosexual. In that case, you will want to have talked about the issue in such a way that your child feels comfortable confiding in you and seeking your support and is not overcome with shame.

Worries about homosexuality and gender confusion. When parents think that their little boy is effeminate or their little girl is masculine, they may wonder whether the child will grow up to be homosexual. Because of prevailing prejudices against homosexuality, this can create worry and anxiety in parents. However, sexual orientation—homosexual or heterosexual—is really a very different issue from gender identity (discussed above). That a girl or boy may want to play with children of the opposite sex and enjoy their activities and toys doesn't tell us anything about his or her future sexual orientation. A small percentage of children, regardless of their gender behavior in their early years, grow up to be gay, and a majority grow up to be heterosexual.

It's normal for boys to enjoy baking, cleaning and playing with dolls, to occasionally play at being mommies, and even to pretend to have babies themselves. If a boy *exclusively* wants dresses and dolls, prefers to play *only* with girls, and says he wants to be a girl, it is reasonable to be concerned about his gender identity. I suspect that most if not all cases of true gender unhappiness will be found to have biological or genetic causes; at present no one knows for sure. Whatever the cause, gender confusion is likely to be a source of great pain for the child and worry for the family. It should be looked into by a professional.

If a girl wants to play a lot with boys and occasionally wishes she were one, she's most likely reacting to taunts that girls are not good, strong or clever enough and is testing her own limits, or she may be showing a positive identification with her father or brother. However, if she wants to play *only* with boys and is *always* unhappy about being a girl, it's wise to take her for a consultation with a professional, who can help clarify the issues and support her and her family.

Is it necessary to reinforce sex roles? The main thing that gives a boy a strong sense of male identity is not the toy cars or cow-boy suits he's given but his positive relationship with his father in early childhood. This relationship makes him want to grow up to be the same kind of person.

If a father anxiously turns down his son's request for a doll or otherwise shows his worry that the boy has girlish tastes, the child's masculinity is not reinforced. In fact, the boy may sense that his and his father's masculinity are doubtful or inadequate. If the father is confident in his masculinity, he can help his son develop the "mothering" side of fatherhood by supporting the doll play.

In the same way, a girl looks to her mother for an image of herself. A mother who encourages her daughter to explore many activities and break through the limits and herself does such things will raise a confident, strong daughter. But a mother who is overanxious about her own femininity and sexual attractiveness to men may put too much emphasis on her daughter's feminine development. If she only gives her dolls and cooking sets to play with and always dresses her in cute, frilly clothes, she sends a distorted message about female identity.

It's also important for girls to forge a positive relationship with their fathers. If fathers neglect or ignore daughters, refuse to play ball games with them, or include them in activities like camping and fishing, they may instill in them a sense of inferiority and reinforce role stereotypes. It is normal for little boys to want to play with dolls and for little girls to want to play with toy cars, and it's all right to let them do so. A boy's desire to play with dolls is parental rather than effeminate, and it should help him to be a good father. There is no harm in boys and girls wearing unisex clothes—jeans and T-shirts, for example—if that's what they want, or for girls to wear dresses, if that's their preference.

As for chores, it's sound for boys and girls to be given the same tasks, just as I think it's wise for men and women to share in the same activities, at home and outside. Boys can do as much bed-making, room-cleaning, and dishwashing as their sisters. Girls can take part in yard work and car-washing. This isn't to say that boys and girls can't swap certain chores or that it all has to come out exactly even; only that there should not be obvious discrimination or differentiation. The example of the two parents will have a strong influence.

◈ CLASSIC SPOCK

In thinking about children's identification with parents it is important to remember that the boy's identification is largely with his father but also usually with his mother to a lesser degree or, more accurately, in a certain respect. I'm sure I became a pediatrician because I identified with my mother's intense love of babies. She had five more after me, and I remember my great pleasure in giving bottles and in soothing a fretful sister by pushing her up and down the porch in her white wicker carriage.

I think of girl patients who identified with a father who was a bird-watcher or an immunologist (the mother had no such interests). So identification is a matter of degree or interest or attitude, rather than 100 percent male or female. In this sense everyone identifies in some respect or degree with the opposite sex. This gives them understanding of the opposite sex as they grow up and a richer, more flexible personality. It also benefits the society as a whole by allowing a mixture of attitudes in any occupation.

Since there is no such thing as a 100 percent identification with one's own sex, it's best to let children grow up with whatever mixture of identifications, attitudes, and interests that has developed in them, as long as they can accept comfortably what they are. This is better than making them feel ashamed and anxious because of parental disapproval.

THE MEDIA

LIVING WITH THE MEDIA

Should you worry? Television, movies, and popular music have been blamed for the decline of everything, including Western civilization as we know it. But are they really a cause of the (alleged) decline in morality in our culture that many lament, or do they merely represent what people want to watch and hear? There are many reasons *not* to worry about the media. Parents in every generation tend to view their children's music and other entertainment with alarm while accepting as harmless the songs and stories of their own youth. People naturally value what they grew up with and reject anything new. Popular music and other media create experiences that can be shared on the school bus and in the halls. This kid's culture is a healthy part of the normal process by which children and adolescents carve out independent identities and search for their own answers to life's eternal challenges.

Nevertheless, it's obvious that the media can have powerful and disturbing effects on children's behavior. The two boys who killed fifteen people, including themselves, in Columbine High School on April 20, 1999, were inspired at least in part by video games and internet sites that glorified killing. When you think about the violence that fills the television universe—eight

465

thousand murders watched by the average child before he gets to high school—and listen to the lyrics of many hit songs, it's hard not to be concerned about the effect of the media on children. Parents need awareness, good sense, and courage to help their children get the best from the media and steer clear of the dangers.

TELEVISION

A high-risk medium. Of all the media, television has the most pervasive influence on children. Young people spend an average of three hours a day watching television and another three hours or more on other screen-based entertainment. According to some estimates, each year they watch an average of ten thousand murders, assaults, and rapes, twenty thousand commercials, and fifteen thousand sexual situations, of which only 175 include birth control. Nearly one-third of children two to seven have a television in their bedrooms; nearly two-thirds of older children do.

There is no question that some programs, usually on public broadcasting stations, provide wonderful learning experiences for children. These are the programs that educate in a fun way, teach values of caring and kindness, and appeal to the child's higher instincts. Unfortunately, these shows are in the minority. Most children's television is meant to sell products and engage the child's attention in fast-paced, often violent buffoonery.

Another subtle and worrisome effect television has on its viewers is its tendency to promote passivity and a lack of creativity. Watching television requires zero mental activity on the viewer's part. You simply sit and let the images flow by. This is very different from reading, which forces you to use your imagination. The viewer becomes a passive receptacle for whatever images television chooses to display. Some believe that nonparticipatory viewing fosters a short attention span, making it hard for children to apply themselves in school.

Obesity—now a national epidemic—is another unwanted

side effect of too much television. Children burn few calories watching television, and while they watch they are bombarded with advertisements for high-calorie fast food and snacks. Research has shown a direct link between television and obesity: the more television a child watches, the greater the chance he'll be seriously overweight. And it's almost impossible to lose weight if much of your day is spent sitting still. Television presents a distorted version of reality in which women are unnaturally thin and men are improbably buff. No wonder so many teens feel unattractive by comparison.

Children who watch a lot of television learn that drinking alcohol and smoking cigarettes makes you cool and attractive. The heroes in popular movies often smoke. Illicit drug use is often portrayed as bold or adventurous, rather than foolish and dangerous.

Violence is another real concern. Many studies show that exposure to violence on the screen results in children acting more aggressively toward their peers while at the same time feeling more vulnerable to attack. Of course, that doesn't mean that *every* child who watches action shows will copy what he sees. But the odds that those children will do something violent are undoubtedly higher. Exposing children to typical television fare puts them at risk just as surely as playing in the street or riding in a car without a seat belt.

ᗌ CLASSIC SPOCK

So here's the situation: We are leaving our children in the care of an electronic babysitter for twenty-three hours of every week. This sitter tells our children that violence is an acceptable way to solve problems; that sex is especially exciting when it occurs without love and, besides, there are no real negative consequences anyway; and that owning the latest products is a measure of success and happiness. There seems to be very little similarity between the world the electronic babysitter is selling to our children and the world we would like to see. Why would parents entrust their children to such a caretaker?

Why is most television so bad? Many people incorrectly believe that the product line of the television industry is the commercials. In fact, the product sold by the television companies is the viewer's attention. The more of this product they accumulate, the more money they make from their commercials. Since television is a means to catch your attention (not to educate, edify, or entertain, unless that catches your attention), it becomes clear why most programs try to appeal to the broadest base of viewers, which usually translates into sensationalism.

That television is designed specifically to capture and hold the viewer's attention explains why watching television is possibly the worst thing to do right before bed. Rather than putting you to sleep, television keeps you up until you are so sleepy you simply cannot keep your eyes open. Most of the children I see with really severe problems falling asleep actually keep themselves awake by watching television.

Do you need a television? Very few parents choose to live entirely without television. But the ones who do always seem happy with that decision. Children who never get into the habit of watching television don't miss it. They fill their days with other activities. Parents often believe that television makes their lives easier, because it keeps their children occupied for blocks of time. But when you figure in all the hours spent arguing about how much children can watch, and what shows they can or cannot watch, then add the hassles of getting the children to stop watching so they can do homework or chores, it probably takes less effort to not have a television at all.

Take control. If you're in the majority who choose to live with television, what's most important is that you take control of it. If there's a television in your child's bedroom, remove it. Put the television out in the open where you can easily monitor what and how much is being watched.

Some children are glued to the set from the minute they come home in the afternoon until they are forced to go to bed at night. They don't want to take time out for supper, homework, or even to say hello to the family. Parents are sometimes tempted to let their children watch endlessly because it keeps them quiet.

It's better for the parents and child to come to a reasonable but definite understanding about which hours are for outdoors and friends, which are for homework, and which are for television viewing. A maximum of one to two hours after homework, chores, or other responsibilities is a reasonable limit for most families.

For very young children the solution is easy, because your control is close to absolute. Pick wonderful videotapes for them to view over and over again. They won't even realize that the television can be used in any other way. When they do watch commercial television, make sure that you approve of the programs. If you use television at all as a babysitter, it is entirely proper for you to make sure that what is watched meets with your approval. For example, you can and probably should flatly forbid your children to watch violent programs.

Young children can only partly distinguish between drama and reality. You can explain that "It isn't right for people to hurt each other and kill each other, and I don't want you to watch them do it." Even if your child cheats and watches such a program in secret, she'll knows that you disapprove. This will protect her to a degree from the coarsening effect of violent scenes. Most likely, your child will be secretly relieved that you keep her away from violent shows. A very large percentage of children report being seriously scared by things they see on television. Who needs that?

For older children, who might watch when you are not there, the V-chip can be a blessing. By law, all new sets with screens thirteen inches or larger come equipped with a device that lets parents block out shows according to published ratings for vio-lence, sex, and adult situations.

An older child is likely to bristle at your attempts at censor-ship: "Everybody else watches these cartoons; why can't I?" When this happens, you should simply stick to your guns. While it's true that children may watch the forbidden programs at friends' houses, you are still giving the message that this pro-gram does not conform with your family's values, which is why you don't want them to watch it.

Watch television with your child. A good way to handle the un-wholesome messages on television is to watch with your child and help her to become a discriminating, critical viewer. You can make comments on whether what you've just seen together bears any resemblance to the real world. If you've just seen a fight where someone is punched and just shrugs it off, you can say, "That punch in the nose must really have hurt. Don't you think it did? Television isn't at all like real life, is it?" This also teaches empathy with the victim of violence rather than identi-fication with the aggressor. When viewing a commercial, you might say, "Do you think what they are saying is true? I think they just want you to buy their product." You want your child to view commercials for what they are and understand their ma-nipulative intent. When viewing a scene with sexual content, you might comment how "that's not what it's like in real life at all. Usually that happens after people have known each other for a long time and really love each other."

You can use television viewing to help your child learn to make sense of the world in a more realistic and wholesome way and to see television for the fantasy it is. As these lessons are learned, your child may become immunized against wholesale acceptance of the media's messages.

Get involved. A simple step is to write letters to the television networks about what you like and don't like in children's programming. When the networks receive one letter, they assume that there are ten thousand people out there who feel the same way. So you can have an impact.

⟨≫ CLASSIC SPOCK

In my opinion, not having a television at all seems to be a logical solution. That way children and the family cannot rely on passive entertainment and, as mankind did for thousands of years, can learn to creatively and actively broaden their interests by reading, writing, or conversing with one another.

VIDEO GAMES

What makes video games so engrossing and potentially dangerous to children is that they provide instant feedback. Point your cursor in the right direction, press a button at the right time, and something blows up—*and* you get points for it. One of the basic concepts in psychology is that a behavior that is consistently rewarded will occur with increasing frequency. Video games provide such rewards. According to education theory, the best way to teach somebody something is to adjust the level of difficulty so that the task is always challenging without being truly frustrating. Video games do this automatically.

In other words, video games are ideal teaching tools. Unfortunately, what they often teach children is how to shoot quickly and accurately. As technology improves and the screens become more and more lifelike, children shoot at images that look increasingly like real people. The more they shoot, the less horror and disgust they feel at the idea of killing people. It's not that they become cold-blooded exactly; just less tenderhearted. When they think of flying bullets, their main emotion is excitement, not fear or revulsion. Video games, much more than violent movies, have the ability to capture children's imaginations and train their emotions to accept violence, because with video games children are active participants.

Is there anything positive about video games? The precise hand and finger movements in response to visual stimuli do seem to develop children's eye-hand coordination in a way that prepares them for jobs that require quick reactions (a fighter pilot, for example, or a New York cabbie). For boys whose social skills are underdeveloped and who are no good at sports, skill at video games is an alternative path to prestige and peer acceptance. If the talk of the playground is all about the latest blow-'em-up video game, it's hard being the one kid who isn't allowed to play.

And, of course, not all video games are violent and destructive. Some allow children to experiment with building things: houses, cities, or roller coasters, for example. Others stretch a child's visual skills or logical thinking, and some even make it more fun to learn math or reading. It's not hard to tell these more peaceful games apart from the shoot-to-kill variety. A glance at the box is usually all it takes.

The key with video games, as with television, is for parents to take control. Most children can probably handle a limited exposure to action videos without ill effects. Parents have to be ready to step in to set a limit, however, so the video playing doesn't get out of hand. If your child is generally inclined to vigorously protest against limits, you may be better off just saying no altogether. If your child is fascinated by force, so that he constantly practices karate kicks or machine-guns the air, I'd suggest that you limit his exposure to violent videos to zero. His head is already working overtime with images of fighting. Better to feed his imagination with nonviolent ideas: roller coasters are exciting, without the bullets.

MOVIES

Scary movies. Movie-viewing is a risky business for children under the age of seven. For example, you hear about an animated feature that sounds like perfect entertainment for your small child. But when you watch it, you find that there is an episode in the story that scares the wits out of him. You have to remember that a child of four or five doesn't distinguish clearly between make-believe and real life. A witch on the screen is just as alive and terrifying to a child as a flesh-and-blood burglar would be to you. The only safe rule is not to take a child under seven to a movie unless you or someone else who knows small children well have seen it and are positive that it contains nothing upsetting. Even then, young children should always be accompanied by a sympathetic adult, who can explain any disturbing scenes and comfort the child when necessary.

What movies are appropriate for children? There are obviously no hard-and-fast rules here. The answer depends on your child's development and maturity, how she responds to scary stories, her desire to see movies, and your family's values. Do you want to avoid violence altogether or only certain kinds, like graphic violence? When do you think a child is mature enough to be exposed to sexual scenes, and what sort of activity is acceptable in those scenes?

If you err, it should probably be on the side of being over-restrictive about which movies you allow your children to see. It is much more harmful for a child to be exposed to an upsetting or inappropriate scene that she is not ready for than to be denied access to a movie she is mature enough to watch. When used as a point for discussion, conflicts about which movies are appropriate allow you to hear your child's side; why she feels she is totally ready and absolutely must see this movie. You can then discuss your view that loveless or brutal sex is not good at any age. Your child still won't be pleased, but you'll be teaching her your values in a direct way and learning more about your child's world.

ROCK AND ROLL AND RAP

⬿ CLASSIC SPOCK
I remember well that in the early days of rock and roll, parents worried about Elvis Presley's dancing on television. He was shown only from the waist up, lest his gyrating hips cor-

rupt the multitudes of youthful viewers. A decade later, the records of the Beatles were burned because of their allegedly depraved effects on the minds of adoring teens.

More recently, the raw and violent lyrics of some songs have been blamed for the surge in violence among teenagers. The more things change, the more they stay the same.

If there is a common thread to the music of teenagers over the decades, it is to turn society's staid old music on its head and rebel against the status quo. If the music of teenagers isn't found offensive by adults, it probably won't be successful. Music, among other things, is a means by which each new generation differentiates itself from the old and provides itself with a bond of shared culture and identity.

This is not to say that offensive music is only in the ear of the beholder. It is distressing to hear lyrics that glorify aggression and disrespect toward women and aggrandize drug use. Is there a way to prevent your children from hearing such songs? You can certainly sit down with them and ask them questions about the songs: "Why does this song call women disparaging names? Why do the lyrics show such disrespect for the police? What do you think these sexy lyrics actually mean?" During such discussions with your child, you can also clarify your view on the song's message: "I don't like songs that say drugs are good." You need to be thoughtful and respectful toward the music, even if you think it sounds like a band of screeching cats, but you should also voice your views in a way that is not disrespectful of your child and his generation. If you appear to reject the music from the start, your child is likely to pigeonhole you as hopelessly out of it and discount anything you say.

In contrast to movies and television, there is little evidence that offensive lyrics have much effect on most children's well-being. Most offensive lyrics go in one ear and out the other. But the coarsening, offensive nature of some lyrics should not go unnoticed and undiscussed by you. It's yet another opportunity to enter into your children's culture and to help them to clarify their ideas and thoughts.

Music videos. The majority of households now have cable television and, with it, music videos. Most of these videos contain sexual images, often bordering on pornography. Violence is common, including violence against women. By pairing these gripping images with catchy tunes, music videos take hold of the imagination in a powerful way. It should not come as a surprise, therefore, that exposure to music videos has been tied to aggression and teen sex. Limiting exposure by not having cable access is one solution; watching with your teen and using the opportunity to educate is another. Some music videos do portray responsible behavior and nonviolent conflict resolution. If you run across them, let your teens know that you approve.

THE INTERNET

Suppose your child says to you this evening: "See you later. I'm going off on my own to a strange and wonderful city. I'll be back in an hour or two." You learn that this city has it all: new people to meet, unlimited places to go, museums on every topic you can imagine and some you can't.

How should you respond? After your initial panic subsides, you'll first take into account your child's level of maturity. Can she really negotiate a big city on her own? If so, do you trust her not to go into dangerous places where she might be harmed? What museums are appropriate for someone her age? How soon should she come back?

The internet is just such a city. As a responsible parent, like it or not, you are going to have to come to terms with it. For children, the internet provides an exciting opportunity for independence and freedom, like a dress rehearsal for a real visit to a real new city but with fewer of the dangers and a lot of friends along for the ride.

Pluses and minuses. Your children know that the internet gives them easy access to information that is almost infinite in scope. Its potential for teaching is immense. There are chat rooms, where people can participate in roundtable discussions on every imaginable subject. For example, there are chat rooms where children with disabilities can talk to children anywhere in the world who have the same disabilities. At other sites, teens can talk together about problems of the world—war or global warming, for example—and share ideas and potential solutions. The internet allows children to break through isolation and create a sort of global village. Some find this aspect alone remarkably helpful and enjoyable.

With these very real advantages comes danger, especially for children. Unfortunately, in the virtual world of the internet there are real individuals who prey on children's innocence and immaturity. A children's chat room, for example, may turn into a lewd monologue by an adult posing as a child. The anonymity afforded by the internet can be used for unsavory ends by exploiters of children. Additionally, websites devoted to violence or pornography are easily accessible.

A less dramatic but in some ways equally concerning risk is the great amount of advertising on the internet. Many of the most exciting sites are built around the advertising of a brand or company. Greater materialism or a reluctance to see big corporations as anything other than benign entities may be a result.

Some parents are so anxious about the potential dangers of the internet that they forbid access to it altogether. But children will have to learn to deal with the information superhighway one way or another. If they are well prepared and responsible, a treasure trove of information awaits them. If they do not become comfortable with using the computer to communicate and to acquire information, they may find themselves at a disadvantage later, in the workplace and socially.

Learn about the internet yourself. Have your child teach you about the internet, if he already knows, or learn about it together. That way, at least for a time, you can surf together, talking about what and where you want to go, discussing what to do and not to do, and stating your expectation of good manners. By sharing this experience, you will have the opportunity to talk things over in a way you'll miss if you never learn the first thing about the internet. You'll get to know what kind of chat rooms and information sites are out there and how they operate. This familiarity will allow you to better judge what sites pose a threat to your child and when you are being unjustifiably old-fashioned or insecure.

Supervise and set limits. It helps for parents to spell out the ground rules for their children, then provide enough supervision to ensure those rules are being obeyed. For a teenager, supervision may mean an occasional glance at the screen while your teenager is online. Preteens require more direct contact and discussion of what they are doing on the internet. When younger children use the internet, you should be at their side for much of the session. Chat rooms, unless well supervised, are not appropriate for young children.

What are fair time limits? As with television, you should set a time limit on how long each day the internet can be accessed. It's unhealthy for a child to be lost in the virtual world of his computer to the neglect of real-life conversations, experiences, and friends. Having the computer in a public room rather than a bedroom makes it easier to supervise and set limits.

Ground rules for internet safety: Just as there are safety rules for crossing the street, riding a bike, or driving in a car, there are rules children need to follow to stay safe online:

1. Never give personal information to anyone online. This means never give your address, your phone number, or the name of your school to someone you haven't already met in person.

2. Don't send photographs of yourself to anyone you haven't met in person.

3. Never tell anyone else your password. Although chat room correspondents may seem like your friends, they are really strangers. You need to be as careful with these strangers as with those you meet on the street.

4. If a message makes you uncomfortable in any way, stop and tell an adult.

5. Use good netiquette: Treat people with politeness and consideration. Inappropriate or rude communications are not acceptable, even when you're anonymous.

Sex on the internet. A great deal of internet content is pornography. You can avoid much of it by using parental control features of commercial online services or purchasing blocking program software. Many online services offer a way for parents to allow a child access only to carefully screened and supervised children's information sites and chat rooms. Similarly, you can buy software that limits what can be accessed, making it difficult, inadvertently or purposely, to access adult chat rooms or information sites. Some software keep logs that allow you to see where your child has been.

It's nevertheless likely that if your child does any amount of surfing, she'll run across sexual material; you can't shield her entirely. Rather than trying to pretend that porn isn't there, take the opportunity to teach. Before your child goes online alone, talk about what she may find. Explain that pornography is a business: Some adults pay money to see pictures of other adults without their clothes on. Help your child understand what's wrong with this mixing of commerce with sexuality. Let your child know what you expect her to do if she runs across a sex site: leave the site, turn off the computer, and tell you.

Remember, talking about sex doesn't make children engage in it. Instead, when you can discuss sex in a matter-of-fact way, it takes away some of the thrill of mystery and discovery that so often surrounds the topic. Also, you let your child know that you are approachable and askable (see page 452 for more on talking about sex).

Technology can help protect your child from much of the worst internet garbage, but there is no substitute for instilling a sense of responsibility and values in your child so that he will make the right choices on his own. For such a child, the internet can be magic carpet to wonderful new worlds of information and experience.

DIFFERENT TYPES OF FAMILIES

As our society has opened up, we've learned that children can thrive in many different kinds of families—families with one parent or many, families with two mommies or two daddies, and many other variations. At the same time, the power of shame and stigma has waned, so that merely being different is less stressful. That people are free now to create families outside the traditional mold means that there are more who can devote their hearts and talents to the raising of children.

When we look past the labels that flag a family as different, we are freed to see children and families as individuals. Still, it can be helpful to consider the special challenges and strengths that come with different family structures and some of the ways parents and children can cope with these issues.

➣ CLASSIC SPOCK
It's been said that the family as an institution in America is dying. I don't think that's true. The family has certainly been changing. Since the mid-1980s, fewer than 10 percent of American families have been made up of a father who goes out to work, a mother who stays at home, and two children. But the family, whomever it may include, is still the center of our daily lives. The family is where the great majority of us get our most important love and nurturance and support. I

think that's what counts most, whether a family has two working parents, only one parent, children from previous marriages, or children only on weekends and holidays.

ADOPTION

Reasons to adopt. People have various reasons for wanting to adopt. A couple should decide to adopt only if both love children and very much want a child. All children, biological or adopted, need to feel that they belong to and are loved by both father and mother deeply and forever. An adopted child can easily sense a lack of love in one or both parents, since she may not be secure to begin with, perhaps having been through one or more previous separations. She knows that for some reason she was given up by her biological parents, and she may secretly fear that her adoptive parents might someday give her up, too.

It's a mistake to adopt when only one parent wants to or when both do it only for practical reasons, such as to have someone to take care of them in their old age. Occasionally a woman who is afraid that she's losing her husband will want to adopt a child in the futile hope that this will hold his love. Adoptions for these reasons are unfair to the children and usually prove to be unwise for the parents, too.

Parents with an only child who is unhappy or unsociable sometimes consider adopting another child to provide company. It is a good idea to talk this over with a mental health professional or the adoption agency before proceeding. The adopted child is apt to feel like an outsider. If the parents lean over backward to show affection for the newcomer, it may upset rather than help their biological child. This is a risky business for all concerned.

There can be pitfalls, too, in adopting to "replace" a child who has died. Parents need time to work out their grief. They should adopt only because they want a child to love. There is no harm in adopting one who is similar in age or appearance to the child who died, but the comparisons should stop there. It is unfair and unsound to want to make one individual play the part of another. She is bound to fail at the job of being a ghost. She should not be reminded of what the other child did or be compared with her either out loud or in the parents' minds. Let her be herself. (This applies also to a child who is born after another one dies.)

At what age should a child be adopted? For the child's sake, the younger, the better. For a number of complex reasons, early placement is not possible for thousands of youngsters living in foster homes and institutions. Research has shown that these older children can also be successfully adopted. That children are older should not prevent their being placed. The agency will help older children and parents decide if adoption is right for them.

⬡ CLASSIC SPOCK

A couple should not wait until they are too set in their ways to adopt. They've dreamed so long of a little girl with golden curls filling the house with song that even the best of children turns out to be a rude shock. It is not a matter of years alone but of an individual's capacity to give a particular child what she needs. This is something to discuss with the agency.

Adopt through a good agency. Probably the most important rule is to arrange the adoption through a first-rate agency. It is always risky for adopting parents to deal directly with biological parents or an inexperienced third person. This leaves the way open for the biological parents to change their minds and try to get their child back. Even when the law stands in the way of the biological parents, the unpleasantness can ruin the happiness of the adoptive family and the security of the child.

A good agency will help the biological mother and relatives to make the right decision in the first place about whether to give the baby up. The agency will also use its judgment and experience about which couples should be dissuaded from adopting. An agency worker can help the child and family during the adjustment period. The goal of all concerned is to help the child become a member of the adoptive family. Wise agencies and wise state laws require this adjustment before the adoption becomes final. One way to find out about the qualifications of an adoption agency is to call your state department of health. All state health departments have a section that licenses adoption agencies.

Gray market adoptions. Most of the children waiting to be adopted are older. This means that most of the people who want to adopt babies or very young children will be unable to do so or will have to wait for a long time. They may be tempted to adopt a baby through a lawyer or doctor, rather than go through an adoption agency. A lot of people think they won't have any trouble if they get a gray market baby this way (as opposed to a black market baby, who is adopted with no legal procedures at all). But these people often discover that they, too, have both legal and emotional difficulties later on, if, for example, the biological mother decides she wants the baby back.

Children with special needs. An increasing number of unmarried parents are keeping and raising their children, so there are fewer very young children who need homes. However, other children are waiting for parents. They are for the most part of school age. They may have a brother and sister from whom they don't want to be separated. They may have some physical, emotional, or intellectual handicap. They may be war orphans. They are as much in need of love and can be as rewarding to parents as any other child.

They do have some special needs, however. Since they are older, they may have been in foster care more than once. Having already lost parents (biological, then foster), they may be insecure and fearful of being rejected again. Children express this in a variety of ways, sometimes frequently testing to see if once again they will be sent back. These anxieties present adoptive parents with special challenges. If parents know about the challenges ahead of time and expect them (instead of expecting a child to be grateful), these children can be especially rewarding. It's the responsibility of adoption agencies to focus their attention on finding homes for these children, even more than on finding babies for adoptive parents.

Nontraditional parents. In the past, most adoption agencies would consider only married, two-parent families without biological children. Now, many agencies welcome single parents, parents in committed gay or lesbian partnerships, parents whose race is different from the child's, and other nontraditional applicants. Childhood passes quickly, and one permanent parent *now* is of more value than the possibility of two parents some time in the future. Furthermore, agencies have learned that successful adoptions depend less on the outward characteristics of families than on the inward character of the parents. There may also be other good reasons: Some children have been emotionally bruised in such a way that it is better for them to have one parent of a particular sex; other children have such a tremendous need for attention and care that the lack of a spouse allows a single parent or a nontraditional family to give the child what he needs.

Open adoption. In recent years, it has become increasingly common for the birth mother (sometimes the birth father, also) and the adoptive parents to learn a lot more about each other. This ranges from getting a general description of each other from the adoption agency to meeting each other at the agency. Sometimes the birth mother can choose which of several possible adoptive parents she prefers. Sometimes an arrangement is made for the birth mother to keep up with the child, for example, receiving a snapshot of the child and a letter from the adoptive parents once a year or more often.

Although the experience with open adoptions is still relatively short, it appears that openness often works out well for everyone. Many children seem able to handle having both a birth mother and "a mother who takes care of me." Knowing their birth mother spares children the pain of wondering "What is she like? What would she think of me?" Even if the reality is sad—the mother may have serious problems, for example—the unhappy reality is often less disturbing to the child than an idealized (or demonized) fantasy.

⟡ CLASSIC SPOCK
We don't yet know how these open arrangements will work out in the long run, particularly the ones that provide continuing contact between the birth mother and the adoptive parents. I think it's good for the birth mother and adoptive parents to know more about each other at the start, because this can prevent a lot of anxious wondering on both sides. But I'm not sure how it will work out emotionally for the child and all the adults involved to have regular contact over the years. It seems to me that this could interfere with the birth mother letting go of her child emotionally, and it could also get in the way of the adoptive parents coming to feel that this is truly their child.

Telling the child. When should an adopted child be told she is adopted? She's sure to find out sooner or later from someone, no matter how carefully the parents think they are keeping the secret. It is nearly always a very disturbing experience for an older child, even for an adult, to suddenly discover that she is adopted. It may disturb her sense of security for years.

The news shouldn't be saved for any specific age. From the beginning, the parents should let the adoption come up naturally and casually in their conversations with each other, with the child, and with their acquaintances. This will create an atmosphere in which the child can ask questions whenever the subject begins to interest her. She will find out what adoption means bit by bit, as she gains understanding.

Some adoptive parents make the mistake of trying to keep the adoption secret, others err in the opposite direction by overstressing it. Most adoptive parents quite naturally have an exaggerated sense of responsibility at first, as if they have to be letter-perfect to justify that someone else's child has been entrusted to their care. If they are too earnest when telling the child she's adopted, she may wonder "What's wrong with being adopted, anyway?" But if they accept the adoption as naturally as they accept the color of the child's hair, they won't make a big deal of it. They should remind themselves that having been selected by the agency, they will probably be darned good parents and the child is lucky to have them. They should not fear the missing biological parent. Adoptive parents need to resolve their fears and anxieties, or they will communicate them to the child.

Answering a child's questions. Let's say that a child around three hears her mother explaining to someone that she is adopted. She asks, "What's 'adopted,' Mommy?" She might answer "A long time ago, I wanted very much to have a little baby girl to love and take care of. So I went to a place where there were a lot of babies, and I told the lady, 'I want a little girl with brown hair and blue eyes.' So she brought me a baby, and it was you. And I said, 'Oh, this is just exactly the baby I want. I want to adopt her and take her home to keep forever.' And that's how I adopted you." This makes a good beginning, because it emphasizes the positive side of the adoption: that the mother received just what she wanted. The story will delight the child, and she'll want to hear it many times.

Children who have been adopted at an older age will need a different approach. They may have memories of their biological and foster parents. Agencies should help both the child and the new parents handle this. It is important to realize that questions will repeatedly surface at different stages of the child's life. They should be answered as simply and honestly as possible. Parents should allow the child to freely express her feelings and fears.

Between the ages of three and four, a child is likely to want to know where babies come from. It is best to answer truthfully, simply enough so that the three-year-old can easily understand. But when you explain that babies grow inside the mother's uterus, it makes an adopted child wonder how this fits with the story of picking her out at the agency. Then or perhaps months later, she asks, "Did I grow inside you?" Then you can explain, simply and casually, that she grew inside another mother before she was adopted. This may confuse her for a while, but she will understand later.

Eventually a child will raise the more difficult question of why her biological parents gave her up. To imply that they didn't want her will shake her confidence in all parents; and a made-up reason may bother her later in some unexpected way. The best answer and perhaps the one nearest to the truth may be "I don't know why they couldn't take care of you, but I'm sure they wanted to." Over the period when the child is digesting this idea, she needs to be reminded, along with a hug, that now she's always going to be yours.

Information about the birth parents. All adopted people are naturally intensely curious about their biological parents, whether they express it or not. In former times, adoption agencies told adopting parents only the vaguest generalities about the physical and mental health of the biological parents. They completely concealed their identities. This was partly to make it easy for the adoptive parents to answer "I don't know" to the extremely difficult questions a child asks about her origin and why she was relinquished, and it was even more to protect the privacy of the biological parents (most were unmarried; many choose to keep the pregnancy a secret).

Today, in recognition of the individual's right to know, the courts sometimes compel an agency to reveal the identity of the biological parents to an adopted youth or adult requesting it. When this leads to a visit, it sometimes has a beneficial effect on the turbulent feelings and obsessive curiosity of the adopted individual; sometimes such a visit disturbs the adopted person, the adoptive parents, and the biological parents. Any such request needs to be discussed, with all its pros and cons, at length with the agency people, whether the case is brought to court or not.

The adopted child must belong completely. The adopted child may have the secret fear that her adoptive parents, if they change their minds or if she is bad, will someday give her up, as her biological parents did. Adoptive parents should always remember this and vow never, under any circumstances, to say or even hint that the idea of giving her up has ever crossed their minds. One threat uttered in a thoughtless or angry moment may be enough to destroy the child's confidence in them forever. They should let her know that she is theirs forever any time the question seems to enter her mind—for instance, when she is talking about her adoption. But it would be a mistake also to worry so much about the child's security that they overemphasize their talk of loving her. What gives an adopted child the greatest security is being loved, wholeheartedly and naturally. It's not the words but the music that counts.

International adoption. Roughly a quarter of the children adopted in the United States began their lives in another country. The opportunity to adopt a baby from overseas is the answer to many parents' prayers. But internationally adopted children and their families face some special challenges. Many of the children arrive malnourished, with missed immunizations and other medical conditions. These can usually be easily dealt with. However, many also have developmental and emotional issues, which can be harder to treat.

Most internationally adopted children have led hard lives. Many have lived in institutions that barely met their physical and emotional needs. Those who had loving foster parents had to endure the pain of leaving them behind. Generally, the longer a child has lived in an orphanage or similar institution, the greater the chance of lasting physical, intellectual, and emotional damage. But it's important to remember that most internationally adopted children grow up to be emotionally as well as physically healthy. They may feel disoriented or experience grief at first, but most eventually make strong, loving connections with their new families. Nearly all show signs of delayed growth and development by American standards, but most catch up in two to three years.

A lot depends on the changing historical and political conditions in the child's country of origin. A country may rule, for example, that foreigners can adopt only children with severe physical disabilities. A few months later, the law may be changed. Because of these variables, an adoption agency that specializes in international adoptions generally or specifically in the country being considered can be a tremendous help to parents.

Internationally adopted children often look very different from their adoptive parents, so they may face insensitive comments or outright prejudice. For children who speak a language other than English, the trauma of suddenly being unable to communicate adds to the stress of the adoption. Because the children's biological heritage links them to a different culture, their relationship to that culture is an issue for the parents to grapple with when the children are young and for the children themselves when they are older.

For many parents, the act of adopting a child from a different country has political and ethical implications, too. The parents understand that they have benefited from the terrible conditions in the child's country of origin. Their child has a chance to lead a better life but at the cost of being taken away from her land and culture. Some families translate these concerns into action, perhaps by sending money and supplies to help other children who are still there.

Many children adopted from overseas end up doing wonderfully. The hard truth is that some do not. Developmental-behavioral pediatricians and other experts can help parents weigh the risks. Only the parents know how strong their need is for a child and how much uncertainty and difficulty they can bear. Parents who decide to raise a child who may have severe problems are heroes. Parents who search their souls and decide that they cannot raise such a child have also acted courageously.

SINGLE-PARENT FAMILIES

ᨆ CLASSIC SPOCK

No question that parenting is a tough job, no matter how you look at it, and being a single parent makes the job that much tougher. You don't have a supportive partner to ease the relentless day-to-day responsibilities of raising children. Everybody and everything depends on you. You don't get a real break or vacation. If you are the only breadwinner, financial worries add to your burden. It sometimes feels as if you just don't have enough physical and emotional energy to keep it all going.

At any given time, more than a quarter of the children in the United States live in single-parent homes. Over their lifetimes, more than one-half of children will spend some time in a single-parent household, either because of divorce (see page 515) or because their parents never married. Nearly nine out of ten single parents are mothers. Most single mothers and their children have incomes below the federal poverty line.

In the past, single and unmarried meant the same thing. But I wouldn't count an unmarried woman with a steady partner as single. By the same token, a married woman whose husband is gone for long stretches of time—on the road, in the military, or in jail—has many of the same challenges as women who have no partners at all.

A successful woman who chooses to raise one or more children on her own takes on a daunting task. Even with a supportive family, good friends, and a good job, the demands of solo parenting can be overwhelming at times, since all the responsibility falls on one set of shoulders. A woman who has single-parenting thrust upon her by divorce, separation, death, or abandonment adds grief and loss to her burdens and very often poverty as well. The support of friends, family, and community can make the difference between a life that is merely very difficult and one that is virtually unlivable.

Being a single parent is no picnic, but it does have its rewards. You and your children may achieve a special closeness. You may discover strengths that you never knew you possessed and come out of the experience a stronger, wiser person. When things go well—as they often do—there is, I imagine, a great sense of accomplishment.

Pitfalls of single parenting. One pitfall for single parents is an unwillingness to set firm limits. Many single parents feel guilty because their children don't have two parents. They worry that their children are missing something essential for their healthy development and regret that they aren't able to spend enough time with their children. The temptation is strong for parents to indulge their children, giving in to their every whim.

It is neither necessary nor sensible for the parent to shower the child with presents and constant attention. In fact, it's unwise for the parent to focus on the child for most of the time they are together, as if the child were a visiting princess. The child can engage in a hobby, do homework, or help with the housework while the parent pursues her own activities. This doesn't mean that they have to be out of touch. If they are in tune with each other, they can chat or comment off and on, as the spirit moves them.

Another pitfall for single parents is to treat their children as their best friends, telling them their deepest feelings. Children need to go through their own emotional growth and development; their having to be substitute adults will interfere with this process. Normal children can all take on extra chores and provide some emotional support to a distressed parent, but no child can take on an adult role without serious consequences to her or his future emotional growth and development.

The mother as single parent. Let's take the example of the child who has no father at home. It would be foolish to say that the father's absence makes no difference to this child or that it's easy for the mother to make it up to him in other ways. But if the job is handled well, the child can grow up well adjusted.

The mother's spirit is the most important element. A single mother may feel lonely, imprisoned, or cross at times and will sometimes take her feelings out on the child. This is natural and won't hurt him too much.

The important thing is for her to go on being a normal human being, keeping up her friendships, her recreations, her career, and her outside activities as far as she can, and not have her life totally revolve around her child. This is hard if she has a baby or child to take care of and no one to help her. But she can ask people in or take the baby to a friend's house for an evening if he is able to sleep in strange places. It's more valuable to him to have his mother cheerful and outgoing than to have his routine be perfect. It won't do him any good to have her wrap all her activity, thoughts, and affection around him.

Children—young or old, boys or girls—need friendly relationships with other men if the father is not there. With babies up to the age of a year or two, a good deal is accomplished if they can be frequently reminded that there are such creatures as agreeable men, with lower voices, different clothes, and a different manner than women. Even a kindly grocer who grins and says hello helps, if there are no close friends. As children become three and older, the kind of companionship men give them is increasingly important. They need chances to be with and feel close to men and older boys. Grandfathers, uncles, cousins, scoutmasters, male teachers, a priest, minister, or rabbi, and family friends can serve as substitute fathers if they enjoy the child's company and see him or her fairly regularly.

Children three or over are likely to build up an image of their father as their ideal and inspiration, whether they remember him or not. The other friendly men they see and play with give substance to the image, influence their conception of their father, and make him mean more to them. The mother can help by being extra hospitable to male relatives, sending her son or daughter to a camp that has some male counselors, picking a school, if she has a choice, that has some male teachers, and encouraging a child to join clubs and other organizations that have male leaders.

The boy without a father in particular needs the opportunity and encouragement to play with other boys every day if possible by the age of two and to be occupied mainly with childish pursuits. The temptation of the mother who has no other equally strong ties is to make her son her closest spiritual companion, getting him interested in her preoccupations, hobbies, and tastes. If she succeeds in making her world more appealing to him and easier to get along in than the world of boys, where he would have to make his own way, he may grow up with predominantly adult interests and have less in common with his peers. It's fine for a mother to have plenty of fun with her boy, provided she also lets him go his own way and provided she shares in *his* interests rather than having him share too many of hers. It helps to regularly have other boys over to the house and to take them along on treats and trips.

The father as single parent. Everything said about a mother raising a child alone also applies to a father raising a child alone. But often there's an additional problem. Few fathers in our society feel completely comfortable in a nurturing role. Many men have been brought up believing that being a nurturing person is soft and therefore feminine. Many fathers will therefore find it hard, at least at first, to provide the gentle comforting and cuddling that children need, especially young children. But with time and experience, they can certainly rise to the task.

STEPFAMILIES

It's no accident that many fairy tales have an evil stepmother or stepfather as the villain. Stepfamily relationships often lend themselves to mutual misunderstandings, jealousy, and resentment. A child whose mother has custody of her after divorce has her all to herself and will form an unusually close and possessive bond with her. Then a strange man comes along and takes away the mother's heart, bed, and at least half of her attention. The child cannot help resenting this intruder, no matter how hard the stepparent tries to form a good relationship. This resentment often takes extreme forms. It can get under the stepparent's skin, and he may feel the urge to respond with equal hostility. The new relationship between the adults quickly becomes strained, because it feels like a no-win, either-or choice. The important thing for a stepparent to realize is that this hostility on both sides is almost inevitable, not a reflection of their worth or an indication of the eventual outcome of the relationship. The tension often persists for months or even years, only gradually lessening. In other, rare situations, the new parent may be much more easily accepted.

ᐳ CLASSIC SPOCK

Years ago, with what I thought was great wisdom, I wrote a magazine article about stepparenting. Then in 1976 I became a stepfather and realized that I was quite incapable of following my own advice. I had advised stepparents to strictly avoid trying to be disciplinarians, but I kept reproaching my eleven-year-old stepdaughter for her consistent rudeness, and I kept trying to make her conform to a few rules of mine. This was one of the most painful relationships I ever experienced and the one that taught me the most.

Why is it so hard? There are plenty of good reasons why life in a stepfamily is stressful, at least initially, for most children:

- *Loss:* By the time they enter a stepfamily, most children will have experienced significant loss: loss of a parent or loss of friends because of a move. This sense of loss affects a child's early response to the new stepparent.
- *Loyalty issues:* The child may wonder, Who are my parents now? If I show affection to my stepparent, does it mean I don't love the parent who is no longer with me? How can I split my affections?
- *Loss of control:* No child has ever made the decision to have a stepfamily. The decision is made for him by adults. The child feels buffeted by forces and people he has no control over.
- *Stepsiblings:* These stresses may be made worse by the presence of stepsiblings. The child wonders, What if my mother or father loves my stepbrother more than me? Why do I have to share my possessions or my room, with this complete stranger?

Positive aspects of stepfamilies. These stresses are fairly universal, but by no means are they the whole picture. There are also potential benefits. First, though difficulty is the rule in the beginning, most family members eventually adapt to the new circumstance. Often stepsiblings and stepparents establish close, long-lasting relationships. After all, they share the experience of a disrupted and reconstituted family. The "dual citizenship" of living in two separate families can also enrich a child's understanding and acceptance of diversity and cultural difference.

Tips for stepparenting. There are some general principles that may be helpful, though they are not always easy to apply. The first is for the parents to agree ahead of time on how they'll handle the children and to have realistic expectations of what the new family will be like.

It's important for the parents to understand that children need plenty of time to get used to the new arrangement. Be consistent with the children about family rules regarding bedtime, chores, and homework and allow time for them to become accustomed to these rules.

It is better for a stepparent to avoid moving into the guiding and correcting role of a full parent too soon. A stepparent who tries to enforce such things as the responsibility for chores, bedtime, and curfews too soon is sure to be judged as a harsh intruder, even if enforcing exactly the same rules as the natural parent.

On the other hand, it's not good for parents to be submissive when the stepchild intrudes into their territory: for instance, abusing one of the parent's possessions. The parent should set a limit in a friendly but firm way: "I don't like it when you hurt yourself or your things, and I don't like it when you hurt my things, either." You can't make an issue of every hostile look; you'd be grouchy all day. So ignore the small slights, and save your comments for major infractions of the rules.

When to seek help. The stresses of stepparenting too often strain marriages to the breaking point or beyond. So it is wise to seek professional help at the first sign of real trouble, rather than wait for the problems to grow. Both adult and child psychiatrists or psychologists are likely to have dealt with stepfamily problems many times and will be able to help. The help may take the form of guidance for the parents on how to proceed, marital or family therapy, or individual counseling for one or more of the children. Stepparent groups, available through many community child guidance centers, can be helpful, too.

For more on stepfamilies, see Divorce, page 515.

GAY AND LESBIAN PARENTS

In the United States, as many as ten million children live with three million gay or lesbian parents. These numbers are likely to increase. A growing number of gay and lesbian couples are choosing to become parents, through adoption, insemination, surrogate parenting, or foster care. Additionally, there are men and women who had children in traditional marriages and subsequently discovered they were gay. While some of these parents remain married until their children are grown up, others divorce and continue to share the job of rearing their children with their former spouse.

If you are not gay or lesbian, you may have asked yourself whether this kind of family is good for children. If you are a gay or lesbian parent, you've learned firsthand some of the difficulties experienced by a nontraditional family. The experience of being a gay or lesbian parent is different in varying degrees, depending on where you live. In some communities it is considered a totally acceptable type of family; other communities so vilify nontraditional families that you may feel uncomfortable even discussing the issue outside the family. That makes your life tougher still.

Effects on children. There have been many studies looking at the development of children of gay and lesbian parents, and much has been learned. Tests of psychological adjustment show no significant differences between the well-being of children raised by heterosexual parents and of those raised by gay or lesbian parents. As in any family, what is most important for children is how loving and nurturing the parents are and whether they are aware of the special needs the children may have. Since gay men and women can be as warm and caring (or as dysfunctional) as heterosexual parents, it is not surprising that the mental health of their children is comparable.

These studies also show that the children of gay and lesbian parents are as likely to be heterosexual as children growing up in more traditional families are. Moreover, these children are often more tolerant of different sexual orientations and more sensitive to minority status. Most studies show that gay and lesbian parents make a special effort to expose their children to strong role models, male and female, heterosexual and gay. Furthermore, sexual abuse occurs less frequently with gay and lesbian parents: Most sexual abuse in families is committed by heterosexual males.

Children of gay and lesbian parents face challenges similar to those faced by other minorities. They may be teased and made to feel ashamed at school when classmates learn that their parents are gay. This torment can be especially cruel when the teacher, other school officials, and the parents of classmates make no effort to educate themselves and their families about gay and lesbian parents.

For children whose identity is in the process of formation, being viewed by peers as abnormal and as a threat to mainstream culture may create emotional conflict. Of course, such childhood trials can also build strength of character and empathy for others (and often do), but the process may be excruciating for parent and child alike. Many schools try to discourage the teasing of children by teaching respect for the values and lifestyles of other cultural groups. In these schools, the teasing of children from alternative families is likely to be much less.

The scientific data are quite clear: children usually do as well in gay and lesbian families as in traditional families. Good parents are good parents. It is most productive to concern ourselves with whether parents are providing their children with love, consistency, and thoughtful care, rather than with the nature of their intimate relationships.

Teasing. As a gay or lesbian parent, one of the issues you (as well as other cultural minorities) have to face is the potential teasing of your children.

Like most parents, you'd like to protect your children from being hurt, even if it's not really possible. I'd suggest talking to them when they are young, explaining casually the nature of your family and how it is different from most other children's families. As your child becomes older, you can discuss how some people are afraid of that which is different and that which they do not understand. When these people are afraid, they may show it by teasing or being mean. You might play out a few scenarios to help your child decide what to do if this occurs and to help your child explain the nature of your family to other children in a way that will win them over. As with every other issue, open and honest communication between you and your child is vital.

I'd also suggest that, assuming you're open about your lifestyle, you go to your child's school to discuss with the teacher how she feels about nontraditional families, if she has noticed any problems with the other children, and if such issues are ever discussed in class.

All parents and all children face special challenges. Your goal should not be to avoid all stress and travail—that's impossible, as you undoubtedly know. Rather, your goal should be to use those negative experiences to teach your child about tolerance, empathy, and consideration toward others.

Legal issues. Recent court rulings have lifted hopes for gay and lesbian parents. In Canada, same-sex marriages are now legal; in the United States, the Supreme Court has affirmed the right of adults to have homosexual relationships without fear of prosecution. Still, legal issues often make things difficult for gay and lesbian parents.

Since the United States does not recognize marriage between homosexuals, decision-making for the child for example, in the hospital emergency room in the absence of the legal parent can be sticky. It's important to consult with a lawyer about legal issues in your state that concern the care of your child. Many states are now addressing this issue, and some are legislating greater rights for gay and lesbian parents. You will do well to keep informed about local, state and federal laws as they evolve.

Finding support. There are many books written for gay and lesbian parents that you might find useful. I particularly like *The Lesbian and Gay Parenting Handbook* by April Martin, Ph.D. (1993, Harper). The Resource Guide at the back of this book includes the addresses and phone numbers of some national gay and lesbian parent groups that can provide you with information and support. Many communities offer support groups for children and parents. There are also terrific books for children that address issues of gay and lesbian families.

Help for heterosexuals. Awareness about gay and lesbian parents has grown so much in recent years that many heterosexual parents feel comfortable with the issue. Others still have concerns. Will it be confusing to a child with a mommy and daddy to be friends with a child who has two mommies or two daddies? I think the answer is, simply, no. Children are remarkably able to accept plain facts when they are plainly presented.

What may be confusing is when a child who has been taught that homosexuality is wrong meets parents who seem very nice, have great kids, and are gay or lesbian. The child may find it difficult to reconcile what she knows from first-hand experience and what she has been taught.

Opposition to gay and lesbian parenting often comes, I think, from the fear that exposure to homosexuality will encourage children to become homosexuals. There is no evidence that this happens. Instead, sexual orientation appears to be mostly a matter of biology (see page 459). Sometimes the opposition comes from a religious conviction that homosexuality is sinful. Children who grow up with those religious beliefs and are homosexual are bound to have a difficult time being comfortable with themselves and their faith.

⬚ CLASSIC SPOCK

The existence of gay and lesbian families offers you an opportunity to teach your child about different types of families and to value what is really important—not whether other families are different from yours but whether they uphold those values your family respects: kindness, consideration, and warmth. Such lessons in tolerance and acceptance of diverse family structures will serve your child well in dealing with the exploding cultural diversity of the world of the twenty-first century.

STRESSES AND TRAUMAS

Ordinary life for a child in the twenty-first century can be extraordinarily stressful. World events intrude into even the most protective of families. Television opens children's eyes to terrorism, earthquakes, wars, and global warming. For many children, the disasters are closer to home. Physical and sexual abuse take a terrible toll. Domestic violence often devastates children, even if they themselves are not physically harmed. Less extreme but still very difficult are such stresses as the death of a family member, a parent's temporarily going away, or the more lasting separation of divorce.

When you think about the stresses and traumas children face, it is amazing that so many grow up strong, loving, and optimistic. This resilience comes from a powerful inner drive toward happiness and health and from relationships—or even a *single* relationship—with adults who care for them and believe in them. We grown-ups do well to remember that as we try to help children cope with our stressful world.

THE MEANING OF STRESS

Stress is a physical response. The body responds to threatening situations by releasing the stress hormones, adrenaline and cortisol. In small doses these hormones help with concentration and endurance (think of doing a long, hard math test). At high levels they trigger the so-called flight-or-fight response (think of being attacked by a vicious dog): the pulse races, blood pressure shoots up, muscles tense, noncritical functions such as digestion shut down, concentration narrows to a pinpoint focus, and time seems to move more slowly.

Stress affects the brain. After severe stress, a special neural connection is forged between the threatening stimulus and the stress response system. As a result, the next time the same stimulus shows up, the response occurs even faster. This special connection also means that anything *similar* to the original threatening stimulus can trigger an inappropriate stress response.

This is what happens in people with posttraumatic stress disorder (PTSD). PTSD is common among soldiers returning from combat (it used to be called shell-shock), and it also occurs in children who have been victims of violence or have witnessed it. With the stress response often come vivid memories of the original traumatic event, which can plague children while awake and create vivid, horrifying nightmares while asleep.

Vulnerability to stress. Not everyone responds to stressful situations in the same way. About one child in seven is particularly vulnerable to stress. Even as babies, they respond to any new person or thing with a release of stress hormones. As older children, they tend to be cautious or shy, taking time to feel comfortable in any new situation, and they often develop fears or other anxiety-related problems. This proneness to stress is inborn and often runs in families. Scientists are close to discovering the responsible gene or genes. Stress-vulnerable children are more likely to develop symptoms in response to any severe stressor, such as being chased by a dog or experiencing an earthquake.

If you know that your child has a special vulnerability to stress, you can help him develop coping skills by limiting his exposure to stresses that he can handle. For example, you might decide to turn off the television when the news is about a war or earthquake and instead talk about the situation over dinner, a much less intense exposure. Each time your child succeeds in handling a mildly stressful situation, his coping skills and confidence grow.

TERRORISM AND DISASTERS

The events of September 11, 2001, are only the most dramatic recent reminders that the world is a dangerous place. Before that, there was the string of shootings in schools and the home-bred terrorism in Oklahoma City. Going further back, there was the fear of nuclear devastation, which still lurks in the background. On a smaller scale, each flood, tornado, and earthquake destroys the illusion of safety for the families and children most immediately affected.

Children who experience disaster, either directly or through the repeated exposure to graphic images on television, are likely to show signs of stress. After September 11, for example, many preschool children drew pictures of airplanes in flames or made block buildings and crashed toy airplanes into them. Play of this kind is one way that young children take control of frightening realities. A sign of *healthy* coping is when the child creates happy endings. The airplane lands safely, the building doesn't fall down, the child comes away looking relieved.

The play of a child who has been traumatized is different: the planes continue to crash, the buildings fall over and over, and the child comes away exhausted and more worried than ever. This kind of repetitive, compulsive play is a sign that a child needs the help of a skilled psychologist or therapist.

Responding to disasters. Disasters, both natural and manmade, threaten the basic contract between parents and children, which is that parents will keep their children safe. It is therefore very important that parents reassure their children that adults—

Mommy, Daddy, the mayor, the president—are doing whatever needs to be done to make sure no one else is hurt. Parents also need to protect their children from being further traumatized by repeated exposure to televised images of the event. As hard as it was to turn off the television after September 11 or during the recent war in Iraq, that is what wise parents did.

The specific reason for a child's anxiety may be different from what you'd expect; a good general rule is listen carefully to your child first, then try to answer the specific questions or concerns your child has. Children take security from familiar surroundings and routines, so a quick return to the comforting patterns of everyday life—breakfast, school, a bedtime story—is very helpful.

Finally, it's important to pay attention to your own response to stress. Children follow their parents' lead. If you are terribly upset, your child will pick up on it. It's good to talk about your feelings in simple terms, so that your child knows what is upsetting you (otherwise, he's likely to imagine that it is him). And it's very important to reach out for help for yourself to friends, family members, clergy, or others in the community. For stress symptoms that persist in you or your child, a professional can often help (see page 620).

PHYSICAL ABUSE

Anger at children. Most parents become angry enough at their children once in a great while to have the impulse to hurt them. You may become angry at a baby who continues to cry for what seems like hours even after you have done everything possible in the way of comforting her or at a child who breaks one of your precious possessions right after you have asked him to put it down. Your justified rage boils up, but you usually have enough control to avoid taking your frustration out on the child. You may feel ashamed and embarrassed after such an incident. Remember that the majority of parents have the same experience.

Talk to your spouse or the baby's doctor to get the support and help you need.

> ### ⊰ CLASSIC SPOCK
> I remember when I was a medical student, picking up my own endlessly crying six-month-old baby in the middle of the night and yelling, "Shut up!" at him, barely able to control myself from physically hurting him. He hadn't slept through the night for weeks, and his mother and I were exhausted and at our wits' end.

The roots of abuse. There has been much study of child abuse in recent years. Abuse may be emotional, physical, or sexual. Child abuse occurs in all economic classes. If a baby is premature or sick, requiring more than the usual amount of care, she is more likely to be abused. Girls are sexually abused more often than boys, usually by heterosexual men.

An adult who hurts a child is usually suffering from a momentary loss of physical and emotional control. Those who repeatedly lose control often were abused or neglected in their own childhood. They may have little physical or emotional support from family and friends and tend to have unreasonably high expectations of the abused child. They profit greatly from counseling, especially from joining a group of parents with similar problems. They need to learn that physically attacking a child teaches the child to use that physical violence to solve his problems. Children who are hit often become hitters.

Laws against abuse. The purpose of the laws on child abuse and neglect is to protect children. The law aims to help parents through counseling to understand and cope with the pressures on their lives. The preference is almost always to keep the child in his home while the parents are in treatment, though if the risk is too great, the child is placed in a foster home until the family is ready to care for him again.

Physical abuse and culture. In many parts of the world, slapping, spanking, and even whipping are considered part of parenting, not child abuse. A parent who fails to use physical punishment is considered a bad parent. When these families move to the United States, the parents are often upset to learn that it is against the law for them to hit their own children. One mother told me, "My children don't respect me, because they know there is nothing I can do."

It may be helpful for immigrant parents to consider that where they grew up *many* things are different from where their children are growing up. Climate, food, housing, dress, jobs are all likely to be new. It makes sense that parenting must be different, too. Ways of disciplining children that work in a small village, may not work well in Boston (see page 418). It is nevertheless very hard for parents to give up parenting practices that feel right and good to them, even though the law says they must.

Other parenting practices can sometimes look like abuse. One example is cupping, a common practice in Southeast Asia, that involves placing a warmed glass over the child's skin. As the air in the glass cools, it sucks the skin into the glass, raising a welt. The purpose of cupping is to take away illness, not to punish. As doctors become more educated about child-rearing in different cultures, they are less likely to mistake traditional treatments for child abuse.

SEXUAL ABUSE

It's very important to realize that the great majority of sexual molestations of children are carried out not by depraved strangers but by family members: stepparents, friends of the family, babysitters, or other people known to the children. Girls are more at risk; boys are also victimized.

What to tell children. One approach is to have talks by police officers in schools, warning children of strangers who offer candy or rides. But such talks, if carried out by authorities without special training, may encourage morbid fears without being of much use. I suggest instead that parents themselves issue any warnings they think wise, depending on their evaluation of the risks.

To make warnings less frightening, you can tell a young child (three to six years old)—preferably when she asks a relevant question or when the mother has discovered her in sex play with another young child—that if an older child tries to touch her private parts (her clitoris or vagina) she shouldn't allow it. (See page 446 on talking about the genitalia.) She can be told to say, "I don't want you to," and to tell her mother about it right away. Then the mother can add, "Sometimes a grown-up may want to touch you. Tell him that you don't want him to. Or he may want you to touch him. You should not. Tell him that you don't want to. Then tell me. It won't be your fault." This last is mentioned because children characteristically fail to report such incidents because they feel guilty, especially if the molester is a relative or family friend.

When to suspect. Sexual abuse is difficult for parents to suspect and doctors to diagnose, because shame, guilt or embarrassment leads to silence and physical signs are usually absent. If there is genital or rectal pain, bleeding, trauma, or signs of infection, you should consider the possibility of sexual abuse and seek a medical evaluation. (It's important to know that most mild vaginal infections in girls before puberty are not a result of sexual abuse.)

Most children who have been sexually abused exhibit unusual behavior, such as sexual behavior inappropriate for the child's developmental age. Some imitate adult sex acts in front of other children. This kind of behavior is not consistent with normal sexual exploration among children (such as, "You show me yours, and I'll show you mine"). A child who masturbates compulsively or in public places is expressing an interest in sexual activity that is abnormally intense (see page 457).

Other behavior associated with sexual abuse in children and adolescents is less specific; it includes withdrawal, excessive anger or aggression, running away from home, fears (especially of situations related to the abuse), changes in appetite, sleep disturbances, a recent onset of bed-wetting or soiling, or a decline in school performance. These behavioral changes can of course occur in children and adolescents as a result of other stresses. Indeed, they are usually *not* signs of sexual abuse. The point is to keep the possibility of sexual abuse in mind but not to obsess about it to the extent that you look for it in every change of behavior. Your child's doctor or nurse practitioner may be helpful in interpreting unusual behavior your child may exhibit.

Getting help. If you suspect sexual abuse, call your child's doctor. In many large cities, there are specialized teams of doctors, psychologists, and social workers who know how to evaluate children who may have been victims of sexual abuse. The point of these evaluations is to find out if abuse has occurred and gather evidence that can be used to convict the abuser—critically important for preventing further victimization—without further traumatizing the child. Part of the evaluation is also to check for medical problems, such as infection, that may need treatment.

After being abused, children often struggle with feelings of shame and guilt. Parents can help by frequent reassurance that the child is not at fault and that the parent will make sure that the abuse never happens again. It is crucially important that a child who has been a victim sees that her parents are standing up for her and doing everything they can to protect her in the future.

A child who has been the victim of sexual abuse should also receive psychological evaluation and treatment. Only brief treatment may be needed or it may need to be repeated later, since the psychological effects of the abuse are bound to resurface. Psychological recovery from sexual abuse is possible but often takes many years.

DOMESTIC VIOLENCE

Every family has disagreements. In all too many, arguments turn into shouting, then to threats, pushing, hitting, or more extreme violence. We have only recently become aware of the effects on children of observing such acts, even when they are not themselves threatened. Children who see one parent hurting the other are likely to be terrified, enraged, and powerless, all at once. During the fighting, they may cower in a corner. Afterward, they often become extremely clinging, as though afraid to let a parent—usually the mother—out of their sight.

Later—this is very hard for parents to understand—the child may take on the characteristics of the abuser, hitting his mother and showering her with the same curses used by the father. Mothers in this situation are understandably horrified and terrified to see their little child seemingly transformed into their abusive partner. Young children who witness violence sometimes lose their appetite (it's hard to feel like eating when you are upset), have difficulty sleeping, fail to pay attention in school, and become aggressive.

What you can do. The first thing is that the violence must stop. That often means that the mother and children must leave the home—a terribly difficult decision but often unavoidable. (I say "mother" here, since mothers are most likely to be the victims, but domestic violence can go in the other direction, too.) The National Coalition Against Domestic Violence has a twenty-four-hour free hotline (800 799-7233) where you can get immediate help and a referral to a program or shelter in your area. Their website, www.ncadv.org, provides specific information to help you stop the violence, find safety, make legal plans, and get support (click on Getting Help). Children who have behavior problems as a result of exposure to domestic violence often need professional help to get past the trauma and recover their ability to feel safe and enjoy life (see page 620).

DEATH

A fact of life. Death is a fact of life that every child must grapple with. For some, the death of a goldfish is their first exposure; for others, that of a grandparent. In many cultures, death is viewed as a natural occurrence, and no attempt is made to isolate it from everyday life. Our culture, on the other hand, remains very uneasy about it.

ᴄ⍲ CLASSIC SPOCK

If adults are uncomfortable with the notion of death, it is no wonder that many are even more perplexed about how to help children deal with it. Some would just as soon deny the whole thing. That dog lying motionless at the side of the road? "He's just resting. He's fine. What did you learn in school today?" Others choose to avoid the concrete and focus solely on the ethereal: "The angels came and took Grandpa and now he's up in heaven with Grandma." Still others duck the question altogether: "Don't you worry about what death is. No one is going to die soon. Where do you get such ideas?"

Helping young children understand death. In the preschool years, children's ideas about death are influenced by the magical tendencies of their thinking. Children this age may believe, for example, that death is reversible, that the dead person will come back someday. They also tend to feel responsible for everything, including death, that happens in their world and may fear punishment for unkind thoughts they had about a dead person or animal. They may also view death as catching, like a cold and worry that soon someone else will die.

Since this is the age when children take everything literally, it's especially important not to refer to death as going to sleep. Many children will then become terrified of going to sleep and themselves dying or else say on hearing that someone has died. "Well, wake him up." Similarly, saying "We lost Uncle Archibald" can strike terror into the heart of any child who has himself gotten lost. I remember one child who developed a fear of flying after hearing that a dead relative had "gone to his home in the sky."

Young children think in concrete terms: "How will Uncle Bob breathe if he's in the ground?" Parents can help a child by being equally concrete: "Uncle Bob won't breathe anymore. He also won't eat anymore or brush his teeth. Being dead means that your body stops working completely; you can't move or do anything. Once you are dead, you cannot become undead." Young children need to hear, sometimes several times, that they in no way caused the death.

Even as young as three or four, children can understand that death is a part of the life cycle. People have beginnings: they start small, they grow up, they become old, and they die.

Death and faith. All religions provide explanations of death. Whether these involve heaven and hell, reincarnation, or spirits moving about the earth, I think it is important for parents to clarify to their children that these beliefs are built on *faith*, which is a special way of understanding the world. Children need to learn to treasure their own faith while at the same time accepting that other people's faiths may lead them to see things differently.

Funerals. Many parents wonder whether to allow a young child to attend the funeral of a relative or close friend of the family. I think that a child of three or more can attend funerals and even accompany the family to the cemetery for the burial if he wants to, if the parents are comfortable with the idea, and if they prepare him for what will happen. Children get from funerals what adults do: confirmation of death's reality and a chance to say good-bye in the company of friends and family.

It's important that an adult the child knows well is with him and emotionally available at all times to answer questions and, if necessary, to take the child home if he becomes upset.

Dealing with grief. Some children show their grief by crying; others may become hyperactive or clinging, others may seem utterly unaffected, although it later becomes clear that they also were grieving. Parents can help their child deal with grief by acknowledging that losing a friend or grandparent is very sad and that it is also sad to realize that person won't be coming back. As a parent, you do not need to pretend that you yourself are not upset or sad. By letting your child see that you have strong feelings, you make it okay for the child to accept her own feelings, too. By handling your feelings appropriately—for example, by talking about them—you teach your child how to deal with sadness and grief in the most powerful way you can, by being a model.

If a child asks about your dying. Probably the scariest thing for a child is the death of a parent. If a death has recently affected the family or your child earnestly asks you about death, you can assume that most likely underlying the question is the concern that *you* might die.

A blanket reassurance is in order here (assuming that you do not have a life-threatening condition). You can say that you will not die until your child is all grown up and (if you're lucky) has children of his or her own. Then, when you are an old, old grandparent, it will be time for you to die. Most children are comforted by having this terrifying event put off into an unimaginably distant future. They know that they aren't grown-ups yet, so they don't have to fear your dying. Although you can't be absolutely certain that you will actually live that long—and therefore your reassurance may turn out to be false—you need to make a definitive statement. Young children cannot grasp the concept of probability. The technically true statement that it is *very unlikely* that you will die any time soon will not meet a child's need for security. It is never right to lie to a child, but the truth must be presented in a way that can be heard. Your confident promise to stay alive is the reassurance your child needs.

SEPARATION FROM A PARENT

Children draw their sense of security from their relationships with their parents. When children have to be separated from a parent, even for a short time, the stress of the separation can cause long-term difficulties. Young children reckon time differently from adults. "Only a few days" can seem like forever.

Traumatic separations. If a mother goes away for a few weeks, to care for her ailing mother, for instance, her baby of six to eight months is likely to go into a depression, especially if the mother has been the only caretaker. The baby becomes visibly depressed, loses her appetite, is unresponsive to known and unknown people, and is more often found to lie on her back just rolling her head from side to side, no longer trying to sit up or explore her environment.

At two to two and a half years of age, separation from the mother no longer produces depression. It instead results in dramatic, severe anxiety. If a mother or father is called out of town by an emergency or decides to take an all-day job without preparing the child for the transition to care by a sitter or at a day-care center, the child may show no marked distress while the parent is away, seeming to like the sitter (in retrospect, the child is too well behaved to be normal), but when the parent returns, the pent-up anxiety breaks out into the open. The child rushes to cling to the parent. She cries out in alarm whenever her mother goes into the next room. She won't let the sitter do anything for her, won't let her come near, in fact, rudely repulses her. At bedtime, she clings to her mother or father with a grip of steel so that she can't be put in her crib. If her parent finally gets free and heads for the door, the child unhesitatingly scrambles over the side of the crib, even if she never dared do it before, and rushes after her mother or father. It's a truly heartrending picture of panic. Even if the parent succeeds in getting her to stay in her crib, she may sit up all night.

If for several days the mother has to be away or the child is put in the hospital, the child may punish her mother by refusing to recognize her when they are reunited. When she decides to recognize her again, she may scream at her in a rage or hit her.

What you can do. For a younger child, tape a photo of the absent parent where it can be seen from the crib; have an article of the parent's clothing for the child to cuddle with (beware, though, of suffocation risks with infants); make a tape recording of the parent telling favorite stories or singing favorite songs. Keep the separation as short as possible. Have a family member rather than a stranger, take care of the child.

For older children, make a calendar and check off each day until the parent returns; talk about what you'll all do together then; have frequent telephone conversations, letters, or email. For separations that are months long, tie the parent's return to an expected change in the seasons or another milestone the child will recognize. Instead of saying "Daddy will be back in June," say "First we'll have winter, then the weather will warm up and flowers will start coming out, and after that, Daddy will be home." Read stories about families that have to be apart, then come together again (my favorite is the classic *Make Way for Ducklings,* by Robert McCloskey.) If the date of the parent's return is uncertain (as when one parent must serve in the military overseas), it is even more important to exchanges emails or letters and phone calls, remember the times together in the past, and talk about the good times to come.

DIVORCE

Separation and divorce have become common. In the United States, there are now about a million divorces a year. You can read about friendly divorces in fiction and see examples of it in movies, but in real life, most separations and divorces involve two people who are angry with each other.

Marriage counseling. Most divorces are disturbing to all members of a family for at least a couple of years. It may of course be less upsetting than continued hostile conflict. There is a third alternative: marriage counseling, family therapy, or family guidance at a clinic, a family social agency, or with a private therapist. It's best, of course, if both husband and wife receive regular counseling to get a clearer view of what has gone wrong and the part each partner is playing. It takes two to make a quarrel, but even if one spouse refuses to acknowledge his or her role in the conflict, it may be worthwhile for the other to receive counseling on whether and how to save the marriage. After all, there were strong positive attractions in the beginning, and many divorced people say that they wish they had tried harder to solve the problems and make a go of it.

It's usually true that when a couple disagree, each feels that the other is mostly to blame. Yet an outsider can often see that the trouble is not that one or the other is a villain but that neither seems to realize how she or he is acting. In one marriage, each spouse may unconsciously want to be pampered like an adored child instead of contributing to the partnership. In another, a bossy spouse has no idea how much she or he is trying to dominate the other and the one who is nagged may be asking for it. Very often an unfaithful partner has not really fallen in love with someone else but is running away from a hidden fear or unconsciously trying to make the spouse jealous.

Telling the children. Children are always aware of and disturbed by conflicts between their parents, whether or not divorce is being considered. It is good for them to feel that they can discuss these situations with their parents, together or singly, to get a more sensible picture than their morbid imaginations may suggest. It is important for children to believe in both their parents in order to grow up believing in themselves, so it is wise for the parents to avoid bitterly heaping blame, which is a natural temptation. Instead, they can explain their quarrels in general terms without pinning blame: "We get angry about every little thing," "We quarrel about how to spend money," "It upsets Mommy when Daddy takes several drinks."

It is wise to keep children from hearing the word divorce shouted in anger. When divorce becomes almost certain, it should be discussed, not just once but again and again. To young children the world consists of the family, which to them is mainly the father and mother. To suggest breaking up the family is like suggesting the end of the world. So the divorce has to be explained much more carefully to them than to an adult: that the children will live most of the time with, let's say, their mother; that their father will live nearby (or far away); that he will still love them and will still be their father; that they will live with him according to some schedule; and that they can telephone him and write him letters anytime. It is also very important to tell the child over and over again that it wasn't anything she did that made her parents divorce. Young children often imagine that it was their actions that caused the parents to separate.

Just as important as telling the children about the divorce is giving them ample opportunities to ask questions. You'll be amazed at some of their mistaken assumptions: for example, that they caused the divorce or that they may lose both parents. It is wise to straighten out these misunderstandings as promptly as possible, but don't be surprised if young children slip back into having weird misconceptions.

All children develop signs of tension. In one study, children under six most often showed fears of abandonment, sleep problems, regression to bed-wetting and temper tantrums, and aggressive outbursts. Children of seven and eight expressed sorrow and feelings of aloneness. Nine- and ten-year-olds were more understanding about the realities of divorce. They expressed hostility toward one or both parents and complained about stomachaches and headaches. Adolescents spoke of the pain of the divorce and their sadness, anger, and shame. Some girls were handicapped in developing good relationships with boys.

The best way to help children is to give them regular opportunities to talk about their feelings and to reassure them that they are normal, that they didn't cause the divorce, and that both parents still love them. If parents are in too much emotional pain themselves to do this with the children, it's important to find a professional counselor the children can see regularly.

Parents' reactions. Mothers who gain custody of the children usually find the first year or two after divorce very difficult. The children are more tense, demanding, and complaining; they are simply less attractive. The mother misses the part that the father played in making decisions, settling arguments, and sharing responsibility for plans. She is likely to be tired from working at a job and caring for the home and the children. She misses adult companionship, including the social and romantic attention of men. Worst of all, most mothers say, is the fear that they will not be able to earn a satisfactory living and run the family. (They may have secured an adequate child-support allowance in the agreement, but this doesn't guarantee that payments will arrive on time.) Many women say they receive great satisfaction in the end when they have proved to themselves that they can support and run a family without help. This gives them a sense of competence and confidence that they never had before in their lives.

One method of limiting expenses, sharing in the care of home and children, and having companionship that has proved practical and satisfying to some divorced women is to share a house or apartment with another divorced woman. They should of course know each other well before moving in together. Fathers who are awarded custody of their children have the same problems as mothers, so there is no reason why they should not consider this alternative.

Some people imagine that divorced fathers without custody, having no family responsibilities except child-support payments and visitations, can have a high old time and all the dates they can handle. However, studies show that most fathers are miserable much of the time. If they have casual affairs, they find them shallow and meaningless. They are unhappy not to be consulted about important and unimportant plans for the children. They miss their company. Even more, they miss having their children ask them for advice or permission, part of what a father is for. Their children's weekend visits often settle into a routine of fast food and movies, which may satisfy the children's needs for pleasure but not their or their father's need for a real relationship. Fathers and children may also find conversation difficult in the new situation.

Custody. It was assumed in the first three-quarters of the twentieth century that children's needs would be best served, at least up to adolescence, by living with and in the custody of the mother (unless she was clearly unfit). (In the nineteenth century and earlier, when divorce was rare, custody was usually awarded to the father, since the children were considered property to which he was entitled.)

In recent years, there is increasing recognition that many fathers are just as capable of nurturing children as mothers, and judges increasingly take this into account in awarding custody. Unfortunately, there is naturally intense bitterness in many divorces. This creates a rivalry between the parents over custody, keeping them from focusing on what is best for the children. Both assume that their having custody is best.

The factors to consider are these: Who has been providing most of the care, especially for babies and small children, who will badly miss their accustomed caregiver? What kind of relationship does each child have to each parent? What is each one's expressed preference, especially of older children and adolescents? How important is it for each child to live with a brother or sister (likely to be very important for twins)?

When a child, especially in adolescence, finds tension building with the custodial parent, she may think that the grass is greener on the other side. Sometimes it is better for this child to live with the other parent, at least for a while. But a child who moves back and forth several times may be trying to leave her problems behind rather than solving them. So it's important to find out what's really troubling her.

Joint custody. In the past, it has usually been assumed that in court the divorcing parents will be adversaries with regard to custody, child support, alimony, and property settlement. The more this battling attitude can be avoided, especially with custody, the better for the children. In recent years there has been a movement for joint custody, to keep the noncustodial parent (more frequently the father) from getting the short end of the stick in visitation rights and, even more important, to keep that parent from feeling divorced from his children and that he is no longer a real parent, a feeling that often then leads to a gradual withdrawal from contact with the children.

When speaking of joint custody, some lawyers and parents mean a fairly equal sharing of the children, such as four days with one, three with the other, or one week with one, then a week with the other. This may not be practical for the parents or comfortable for the children. Children should continue going to the same school, day care, or preschool. Children like and benefit from routine schedules.

It's more positive to see joint custody as a spirit of cooperation between the divorced parents for the children's welfare. They should consult with each other about plans, decisions, and responses to the children's major requests so that neither parent feels left out. (It may be very helpful to have a counselor, one who knows the children, to help the parents come to some decisions.) They should share the children's time in such a way that each parent keeps as closely in touch with them as possible. This will depend on such factors as the distance between the parents' dwellings, their capacity, the location of the school, and the preferences of the children as they grow older. Obviously if one parent moves across the continent, visits will have to come at vacation times. The parent can of course still keep in touch by email, letter, or phone.

Joint custody is practical only when both parents believe that they can subordinate any bitterness they have toward each other for the benefit of their children. Otherwise, the wrangling will be continuous. Then it's better for one parent to have custody and the judge to set the rules for visitation.

> ◁ **CLASSIC SPOCK**
> Joint custody lets both parents know that they are important in their child's life. Although it is a contract bound by the legal system, the most important thing here is the spirit of cooperation between the parents.

Details of joint custody arrangements. Parents can divide up the time the child is actually with each parent. This is referred to as joint physical custody. It is also possible when the parents have joint custody for a child to live primarily with either the mother or father. This is often referred to as joint legal custody. In joint legal custody, the parents consult each other about major decisions in the child's life—school, camp, health, and religion.

If the parents can work together, joint custody can have significant positive ramifications for the children. Research on divorce has found that in general children have a better social, psychological, and academic adjustment when both parents remain part of their lives.

Scheduling visitation. Five days with the mother and weekends with the father sounds practical and is common, but the mother may well want some weekend time with the children, when she can be more relaxed, and the father may want an occasional weekend without them. Much the same considerations may apply to school vacations. As the children grow older, friends, sports, or other activities may draw them to one home or the other. So any schedule requires flexibility.

It is vital that the noncustodial parent not casually break appointments for visits. Children are hurt when they receive the impression that other obligations are more important. They lose faith in the negligent parent and in their own worth. If appointments have to be canceled, it should be done well ahead of time and substitutions made if possible. Most important is that the noncustodial parent not frequently or erratically break contact.

Keeping visitation time comfortable. Some noncustodial parents feel shy or awkward when visitation time comes. They often respond by simply providing treats—meals out, movies, sporting events, excursions. There is nothing wrong with these occasionally, but they shouldn't think of treats as essential on every visit; such behavior signals that they are afraid of silences and makes these treats obligatory every time.

The children's visits can generally be as relaxed and routine as staying in their regular home is. That means opportunities for such activities as reading, doing homework, bicycling, roller skating on the sidewalk, shooting baskets, playing ball, fishing, and working on hobbies. The parent can participate in those activities they enjoy, which provide ideal opportunities for casual conversation. The children can watch their regular television programs (though I would discourage a whole weekend of viewing). Part of the time, the parent can pursue his own interests.

Parents often find that the children, especially younger ones, are irritable when they make the transition from one parent to the other. Especially on their return from a visit with the noncustodial parent, children may be cranky from fatigue. Sometimes it's simply that the child has difficulty shifting gears from one setting to another. Each departure and return may remind the child, at least subconsciously, of the original departure of the noncustodial parent.

Parents can help by being patient during the transitions, by being absolutely reliable about time and place of pickup or drop-off, and by keeping these exchanges as free of conflict as possible.

Grandparents after a divorce. It's also important for the children to maintain as much contact with their grandparents as they had before the divorce. It can be very difficult to stay in touch with the parents of your former spouse, especially if you or they are hurt or angry. Sometimes the custodial parent will say, "The children can see your parents during their visitation time with you. I won't have anything to do with your parents." But birthdays, holidays, and special occasions can seldom be so conveniently arranged. Remember that grandparents can often be a great source of support and continuity for the children, so keeping in touch will be worth the extra effort. The grandparents' own emotional need to stay in touch with their grandchildren should also be respected.

Avoid trying to bias the children. It's vital that one parent not try to discredit the other to the children, though it is tempting to do so. Both parents feel guilty about the failure of the marriage, at least unconsciously. If they can get their friends, relatives, and children to agree that the ex-spouse is at fault, they can lessen their feelings of guilt. So they are tempted to tell the worst possible stories about their ex, leaving out any mention of their own contribution. The trouble is that children sense that they are made up of both parents; if they accept the idea that one was a scoundrel, they'll assume that they've inherited some of that quality. Besides, they naturally want to retain two parents and be loved by both. They feel uncomfortably disloyal listening to criticism. It's equally painful for children if one parent involves them in keeping secrets from the other parent.

By adolescence, children know that all people have imperfections and are therefore not so deeply affected by the faults of their parents, though they can be plenty critical. Let them find the faults for themselves. Even at that age, it's better policy for one parent not to try to win the children's allegiance by criticizing the other. Teenagers are prone to turn hot or cold on slight provocation. If they become angry at the parent they've favored, they may do an about-face and decide that all the unfavorable things they've heard in the past about the other parent are unfair and untrue. Both parents will have the best chance of retaining their children's love for the long haul if they let them love both, believe in both, and spend time with both.

It's a mistake for one parent to pump the children about what happened while they visited the other parent. This only makes children uneasy; in the end it may backfire and make them resent the querying parent.

Dating by the parent. Children whose parents have been recently divorced consciously or unconsciously want them to get back together and think of them as still being married.

They are likely to feel that dating represents faithlessness on the part of their parent and that the date is an unwelcome intruder. So it is best for a parent to go slowly and be tactful in introducing a date to their children. Let the fact that the divorce is permanent sink in for a number of months. Be alert to the children's remarks. After a while, you can bring up the topic of your loneliness and introduce the idea that you may want to have dates. It's not that you are allowing your children to control your life forever; you are simply letting them know that dating is a possibility, doing so in a way that is more comfortable for them than being presented with a person in the flesh.

If you are a mother living with young children who rarely or never see their father, they may beg you to marry and give them another daddy, but they also may, and probably will, show evidence of jealousy as soon as you let them see the growing closeness between you and a man, especially when you marry again.

The same happens to a father who's had custody of his young children, who want him to give them another mommy.

Long-term effects on children. Children who have been through a divorce never come out untouched. Some struggle for a long time with feelings of anger, loss, or uncertainty, but many go on to have happy, fulfilled lives. Children who continue to have loving relationships with both parents do the best. Where this is not possible, professional counselors or therapists can often help.

Common Developmental and Behavioral Challenges

SIBLING RIVALRY

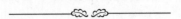

JEALOUSY BETWEEN SIBLINGS

There is bound to be some jealousy between siblings. If not severe, it probably helps children to grow up more tolerant, independent, and generous. One way children learn to deal with
their jealous feelings is take on some of the nurturing qualities
of their parents. In many families, jealousy is turned into
friendly competition, mutual support, and loyalty.

You may know other families where the children never really
liked each other very much and may not have much to do with
each other even as adults. Parents affect how sibling relationships develop, and luck also plays a role. Some siblings naturally
enjoy each other's company: They'd be friends even if they
weren't from the same family. Other siblings start out with very
different personalities—one likes noise and excitement, the
other craves peace and quiet—so have a harder time getting
along.

Equal love, different treatment. In a general way, the more
agreeably parents get along with each other, the less jealousy
there is. When all the children are satisfied with the warm affection they receive, they have less reason to begrudge the attention
their parents give to their brothers and sisters. What makes each

529

child secure in the family is the feeling that his parents love him and accept him for who he is.

Parents can love their children equally without treating them exactly the same. A useful principle is "Everybody in the family gets what they need—and sometimes we all need different things." A younger child needs an earlier bedtime. An older child needs more responsibility for chores.

When parents or relatives try to treat different children equally rather than individually, jealousy often intensifies. A harassed mother who is trying hard to treat her jealous children with perfect justice may say, "Now, Susie, here's a little red fire engine for you. And, Tommie, here is one exactly like it for you." Each child, instead of being satisfied, suspiciously examines both toys to see if there is any difference between them. It's as if the mother said, "I bought this for you so you wouldn't complain that I was favoring your brother," instead of implying "I bought this for you because I knew you'd like it."

Avoid comparisons and typecasting. The fewer comparisons, complimentary or uncomplimentary, between siblings, the better. Saying to a child, "Why can't you be polite like your sister?" makes him resent his sister and the very idea of politeness. If you say to an adolescent girl, "Never mind if you don't have dates like your sister; you're much smarter than she is, and that's what counts," it belittles her unhappiness at not having dates and implies that she should not be feeling what she is, in fact, feeling. This is a setup for further rivalry.

It's tempting for parents to typecast their children. One child is "my little rebel"; the other is "the angel." The first child may begin to believe that she always has to buck authority or risk losing her identity in the family. And even though the "good child" may sometimes feel like doing something naughty, she may fear that she has to continue to play her assigned role or risk losing her parents' love. She may resent the rebel for having a freedom she lacks.

Sibling fights. It generally works better if parents keep out of fights between children who can stand up for themselves. When parents concentrate on pinning the blame, it leaves one warrior feeling more jealous.

To a greater or lesser degree, children's jealous squabbles come about because each would like to be favored by the parents. When parents are quick to take sides, deciding who is right and who is wrong, it encourages the children to fight again soon. The fight becomes a tournament to see who can win Mom's allegiance, at least this time. Each wants to win the parents' favor and see the other scolded.

If you do feel that you have to break up a fight—to protect life and limb, prevent rank injustice, or restore quiet—it's better to demand an end to the hostilities, refuse to listen to arguments, act disinterested as to right and wrong (unless a flagrant foul was committed), concentrate on what's to be done next, and demand that bygones be bygones. You may suggest a compromise, distraction might save the day, or the children may need to be separated and sent to neutral, boring, and very separate locations.

When sibling fighting is severe and becoming increasingly more so, that is often a sign that family therapy may be needed (see page 623). Older children left to take care of their younger brothers and sisters may resort to violence or threats to keep control of them. If this happens, it's important to put someone else—a hired sitter, or an adult relative—in charge or find childcare or after-school programs for the children (see page 403).

THE MANY FACES OF JEALOUSY

Recognizing sibling jealousy. If a child picks up a block and swats the baby with it, the mother knows that he's jealous. Another child may be more subtle. He simply observes the baby with little enthusiasm or comment. One child focuses his resentment against his mother, grimly digging the dirt out of the houseplants and sprinkling it on the living room rug in a quiet, businesslike way. Another with a different makeup mopes and becomes dependent, loses his joy in the sandpile and his blocks, and follows his mother around, holding on to the hem of her skirt and sucking his thumb.

Occasionally you see a small child whose jealousy is turned inside out. He becomes preoccupied with the baby. When he sees a dog, all he can think of to say is, "Baby likes the dog." When he sees his friends riding trikes, he says, "Baby has a tricycle, too." In this circumstance, some parents may say, "We found that we didn't have to worry about jealousy at all. Johnny is so fond of the new baby." It is fine when a child shows love for the baby, but this doesn't mean that jealousy isn't there. It may show up in indirect ways or only in special circumstances. He may hug the baby a little too tightly. Perhaps he acts fond of her indoors but is rude when strangers admire her on the street. A child may show no rivalry for months until one day the baby creeps over to one of his toys and grabs it. Sometimes this change of feeling comes on the day the baby begins to walk.

Being oversolicitous of the baby is just another way of coping with the stress. At its root is the same cauldron of mixed feelings—love and jealousy—that drive other children to regress or indulge in wrathful fits. It's wise to go on the assumption that there is always both some jealousy and some affection, whether both show on the surface or not. The aim is not to ignore jealousy, forcibly suppress it, or to make the child feel deeply ashamed about it; it is to help the feelings of affection to come out on top.

Handling different kinds of jealousy. When the child attacks the baby, a parent's natural impulse is to be shocked and shame him. This doesn't work out well for two reasons. He dislikes the baby because he's afraid that his parents love her instead of him. The parents' shock is seen as a threat that they don't love him any more and makes him feel more worried and cruel inside. Shaming also may make him bottle up his feelings of jealousy. Jealousy does more harm to his spirit and lasts longer if it is suppressed than if it is allowed to stay out in the open.

As a parent in this situation, you have three aims: to protect the baby, to show the older child that he is not permitted to put his jealous feelings into action, and to reassure him that you still love him and that he is really a good boy. When you see him advancing on the baby with a grim look on his face and a weapon in his hand, obviously you must jump up and grab him, telling him firmly that he must not hurt the baby. (Whenever he succeeds in being cruel, it makes him feel guilty and more upset inside.)

In this situation lies the opportunity to teach the child that his feelings are understandable and acceptable; it is acting on those feelings that is not permitted. You might turn your grab into a hug and say, "I know how you feel sometimes, Johnny. You wish there weren't any baby around here for Mommy and Daddy to take care of. But don't you worry, we love you just the same." If he realizes at a moment like this that his parents accept

his angry feelings (but not his angry actions) and still love him, it is the best proof that he doesn't need to worry, let alone act out on that worry.

As for the child who intentionally spreads dirt around the living room, it's natural for you to feel exasperated and angry, and you will probably reprove him. But if you realize that he did it from a deep sense of despair and anxiety, you may later feel like reassuring him. Try to remember what may have happened to send him over the edge.

Withdrawal is a concern. The child who, being of a more sensitive and introspective nature, mopes in his jealousy needs affection, reassurance, and drawing out even more than the child who eases his feelings with aggression. With the child who doesn't dare show directly what's bothering him, it may actually help him to feel better if you can say understandingly, "I know that sometimes you feel mad at the baby and angry with me because I take care of her," and so on. If he doesn't respond after a while, consider hiring a temporary helper for the baby for a short while to see if he can recover his old zest for life by being given more individual attention.

It is worthwhile consulting a children's psychiatrist or psychologist or a pediatrician with special expertise in child behavior and development about the child who cannot seem to get over his jealousy, whether it takes the form of constantly misbehaving, moping, or obsession with the baby. The therapist may be able to draw the jealousy to the surface so the child can realize what's worrying him and get it off his chest.

If the jealousy comes out strongly only after the baby is old enough to grab the older child's toys, it may help a great deal to give the latter a room of his own, where he can feel that he, his toys, and his buildings are safe from interference. If a separate room is out of the question, find a big chest or cupboard for his things, one with a latch that the baby can't work. This protects his toys, and his having a latch that only he can operate gives him a sense of importance and control. (Beware of toy chests with heavy lids, or cupboards in which a child might become trapped; see page 134.)

Sharing toys. Should an older child be urged or compelled to share her toys with the baby? If you force your child to share her toys, chances are her resentment will grow, even if she does what you tell her to. Instead, try suggesting that she give the baby a plaything she has outgrown. This may appeal to her pride in her relative maturity, allowing her to demonstrate a generosity of spirit toward the baby that is not really there yet. For generosity to have any meaning, it must come from inside: the person must first feel secure, loving, and loved. Forcing a child to share her possessions when she feels insecure and selfish only makes her feel more put-upon and undervalued.

Generally speaking, jealousy of the baby is strongest in a child under five, since he is much more dependent on his parents and has fewer interests outside the family circle. The child of six or more is drawing away from his parents and building a position for himself among his friends and teachers, so being pushed out of the limelight at home doesn't hurt so much. It would be a mistake, though, to think that jealousy cannot exist in an older child. He, too, needs consideration and visible reminders of love from parents, particularly in the beginning. The older child who is unusually sensitive or has not found his place in the outside world may need just as much protection as the average young child. Stepchildren, whose relationships in the family may be shaky anyway, probably need extra help and reassurance. An adolescent girl, because of her growing desire to be a woman, may be unconsciously envious of her mother's new pregnancy or parenthood. Teens are often scandalized that their parents have a sex life. A typical remark is "I thought my parents were beyond that sort of thing."

Feeling guilty doesn't help. There's one caution to add here that may sound contradictory. Conscientious parents sometimes worry so much about jealousy and try so hard to prevent it that they make the older child less rather than more secure. They may reach the point where they feel guilty about having a new baby, are ashamed to be caught paying attention to her, and fall all over themselves trying to appease the older child. If a child finds that his parents are uneasy and apologetic toward him, it makes him uneasy, too. His parents' guilty behavior reinforces his own suspicion that there is dirty work afoot and inclines him to be nasty to both baby and parents. In other words, the parents should be as tactful as possible to the older child but not be worried, apologetic, submissive, or lacking in self-respect.

JEALOUSY OF THE NEW BABY

ᝃ CLASSIC SPOCK

Imagine this scenario: Your partner comes home one day with another woman and says to you: "Dear, I love you as much as I always have, but now this person is going to live with us too. By the way, she is also going to take up a lot of my time and attention because I'm crazy about her, and she is more helpless and needy than you are anyway. Isn't that wonderful? Aren't you delighted?" How nice do you think you would be?

I heard of a child who ran to the door when the visiting nurse was leaving and called out, "You forgot to take your baby."

Rivalrous feelings are often more intense in a firstborn child since he is used to the spotlight and has had no competition. A later child has had to learn to share his parents' attention after his birth. He sees that he's still just one of the children. This doesn't mean that second and third children don't have deep feelings of rivalry toward the next child; they do. More depends on how the parents handle the situation than on whether the child is firstborn.

Jealousy can be helpful as well as hurtful. Jealousy and rivalry invoke strong emotions, even in grown-ups. They can be more disturbing to the very young child, because she doesn't know how to deal with them. Though it can't be completely prevented, you can do a great deal to minimize jealousy or even convert it into positive feelings. If your child comes to realize that there is no reason to be fearful of a rival, it will strengthen her character, and prepare her to cope better with rivalry situations later in life, both at work, and at home.

What is important is not that the child feels jealous, which is normal, but how he resolves the feeling. Putting his feelings into words will help him master them. You can say, "I know you are angry and jealous, but hurting the baby won't help." You can add, "And I love you, too. I love you *and* the baby." If a two-year-old slaps the baby, for example, you can guide his hand into a caress and say, "He loves you." At any age, the child's feelings are a mixture; you can help the love to come out on top.

The first weeks and months. Ways to prepare a child for the birth of a sibling have been discussed in an earlier chapter (see Helping Siblings Cope, page 31). The first weeks and months are times when tactful parenting can also help. Play down the new baby in the early weeks. Don't act too excited about her. Don't gloat over her. Don't talk a lot about her. As far as is convenient, take care of her when the older one is not around. Fit in her bath and some of her feedings when he is outdoors or taking his nap.

A very young child may feel the greatest jealousy when he sees his mother feeding the baby, especially at the breast. Give him a bottle or a turn at the breast, if he wishes. It's a little funny to see an older child trying a bottle from envy of the baby. He thinks it's going to be heaven, but when he takes a suck, disappointment spreads over his face. It's just milk, after all, that comes out slowly, and has an odd, rubber taste. He may want a bottle on and off for a few weeks, but there's not much likelihood that he'll want to go on with it forever if his parents give it to him willingly and do other things to help him deal with his jealousy. If he's around when you feed the baby, he should be allowed in. But if he is playing happily downstairs, don't attract his attention to what's going on. The goal is not to avoid rivalrous feelings altogether—that is impossible—but to minimize them in the first weeks, when the awful reality for the older sibling is sinking in.

Other people play a part in jealousy, too. When a family member walks into the house, he should suppress the impulse to ask the child, "How's the baby today?" Better to act as if he has forgotten there is a baby, sit down, and pass the time of day with the child. Later he can drift on to have a look at the baby when the older one is interested in something else.

Grandparents who make a big fuss over the baby can be a problem, too. If the grandfather meets the older sibling in the front hall with a big package tied up in satin ribbon, and says, "Where's that darling baby sister of yours? I've brought her a present," the brother's joy at seeing his grandad turns to bitterness. If parents don't know a visitor well enough to coach her in how to act, they can keep a box of inexpensive presents on a shelf and produce one for the older child any time a visitor comes with a gift for the baby.

Helping your child feel more grown up. Playing with dolls may be a great solace to the older child, whether girl or boy, while the mother cares for the baby. He wants to warm his doll's bottle the way his mother does the baby's and have reasonable facsimiles of the clothing and equipment that his mother uses. But playing with a doll shouldn't take the place of having the child help care for the real baby; it should only supplement it.

Young children often react to a baby's arrival by yearning to be babies again, at least part of the time. This developmental regression is normal. They may, for example, lose ground in toilet training, resuming wetting or soiling themselves. They may lapse into baby talk and act helpless about doing things for themselves. I think parents are wise to humor the craving to be a baby at those moments when it is very strong. They can even good-naturedly carry the child up to his room and undress him, as a friendly game. Then he can see that he is not being denied these experiences, which he imagines are delightful but which may prove disappointing.

The drive to continue to grow and develop usually soon overtakes the desire to regress, if the temporary regressions are handled sympathetically and good-naturedly. You can help by paying little attention to these episodes of regression and by appealing most of the time to the side of your child that wants to grow up.

You can remind him of how big, strong, smart, or skillful he is, how much more he is able to do than the baby. That's not to say that you should constantly give him overenthusiastic praise, but you should remember to hand him a sincere compliment whenever appropriate. And I'd avoid pushing him too hard to be a grown-up. After all, if you are constantly calling everything the child temporarily yearns to do babyish and everything he's temporarily reluctant to do grown-up, he can only conclude that he wants to be a baby.

It's also important to avoid making comparisons that imply that you prefer the older child to the baby. To feel that he is favored may temporarily gratify a child, but in the long run he will feel insecure with parents who are partial, feeling that they might change their preference. The parents should of course let their love for the baby be evident. All the same, it is very helpful to give the older child chances to feel proud of his maturity and to remember that there are many disadvantages to being a baby.

Turning rivalry into helpfulness. One way a young child tries to get over the pain of having a younger rival is to act as if he himself is no longer competing in the same league as the baby.

Instead, he becomes a third parent. When he's very angry with the baby, he may act the role of the disapproving parent; when he feels more secure, he can be the kind of parent you are, one who teaches the baby how to do things, gives him toys, wants to assist in feeding, bathing, and clothing him, comforts him when he's miserable, and protects him from dangers.

You can assist his role-playing by suggesting how he can help you at times when it doesn't occur to him and showing real appreciation for his efforts. Sometimes it's not even pretend help: Parents of twins, who are often desperate for assistance in caregiving, are often amazed to find how much help they receive from a child as young as three years with tasks like fetching a bath towel, a diaper, or a bottle from the refrigerator.

A small child almost always wants to hold the baby, and parents hesitate for fear he may drop her. But if the child sits on the floor (on a carpet or blanket), in a large stuffed chair, or in the middle of a bed, there's little risk if the baby is dropped.

In such ways parents can help a child to transform resentful feelings into cooperativeness and genuine altruism. The stress of coping with a new sibling can be transformed into new skills in conflict resolution, cooperation and sharing. Learning to cope with the challenges of not being the only show in town is a lesson that may pay off all through life.

SIBLINGS WITH SPECIAL NEEDS

If the new baby has colic or for some other reason needs lots of extra attention, the older child will need extra reassurance that his parents love him just as much as before. It may be helpful for the parents to divide their chores up to be sure that one parent is always available to the older child. He'll also need to be reassured that nothing he did or thought is responsible for the baby being sick. Remember that young children are prone to think that everything that happens in the world is because of them.

Siblings of children who have special needs—a chronic medical condition, say, or a developmental problem, such as autism—also need special attention. Parents need to take care that the siblings *without* special needs feel included in the family and important in their own right. It is good for a healthy child to be able to help out in the care of a brother or sister with a chronic illness, but the healthy child also needs time and support to do normal childhood things: to have friends, play baseball, take piano lessons, just goof off. The healthy child needs at least some of the parent's time all to himself.

Meeting the special needs of one child and the everyday needs of his siblings puts great demands on a parent and on a marriage. There will be times when *someone's* needs aren't met. The point is that it shouldn't always be the healthy child who has to make that sacrifice. Finding the right balance is a great challenge. Help from outside the nuclear family—other relatives, friends, professionals, and community programs—often makes it possible.

Siblings of children with special needs sometimes grow up angry or sad, burdened with emotional or behavioral problems. Many, however, develop maturity, generosity, perspective, and a sense of purpose that serve them well throughout life.

ACTING OUT

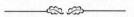

TEMPER TANTRUMS

Why tantrums? Almost all children have temper tantrums between one and three years (see pages 143 and 158). They know their desires and have a sense of their own individuality. When they're thwarted, they know it and become angry. Yet they don't usually attack the parent who interfered with them, perhaps because that grown-up is too important and too big. Also, their fighting instinct isn't very well developed yet.

Instead, when fury boils up in them, they can think of nothing better to do than take it out on themselves and the floor. They flop down, yell, and pound with their hands, feet, and maybe their heads.

A temper tantrum once in a while doesn't mean anything; a child is bound to be frustrated sometimes. A surprising number of tantrums are a result of fatigue or hunger or of putting a child in a situation that exceeds his capabilities. (Most shopping mall tantrums fall into this category.) If the tantrum is of this sort, a parent can ignore the apparent cause and deal with the underlying problem: "You're tired and hungry, aren't you? Let's get you home, fed, and to bed, and you'll feel a lot better."

You can't dodge all temper tantrums. Parents would be unnatural if they had that much patience and tact. When the storm breaks, try to take it casually and help to end it. Don't give in and meekly let the child have her way; otherwise she'll be throwing tantrums on purpose all the time. Don't argue with her, because she's in no mood to see the error of her ways. Becoming angry yourself only forces her to keep up her end of the row. Give her a graceful way out. One child cools off quickest if the parents fade away and matter-of-factly go about their own business, as if they can't be bothered. Another, with more determination and pride, continues to yell and thrash for an hour unless her parents make a friendly gesture. As soon as the worst of the storm has passed, they might pop in with a suggestion of something fun to do and a hug to show they want to make up.

It's embarrassing to have a child throw a tantrum on a busy sidewalk. Pick her up, with a grin if you can manage one, and lug her off to a quiet spot where you can both cool off in private.

Frequent tantrums. A child who has frequent temper tantrums often has inborn traits of temperament that lead to frustration. For example, she may be very sensitive to changes in temperature or noise level or to the feel of different clothes on the skin. She may have a tantrum every time her parents put her socks on, unless the seams at the toes are in exactly the right place. Another child is very persistent. Once she is doing something interesting, it's very hard to tear her away. This child might be very successful later on in school, when persistence is often rewarded by high grades. But when she is young, her persistence guarantees a couple of tantrums a day.

Another temperament trait that results in frequent tantrums is high intensity of expression. Children with this trait are very dramatic. When they're happy, they shout with glee; when they're upset, they wail in despair. Another kind of tantrum-prone child is very sensitive to new people and places. It takes this child several minutes before he feels comfortable. If he's pushed to join the group before he's ready, he may throw a tantrum.

If your child throws frequent temper tantrums, ask yourself

the following questions: Does she have plenty of chances to play
freely outdoors? Are there things for her to push and pull and
climb on there? Has she enough toys and household objects indoors to play with, and is the house childproof? Do you arouse
balkiness without realizing it, by telling her to come put her shirt
on instead of slipping it on her without comment? When you
know that she needs to use the toilet, do you find yourself asking
her if she wants to go to the bathroom instead of leading her
there? When you have to interrupt her play to get her indoors or
to meals, do you give her a minute or two to find a good stopping
place? Do you get her mind on something pleasant that you're
about to do? When you see a storm brewing, do you grimly meet
it head-on, or do you distract her with something else?

Learned tantrums. Some children have learned that tantrums
are the best way to get what they want. It's hard to sort these
manipulative tantrums from tantrums caused by frustration,
hunger, tiredness, or fear. One hint is that manipulative
tantrums tend to stop right away once the child gets what he
wants. Another hint is that the child may work up to the
tantrum by whining in a demanding way. The answer to these
tantrums, of course, is for parents to stick to their guns. When
they say, "No cookies now," the cookies should not appear two
minutes later in response to a tantrum.

To make this strategy work, you have to pick your battles
carefully. If you feel strongly that cookies before dinner are a bad
idea, by all means lay down a "no cookies" rule, and stick to it. If
you *don't* feel strongly, consider saying yes *before* the tantrum,
because if you wait until *after* the tantrum to say "Yes," your
child will have learned that tantrums work!

A lot of parents find that their children throw tantrums about
cookies but rarely if ever when they're getting buckled into their
car seats. Why? Because the parents are absolutely consistent
with the car seats, so the children know there is no point in
protesting that rule.

Tantrums in older children. Tantrums are a normal part of being two. And everybody, child or adult, loses it once in a while. By age four or five, most children are down to the rare tantrum, maybe one or two a week. One child in five, though, continues to throw frequent tantrums, three or more a day, or long ones, lasting more than fifteen minutes. Often, the cause is one of those described above: difficult temperament traits or a bid to exert power. Sometimes, however, frequent tantrums are a sign of a more serious problem.

A common cause is delayed language development. Such children often become frustrated because they can't make their needs and wants known. They may feel cut off from other children and adults, a lonely and frustrating feeling. Since they can't let their frustrations out in words when they are upset, all they can do is *show* their anger.

As children grow older, they learn to talk to themselves to calm themselves down. If you think about it, you probably talk to yourself, too, either out loud or silently, when you need to calm or reassure yourself. A child who has underdeveloped language skills can't use this very powerful self-comforting and self-control strategy. So, negative emotions are more likely to be expressed in tantrums.

Other causes of frequent tantrums in older children include developmental problems, such as mental retardation, autism, and learning disabilities. When children have been seriously ill, parents often have a hard time setting limits. Frequent tantrums may be the unhappy result. For these problems—or any time tantrums are out of control and not responding to basic good parenting and the passage of time—it makes sense to seek the help of an experienced professional (see page 620).

SWEARING AND BACK TALK

Potty talk. Around four years of age, children may go through a phase of reveling in bathroom words. They cheerfully insult each other with expressions like "You great big poop" and "I'll flush you down the toilet" and think they are very witty and bold. You should consider this a normal development, one that usually passes soon. In my experience, young children who continue to delight in using naughty words are those whose parents are openly shocked and dismayed and who threaten dire consequences for continued use of bathroom language.

This often has the opposite of the intended effect. The child thinks to herself: "Hey, this is a pretty good way to stir things up. This is fun! This gives me power over my parents." Her parents, in turn, become increasingly upset with her.

The easiest way to stop a young child from using naughty words is to simply ignore them. If the words float out into space and nothing comes back, the child is likely to lose interest.

School-age swearing. As they grow older, all children learn swearwords and dirty words from their friends. Long before they know what the words mean, they know that they are naughty. Being human, they repeat them to show that they are worldly wise and unafraid to be a little bad. It's usually a shock to conscientious parents to hear these words coming from the mouths of their supposedly sweet innocents.

What's a good parent to do? As with the three- or four-year-old, it's better not to be horribly shocked. On timid children, this has too strong an effect; it worries them and makes them afraid to be around children who use bad words. But most children who have shocked their parents are delighted, at least secretly. Some of them go on endlessly cussing at home, hoping to get the same rise. Others, stopped at home by threats, use their bad language elsewhere. The point is that when you show children that they have the power to scandalize the whole world, it's like handing them a firecracker and telling them, "For goodness' sake, don't set it off."

On the other hand, you don't have to sit mute and just take it. You can firmly tell your child that you and most other people don't like to hear those words and that you don't want them to use them. End of discussion. If your child persists in challenging you, you can use time-out as a reasonable consequence (see page 418).

Teenagers. Last comes the cursing of some teenagers, who liberally interject curse words into many of their conversations. These expletives serve multiple purposes: to express disgust or contempt (a common feeling in many teens), to underline the importance of the topic, to discharge emotion, to show frank disregard for arbitrary and old-fashioned societal taboos. But cursing at this age serves primarily as a mark of belonging to one's peer group.

You will lose any debate about whether swearing is good or bad, and your child already knows that some behavior makes you unhappy. But it is reasonable for you to request that your teen limit his swearing to times when it won't offend others or prove harmful to himself. For example, no swearing in your presence, no swearing in front of his little brother, no swearing at school. As with younger children, if you make a big deal about the swearing, you will probably only end up giving your teen an easy way to show his independence and feel powerful. With teens in particular, it's helpful to focus on what they are saying, rather than how they are saying it.

Back talk. With back talk, as with swearing, the key is to focus on what the child says, not how she says it. Young children often try talking back as a way to test limits and exert power (see page 418). It's helpful to let the child know that you have heard her, but then make sure that your rules still stand: "I know you don't want to stop now, but it's time to pick up" (while helping the child to start picking up).

If you are reasonably polite to your child, you have the right to expect reasonable politeness in return. Sometimes children need to be told or reminded that the way they are expressing themselves is, in fact, rude. A clear, unemotional statement often works best: "When you talk to me in that tone of voice, it makes me feel that you don't respect me. That makes me angry." Another approach is to ask the child what he meant by his tone of voice: "Were you meaning to sound sarcastic just now? I just want to be sure I really understand what you want to tell me."

BITING

Biting babies. It's natural for babies around one year to take a bite out of their parent's cheek. Teething makes them want to bite anyway, and when they feel tired they're even more in the mood for it. It also doesn't mean much when a child between one and two bites another child, whether in a friendly or angry spirit. Children at that age can't express their feelings in words, so their frustration or desire to dominate comes out in primitive ways, like biting. Additionally, they can't really put themselves in their victim's shoes; they usually don't realize how much it hurts the other child.

A parent or other caregiver can say firmly, "That hurts! Be gentle," then briefly put the child down on the floor or remove him from the playgroup for a moment. The idea is simply to give him the message that this behavior makes you unhappy, even if he is too young to understand exactly why.

Toddlers and preschoolers who bite. If biting is a problem between ages two and three, you have to decide if it is an isolated one. Consider how often the biting occurs and how the child gets along otherwise. If he is tense or unhappy much of the time and bites other children, it's a sign that something is wrong. Perhaps he is disciplined or restricted too much at home or is frantic and high-strung. Perhaps he has had too little chance to get used to other children and imagines them to be dangerous and threatening. Perhaps he is jealous of a baby at home and carries over the fear and resentment to all other small children, treating them as competitors, too.

When biting is accompanied by other aggressive and worrisome behaviors, it is a symptom of a larger problem. It is that larger problem, rather than the biting, that should draw your attention.

Usually, however, biting comes like a thunderbolt out of the blue in an otherwise model citizen and is a normal developmental challenge, not a psychological problem. Still, most parents of biters worry a lot, imagining that their sweet child may grow up to be a cruel adult. But biting is usually a temporary behavior that even the gentlest of children engage in.

What to do about biting. The first thing to do is to prevent biting before it starts. Are there predictable times when it occurs? If so, adult supervision at those times is often useful. Is your child often frustrated because he is the least competent member of his playgroup or because your limit-setting is inconsistent? You may need to consider changing his daily routine. Also, be sure to give him lots of positive attention when he behaves well. Some children only receive really intense attention from their parents after they've broken something or bit someone. It's much more effective to give high-intensity attention in response to positive behavior.

When you see your child's frustration growing, redirect his attention to another activity. If your child is old enough, you can discuss the problem at another time, asking him to think about how it hurts and what else he can do when he has the urge to bite.

If the biting has already occurred, it's helpful to turn your attention first of all to the child who was bitten, ignoring the biter. After comforting the victim, give your child the firm message that biting makes you unhappy. Tell him not to do it again. Then sit with him for a few minutes while the message sinks in. Hold his hand or hug him firmly if he tries to go away. Avoid long lectures.

Bite back? Some parents who have been bitten by an infant or a one-year-old ask if they should bite back. Parents can control their child better by staying in charge as a friendly boss than by descending to the child's age level with bites, slaps, or shouts. Besides, when you bite or slap a very young child, he's likely to bite or slap back, as a fight, or a game, or because he believes that if you are capable of such behavior, why shouldn't he be? The best response is to keep from being bitten again by drawing back when he gets that gleam in his eye, clearly showing him that you don't like it and won't let him do it.

Biting after three. Biting usually stops by the third birthday or a little after. By that time, the child has learned to use words to express his desires or vent his frustrations. He also is better able to restrain his impulses. Children this age continuing to bite may be a sign of a bigger developmental or behavioral problem. An experienced doctor, nurse practitioner, or other professional can be very helpful (see page 620).

HYPERACTIVITY (ADHD)

What is hyperactivity? Most people use hyperactivity to mean the same thing as attention deficit hyperactivity disorder (ADHD). The most widely accepted definition of ADHD has three main parts: inattention, impulsivity, and hyperactivity. That is, a child with ADHD has poor ability to focus and sustain attention on tasks that aren't terrifically interesting; difficulty controlling impulses, such as calling out in class with an answer or hitting someone who rubs him the wrong way; and difficulty sitting still in class or at the dinner table, being constantly on the go, or fidgeting. To be ADHD, these problems need to be severe enough to interfere seriously with the child's life. A child who has a lot of energy, is the class clown, or is spacey but who is doing okay in school and getting along okay at home does not have ADHD.

Does ADHD exist? Despite ongoing controversy, nearly every professional agrees that there are *some* children who have a condition of the brain that makes them extremely hyperactive, impulsive, and inattentive. Where experts disagree is in the matter of how many such children there are. Using the criteria for diagnosing ADHD published by the American Psychiatric Association, a great many children in the United States—from one in twenty to one in ten—have ADHD.

The problem is that the published criteria for diagnosing ADHD rely on the answers parents and teachers give to fuzzy questions. For example, one of the criteria is that a child—in the opinion of a parent or teacher—"often has difficulty organizing tasks and activities." There is no clear definition of the terms "often," "difficulty," and "tasks and activities." Does "often" mean once a day or all day long? Is fixing a lawn mower a "task or activity"—something many children with ADHD can do handily—or does the term apply only to school work? It's not surprising that teachers and parents often disagree in their assessments of whether a given child is hyperactive.

So, although it is clear that there are many children who struggle in school and at home and whose problems fall into the three areas that define ADHD—hyperactivity, inattention, and impulsivity—it's not clear how many of them have abnormal brains. I suspect that many of them have brains that are perfectly healthy but are simply not well suited to doing what we now require all children to do: sit still, listen, and follow directions for paper-and-pencil tasks all day long.

Does bad parenting cause ADHD? There is no question that children who are inattentive, overactive, and impulsive put great strains on their parents. Some parents of children with ADHD have excellent parenting skills, many are average, and a few have very limited skills. There's no evidence, though, that parenting *causes* ADHD. A child who is spoiled—one who has never learned to take no for an answer or to wait for what he wants—can act in ways that look like ADHD. But most children with ADHD have grown up under reasonable limits and discipline but have not responded the way most children do.

Things that look like ADHD. Many children have conditions that make it appear that they have ADHD, but they don't. Some of these problems are inside the child; for example, seizures that cause a child to black out for a few seconds many times a day. Other problems that look like ADHD are outside the child, such as school curriculum that is either much too hard or much too easy for that child. More often than not, many different things are going on all at once: children who have emotional and learning problems and live in stressful homes and whose school classrooms are out of control. It's hard for anyone, even a skilled doctor, to sort through this puzzle, and it's often tempting to simply call it ADHD and prescribe medication. But the usual medications for ADHD are likely to make some conditions—such as seizures or anxiety—worse and not help others. So it is very important that parents and doctors take time and care when diagnosing ADHD.

Some of the conditions that can look like ADHD include:

- Psychiatric problems, including depression, obsessive-compulsive disorder, and response to trauma or grief;
- Hearing and vision problems;
- Learning disabilities (children with reading difficulties often act out in classes; see page 673). Learning disabilities often occur together with ADHD; at other times, learning disabilities are mistaken for ADHD.
- Sleep disorders (overtired children are often inattentive and may act impulsively; see page 200, sleep in adolescents).

- Medical problems, such as seizures or side effects of medication.

How doctors diagnose ADHD. There is no blood test or brain scan for the diagnosis of ADHD. Children with ADHD sometimes act normally in the doctor's office because they are on their best behavior. (Children with ADHD *can* behave appropriately; they just can't do it consistently.) So doctors have to rely on information from parents and teachers as well as their own observations. According to professional standards published in 2000 by the American Academy of Pediatrics, a doctor attempting to diagnose ADHD should obtain information from at least one parent and one teacher, by interview, questionnaire, or a written description. The doctor should review the child's developmental and psychiatric history, review the family history, interview the child, and carry out a thorough physical examination. A doctor who makes a diagnosis of ADHD after spending only fifteen minutes with a child is not acting properly.

Often, a pediatrician or family doctor will work together with a psychologist or psychiatrist to diagnose ADHD, perhaps using psychological testing and a detailed learning assessment.

Treatments for ADHD. There are many kinds of treatment available to children with ADHD. Most benefit by having more than one. It's usually a mistake, for example, to treat the child only with medication without trying to change the way parents and teachers deal with his challenging behavior.

The diagnosis of ADHD does *not* automatically mean that a child has to be on medication. There is, however, plenty of evidence that medication is the most effective treatment for the core symptoms of ADHD: inattentiveness, impulsivity, and overactivity. In a recent large study, children who were given both medication and psychological treatment did no better (in terms of their core ADHD symptoms) than children who were given medication alone.

But psychological counseling and other nonmedication therapies are still very important for two reasons. First, they help
children cope with problems brought on by the ADHD, such as
difficulty making friends and dealing with frustration. Second,
nonmedication therapies are important to help children with
the learning and behavior problems that often go along with
ADHD but are not the core symptoms. Medication for the
ADHD does not treat learning disabilities; for those, special education is required.

Medications for ADHD. The medications most often used to
treat ADHD are stimulants. Like caffeine, stimulants increase
alertness by stimulating parts of the brain that are active during
focused attention. Also like caffeine, stimulants cause the heart
to beat faster and can create a feeling of anxiety or being wired,
especially at higher doses. The two main stimulants used are
methylphenidate (the medication in Ritalin, Concerta, and
Metadate, among others) and amphetamine (the medication in
Adderall, Dextrostat, Dexedrine, and others). Stimulants have
been researched extensively, and found to work for nearly eight
out of ten children with ADHD.

Are stimulants safe? Many parents are afraid to use medication
to treat ADHD. It is reasonable to be concerned about any substance that affects how a child's brain works, especially if the
child may need to take it for many years. Moreover, a lot of misinformation about Ritalin and other ADHD medications has
been spread around, and many of the fears that parents have are
unfounded.

It appears that stimulants are not addictive the way drugs
such as heroin or cocaine are. Children who suddenly stop taking Ritalin, for example, do not crave it or have withdrawal
symptoms. Some people abuse stimulants to get high, but children who take stimulants to treat ADHD are calmed by the
medication, not jazzed up. Children with ADHD do go on to de-

velop alcoholism and other addictions more often than other children, but it's doubtful that the medication causes that. In fact, children with untreated ADHD may turn to alcohol or drugs as a way to deal with feelings of sadness and hopelessness that result from their endless troubles in school, at home, and with peers. Medication treatment for ADHD may make it less likely that teens abuse illegal drugs.

Stimulants do have side effects, such as stomachaches, headaches, reduced appetite, and sleep problems. But for the most part, these are mild and go away after the dosage is adjusted. Children taking stimulants should not be either spacey or act like zombies. These are symptoms of overdosing. Either the dose needs to be lowered or a different medication found. I know medication is working when I ask a child how it makes him feel and he responds, "I feel like myself." A key to the safe use of medication—any medication—is close monitoring by a doctor. Children on medication for ADHD should see the doctor at least four times a year, more often in the beginning while the dose is being adjusted.

Children who take medication for ADHD do not have to stay on it for their entire lives, although many do choose to continue through adolescence. As children get older, their physical hyperactivity tends to wane but their difficulty in focusing often continues and medication continues to help them. Others, by exercising a great deal of self-discipline, do well without medication.

What happens to children with ADHD? With good medical care and education, children with ADHD should be able to succeed. As they grow, the traits that caused them so much trouble in school—spontaneity, energy, the ability to think about three things at once—may serve them well in the workplace. Children who have other problems in addition to ADHD, such as depression or severe learning disabilities, face a tougher road and need more support.

A good way to know if your approach to ADHD is working is to pay attention to your child's self-esteem. A child who feels good about himself has friends, likes school, and does well. A child who feels bad about himself, who frequently says that he's "stupid" or that the other kids don't like him, needs more help. Over time, low self-esteem may become a bigger problem than the ADHD itself.

What you can do. If you think your child might have ADHD, talk with your child's doctor or another professional (see page 620). The Resource Guide (page 917) lists parent support organizations and books that may be helpful. As with any chronic developmental or medical condition, the more you know, the better you'll be able to work with doctors, teachers, and other professionals to support your child's healthy development.

MESSINESS, DAWDLING, AND WHINING

MESSINESS

Let them get dirty sometimes. Children want to do a lot of things that get them dirty, and doing them is often good for children, too. They love to dig in earth and sand, wade in mud puddles, splash in water in the sink. They want to roll in the grass and squeeze mud in their hands. When they do these delightful things, it enriches their spirit and makes them warmer people, just the way beautiful music or falling in love improves adults.

Small children who are sternly warned against getting their clothes dirty or making a mess and who take these warnings to heart become inhibited and mistrustful of the things they enjoy. If they become really timid about dirt, it makes them too cautious in other ways also and keeps them from developing into the free, warm, life-loving people they were meant to be.

I don't mean to give the impression that you must always let your children make any kind of mess that strikes their fancy. But when you do have to stop them, don't try to scare them or disgust them; just substitute something else a little more practical. If when they have their Sunday clothes on they want to make mud pies, have them change into old clothes first. If they get hold of an old brush and want to paint the house, set them to work with a pail of water for paint on the woodshed or the tile floor of the bathroom.

Messes around the house. Once children are old enough to make a mess, they're old enough to learn to clean it up. At first they'll need a lot of help; later, they can take on more of the task themselves. A child who leaves a mess may have learned that someone else—Mommy, perhaps—will clean it up. Another child is simply overwhelmed, needing directions and help in breaking the task into manageable pieces: "First, find all the wooden blocks and put them in the block box."

If children refuse to clean up messes, it's reasonable to deprive them of the privilege of playing with the toys that were left around for a few days (see page 429 for nonphysical punishments). If you've stored away a lot of your child's toys there are simply fewer toys to trip over. If you store toys for longer periods, when they come out of the closet they are "new" again, and therefore much more fun for a while.

The messy room. A child's bedroom is a different story. If a child has her own room, it's good for her to take responsibility for it. From a parent's point of view, that may mean keeping quiet about a level of disorder that would be unacceptable in other parts of the home. Setting aside vermin, fire hazards, and a floor so cluttered that it's impossible to walk, a messy room harms no one but its occupant. A child who always has to search around for her favorite pants or socks that match eventually learns to put things where they belong.

Giving your child responsibility doesn't mean that you shouldn't remind her gently from time to time about the room or even offer to help out. After a certain level of messiness, many children simply don't know where to start. But the problem belongs to your child, so the solution should, too.

DAWDLING

If you've ever watched a parent trying to jump-start a dawdling child in the morning, you probably vowed that you would never get into that fix. The parent urges him and warns him; scolds him to get out of bed, get washed and get dressed, eat his breakfast, start for school.

The dawdling child wasn't born that way, although some children were clearly born less self-directed than others. Most dawdlers were gradually made that way by constant pushing: "Hurry up and finish your lunch." "How many times do I have to tell you to get ready for bed?" It's easy to fall into the habit of prodding children, but it may build up an absentminded balkiness in them. Parents say they have to nag, or the child won't get anywhere. It becomes a vicious circle, but the parent usually starts it—especially an impatient one or one who doesn't leave enough time to allow for children's naturally slow pace.

⤜ CLASSIC SPOCK

You may have the impression that I think children should not be held to any obligation. On the contrary. I think they should sit down at the table when the meal is ready and get up in the morning at the proper time. I'm only making the point that if they are allowed to use their own initiative most of the time, are reminded in a matter-of-fact way when they've clearly failed to do something on their own, are not prodded unnecessarily in advance, and are not hurried all the time, they usually find strategies to overcome their slow-starting nature.

Early teaching. In the early years, before a child is capable of carrying out directions, lead him through his various routines. As he gets old enough to want to take over responsibilities, step out of the picture as fast as you can. When he forgets and slips back, lead again. When he goes to school, let him think of it as his job to get there on time. It may be better to quietly allow him to be late to school once or twice or to miss the bus and school altogether and find out how sorry he feels. A child hates to miss things even more than his parent hates to have him miss them. That's the best spring to move him along.

Dealing with dawdling. An older child who dawdles may be disorganized or distractible. She starts out with the intention of getting dressed, then on the way to her dresser she finds a toy that needs playing with, a doll that has to be put to bed, and a book that needs reading. Fifteen minutes later she's still in her pajamas, happily playing. One strategy is to help the child make a chart, using pictures or, if she can read and write, words, outlining the different steps that must be done, say, to get ready for school in the morning. Cover the list with clear plastic so that the child can use a dry-erase marker to check off each step as she completes it. Set a timer, and have her try to get through her list before it dings. Give her a small reward for beating the clock. The best rewards follow naturally: getting dressed and ready on time without having to be nagged means that there is time for a few minutes of your reading aloud to her or video gaming, even television, before it's time to leave for school.

WHINING

The whining habit. Whining is common in the preschool and early school years (see page 159). Here the focus is on the special problem of the chronic, continual whiners who make themselves and their parents miserable. It's a pattern of excessive demandingness that takes weeks or months to become fully established and quite a while to overcome.

The whiner's words may vary—"There's nothing to do," she keeps complaining on a rainy day, or "Why can't I stay up for this program?"—but the wheedling, whining, nagging tone is unmistakable. The same request is repeated again and again. Most

of the requests are for things or activities that all children enjoy—but are made repeatedly and in an unreasonable way.

Many children whine at only one parent. This whining often expresses not simply a habit or a mood in a child but also an attitude toward, or a slightly disturbed relationship with, that parent. Often, too, a parent with two or more children tolerates whining in only one.

ᏇᏗ CLASSIC SPOCK

I remember spending a day with a family in which the mother was a no-nonsense person with three of her four children. They were polite, cooperative, independent, cheerful individuals, but the five-year-old girl bugged her mother endlessly. She complained of boredom, hunger, thirst, and cold when she herself could easily have found remedies for these small needs.

The mother would ignore her for a while. Then she'd suggest that the girl get what she wanted. But she'd say it in an indecisive or apologetic tone. She never got masterful, even after an hour of steady whining. Sometimes she would even begin to whine back to "quit the whining." The end result: a nonproductive, mewling duet.

In one sense, such whining is not a serious disturbance. But it's certainly a pain in the neck to the other members of the family and to their friends, and it can lead to a mountain of frustration in the parent who hears it most often.

Why do some parents tolerate whining? Some parents may feel that they have to accept whining because they have been guilty of something: not giving the child what she needs, perhaps, or not loving her enough. Extremely conscientious parents who were brought up with a lot of criticism from their parents and as a result are easily made to feel inadequate, often begin child care with at least a mild sense of guilt about their lack of knowledge on the subject and a fear that they'll do the wrong thing.

There are various reasons for parents to feel unconsciously guilty toward only one of their children. The parent may not have been fully ready for the pregnancy, may have resented the unborn child, may have gotten off on the wrong foot with a baby who was very fretful or demanding, or may be reminded of a family member who made the parent's life miserable and aroused a great deal of both hostility and guilt, emotions that now color that parent's behavior toward the child. Parents who were abused in their own childhoods often worry that they will be too harsh to their children. This can make it hard for them to set reasonable limits.

How to stop the whining. There are definite, practical steps you can take if your child is an habitual whiner. First, ask yourself whether your attitude feeds the whining. You may be using an expression of evasiveness, hesitation, submissiveness, or guilt mixed with the irritability that inevitably comes from feeling victimized. This is the most difficult step, because parents are usually unaware of anything except the child's constant demands and their impatience.

If you see no uncertainty in your behavior, ask yourself how you may be unwittingly rewarding the whining: for example, by paying too much attention to it or finally giving in to stop it.

Make as many rules as necessary to cover all the usual pleas, then stick to them with determination and consistency. Bedtime is always to be at a specific hour, only certain television programs may be viewed, friends may be invited for a meal or an overnight only at a specific frequency. These are the family rules, carved in stone by benevolent dictators. There can be no arguments about them.

If your child whines that he has nothing to do, it's smarter not to be drawn into suggesting a variety of possible activities, since a child in this mood will scornfully and with relish shoot them down, one by one. You can toss the responsibility back to the child without getting bogged down in a futile argument by saying, "Well, I've got a ton of work to do, then I'm going to do some fun stuff afterward." In other words, "Follow my example: find things to do for yourself. Don't expect me to argue with you or amuse you."

You can also tell your child that you don't respond to requests made in a whining tone of voice. You can say simply, "Please stop whining right now." If your child persists in annoying you, threatening to make you miserable unless you give in, you can impose a time-out (see page 429).

It's fine to give children reasons: "We're not having pizza for dinner because we just had pizza for lunch" or "We have to go home now, so we can take our naps." But sometimes (often!) parents just have to make decisions and children just have to live with them. "We're not buying that toy today because we're not buying toys today." Confident parents don't engage in endless arguments with their children about the limits they've set. If allowed to do so, children will keep such conversations going forever, probably outnegotiating the parent at every turn. State your case, set your limits, and end the conversation pleasantly but decisively.

It's fine for children to occasionally ask for something special and fine for parents to give freely what they ask for if they think the request is reasonable. But it's also important for children to learn to accept no or not today as an answer. Demanding whining is a sign that your child has yet to learn this key lesson.

HABITS

THUMB-SUCKING

What thumb-sucking means. Thumb-sucking means different things in babies than in older children. Many babies suck their thumbs, fingers, or fists even before they are born. Sucking, after all, is how babies get nutrition, and it also helps them relieve physical and emotional tension. Babies who nurse more tend to suck their thumbs less since they already do plenty of sucking. Not all babies are born with the same urge to suck. One baby never nurses more than fifteen minutes at a time yet never puts a thumb in her mouth. Another baby, whose bottles always take twenty minutes or more, needs still more time sucking. A few begin to thumb-suck in the delivery room and keep at it; others thumb-suck early then soon give it up. Most babies who thumb-suck start before they are three months old.

Thumb-sucking is different from the thumb-, finger-, and hand-chewing that almost all babies do from the time they begin to teethe (commonly at three to four months). The baby who is a thumb-sucker naturally sucks at one minute and chews at another during his teething periods.

Thumb-sucking in the older baby and child. By the time a baby is six-months-old, thumb-sucking has turned into something different. It is a comforter that she needs at special times. She sucks when she is tired, bored, or frustrated or to put herself to sleep. When she can't make a go of things at a more grown-up level, she retreats to early infancy, when sucking was her chief joy. It's very rare for a child beyond the age of a few months or a year to thumb-suck for the first time.

Is there anything the parents need to do? Probably not, if the child is generally outgoing, happy, and busy and sucks mainly at bedtime and occasionally during the day. Thumb-sucking by itself is not a sign of unhappiness, maladjustment, or lack of love. In fact, most thumb-suckers are very happy children; children who are severely deprived of affection don't thumb-suck.

If a child sucks a great deal of the time instead of playing, parents should ask themselves whether there is anything they ought to do so that she won't need to comfort herself so much. Another child may be bored from not seeing enough of other children or from not having enough things to play with. Or perhaps she has to sit for hours in her playpen. A boy of a year and a half may be at loggerheads with his mother all day if she always stops him from doing the things that fascinate him instead of diverting him to playthings that are permissible. Another boy has children to play with and freedom to do things at home but is too timid to throw himself into these activities. He thumb-sucks while he watches. The point of these examples is to make it clear that if there is anything that needs to be done for excessive thumb-sucking, it is to make the child's life more satisfying.

Health effects of thumb-sucking. The physical problems caused by thumb-sucking are mild: thickened skin on the favored thumb or finger is common (it will go away on its own). Minor infections around the finger nail may occur; they are usually easy to treat (see page 781). The most serious problems are orthodontic. It is true that thumb-sucking often pushes the upper front baby teeth forward and the lower ones back. How much they are displaced depends on how much the child sucks her thumb and even more on the position she holds her thumb in. Dentists point out that this tilting of the baby teeth has no effect on the permanent teeth that begin coming in at about six years of age. If the child gives up thumb-sucking by six years of age, as usually happens, there is very little chance of the displacement of permanent teeth.

Preventing thumb-sucking. You don't need to be concerned when babies suck their thumbs for only a few minutes just before their feeding time. They probably do this only because they're hungry. It's when babies try to suck their thumbs as soon as the feeding is over or when they suck a lot between feedings that you might try to think of ways to satisfy the craving for sucking.

If your baby begins to try to suck her thumb, finger or hand, it's best not to stop her directly. Instead, give her more opportunity to suck at the breast, bottle, or pacifier. If your baby hasn't been a confirmed thumb-sucker from birth, the most effective method by far of preventing the habit is ample use of the pacifier in the first three months. If you're bottle-feeding, use a nipple with a smaller hole so that your baby does a lot of sucking in feeding. If you're breast-feeding, let your baby nurse longer, even after she's gotten the milk she needs.

With a thumb-sucker, it's better to go more slowly when omitting feedings. It's not just the length of each feeding but also the frequency of feedings that determine whether a baby satisfies the sucking instinct. So if a baby still thumb-sucks even though you make each breast- or bottle-feeding last as long as possible, it is sensible to go slowly in dropping feedings. For example, if a three-month-old baby seems willing to sleep through the late evening feeding at the parents' bedtime but does a good deal of thumb-sucking, you might wait a while longer before dropping the late evening feeding, perhaps a couple of months, provided the baby is still willing to drink when awakened.

Methods that don't work. Why not tie babies' arms down to keep them from thumb-sucking? This would frustrate them a great deal and produce new problems. Furthermore, tying down the hands usually doesn't cure the baby who thumb-sucks a lot since it doesn't address the baby's need for more sucking. A few despairing parents use elbow splints or put bad-tasting liquid on the baby's thumbs, not just for days but for months. But on the day they take off the restraint or stop putting the liquid on the thumb, the thumb pops back in the mouth.

To be sure, some parents say they have had good results from using such methods. Most likely the thumb-sucking was very mild to begin with. Many babies do a little thumb-sucking off and on. They quickly get over it whether you do anything or not. In confirmed thumb-suckers, restraints, bad-tasting liquids, and other deterrents rarely solve the problem in the long run.

Breaking the habit. Elbow splints, mitts, and bad-tasting stuff on the thumb won't stop the habit any better in older children than in small babies. They may even prolong the habit by setting up a power struggle between the determined sucker and his parents. The same applies to scolding a child or pulling his thumb out of his mouth. What about the common ploy of handing a child a toy when he starts to thumb-suck? It certainly is sound to have interesting things to play with so that he won't be bored. But if every time his thumb goes in the mouth you jump toward him and poke an old toy into his hands, he'll soon catch on.

What about bribery? If your child is one of the rare ones who still thumb-sucks at the age of five and you worry about what it will do to the permanent teeth when they come in, you will have a fair chance of succeeding if the bribe is a good one. A girl of four or five who wants to get over her thumb-sucking may be helped by having her fingernails painted like a woman's. But hardly any child of two or three has the willpower to deny an instinct for the sake of reward. You're apt to make a fuss and get nowhere.

If your child is thumb-sucking, see to it that his life is good. In the long run, it will help to remind him that someday he will be grown up enough to stop. This friendly encouragement makes him want to stop as soon as he is able, but don't nag him.

Most important of all, try to stop thinking about it. If you continue to worry, even though you say nothing, the child will feel your tension and react against it. Remember that in time thumb-sucking goes away by itself. It is almost always over before the permanent teeth appear. It doesn't go away steadily, though. It decreases rapidly for a while then comes back partway during an illness or when the child has a difficult adjustment to make. It usually peters out between three and six.

Some dentists use metal wires attached to the upper teeth to make thumb-sucking not only unpleasant but virtually impossible. This should be a last resort. It is expensive, and it takes all control away from the child at an age when it's important for children to feel that they are in control of their bodies.

OTHER INFANT HABITS

Stroking and hair-pulling. Most of the babies who thumb-suck until they are one or more years old do some kind of stroking at the same time. One little boy rubs or plucks a piece of blanket, diaper, silk, or a woolly toy. Another strokes his earlobe or twists a lock of hair. Still another holds a piece of cloth close to his face, perhaps stroking his nose or lip with a free finger. These motions remind you of how younger babies gently felt their mother's skin or clothing when they sucked at the breast or bottle. When they press something against their faces, they seem to be remembering how they felt at the breast.

Occasionally, an infant gets into the habit of stroking and tugging on strands of his hair. The result can be unattractive bald spots and worry for the parents. The best explanation for his behavior is that it is just a habit, not a sign of emotional or physical disturbance. The best treatment is to cut the hair short so that there is nothing for the baby to grab hold of. By the time the hair grows back, the habit is usually gone.

In older children, compulsive hair-pulling is more likely to be a sign of anxiety or psychological tension, so consultation with a psychologist or other professional makes sense (see page 620).

Ruminating. Sometimes a baby or young child gets into the habit of sucking and chewing on her tongue until her last meal comes up, somewhat the way a cow does, a practice known as ruminating. This is rare. It may begin when thumb-sucking babies have their arms restrained. They turn to sucking their tongues instead. I advise letting such babies have the thumb back immediately, before the ruminating becomes a habit. Be sure that the baby has enough companionship, play, and affection as well. Rumination may also be a signal of unusually high tension in the infant-parent relationship. Professional guidance can often help (see page 620).

RHYTHMIC HABITS

Body-rocking, head-banging. Between eight months and about four years, up to one in seven healthy babies rocks his body, bangs his head, or regularly engages in another rhythmic habit. Teething or an ear infection may cause a sudden onset of rocking or banging. A baby sitting in a chair or couch may rock hard against the back then rebound. Another baby gets on all fours and jounces back and forth against her heels. Another baby rolls her head from side to side while lying in the crib or bangs her head repeatedly against a hard surface, like the head of the crib. Headbanging is the most distressing of rhythmic motions to parents; they understandably fear that the child may injure herself. She won't; rhythmic habits are common, but they're rarely severe enough to injure a child.

What's the meaning of these rhythmic movements? They usually appear during the second half of the first year, by which time babies have naturally acquired a sense of rhythm. The movements usually occur—like thumb-sucking or the stroking of a soft toy—when the child is tired, sleepy, or frustrated. They are self-comforting behaviors. Perhaps they represent the desire to reproduce the experience of being rocked and carried by a parent in very early infancy.

The same movements, especially head-banging, occur frequently and intensely in some children who are emotionally neglected or physically abused and in some with autism or other severe developmental disorders. If you see such behavior occurring with great regularity in your child, it's wise to discuss it with your child's doctor or nurse practitioner.

NAIL-BITING

What it means. Sometimes nail-biting is a sign of tenseness, sometimes it's just a habit that means nothing in particular. Nail-biting is more common in high-strung children who are inclined to worry a lot, and it runs in families. Children often bite their nails when they are anxious: for instance, while waiting to be called on in school or watching a scary episode in a movie.

A good general approach is to find out what pressures your child has and try to relieve them. Is she being urged, corrected, warned, or scolded too much? Are you expecting too much in her school work? Consult the teacher about her school adjustment. If movie, radio, and television violence makes her jittery, it's wise to make such programs off-limits. (That's probably a wise decisions for most children.)

Antibiting strategies. School-age children are often motivated to stop nail-biting when they sense disapproval from peers or want nicer-looking nails. You can support this positive motivation by offering suggestions, but it's best to let your child be in charge of the antibiting campaign. The problem belongs to your child, so the solution should, too.

Nagging or punishing nail-biters usually doesn't stop them for longer than half a minute since they seldom realize they are doing it. In the long run it may increase their tension or encourage them to think of the biting as their parents' problem, not their own. Bitter-tasting liquids on the nails may work if the child asks for it to remind himself that he wants to stop the nail-biting. But if it's put on against his will, the child is bound to think he's being punished. That only gives him another thing to be tense about and may prolong the habit.

Take a broader view. If your child is otherwise reasonably happy and relaxed, you don't need to make too much of nail-biting. But when nail-biting is one of a host of worrisome behaviors, it makes sense to seek professional help (see page 620). It is the cause of the child's anxiety, not the nail-biting itself, that should be of most concern.

STUTTERING

What causes stuttering? Almost every young child goes through a period when talking is an effort and the words sometimes don't come out right; he may repeat words or hesitate then rush ahead too fast. This is part of normal speech development. About one child in twenty has more difficulty, repeating many words or part words, lengthening some, entirely blocking others. Some children show signs of facial stress. Fortunately, mild or moderate stuttering like this usually goes away by itself. Only about one child in a hundred ends up with a severe long-standing stuttering problem.

We don't really know what causes stuttering. It's likely that some children are born with a tendency to stutter. Like many other speech and language problems, stuttering is much more common in boys than in girls. It often runs in families, suggesting that genetics plays a role. And brain scans have found some differences in the size of certain brain areas in adults who stutter.

It used to be thought that stuttering was a sign of stress. That makes sense: Children who stutter almost always stutter more when they are under stress. But many children experience very severe stresses yet never develop stuttering, so stress can't be the only cause.

A tongue tie (when the frenulum, the fold of skin that runs from the middle of the underside of the tongue to the floor of the mouth, is too short to allow free movement of the tongue) has nothing to do with stuttering.

Why is stuttering so common between two and three? There are two possible explanations. This is the age when a child works very hard at talking. When he was younger, he used short sentences that he didn't need to think out: "See the car." "Want to go out." When he gets past two, he tries to make up longer sentences to express new ideas. He may start a sentence three or four times, only to break off in the middle because he can't find the right words. His parents, worn out by his constant talking, pay little attention. They say "Uh-huh" in an absentminded way while they go about their business. The child is further frustrated by being unable to hold his audience. The balkiness that's a part of this tense stage of development may affect his speech, too.

⬳ CLASSIC SPOCK

One little boy began to stutter when a new baby sister was brought home from the hospital. He didn't show his jealousy outwardly. He never tried to hit or pinch her. He just became uneasy. A girl of two and a half began to stutter after the departure of a fond relative who had been with the family a long time. In two weeks her stuttering stopped for the time being. When the family moved to a new house, she was quite homesick and stuttered again for a period. Two months later her father was called into the army. The family was upset, and the little girl started stuttering again. Parents report that their children's stuttering is definitely worse when they themselves are tense. I think children who, during too much of the day, are talked to and told stories, urged to talk and recite, and shown off are especially likely to stutter. Stuttering may also start when a parent decides to be stricter in discipline.

Responding to stuttering. When your child talks to you, give him your full attention so he doesn't get frantic. Telling a child to "slow down" or asking him to repeat himself often just increases the child's self-consciousness, making the stuttering worse. Instead, try to respond to what the child is saying rather than how he says it. Train yourself to speak in a relaxed, unpressured way, and help others in the family to do the same. (Slowing *way* down doesn't help, though; it's best to be natural.) Stuttering becomes worse when children feel they have only a few seconds to make themselves heard. Make it a family rule that everyone takes turns and gives the others time to express themselves.

Anything you can do to lower your child's stress level is likely to help. Does he have plenty of chances to play with other children he gets along with easily? Does he have enough toys and equipment, indoors and out? When you're with him, relax and let him take the lead. Play with him by doing things instead of by always talking about things.

A regular daily schedule, less pressure to perform, and less rushing around are all helpful. If he was upset by being separated from you for several days, try to avoid further separations for a couple of months. If you have been talking to him or urging him too much to talk, train yourself out of it.

When to get help. Since most children go through a stage when speaking is difficult or effortful and many who stutter for a time get over it on their own, it can be hard to know when to refer a child for special help. A good rule of thumb is to get help right away for severe stuttering and get help for *any* stuttering that hasn't shown signs of getting better after four to six months.

How can you tell mild stuttering from the more severe variety? In mild stuttering, the child isn't terribly concerned or self-conscious; there isn't a lot of muscle tension in the face, and the pitch of the voice is normal; he stutters only when under stress, not when he is relaxed.

In severe stuttering, the child is often very concerned and self-conscious and may avoid speaking altogether; there's usually a lot of muscle tension in the face, and the voice's pitch may go up (another sign of tension); and he stutters pretty much all the time, even when relaxed. When you're with a child who stutters severely, you probably feel tense yourself.

Here, as with so many parts of parenting, it's wise to follow your heart (or your gut): If a child's speech difficulty makes you feel uncomfortable, that's a sign to get help.

The sooner a child with severe stuttering gets help from a trained speech and language pathologist, the better (see the Resource Guide, page 917). There are techniques to teach a child to speak more fluently. Even if speech therapy doesn't stop a child's stuttering, it may keep it from getting worse. Severe stuttering can be terrible for a child and have lifelong consequences. A good therapist can help the child and the family understand the problem and adapt to it in healthy ways.

TOILET TRAINING, SOILING, AND BED-WETTING

READINESS FOR TOILET TRAINING

Getting yourself ready. Everyone talks about the child's readiness to be trained. Parents have to be ready, too. Many are anxious about the whole business. I think the anxiety is partly because we live in a society that teaches us to be ashamed of and disgusted by our bowel and bladder functions.

Anxiety can also come from an internal pressure to have your child succeed with toilet training the "right" way at the "right" time. For working parents, there's often external pressure to toilet train as early as possible to ease the burden on a full-time babysitter or to get a toddler into a day-care center or preschool that doesn't accept children in diapers.

Some parents have misinterpreted *don't push* and *don't force* as *don't train*. But you can train without pushing. The key is to adjust your training to your child's motivation and level of maturity.

A good first step in toilet training your child is to sort out your feelings on the matter of, well, poop. If they are negative, it helps to be aware of them so than you can work around them. For example, imagine that you're changing your two-year-old's diaper and she's really made a big mess. Instead of making comments about how dirty and smelly it is, it helps to say something like "Oh, my, what a big poop you made today! If you had made it in your potty seat, you wouldn't have to lie still all this time while I clean you up and change you. Next time you have to go, tell me; and I'll help you use your special potty seat." This cheerful, matter-of-fact approach works only if you train yourself to use a neutral, interested tone of voice rather than one dripping with disgust (which your child may think is directed against *him* rather than his by-products).

An important step. The start of toilet training normally overlaps young children's growing sense of themselves as separate, independent beings. At this age they want more independence and control over everything they do. They are just learning what's theirs and that they can decide whether to keep it or give it away. They are naturally fascinated by what comes out of them and pleased by their growing mastery over when it comes out and where it goes.

With toilet learning, children gain control of two orifices of the body that previously functioned automatically. This gives them a lot of pride. Indeed, they're so proud that at first they try to perform every few minutes. They are accepting the first serious responsibility their parents have assigned to them. Successful cooperation on this project will give parents and child new confidence in each other. And the child who previously lightheartedly messed with food and BM will now take satisfaction in cleanliness.

You may think of this shift as meaning primarily no more soiled diapers. That's important, all right. But the preference for cleanliness that a child gains at around two years means a lot more than that. It's the foundation for a lifelong preference for unsticky hands, clean clothes, a neat home, an orderly way of doing business. It's from their toilet training that children get some of their feeling that one way of doing things is right and another is not. This helps them to develop a sense of responsibility and become systematic people. This is how toilet training plays a part in the formation of a child's character and in building the trust between child and parents. So if you take advantage of your child's natural desire to become more grown up and self-sufficient, toilet training will be a lot easier for both of you.

Bowel control, the first year. In the first year, a baby shows little awareness of bowel function and doesn't voluntarily move her bowels. When her rectum is full, particularly right after a meal when the intestines are active, the movement presses against the inner valve of the anus and causes it to open somewhat. This stimulates a squeezing, pushing-down action of the abdominal muscles. The baby, in other words, does not *decide* to push as an older child or adult does but does so automatically.

Some babies during the first year always have their first movement of the day at the same time of day, often soon after eating. An alert parent may notice the small changes in behavior that signal that a BM is about to happen. The parents may sit the baby on the potty seat at that time every day to "catch" the movement. After a few weeks, the baby's nervous system will have been conditioned to push as soon as she feels the toilet seat under her. This is training but not learning: The baby is not conscious of the bowel movement or what she is doing. She's not knowingly cooperating. It takes a lot of attention and persistence to train a child in this manner, and it's important that the parent remain calm and positive. If the parent becomes frustrated or impatient, the negative emotion is bound to become attached in the child's mind with being put on the potty—just what you don't want to have happen.

Bowel control between twelve and eighteen months. At this age, children gradually become conscious of when a bowel movement occurs. They may pause in what they are doing or their facial expression momentarily changes, though they are nowhere near ready to notify a parent.

As they gaze fondly at their BM in the diaper, on the floor, or accidentally in the potty, they are likely to develop distinctly possessive feelings for it. They are proud of it as a fascinating personal creation. They may sniff the smell appreciatively, as they have been taught to sniff a flower. Such positive pride in the movement and its smell and the enjoyment of messing in it if the opportunity arises are characteristic reactions in this period.

One aspect of this possessiveness, as those parents who succeeded in catching movements early in the second year have discovered, is a reluctance about giving up the BM to the pot or the parent. Another aspect is anxiety at seeing the BM flushed away; to some small children this is as disturbing as if they saw their arm sucked down the toilet.

Later, after about eighteen months, a child's possessive feeling toward his BMs naturally gives way to a preference for being clean. You don't need to teach a child to be disgusted by body functions. The natural preference for being clean helps motivate a child to become trained and stay trained.

Indirect signs of readiness. Beginning in the second year, other aspects of readiness appear, ones we don't ordinarily associate with toilet training. Children now feel an impulse to give presents. They get great satisfaction from this, though they usually want them right back again. Their contradictory feelings may show in the way they hold out one of their toys to a visitor but refuse to let go of it. It's at this age that children become fascinated with putting things in containers, watching them disappear then reappear. Toddlers take great pride in learning any skill they can carry out independently, and they enjoy being praised for the accomplishment. They gradually imitate more of the activities of their parents and older brothers and sisters. This drive may play an important part in training.

Balking. Children who took to using the potty seat early in the second year often suddenly change their pattern. They sit down willingly but don't have a movement. Then, right after getting up, they move their bowels in a corner of a room or in their pants. Parents sometimes say, "I think my child has forgotten what it's all about."

I don't believe children forget that easily. I think that their possessive feelings about their BMs have become temporarily stronger and that they are simply unwilling to give them up. Early in the second year, they have an increasing urge to do everything for themselves in their own way. Toileting may seem too much like the parents' scheme. So they hold the movement in until they can get away from the seat, which symbolizes giving it up and giving in.

If this resistance persists for many weeks, children may hold back not only when on the seat but, if they can manage it, for the rest of the day. This is psychological constipation. Balking can occur at almost any point in the toilet training process, but it occurs most often between twelve and eighteen months, rather than later. Balking may be a signal for you to wait at least a few months, to let your child feel that he himself has decided to control his bowel and bladder rather than that he is giving in to parental demands.

Readiness between eighteen and twenty-four months. At this age, most children show more definite signs of readiness. They are more aware that they are separate from their parents. As a result, many become clinging; they often also show a new desire to please the parents and fulfill their expectations, very helpful for toilet training. At this age, children take great pride in learning any skill they can carry out independently, and they enjoy being praised for their accomplishments. They gain the idea that things belong in their places and begin to take an interest in putting away their toys and clothes.

Body awareness is increasing, so they have a greater sense of when a movement is coming or being passed. They may stop playing for a few seconds or act uncomfortable afterward. They may make a sign or sound to the parent to indicate that the diaper is soiled, as if asking to be cleaned up. You can help by gently reminding your child to tell you if he has had a BM. At first, of course, he's apt to tell you after the fact. With practice, he'll notice the feeling of pressure in the rectum that signals that a BM is ready. Without this body awareness, it's hard to learn to use the toilet independently.

In addition, children now have greater ability to move around. They can walk and climb almost anywhere, so they can certainly get onto the potty chair and sit there. They can pull down their diaper or pants by themselves.

A child who has arrived at these developmental milestones is probably ready to begin the fine art of bowel and bladder control.

A GENTLE TRAINING APPROACH

Training without force. If you wait until they are ready, children can learn to use the potty without being forced. Research done in the 1950s by T. Berry Brazelton, the great pediatrician, showed that children trained in this way had a low risk of subsequent bed-wetting and soiling. Such problems were common in children who were subjected to the harsher, more controlling training approaches that were then standard practice.

Training children when they are ready results in the process being more relaxed and pleasant for parents and children with few power struggles. Children who train this way often end up being proud of themselves and ready to take on the next developmental challenge.

How do you do it? Have your child become familiar with the potty without any pressure to perform. If you let your child see you use the toilet, he'll know what it's for and may develop a desire to mimic this grown-up activity. You can make tactful suggestions and use flattery, but don't show disapproval of failure. If your child does sit on the potty, don't try to make him stay any longer than he wants to; that's a sure way to make the potty seem like a punishment. More specific directions are given in the paragraphs that follow.

Following this approach, most children are out of diapers somewhere around two and a half and are dry at night around three to four. The key is that when they are able children decide of their free will to gain control over their bladders and bowels because they want to be grown up. This method requires that the parents trust their children's desire to mature and that they be willing to wait.

This does not imply an absence of expectation on the parents' part. Once a decision to train the child is made, when he is two to two and a half, the parents' attitude should always be the same; a consistent expectation that the child will use the toilet as older children and adults do. This should be expressed as mild praise when the child is successful and encouragement, not anger or criticism, when he doesn't comply or has an accident.

The adult toilet or a potty seat? You can buy a child-size toilet seat that fits over the regular ones. But this puts the child high up in the air, an uncomfortable position in which to try to relax and let go. A seat with footrests and a sturdy step stool so your child can climb up by himself can help.

A better solution is to use a child's small plastic potty. Children are friendlier toward a small piece of furniture that is theirs and on which they can sit down by themselves. Their feet stay on the floor, and the height won't make them insecure. For boys, don't use the urine guard that comes with the seat. It can hurt him when he gets on or off. If it does, he won't use the seat again.

The first stage. The first step in training should *not* be to take the child's diaper off and sit him on the seat. That's too strange and sudden. It's much better for at least a few weeks to have him get used to the seat as an interesting piece of furniture to sit on with all clothes on rather than a contraption to take his BMs away.

The second stage. When your child has accepted the seat, you can suggest casually that he use it with the lid up for BMs, the way his parents use the toilet seat. (Children at this age are easily alarmed by being hurried or pushed into an unfamiliar situation.) Show how you sit on the grown-up toilet seat, and he can sit on his potty while you sit on the toilet.

Let your child get up from the seat and leave immediately if he wants. No matter how brief it is, the experience of sitting will be helpful. The child should think of sitting on the seat not as imprisonment but as a voluntary ritual carried out with pride.

If the child is unwilling to sit down without diapers, wait a week or so before suggesting it again. You can explain again how Mommy and Daddy—and perhaps one or two of the child's older acquaintances—use their toilet that way. It often helps to have your child watch a friend perform. (If he has an older brother or sister he will probably already have watched.)

After the idea of depositing the BM or urine in the potty has been discussed a couple of times, take off the child's diaper at a time when a movement is most likely, lead him to the seat, and suggest that he try it. It is okay to encourage the child to sit by praise or small rewards, but don't spend time urging or pushing him if he doesn't want to. Try another time or another day. Some day, when the movement does go into the potty, it will help him understand and cooperate.

After a movement in the diaper, take it off, lead the child to the seat, and show him the movement as you put it in the potty. Explain again that Mommy and Daddy sit on their seat to have their BMs, that he has his own seat, and that someday he will do his BM in it just like them.

If you have had no success in catching a movement or urination, wait for a few weeks, then gently try again. Take an upbeat attitude without making it a big deal or applying a lot of pressure.

At this stage, don't flush the BM from the diaper down the toilet until the child has lost interest and gone on to something else. Most one- to two-year-olds are at first fascinated with the flushing and want to do it themselves. Later some become frightened by the violent way the water flushes the movement away and become afraid to sit on the seat. They probably fear that they might fall in and be swirled away in a watery rush. Until two and a half years, it's a good idea to empty the potty and flush the toilet after the child has left the room.

The third stage. When your child becomes interested and cooperative, take him to the seat two or three times a day, especially if he gives the slightest signal of readiness to urinate or have a BM. Even if a boy has only to urinate, I recommend that he sit rather than stand at this stage. If he allows himself to be caught, for example, after a meal or when he has been dry for a couple of hours, praise him for being so grown up—"just like Daddy" or Mommy, brother, sister, or admired friend—but don't overdo it. At this age, a child doesn't like to be too compliant.

When you're sure your child is ready for the next step—going by himself—have him play for periods with no clothes on from the waist down. Put the potty seat nearby, indoors or out, explaining that you did this so he can go by himself. If he isn't resistant, you can remind him every hour or so that he may want to go by himself. If he becomes bored or resistant or has an accident, put him back in diapers and wait.

Is this the right method for you? There is now a small industry in books on toilet training. Many promise fast results. Why wait patiently when you can get the process over with right away? Why not just tell your child what you want him to do and expect him to do it?

If your child is very obedient, a simple demand for potty performance may work. However, if your child often tries to resist your demands—normal behavior for toddlers and young preschoolers—toileting can easily become a power struggle.

It's a struggle that you, the parent, are bound to lose. Young children are more powerful than their parents in two areas: what goes in their bodies and what comes out. If a child is determined to refuse the food in front of him or to hold on to his bowel movements, there is little a parent can do about it. When a child holds back, the movement often becomes hard and dried out and therefore painful to pass (see below). The child then has a new motivation to resist the toilet, and the problem gets worse.

Many parents feel they have to train their children early so that the children can go to day care. On the other hand, day-care providers who take care of young children are often experienced in toilet training and can be a great help. Toilet training is a perfect example of a developmental challenge that is easier to tackle when parents and day-care providers work as a team.

Of the many techniques for quick toilet training, one is actually research-proven. The psychologists Nathan Azrin and Richard Foxx describe their method in detail in the book *Toilet Training in Less Than a Day* (Pocket Books, 2000). I suspect that many parents find the instructions hard to follow, especially since real-life children don't always respond the way they're supposed to. Resistance and tantrums can be a problem. The approach might work best if in addition to the book the parents have an experienced professional available to coach them through it.

Fear of painfully hard movements. Sometimes a child has a spell of unusually hard movements that are painful to pass. Collections of small, hard pellets are rarely painful, it's usually the hard movement in one large piece with a large diameter that is to blame.

As it is passed, this movement may tear a tiny slit or fissure in the rim of the stretched anus that may bleed a little. (If you notice blood in your baby's diaper, tell the doctor.) If a fissure occurs, it is likely to be stretched open again each time another movement is passed. This is painful and may keep the fissure from healing for many weeks. You can easily understand that a child who has been hurt once may dread a repetition and so fight against toileting again. It may become a vicious circle: If the child holds back the movement for several days, it even is more likely to be large and hard.

If a child has constipation, it's likely to be very hard to toilet train him, so take care of the constipation first (see page 844). Adding prunes or prune juice to the diet every day usually works, or try a slurry of bran, applesauce, and prune juice. Children love it, and it moves things along very nicely. Cereal, bread, and crackers with whole-grain wheat or oats may help some. It may also help to have the child sit cross-legged in warm water in the bathtub a couple of times a day for ten to fifteen minutes. An ointment of petroleum jelly and lanolin may be gently dabbed onto the anal area as often as necessary.

If these simple approaches don't soften the stool, ask the child's doctor or nurse practitioner to prescribe a lubricant or stool softener. Some parents turn quickly to enemas, perhaps because they worked for them. But enemas often upset a child and, if used repeatedly, can cause medical complications. Gentler approaches are likely to be effective. I recommend talking with the doctor first.

Reassure the child that you know he is worried that another movement will hurt the way the previous one did but that he doesn't need to worry anymore because the movements will now be soft. A child who remains frightened and resistant or continues to have pain should be examined by the doctor to see whether there is a fissure.

BLADDER CONTROL

Simultaneous bowel and bladder control. One of the advantages of the gentle approach described above is that when children feel ready to control themselves, they usually achieve bowel and bladder control almost simultaneously. By the first part of the third year, there is sufficient awareness and physical competence for both bowel and bladder control. All that is then necessary is the child's wish to be grown up in these respects; little special effort is required on the parents' part to achieve bladder control.

Attitudes toward BMs and urine. Children rarely make an issue of daytime urination. They don't become possessive about urine, as they do BMs. In most children, complete bladder control comes at the same time or slightly later than bowel control. It may be that it's easier to hold on to a solid than a liquid (bowel control is much less effective during diarrhea, as you know). Bladder function tends to mature by itself, irrespective of training efforts. The bladder empties itself frequently in the first year, then by fifteen to eighteen months it retains urine for a couple of hours, even though training has not been started. In fact, an occasional baby spontaneously stays dry at night by a year of age.

The bladder retains urine for longer periods during sleep than wakefulness, and a baby may stay dry after a two-hour nap months before daytime control is achieved.

There may continue to be occasional accidental wettings in the daytime for several months after children have gained general control of urine. This happens when they are preoccupied with play and don't want to interrupt it.

Training pants. When your child successfully controls his BMs and bladder, put him in training pants that he can pull down by himself. This further step toward independence will lessen the chance of backsliding. But don't use pants before the child is generally successful; they won't do any good for a child who isn't, and you will have wasted their value as a mark of independence.

Inability to urinate away from home. It sometimes happens that a child around two has become so well trained to his own potty chair or toilet seat that he can't perform anywhere else. You can neither urge him nor scold him into it. He will probably eventually wet his pants, for which he shouldn't be scolded. Keep this possibility in mind when you take him traveling, bringing his own seat if necessary.

If he is painfully full and can't let go and you can't get home, have him sit in a warm bath for half an hour, letting him know it's okay to urinate in the bathtub. This will probably work.

It's better to get a child used to urinating in different places early. There are portable urinals for boys and girls to which they can become accustomed at home that can be taken along when they visit. Some children are more comfortable in diapers when they're away from home, so you may want to give them that choice.

Standing up to urinate. Parents are sometimes worried when a two-year-old boy won't urinate standing up. It's fine for boys to sit down to urinate until they are very comfortable on the potty. When they sit for urinating, they are less likely to miss the toilet. A boy will get the idea sooner or later when he sees his father or older boys standing.

Staying dry at night. Many parents assume that children learn to stay dry through the night only because the parent takes him to the toilet late in the evening. They ask, "Now that he is reasonably dry in the daytime, when should I begin to toilet train him at night?" This is a mistaken idea, making night dryness sound like too much of a job. It's closer to reality to say that a child naturally stays dry at night when his bladder becomes mature enough (provided he isn't nervous or rebellious). This is shown clearly by the fact that one baby in a hundred regularly stays dry at night from the age of twelve months, even though the parents made no training effort at all and the child wets throughout the day. A few children, late in the second year or early in the third, stay dry at night before they exercise control in the daytime. The bladder can retain urine for longer periods during sleep because the kidneys automatically produce less urine and concentrate it more when a person is asleep.

Most children begin staying dry at night around three years

of age, although roughly one in five still wets the bed at age five. Boys tend to be later than girls, high-strung children later than relaxed ones. Slowness in staying dry at night is often a family trait (see page 592 on bed-wetting).

> ◈ **CLASSIC SPOCK**
> I don't think it is necessary for parents to do anything special about night training beyond expressing the consistent expectation that the child will make an effort to be dry at night. The natural maturing of the bladder plus the idea that urine belongs in the toilet will take care of most cases. Of course, it helps a little if the parents share in children's pride when they begin to have dry nights. If, six or eight months after daytime control is achieved, your child expresses a wish to leave his diaper off at night, you can act pleased that he wants to try and let him.

Teach proper wiping and hand-washing. When your daughter shows an interest in wiping, you'll have to negotiate letting her wipe first with you finishing up until she can do a complete job by herself. This is the time to start teaching little girls to wipe from front to back to prevent urinary tract infections. Boys often need help with hygiene, too.

Hand-washing is part of going to the bathroom. A step stool helps young children reach the sink. Little hands need small bars of soap, the size you find in hotel rooms. To wash effectively takes at least fifteen seconds of brisk rubbing with soap suds, a fairly long time. To make the time pass pleasantly and get your child into the habit of washing for long enough, make up a hand-washing song to sing while washing or tell a story about each finger.

SETBACKS IN BOWEL AND BLADDER CONTROL

Expect setbacks. Mastery of bowel and bladder functions occurs in little steps for most children. You can expect plateaus and setbacks to be scattered among the gains. Emotional upsets, illness, traveling, a new baby: These can cause setbacks even in a child who seems fully trained. Avoid scolding and punishing when this happens. When accidents occur, your child will need reassurance that he'll soon regain control and that you know he still wants to be grown up in this respect.

Backsliding on BMs. Many children, more often boys, when they train themselves to urinate, refuse to have their BMs on the potty as well. They may hide in a corner when they have to have a BM or insist on wearing a diaper. Some appear afraid of the toilet or become constipated; many simply cannot give in to all their parents' requests at once.

It can be terribly frustrating to parents who know that their child can use the potty, if only he *would*. Sticker charts, rewards, threats, bribes, pleading: all are likely to fail. At worst, the child may hold back his stool, leading to large, hard painful bowel movements that further convince him not to go (see page 584). This problem often develops after parents refuse to let the child have his BMs in a diaper as is comfortable for him.

The best method I know of is for the parent to take away the pressure for potty performance. Instead, have the child wear his diapers or pull-ups all the time. Let him know that you're confident he'll use the potty when he's ready to. And leave it at that. In one study, this approach worked within a matter of a few months in the great majority of cases. If this behavior continues past four years of age, it's reasonable to consult a pediatrician or psychologist with experience in helping families with toilet training

SOILING

Normal accidents. It's normal for a young child to have an occasional accident, staining their underwear or even having a whole poop in the pants. The child may have forgotten to wipe sufficiently. Or he may have been so busy playing that he ignored the feeling of fullness in his rectum until it was too late. The answer for these problems is simple: A gentle reminder about wiping and the habit of taking a toilet break a couple of times a day ought to do the trick. For a very busy child, it helps to have a magazine rack or a small stack of picture books in the bathroom, so that there's something to do while sitting on the potty.

Soiling by an older child. After about age four, soiling (encopresis is the medical term) is a more serious problem. Typically, a school-age boy begins to stain his underpants with stool long after having been toilet trained. What is bewildering to the family is that he fails to notice it and claims to have had no sensation of passing the stool; even more incomprehensibly, he even denies smelling it. This denial is not psychological. When the rectum and the muscles (called sphincters) that usually hold in the stool are chronically stretched out, they lose their ability to contract effectively, and the child loses the sensation of fullness. People do not normally smell their own body odors (bad breath, for example), so it is not unusual for a child not to smell the bowel movements in his pants.

Other children of course notice the odor and may tease the child unmercifully, call him Stinky, and shun him. So soiling is really a psychological and social emergency because of the shame and humiliation it may cause. A child with this problem who says that he does not care is just trying to protect himself from the very distressing reality.

Causes of soiling. Soiling is usually the result of severe constipation (see page 844). As the stool sits in the intestines and the rectum, it builds up into large chunks of dry, claylike material that stretch out the muscles of the intestines. The stretched muscles don't push the stool along well, so more and more builds up. Occasionally a large chunk comes out, painfully, perhaps clogging up the toilet. At other times, liquid stool drips down between the "rocks" of stool, and makes its way out of the overstretched rectum. The child is truly unaware that this is happening.

The cause of the underlying constipation may be any number of things: reduced fluid intake during an illness, a single painful bowel movement that set up a cycle of withholding, forced toilet training, some medicines, the birth of a sibling, a divorce or death in the family, or another stressful event. Other changes, such as going to a new school or camp, may make some children uncomfortable if the bathroom does not allow for privacy. The trigger may have happened long enough ago to have been forgotten. All that remains is the constipation.

On rare occasions, soiling occurs without constipation. The child passes formed, not rock-hard stools into his pants. This form of encopresis is more likely to reflect an underlying emotional disturbance or response to severe stress. Getting help from a child behavior professional (see page 620) can make a big difference in children with this problem.

What you can do. Successful treatment starts with helping the child to understand that the problem is faulty plumbing, not a personal failure on his part. A doctor or nurse practitioner can help by taking time to explain the problem to the child in simple terms. Drawing a picture and labeling all the important parts—mouth, stomach, intestines, poop in the intestines, rectum, and the sphincter muscles that hold the poop in— enables a child to see what is going on and gives him the right words to talk about it.

The next step is to treat the constipation with a combination of diet changes, planned time on the toilet, exercise, and often medications (see page 844). When the constipation has gone on for a long time, with much family stress and a poor response to medical treatment, it often helps for the child and parents to be seen by a child psychiatrist, psychologist, or social worker.

It's important for parents to maintain a realistic optimism. Soiling *is* a problem (even if the child denies it), but it's also

treatable. On the general principle that family is about supporting each other, not hurting, no one in the household should be
allowed to shame, embarrass, or criticize the child. A "we're in it
together" attitude, with the child, parent, and doctor playing on
the same team, is most helpful.

BED-WETTING

Everybody wets the bed until they learn how to stay dry. The age
by which most children have mastered nighttime dryness is
about four for girls, five for boys. No one knows why girls are
earlier (they also tend to be earlier in language development and
controlling their tempers, so perhaps faster brain maturation is
the answer). At age eight about 8 percent of children—one in
twelve—still wet the bed. So if I see a third-grader who wets the
bed, I can assure him that there is most likely at least one other
child in his classroom who has the same problem.

Various wetting problems. The medical term for wetting is
enuresis. There are three main types of wetting problems. In the
most common, children stay dry during the day but not consistently at night. Doctors call this problem primary nocturnal
enuresis. In the second, children who have stayed dry at night for
a long time—five to six months at least—suddenly start wetting
again. Doctors call this secondary nocturnal enuresis. The third
is wetting during the day, which doctors call diurnal enuresis.

It helps to keep the types separate, since they often have
different causes and require different treatments. In particular,
secondary nocturnal enuresis (wetting after a period of dryness) and diurnal enuresis are more likely than primary nocturnal enuresis to be caused by medical problems, such as
infections or diabetes. Occasionally, severe psychological stress,
such as sexual abuse, can also cause a child to start wetting. For
these reasons, I think that any child with secondary or diurnal

enuresis should be under the care of a well-trained doctor or nurse practitioner.

There is one exception to this: A young child, say four or five, who has been dry at night for several months may start wetting at night again in response to stress. It might be the birth of a sibling, a move, or another change. Patience and reassurance often do the trick. In a few weeks, the child feels better and is able to stay dry at night again.

The rest of this section deals with primary nocturnal enuresis.

Causes. Genetics plays a role. There is often a history of bed-wetting until middle childhood or adolescence in the parents. If both parents wet the bed as children, there is a 75 percent chance that their children will, too. Parents often believe that their children who wet the bed are deeper sleepers or harder to wake up than other children, but doctors who study children's sleep patterns have found no evidence of this. Children who wet the bed do not appear to have smaller bladders than other children. But it may be that their bladders are more prone to empty before they are completely full.

Rarely, bed-wetting is caused by a medical illness, such as a urinary infection. For the most part, children who wet the bed are healthy. However, it's not uncommon for a child with bed-wetting to have constipation also. The bladder sits right next to the rectum in the pelvis. If the rectum is packed full of hard stool, it puts pressure on the bladder, making it difficult for the urine to get out. As a result, the bladder squeezes extra hard in response to a small volume of urine rather than stretch to hold more. Treating the constipation (see page 844) often fixes this, and the bed-wetting ceases. By the same token, attempts to treat the bed-wetting without first dealing with the constipation often fail.

For the most part, though, the cause of bed-wetting is simply that the child has not yet learned how to stay dry at night. With the passage of time, in any given year, about one in seven children who wets will stay dry on his or her own. For those who don't, there are effective ways to speed the process along.

Learning to stay dry. The first step in learning to stay dry is for the child to understand the problem. People normally stay dry in one of two ways. Either they wake up in the middle of the night and use the bathroom or hold their urine in tightly. Holding the urine in requires the action of two muscles, called sphincters. When they tighten, they block the urethra so urine can't flow; when they relax, the urethra opens up. One sphincter is under conscious control: the muscle you tighten when you're trying to hold on until you get to the next highway rest stop. The other is under unconscious control, like many other muscles in the body that function on autopilot. During sleep, this muscle needs to keep squeezing or the bed will become wet. Staying dry at night depends on the brain's paying attention to the signals that the bladder is filling up with urine and sending the message to the unconscious sphincter to keep squeezing.

If a child knows how to ride a bicycle, he can use that experience to help understand the process of staying dry. Like riding a bike, staying dry requires practice. Once the brain has been trained to balance the bike, you don't have to think consciously about it anymore; you simply hop on and ride. It's the same with staying dry. Once the brain has been trained, you simply fall asleep. The autopilot does the rest.

Treatments for bed-wetting. Commonsense treatments include putting a night-light in the hall, so that it's easy for your child to get to the bathroom and reminding your child not to drink a lot in the hour or two before bedtime. Some parents insist that their child not drink anything at all after dinner; but this more drastic measure is often uncomfortable and rarely works anyhow. Avoiding caffeine-containing drinks such as cola and tea is also very helpful, since caffeine increases urine production.

A sandwich bed is a nice technique to help your child sleep in a dry bed while letting him be independent. Make up your child's bed with a plastic mattress cover, covered by a cloth sheet, covered by another plastic sheet, and covered by a final cloth sheet. If the top sheet becomes wet during the night, the child removes it and the plastic one under it and goes back to sleep in dry pajamas on the bottom cloth sheet.

Many doctors treat bed-wetting with medication. One medication, imipramine, is sometimes used in much higher doses to treat depression in adults. Another one, desmopressin, contains a hormone that slows down the production of urine in the kidney. Both can be effective in temporarily reducing bed-wetting. But there are disadvantages. An overdose of either can be very dangerous. Desmopressin is expensive. And neither actually solves the problem. Once a child stops taking the medication, there is a very strong chance that the bed-wetting will return.

A better solution relies on the brain's ability to learn. It often helps for children to visualize what they want to happen during the night. As their bladders fill up with urine, a message goes up to the brain, which responds by either waking the child up or tightening up the sphincter that holds the urine in. An imaginative child might visualize a little man at a switchboard up in the brain. When the message comes over the wire (the nerves) that the bladder is full, the little man jumps up and rings a bell or does something else to alert the brain to keep the body dry. A child who visualizes this scene several times before bed stands a better chance of staying dry in the night.

Another technique uses a bed-wetting alarm. These devices have an electronic sensor that detects the presence of urine. One kind rings a buzzer, another activates a device that vibrates. Either wakes the child at the very first sign of wetting. A bed-wetting alarm can help nearly three-quarters of children become dry, usually permanently. There is no risk. A bed-wetting alarm costs about the same as one month of desmopressin. A doctor familiar with the treatment of bed-wetting can help make sure the alarm is used correctly. For sources for bed-wetting alarms, see the Resource Guide (page 917).

A final advantage of the nonmedication approaches is that they let a child take full credit for solving his problem. The next time he faces a difficult challenge, remind him of his past success. In this way, bed-wetting becomes an opportunity for growth.

CHILDREN WITH DISABILITIES

———— ⌇ ⌇ ————

AN UNEXPECTED JOURNEY

Having a child with a disability or chronic medical condition sends a family on an unexpected journey. The road is steeper, the signposts less clearly marked, and the destination less familiar than for families with typical children. The journey may begin with an unsettling worry that something is not as it should be, or it may begin with the shock of a completely unexpected diagnosis. Either way, the first steps take parents through a bleak landscape of loss: the loss of the healthy baby or child of their dreams. The features of this landscape differ from person to person. Many find sharp peaks of anger, quicksands of guilt, valleys of sadness, and plains of numbness.

Parents who find their way through this desert—and most do—confront new barriers, both practical and emotional. On the practical side, there is the challenge of finding good medical and educational care for a child with special needs and the resources to pay for it. On the emotional side, there is the challenge of throwing one's whole heart into the care of a special child while still having emotional energy and time for one's other children, one's partner, and oneself.

The journey can be lonely, but it doesn't have to be. Approximately one-third of children in the United States have a chronic medical or developmental condition, one child in ten has a condition of at least moderate severity, and one in a hundred has a severe disability. One in one hundred may not sound like a lot, but it means that many thousands of children and families have already gone down the road. These families and the professionals who support them make up a strong and accepting community, rich in knowledge, wisdom, and commitment. If there is one piece of advice that surely applies to any parent of a child with special health or developmental needs, it is to reach out to this community for help and support. Each family has to follow its own path, but the way can be smoother if you let families that have gone before serve as guides.

One other word about the journey: The terrain may be stark and rough, but you may discover spots of startling beauty and deep springs of sweetness to sustain you. The chances are that you will find that you and your family have strengths you had not imagined.

Who are the children with disabilities? In the past, it was common to talk about handicapped children or to label a child by the name of his condition: a Down syndrome kid or autistic child. Newer ways of thinking put more emphasis on the child. So we talk about a child with a disability rather than a disabled child or a child with special health-care needs (CSHCN for short).

A wide range of children fall under this heading. They include children with common medical conditions, such as asthma and diabetes, moderately uncommon conditions, such as Down syndrome and cystic fibrosis, and extremely rare conditions, such as maple syrup urine disease. They include children with complications of prematurity, such as cerebral palsy, deafness, or blindness; children whose brains were damaged by trauma or infection; and children with physical malformations, such as cleft lip, cleft palate, dwarfism, or disfiguring birthmarks. Altogether, there are probably three-thousand different conditions that make up the universe of special health-care needs.

Each carries its own set of problems and therapies. And of course, the children who have these conditions and their families all have their unique strengths and weaknesses, so that it is often unrealistic to talk about children with disabilities as though that were a single large group. Still, there are some generalizations that apply.

COPING WITHIN THE FAMILY

Different parents cope differently. One parent becomes analytical, learning everything possible about her child's condition; another is content to let somebody else be the expert. One parent shows a lot of emotion, another puts on a stoic face and seems to feel very little. One parent blames himself and becomes depressed; another blames others or the world at large and is furious. One feels hopeless; another dives into political advocacy.

Within a family, parents' different coping styles may complement each other or become an added source of stress. Although it's changing somewhat, there's still the expectation in our culture that real men don't cry. Mothers are often upset because they feel that the fathers don't care: That is, they don't show much outward emotion in response to the discovery of a disability. Fathers, on their part, may feel that the mothers are being overemotional and dramatic, just making things worse. It's important to be aware of differences in style and to be able to look past them to the underlying reality, which is that both parents care deeply. When parents understand and accept each other's different coping styles, both feel supported and stronger.

Expect grief. All parents whose child has a disability grieve. This is entirely normal and understandable. Parents have to mourn the loss of the imagined perfect child they expected before they can learn to accept the actual child they have.

It's common to read about stages of grief—shock, denial, sadness, and anger—as though everyone passed through all of them, one at a time, in neat order. The reality for most parents is that all of these stages of grieving are always there, less intense at some times than at others, perhaps, but present all the same. So you may find yourself feeling angry or depressed for no apparent reason—at the supermarket, say—until you realize that your grief has for some reason emerged at this moment.

Grief becomes worrisome when a father or mother seems to be locked into it with no room to move on: the parent who is angry at everybody, is so depressed as to be unable to get out of bed in the morning, or persistently refuses to acknowledge the reality of the child's circumstances. Such responses are common early on but it's a concern if they render the parent unable to function or persist for many months without fading.

Part of grief is turning inward; it's normal to need to be alone for a time. But it's not healthy to be isolated. Grief starts to pass once it is shared. The ability to grieve together with a partner, friends, family, fellow church goers, or a professional is a good sign of resilience. People are not meant to suffer alone.

Watch out for guilt. Another common reaction is guilt. A parent thinks, "It must be something I did wrong," and is endlessly preoccupied with that notion, despite assurances from professionals that what happened was simply a matter of bad luck. One parent believes deep down inside that her child's malformed hand was caused by the aspirin she took during her pregnancy (it had nothing to do with it). Others recurrently relive the scene of an accident and berate themselves: "If only I had not let him ride his bicycle on that street, this would never have happened."

The problem with guilt is that it leaves no way to move forward. The preoccupation with the past saps the energy that a parent needs to cope with the present. Guilt can even become a handy excuse: "It's all my fault, so I can't be expected to do anything about it." Don't fall into this trap, and if your partner has, confront him and drag him out.

⟳ CLASSIC SPOCK
There is no perfect way to be a parent of a child with disabilities. There are always trade-offs: sometimes you just need to get away for your own peace of mind; sometimes you feel that you're neglecting one family member while you attend to the needs of another; sometimes you feel as if you're just not up to the task. This is all par for the course; you can't do it all. The good news is that you don't need to do it all—after all, no one ever has.

Beware of specialization. It often happens that one parent takes the lead in the care of the child with a disability, going to all the appointments and parent support group meetings and learning everything about the condition. The problem with this kind of specialization is that the other parent—often the father—may feel increasingly left out and less comfortable providing care for the child. The "nonspecialist" may also find that he has less to say to the "specialist," who is wrapped up in the world of the disability. If this unhealthy situation persists, it may destroy a marriage.

The best way to avoid this trap is for each parent to take turns providing care for the child with special needs. If one parent stays home to care for the child during the day the other parent should make sure that he (or she) cares for the child for blocks of time after work and on weekends and takes time from work now and then to go to appointments and meetings. It may seem unfair—after all, the parent with the job probably works hard all day long, too, and deserves to relax—but unfair or not, it's necessary if the parents are to stay together and function as a team.

Save time for siblings. Children with disabilities require extra effort, physically and emotionally, but if one child's disability becomes the sole focus for the family, the other siblings are bound to feel resentment. They may wonder why it takes a problem to engage their parents' attention. Some cause trouble, as if to say, "Hey, I'm your child also. What about me?" Others become hyperresponsible, as though by being perfect they can somehow make up for their sibling's imperfection and win their parents' love. Neither of these responses leads to long-term mental health.

All children have needs, even if they aren't "special" needs. They need love and attention every day. That doesn't mean parents necessarily have to spend lots of time, just enough to let each child know that he is important. Many times a school play or softball game has to take back seat to an emergency medical appointment. But it's good if *sometimes* the routine doctor's appointment is what ends up being rescheduled.

It's also helpful to offer to bring healthy siblings, if they wish, to some of a child's evaluation or therapy sessions. This takes some of the mystery out of the attention the child with a disability receives, and the siblings get to see the boredom and tedium in these processes. But if a sibling doesn't want to tag along to the clinic or therapist's office, honor that preference when you can. A child who has some say in the matter is much more likely to offer his assistance freely and with a good heart.

It isn't easy being the sibling of a child with a disability. But it can be a positive experience, teaching empathy and compassion, tolerance for differences in people, courage, and resilience.

Nurture your adult relationships. Your relationship with your spouse requires care and attention. The statistics are thought-provoking: When a severe disability makes its appearance, about a third of marriages crumble under the strain, a third remain the same, and a third are strengthened and enriched, as parents meet the challenges together. For relationships to grow requires open communication and mutual trust. Most of all, it takes work and a commitment to invest energy in the relationship itself.

Your relationships with friends and your community are likely to change also. If you let it, having a child with a disability can be a profoundly isolating experience. Or it can enrich your relations with your circle of friends. Many parents learn who their real friends are: those who offer love and support, not those who shy away. You will be the best possible parent only when you don't neglect the other important things in your life. You need and deserve to have friends, to go out with them and have a good time, to get away from your daily responsibilities.

Respite equals freedom. In one study, parents of a child with a disability were asked what the biggest need in their lives was. It was respite: someone to take care of their child for a time so that they could go to a movie, the shopping mall, or visit friends or family. Respite can come from professional agencies, friends, church or synagogue, and family. Don't feel that you should never leave your child. She needs to learn to separate from you, as any child does, and you need to be comfortable leaving her in the care of others.

Take care of yourself. To be the best parent you can be you must be the best person you can be. Most martyrs eventually come to resent both their martyrdom and its cause. You can provide the best care for your child when you feel happy and fulfilled as a person. No one can tell you what that will take. For some parents, it's finding excellent services for their child and going back to work. Others choose to devote more of their time to their children. Regardless of how you decide to focus your energies, there are bound to be family members and friends who think you ought to make different choices. You can't please them all, so don't put much weight on their opinions. There is no right or wrong decision here, just whatever works best for you.

TAKING ACTION

Having a child with a disability or special health-care needs can easily bring on feelings of helplessness and despair. The antidote to those feelings is to take action. There is a lot you can do.

Learn all you can about your child's condition. The more you understand it, the less mysterious it will be, the better you will be able to understand the doctors, and the more you will be able to help the therapists. Write to the national organizations that deal with this problem. Check out books from the library. And talk to your child's doctor, nurse practitioner, or social worker.

Get organized. The demands on parents of children with disabilities can be overwhelming: doctors' appointments, therapy sessions, diagnostic tests, school visits, and so on. You will need to be efficient if these responsibilities are not to take over your life. Many parents keep a loose-leaf binder with information about what has been done and what has happened. They bring it with them to all appointments. Schedule as many visits on the same day as possible, and look for clinics or hospitals that arrange for multiple visits close together in time and space (one-stop shopping).

Find a medical home. Children with special health-care needs benefit if they have one doctor—usually a primary-care physician—who understands the child's condition, knows the available medical and social-service resources, and can coordinate the child's care. This doctor should know the child and family well, it's strengths and weaknesses and should help the parents take steps that support the health of the entire family. In recent years, the American Academy of Pediatrics and other professional organizations have been referring to this special doctor as a child's "medical home." Of course, every child deserves individualized, supportive, family-centered care. For children with special health-care needs, a medical home is a necessity.

Doctors who are able and willing to serve as medical homes often have special training. They may be members of the Society for Developmental and Behavioral Pediatrics (SDBP). Contact this national organization to find members in your area. If you already have a doctor for your child, ask her openly whether she is able to serve as a medical home for your child. If not, she will probably be able to give you the names of others who regularly provide this sort of care.

Join a parent support group. Parent groups can provide education, tips for finding the best doctors and therapists, and personal support. There are national organizations for most medical and developmental conditions. Some are listed in the Resource Guide (starting on page 917), or you can find them by asking your child's doctor, inquiring at your local library, or searching the internet. There may be a local branch near your home. Even if there is no group dedicated to your child's specific condition, there may be a group for parents of children with a variety of special needs.

Another great resource is *Exceptional Parent* magazine, which regularly runs reliable, informative, and inspirational articles. The magazine's website, www.eparent.com, is a good place to start.

Advocate for your child. You may find that you have to negotiate between large bureaucracies and multiple professionals. The school system may not offer what you believe to be an optimal program, one that is tailored to your child's special needs. Insurance companies may balk at paying for some tests or therapies. Some communities are insensitive to the needs of people with disabilities, failing to provide appropriate support.

In such cases an insistent, knowledgeable parental voice can make a difference. Many communities have organizations whose main purpose is to educate and empower parents to be effective advocates. Ask your child's doctor, or go through the national organizations listed in the Resource Guide.

Don't be discouraged if your first efforts meet resistance. With practice, you'll become increasingly effective. You also don't have to do it alone. The only voice more powerful than that of a persistent parent is the voice of a *group* of persistent parents.

Join with a national coalition of parents to make your single voice part of a chorus to influence legislators and the courts.

Get involved in your community. Many communities and religious groups rally in support of their members with disabilities. Introduce your child to your neighbors, to the people in your place of worship, to the community as a whole. Help them to understand the needs of children with disabilities. You will be gratified at the outpouring of support from your community when they learn about and get to know your child as a person.

EARLY INTERVENTION AND SPECIAL EDUCATION

Early intervention. Under federal law, every state is required to have a system in place to coordinate early intervention (EI) services for children with special needs. These services include such things as occupational, physical, and speech and language therapy. EI also includes assistance to families in finding and paying for these services, either through private insurance or publicly funded programs. For each identified child, the state-funded co-ordinating agency is supposed to work with the parents to create an individual family service plan (IFSP) that spells out the needs of the child and family and how they will be met. Clearly, if your physician is a medical home (see page 604), he or she can participate in the planning and ongoing case management.

What's remarkable—and remarkably positive—is that the law specifically recognizes that children exist in *families,* so in order to meet a child's needs, the whole family has to be taken into consideration. For any child under age three, the early intervention system is a crucially important resource. Your child's doctor ought to be able to connect you with it.

IDEA and special education. For children with special needs who have reached age three, another part of the federal law governs how states educate them. The individuals with disabilities Education Act (IDEA) grew out of a movement, led by parents of children with special needs, to see that their children were not ignored or abused by the education system. IDEA states that all children have a right to a "free and appropriate public education" provided in the "least restrictive environment." According to this standard, schools are supposed to provide whatever supports are necessary to make it possible for children with disabilities to participate to the greatest extent possible in mainstream academic and social activities. For example, if a child has a hearing deficit, the school has to provide hearing aids if that will make it possible for the child to participate fully in school.

IDEA gives parents the right and responsibility to assure that their children's special needs are being met. Parents have the right to request an evaluation of the child; if the child is found to have special needs, the school has to create an individualized education plan (IEP), which spells out his needs and how the school proposes to meet them. Parents sign off on those plans and have the right to appeal if they disagree. (See page 676 for more on special education law.)

Mainstreaming. In the past, it was believed that children with disabilities that interfere with ordinary classroom learning–impaired hearing or vision, for instance—should from the start be sent to special day schools in their own community or, if unavailable, to specialized boarding schools. In the last twenty years, there has been an increasing effort to integrate children with disabilities into mainstream school activities.

When it's done well, mainstreaming benefits all children, both those with disabilities and those without. When it's done poorly, with inadequate provision for children's special needs, the result may be that a child with special needs does not have his needs met and therefore does not learn. The IDEA law described above (and see page 676, **the federal IDEA law**) gives parents the power to assure that their children are appropriately educated.

MENTAL RETARDATION

Labels and stigma. More than almost any diagnosis, mental retardation carries a stigma. It sounds like an insult. Over the years, people have used many different terms to describe children and adults whose intellectual abilities are below average: slow, delayed, cognitively impaired, and so on. These terms strike me as weak attempts to disguise what's being talked about. The answer, I think, is not to change the words we use but to change how we think about the thing itself. Mental retardation is a condition, like blindness or deafness, that makes it difficult for people to function in society without special assistance. When they receive that assistance, they can live lives that are full, satisfying, and productive. They can love and be loved. They can contribute to their communities. There should be no shame attached to the term mental retardation.

Developmental delay and mental retardation. Many typically developing infants and young children are slow to reach milestones, such as walking independently or using full sentences. A child who is very slow may be labeled developmentally delayed. The label doesn't say much about why the delay exists or what it portends for the future. Young children often show uneven progress in their development, and many children with developmental delays eventually catch up, often without help from therapists or other professionals.

Others remain delayed and over time, it becomes clear that they are learning and developing many skills at a slower rate than most other children. These children are eventually likely to be diagnosed as mentally retarded. Young children with more severe delays or with medical conditions known to affect brain development may be diagnosed as mentally retarded in the first year or two of life. Many children are not diagnosed as mentally retarded until they are in school.

Definition of mental retardation. The definition of mental retardation (MR) has changed over time. Professionals no longer look only at the results of an IQ test; they also look at how well a child carries out everyday activities, such as self-care (feeding, grooming, dressing), communicating needs and ideas, school work, and chores. In the past, children were categorized as having mild, moderate, or severe MR. Although it's hard to entirely avoid these terms professionals now focus more on the amount of support a child needs to get along in life. Does the child need special support only some of the time and only in some situations (for example, in school) or most of the time in most settings? Instead of being just a label, the diagnosis of MR becomes a description of the kind and intensity of help a child needs to make progress and function in life.

Causes of MR. When mental retardation is severe, it's often possible to find an underlying cause. Examples include lissencephaly, a condition in which the brain fails to form normally, or rubella (German measles), a viral infection that in childhood is mild but can cause brain damage to the developing fetus when contracted by a pregnant woman. Many genetic conditions, such as Down syndrome (see page 617), result in mental retardation.

When mental retardation is mild however, it is often impossible to pin down a cause. We know that various things can affect the developing brain, such as exposure to lead or mercury (see page 764) or malnutrition early in life. Exposure to alcohol during pregnancy is a well-known cause of MR, and it appears that smoking during pregnancy has similar, if less dramatic, effects. We know that on average these exposures lower IQ. But for a specific child, we can't say that this or that exposure was *the* cause of the MR. A lot of mental retardation remains idiopathic, which simply means that we don't know the cause.

Children with mild mental retardation often come from homes that offer little intellectual stimulation. It's not clear that the lack of stimulation *causes* the retardation; it's more likely that several factors are at work. But it is clear that high-quality preschool programs promote the intellectual development of children from less stimulating homes. Encouraging parents to read aloud to their babies, and giving them picture books to get them started, also stimulates young children's language development, a key part of IQ. That extra stimulation helps does not mean that parents are to blame for their children's mental retardation. It means only that the brain is a very adaptable organ; given the right stimulation, it can grow in surprising ways.

What children with MR need. Being accepted and loved enables *all* children to make the most of their abilities. Like all children, children with MR need stimulation and challenges that fit their level of ability, even if that means challenges below a child's chronological age. For example, a child of seven or eight may need opportunities to play make-believe while his typically developing age mates have moved on to board games. Children with MR need playmates they enjoy and can keep up with, even if they are much younger. In school, they need to be placed in classes where they feel that they belong and can accomplish something.

⟨⟩ CLASSIC SPOCK

The slow child whose parents have had only an average amount of schooling and are living happily on a modest scale often makes out better than the child who is born into a college-educated family or one that has high ambitions for worldly success. The latter are more likely to assume that it's vital to get good marks at school, to go to college, to get into a profession. Many useful and dignified jobs can be performed well by people who have less than average intelligence. It's the right of every individual to grow up well enough adjusted and well enough trained to be able to handle the best job that he has the intelligence for.

Anyone who has observed groups of slow children knows how natural and friendly and appealing most of them are, particularly the ones who have been accepted naturally at home. And when they are busy at play or schoolwork that is right for them, they have the same eager, interested attitude that average and superior children do. In other words, the "dumb" look comes more from feeling out of place than from having a low IQ. After all, most of us would have a dull look in an advanced lecture on relativity.

Parents of a child of average intelligence don't have to ask a doctor or read a book to find out his interests. They simply watch him playing with his own possessions and with the possessions of neighbors and sense what else might appeal to him. They observe what he is trying to learn and help him tactfully. The same should hold true for children with mental retardation. You watch to see what he enjoys. You get him the playthings that are sensible. You help him locate the children he has fun with, every day if possible. You teach him the skills he wants assistance with.

School placement. Placement in the right school is vital. It is wise to get the opinion and guidance of a psychologist or child psychiatrist, privately or through a child guidance clinic or the school system. A child should not be placed in a class that is way beyond him. Every day he is unable to keep up his self-confidence will be reduced a little, and having to be left back a grade or demoted will discourage him greatly. It is not ideal to delay a child's school attendance because of mental retardation. In fact, preschool programs can be extremely helpful for children with developmental delays or mental retardation.

The child with more severe MR. A child who at eighteen months or two years is still unable to sit up, who shows little interest in people or things, presents more complicated problems. She will have to be cared for like a baby for a long time. Whether she continues to be cared for at home or in a residential setting depends on the degree of retardation, the temperament of the child, how she affects other children in the family, and whether by the time she is active she can find playmates and activities to keep her happy. It depends on whether there is a special class in one of the local schools that will accept and suit her. Most of all, it depends on whether her parents can manage the strains of caring for her and find enough satisfaction to keep at it year after year. In the past, the assumption was that children with mental retardation would be sent to special schools or attend separate classes. Now the assumption is that children with mental retardation will live at home and attend regular schools with the supports they need to succeed.

Adolescence and the transition to adulthood. Children with mental retardation grow up. In adolescence, a child with mental retardation is likely to face the same conflicting desires and fears that bedevil and enchant other teens, but with added challenges. With his limited independence, the mechanics of socializing— going to a movie, hanging out with friends—may be harder. And it may be difficult for the teen to understand the social rules that govern relationships between the sexes. It doesn't help that many people assume that a person with intellectual impairments doesn't or shouldn't have sexual feelings. Early and continuing education about sexuality and human relationships is important for typically developing children (see page 446), and it is especially important for children with cognitive disabilities.

Worries about how a child with mental retardation will find a place in the adult world haunt many parents. Schools are increasingly providing special education to children through age twenty-one and also services to help young adults make the transition to appropriate jobs and living arrangements.

You can find much more information on all of the topics touched on above; the Resource Guide (page 917) is a good place to start.

AUTISM

A time of hope and concern. Awareness of autism has never been greater. It is now understood that autism is caused by abnormal development of the brain, not abnormal parenting. There is promise that early, intensive special education can help children with autism learn to communicate and think more flexibly. With greater awareness and optimism about treatment and with more high-quality treatment programs available, professionals are making the diagnosis at increasingly earlier ages, thereby greatly increasing the chances of improvement.

On the negative side, the number of children with autism seems to be rising. I say *seems*, because we aren't sure how much of the rise is the result of increased awareness and how much may be the result of actual changes in children. The popular theory that autism is caused by immunizations seems very unlikely (see page 726). But there are many other possible causes, and not all have been thoroughly researched. And while early, intensive education helps more children make gradual progress, many parents still cling to hopes that miracle treatments can deliver an instant cure. When those hopes turn out to be false, as they always have so far, the disappointment may be severe. The realistic likelihood is that a child with autism will continue to experience special challenges throughout life.

We know more about autism now than ever before, but we still have a great deal to learn. The paragraphs that follow can provide only a brief introduction. If a child of yours or one you love has autism, you'll want to learn much more. The Resource Guide should get you started (see page 917).

What is autism? Children with autism have abnormal development in three main areas: communication, relationships, and behavior. Typically developing children sometimes have difficulties in one or another of these areas; it is the pattern of problems that constitutes autism. Here are some examples:

Communication. Children with autism may not babble at the expected time (around six to twelve months), and are often late to say words. If they do speak, they often repeat words meaninglessly and have great difficulty carrying on a back-and-forth conversation. Children with autism also have problems with nonverbal communication. They don't use eye contact to show that they are listening or point to things to show that they find them interesting.

Relationships. Infants with autism may not cuddle normally or reach out to be picked up; some are upset by tickle games such as "s-o-o-o big" that most babies find delightful. Children with autism often ignore peers, or they interact in unwanted ways because they can't read the social cues that mean "I'm ready to play now" or "Leave me alone." They may be affectionate with their parents but in odd ways, such as backing into someone to request a hug.

Behaviors. Children with autism often become fascinated by one or two behaviors which they repeat over and over. One child lines up toy cars in the same order or perpetually flicks the lights off and on. Another child puts a tape into the VCR then takes it out again, for hours at a time. Any attempt to change the routine may bring on a tantrum. Spinning objects often seem to hold a special fascination. Children with autism often spin their own bodies, flap or twist their hands, or rock back and forth repetitively. They may react unexpectedly to sounds, odors, or touch. For example, many love the feeling of being held tightly but hate being touched lightly.

The range of autistic problems. Experts recognize a spectrum of autistic disorders, from mild to very severe. The terminology can be confusing: Pervasive developmental disorders is sometimes used to describe the whole autism spectrum; but pervasive developmental disorder (PDD or PDD-NOS) also refers to a particular autistic disorder that does not have all the symptoms of full-blown autism.

Asperger's syndrome is a type of autism in which children speak correctly but struggle with the finer points of social language use. For example, the intonation of their speech is flat or singsongy, or they speak like little professors but find it next to impossible to make small talk.

At the more severe end, autism often exists with severe mental retardation, hearing problems, or persistent seizures. Although such children may never learn to communicate verbally, sensitive teachers and therapists can often help them establish other means of communication and connection.

Is there a basic problem in autism? There are many theories. One that makes sense to me is that autism affects the way the brain processes information from the senses, perhaps like a television set with bad reception. Some of the signal gets through okay, other bits are distorted, and other bits are lost altogether. It's possible that the core difficulties in autism—with communication, relationships, and behaviors—are responses to these mixed-up signals, the child's attempt to cope with a confusing, frightening world.

Some of the more dramatic symptoms, such as violent temper tantrums, may be expressions of the extreme frustration and unhappiness that comes from being cut off from other people. The love of spinning, another common symptom, may reflect abnormalities in the child's vestibular sense, the sense that normally controls balance. The child may avoid eye contact, preferring instead to look at a small number of very familiar objects, because the human face provides too much information at once, something the child with autism finds overwhelming and upsetting.

If autism distorts the way a child sees, hears, feels, and tastes, all of the everyday sensations that normally connect children with their parents—shared glances, cookies, music—may instead set the child with autism apart. The challenge in treating autism is to get past the garbled sensory input and connect with the child, overcome the child's defensive behaviors, such as gaze avoidance, and teach the child the skills to communicate ideas and feelings.

Early signs of autism. Early detection of autism greatly improves the outlook. Very early in infancy, parents may have a vague feeling that something just isn't right. Looking back later, they may realize that their baby didn't gaze into their eyes like other infants, or never really liked tickling games. Other early signs include, by twelve months, not pointing at objects with a single digit in order to direct the parent's attention; by fifteen months, not using any words to communicate wants or simple ideas; or by age two years, not putting two words together to make simple sentences. None of these warning signs is definitive for autism (hearing loss, and other developmental problems and variations of normal development sometimes look the same). Still, if you notice any of them, you should seek a developmental evaluation for your child and not simply accept reassurance that he will "grow out of it."

Therapies for autism. The mainstay of autism therapy is early intensive education with a focus on communication. Programs shown to improve children's language and relationship skills usually require effort several hours a day, seven days a week. Children may be in more than one program and also have tutors or hired assistants working with them. Because of the great intensity of this effort, it is almost inevitable that one parent will devote full time to the care and education of the child with autism. Finding a balance, so that others in the family stay involved and family relationships are nurtured, is a critical challenge.

No medication has been found to cure the underlying problems of autism. Various medications are used, however, to reduce the symptoms of rage, anxiety, or obsessiveness that may make family life intolerable or interfere with the child's education.

Parents of a child with autism need to learn a great deal to manage their children's education. The Resource Guide (page 917) lists some reliable starting points.

DOWN SYNDROME

A child born with Down syndrome faces both developmental challenges and medical risks. Early on, feeding problems and developmental delays are common. Most children with Down syndrome have mental retardation, ranging from mild to severe. They grow slowly and are prone to hearing and vision problems, ear and sinus infections, disturbed sleep, low thyroid hormone, heart problems, severe constipation, joint problems, and others. A specific child may have none, a few, or many of these problems.

Still, life can be full and satisfying for a child with Down syndrome and his family. This positive outlook is due, in large part, to courageous parents who have refused to hide their children away, demanding that society grant full rights to children and adults with Down syndrome and all other disabilities.

Definition and risk. A syndrome is simply a group of symptoms that often occur together. "Down" refers to a person, not a direction: John Langdon Down first described the syndrome back in 1865. Nearly a hundred years later, the cause was discovered: extra genetic material from chromosome number 21. Most people with Down syndrome have three copies of chromosome 21 rather than the normal two. The term trisomy 21 simply means three copies of chromosome 21, another name for Down syndrome. Rarely, the cause is a small piece of an extra chromosome 21 that has moved over to another chromosome—in genetics terms, a translocation. A translocation increases the chance that a second child in the same family will have Down syndrome.

One child in eight hundred is born with Down syndrome, making it common, as genetic disorders go. As women grow older, the chance that one of their eggs will contain an extra chromosome 21 rises, increasing the chance that their children will have Down syndrome. There is one chance in two hundred-fifty that a child born to a mother of thirty-five will have Down syndrome.

Diagnosis of Down syndrome. Diagnosis can be made during the first trimester of pregnancy by testing the amniotic fluid (amniocentesis) or part of the placenta (chorionic villus sampling, or CVS). Most obstetricians recommend that pregnant women age thirty-five and over have one of these tests. Prenatal ultrasound tests may also show features suggesting the diagnosis.

At birth, facial features and other findings of a physical examination can also suggest Down syndrome, but a final diagnosis depends on a blood test. It can take a week or two for the results to come back from the lab.

Treatment. No medication, diet, supplement, or other treatment can cure Down syndrome. Wonder drugs and revolutionary therapies appear with regularity; so far none has stood up under scientific study. Parents have to balance the resolution to try every possible treatment against the emotional drain and expense of one disappointment after another. It's important that parents accept the children they have, even as they look for ways to make their lives better.

Children with Down syndrome benefit from having a medical home (see page 604): a committed doctor who can help the parents anticipate the various health issues that are bound to come up and find the specialists and therapists they need. It's worth the effort to find a doctor who has expertise and experience working with children with disabilities, Down syndrome in particular. Such a doctor is more likely to have access to special growth charts that can aid in the detection of growth difficulties in children with Down syndrome (they grow differently from average children).

Educational planning should be tailored to a child's interests, temperament, and learning style. This is true for all children, of course, but it's especially critical for children with Down syndrome. Inclusion of children with Down syndrome in regular classes often works well though it usually requires special support from a knowledgeable educational specialist or school psychologist.

The care of children with Down syndrome works best when it is a team effort, with parents, doctors, and teachers working together. The leaders of the team are inevitably the parents. Their participation in a parent-support group can give them the information and encouragement they need to be effective leaders for their children's care. The Resource Guide (page 917) can help you find groups in your area.

OTHER SPECIAL NEEDS

This chapter describes the most common conditions that create special medical and developmental needs. Attention deficit hyperactivity disorder, a very common condition, is discussed in the chapter on Acting Out (page 542). Learning disabilities are tackled in the section on Learning and School (page 629). For many other common and uncommon problems, such as deafness, Tourette's syndrome, and cystic fibrosis, the Resource Guide (see page 917) can get you started.

GETTING HELP

WHY PEOPLE SEEK HELP

Many different professionals are trained to understand and treat the behavioral and emotional problems of children. In the nineteenth century, psychiatrists cared mainly for the insane, and some people still hesitate to consult any mental health professional. But as we have learned how serious troubles develop from mild ones, mental health professionals have paid their attention more to everyday problems. This way they can do the most good in the shortest time. There's no more reason to wait until a child is severely disturbed before seeing a child mental health professional than there is to wait until he is in a desperate condition from pneumonia before going to the doctor.

FIRST STEPS

When you need help, it may be hard to know where to turn. Your child's doctor may be the best place to start, assuming that you trust his or her judgment. Many communities have clinics that provide counseling for children and families. You may find them in the phone book under family services, counseling, or mental health. Religious leaders often provide counseling or will help connect families with other professionals. Or you can call a nearby hospital and ask the switchboard to connect you with the right department.

Depending on your particular needs, one type of professional may be better than another. The paragraphs below give brief descriptions of many of the professionals most likely to be of help. To learn more and to locate professionals in your area, contact the professional societies for each field; contact information is listed in the Resource Guide (page 917).

Choosing a professional. When medication is the main treatment, it's usually best to see a child psychiatrist or a behavioral and developmental pediatrician. In most circumstances, however, the professional title is not nearly as important as the individual in front of the academic degree. Ask friends and family for a recommendation. Talk with the professional before bringing your child. It's important that both you and your child feel comfortable.

Many community-based services are provided free or on a sliding scale, based on income. Private insurance providers may offer limited choices. Find out what mental health benefits your plan allows before you begin treatment.

Family social service agencies. Most cities have at least one family social service agency; larger cities often have several. Agencies may identify themselves with a specific religion; all provide services regardless of a family's faith. These organizations are staffed by social workers trained to help parents with all of the usual family problems: child management, marital adjustment, budgeting, chronic illness, housing, finding a job, and medical care. They often have consultants—psychiatrists or psychologists—to help with more difficult cases.

Many parents have grown up with the idea that social agencies mainly provide charity and are only for destitute people. In fact, the modern family agency is as glad to help solve small problems as it is to treat large ones and as glad to assist families who can afford to pay a fee as it is to lend a hand to those who can't.

Developmental and behavioral pediatricians. These are doctors who have the training usual to pediatricians plus two or three years studying and taking care of children with developmental and behavioral problems. Some specialize in developmental problems (such as mental retardation or autism; see pages 608 and 613; others specialize in behavioral problems (such as bed-wetting or ADHD; see pages 592 and 550). If you find this distinction confusing, you are not alone. The best thing to do is to ask about a doctor's training and expertise.

Most developmental and behavioral pediatricians have experience in assessing and treating the common behavioral and emotional problems of children. Like psychiatrists, they are trained in the use of medications to treat behavior. (Some very severe problems, such as schizophrenia, are probably best handled by psychiatrists.)

Psychiatrists. These are medical doctors who specialize in mental and emotional disorders. They are most likely to be helpful to children with severe problems, such as schizophrenia. A child and adolescent psychiatrist has additional training in handling the specific problems of children and adolescents. Psychiatrists often work as part of teams, prescribing medications while other professionals—psychologists or social workers—provide counseling or talk therapy.

Psychologists. Psychologists who work with children are trained in such areas as intelligence and aptitude testing and the causes and treatment of learning, behavior, and emotional problems. To be a licensed psychologist, a person must have earned a Ph.D. and had a clinical internship (working with clients under supervision).

Social workers. These professionals have had at least two years of classroom and clinical training after college, leading to a master's degree. To earn a LCSW (licensed clinical social work) degree, a master's level candidate must provide counseling or therapy to clients under supervision and pass a state licensing examination. Social workers can evaluate a child, his family, and his school situation and treat behavioral problems in both the child and family.

Psychoanalysts. These are psychiatrists, psychologists, or other mental health professionals who treat emotional problems through the exploration of unconscious conflicts and defenses and through the patient's relationship with the analyst. Many analysts apply other therapies and medication as well. Child psychoanalysts (like psychologists) often use play and art as well as conversing to communicate with their young patients, and they often work with the parents as well. Legitimate psychoanalysts have advanced degrees, have studied psychoanalysis and undergone psychoanalysis, and worked under supervision for years. However, there is no national licensing of these professionals, and anyone can legally call himself or herself a psychoanalyst. So it's important to look carefully at a person's credentials before entering into psychoanalytic treatment. *The American Psychoanalytic Association* website provides a detailed and clear description of psychoanalysis and a national listing of psychoanalysts (see Resource Guide, page 917).

Family therapists. The main insight of family therapy is that everyone in the family is connected. A child's difficult behavior often causes difficulties in the family as a whole, and problems in the family often result in troubled behavior in a particular child. The best way to improve the child's behavior is often to help the whole family function better.

Family therapists may be psychologists, psychiatrists, social workers, or other professionals who have completed additional

training in family therapy. Most states have licensing requirements that include at least a master's degree, two years of family
therapy practice under close supervision, and passing a standardized exam.

Licensed professional counselors and school counselors. The
qualifications for a professional counselor in most states are a
master's degree in counseling and two or three years of supervised practice: from two thousand to four thousand hours.
School counselors are specially trained to provide counseling in
schools. The training to become a licensed professional counselor (LPC) or school counselor is similar in scope to the training of many family therapists or master's-level psychologists.

TYPES OF THERAPY

It's important to realize that there are many different types of
therapy. The old cliché of lying on a couch and talking about
your dreams while a bearded psychoanalyst takes notes is just
that: an old cliché. Insight-oriented therapies do attempt to
bring patients to a deeper understanding of their personal histo-
ries and motivations, including early childhood experiences.
Other therapies focus much more on the here and now, seeking
to change behavior by changing how patients think about themselves and others, an approach known as cognitive-behavioral
therapy (CBT). Research in the past few years has shown that
CBT can be surprisingly powerful. For example, a child suffering
from depression may learn to recognize the negative, overcriti-
cal thoughts he repeats to himself and substitute more realistic
and hopeful ones.

Young children, who have a hard time putting feelings into
words, often benefit from play therapy. Older children may benefit from art therapy or narrative therapy, in which they learn to
create narratives or stories that help them cope. For children

with problematic behaviors, a behavioral approach, focusing on identifying triggers and consequences to negative and positive behaviors, can be very effective. Most behavior therapies include a component of parent training: that is, specific instructions and coaching to help parents intervene effectively to change their children's behavior.

Family therapy can often be extremely helpful, in combination with one of these individual approaches. The point is that there are many options out there. When you are considering a therapist, ask about her therapeutic approach to make certain it is something that is comfortable for you.

WORKING TOGETHER

Parents should plan to work together with the professionals they choose. Some therapists limit a parent's involvement to bringing the child and taking him home again. Most, however, invite parents to take a much more active role. In family therapy, the whole family is the patient.

You should agree early on with the professional on the main goals of the therapy. What changes can you expect and when? Then, from time to time, you can check in to see if you are getting where you hoped to. For specific issues, such as bed-wetting or tantrums, a few sessions may be all that's needed; other problems may take longer. Children and parents often benefit from working with the same professional from time to time over a period of years.

One of the advantages of clarifying your expectations early on is that it helps you make decisions when things aren't going well. You can't expect instant solutions for problems that developed over a long time, and problems often get worse before they get better. Once you've chosen a professional to work with, it makes sense to stick with that person for a time, even if there are periods of uncertainty. On the other hand, if months have gone by without positive change and your expectation was that change would come about, it's fine—necessary, really—that you talk with the therapist about trying a new approach or a new therapist.

A setback, even a change from one professional to another, is not the end of the world. What's most important is that you and your child maintain an optimism that things will get better. I think that such an attitude often makes all the difference in the long run.

SECTION V

<hr />

Learning and School

LEARNING AND THE BRAIN

―――――――――∞ ∞―――――――――

THE NEW BRAIN SCIENCE

We now know enough about the brain to begin to understand how babies and children learn. We understand, for example, why babies learn best when they have a chance to use all their senses. We understand why they repeat a certain behavior over and over—shaking a rattle, or listening to the same story—then suddenly lose interest. And why it is easier for them to learn certain skills at certain ages, such as learning a second language before age ten. We are also beginning to use our knowledge of how the brain changes to design new therapies for children with learning disabilities.

The new brain science can be boiled down into a few principles. All thinking is an activity of the brain. As the brain acts, it changes to become more efficient at whatever it is doing. Although it never stops changing, the brain becomes less flexible with age. Experiences in the first years of life are therefore important in getting the brain off to a good start, setting the stage for learning throughout life.

Genes and experience. For decades, scientists believed that a baby's brain developed according to a detailed plan carried in her genes. Now we know that genetics draws only the outline;

experience fills in the details. A child's experiences shape how her brain is put together and, therefore, how it functions.

One reason that experience, and not genes, must determine how the nerves in the brain connect up with each other is that the brain is too complicated. The human brain contains about a hundred billion nerve cells (neurons), and each connects to about ten thousand other neurons. If you multiply these numbers together, you come up with ten trillion connections. The twenty-six chromosomes that make up the human genome simply cannot contain enough information to spell out each of those connections.

Instead, genes are responsible for creating the overall structure. Early in development, they cause neurons to divide and grow at an enormous rate, move out to their approximate final positions, and begin to connect up with each other. The parts of the brain that control basic body functions, such as breathing or heartbeat, develop early—they have to. But other functions, such as the ability to understand language and to speak, develop much later. These functions and the complicated neural circuits that make them possible develop under the control of experience.

In other words, we are born with unfinished brains. This is a good thing. If our brains were finished at birth, they wouldn't be able to adapt as readily to different surroundings. For example, a child who grows up hearing Chinese develops the neural circuits required to process the sounds of Chinese; and by twelve months of age, he has already largely lost the ability to perceive some sounds used in English that are not used in Chinese. In the same way, the child who grows up hearing English loses the ability (the circuits) to process sounds used in Chinese that are not used in English, even as he becomes much more skillful in handling the sounds of English. This kind of adaptation occurs in other senses, as well. For example, children who grow up in modern houses become better at perceiving straight lines and right angles than children who grow up in rounded huts.

Use it or lose it. How is the brain able to adapt itself so well? An important part of the answer lies in a simple rule that affects the connections between neurons: Use it or lose it. All thinking depends on nerve cells connected with each other across tiny gaps called synapses. Each time two nerves make a connection, that synapse grows stronger. Stronger synapses remain while weaker ones are pruned away, as a gardener prunes a rosebush.

Early on, the brain makes many more synapses than it needs. In the course of learning, many are pruned away. A twenty-two-year-old college graduate has fewer synapses than a two-year-old baby. By cutting out unnecessary unused synapses, the brain makes itself faster and more efficient. At the same time, though, it becomes harder for the brain to adapt in completely new directions. So, for example, our college graduate can readily learn complicated concepts in history (an area she has studied) but has a very hard time learning the sounds of Mandarin Chinese, something that requires her brain to work in an entirely new way (something our two-year-old can do with ease).

The point about use it or lose it that is so important for raising children is that babies need to be exposed to a wide range of experiences for their brains to develop with the greatest flexibility. They need things to feel, bang, taste, draw with, build with, take apart, jump on, jump off, hold, throw—a full range of experience. They need to hear lots of language and have the experience of being listened to. As they grow, the neural connections strengthened by their early experiences allow them to acquire all kinds of new information.

Again! Again! The use it or lose it principle helps to explain why babies and young children tend to get stuck on certain activities, doing them again and again. At ten months, for example, a baby grabs the bars of his crib and, using all the strength in his chubby arms and legs, pulls himself up to standing position. Unsure of what to do next, he lets go and bumps back down on his bottom;

a minute later he pulls up again. This continues until he starts to fuss or falls asleep exhausted.

This baby is exercising more than his muscles; he's exercising his brain. Each time he repeats the process of pulling up and standing, he strengthens a set of synapses that eventually will give him the balance and coordination he needs to walk. Of course, once the baby has mastered the skill of standing on his own, the pulling-up routine loses all interest, and he moves on to his next project.

You can see this sort of repetition in every area of development. Babies have a strong internal drive to learn. It's helpful for a parent to know that your baby's obsessive interest in putting blocks into a bucket or hearing the same story five hundred times is evidence that his brain is busy wiring itself.

Learning and emotion. We're used to thinking about emotions as being very different from logic. In fact, they are closely connected. When a baby is learning, he's generally attentive, involved, and happy. Positive emotions are the fuel that power children's exploring and learning. In another way, emotions both positive and negative make learning possible. Children pay attention only to new things and therefore learn from them, because they evoke positive or negative emotions. (Later, we may make ourselves pay attention to things because we know we have to, but we never learn them as well as when we're emotionally involved.) In the brain, the neural systems that produce emotions are closely connected to the systems that produce logical thought. When (as rarely happens) those systems are disconnected, so that a person now thinks purely logically, it creates a very severe learning disability.

In babies and young children, a good sign that they are learning is that they laugh, smile, and coo or simply gaze intently. All of the loving you give a baby—the rocking, holding, tickling, singing, and talking—feeds her emotional growth and at the same time strengthens her desire and ability to learn.

HOW CHILDREN THINK

Piaget's insights. How do babies and children learn to make sense of the world? Some of the earliest, and still best, answers came from a Swiss psychologist named Jean Piaget (Pee-a-zhay). Piaget initially developed his theories after making careful observations of his three young children. He then spent the rest of his life trying to prove these theories through scientific study, but it was watching the day-to-day development of children that got him started. You can do the same.

Piaget believed that human development proceeds in stages that are the same for everybody. Through a careful description of these stages, he explained how an infant with little ability to think abstractly comes to be able to reason logically, create hypotheses about how things work, and invent new ideas and behaviors that he has never seen or heard before.

Little scientists. Piaget viewed infants and children as little scientists. He believed we are born with a drive to make sense of the world and that we do so by constantly conducting experiments. Take, for example, a four-month-old who keeps dropping food off the high chair then looking for it. He is experimenting with the idea of gravity. He's also experimenting with the idea that objects continue to exist even if they're out of sight, a concept psychologists call object permanence.

Until the baby does this experiment, repeating it many times, nothing really exists for him except what he sees, hears and touches at that moment. Out of sight is out of mind. Infants begin to learn object permanence in the first months, doing so by trial and error. At three months, the infant drops the pacifier or bottle by accident and is surprised to see it on the floor a second later. This happens again and again. Slowly it begins to dawn on him that the object on the floor is the same one that was just in his hand.

The little scientist goes into action. He begins to purposely drop things on the floor. He looks down and sees them. He repeats the experiment. Success! He continues to drop things on the floor, over and over and over.

Finally, when his research on dropping things is completed to his satisfaction, he has the idea that if he just saw something that's now gone, it must be on the floor. If it's not on the floor, it probably no longer exists. It is not until the next stage, at about eight months, that the infant's ideas about object permanence become more sophisticated, and he searches elsewhere for missing objects.

Infants love to play peekaboo for the same reason: The face is there, then it's not, then it is. The infant's capacity for continuing this game is boundless because it is one of the questions he is working on at that stage of his development. Once he is satisfied that faces continue to exist even when he can't see them, peekaboo falls by the wayside, and a new game, one appropriate to his current developmental questions, arises.

Sensorimotor thinking. Piaget called the first two years of life the sensorimotor period. By this he meant that infants and toddlers learn by doing, by exercising their senses and motor (muscle) abilities. If a baby learns to hold a rattle, she has the idea that rattles are for holding. When she shakes the rattle, bangs it on her high chair, and puts it in her mouth, she's showing that she has additional ideas about rattles. If you take the rattle and hide it under a cloth, does she pull the cloth away to get at the rattle? If so, she has the idea that objects (or at least rattles) can be hidden then found. (At this point, it becomes harder to take things away from her when you no longer want her playing with them.)

Another principle babies learn about is cause and effect. At four or five months, if you tie one end of a string to a baby's ankle and the other to a mobile hanging over the crib, the baby will quickly learn to move his leg to make the mobile move. (Be sure you take the string with you when you go: it poses a strangulation risk.) This is what Piaget did in one of his most famous experiments. Babies later learn to use objects to achieve desired effects, such as using a stick to get a toy that is out of reach. In a yet later stage they discover that *hidden* causes can have effects. Windup toys are a good example of hidden causes. Somewhere between eighteen and twenty-four months is when most babies figure out how to make them work.

During the sensorimotor period, babies begin to understand words and use them to refer to objects and communicate their needs. But it's not until toddlers are able to put words together into interesting combinations—"Block in!" or "Cookie all gone!"—that words become a flexible tool for thinking. When that happens, the sensorimotor period comes to an end.

What's important for parents to understand is that thinking develops in stages. It's a mistake to try to rush the process by skipping over sensorimotor learning and going straight to more advanced verbal learning. All the banging, smearing, and messing around that babies do is necessary to prepare their brains to take the next step.

Preoperational thinking. Piaget used the word operation to mean thinking based in logical principles. He thought of preschool age children, from two and four, as preoperational because children that age don't think logically. For example, a three-year-old may well think that rain falls because the sky is sad or that she became sick because she was bad. A child in the preoperational stage can see things only from her own point of view. She's self-centered though not necessarily selfish. If her father is unhappy, she may bring over her favorite stuffed animal to try to comfort him (after all, it works for her).

A young child's ideas about quantity are also not well developed. Piaget showed this in a famous experiment in which he gave young children a low, wide dish full of water. Then he poured the water into a tall, narrow glass. Almost all of the children said that the glass held more, because it looked bigger. That the same water was poured back and forth between the dish and the glass didn't change the children's minds. Any doctor who has tried to convince a two-year-old that the needle he is about to use is really very small knows that to a child in the prelogical phase, the *actual* size of an object is not nearly as important as how big it *seems*. The same sort of confusion causes many young children to fear that they may be swept down the bathtub drain.

Concrete operations. Most children during the early school years, from about age six through perhaps nine or ten, are capable of logical thinking but not abstract thinking. Piaget called this early logical thinking concrete operations, that is, logic applied to things you can see and feel. This kind of thinking shows up in children's approach to right and wrong. A six-year-old, for example, is likely to feel that a game can be played by only one set of rules. It wouldn't be right to change the rules, even if all the players agreed, because that would be breaking them. A nine-year-old might consider breaking a window with a wildly thrown baseball to be a more serious crime than stealing a candy bar because the window costs much more. That the window-breaking was completely unintentional while the candy theft was deliberate would not necessarily figure in this concrete-operational thinking.

Another area where a concrete-operational child may have difficulty is in figuring out other people's motivations. It's fascinating to read a story to a young school-age child and ask her to explain *why* certain characters did what they did. You'll quickly discover that what is obvious to you is actually very hard for your bright eight-year-old to grasp. I recommend trying this with a classic like *Charlotte's Web* by E. B. White or *Homer Price* by Robert McCloskey.

Abstract thinking. Toward the end of grade school, children begin to think more about abstract concepts such as justice or destiny. Their thinking becomes much more flexible, and they can imagine many different solutions to a physical or social problem. They are able to reason from principles to particulars and back again. Abstract reasoning of this sort often leads teens to question their parents' teachings and values, making for sometimes heated dinnertime conversation. It may also lead teens to develop a high level of idealism, which can become a powerful political force.

Not all teens reach this state of formal operations, as Piaget terms it. They may use abstract thinking in some areas but not in others. For example, a fifteen-year-old who loves computers may think abstractly about firewalls and file-sharing protocols but concretely about friendships with girls. In some ways, he might even be *pre*operational. For example, he may harbor the utterly illogical belief, common in teens, that he is invulnerable. Therefore, he smokes cigarettes and gets into cars with other teens who have been drinking.

As a parent, paying attention to your child's level of thinking—preoperational, concrete-operational, or formal-operational—may allow you to communicate more effectively.

Children are different. An understanding of cognitive development leads to an important point: Children are not merely little adults. Rather, they understand the world in a fundamentally different way from the way most adults do. Depending on their cognitive stage, they may be more self-centered, more rigid, or more idealistic. What makes perfect sense to us may make little or no sense to a child.

✐ CLASSIC SPOCK

In my experience, parents sometimes have problems with their children because they don't really appreciate how fundamentally differently they and their children see the world. Consequently they think their child is capable of more understanding than he really is. This is why they sometimes offer a long intellectual explanation to a two-year-old of why she should share. Although sharing is not part of any child's way of seeing the world at that stage, that doesn't mean that it won't be later on. This same misunderstanding causes some adults to tell teenagers not to smoke because they might get lung cancer and die in forty years. Much better to speak to teens about immediate consequences, like bad breath, decreased endurance, and looking stupid. That's what really counts in their world.

MULTIPLE INTELLIGENCES

The theories of Piaget, described above, explain a lot about children's thinking, but they don't tell the whole story. We now know from very ingenious experiments that very young babies are capable of feats of memory and even of simple mathematics that we never thought possible.

Another great advance has been the realization that the verbal-analytical intelligence Piaget talked about, which is the kind measured by the standard IQ tests, is only one of several kinds of intelligence. In fact, everyone has multiple intelligences. Other types include spatial, musical, bodily kinesthetic (movement), interpersonal (relationships with others), intrapersonal (self-understanding and insight), and naturalist (understanding and classifying objects in nature).

Uneven intelligence. The key to the understanding of multiple intelligences is to realize that intelligence is the processing of information by the brain. Information of all sorts flows through the brain all the time: for example, information about tones and rhythms in speech or music or the position of one's body in space. Different parts of the brain process this information, combining it in different ways. It's possible for one area of the brain to be working well while another is not. People who have damage to the part of the brain that controls speech may not be able to talk but may be able to sing words since their musical ability is housed in another location and is unimpaired.

Even people without brain damage aren't equally endowed in all the different intelligences. One child learns best by listening, another by watching, another by holding something physical in her hand, and still another by acting out a concept with her whole body. Someone can be verbally gifted but completely at a loss at figuring out what to tip a waiter at lunch. When these inequalities in intelligence are very marked, they may create learning disabilities (see page 673).

Think about your own abilities and limitations and you're sure to realize that you're much more gifted in some areas than others. In my case, I am a good talker but can't hit a baseball to save my life. I can play a musical instrument, but I've never been able to draw a horse that looks like one (although once I tried for several months).

As you pay attention to your child's different intelligences, you may realize that some of the things you thought he was avoiding out of laziness are in fact more difficult for him than you suspected. You may also recognize areas in which your child is gifted, though these gifts may not translate to higher grades. By expanding your focus to include multiple intelligences, you can appreciate and nurture more of your child's strengths, and your own.

READY FOR SCHOOL

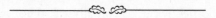

Everything you do to keep your child safe and healthy, teach reasonable behavior, and have fun together prepares your child to succeed in school. It's important, too, for young children to have opportunities to play with their peers and feel comfortable with adults who are not their parents. Beyond this, the qualities that make a child ready for school include a basic level of developmental maturity, especially listening and speaking skills, and an eagerness to find out things. Children also need a familiarity with letters and sounds, a love of stories, and a strong desire to master the printed word.

A few children go straight to kindergarten, having spent their first five years entirely at home. But for most, school readiness is a team effort, with parents and preschool teachers working together to help children get off to a good start.

READING ALOUD

The goal of education is not just for children to be able to read and write but for them to become literate. Literate adults use reading to learn about things that interest them and use writing to share their ideas. Literate children view reading and writing as exciting and worthwhile in their own right. They tend to have rich imaginations and many interests. Literacy widens a child's world. And, very often, literacy starts with a parent's reading aloud.

If you were lucky enough to have been read to when you were a child, there's a good chance that you will share the pleasure with your child. Even if you weren't, you've probably heard that reading aloud is a good thing to do. But the details—why, when, and how—may be less clear.

Why read aloud? It is true that some children do well in school without ever having been read to by their parents. But the chances that a child will succeed at reading and writing go way up if that child starts school having already had a lot of experience with the printed word and feeling very positively about books.

When you sit down with your child and a book, many wonderful things happen. By talking about the pictures, for example, you expose her to lots of new and interesting words. By reading and rereading, you give her many opportunities to learn how the words come together in interesting sentences. You build up her listening and attention skills. You help her begin to see the connections between the letters she sees and the words she hears. Most of all, it's the joyful interaction with a loving parent that brings picture books to life for children and makes being read to such as powerful experience.

Bilingual families. Children who grow up hearing two languages have a real advantage. While they often take a bit longer to express themselves clearly, once they get going they quickly become fluent speakers of both languages.

Parents living in the United States who don't speak English well themselves should talk with and read to their children in their native language. It's much more helpful for a child to hear a language—*any* language—spoken well than to hear English spoken badly. A child who learns Spanish or Russian at home can quickly pick up English in preschool or the child-care center. A child who never learns to speak any language well (because he did not have the chance to hear one spoken well) has a much, much harder time.

Many picture books are now available in Spanish translation and other languages. Also, many that are in English have a second language printed on the same page: a great way for parents and children to learn.

Reading to newborns. Babies who are read to enjoy the sound of the reader's voice and the feeling of being held. Most parents who read to their babies starting at birth also read to them for many years afterward. Those children often grow up to love books, although I'm not sure how much the newborn experience has to do with it.

What reading to newborns does do is expose babies to much human speech. Listening as their parents talk to them is one very important way that babies begin to learn language. Strong language skills are among the best predictors of reading and writing ability. Listening also helps calm babies down.

If you want to read to your new baby, it doesn't much matter what you read. Choose something that interests you—gardening, sailboats, or a novel. Even better, choose something that both you and your spouse or partner enjoy, and take turns reading to each other while you cuddle with your new baby.

Sharing books with babies. By six months, your baby is likely to be excited by a new, brightly colored book. He might reach for it, pat it, and growl. He might want to hold it, wave it, bang it, or chew on it. He might "talk" in an excited way. Don't be put off by your child's gleeful manhandling of her reading materials: Children gradually learn to respect and take care of books as they come to understand their special value.

Pick board books with simple, bright pictures. Photos of other babies are a favorite. Pick some simple rhyming poetry. If your baby likes it (many do), read your own grown-up book out loud, stopping frequently to talk with your baby. Babies this age don't understand the words, but they like the sounds.

Somewhere around nine months of age, babies begin to develop wills of their own. Just as they want to feed themselves, so they often want to be in charge of their books. If reading time begins to resemble a battle, change your tactics. Use two books, one for your baby and one for you. Read for shorter periods. It's okay to use the book as a plaything for some of the time, letting your child take it, flip the pages, bang it. As you do that, you may discover a special picture now and then to show to your baby, letting your voice convey your excitement.

Play peekaboo with the pictures by covering a favorite character then asking, for instance, "Where's the doggie?" If there's a poem, read it rhythmically. Move your body (and the baby in your arms) in time with the words. If the book has pictures of babies, touch a picture then your baby in the same place.

Some babies love to listen for a long time (five to ten minutes or more). More active babies may pay attention for only a minute or less. The amount of time is not important. Enjoying each other and the book is. If your baby seems bored (or if *you* are), pick a different book or do something else.

Toddlers and books. Between nine and twelve months of age, some babies begin to understand that things have names. Once they have this idea firmly established, they want to hear the names of everything. A picture book is the perfect vehicle for naming games. With a familiar picture book, ask, "What's that?" Pause for an instant, then give the answer. If your baby loves this game, it is because his mind is open to learning. You won't hear him saying all these new words right away, but over the next year or two, you're likely to be amazed at his vocabulary.

As time goes by, toddlers pay more attention to what the pictures show. A twelve- to fifteen-month-old may be content to hold the book upside down. Starting around eighteen months, many children will turn the book around so that the pictures are right side up.

Many younger toddlers are in love with movement. Those who are not yet walking still love the rocking, tickling, and hugging that go along with reading aloud. Those who are walking may sit still for only a few minutes at a time, but they often enjoy listening from across the room. Mobile toddlers will often carry a book around or bring it to a grown-up to read. A toddler who has discovered his own will may insist on picking the same book over and over, protesting if you make a different selection.

To avoid a power struggle, store books on a low shelf so that your toddler can get them out and put them back herself. Put only three or four books out at a time; too many makes the choice overwhelming and increases the number of books you'll have to pick up off the floor.

By eighteen months many toddlers are walking steadily. A favorite activity now is walking while carrying something, often a book. A toddler who knows that a book is a ticket to attention from parents will walk over and deposit one on a parent's lap, often accompanied by the demand "Read!"

Reading with an older toddler. As they approach their second birthday, toddlers are making great strides in language development. Books help teach language by giving the older toddler many opportunities to name things and to get feedback from a grown-up. The parent points at a picture and asks, "What's that?" Then, depending on the toddler's response, the parent either says the name of the object, praises the child, or offers a kind correction: "Nope, that's not a dog; that's a horse."

What makes this sort of back-and-forth teaching so powerful is that it happens over and over. For a young child, repetition is a key to learning. That the same pictures come up again and again paired with the same words on the same pages allows him to feel a measure of control over the book. The child expects a particular picture or word to show up on the next page—and it does!

At the same time your toddler is conquering new words, he is also figuring out how they come together to make sentences and how sentences make stories. You won't see the results of this learning for many months. But by two and a half to three years, you may notice your child using complex, storylike phrases in his play, such as "Once upon a time" or "What's going to happen next?" The seeds of rich language are planted early through much experience with books and stories.

The wrecking crew. Babies and toddlers are rough on books. Many bent pages, even a tear here and there, can be expected. Scribbling on the pages of a book is something almost every toddler does at least once or twice in her literary career. While it looks destructive, it's often a toddler's way of getting into the book, sort of like becoming an author.

A gentle reminder that books need tender loving care works better than scolding (which might convince your toddler that books are too much trouble altogether). Even better, get some scrap paper and crayons and let your toddler scribble to his heart's content on those pages. The first step on the road to writing is scribbling. If you look at your toddler's scribbling over time, you may well start to see letterlike shapes.

Different learning styles. One toddler who is very visual in her approach to the world may spend long minutes studying the pictures in a book. Try a book with partially hidden characters. A visually oriented toddler will delight in finding the duckling on each page.

A verbally oriented toddler will love to listen to the sound of words. Poetry is especially attractive because of the rhyme and rhythm. A story with a repeated chant ("Fee-fi-fo-fum" in "Jack and the Beanstalk") delights many toddlers and, because it is predictable, they can join in the reading of the book. Knowing what is coming gives them the sense that the book is theirs.

Many young children learn best by touching and through

body movement. If there is motion in the story (a boat rocking on the waves, a baby on a swing, a horse galloping, or a mom stirring soup), you can act out the motion with your toddler. Talking, touching, moving, and playing make the book come alive to all of your toddler's senses.

Children learn best when they are actively involved. They love the opportunity to act out parts of the books they're listening to. So if you're reading a story about magic genies and flying carpets, you might want to dig out an old teapot and rug (or sheet). Your child will know just what to do.

Reading with preschoolers. Preschool children have wonderful imaginations. In their minds, magic really can and does happen. Feeling happy makes the sun come out. Because they don't have much experience of how the world works, young children are able to believe many things that older children reject (Santa Claus, for example). In a sense, they live in a world that their imagination creates.

It's natural, then, that preschoolers love story books. When a young child listens to a story, her face is utterly absorbed, her eyes wide. Another child needs to keep moving around (the restless energy of some preschoolers is really a force of nature) but still manages to catch every word. You know that a child is caught up in the imaginative world of a book when she responds with real emotions to events in it. Characters from the book are likely to come alive in her play. Words from the book sneak into her vocabulary.

Like all of us, preschool children want to feel a sense of control. One way is to choose the book. Although some preschoolers have no trouble choosing one book from a shelfful, many need fewer choices (from three books, say) to be comfortable. Another way preschoolers enjoy a sense of control is by memorizing books. They may not recall every word but can often fill in a word at the end of a line, especially if there is a rhyme.

When a child chooses the same book over and over, it's a sign that something in that book is very important to her. It may be an idea (for example, the idea of overcoming an obstacle, as in *Three Billy Goats Gruff*), a visual image (perhaps the picture of a troll under a bridge), or even just a single word. Whatever it is, once the child completely understands it, she usually moves on to a new book.

There are many ways to enjoy books with your preschool child:

- Have books all over the house: in the living room, the bathroom, by the kitchen table, and especially in her bedroom.
- Make bedtime, waking up in the morning, or both regular times for reading together. Let your child tell you when she's had enough. (Also, stop when you have had enough.) It's great if children love books, and it's also important that grown-ups set limits on reading, as on everything else.
- Limit television viewing. I personally feel that a no-television diet is perfect for preschoolers. The vivid images on television (even, or especially, in cartoons) overwhelm their sensitive imaginations so that there is no space left for the quieter, but still compelling images from books.
- Use your public library. Many libraries have story hours and playgroups, small child-size tables and chairs, and a huge selection of books to choose from. An outing to the library can feel special, even if it happens every week.
- Don't feel that you have to keep reading to the bitter end. If your child loses interest, it's best to stop or perhaps try a different book. It may be that the book touched on issues that are emotionally charged for your child. Squirming or falling asleep may be your child's way of saying, "I've heard enough for now."
- Invite your child to participate. Children learn the most from reading aloud and probably benefit emotionally the most if they actively participate. They may make com-

ments or even interrupt the reading to talk about an idea or feeling that comes up. Reading aloud shouldn't be a performance; it should be more like a discussion.

- Make up stories and encourage your preschooler to help you. If you come up with a story you really like, write it down. You can make your own story book, then read it aloud.

Reading aloud with an older child. Reading aloud doesn't have to end when your child gets older. If it's something you both love to do together, there are many good reasons to continue. Sharing pleasant and interesting experiences makes your relationship stronger. Having a reservoir of positive feelings helps you and your child cope with disagreements and other tensions that are an inevitable part of growing up.

Reading aloud keeps interest high. Between first grade and third or fourth, children are still developing their basic reading skills. During that time, most of the books simple enough for them to read themselves are too simple for them to find interesting. By reading aloud together, you can help your child enjoy more difficult books that are likely to keep her engaged until her reading ability catches up with her interests.

Reading aloud is especially important if your child is having difficulty learning to read. Some children find reading easy. Others, equally bright, find it challenging at first, often because their brains are taking longer to reach the level of maturation needed for reading. In time—most often by the end of third grade—they catch up and do just fine. But until that happens reading is likely to be difficult, and many children decide that it is not for them. If they have parents who read to them, however, they're much more likely to stay open to the pleasures that books can bring to their lives. They'll stick with it, work hard, and eventually gain the skills they need for independent reading.

Reading aloud builds listening skills. It's a good idea to stop from time to time and talk about the story with your child. First of all, you want to make sure that she really understands what is going on. If not, you can explain the plot, a character's motivations, a new word, or whatever else is puzzling her. Also, when you ask open-ended questions, you strengthen your child's ability to think about what she hears and make sense of it. Ask why a particular character did what he did, or ask your child what she thinks is going to happen next.

Reading aloud also builds vocabulary. There are words in books that you almost never hear in everyday speech. One of the best children's books, *Charlotte's Web* by E. B. White, is written mostly in plain English. But even here, you find interesting words like injustice, terrific, and humble. Don't be surprised if you hear your child using some of these "book words" when she speaks. Many children love to play with new words. In the process, they build skills that will help them throughout their school careers.

Stories are the building blocks of imagination. Children take bits and pieces of the stories they hear and use them in their own make-believe. If you want your child to have a rich imagination, let her hear lots of good stories. The same thing happens when children watch television. They build the stories into their play. But because the images are so much more vivid than the word images in books, children don't need to use their imagination as much. Consequently they often simply copy what they see on television rather than create their own stories.

Books help build character. Many educators and psychologists believe that books are one of the best ways children learn about right and wrong. As they see how different characters react—how they treat their friends, for example, or what they do when they want something that isn't theirs—they get a clearer picture of what's admirable behavior and what's not. The messages in the books can be a compelling and enjoyable way to reinforce the values you're teaching your child at home.

Choosing nonracist, nonsexist books. Books carry powerful messages, both in what they say and how they say it. Books that portray people of all colors, cultures, and ethnicities with respect and avoid sexual stereotypes help children develop an accepting and positive view of themselves and the rest of humanity. An increasing number of children's books embrace the reality of our multicultural society.

When judging a book, look at the story line. Do people of color or females play subservient roles? Are cultural beliefs and practices portrayed accurately? Are negative judgments implied in the way different lifestyles are depicted? Look at the illustrations. Are characters drawn stereotypically? Do people of color have tinted skin, but Caucasian features? This token concession doesn't help your child realize that people have many different physical characteristics. Look at the characters. How are individual characters presented? Who has the power? Who are the heroes? Who are the villains?

What messages does the story send? Does it glorify violence or revenge? Stories in which the hero's only virtue is brute strength do not help children value their own positive qualities. By contrast, heroes who also show compassion, resourcefulness, and courage allow children to feel that they might be like those heroes in their own small way.

PRESCHOOL

The philosophy of preschool. The purpose of preschool is not just the custodial care of children, just to prepare them for the three R's of elementary school. The aim is to give young children a variety of valuable experiences to help them grow up in all respects and to make them more sensitive, capable, and creative people. These experiences often include dancing, making rhythmic music, painting pictures, finger painting, clay modeling, building with blocks, vigorous outdoor play, and playing house, which is really playing family. Ideally, there are quiet corners for individual play and for when a child needs to rest. Preschool tries to nurture a broad variety of capabilities: academic, social, artistic, musical, and muscular. The emphasis is on initiative, independence, cooperation (discussing and sharing play equipment instead of fighting over it), and on incorporating the child's own ideas into play.

The term preschool means, literally, before school. But preschool isn't really something that occurs before school; it *is* school. The focus of preschool shouldn't be on preparing a child to succeed at "real" school later but rather to concentrate on her educational needs right now. (The terms preschool and nursery school mean the same thing.)

Preschool is not the same as child care. Child care refers to the day-to-day care of children from birth to three years and to those parts of an older child's day in which the primary focus is not on education. Preschool refers to the portion of the day in which the main goal is developmentally appropriate education. (Of course, much of what goes on in a preschool classroom is taking care of a child's physical and emotional needs, and much of what goes on in a good child-care setting is educational.)

What do children learn in preschool? Many three- and four-year-old children are already old hands at child care; others must learn to feel comfortable away from home. Regardless of their past experiences with care outside the home, children face similar challenges when they enter preschool. They all need to learn to control their feelings and also to express them. They need to get along in a group and also to take their own ideas and run with them. They need the opportunity to be leaders, and also to let others lead. Preschools that include mixed-age groups especially encourage this sort of natural learning.

Three- and four-year-olds are naturally very curious about the world around them, and they are capable of learning a great deal about its workings: how seeds sprout, how water flows, how clay feels when it's pushed and pulled, how colors change when paints are mixed together, what makes one block tower balance and another fall over, and so on. Good preschools give students plenty of hands-on opportunities to explore their world.

More fundamentally, children in preschool learn how to learn. In a good school they come to view learning as creative exploration, not dull memorization, and they come to view school as a place where they are comfortable and safe.

Readiness for preschool. Good preschools welcome diversity. Not every child has to be verbally precocious, artistically gifted, or extraordinarily well behaved. Every child faces unique challenges in growing up. Skilled preschool teachers are trained to work with children with different strengths and needs.

At the beginning of preschool, many children use simple three- to five-word sentences. They can express their needs and tell what happened in the recent past. They understand most of what's said to them and can follow three-part directions. They can listen to a story for several minutes then talk about it. However, they are apt to misunderstand many phrases that make perfect sense to adults. For example, if you say you are "hungry enough to eat a horse," a three-year-old might point out seriously that there aren't any horses around.

At age three, children often mispronounce words. In general, you should be able to understand about three-fourths or more of the words they say. Children who have articulation problems or who stutter (a common difficulty at this age, see page 571) may become frustrated when people don't understand them. An understanding and patient teacher can be very helpful.

Some but not all preschools require children to be comfortable using the toilet before starting in school. Being around peers who all go to the bathroom like grown-ups is a huge incentive for children who still rely on diapers. Most work hard at mastering toilet skills within a few weeks. Many young children still need help with wiping, or they at least need a reminder to wipe well and wash their hands. Preschool teachers understand that being able to use the toilet independently is a major milestone for a young child and will gladly work with parents to help him achieve this goal.

Eating is a part of every preschool day. By age three, children are usually able to manage finger foods and drinking from a cup and understand basic table manners. Children with developmental disabilities (such as cerebral palsy) may need individual help during snacks as part of their educational program.

It helps if a child is interested in learning basic dressing and undressing: putting on a coat for example, or slipping on boots. Teachers expect to help with buttons, zippers, and snaps. It's okay if some children need more assistance for a while.

What an excellent preschool looks like. A good preschool teacher is many things: a nurturing caregiver, an instructor sowing the seeds of learning, a physical education coach, a guide to the creative worlds of art, music, and literature. The more you understand about what a preschool teacher does, the better able you'll be to find excellence and appreciate it when you do. One important clue to a teacher's approach to learning is evident even before her young charges set foot in the preschool: the setup of her classroom.

A preschool classroom shouldn't look like a classroom for older children. Instead of desks or tables in rows, there should be areas for different activities: painting, block-building, make-believe, reading, and playing house.

In a typical preschool, children have ample opportunities to move from space to space according to their interests. An important part of their education is to learn how to decide on an activity, then stick with it for a while. The good teacher keeps tabs on her students, knowing where every child is and how engaged they are in their activities. If a child is having a hard time choosing, the teacher helps him settle into an activity. If a child is stuck in the same activity for too long, the teacher helps him make another choice.

Many aspects of the room change daily. One day, the art area features finger paints. A day or two later, there may be an assortment of materials for mosaics. Another day there are sheets of paper stapled together to make books. How long an activity lasts depends on the children's interest.

In addition to the regular activity areas, some parts of the room reflect projects or special areas of focus for the class. One month there is a grocery store, with children shopping, making change, and taking inventory; the next month, a post office appears; after that, there might be a bakery.

The different areas in the room connect with other things the class is doing. For example, after a visit to a pizza parlor, the children might transform a part of the room into a restaurant. These special areas also reflect the values and concerns that the children are developing: a focus on the environment, perhaps, with an indoor garden and items collected on a nature walk around the neighborhood.

In planning and making these changes, the teacher listens to the children. She understands that the classroom is not hers but theirs. As the children think and talk about their space and how they use it, they learn important lessons about negotiation and cooperation.

The teacher arranges the environment outside the classroom as well. Preschools need to have outdoor space for active play. A thoughtfully designed yard has safe areas for running, climbing, riding, and imaginative play. The teacher keeps track of each child, noting who is doing what and for how long. She offers direction where needed, sometimes joins in the play, knows when to observe quietly.

The teacher also makes creative use of the neighborhood and beyond. A walk around the block becomes an opportunity to observe the different shapes of leaves, the materials buildings are made of, or the appearance of street signs and what they mean. These observations feed into discussions and other projects in the classroom, making the neighborhood a useful and interesting extension of the preschool.

The first days at preschool. An outgoing four-year-old takes to preschool like a duck to water and doesn't need a gentle introduction. It may be different with a sensitive three-year-old who still feels closely attached to his parents. If his mother leaves him at school the first day, he may not make a fuss right away, but after a while he may miss her. When he finds she isn't there, he may become frightened. The next day he may not want to leave home.

With a dependent child like this, it's better to introduce him to school gradually. For several days his mother might stay nearby while he plays, then take him home again after a time. Each day, the mother and child stay for a longer period. Meanwhile, he is building up attachments to the teacher and other children that will give him a sense of security when his mother no longer stays.

Sometimes a child seems happy for several days, even after his mother has left him at school. Then he gets injured and suddenly wants her. In that case, the teacher can help the mother decide if she should come back for a few days. When a mother stays around the school, she should remain in the background. The idea is to let the child develop his desire to enter the group so that he forgets his need for his mother.

Sometimes the mother's anxiety is greater than the child's. If she says good-bye three times over with a worried expression, he may think, "She looks as if something awful might happen if I stay here without her. I'd better not let her go." It's natural for a mother to worry about how her small child will feel when she leaves him for the first time. Teachers can often provide good advice in this situation; they've had lots of experience with it. A parent-teacher conference before the beginning of school will give the teacher a head start in getting to know your child and help you and the teacher trust each other and work together smoothly right off the bat.

A child who starts with genuine anxiety about separating from the parent may learn that this gives him control over a highly sympathetic parent. He may then progressively exploit this control.

When a child becomes reluctant or fearful about returning to a school with understanding teachers, I think it is usually better for the parents to act confident and firm, explaining that everybody goes to school every day. In the long run, it's better for the child to outgrow his dependence than to give in to it. If the child's terror is extreme, the situation should be discussed with a child mental health professional.

Reactions at home. Some children make hard work of preschool in the early days and weeks. The large group, new friends, and new things to do key them up and wear them out. If your child is too tired at first, it doesn't mean that she can't adjust to school, only that you have to compromise for a while until she is used to it. Discuss with her teacher whether it would be wise to cut down her school time temporarily. Coming to school in the middle of the morning may be the best answer. Taking the easily tired child home before the end of the school day works less well: she'll hate to leave in the middle of the fun.

The problem of fatigue in the early weeks is further complicated in an all-day school by those children who are initially too stimulated or nervous to go to sleep at naptime. Keeping the child at home one or two days a week may be the answer to this temporary problem. Some small children starting preschool maintain their self-control in school in spite of fatigue then let loose on the family when they come home. This calls for extra patience and a discussion with the teacher.

A well-trained preschool teacher ought to be—and usually is—a very understanding person. A parent shouldn't hesitate to talk over the child's problems with the teacher, whether or not those problems are connected with school. A teacher gets a different slant and has probably faced the same problems before.

Pressures in preschool. Education is competitive, and preschools are not immune. Ambitious parents often see the right preschool as the necessary first step on the path to an Ivy League diploma. Some preschools have responded to the pressure for future success by incorporating more academic structure, curriculum, and teaching practices. Children are taught to memorize the alphabet and to spell simple words. They have mimeographed sets of math problems to do. A part of each day may be set aside for what is often called seat work (staying in your chair for an extended period of time to concentrate on an assigned task). These efforts are intended to prepare children for the next rung of the educational ladder.

What's wrong with this approach? Most young children are eager to please their teachers. Given a set of letter names to recite, they'll dutifully go along. Many will actually learn them. After much repetitive drilling, they will even be able to read several words by sight. Some of the more advanced will be able to sound out simple words. Many of the children will be very impressive when they start in kindergarten.

However, research shows that by the end of second grade, they won't be any better at reading than other children. They will have spent a lot of time and effort with no long-term benefit. Moreover, many of them may have decided that reading and math are terribly boring and hard, nothing they would ever do voluntarily.

This is not to say that letters and numbers shouldn't be taught, but these academic elements need to be part of experiences that are meaningful to children. For example, rather than doing drills with alphabet flash cards, listening to stories read aloud and talking about them naturally sparks children's interest in letters and words. With encouragement, children pay attention to signs and labels, things they encounter in real life that are interesting and important. They make up stories. The teachers may write the stories down and read them back. There's active participation and a gratifying sense of accomplishment.

Preschool teachers know how to call attention to the writing and counting that are part of almost any activity. For example, if the classroom has a pet hamster, every child will learn to read the animal's name on the sign above the cage. The teacher might make a calendar showing feeding times then have the children sign up to feed it, counting the days until it's their turn. In such ways, children learn print and number concepts in the course of real-life experiences.

One problem with an overacademic approach to preschool is that it gets in the way of play, which is the way children *really* learn, develop social skills, and spark their creativity. A skill-and-drill approach to preschool education teaches young children that learning is something you do from a sense of duty or obedience. A play-centered approach teaches children to love learning.

SCHOOL AND SCHOOL PROBLEMS

A dedicated school principal once said to me, "Every child has gifts; it's our job to help discover and nurture them." I think this comes close to defining the heart of education. In fact, the word education stems from Latin words that mean to lead out, that is, to draw out the child's inner qualities and strengths. That is very different from the notion that teachers need to pour knowledge into children, who are like empty jars waiting to be filled. John Dewey, a famous educator of a century ago, said, "True education frees the human spirit." I believe that.

WHAT SCHOOL IS FOR

The main lesson learned in school is how to get along in the world. The various subjects are merely means to this end. One job of a school is to make subjects so interesting and real that children want to learn and remember information for the rest of their lives.

There's no use in knowing a lot if you can't be happy, get along with people, and hold the kind of job you want. The good teacher tries to understand each child to help him strengthen weak points and develop into a well-rounded person. The child who lacks self-confidence needs chances to succeed. The troublemaking show-off has to learn to gain the recognition he craves by doing good work. The child who doesn't know how to make friends needs help in becoming sociable and appealing. The child who seems to be lazy needs to have her enthusiasm kindled.

◈ CLASSIC SPOCK

In the old days, it used to be thought that all a school had to do was teach children how to read, write, figure, and memorize a certain number of facts about the world. I heard a teacher tell how, in his own school days, he had to memorize a definition of a preposition that went something like this: "A preposition is a word, generally with some meaning of position, direction, time, or other abstract relation, used to connect a noun or pronoun, in an adjectival or adverbial sense, with some other word." Of course, he didn't learn anything when he memorized that. You learn only when things have meaning for you.

How teachers make school interesting. A school can go only so far with a cut-and-dried program in which everyone in the class reads from page seven to page twenty-three in the textbook at the same time, then does the examples on page one hundred twenty-eight of the arithmetic book. This works well enough for the average child. But it's too dull for the bright pupils, too speedy for the slow ones. It gives the boy who hates books a chance to stick paper clips in the braids of the girl in front of him. It does nothing to help the boy who is lonely or the girl who needs to learn to cooperate.

When teachers start with a topic that children are interested in, they can use it to teach all manner of subjects. Take the case of a third-grade class in which the work of the term centers on Native Americans. The more the children find out about the various tribes, the more they want to know. The textbook tells a story, and the children really want to know what it says. For arithmetic they study how the Native Americans counted and what they used for money. This way arithmetic isn't a separate subject at all but a useful part of life. Geography isn't spots on a map; it's the lands tribes lived on or traveled through. In science, the children make dye from berries and use it to dye cloth or discuss how Native American societies adapted to different ecosystems.

People are sometimes uneasy when schoolwork is too interesting, believing that a child needs to learn mostly how to do what's unpleasant and difficult. But if you stop to think of the people you know who are unusually successful, you'll see that they are usually the ones who love their work. In any job there's plenty of drudgery, but you do it because you see its connection with the fascinating side. Darwin was a wretched student in school. Then he became interested in natural history, performed one of the most painstaking jobs of research that the world has ever known, and worked out the theory of evolution. A boy in high school may see no sense in geometry, hate it, and do badly in it. But if he is studying to be a airline pilot, sees what geometry is for, and realizes that it could save the lives of the crew and passengers, he works at it like a demon.

Effective teachers understand that every child needs to develop self-discipline to be a useful adult. But you can't snap discipline onto children from the outside, like handcuffs; it's something they have to develop inside, like a backbone, by first understanding the purpose of their work then feeling a sense of responsibility to others in how they perform it.

Linking school with the world. A school wants its pupils to learn firsthand about the outside world so that they will see the connection between their schoolwork and real life. It arranges trips to nearby industries, asks people from the community to come give a talk, encourages classroom discussion. A class studying food may have an opportunity to observe some of the steps in the growing, harvesting, transportation, and marketing of vegetables. A class studying government might visit City Hall and sit in on a session of the City Council.

Another thing that a good school wants to teach is democracy, not just as a patriotic ideal but as a way of living and getting things done. A good teacher knows that she can't teach democracy from a book if she acts like a dictator in her classroom. She encourages her pupils to decide how to tackle projects and overcome the difficulties they will encounter. She lets them figure out who is to do this part of the job, who that one. That's how they learn to appreciate each other. That's how they learn to get things done, not just in school but in the outside world, too.

When teachers tell their pupils what to do every step of the way, the children will work while she is in the room. When she leaves, though, a lot will fool around. They figure that lessons are the teacher's responsibility, not theirs. Children who help to choose and plan their own work and cooperate with each other in carrying it out accomplish almost as much when the teacher is out of the room as when she is present. They know the purpose of their work and the steps to accomplish it. Each wants to do a fair share because each is proud to be a respected member of the group and feels a sense of responsibility to the others.

This is the very highest kind of discipline. This training, this spirit, is what makes the best citizens and the most valuable workers.

How school helps a child with difficulties. A flexible, interesting program does more than make schoolwork appealing. It can be adjusted for the individual pupil. Take the case of a girl who spent her first two years in a school where teaching was done by separate subjects. She had great difficulty learning to read and write, fell behind the rest of the class, and was ashamed to be a failure. She wouldn't admit anything except that she hated school. She had never gotten along easily with other kids anyway, even before her school troubles began. Feeling that in the eyes of the others she was stupid made matters worse. She had a chip on her shoulder. Once in a while she would show off to the class in a smarty way. Her teacher thought that she was just trying to be bad. In fact, in this unfortunate way she was attempting to gain attention from the group. It was a healthy impulse to keep herself from being shut out.

She transferred to a school that wanted to help her not only to read and write but also to find her place in the group. The teacher learned in a conference with her mother that she used tools well and loved to paint and draw. He saw ways to use her strong points in the class. The children were painting a large picture of Indian life to hang on the wall and were working cooperatively on a model of an Indian village. The teacher arranged for the girl to have a part in these projects. Here were things she could do well without nervousness.

As the days went by, she became more fascinated with Indians. To paint her part of the picture well, to make her part of the model correctly, she needed to find out more from books. She wanted to learn to read so she tried harder. Her new classmates didn't think that because she couldn't read she was a dope. They thought more about what a help she was in creating the painting and model. They occasionally commented on how good her work was and asked her to help them. She warmed up. After all, she had been aching for recognition and friendliness for a long while. As she felt more accepted, she became more friendly and outgoing.

LEARNING TO READ

The question of how best to teach children to read is extremely controversial. Early in the twentieth century, the received wisdom was that children should not be exposed to reading too early, lest it confuse their immature brains. In the 1960s, researchers realized that even very young children learned a lot about literacy by observing their parents. Furthermore, children given crayons and paper often experimented with making letters and words. They also learned to read familiar words on cereal boxes and street signs long before they received formal lessons. So enamored were educators of this idea of emergent literacy or whole language that some even thought that formal teaching was altogether unnecessary.

In the past decade, however, educational research has come back to the idea that children need to be taught how the alphabet works. What's very positive is that this new emphasis on phonics has not *replaced* the insights of emergent literacy. Instead, educators realize that children need exposure to both kinds of learning. They need to be read to, to make up their own stories and dictate them to parents and teachers then read them back, and to have lots of time to play with letters and words. They also benefit from direct teaching—although not boring skill-and-drill memorization—about how letters stand for sounds and how those sounds come together to form words. These are the lessons of a landmark 1998 report from the National Research Council, *Preventing Reading Difficulties in Young Children.* We can hope that this report finally ends the reading wars that have confused teachers for so long and makes it possible for more children to master reading and writing.

PHYSICAL EDUCATION

Physical health means more than just the absence of disease. It means having a body that is strong, flexible, and coordinated and having the skills to use it in joyful ways. Many three- and four-year-old children already demonstrate these fundamentals of physical health. But as children get older and spend long hours sitting in school or doing homework, physical fitness often declines.

In the past, it was common for public schools to require daily physical education. Recently, however, the number of children who have daily P.E. has dropped. Few high school students now have daily physical education, and fewer than half of middle schools require three years of it.

Benefits of physical education. In the past, the focus of P.E. classes was to train children to participate in competitive sports. More recently, the focus has shifted to developing healthy habits and to fitness. The hope is that children will adopt regular physical activity as a part of their lifestyle. Regular physical activity also increases children's attention, whether or not they have attention deficit disorder. Regular exercise is a safe and effective treatment for mild degrees of depression, and it also seems to boost the mood of people who aren't depressed. Exposure to a variety of different physical activities—swimming, running, gymnastics, and other sports—helps children discover the activities that most appeal to them. With increasing coordination and endurance, they enjoy the activities even more and are more likely to continue them.

Children also learn sportsmanship, teamwork, and tolerance for others who may not be as skilled as they are and even for their own limitations. For children who have academic difficulties or learning disabilities, physical education provides an opportunity to excel and build their self-esteem. For many children, vigorous, skillful physical activity provides an important avenue for self-expression. While some children draw pictures or write in their diaries, others find a more physical outlet for powerful emotions. Children benefit greatly from a P.E. teacher or coach who understands this emotional side of physical activity and sports and forms a supportive relationship with the child.

PARENTS AND SCHOOLS

Fifty years ago, educating children was seen as solely a job for professionals; parents were supposed to parent and leave teaching to the teachers. But educators increasingly understand that they can't do it alone. Parents are crucial. Study after study shows that parent involvement is important for their children's achievement, not just early on but throughout the school years.

Parent involvement. When parents are involved in their children's education, the students are more comfortable at school and see it as an extension of the values of their homes. Teachers communicate more easily with involved parents and are more likely to inform them of academic, behavioral, or social difficulties early on, when they are easier to fix. Moreover, solutions that include both parent and teacher input are almost always more effective. Involvement can include volunteering at school in addition to what you do at home to support your child's education. Besides attending parent-teacher conferences (which are important), involved parents make an effort to get to know their children's teachers. They volunteer to help in the classroom and participate in field trips and special events.

Parent groups, such as PTAs and site councils, make great contributions to schools. Parents working together can provide the school with vital feedback about the lives of the students. What concerns do their children voice at home? What parts of the school experience are strong, and what could be stronger? Also, if something traumatic has happened at home, such as the death of a grandparent or a divorce, let your child's principal and teachers know so they can be supportive and watch for signs of stress.

Create a home environment that supports learning. Most children need a well-lit, quiet place to work (although some children do, in fact, concentrate better with noise around them), and they need sufficient time. That may require limiting social engagements or even other learning activities. Some children are so overscheduled with music lessons, sports practice, art lessons, religious schooling, and other obligations that homework is compressed into a last-minute, late-night rush. It also may require limiting television, video games, and recreational use of the computer.

Be a role model for learning. Children approach learning more positively when they see their parents make efforts to continue to learn. Set high but realistic expectations. As one colleague put it, "My children know that they have to do their best. Since their best is A's, they know I expect A's." For other children, realistic high expectations means earning solid B's or working hard in special education courses. Regardless of their level, children succeed when they set rigorous but attainable goals for themselves.

Parents as advocates. Some parents feel helpless in the face of an educational system that seems big, impersonal, and unresponsive. Other parents feel empowered to take a leadership role when it comes to their children's education. Leadership doesn't necessarily mean being completely in charge. Effective parents know that they need to work with teachers and principals and, sometimes, with doctors or therapists. They are pleasant and thoughtful but insist that their children receive an excellent education. They know their rights and join with other effective parents. They become a force for the positive education of their children. Not all school personnel are happy with empowered parents (they make demands and ask a lot of questions, after all), but administrators usually respect them and work hard to meet their expectations.

Your educational past. As a parent, your point of reference is bound to be your own school days. Many things have changed, of course, but it is natural for you to make comparisons. If you were lucky enough to go to a good school, you may have very high standards for your child's school. I think some adults are tempted to idealize their school memories, so nothing in their child's present ever lives up to the ideal. On the other hand, your school experiences may have been largely negative, giving you a pessimistic attitude toward the educational system. It's important to remain open-minded and optimistic that your child will have a better experience. And she can. Your active, committed, thoughtful cooperation with the school can help bring that about.

HOMEWORK

Homework does not have to result in a war. If you can see your role as a coach rather than a taskmaster, homework can teach your child the value of hard work and teach you a lot about your child. To be an effective coach, though, you have to know the rules of the game. And that means understanding homework from the teacher's point of view.

Why homework? Teachers assign homework for three reasons: to get children to practice skills or concepts they have learned in class, to prepare children for the next class, or to give children the chance to work on a project that is time-consuming or requires outside resources (such as the library, the internet, or you, the parents). Early on, the main purpose of homework is to get children used to the idea of working outside the classroom and to help them develop time-management and organizing skills. Later in elementary school and especially in high school, children who do more homework score higher on standardized tests. It stands to reason that when teachers set high expectations for learning, including high homework demands, children learn more.

How much is enough? There are no hard and fast rules about how much homework should be assigned. The National Education Association and the National PTA have issued these recommendations: about twenty minutes a night in early elementary grades (first through third); about forty minutes in fifth through sixth grade; about two hours in seventh through ninth.

Some schools assign much more than others, but this doesn't guarantee higher achievement, especially early in elementary and middle school. Beyond a point homework may not only be overwhelming but may squeeze out other valuable activities, such as play, sports, music lessons, hobbies, and relaxation. More is not always better.

Helping with homework. What should you do if children ask for help with their homework? If they are puzzled and turn to you for clarification, there's no harm in straightening them out. (Nothing pleases parents more than to prove to a child that they really know something.) But if your children ask you to do their work for them because they don't understand it, you'd better consult the teacher. A good teacher prefers to help children understand then have them rely on themselves. If the teacher is too busy to give your child extra time, you may have to lend a hand; even then you should just help him to understand his work, not do it for him. Your child will have many teachers but only one mother and father. Your role as parent is more important.

Sometimes a teacher will advise parents that their child is falling behind in a subject and needs tutoring. Sometimes the parents themselves get the idea. This is something to be careful about. If the school can recommend a good tutor, whom you can afford, hire him. Too often parents make poor tutors, not because they don't know enough or try hard enough but because they care too much and are upset when their child doesn't understand.

If a child is already confused by his lessons, an impatient parent may be the last straw. Another trouble is that the parents' method may be different from that of the teacher. If the child is already baffled by the subject as presented in school, the chances are that he will be even more baffled when it's presented in a different way at home.

It's not that a parent should never tutor a child; it sometimes works very well. Talk it over thoroughly with the teacher first, and consider making a change if it doesn't go well. Whoever tutors the child should keep in touch with the teacher at regular intervals.

PROBLEMS IN SCHOOL

Developing capability in school is the first big responsibility we put on our children. That's why we should view school problems with the same urgency with which we view a high fever: It's an indication that something is wrong, and that steps should be taken promptly to discover the cause and make things better. Whatever the cause, when problems persist, a child is bound to believe the worst about himself. Once a child becomes convinced that he is stupid, lazy, or bad, it becomes much harder for him to change.

Causes of school problems. Often there isn't a single cause but rather several problems that combine to undermine a child's ability to do well in school. An average student may do poorly in a class that is too high-powered and pressured; a bright student may find herself bored and unmotivated in a class that moves too slowly. A child who is bullied may develop a sudden aversion to school, and her grades may drop. Hearing or vision difficulties, chronic illness, learning disabilities (see page 673), and ADHD (see page 550) may all lead to serious problems. Children with sleep disturbances may be chronically overtired and fail to pay attention. An unforgivably high number of children go to school hungry. Among psychological causes are worries about ill or angry parents, divorce, or physical or sexual abuse.

It's rare for a child to fail purely because of laziness. Children who have given up trying aren't lazy. Children are naturally curious and enthusiastic. If they have lost their eagerness to learn, it's a sign that there is a problem that needs to be addressed.

School problems are not just a matter of grades. A child who gets all A's but is so perfectionistic and anxious that his stomach hurts and he dreads going has a school problem. A child who gets mostly B's only by working so hard that she has no time for friends or fun may also need help learning how to commit to school in moderation.

Sorting it out. Have a friendly, nonscolding discussion with your child about her school problem. Do this in a gentle and supportive manner. What does she think is the problem? Ask for details about what happens in school and how she thinks and feels. Meet with the teacher and principal. It's best to approach them as collaborators, not an enemy. Though the teacher or school may contribute to the problem, start out by assuming they are on your side. Talk with your child's doctor and with a developmental and behavioral pediatrician, child psychologist, or other professional who works with children with school difficulties (see page 620). There should be one doctor—your child's primary care doctor or a specialist—who helps you to put the information together to come up with a better idea of what the problem is and where to go next.

School intervention. There are many approaches that educators and parents can take to minimize or eliminate school difficulties. When academic pressure is the problem, you may want to try a nongraded class. For teasing or bullying, teachers need to intervene with the whole class, teaching that classmates are expected to take care of each other, never hurt one another's bodies or feelings, and speak up by if another person is hurting one of their classmates. Positive education of this sort helps a great deal, especially if done throughout the school (see page 182, **Bullies**). For learning disabilities, special education is often helpful (see page 677); for ADHD, a combination of medication and behavioral therapy (see page 550). Better parent-teacher communication often helps with behavior problems.

It may be helpful for a child who is immature to repeat kindergarten or first grade. After that, however, simply repeating a grade is not an effective treatment for serious school problems. More often, it is a painful disaster. The social and emotional consequences and the blow to self-esteem often result in a child's eventually dropping out of school, especially when he reaches junior high school.

Helping children outside school. There is much that parents can do outside the school setting to help the child who is having serious academic problems. Most children are curious about the world around them. When you share and encourage that curiosity, the child's interest in learning grows. Explore your child's special interests with her. Allow the child to guide you, and listen for eagerness in specific subjects. Follow up such interest with field trips, reading materials, and projects of the child's choice.

Relations between parents and teachers. It's easy to get along with a teacher if your son is her pride and joy and does well in class. But if your child is having trouble, the situation is more delicate. Even the best parents and teachers are all too human. All take pride in the work they do and have possessive feelings toward the child. Each, no matter how reasonable, secretly feels that the child would do better if only the other would handle him differently. Parents should realize at the start that the teacher is just as sensitive as they are and that they will get more from a conference by being friendly and cooperative.

Some parents are afraid to face a teacher, forgetting that just as often that the teacher is afraid of them. The parents' main job is to give a clear history of the child's past, what his interests are, and what he responds to, well or badly, then to work with the teacher on how best to apply this information in school. Don't forget to compliment the teacher on those parts of the class program that are a great success with the child.

Occasionally a child and teacher just don't fit temperamentally, no matter how hard they work at it. The principal should be involved in the question of whether to move the child to another class.

Parents should avoid blaming the teacher if their child is unsuccessful in class. If the child hears the parents bad-mouthing his teacher, he will learn to blame others and avoid taking responsibility for his own contribution to his problems. You can still be sympathetic: "I know how hard you are trying" or "I know how unhappy it makes you when your teacher is dissatisfied."

LEARNING DISABILITIES

There was a time, not so long ago, when only two reasons were given for why a child was having difficulty with reading, writing, and arithmetic. Either he wasn't trying or he was not as bright as other children. Now we know that many such children have learning disabilities.

What is a learning disability? There are many bright children who, despite trying hard, do poorly in school. Both boys and girls have this problem. More often, it is boys who come for professional help. These children often speak well and have talents in nonacademic areas, such as art or mechanics. Most of the time, the main problem is with reading; occasionally a child reads well but struggles with math.

Many of these children are terribly frustrated by schoolwork and are convinced that they are stupid. They are not. Sometimes, in their frustration, they give up on school, adopting the attitude that the school is stupid.

Learning disabilities (LD) are problems in a child's brain development that prevent a child from succeeding academically. Not counted among LD are problems that arise from inadequate schooling, serious vision and hearing problems, emotional problems such as depression or anxiety, and physical disabilities such as cerebral palsy. Such problems often do coexist with LD.

Many children with LD are intellectually bright, but some have lower than average general intelligence (IQ). A child with a low IQ may still have an LD, if the level of his accomplishment in reading or math is below what could be expected based on his IQ.

What it feels like to have an LD. Children with an LD know that there is something wrong with them but not what it is. Their teachers and parents tell them to try harder. Sometimes, through great effort, they have some success. One day a child may spend five hours on a thirty-minute homework assignment and get a good grade. His teacher may wonder why he doesn't always perform up to this standard and concludes that he is lazy. On his part, he is exhausted and probably suspects that he is stupid. Also, he may understandably come to resent a teacher who never seems satisfied.

I think you can see how what starts as a learning disability can easily grow into an emotional or behavioral problem. Some children decide to be class clowns or rebel against teacher discipline to draw attention away from their disability. In their view, it is better to be bad than stupid. Other children suffer in silence. They "forget" to turn in homework and never volunteer in class. They may act out their frustration by getting into fights on the playground.

Dyslexia. The most common learning disability is in reading and writing. This problem is sometimes called dyslexia, sometimes specific learning disability for reading. These terms essentially mean the same thing. I'll use dyslexia because it's shorter.

Dyslexia is the condition of a child who has more difficulty learning to read than is expected from his general intelligence. If new glasses solve the problem, it's not dyslexia. If treatment of attention deficit hyperactivity disorder (ADHD) or an emotional disorder solves the problem, it's not dyslexia, either.

Some children with dyslexia transpose letters when they write or complain of eyestrain when reading. These problems are the result of dyslexia, not its cause. Many children without dyslexia also have these problems. Transposing letters in particular is entirely normal in children learning to read and write, up to age seven or eight.

Other learning disabilities. Every ability needed to succeed academically has a corresponding disability. This is a partial list of academic abilities and what happens when they are lacking:

- *Reading:* Children need to be able to relate written symbols (letters and groups of them) to the sounds they represent then connect those sounds and relate them to words they know. Problems handling word sounds underlie most cases of dyslexia.

- *Writing:* Children have to be able to form all letters automatically, that is, without thinking about their shapes. If they have to stop to think about each letter, their writing will be slow and choppy, and they will be unable to keep up with writing assignments.

- *Math:* The ability to handle basic math processes—addition and subtraction—is related to the underlying ability to visualize things in space and gauge their quantity. Children with problems in this area may have dyscalculia, a learning disability specific to math.

- *Memory:* Memory skills include taking information in, holding on to it, and retrieving it in response to a question, such as "Who invented the light bulb?" Problems with any of these processes—intake, storage, and retrieval—result in a learning disability.

There are many other specific skills that may become problem areas, such as understanding or expressing spoken language, keeping things in order (sequencing), rapid recall, planning physical movements, and so on. Often a child has difficulties with more than one skill (and may have strengths in other areas).

None of us is equally good at all things. When the gap is *very* wide between what you are good at and what you're not good at, you may have a learning disability.

LD assessments. If you suspect an LD, arrange a private assessment or go through your child's school. Most large hospitals have a learning clinic where a team of specialists provides comprehensive evaluations. The team usually includes a pediatrician with expertise in child development along with a learning specialist, psychologist, and social worker. A comprehensive assessment often takes several hours. You should receive a detailed report that spells out your child's problems and diagnosis and gives detailed suggestions for educational planning or treatment. These assessments can cost several hundred dollars and may not be covered by insurance.

Another way to get a learning assessment is through the school. The federal IDEA law (see below) orders schools to provide a multifactored evaluation for any child suspected of an LD. The multifactored evaluation includes tests of academic achievement (how well a child reads and does math), intelligence (a standard IQ test), and other aspects, such as vision, hearing, and speech. The assessment team typically includes the child's teacher, a psychologist, a learning specialist, a speech therapist, and the parents. If there are medical issues, a doctor is asked to participate. This team is responsible for coming up with a detailed plan to support the child's learning. By law, the plan cannot take effect until the parent agrees. The plan also has to be reassessed at regular intervals, with changes made to meet the child's changing needs.

The federal IDEA law. Since the 1970s, there has been a series of federal laws that spell out the responsibilities of schools for teaching children with special needs. The most recent version is the Individuals with Disabilities Education Act (IDEA) of 1997. IDEA covers children with the full range of medical and developmental problems, including ADHD, dyslexia, and speech and language problems, all very common. It also covers less common conditions, such as severe vision and hearing impairments, and such neurological problems as cerebral palsy, and many mental and emotional problems. Any problem that makes it impossible for a child to function in a typical classroom comes under IDEA.

The main principle of the IDEA law is that every child has

a right to a "free and appropriate public education in the least restrictive environment." It's useful to take a close look at this sentence. "Free" means that the county, state, or federal government pays for the education. (Often it is some combination of the three). "Appropriate" means that the child gets what he needs to learn. If he needs an expensive hearing aid, he should get it. If he needs a special chair to supports his body as he learns, he gets it. If he needs an aide to function in the classroom, the law says that the school has to provide one. "Least restrictive environment" means that a child should not be sent off to a separate place, away from his classmates, because of a disability. It used to be common practice to send children who were not "normal" to a single "special needs" classroom. Today, that is a violation.

Treatments for LD. The first and most important step in treating a learning disability is for everyone to acknowledge that it exists. Then teachers and parents can recognize how hard the child is really working and praise the effort rather than criticizing the product. Children need to hear that they are not stupid; they have a problem that they need to work on. With the help of parents and teachers—they don't have to deal with it alone—their situation can get better.

Specific educational treatments depend on the type of LD. For dyslexia, the most effective treatments center on the intensive teaching of letters and the sounds they represent. The child may use all of his senses, feeling wooden letters; cutting them out of paper; making them from cookie dough, baking, and tasting them. New, experimental treatments are being tried all the time, and many show promise. In addition to attacking the problem head-on, special educators teach children how to work *around* learning difficulties. So a child who struggles with reading might listen to books on tape; a child with extremely poor handwriting might do his writing assignments on a computer. Teachers also help children focus on, and develop, their strengths.

For more information on LD, you can begin with the books and websites in the Resource Guide (page 917).

THE UNPOPULAR CHILD

From a child's point of view, getting good grades is rarely as important as being accepted by peers. Every child probably has days when he comes home and announces, "Nobody likes me." The child who feels this way day after day is in real trouble. To the unpopular child, every day brings new trials. He's belittled and teased, victimized by bullies, the last to be picked for any sport. The unhappy result in the worst cases is an increasing sense of isolation and alienation, meager self-esteem, depression, and hopelessness about the future.

A child who is unpopular is often one who does not fit the expectations and patterns of behavior of his classmates and peers. He may not understand what is expected of members of the peer group, and may be unaware of how his actions and words are perceived by them. In other words, markedly unpopular children often have limited interpersonal intelligence. Other children do not understand this. They simply know that the unpopular child does not know how to play as they do, that he won't follow the rules in games, or that he insists on having things his way all the time.

As cruel as his peers may be, their judgment is taken seriously by professionals as an indication that something may be significantly wrong with the unpopular child and that the problem needs to be investigated.

Helping the unpopular child. If your child is unpopular, it's important that you take it seriously. Do not shrug it off. Observe his behavior with other children and try to determine how often he acts differently or provokes or withdraws from the others. If your concerns remain, speak to other parents, teachers, and caring adults who will be honest with you about your child's behavior. If a child's isolation and unpopularity are extreme, evaluation by a child psychiatrist or psychologist is usually indicated. The best way to solve the problem is usually a combination of therapy and efforts on the part of caring parents and involved adults (such as teachers and friends) to minimize the harmful effects of the isolation and abuse until the child changes.

Some of the following suggestions may help you and your child. Invite one of your child's classmates to your home to play, or take him and your child to the park, a movie, or some other place of mutual interest. Taking just one prevents your child from being the odd man out. Watch your child's behavior on these excursions. After the potential friend has left, gently suggest ways your child might behave more appealingly.

The unpopular child of any age always is treated better when adults supervise play activities. For this reason, enroll your child in group activities, such as sports, religious events, or dance classes. Explain your problem to the group leader and ask for her help. It will not be a new or unusual problem to anyone who has worked extensively with children. By adolescence many children will have found one or two friends who have similar interests. This is a great comfort and will help them to make other friends.

When your child has had a difficult experience with other children, be available and listen empathetically. Do not scold or reprimand. Always make your home a safe refuge and your interactions with him an unshakable source of comfort, love, and self-esteem. Remember that parental understanding and unequivocal love, the support of other adults, and, in some instances, professional evaluation and treatment can go a long way to help an unpopular child get along.

SCHOOL AVOIDANCE

School avoidance is a term used for a child's reluctance to go to school regardless of the reason. Some children throughout the elementary grades and even in high school may have severe difficulty with, or even genuine fear of, going to school. The specific reason must be discovered in each case.

Separation anxiety. The most common cause of school avoidance in kindergarten is separation anxiety. Not all children of this age have progressed far enough developmentally to be comfortable away from their mothers for long periods of time. And yet, we ask our five-year-olds to come to a strange, very big building in which they may at first feel lost. In addition, we expect them to give themselves up to strange adults and to share these grown-ups with a roomful of children who are also strangers. Most children readily adjust, but some do not.

How should this be handled? If parents and teachers see that their aim is to help the child separate from home and adjust to school and the outside world, much can be done. If, on the other hand, their only interest is in formal learning, they may miss an opportunity to help the child grow emotionally.

As in all cases of problem behavior, an attempt should first be made to understand the meaning of the child's behavior. It may simply be that the child is immature or it may be a reaction to the anxiety of overanxious parents. Or the child may be chronically ill. If you recognize that the behavior may be due to various factors, it follows that your response must vary accordingly. Some teachers insist that the boy or girl be left at school despite a flood of tears; others request that the child's mother or father spend several days in the classroom until their child becomes familiar with the new surroundings and people. (I hope that the policy of banning mothers and fathers from the classroom on the first day of kindergarten or first grade will soon be replaced by a more flexible approach based on an understanding of the individual child.)

Fears and worries. During the early elementary school years and after, it is not unusual for children to have difficulty remaining in school as a result of fears and worries. Some children don't want to go to school because they have no friends or are teased on the playground. If your child does not fit in because of marked racial or cultural differences, a consultation with the teacher or a change of classroom or school may be in order. But if the child is overreluctant to join the group or her behavior is seen as odd by most of the other children, referral to a child psychiatrist, psychologist, or other mental health professional should be considered. Failure to be accepted by elementary school classmates is one of the most common signs of emotional problems.

Children may also avoid school because they are worried about what is happening at home. If parents are fighting or absent or if caretakers are unkind, a child may cling to his parents. In other instances, a child's worries about his parents' safety and well-being while away at school may be based not on reality but on his guilt for hostile feelings he harbors toward them. Unlikely as it sounds, psychiatrists have found this to be fairly common.

Adolescents. Their changing bodies are a cause of constant preoccupation and concern to all adolescents and may result in school avoidance. In those who develop early or late or stand out because of an unusual physical characteristic, this preoccupation can overshadow everything else. One tall twelve-year-old girl was mortified when a male teacher casually mentioned that she was taller than he. This confirmed her feelings that she was unattractive and peculiar, making going to school each day a torture. Considerable support from her parents and counselors helped her to remain in school, though not without emotional pain. Her concern with her height continued through the high school years. She was sure that boys found her unattractive.

Absenteeism may be higher on days when there is gym. To the child going through puberty and also struggling with other emotional issues that undermine his confidence and self-esteem, the thought of dressing and undressing in front of others and being forced to perform physical activities that will expose real or imagined inadequacies is more than he can bear. For him, avoiding school is the only solution.

Older adolescents may also avoid school. Some of the most common reasons are obesity or other unacceptable physical characteristics, lack of friends, shame over severe academic difficulties, and fear of rejection by the opposite sex.

What to do. A child's persistent avoidance of school, regardless of age, is an emergency requiring prompt attention. Every effort should be made by parents, educators, and school counselors to determine the cause. Professional help may be required. Once the cause is determined, specific corrective measures can be started. Meanwhile, you should insist that your child stay in school. If she is allowed to avoid school, she will probably find it even more painful and difficult to go back later on.

PLANNING FOR COLLEGE

⊰ ⊱

WHAT COLLEGE IS FOR

College represents different things to different families. For some, that a child even gets into college—any college—and comes away with a diploma is a major triumph. For other families, acceptance by anything less than the most prestigious university is a disappointment. The actual education that a college student acquires depends at least as much on the individual as it does on the school and its faculty. It is easy to find highly educated people who went to obscure schools just as there are others who attended famous universities without taking away much.

In today's technological society, a college diploma is the admission ticket to most jobs that pay decent wages. For children who grow up in lower-income homes, college holds out the most reliable hope for social advancement. Ideally, college also presents an opportunity for young adults to stretch their intellectual wings, to explore the world of ideas, and to find themselves.

CHOOSING A COLLEGE

The process of choosing. As a parent, you care about the result: You want your child to go to a good school, one where she'll be happy as well as successful. The process of making the decision is also important. For most adolescents, choosing a college is the first major life decision in which they have a real say. It's an opportunity for them to examine their goals and weigh their priorities. You'd like your teen to take the decision seriously, though not so seriously that he becomes overwhelmingly anxious.

Start by helping your teen get organized. The first step is to obtain a calendar of application deadlines from the high school guidance office. Your teen can then visualize the available time and plot what tasks to do when. It's easy to find out almost anything you want about nearly any college in the United States. The standard college guidebooks—available in many high school guidance offices and most public libraries—provide information about courses, students, faculty, and financial aid for more than two-thousand institutions. (There's little point in buying the guides, as they quickly become outdated.) Virtually every college and university also has a website.

What if your child makes a mistake? Choosing the right school can make for a happier, more successful college experience; choosing the wrong school can be a learning experience as well. In fact, many students start at one school then, after finding that it does not meet their needs, complete their degrees at another institution. Changing colleges is inconvenient, but it's not the end of the world. Knowing this should take some of the pressure off your teen and you.

Factors to consider. The main question when choosing a college is "What do I want to get out of college?" It helps to break down this big question into smaller, more manageable pieces. The list that follows is intended to introduce you to the range of issues involved in college selection and help you in discussions you have with your teen. (But remember, the choice is your teen's to make.)

What type of school? Most students choose a four-year college leading to a B.A. (bachelor of arts) or B.S. (bachelor of science) degree. But there are other options, such as the shorter programs offered by many community colleges and vocational schools. A four-year college offers the greatest amount of flexibility in future education and careers, but even so it's not always the best choice for every student. Also keep in mind that your child's decision is not carved in stone: students who initially earn an associate's degree may later decide to transfer to a four-year program.

How big? Large schools offer a broad range of academic subjects and extracurricular activities. Although many big universities boast a number of top-rank professors, the average student may see them only in large lecture halls; most of the hands-on teaching is done by graduate students. Smaller schools have fewer famous professors but may offer more access to them. Big schools provide a wider range of extracurricular and social activities, but it may be easier to get to know classmates on smaller campuses. Some students feel lost at a big school; others feel too confined at a small one.

Cost. In principle, financial aid is intended to make all colleges accessible to all students, but the reality is that going to a more expensive school may require a greater financial sacrifice. From a strictly financial point of view, state universities may seem to be an obvious bargain compared with most private schools, which may cost three times as much or even more. However, if a student qualifies for a substantial scholarship or other types of financial help at a private college, it might end up being affordable, perhaps even cheaper than a state school.

Location. Some students thrive in the excitement of a big city; others immerse themselves in their studies and pay little attention to the world outside their classroom walls. Your teen may have strong feelings about which part of the country she'll go to. If she loves skiing, for example, that will eliminate a lot of places. If she's prone to seasonal depression, a place with long, cloudy winters may be out. Closeness to family is another key issue. How important is it to you and your teen to be able to spend time together more than once or twice a year?

Academic majors. While many teens enter college without a clear-cut academic major in mind and a lot of students change majors in the course of their schooling, most have at least a general idea of what they're interested in. A school that is strong in humanities but weak in natural sciences may be perfect for a student whose passion is Renaissance poetry. On the other hand, it's not unheard of for a poetry lover to switch to, say, premed and develop a sudden interest in physics and chemistry. A college with all-around strengths gives students more flexibility to change their minds without having to change schools.

Extracurricular activities. Students who want a specific athletic or extracurricular activity are often tempted to choose a school that excels in that area. It's better, however, if there are several areas where the school's strengths and the student's interests overlap. Otherwise, he may find himself unhappy for the many hours of each day when he is not pursuing his favorite activity.

Religious identification. Some students know without doubt that they will attend a school with a specific religious identity. Others need to decide how important it is to them to combine religious training with secular studies. They may decide that an active religious community at a secular university is what they need. Or religion may not factor into their choice at all.

Diversity. One of the virtues of a college education is the opportunity for students to learn from and about each other. Counterbalancing the benefit of diversity is the support some students derive from having peers with similar values and worldviews. This applies equally to racial or ethnic diversity, geographic and political diversity, and sexual diversity (coeducational versus single sex or whether there is a sizable gay or lesbian community).

Reputation. Some colleges have a reputation for being party schools; others see themselves as serious or politically progressive. It is hard to determine this from the college catalog, but guidebooks note each school's special flavor—and this is of course one of the main things to look for on a campus visit.

Other questions. In addition to questions about personal values (above), it helps to have the answers to several factual questions:

- How many students apply, and how many are accepted?
- What are the grade-point averages and average (or minimum) SAT or ACT scores?
- How many applicants receive financial aid, and what is the typical aid package?
- What does the typical aid package consist of in terms of grants, loans, and work-study programs?
- Is the campus safe? Colleges are required to report campus-crime statistics.
- What does the campus look like? Architecture that is inspiring to some may be gloomy to others.
- How is the campus housing? Some schools require freshmen to live in dorms; some have mandatory meal plans. It can be hard to assess the appearance—not to mention the plumbing—of dormitories except on a visit.
- Are fraternities and sororities an important part of college life?
- What is the availability and cost of off-campus housing?
- How many students enroll, and how many complete their degrees in how many years, on average?
- Of those who look for jobs in their chosen field how many get them? Ask about specific jobs, too.
- Of those who apply to graduate schools how many are accepted? Ask this about specific majors, too.

Guidance counselors. A good high school guidance counselor can help your teen assess her life goals and plan an academic course to reach them; based on her goals, he can help her select the right courses and extracurricular activities; and he can help her ask the questions and find the facts she needs to make the best college choice. If this sounds precisely like the sort of help you yourself are planning on giving your child, it is. Precollege counseling shouldn't replace a parent's input, it should supplement it.

COLLEGE ENTRANCE EXAMS

Our competitive culture puts a tremendous value on high test scores. It's no wonder then that college entrance examinations—the SATs, ACTs, and others—so often cause intense anxiety in teens. Many parents pay hundreds, even thousands, of dollars for private coaching in hopes that their child will achieve higher scores.

The various names of the tests can be confusing. SAT used to stand for Scholastic Aptitude Test. ACT originally stood for American College Testing. But recently, the nonprofit companies that produce the tests decided that the tests' official names would be simply SAT and ACT, not standing for anything.

To further confuse the issue, there is now the SAT I and the SAT II. The SAT I and ACT are aptitude tests. The SAT II is an achievement test. (In fact, before the name was changed, it was called the Achievement Test.)

Aptitude versus achievement. Aptitude tests are intended to measure a student's ability to reason verbally and mathematically, independent of specific facts. For example, aptitude tests typically require students to understand the relationship between two words (say, between amusement and laughter) then pick out a pair of words that are related to each other in the same way (say, sorrow and tears).

Achievement tests measure a student's knowledge in a specific subject: say, Math, Spanish or history. For example, does the student know the central ideas put forth in the Gettysburg Address? Advanced Placement (AP) tests, which are increasingly popular with students and admissions offices, are also achievement tests.

What's wrong with these tests? Even as test prep companies multiply, the tests themselves have come under fire. Many experts argue that both the SAT and the ACT discriminate against women and minorities. For example, women as a whole score lower than men on the SAT but earn higher grades their freshman year.

Most admissions officers put more weight on high school grades than on the standardized test scores. They also take into account the difficulty of a student's high school courses, the application essay or personal statement, and recommendations from teachers and coaches. When admissions officers take all that information into account, it's debatable how much the standardized tests contribute to the decision.

More than four hundred colleges no longer require SAT or ACT test scores. (For a list, see www.FairTest.org.) Students instead have the option of submitting a report or essay they wrote for a high school course, which allows the admissions office to see both the quality of the student's work and the toughness of the school's grading.

Nonetheless, the majority of colleges still rely on standardized tests, so your child may have to take them even if you're philosophically opposed to then. To find out which tests are required at which schools, look in college catalogs, printed college guidebooks, or online.

Test preparation. The College Board (which produces the SAT I, the SAT II, and AP tests) maintains that coaching doesn't raise SAT I scores very much—only twenty-five to forty points, on average. However, critics of the SAT argue that students who can afford extensive coaching do raise their scores significantly, giving them an unfair edge.

Both sides agree that taking the test more than once does raise your score considerably. (The test fees are about $25, so many students can afford to take them twice.) For motivated students, public libraries often provide free or low-cost opportunities to gain and practice test-taking skills.

SAVING FOR COLLEGE

It's true that the purpose of financial aid is to make college affordable to everyone. However, most financial aid—some 60 percent—comes in the form of loans, so many students finish college with a load of debt, as well as a diploma.

The key to college savings is to start putting money away early to take advantage of compounded interest. When assessing a student's financial need, the federal government calculates that approximately 5 percent of parents' savings should go toward college expenses each year; the estimated financial need—and thus the value of the financial aid you receive—is therefore reduced by that amount. The government does not count savings in the form of home equity or any savings at all of a family whose income is less than $50,000 a year.

In one sense, if you qualify for financial aid, having money in the bank costs you, since the federal government counts it against your financial need. On the other hand, if you don't save ahead of time, you may have to take out student loans. If you do, you—or your child—may end up paying more in interest than it would have cost to have saved the money in the first place.

Putting money away in your child's name may save money in taxes, since your child's tax rate is likely to be lower than yours. However, money saved in your child's name dramatically reduces any financial aid award. This is because the federal government considers that 35 percent of a child's savings is available to pay for college in a given year. So saving money in your child's name probably makes sense only if you are sure that you earn too much to qualify for financial aid.

There are also several government-sponsored savings plans that offer tax incentives for college savings. See the Resource Guide (page 917) for information on these and other programs that can help with college savings, scholarships, and loans. College is expensive, but financial aid and loans should make it possible for every child to afford a college education.

Health and Safety

GENERAL MEDICAL ISSUES

❧ ☙

YOUR CHILD'S DOCTOR

Children receive health care from pediatricians, family doctors, nurse practitioners, and physician's associates. To keep things short, I'll refer to all of these professionals simply as doctors.

You are partners. The doctor is the medical expert, but you are the expert on your child. The doctor's ability to give you advice and offer treatment often depends on the information you supply. Your ability to supply good information depends, at least in part, on your feeling comfortable with asking any question without fear of offending the doctor or being looked down on. Communication is a two-way street. Remember, you and the doctor have the same goal: to help your child to grow up healthy, happy, and successful.

Asking questions. Most new parents hesitate to ask questions that they think may be too simple or silly. But if there's a question on your mind, you're entitled to an answer. Most doctors and nurse practitioners are pleased to answer any questions they can, the easier the better. If you write down your questions before each visit, you won't have to worry that you'll forget any.

It often happens that when a parent asks about a problem, the doctor explains part of it then is sidetracked before answering the most important part. If a mother is shy about speaking up, she may hesitate to come back to that point and go home unsatisfied. It's better to be bold and make clear exactly what you want to know so that the doctor can give you the answer or, if necessary, refer you to another professional.

On getting home from an office visit, parents often find that they forgot to bring up their most important question or questions and are ashamed to call back so soon. Doctors are not bothered by this; indeed, they are used to it.

Questions also come up in between visits. If you are certain that the question can wait, by all means wait. But if you have any concerns at all, you should call, even if you are pretty sure that the issue is really trivial. It's much better to ask and be reassured than to sit and worry.

Disagreements with the doctor. Usually the parents and doctor soon come to know and trust each other and get along fine. But occasionally, since they are human beings, there are misunderstandings and tensions. Most are avoidable or easily cleared up by frankness on both sides.

It's best to lay your feelings on the table. If you are upset, anxious, or concerned, let the doctor know how you feel. Some parents are too intimidated to express their misgivings about a diagnosis or the way the doctor handles their child during a physical examination. If these feelings are out in the open, they can be addressed. If you keep them inside, your concern will probably grow and you'll have missed an opportunity to improve the channels of communication. Most doctors and nurse practitioners aren't so insecure and thin-skinned that they require absolute obedience and compliance.

Asking for a second opinion. If your child has an illness or condition that worries you intensely and you would like another expert opinion, it is always your right to ask for it. Many parents are hesitant about doing so, fearing that it expresses a lack of confidence in their doctor and may hurt his feelings. But it is a frequent procedure in the practice of medicine, and the doctor should take it in stride. Actually, doctors, like other human beings, sense any uneasiness in the people they deal with, even if unspoken. It makes their job harder. A second opinion usually clears the air for them as well as for the family.

✍ CLASSIC SPOCK

Frankness works best. I think the main point to remember in all these situations is that if you are unsatisfied with your doctor's advice or care, you should bring the problem out into the open right away in the most matter-of-fact manner you can muster. An early meeting of minds is easier for both of you than allowing your tension and irritation to accumulate.

Sometimes, though, a parent and doctor find that they can't get along together, no matter how frank and cooperative they try to be. In this case it's better all around to admit it openly and find a new doctor. All health professionals, including the most successful, have learned that they don't suit everybody, and they accept this fact philosophically.

REGULAR CHECKUPS

The best way to be sure that your baby is doing well is to have her regularly checked by a doctor. Most practices suggest a visit in the first two weeks after delivery, then at two, four, six, nine, twelve, fifteen, eighteen, and twenty-four months, and yearly thereafter—a schedule recommended by the American Academy of Pediatrics. If you'd like additional visits, ask for them.

During a regular checkup, the doctor will ask you how your baby is doing. Your baby will be weighed and measured to see how she's growing. She'll be given a full physical examination to make sure she's healthy. For the first eighteen months, she'll receive immunizations at almost every visit (see page 722). Even if your baby is perfectly healthy, these visits allow you to develop a relationship of trust and familiarity with the doctor, ask any questions you have, and hear any words of wisdom the doctor has to offer. Doctors generally address feeding and nutrition, behavior, sleep, and safety—all topics in this book.

TELEPHONE CALLS TO YOUR DOCTOR

Phone policies. Find out the policy of your pediatric practice on taking calls about ill children. Most practices have a nurse during the workday who answers questions about illness and decides if the child needs to see a doctor. Find out if there is a preferred time to phone, especially about a new illness that may require a visit to the office. Many children first develop definite symptoms of illness in the afternoon, and most doctors would like to know about them as early in the afternoon as possible so they can plan accordingly.

At night or on weekends, it's a different story. All practices have a number to call if you are worried about your child. Usually you will reach an answering service, which will notify the doctor or nurse on call that night. The on-call professional might be your doctor (if you're lucky) but is more likely to be someone who doesn't know you or your child at all. This can lead to trouble, especially if the severity of the child's illness is underestimated by the on-call doctor or nurse.

When to call, in general. After you've raised a couple of babies, you'll have a good idea of which symptoms or questions require prompt contact with the doctor and which can wait until the next morning or the next routine visit.

New parents often feel more comfortable with a list of symptoms that require a call to the doctor. No list, however, can be anywhere near complete. After all, there are thousands of diseases and injuries. You always have to use your own common sense. A good rule is that if you're really concerned, you should

call, even if you think the call may be unnecessary. It's much better to call too often in the beginning when it isn't really necessary
than not to call when you should have.

By far the most important rule is to consult the doctor
promptly, at least by telephone, if a baby or child looks or acts
sick. By this I mean such signs as unusual tiredness, drowsiness,
or lack of interest; unusual irritability, anxiousness, or restlessness; or unusual paleness. This is particularly true in the first two
to three months of life, when a baby can be seriously ill with no
fever or other specific symptoms and signs of illness.

If your child looks sick, you should contact your doctor,
whether or not there are specific symptoms. The flip side is also
usually true: If a child looks well, is playful, active, alert and
bright, serious illness is unlikely, no matter what the other
symptoms are.

Specific symptoms to call about. In spite of what I just said,
there are a few symptoms that should trigger a call to the doctor,
no matter what else is going on.

Fever. If your baby is less than three months old, call right
away for any temperature of 100.5 or higher (taken rectally: see
page 702), even if your baby looks fine. Infants with a low fever
or none at all can become ill very fast. In older children, fever is
usually less important than whether the child seems really sick.
After the age of three or four years, a high fever often accompanies a mild infection. As a rule, consult the doctor if your baby
has a temperature of 101 or more. You don't have to call in the
middle of the night if your baby has a 101 fever with a mild cold
but otherwise seems happy.

Rapid breathing (tachypnea). Children normally breathe
faster than adults. Infants normally don't breathe more than
forty times a minute; thirty for young children; twenty for children age ten and above. It's best to count the breaths for a full
minute, with each in and out being one breath. If you count your
child's breathing rate, both asleep and awake, when she is well,

you'll know how she normally breathes and be in a better position to decide if the rate is different when she's sick. Sometimes a child will breathe a little faster for a short time then revert to normal. Children who are really ill—for example, with pneumonia—often have a respiratory rate that stays high. So unless your child looks sick, don't panic after one measurement. Wait a bit; try to bring her fever down, if she has one; and recheck her breathing.

Retractions. The child is working very hard to breathe, drawing in the muscles in the stomach, chest and neck. Retractions are a sign that it requires extra effort to get air into his lungs. Something is wrong. Some infants may also make grunting noises when they exhale, or exhaling may be prolonged with increased effort.

Noisy breathing. Children with chest infections or asthma often breathe more noisily than usual. It may be hard for you to tell exactly where the noise is coming from. Sometimes it's just from mucus in the nose, not really a lung problem. At other times, it may come from the windpipe (stridor) and is loudest when the child breathes in. Sometimes the noise comes from farther down in the lungs. If these are high-pitched, almost musical noises, usually louder when breathing out, they may be wheezes, which children with asthma are prone to. If a child continues to have retractions and tachypnea but his breathing becomes *less* noisy, there may be too little air moving around the obstructed area. This is a true medical emergency. Hoarseness of voice accompanied by difficulty in breathing should always be reported immediately, especially if there is drooling.

Pain. Pain is the body's internal alarm that something is wrong. If pain is not severe and there are no other symptoms (such as fever), you can probably safely wait and watch. If the pain seems unduly severe, the child cannot be consoled, or he seems very ill, call the doctor. When in doubt, call.

Vomiting of any unusual type should be reported promptly, especially if the child looks sick or different in any way. Call right away if there is bloody vomit. This does not apply, of course, to the spitting-up after meals common in infants.

Diarrhea of the more serious sort, such as bloody diarrhea or unusually large quantities of loose or watery stools in infants, should be reported to the doctor immediately. The milder kinds can wait. If you see signs of dehydration (tiredness, reduced urine output, dry mouth and reduced tears), report them to your doctor. Call right away if there's blood in bowel movements or urine.

Injury to the head should be reported if your child loses consciousness, isn't happy and healthy looking within fifteen minutes, looks more lethargic and dazed as time goes by, or vomits after the head injury.

Ingestion of poisons. If your child has eaten anything that may be dangerous, call the poison hotline immediately (800 222-1222; see page 761).

Rashes. Consult the doctor about all persistent or unusual rashes. It's easy to be mistaken. If a child seems sick with a rash or it is extensive, you should call the doctor right away.

Remember, this is only a partial list of situations when you should call your doctor. When in doubt, call!

Before you call. It's sometimes hard for the doctor or nurse to tell if your child is really sick and should be seen right away or can wait until the office opens the next day. That's why the information you relate to the on-call doctor or nurse is vital. Before calling, make sure you have the following information handy (write it down if you need to):

1. What are the troubling symptoms? When did they start? How often are they occurring? Are there any other symptoms?

2. What are your child's vital signs: temperature, trouble breathing, pallor? (You should take her temperature whenever your child is sick; see page 702.)

3. What have you done for this problem? Has it worked?

4. How sick does your child appear to be? Is she alert or lethargic? Bright-eyed or dazed? Happy and playful or miserable and crying?

5. Does your child have any past medical problems that may relate to your current concern?

6. Is your child on any medications? If so, what are they?

7. How worried are you about the situation?

The quality of the phone diagnosis will depend on the quality of the information you provide. Doctors and nurses, being human, sometimes forget to ask everything, especially late at night. It's up to you to make sure that the information is related over the phone so an appropriate decision can be made.

FEVERS

What's fever and what isn't? The first thing to realize is that a healthy child's body temperature doesn't stay fixed at the "normal" temperature of 98.6 degrees Fahrenheit (37 degrees Celsius). It is always going up or down a little, depending on the time of day and what the child is doing. It's usually lowest in the early morning and highest in the late afternoon. This change during the day is only a slight one, however. The change between rest and activity is greater. The temperature of perfectly healthy small children may be 99.6 or even 100 right after they have been running around.

In a newborn, up to three months of age, any temperature of 100.5 or more may be a sign of illness and should be reported to the doctor. (If your baby has been wrapped oversnugly, unwrap her and take the temperature again.) In an older child, a temperature of 101 or higher probably means illness. In general, the higher the fever, the more likely the illness is a serious infection rather than a mild cold or viral infection. But some children with only mild infections run high temperatures, and some children with serious infections run lower ones. Fever itself is harmful to a child only at temperatures of 106 or more, higher than most children ever go.

What causes fever with illness? Fever is part of the body's response to infections and some other illnesses as well. Fevers may actually help the body fight off infections, since some germs are more easily killed at higher temperatures. Normally, body temperature is controlled by a small area in the brain called the hypothalamus. When the body becomes too warm, the hypothalamus calls for sweating, which cools the body by evaporation. When the body becomes too cold, it calls for shivering, which generates heat through muscle activity. The system works very much like the thermostat for the furnace in a house. In response to an infection, the immune system releases chemicals that "turn up" the thermostat in the brain. So even though body temperature may be 100, if the new thermostat setting is 102, the child will feel chilled and may even shiver. Medicines like acetaminophen (Tylenol) work by blocking the production of these fever-inducing chemicals, allowing the body's thermostat to return to normal. When the fever breaks the child may sweat, a sign that the brain now recognizes that the body is overheated.

Many parents assume that the fever itself is bad and want to give medicine to bring it down. But it's good to remember that the fever is not the disease. The fever is one of the methods the body uses to overcome the infection. It is also a help in keeping track of how the illness is progressing. A doctor may want to bring a fever down because it is interfering with the child's sleep or exhausting him, or the doctor may be willing to leave the fever alone and concentrate on curing the infection.

In most feverish illnesses, the temperature is likely to be highest in the late afternoon and lowest in the morning, but don't be surprised if a fever is high in the morning and low in the afternoon. There are a few diseases in which the fever, instead of climbing and falling, stays steadily high. The most common of these are pneumonia and roseola (see page 864). An infant who is very sick may have a *below*-normal temperature. Slightly low temperatures (as low as 97) sometimes occurs at the end of an illness and also in healthy babies and small children in the morning. This is no cause for concern if the child feels well.

Taking the temperature. Experienced parents often feel that they can tell a child's temperature by touching the back of their hand or their lips to the child's forehead. The problem is, of course, that it's impossible to communicate to a doctor (or anyone else) just how warm the child feels.

I am a strong advocate of digital electronic thermometers. They are faster, more accurate, and easier to read than traditional glass thermometers. They're inexpensive, only about $10. And there is no risk that they will break and release toxic mercury into the environment. If you own a glass thermometer, you should get rid of it, but don't simply throw it in the garbage. Mercury is a poison that should never go into landfills. Instead, give it to your child's doctor to dispose of or turn it in to your

municipal solid waste system, following the procedure for toxic waste (which is what it is).

With a digital thermometer, all you do is wipe it off, turn it on, and pop it in. A friendly beep lets you know when it's time to read the temperature. With infants, it's most accurate to take a rectal temperature. Use a little petroleum jelly (Vaseline) or other mild lubricant, lay your baby over your knee or hold her legs up with one hand, and slide the thermometer tip in about a half inch. After age five or six, most children can cooperate by holding the thermometer under their tongue with their lips closed for a minute or so. You may also take the temperature under your child's armpit (axillary temperature), but this is not as accurate as either rectal or oral. In one child, the blood vessels may lie close to the skin so the axillary temperature reads higher; in another, they may lie farther from the skin so the temperature reads lower. When accuracy matters, either rectal or oral is best.

High-tech electronic thermometers that read the temperature through the ear are expensive and offer no real advantage, except for the rare child who will not hold still. Thermometers that read temperature by scanning the skin may not be particularly accurate.

You clean a thermometer by washing it with lukewarm water and soap. You can then wipe it with rubbing alcohol, but be sure

to rinse it with cold water to get rid of the alcohol taste before using it again.

When reporting the temperature to your child's doctor, pay attention to the decimal point. Sometimes parents say "one hundred and three" (103) when they mean "one hundred *point* three" (100.3). The more precise you are, the better advice you'll get.

TEMPERATURE EQUIVALENTS

Fahrenheit	Centigrade (Celsius)
98.6	37.0
100.4	38.0
102.2	39.0
104.0	40.0

How long to keep taking the temperature? Here is what occasionally happens. A child has a bad cold with a fever. The doctor sees the child or gets regular reports and has the parents take the temperature twice a day. Finally the fever is gone and the child is convalescing well, with only a mild cough and running nose. The doctor tells the parents to let the child go outdoors as soon as the cold is completely gone. Two weeks later, the parents telephone to say that they and the child are getting desperate staying indoors, that the running nose and cough have been completely gone for ten days, that the child looks wonderful and eats well, but that the fever is still going to 99.6 each afternoon. As I explained earlier, this is not necessarily a fever in an active child. The ten days of staying indoors and worrying over the temperature was a waste and a mistake.

Under most circumstances, when the temperature has stayed under 101 for a couple of days, it's a good general rule to forget about the thermometer unless the doctor asks you to continue or the child seems sicker in any way. Children should be kept home from school until the temperature has been normal for twenty-four hours and they feel better. Not all the cold symptoms have to be gone. Don't get in the habit of taking the temperature when a child is well.

Treating a fever (until you reach the doctor). Between the ages of one and five years, children may develop a fever as high as 104, sometimes even higher, with the onset of a mild infection, such as a cold, a sore throat, or the flu. A dangerous illness, on the other hand, may not bring a temperature higher than 101. So don't be influenced too much one way or the other by the height of the fever. Get in touch with the doctor when your child looks sick or different, whatever the temperature.

Sometimes a child feels especially uncomfortable with a high fever. If on the first day of an illness a child's temperature is 104 or higher, you can bring the fever down a little with an antifever medication such as acetaminophen (Tylenol) or ibuprofen (Motrin) (not aspirin: see page 872). These come in both solid and liquid. Follow the directions on the package for the correct dose. Remember that doses change with age and weight.

The medicine to bring the fever down should be given one time only, unless you still haven't reached the doctor after three to four hours, in which case you can give a second dose. (Be sure to keep these medications out of your child's reach and in a childproof container. Even though they are sold without prescription, they are not harmless; large overdose can be fatal.)

You may want to give your child a bath or wipe his skin with a damp cloth or sponge. The purpose of the tepid bath or wet rub is to bring blood to the surface by rubbing and to cool it by the evaporation of the water from the skin. Traditionally, alcohol has been used in a wet rub, but if it is applied very freely in a small room, too much may be inhaled. Water works just as well and is free and safe. These methods provide only temporary relief, however, because the body's thermostat remains set at a higher temperature and will quickly cause the fever to return.

When a child's fever is very high and he is flushed, use only light covers at ordinary room temperature, perhaps as little as a sheet. Your child will be more comfortable that way, and it may help his temperature come down.

◈ WARNING

Never give aspirin to a child or teenager for fever or for cold or flu symptoms unless the doctor recommends it. Only acetaminophen (Tylenol), ibuprofen (Motrin), and other nonaspirin products should be used for these symptoms in children and teenagers. If it turns out to be a viral illness, especially influenza or chicken pox, aspirin can make the child more susceptible to Reye's syndrome, an uncommon, very dangerous condition (see page 872).

Fevers and seizures. Parents often worry that prolonged high fever can cause a convulsion or seizure. This isn't true. It's usually the abrupt increase in temperature at the onset of an illness that occasionally causes a convulsion in small children (see page 879). The reason for trying to bring a high fever down is to help the child feel less miserable, not to prevent a convulsion.

DIET DURING ILLNESS

Your doctor will advise you what diet to use in each of your child's illnesses, taking into account the nature of the disease and the child's taste. What follows are some principles to guide you until you are able to get medical help.

Colds without fever. The diet during a cold without fever can be entirely normal. However, children may lose their appetite with even a mild cold because they're indoors, not taking the usual amount of exercise, a little uncomfortable, and swallowing mucus, which nauseates them. Don't urge them to eat more than they want. If they're eating less than usual, offer them extra fluids between meals. Some people have the idea that the more fluid, the better the treatment. There is no harm in letting children drink all they want to, but excessive amounts of fluid don't do any more good than reasonable amounts.

Diet during fever until you can consult the doctor. When children have fever above 102 with a cold, flu, sore throat, or one of the contagious diseases, they usually lose most of their appetite in the beginning, especially for solids. In the first day or two of such a fever, don't offer solid food at all if they don't seem hungry, but do offer fluids frequently. Orange juice, pineapple juice, and water are the most popular; don't forget water. It has no nourishment, but that's unimportant for the time being. It's for this very reason that it often appeals to the sick child the most. Her receptivity to other fluids depends on her taste and the illness.

If a child has an infection that causes sores in his mouth, he may not want citrus drinks that are acidic and make the sores sting. Some children love grapefruit juice, lemonade, pear juice, grape juice, and weak tea. Popsicles are also a good source of fluid. Older children like carbonated drinks, such as ginger ale and fruit-flavored sodas. Cola drinks often contain caffeine, so it's better to avoid them. Dairy products may cause more mucus and discomfort in upper respiratory infections.

The most important rule is: Do not urge a sick child to eat anything that she doesn't want unless the doctor has a special reason for urging it. It's only too likely to be vomited, cause intestinal upset, or start a feeding problem.

Diet when there is vomiting. Vomiting occurs in many different diseases; it occurs because the stomach is upset by the disease and is unable to handle food. The diet depends on many factors and should be prescribed by the doctor. However, if you cannot reach the doctor immediately, follow these suggestions.

Start with small sips of water or Pedialyte, which is water with the amount of salt and sugar that is absorbed best (see page 912, **Electrolyte Solutions**). At first, give only half an ounce every fifteen to twenty minutes. Gradually increase the amount, as the child tolerates it, up to four ounces (half a glass) every half hour or so. If she goes this far without vomiting, try a little diluted apple juice or herb tea (peppermint or chamomile often stay down well). Many children tolerate Popsicles well, too.

It's okay to offer solid foods, too. Start simple, with a cracker or a piece of toast, some banana, or a tablespoon of applesauce. Avoid milk or milk products, which may be harder to digest.

Diet when there is diarrhea. By the time a child is two or more, there is much less chance of severe or prolonged diarrhea. Until the doctor can be reached, the best treatment is as much of his normal diet as he is hungry for. Research has shown that the traditional diarrhea diet of sugary fluids, such as Jell-O water, soda drinks, or apple juice, actually increases and prolongs diarrhea, so this approach is no longer recommended. With significant diarrhea, consider using Pedialyte (see page 912); it's best, though, to talk with the doctor first. A child who is ill enough to need Pedialyte probably should be medically evaluated.

The key feature of diet during diarrhea is to make sure your child takes in sufficient fluids so as not to become dehydrated. Dehydration occurs when what the child takes in by drinking is less than what goes out in diarrhea and vomiting. The first sign is listlessness. Dry mouth, sunken eyes, and skin that feels doughy are all signs of dehydration. If a rehydration solution (Pedialyte, for example), taken in frequent small sips, doesn't stay down, the child may need fluid through an IV in the doctor's office or the hospital.

Feeding problems at the end of illness. If a child has a fever for several days and eats little, he naturally loses weight. This worries parents the first time or two that it happens. When the fever is finally gone and the doctor says it's all right to work back to a regular diet, they are impatient to feed the child. But it often happens that the child turns away from food. If the parents urge him to eat, meal after meal, day after day, his appetite may never pick up.

Such a child has not forgotten how to eat, nor has he become too weak to do so. At the time the temperature went back to normal, there was still enough infection in his body to affect his stomach and intestines. As soon as he saw that first food, his digestive system warned him that it was not ready yet.

When food is pushed or forced onto a child who is already nauseated from illness his disgust builds up more rapidly than if his appetite were normal. He can develop a long-lasting feeding problem in a few days' time.

As soon as the stomach and intestines recover from the effects of illness and are able to digest food again, children's hunger comes back with a bang—and not just to what it used to be. Children are usually ravenous for a week or two in order to make up for losses. You sometimes see such children two hours after a large meal whimpering for more. By age three, they may demand the specific foods their starved system craves most.

The parents' best course at the end of illness is to offer children only the drinks and solids they want with no urging and to wait patiently and confidently for signs they are ready for more. If their appetite has not recovered in a week, the doctor should again be consulted.

GIVING MEDICINE

It's sometimes quite a trick getting a child to take medicine. The first rule is to slip it into her in a matter-of-fact way, as if it occurred to you that she won't take it. If you go at it apologetically with much explanation, you'll convince her that she's expected to dislike it. Talk about something else when you put the spoon into her mouth. Most young children open their mouths automatically, like young birds in a nest. With babies, it often works to draw up the medicine in an oral syringe (available in drug stores) and gently squirt it into the mouth, alongside the cheek, toward the back.

Tablets that don't dissolve can be crushed to a fine powder and mixed with a coarse, good-tasting food, like applesauce. Mix the medicine with only a teaspoon of the applesauce, in case she decides she doesn't want much. Bitter pills can be mixed in a teaspoon of applesauce, rice syrup, or rice milk. (Some foods interfere with the absorption of specific medicines; check with a pharmacist before you give your creativity free reign.)

When giving medicine in a drink, it's safer to choose an unusual fluid that the child does not take regularly. If you add a strange taste to orange juice, you may make the child suspicious of it for months.

Eye ointments and drops can sometimes be applied while the child is asleep. They can also be given to a small child by placing him on your lap with his legs around your waist out of kicking range. Place his head gently but firmly between your knees, holding it with one hand while giving the medicine with your other. (This position is also good for suctioning the nose or inserting nose drops.)

Cathartics and laxatives (drugs to make the bowels move) should not be used for any reason—especially stomachache—before consulting a doctor. Some people have the mistaken idea that stomachache is frequently caused by constipation and want to give a cathartic or laxative first. There are many causes of stomachache (see page 836) and some, such as appendicitis and obstruction of the intestines, are made worse by a cathartic or laxative. It is dangerous to treat stomachache with a strong medicine since you don't know what is causing it.

Check with the doctor. It's always safest to check with a doctor before giving any medication or before continuing to give a medicine for longer than the original prescription. Here are some examples of why either is inadvisable: A child has a cough with a cold for which the doctor prescribes a certain cough medicine. Two months later the child develops a new cough, and the parents have the prescription renewed without consulting the doctor. It seems to help for a week; then the cough becomes so bad they have to call the doctor anyway. The doctor realizes right away that the disease this time is not a cold but pneumonia; he would have suspected it a week earlier if the parents had called.

Parents who have treated colds, headaches, or stomachaches a few times in the same way come to feel like experts, which they are, in a limited way. But they're not trained, as a doctor is, to first consider carefully the diagnosis. To them, two headaches (or two stomachaches) seem the same. To the doctor, one may have an entirely different meaning from the other and call for different treatment.

People whose children have been treated by a doctor with one of the antibiotics (such as penicillin) are sometimes tempted to use it again for similar symptoms. They figure that since it produces wonderful results, is easy to take, and they know the dosage from the last time: Why not? First, the medicine may no longer be effective or the child may need a different dosage or a different medication entirely. Second, the antibiotics may interfere with a diagnosis when the doctor is finally consulted. Finally, children occasionally have serious reactions to these drugs: fevers, rashes, anemia. These complications, fortunately, are rare, but they are more likely to occur if the drugs are used often, especially if improperly used. That is why they should be given only when a doctor has decided that they are needed. Even the continued use of as common a drug as acetaminophen can occasionally cause serious trouble. For the same reasons, you should never give a neighbor's, friend's, or relative's medicine to a child.

Antibiotic resistance. Overuse of antibiotics has led to the emergence of bacteria that are resistant to many common medications. In day-care centers, for example, where in the course of a year the average child may have ten or more bouts of illnesses with fever, many ear infections don't respond to standard doses of antibiotics. We have to *double* the dose to kill off the supertough bacteria causing these infections. Often, a doctor may not be certain whether a particular infection is caused by a bacteria or by a virus. In these cases, it's often wise to wait and watch, rather than dive in with an antibiotic that might not do any good (since viruses don't respond to antibiotics), but that is bound to stimulate the growth of resistant bacteria.

Antibiotic resistance also grows when children are given partial doses of antibiotics—enough to kill off the weaker bacteria, while allowing the stronger, more resistant bacteria to take over. To prevent this unwelcome development (and protect your child from becoming the host to super-hardy bacteria), when you do give your child an antibiotic, always give it at the full prescribed dose, for the full course of treatment.

Generic prescriptions. A generic prescription is one that uses not the trade name for a medicine but the chemical name instead. Most medicines prescribed this way are cheaper than those prescribed by the advertised trade name, even though it's exactly the same medicine. You should ask your doctor about using generic prescriptions. Most of the time—though not all—it's a good idea.

ISOLATION FOR CONTAGIOUS DISEASES

There are many ways an infectious disease can pass from one person to another. Some are transmitted by coughing, some by touching the person. You won't catch something just by being in the room unless that germ has somehow made its way from the sick individual to your body. Some infectious diseases, like chicken pox, are very contagious; others, like HIV, are transmitted only through the blood or other body fluids.

As a general principle, it's a good idea to keep a child with a contagious disease in the house until he no longer has a fever and the doctor says that he is no longer contagious. It's sensible to keep the amount of intimate contact (kissing, hugging, and cuddling) to a minimum, except for the one person who is taking care of the sick child. This precaution helps to prevent others from catching the disease. Another reason for keeping sick children isolated is so they will not pick up new germs from others to complicate their illness.

Grown-ups in the family are generally not restricted to home when a member of the household has a contagious disease. You have to use your own good sense, though, about visiting families who have susceptible children. The chances of your carrying the germs to other children are practically zero so long as you keep away from them. Just the same, you may be blamed if anyone in those families catches your child's disease any time in the next year.

The best way to limit the spread of disease is through frequent and thorough hand-washing. Teach children to wash up to their wrists and between the fingers, scrubbing for a minute or more—a long time, actually. A stepstool makes it easier for a child to reach the sink comfortably; small bars of soap, like the ones in hotel bathrooms, make it easy for small hands. Put boxes of tissues around the house to inspire frequent nose-blowing and paper garbage bags so that used tissues don't end up on the floor.

CARING FOR A SICK CHILD

Beware of spoiling. When children are sick, it's natural to give them lots of special care and consideration. You don't mind preparing drinks and food for them at frequent intervals or even putting aside a drink they refuse and making another kind right away. You are glad to get them new playthings to keep them happy and quiet. A child easily gets used to this arrangement and may boss his parents around and expect instant service. Fortunately, most children are on their way to recovery in a few days. As soon as the parents stop worrying, they stop putting up with the child's unreasonable demands. After a couple of days, things are back to normal.

With longer illnesses, the persistent high level of concern and special treatment may have a bad effect on a child's spirits. He's apt to become demanding. If he's too polite for that, he may become excitable and temperamental, like a spoiled actor. It's easy for him to learn to enjoy being sick and receiving sympathy. His ability to make his own way agreeably may grow weaker, like a muscle that isn't being used.

Casual caring. It's wise for parents to get back into normal balance with the sick child as soon as possible. This means such little things as having a friendly, matter-of-fact expression rather than a worried one when entering the room; asking him how he feels today in a tone of voice that expects good news rather than bad; and perhaps asking only once a day. When you find out by experience what he wants to drink and eat, serve it up casually. Don't ask timidly if he likes it or act as if he were wonderful to take some. Keep strictly away from urging unless the doctor feels it is necessary. A sick child's appetite is more quickly ruined by pushing and forcing.

If you buy new playthings, look especially for the kind that encourages children to take an active role and use their imagination: blocks and building sets; sewing, weaving and bead-stringing kits; painting, modeling, and stamp-collecting supplies. Deal out one new plaything at a time. There are many homemade occupations, like cutting pictures out of old magazines, making a scrapbook, sewing, building a farm, town, or doll's house of cardboard and masking tape. A little extra television and videogame playing is fine; too much may make your child feel listless or encourage him to stay sick longer to continue indulging his obsession.

If a child will be laid up for a long time but is well enough to study, get a teacher or a tutor or the best teacher in the family to start him on his schoolwork again for a regular period each day as soon as possible. It's fine to spend time each day keeping your sick child company, but you don't need to be there every minute. It's healthy for a child to know that there are times when his parents will be busy elsewhere, as long as they are available in an

emergency. If the child has a disease that isn't catching and the doctor lets him have company, regularly invite other children in to play and stay for meals.

The hardest part may be when the child is over her illness but not yet fully back to her old self. You have to use your best judgment about how much special consideration she still needs. The best policy, in short, is to let your child lead as normal a life as is possible under the circumstances. You should expect reasonable behavior toward you and the rest of the family. Avoid worried talk and looks.

GOING TO THE HOSPITAL

A child who ends up in the hospital after a sudden illness or trauma is bound to be disoriented and scared. Having a parent or other close family member nearby at all times can make a huge psychological difference. Children who go to the hospital for planned procedures, such as surgery to remove enlarged tonsils and adenoids, may become terribly anxious in anticipation of what will be done to them. A chance to voice their fears and receive reassurance may help tremendously. Children with chronic illnesses and special health-care needs may be frequently hospitalized. For them and their families, the expertise of child life specialists—professionals who are trained to help children adapt to hospitals and medical procedures—can be invaluable.

Why the hospital is upsetting. Between the ages of one and four years, the child worries most about being separated from the parents. He feels as if he is losing them forever when they leave him after each hospital visit. Between visits he may remain anxious and depressed. When the parents come to see him, he may silently reproach them by at first refusing to greet them. To avoid these fears and strains, it's important for parents to stay with their young children throughout the hospital stay. When this isn't possible, a grandparent or other trusted adult should step in.

After the age of four, the child is likely to be more fearful about what's to be done to him, the injury to his body, and the pain. It won't do for the parents to promise that the hospital will be a bed of roses. If unpleasant things happen, as they surely will, the child will lose confidence in his parents. On the other hand, if he is told everything bad that might happen, he is likely to suffer more in expectation than he will when he is there.

The most important thing is for the parents to show all the calm, matter-of-fact confidence they are capable of, without forcing it so much that it sounds false. Unless the child has been a hospital patient before, he is bound to imagine what it will be like, perhaps fearing the worst. The parents can set his mind at rest better by describing hospital life in general rather than by arguing with him about whether it's going to hurt a lot or a little.

It also helps for parents to mention some of the fun things about the hospital: the books and toys brought from home, the television over the bed, and the button that calls the nurse. Many children's wards also have playrooms, stocked with all sorts of great games and toys.

It's fair to dwell on these more pleasant everyday aspects of hospital life, because even at the worst, the child will spend most of his time amusing himself. I wouldn't avoid discussing the medical program altogether, but let the child see that it's a small part of hospital life.

Many children's hospitals also have hospital preview programs for children whose hospitalization is planned ahead of time. The child and parents can come to the hospital a few days before the actual admission to see various parts of the hospital and have their questions answered. In many hospital preview programs, slide and puppet shows demonstrate what the hospital experience will be like.

Let them tell you their worries. Most important is giving your child the opportunity and license to ask questions and tell you what he imagines. Young children view these things in ways that would never occur to adults. In the first place, they often think they have to be operated on or taken to the hospital because they have been bad: haven't worn their boots, stayed in bed when sick, or been angry with other members of the family. A child may imagine that his neck has to be cut open to remove his tonsils or his nose removed to get to the adenoids. So make it easy for your child to raise questions. Be ready to hear about strange fears, and try to reassure him about them.

⟨⟨ CLASSIC SPOCK
When to tell your child. If there is no chance of his finding out, I think it is kinder to wait to tell a small child until a few days before it's time to leave. It won't do him any good to worry for weeks. It may be fairer to tell a seven-year-old some weeks ahead if he's the kind who can face things reasonably, especially if he has some suspicions. Certainly don't lie to a child of any age if he asks questions, and never lure a child to a hospital pretending it's something else.

Anesthesia. If your child is going to have an operation and you have a choice in the arrangements, you can discuss the matter of anesthetists and anesthesia with the doctor. How a child accepts the anesthesia may make the biggest difference in whether he becomes emotionally upset by an operation or goes through it with flying colors. Often in a hospital there is one anesthetist who is especially good at inspiring confidence in children and getting them under without scaring them. It is worth a great deal to obtain the services of such an anesthetist if you have a choice. There is sometimes a choice of anesthetic; this also makes a difference to the child psychologically. Generally speaking, it is less frightening to the child to start with gas. Naturally, the doctor is the one who knows the facts and has to make the decision, but if the doctor feels that medically it makes no difference, the psychological factor should be carefully considered.

You shouldn't use the expression "put to sleep" when you explain anesthesia to a child. That can lead to a child's developing sleep problems after surgery. Instead, explain that anesthesia causes a special kind of sleep, from which the anesthetist will awaken the child as soon as the operation is over. Stay with your child until he is under. It's been shown that having a parent present when anesthesia is given makes a child much less frightened and nervous about the surgery and cuts down on the need for drugs to calm him.

Visiting. The parent should stay in the hospital with a child between the ages of one and five years if at all possible, especially in the daytime. At the very least, a parent should visit daily. Most hospitals now have rooming-in facilities so that a parent or other adult well known to a child can stay overnight in the room.

If the parents are able to visit only intermittently, the visits may create temporary difficulties for the small child. The sight of his parents reminds him how much he has missed them. He may cry heartbreakingly when they leave or even through the entire visiting period. The parents may get the impression that he is miserable all the time. Actually, young children adjust surprisingly well to hospital life when the parents are out of sight, even though they feel sick or are undergoing uncomfortable treatments.

None of this, however, should be taken to mean that the parents should stay away. The child gets security from realizing that after his parents leave, they always come back. But if you have to go, act as cheerful and unworried as possible. An anguished expression makes the child more anxious.

Late reactions to hospitalization. A young child may seem to pull through a hospitalization all right, only to show disturbing behavior once back home, either clinging and being excessively fearful or acting aggressively. These are normal, if unpleasant, responses. Patience, reassurance, and calm insistence that the child will soon feel more comfortable are usually all a child needs to put the hospitalization in the past and move on with the business of being a child.

IMMUNIZATIONS

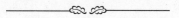

I grew up in a time when every parent was worried sick about their child contracting polio, a paralytic virus. This illness killed about twenty-five thousand people, mostly children, each year. We were warned not to drink from drinking fountains, to avoid crowds in the summer, and to fret about every viral infection. But no more. There has not been a naturally occurring case of polio in the United States since 1979. The rest of the world is a little behind us but on the same track. Smallpox has been totally eradicated from our planet.

The elimination of these illnesses is nothing less than a medical miracle, one of mankind's proudest achievements, and it came to pass because of vaccines.

HOW VACCINES WORK

Vaccines stimulate the body's immune system to make antibodies against viruses and bacteria. Normally, after a person fights off an infection, the immune system remembers and is better able to defeat that infection in the future. Vaccines create the same beneficial responses without the illness.

Infections prevented by vaccines. Currently, most children in the United States are vaccinated against eleven different diseases, and many receive a twelfth. By age two, children should have protection against the following infections, listed along with some of their more serious complications:

- *Diphtheria,* in which a thick covering forms in the throat, leading to severe breathing problems;
- *Pertussis* (whooping cough), which often includes coughing spells so bad that a child can't eat, sleep, or breathe well for weeks;
- *Tetanus* (lockjaw), in which muscles involuntarily tighten, so that breathing becomes difficult or impossible;
- *Measles,* which includes not only an uncomfortable rash, but also high fevers, pneumonia, and brain infections;
- *Mumps,* which can include fever, headaches, deafness, swollen glands, and painful swelling of the testes and ovaries
- *Rubella* (German measles), which is generally mild during childhood, but can result in severe birth defects when contracted during pregnancy;
- *Polio,* which can cause paralysis;
- *Hib* (short for Haemophilus influenzae type B), which can result in deafness, brain damage, or suffocation caused by blockage of the windpipe;
- *Hepatitis B,* an infection of the liver that can result in chronic liver damage and ultimately liver cancer;
- *Pneumococcal* infections of the lungs (pneumonia) or brain (meningitis);
- *Varicella* (chicken pox), which typically causes an uncomfortable rash, but can also lead to severe pneumonia or meningitis;
- *Influenza,* which normally includes fever with aching muscles and other symptoms (the flu), but can also include severe pneumonia, particularly in children with chronic illnesses and in elderly people.

This list, long as it is, doesn't describe all the illnesses caused by the bacteria and viruses targeted by vaccines. For example, Hib and pneumococcus can infect any organ in the body. Varicella (chicken pox) often causes shingles, an itchy and painful rash that can return repeatedly through life. I could go on. The point is that the infections prevented by vaccines are worth preventing. (You can read more about many of these diseases in "Common Childhood Illnesses."

Influenza vaccine, the last on the list above, is strongly recommended for children with certain chronic illnesses, including asthma and heart conditions. It is available to any child whose parents decide that the extra protection is worth the pain, and for all children under age two years.

Other vaccines. There are many other immunizations not listed above. For example, children living in some areas benefit from vaccination against Hepatitis A, a virus that infects the liver. Children who travel to countries in Africa, Asia, and South and Central America often need additional immunizations. Your child's doctor can tell you if your child has special immunization needs.

RISKS OF IMMUNIZATION

Weigh risks and benefits. A lot of information is available about the risks of immunization. Unfortunately, there is a lot of misinformation out there, too. Many parents are concerned, some are frightened. The bottom line, however, is that the benefits from preventing these diseases far outweigh the risks of receiving the vaccines. Every expert panel and every responsible physician stands behind this conclusion.

Take one of the newer vaccines: Before the Hib vaccine, twenty thousand children under age five got severe Hib infections in the United States, including meningitis. In 2000, that number was down to approximately fifty. The first child I took care of as a medical student was a beautiful baby who lost her hearing as a result of Hib infection. Another child came into the emergency room with his throat swollen nearly shut and had to go to the operating room to have a tube placed in his windpipe. He was in the hospital for two weeks. In the last ten years, I have not seen a single Hib infection.

The risks of vaccines are usually very mild. Injections hurt more than a pinch but less than a stubbed toe. Some children develop soreness at the injection site and occasionally a firm swelling that can take weeks to go away. Rarely, a high fever develops. Very rarely (about one in one hundred thousand) children show worrisome behavior, crying hour after hour, not responding normally, or having a seizure. These reactions are frightening and in very rare cases do lead to serious long-term problems. But—and I can't say this too many times—the diseases being prevented would be *much* more common and much worse.

How vaccines are made. Most vaccines are made from viruses or bacteria that have been killed (inactivated polio virus, or IPV) or chopped into pieces (accellular pertussis, Hib, hepatitis B, and pneumococal vaccines). Some vaccines are made for use against the poisons or toxins produced by bacteria (diphtheria, tetanus); antibodies against the toxins also help fight off the bacteria. A few vaccines—for measles, mumps, rubella, and varicella—are made from live viruses that have been weakened to the point that they cannot cause disease in healthy children or cause only very mild illness. These vaccines are not safe for children who have seriously weakened immune systems (such as children receiving some cancer treatments) or children who live with other people with weakened immune systems.

Vaccines are getting safer. Polio vaccine used to be given by mouth. But this form of the vaccine used live virus, which resulted in a few cases of polio each year. To prevent these rare reactions, we now use a killed-virus vaccine. (Unfortunately, this vaccine has to be injected.)

Pertussis vaccine used to be notorious for causing pain, swelling, redness, and fever. The new version of the vaccine, acellular pertussis vaccine, or aP, is much gentler.

Exposure to mercury before birth or in the early years can cause brain damage (see page 764). In the past, several vaccines contained a preservative called thimerosal, which contains mercury. The thimerosal in vaccines was never shown to be harmful. Still, just to be safe, vaccines commonly used for children are now thimerosal free and contain at most only tiny traces of mercury.

Vaccines and autism. The number of children with autism appears to be rising fast, and no one knows why (see page 613). It seems reasonable to ask whether vaccines or something in them might be the cause. Many theories and rumors have focused on the measles, mumps, and rubella vaccine (MMR). However, carefully done studies have failed to find any connection between MMR and autism. For example, there is no difference in the rate of autism in children who have received MMR from those who have not.

In 2001, an expert panel of the Institute of Medicine concluded that MMR is *not* responsible for the vast majority of cases of autism, although the research leaves open the possibility that it causes some rare cases. Without MMR, the number of cases of measles would skyrocket, resulting in many more children with brain damage than ever could have been caused by the vaccination. The panel recommended that children continue to get MMR vaccine. Expert committees of the American Academy of Pediatrics and the U.S. Centers for Disease Control (CDC) agree.

Vaccines have also been blamed for other diseases, one a serious condition called inflammatory bowel disease (IBD). Again, careful study has shown no connection between vaccines and IBD.

Where to learn more. Every doctor who gives vaccines is required by law to give parents a fact sheet about each shot, called a vaccine information statement. These sheets, created by the Centers for Disease Control (CDC), are very clear and accurate. Ask your child's doctor for these handouts ahead of time so that you can read about upcoming immunizations. There are also several excellent websites listed in the Resource Guide (see page 917).

THE IMMUNIZATION SCHEDULE

So young, so many shots. To most of the illnesses prevented by vaccines, little babies are the most vulnerable. So it makes sense to start immunizing as soon as possible. But with many vaccines, children require more than one exposure to develop a full-strength immune response. That's why many of them are given several times in the first year to get the maximum protection as early as possible.

The standard schedule of immunizations that most doctors follow comes from the U.S. Centers for Disease Control (CDC) and is approved by the Advisory Committee on Immunization Practices of the United States Public Health Service (ACIP), the American Academy of Pediatrics (AAP), and the American Academy of Family Physicians (AAFP). The CDC also publishes specific guidelines for which babies should *not* be immunized and which ones should receive special immunizations, such as influenza vaccine.

Alphabet soup. Many of the shots are referred to by their initials or brand names. The following glossary should help (see page 862 for more about the diseases themselves):

- *DTaP* (diphtheria, tetanus, and pertussis, a three-in-one multiple vaccine combination)
- *HepB* (hepatitis B)
- *Hib* (Haemophilus influenzae, type B)

- *ComVax* or *PedvaxHIB* (two-in-one combinations of Hib + Hep B)
- *IPV* (inactivated polio vaccine)
- *MMR* (measles, mumps, and rubella, another three-in-one combination)
- *Varicella* or *Varivax* (chicken pox vaccine)
- *PCV* or *Pneumovax* (pneumococcal vaccine)
- *Td* (tetanus vaccine with a small dose of diphtheria vaccine, formulated for children over seven)

A typical immunization schedule. For maximum protection, children need to get their immunizations on time. The schedule allows some flexibility. Doctors and parents can choose to delay some of the immunizations by up to several months, either to spread out the shots or because a child is ill when an immunization is due. If children fall far behind, doctors can help to catch

PRIMARY SERIES

Age	Vaccines	Needles
Birth	Hep B	1
2 months	DTaP, IPV, PCV, Hib+Hep B	4
4 months	DTaP, IPV, PCV, Hib	4
6 months	DTaP, IPV, PCV, Hib+Hep B	4
12 to 15 months	MMR, PCV, Hib, Varicella	4
15 to 18 months	DTaP	1

BOOSTERS

Age	Vaccines	Needles
4 to 6 years	DTaP, IPV, MMR	3
11 to 12 years	Td	1

them up quickly. The goal is to have the primary series completed by the time your child is two years old.

The immunization schedule is sure to change as new vaccines are developed and approved. By the time you read this, more may be available in multivaccine formulas that lower the number of needles. Eventually vaccines may be given in edible form, with no pain at all. In the meantime, there are many things you can do to help your children cope.

COPING WITH SHOTS

⟨⟩ CLASSIC SPOCK

The best way to get your child ready for each immunization is to be as honest and simple in your explanations as possible, considering his age and understanding. Tell him that the shot will hurt a little ("like a hard pinch"), but that it will protect him from sickness that would hurt much more than the shot. Reassure him that it's okay to cry if he wants to and it's okay to feel angry at the doctor and you. I think that even little babies, who won't understand your words, are still soothed by your tone of voice when you're holding them and explaining why they have to have a shot.

Body comfort. Babies feel safe in their parents' arms. One-day-old infants getting their heels stuck for blood cry less and show fewer physical signs of stress if their mothers hold them close during the stick. A good position is with your child facing you, chest to chest, arms and legs wrapped around your body. This position works for children up through five or six years old.

Sucking on a pacifier, rocking, and being stroked are effective comfort measures for babies.

Use your voice. For infants, it doesn't matter what you say. The tone of your voice will make them feel safe. For toddlers and preschool children, the fear of the shot is often worse than the actual feeling. To reduce fear, tell your child what is going to happen just before it does. For example, "Now you'll feel the alcohol wipe—does it feel chilly?"

By the way, you might want to use words other than shot, such as vaccine or medicine. For some literal-minded preschoolers, shot sounds like something done by a gun.

When children are scared, they often ignore negative phrases. That is, if parents say "Don't *scream!*" they hear "scream!" If parents say "Stop *crying!*" they hear "crying!" It's better to use only positive words: "You're okay; there, there; over soon."

Give your child choices. Some children want to see what the nurse or doctor is doing; others don't. A child who has a choice feels more in control. Also, you can give your child permission to scream if it helps. "It's okay to yell, if you want to, but you need to hold still. Why not wait till you feel the pinch?"

Distraction. A very effective technique for toddlers and preschoolers is to tell a story, sing a song, or look at a picture book. Children have strong imaginations. A child who imagines herself doing a favorite activity—running, riding a bike fast, or jumping on a bed—will feel less pain. Two powerful distraction techniques, great for four and five year olds, are blowing at a pinwheel or blowing bubbles. If your child loves bubbles, bring a bottle of bubble soap and a plastic wand to the doctor's when you go for the checkup (a lot of clever doctors have their own bubble wands).

Helping a fearful child. If your child is especially fearful of shots, ask him to draw a picture of what he thinks is going to happen. Don't be surprised if the picture shows a very small person next to a huge, terrifying needle! Help your child to realize that the needle is really very small.

Children often cope with scary things through play. Give your child a toy syringe and stethoscope, and let him practice being the doctor to a doll who needs "medicine." By giving shots, your child may come to feel more control and therefore less fear.

If severe fears persist, talk with your child's doctor or nurse. There are professionals called child life specialists in most children's hospitals who are experts at helping children cope with medical procedures. It's worth a visit with one to have your child feel more comfortable. Getting a needle and coming away feeling all right helps a young child realize that he can handle things that make him afraid: a great lesson at any age.

A PRACTICAL TIP

Keep a record with you. It's a good idea to have a record (signed by your doctor or nurse practitioner) of all your children's immunizations and also allergies to medications to carry with you when the family goes on trips or changes doctors. The commonest emergency occurs when a child away from home receives a wound that calls for extra protection against tetanus (lockjaw). Then it is very important for the attending doctor to know whether the child has been immunized against tetanus. Immunization records are also needed for children entering day care, school, college, and the military.

PREVENTING INJURIES

———— ❦ ❦ ————

KEEPING CHILDREN SAFE

Safety is a parent's first and most important job. The other aspects of parenting—love, limits, values, fun, and learning—don't mean a thing without safety. We promise our children that we will keep them safe, and our children expect this of us. The beginning of psychological health is the deep-down belief that there is a big person out there who can provide security.

Our most basic instincts center on safety: Infants cry, and parents have the urge to pick them up. It's easy to imagine that these protective responses helped our prehistoric ancestors survive in a hostile environment. But even in our modern world, dangers abound. Unintentional injuries cause more deaths in children over age one than all illnesses combined. Each year, more than ten million children require medical care for unintentional injuries. One out of six children hospitalized because of injury comes away with a permanent disability. More than five thousand die.

Bad as these numbers are, they represent a dramatic improvement over previous years, largely from public-awareness campaigns and tougher safety standards. Even so, it's clear that the world remains a very dangerous place for children.

The point of telling you this, of course, is not to frighten you but to help you take reasonable precautions. The more you know about the dangers out there—and in your own home—the better you'll be able to keep your children safe while you go about the other important parts of living.

Why not just call them accidents? For many people, the word accident implies something that is unavoidable, as in "I couldn't help it, it was an accident." The truth is that many childhood injuries that are called accidental really *can* be avoided. They don't just happen; they happen because adults tolerate the conditions that make them possible. Consider, for example, a car with seat belts not made to fit small bodies, that is, *any* car without a car seat. If a child riding in such a car is killed in a crash, his death is not truly accidental. It was predictable and most likely could have been prevented.

Who is injured, and how. In sheer numbers, injuries to children riding in cars top the list. Injuries to pedestrians and bicyclists are also common, as are burns, suffocation, poisoning, choking, falls, and unintentional shootings. A child's age determines which form of unintentional injury is most likely to be deadly. Under age one, suffocation and choking are the most common. From one to four, drowning kills more children. After age five, it is children riding in cars who are most likely to die from unintentional injuries.

An entirely different set of unintentional injuries typically cause health problems but not death. Falls from heights, for example, or collisions with coffee tables commonly result in cuts, bruises, and broken bones. Falls from bicycles often result in serious brain injury, unless the child is wearing a helmet. Lead poisoning, another very common form of unintentional injury, rarely kills children but causes learning problems that can limit a child's life success.

It isn't possible to prevent absolutely every injury, but we know enough now to bring the risks way down for most children.

Principles of prevention. It's a natural human tendency to go through life with an attitude of "It can't happen to me." So the first step is to stop denying the possibility of an injury. Then practice the three basic principles of effective injury prevention.

Childproof your child's environment. Certain dangerous items simply don't belong in a house with young children: for example, coffee tables with sharp corners, unguarded stairs, and furniture and beds next to open windows. Use a checklist (see page 762) to systematically identify hazards then remove them.

Supervise your child closely. Even in a childproofed environment, children require close supervision. Toddlers especially take chances, lack judgment, and need the protection of an adult. Of course you can't spend every waking minute keeping track of your child, but some environments are inherently more dangerous than others. If a playroom has been well childproofed, you can relax a little there. Out in the big world—and in the bathroom and kitchen—you must be more vigilant.

Be particularly careful during stressful times. Injuries happen when routines change and parents' attention is diverted. When the in-laws come for a surprise visit and you have a critical deadline at work is when you need to force yourself to think about where you left the scissors, whether your father-in-law put away his bottle of heart pills, and if the cup of hot coffee you desperately need is sitting too near the table edge.

Safe, outside and in. In planning for your child's safety, it may help to think about safety issues in two settings: outside and inside. The topics that follow are organized into two parts, roughly corresponding with those two settings. Of course, no list of safety topics can be absolutely complete, because dangers pop up in so many different ways. So consider the advice that follows, and use your own good sense, too. Also, refer to the chapters in section I of this book, Your Child Age by Age, which describe safety precautions that apply to children at specific ages.

Part 1: Safety outside the Home

RIDING IN CARS

Injuries to passengers. More children die in automobile crashes than by any other unintentional injury. It's hard to overestimate the importance of seat belts with shoulder harnesses for adults and older children and properly installed child safety seats for infants and young children. All fifty states have laws requiring that children under age four be properly restrained in a child safety seat when a car is in motion. More than half the states now require that everyone riding in the front seat be buckled up. Some parents claim that their children refuse to wear them. This excuse isn't worth a nickel. All children will do whatever their parents really insist on. If you begin making exceptions, a child will argue every time; that's exhausting for both child and parent. The safest policy is not to operate any vehicle unless everyone in it is secured in a car seat or with a seat belt.

There's an added benefit to keeping children in car seats or seat belts: They behave better when they're secured than when they're not.

Car seat choice and installation: There are rear-facing seats for infants, forward-facing for toddlers, and booster seats for preschoolers and young school-age children (see the sections that follow). A seat that has been through a crash may look fine then fall apart at the next impact. So before you buy a used seat, be sure to find out if it's ever been in a crash. Read the instructions that come with the seat and do your best putting it in; then if possible, go to an official child safety seat inspection station and have a free inspection by a certified child passenger safety technician. To find an inspection station, look on the internet at www.nhtsa.gov. NHTSA (Nitsa) is the National Highway Traffic Safety Administration, the best source for reliable information about auto safety for both children and adults. You can also ask at your local fire station.

I recently took a course to become a NHTSA-certified car seat technician. After a whole week of study and practice, I still had a hard time getting some of the car seats to fit right. Inspectors find problems with eight out of ten seat installations. In other words, if you show up for a free car seat check, chances are that your children will be safer when you leave than when you came.

Infant seats. Your baby's first ride home after birth and every ride thereafter should be in a car safety seat that conforms to federal motor vehicle safety standards. Car seats are required by law and also by common sense. While it may seem that you can hold a baby safely in your lap, you can't. In a sudden stop from

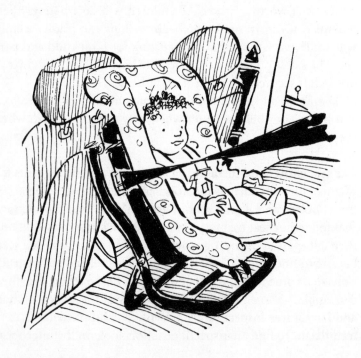

forty miles per hour, a ten-pound baby can pull away with a force of two hundred pounds or more. Placing a baby under your own seat belt or shoulder belt is even more dangerous, as the baby may be crushed by your body in a crash.

Up until a baby is twelve months old and weighs twenty pounds or more, the only safe way to ride is in a rear-facing infant seat secured in the back seat of the car. (For safety, the rear center seat is the best seat in the house for people of all ages.) A ten-month-old who weighs thirty pounds should still face backward, as should a fourteen-month-old who weights nineteen pounds. Children under the twelve-month, twenty-pound floor are at risk of serious spine and neck injuries if they are seated facing forward. You can choose a rear-facing-only seat, some of which double as infant carriers, or a convertible seat that can be turned to face forward once your baby is old enough and big enough.

It's critically important that infants and children twelve years and under *never* ride in the front passenger seat of a car equipped with airbags (and almost all new cars are). Airbags save adult lives, but they explode with a force that can severely injure or kill a child.

Toddler seats. When a baby is twelve months old and at least twenty pounds, he's ready to graduate to a forward-facing toddler seat. If you bought a convertible infant seat, turn it around. Be sure to follow the instructions for changing the straps, and anchoring the seat. Newer seats use a system called LATCH, which uses a strap to hold the seat from pitching forward. If you're buying a toddler seat, you may choose one that converts to a booster seat, so that you save making yet another purchase later.

The best toddler seats use what is called a five-point harness, with straps that go over each shoulder, each hip, and between the legs. A few seats are still made with solid plastic shields; these aren't as good. For one thing, if a child pitches forward during a crash, the shield may hit him in the face.

The best way to install a toddler seat is to follow the instructions and have a certified car seat inspector check your work. Children should use the toddler seat until they weigh about forty pounds. They are then ready for a booster seat.

Booster seats. Booster seats are for children who have outgrown child safety seats. The official guidelines are for children to use booster seats until they weigh eighty pounds or measure four feet, nine inches tall. Here's why: without a booster seat, a child will tend to slouch down in the seat so that the lap belt runs across her abdomen; in a crash, the belt may injure her internal organs or spine. With a booster seat, the belt runs across the child's pelvic bones; in a crash, these strong bones get the pressure, rather than the soft internal organs. A booster seat also makes the shoulder strap fit comfortably over the shoulder rather than against the neck, so the child is more likely to keep the shoulder belt on. In fact, booster seats *have* to be used with lap-shoulder belts. With a lap belt alone, they don't do a good job of holding the child in place during a crash. Many parents skip the booster seat because they don't want to buy another restraint system. But booster seats are the cheapest type of car seat by far, and they make a huge difference in a child's safety and comfort.

Key points to remember:

✔ Never place a child twelve or under in front of a working airbag.

✔ The safest place at any age is the center of the back seat.

✔ A good rule is "The car doesn't move unless everyone is buckled up."

✔ It isn't safe (or legal) to hold a child on your lap when the car is moving or to put your own seat belt around the child.

✔ Even when you think you've got the car seat installed correctly, chances are you don't (it's a lot harder than it looks).
Let a certified car seat technician do a free check to be sure.

On airplanes. The recommendations for safe travel and the use
of child safety seats on airplanes are confusing. Children under
age two can fly for free but are not given a seat. As a result, you
may not be able to use a child safety seat unless there is a vacant
seat next to you. Of course, holding a child in one's arms on an
airplane is not as safe as securing a child into a safety seat, but it's
not as dangerous as doing the same thing in a car, because planes
don't usually make sudden stops. Even if you choose not to pay
for an extra seat for your baby on the plane, it's still safer to fly
than drive to your destination. Take your car safety seat along,
whether you use it on the plane or not so you'll have it for travel
when you reach your destination.

Beds are available on airplanes for use by infants under two,
but they may be used only in the bulkhead seats. For children
over age two, a ticket is required, and it is recommended that you
bring a toddler seat on board for children under forty pounds.
Harnesses and inflatable seat vests are not recommended by
the FAA.

STREETS AND DRIVEWAYS

Injuries to pedestrians. The most common cause of death by
injury in children between the ages of five and nine is being hit
by a car. School-age children are especially at risk because they
are frequently exposed to traffic and do not have the skill to handle it. Their peripheral vision isn't fully developed, they can't accurately judge the speed and distance of oncoming cars, and
many don't know when it's safe to cross.

Research shows that adults generally give their children credit
for more street smarts than they actually have. The hardest job
for parents is to teach children that drivers regularly ignore red

lights and that crosswalks are not automatic safety zones. One-third of pedestrian injuries occur when the child is in a marked crosswalk. Parking lots are another high-risk zone; drivers backing out of spaces may not be able to see children behind them.

Guidelines for pedestrian safety

✔ From the time your child begins to walk on the sidewalk, teach him that he can step off the curb only when you are holding his hand.

✔ Always supervise the outdoor play of preschoolers, and make sure they never play in driveways or streets.

✔ Explain to five- to nine-year-olds over and over again the rules of crossing residential streets. Model safe pedestrian behavior yourself when you walk with them. Point out how traffic lights and crosswalks work and why they need to look left, right, and left again, even when they have the traffic light in their favor and even when they are in a crosswalk.

✔ Remember that children aren't developmentally ready to cross a heavily traveled street without adult supervision until they're at least nine or ten years old.

✔ Together with your child, find safe places to play in your neighborhood. Explain repeatedly that he must never run into the street when playing, no matter how important the game may seem.

✔ Think about where your child walks, especially on the way to school, to playgrounds and playmates' houses. Walk with him, as if you are explorers, and find the safest route with the easiest street crossings. Then help him learn that the safest route is the only one he should use.

✔ Find the time to get involved in community safety. Find out if there are enough traffic signals and crossing guards on the way to your child's school. If a new school is being built, look into the traffic pattern in that area. Will there be enough sidewalks, lights, and guards?

✔ Be especially cautious with toddlers in parking lots and insist that they hold your hand. Keep toddlers in a shopping cart or put them in the car while loading bags.

Driveways. Driveways are a natural place for children to play, but they can be very dangerous. Children need to be taught that as soon as they see a car pulling in or pulling out to get off the driveway immediately. Drivers should *always* walk once around their cars before backing out to make sure there are no small children playing behind the car. Just looking back isn't good enough: a child can easily be overlooked.

BICYCLE INJURIES

Cycling hazards. In children ages fourteen and under in the United States, bicycle injuries cause more than two hundred fifty deaths and three hundred fifty thousand emergency room visits every year. These injuries are especially common in the after-school hours before darkness. Following basic safety rules can prevent the majority of serious injuries. Remember that 60 percent of serious bike injuries are head injuries. And a head injury potentially means a brain injury, which always carries the possibility of permanent brain damage. Proper use of bicycle helmets can reduce the incidence of head injuries by 85 percent.

Choosing helmets. A helmet should have a solid, hard outer shell and a firm polystyrene liner. The chin strap should be attached to the helmet at three points: beneath each ear and at the back of the neck. Look for the label that says that the helmet meets voluntary ASTM, ANSI, or SNELL safety standards.

The helmet should fit properly. It should sit on top of the child's head in a level position, not rock back and forth or from side to side. Measure your child's head with a tape measure and select the appropriate size according to the information on the box. Be sure the box tells you the head size in inches to ensure proper fit; do not rely on the age recommendations on the box. A general guideline to follow is that infant-size helmets are recommended for children ages one and two years, child-size for three to six, and youth helmet for seven to eleven. After that, an adult size will be required. Adult helmets come in small, medium, large, and extralarge.

Replace the helmet if it is involved in a crash or serious head thump. Most companies will replace the impact-absorbing liner free if you send them the helmet. You should be able to get a safe helmet for $20 or less.

Bike safety tips and rules. The most important rule is "No riding without a helmet, ever." When parents ride, they should wear helmets too. You can't expect your children to follow this rule if you don't set an example. Children should ride only on sidewalks until age nine or ten, when judgment is mature enough to

handle traffic while riding in the street. Then teach them the basic rules of the road so they can obey the same traffic rules that automobile drivers follow.

It's safest to get your child a tricycle or bicycle that fits her, not one that she will grow into. Children generally aren't ready for a two-wheeler until they're five to seven years old. Choose bikes with coaster brakes for children up to age nine or ten; after that, they will have developed the strength and coordination to manage hand brakes. Put reflective materials on the bike, the helmet, and the child for better visibility. This is especially important for children who ride at dawn or dusk. Headlamps are required for night riding, but night riding is not recommended for children.

Bicycle carrier seats. Parents bicycling with a child in a carrier should follow these additional rules: Select a child carrier with headrest protection, spoke guards, and shoulder straps. Never use a backpack to carry your child on a bike. Practice with your bike and a weighted carrier before biking with your child. Practice riding in an open area, free of traffic and other cyclists, to get used to the extra weight and gain confidence balancing a child in a carrier. Never carry a child who's less than a year old or who weighs over forty pounds.

A child should wear a helmet at all times while strapped in the carrier seat. Never leave your child unattended in the carrier. Bikes are not made to stand with loaded carriers, and many injuries are caused by falls from a standing bike. Ride on safe, uncongested bike paths, not in the street. Don't ride after dark. Be sure to wear a helmet yourself.

PLAYGROUND INJURIES

More than two hundred thousand children end up in hospital emergency rooms each year as a result of playground injuries. Many of these injuries are severe: broken or dislocated bones, concussions, and injuries to internal organs. A small number result in death. The cause of fatal playground injuries is often strangulation: a lose drawstring or hood becomes caught on the climbing structure in a fall and chokes the child. Nonfatal playground injuries (broken bones and the like) often occur in school playgrounds and public parks; fatal injuries are more likely to happen in the backyard. Children age five through nine are most at risk.

What can you do? Check the playgrounds in your neighborhood, both in parks and at schools. Make sure the equipment is well-maintained and that there are energy-absorbing surfaces, such as rubber mats, sand, pea gravel, or wood chips under the climbing structures and swings. Check that the surfaces have not become packed down or dispersed with use. If the playground needs improvement, talk to the local parks department or school district. If necessary, consider joining or organizing a group of citizens to tackle the problem. It's remarkable what people can do together.

At home, be sure that any playground equipment is sturdy and well-maintained. Make sure that children take off all loose clothing before going to play, including drawstrings on hoods of jackets and sweatshirts. Several clothing manufacturers have voluntarily discontinued using drawstrings in children's garments because of recommendations by the Consumer Product Safety Commission.

Toddlers test their limits and learn new skills on the playground. Many sustain injuries on playgrounds because of their lack of balance and coordination; adult supervision is a must. For those fearless toddlers who take physical risks, an adult should always monitor their activity on the equipment.

SPORTS AND RECREATION SAFETY

An estimated twenty million children play organized sports outside of school, and twenty-five million participate in competitive school sports. Participation in sports improves physical fitness, coordination, self-discipline, and teamwork. But injuries take a heavy toll in pain, missed practices, and games, and long-term disability or worse.

Who is most at risk? Young children are especially susceptible to injury while training and competing, because their bodies are still growing. Before puberty the risk of sports-related injury is the same in boys and girls, but after puberty, as boys grow in strength and size, they are more frequently and severely injured than girls. Boys incur 75 percent of sports injuries.

Collision and contact sports have the highest rate of injury: Football, basketball, baseball, and soccer top the list for boys, and softball, gymnastics, volleyball, and field hockey top the list for girls. Basketball injuries are sure to rise as more girls play competitively. Overuse injuries from playing while injured or tired may cause chronic conditions like tendonitis and arthritis. Head injuries, though less frequent, may result in more serious problems.

Protective gear. Equipment to protect the eyes, head, face, and mouth is a must in many sports. Mouth guards help to prevent dental injuries, which are the most common sports-related facial injury. Mouth guards also cushion blows that might cause a concussion or jaw fracture. Eye protection makes sense for ball sports, including basketball.

Specific sports. *Baseball* safety includes wearing the proper gear to prevent eye, head, face, and mouth injuries. Ballplayers should wear shoes with rubber, not metal, spikes. Injuries can be reduced by using safety bases and installing safety fencing by dugouts and benches. Youngsters should be taught to slide properly and should not be allowed to slide headfirst. Softer-than-standard baseballs and softballs can reduce the severity of impact injuries to the head and chest. Young players should be restricted in the amount of pitching they do so as to prevent permanent arm or elbow injury.

Soccer: Heading is not recommended for young children just learning to play the game; it's probably not good for anyone to clobber their heads over and over, which is what heading is. Soccer goals need to be anchored to the ground so that they cannot tip over on players, and children should not be allowed to climb on movable goals.

In-line skating and skateboarding: These sports result in thousands of injuries each year, mostly sprained or broken wrists, elbows, ankles, and knees. They can be minimized by wearing knee pads, elbow pads, and wrist guards. Head injuries, which tend to be more serious, can be prevented by wearing a helmet. Multisport helmets are now available; they provide extra protection to the back of the head. The current safety label to look for on a multisport helmet is N-94. If your child does not own a multisport helmet, a bicycle helmet worn while in-line skating or skateboarding will provide adequate protection. Be sure that

your child skates only on smooth, paved surfaces with no traffic; warn her to avoid streets and driveways. Make sure she learns to stop safely using the brake pads on the heels of her in-line skates.

Sledding: Wintertime fun includes sledding down snowy hills. It is a surprisingly hazardous pastime. Before you begin, review these safety tips:

- Survey sledding areas before letting children use them. Look for such hazards as trees, benches, ponds, rivers, rocks, and excessive elevation.
- The bottom of the hill should be far from traffic or bodies of water.
- Inflatable snow tubes are fast and unsteerable; use extra caution when children use them. Sleds with a steering mechanism are safer.
- Never allow a child under four years to sled unsupervised. The steepness of the hill should be your guide as to whether older children should be allowed to sled alone.
- Avoid crowded hills, and don't overload a sled with children.
- Do not sled alone or after dusk without adequate light.
- Consider having your child wear a helmet for head protection, but warn him not to let it be an excuse for recklessness.

COLD- AND HOT-WEATHER INJURIES

Cold weather. When the weather turns cold, children should stay dry and dress warmly preferably in multiple layers with special attention to hands and feet. Below 40, infants should stay outdoors for only short periods of time. Pay attention to shivering. Persistent shivering is a sign to head indoors. Serious health risks from cold weather include hypothermia and frostbite.

Hypothermia results from the loss of body heat due to prolonged exposure to cold temperatures. Warning signs in infants include cold, red skin and very low energy. Shivering, drowsiness, and confusion or slurred speech are danger signs in older children. If a child's temperature falls below 95°, seek medical attention immediately and warm the child. Warm drinks and a warm bath work well, or dry the child thoroughly and have him stand by a fire or heater.

Frostbite most often affects the nose, ears, cheeks, chin, fingers, and toes. Signs of frostbite are a loss of feeling and color; a white or grayish-yellow patch may appear. Frostbite can cause permanent damage. To treat frostbite, immerse the affected area in warm—not hot—water, or warm the affected area with your body heat. Skin damaged by frostbite is very delicate. Massaging, rubbing, or walking on it can cause further injury; heating it with a stove, fireplace, radiator, or heating pad can cause burns on top of the frostbite. The best treatment is really prevention. Wet gloves or socks increase the risk of frostbite, so staying dry, as well as reasonably warm, is important.

Hot weather. Infants and children up to the age of four are sensitive to high temperatures. They should drink liquids frequently through the day, wear sun hats, avoid overexertion, and stay indoors during the hottest part of the day—10 A.M. to 2 P.M.—if possible. No matter what the color of their skin, all children should wear sunscreen to protect them from the harmful rays of the sun (see next page). Besides sunburn, heat rash is the most common heat-related illness in young children; heat exhaustion and heatstroke are the most serious.

Heat rash is an irritation caused by excessive sweating in hot, humid weather. It looks like a red cluster of pimples or blisters. The best treatment is to keep the area dry and avoid creams; they keep the skin moist, making the condition worse.

Heat cramps, heat exhaustion and heat stroke are most likely to affect children under five and the elderly. Even healthy teens are vulnerable if they exercise in the heat for long periods of time while drinking little water. Signs of heat exhaustion include heavy sweating, paleness, muscle cramps, tiredness or weakness, dizziness or headache, nausea or vomiting, and faintness. Heatstroke, an even more serious condition, appears as red, hot, and dry or sweaty skin, a strong, rapid pulse, throbbing headache or dizziness, confusion, and unconsciousness.

Prevention is the key: Make sure children take frequent breaks for shade, rest, and fluids. Stop them altogether at the first signs of weakness, nausea, or excessive sweating. Be especially careful when children are dressed heavily or when the humidity is high, two factors that increase overheating. *Never* leave an infant or toddler alone in a car. Even on a cloudy day, the inside temperature can rise to dangerous levels in less than the time it takes to pick up a tube of sunblock.

SUN SAFETY

Most of us grew up thinking that sun exposure is a healthy thing. The glow of a suntan makes us look great and feel terrific. Now we know better. We lament our wrinkles, sunspots, and freckles, which we now know were caused by too much sun exposure in our youth. We have learned that many adult skin cancers are caused by sunburns in childhood. Even the cataracts of the eye that many of us will develop later in life are partly due to exposure to the ultraviolet rays of the sun. To prevent later trouble, you need to protect your child from too much sun exposure. This is not that hard to do, but it takes constant mindfulness.

Who is at risk? The fairer the skin, the greater the danger. African Americans and others with darker skin have more natural protection from the sun because of the melanin—the dark pigment—in their skin, but they should still exercise caution. Infants, because their skin is thin and has less pigment, are also at risk. Any activities in or near water—sitting by a pool, lying on the beach, boating—double the risk of sunburn, because children are hit by UV rays reflected up off the water as well as those streaming down from above. By the time a child's skin begins to feel warm and red, it's too late to prevent the sunburn. You have to think ahead and limit sun exposure before symptoms appear.

Made in the shade. First, protect your child's skin from direct exposure to sunlight, especially between 10 A.M. and 2:00 P.M., when sunlight is strongest and most harmful. Make sure your child wears protective clothing and a hat. A good rule is that if your shadow is shorter than you are, the sun is strong enough to burn you. Remember that ultraviolet rays can damage the skin and eyes even on hazy or cloudy days. Use an umbrella at the beach. Find a shady tree at a barbecue. Wear long-sleeve shirts, long pants, bonnets and caps, anything that will come between the skin and direct sunlight. Not all clothing blocks the sun well, and it is possible to get burned through a shirt. Water does not block the sun well either, so be especially cautious while swimming.

Sunscreen is a must. There are three effective chemicals in sunblocks or sunscreens: PABA esters, cinnamates, and benzophenones. Be sure that one or more of these are listed on the container. Sunscreens can irritate the skin of babies less than six months; it's best to keep them out of the sun. After six months, use one with a sun protection factor (SPF) of at least 15. This means that only one-fifteenth of the harmful rays get through, so fifteen minutes of sun exposure with sunscreen is the equivalent of one minute in the sun without it.

Use a waterproof sunscreen. Slather it on liberally at least a half hour before sun exposure, being sure not to miss any spots. Avoid the eyes, however; sunscreen stings. Reapply it frequently, every half hour or so. For a fair-skinned child who lives in a sunny climate, putting on sunblock cream or lotion should be part of his daily routine before leaving the house in the morning. And a second application should be done before he goes out to play after school.

Sunglasses. Everybody should wear sunglasses, even infants. The harmful effects of ultraviolet light on the eyes don't show up until much later in life, so you can't wait for problems to appear before practicing prevention. You don't need to buy expensive sunglasses, just so the label states that they block UV rays. The darkness of the lens has nothing to do with UV protection; the lenses must be coated with a special compound that specifically blocks out UV light. Baby shades are well tolerated by most infants, and the child gets used to wearing sunglasses.

PREVENTING INSECT BITES

Insect bites are always unpleasant and occasionally dangerous. West Nile virus is one example of an illness transmitted by mosquito bites that is spreading in the United States (see page 886.)

What you can do. Protect your child against insect bites by making sure his clothing covers as much skin as possible when the bugs are out in full force. Light-colored clothing is less attractive to bugs. Avoid heavily scented detergents and shampoos during the bug season. Use insect repellents designed for children. If the product contains DEET, the concentration for children should not exceed 10 percent. Keep the child's hands free of repellent so it doesn't get in his eyes or mouth. DEET may be harmful if ingested. Wash all repellent off when the child is back indoors.

Mosquitoes: Drain any standing water on your property to cut down on mosquitoes. Keep toddlers indoors at night, when mosquitoes arrive in full force. Keep doors closed, and repair damaged or missing screens.

Bees and wasps: When bees are about, avoid eating outdoors. Wash your children's hands after snacks to avoid attracting bees. It's safest to have nests removed professionally.

Ticks: Deer ticks, the carriers of Lyme disease, are very tiny creatures, the size of a pinhead. (Wood ticks, about the size of a small nail head, are more common and not harmful.) If you're not sure whether there is Lyme disease in your area, check with your doctor. You can also find a great deal of information on Lyme disease on the Centers for Disease Control (CDC) website, www.cdc.gov; click on Health Topics (and see page 859).

Protective clothing and DEET-containing repellants help, but you'll still need to check carefully for ticks after your child has been playing outside, especially in tall grass or near wooded areas. If you find one, the chances are good that it has not had a chance to transmit the disease. The best method for removing ticks is to use a tweezers to grab the tick as close to the skin as possible, then pull straight out. Don't use petroleum jelly (Vaseline), nail polish, or a hot match. Wash the skin with an antiseptic, and ask your child's doctor whether your child needs to take antibiotics.

PREVENTING DOG BITES

Children need to learn to leave strange dogs alone. Small children may be more likely to startle or hurt the animal and so are more likely to be bitten. Most of the people injured by dog bites are ten years old and younger.

The breeds most commonly associated with dog-related injuries, in order of frequency, are pit bulls, Rottweilers, and German shepherds. A combination of factors contributes to these injuries, including the behavior and upbringing of the dog, whether the dog is leashed, and the behavior of the child.

What you can do. Before you choose a family dog, read about the various breeds. Steer clear of aggressive or high-strung breeds. Spay or neuter your dog to reduce aggressive tendencies related to territorialism. Never leave infants or young children alone with any dog. (There is a series of wonderful wordless picture books about a dog named Carl who proves to be an excellent babysitter. Enjoy the books, but don't try it at home.)

Dog rules for children. A sensitive, anxious child may need lots of reassurance before he goes anywhere near a dog. A bold, fearless child may need to be taught specific rules for dealing with dogs. Here are some commonsense ones:

- Keep away from dogs you don't know, even if they're tied up.
- Always ask the owner before petting or playing with a dog.
- Never tease a dog, or stare directly into the eyes of a dog you don't know. Many dogs take staring as a threat or challenge.
- Don't disturb a dog who is sleeping, eating, or caring for puppies.
- If a dog comes near you, don't run away; he probably just wants to sniff you.
- If a dog knocks you over, curl up in a ball and stay still.
- Beware of dogs while biking or skating.

FIREWORKS AND TRICK OR TREAT

Holidays are exciting and often memorable but can also bring special hazards. Consider the Fourth of July and Halloween.

The Fourth of July. The use of fireworks on the Fourth of July results in almost six thousand injuries to children each year. These injuries usually involve the hands, fingers, eyes, or head, sometimes resulting in the loss of a finger or limb or in blindness. Children and fireworks are a bad combination. Fireworks are illegal in many states and are not recommended for personal use. Even sparklers, which seem so harmless, are a tragedy waiting to happen. Why take the risk? When viewing public fireworks displays, stay far away and protect the ears of small children from the loud explosions.

Halloween. Injuries on October 31 are often caused by falls, pedestrian mishaps, and burns and rarely by vampires and witches. Most important, make sure that costumes and masks don't obstruct your child's vision. Face paint or makeup is often safer than a mask. Trick or treaters should carry flashlights and not cut through yards where they may trip on items they cannot see. Shoes and costumes should fit so as not to cause tripping, and such items as fake swords and knives should be of flexible material that cannot cause injury. To prevent burns, make sure costumes, masks, beards, and wigs are made of flame-resistant materials. Clothing that is very loose is more likely to come into contact with candles (in a jack-o'-lantern, for example). Put reflective tape on bags and costumes so that cars can see trick or treaters. Remind children to obey all traffic rules and not to dart out between parked cars. Accompany young children and wait until arriving home before eating any treats. Children under age eight should not trick or treat without the supervision of an adult or older sibling. Instruct children to travel only on well-established routes, stop only at homes with outside lights on, and not to enter a home unless accompanied by an adult. In many neighborhoods, trick or treating is no longer considered safe. Halloween parties have become a popular alternative.

Part 2: Safety at Home

DANGERS AT HOME

Homes can be dangerous places for children. Drowning, after car crashes (the second-most common cause of injury-related death), often occurs in bathtubs and backyard pools. Burns, poisons, medications, choking, falls: it's enough to scare anyone. Of course, there's no point being scared; instead, be prepared. By childproofing your home, you can significantly lower your child's chance of injury. Close supervision is of course a must. Planning ahead is also critical. (Refer, too, to chapters "The First Year" and "Your Toddler" in Section I for additional detailed safety strategies for infants and toddlers.)

DROWNING AND WATER SAFETY

Drowning takes the lives of nearly a thousand children under age fourteen each year, ranking as the second leading cause of injury death to children in this age group. For every child who drowns, four are hospitalized after nearly drowning, many with permanent brain damage. Children under age four drown at a rate that is two to three times greater than other age groups.

For preschoolers, the bathtub is a major cause of drowning. Children have been known to crawl into a dry bathtub, turn on the faucet, and drown. Children can fall into a toilet or a pail of water headfirst and facedown and drown in just a few inches of water. Empty five-gallon buckets should not be left outside; they may collect rain water (breeding mosquitoes), and a child who falls in can drown. Keep toilet seats down; plastic latches can also keep out curious hands and heads.

Water safety. Prevention of drowning requires constant parental awareness and supervision. Emphasize these points with a babysitter as well.

- Never leave a child age five or younger alone in the bathtub, even for an instant. A child can drown in as little as an inch of water. Do not leave her in the tub in the care of a child who's under age twelve. If you absolutely must answer the phone or the doorbell, wrap the wet, soapy child in a towel and take her with you.

- Keep your eyes on your child when he is near the water, even if a lifeguard is present. If your child is an accomplished swimmer with enough skill and judgment to stay out of trouble, she can, at ages ten to twelve, swim without adult supervision if she always swims with a buddy. Do not permit her to dive unless the water is at least five feet deep and an adult is present.

- If you have a backyard wading pool, be sure to empty it and turn it upside down when not in use to prevent small children from drowning.

- If you have a swimming pool, it should be fenced on all sides. The fence should be at least five feet high with slats no more than four inches apart, and there should be a lock on the gate. The gate should be self-closing and self-latching. Don't consider a wall of the house as the fence on one side; it's too easy for a child to slip out through a door or window.

- Do not rely on pool alarms to warn you; they don't go off until someone is in the water, which may be too late. A better warning system is an alarm on the gate.

- Keep everyone away from pools or other bodies of water during thunderstorms.

- Stay away from frozen ponds and lakes unless the ice has officially been announced as safe for skating.

- Do not allow children to sled near water. Golf courses, a popular spot for sledding, often have bodies of water that are potentially dangerous.
- Wells and cisterns should be securely protected.

Swimming lessons. You might think that swimming lessons would protect infants, toddlers, and preschoolers from drowning, but there is no evidence that they do. Even with lessons, children up to age five just don't have enough strength and coordination to float or swim out of danger. Early lessons may even increase the risk of drowning by giving parents and children a false sense of security.

FIRE, SMOKE, AND BURNS

Fire is the second most common cause of death from injury in childhood. Children under five are at the greatest risk. Some 75 percent of fire-related deaths are actually from smoke inhalation, not burns. Approximately 80 percent of fire-related deaths occur in house fires. Half of house fires are due to cigarettes, another good reason not to smoke. Fire spreads rapidly, so don't leave young children alone in the house, even for a few minutes. If you have to go out, take them with you.

The most common nonfatal burn injuries are from scalding. About 20 percent are from tap water; 80 percent from spilled food or liquid. Half of scald burns are serious enough to require skin grafting.

What you can do. Take these simple steps to ensure long-term protection:

1. Install smoke detectors on each floor of your home in the hallways just outside sleeping areas and outside the kitchen. Change the batteries yearly (or when you reset your clocks for daylight saving time).

2. Keep a dry-chemical fire extinguisher in the kitchen.

3. Turn the temperature of your water heater down to 120. At 150 to 160 (most manufacturers' preset temperature), a small child will receive a third-degree burn in less than two seconds! At 120, it takes five minutes to produce a scald burn. (You'll also reduce your energy bill.) If you live in an apartment or condominium, ask your landlord or condominium association to turn the water heater down. You can still get your dishes clean in water at a temperature of less than 130. Antiscald devices can be installed in your shower, bathtub and sink fixtures to stop the flow when the temperature exceeds 120.

4. Open heaters, woodstoves, fireplaces, poorly insulated ovens, and easily opened broilers are dangerous. Place grilles or guards around or in front of woodstoves, fireplaces, and wall heaters. Install radiator covers to prevent burns.

5. Put electric outlet covers on all outlets to prevent children from shock if they insert something in them. Don't overload outlets.
6. Replace worn electric cords. Tightly tape the connections between cords and extension cords. Don't run cords under rugs or across walkways.

You can also lower the risk of fire and scald burns by adopting these prudent habits:

1. Always feel the temperature of bathwater immediately before putting the child in even if you did it earlier. Also, feel the faucets to make sure they're not hot enough to burn.
2. Never drink hot coffee or tea with a small child in your lap. Be sure that cups of hot coffee aren't near the edge of the table where a small child can reach up to pull them off. Avoid using tablecloths or placemats, which a small child can pull off the table.
3. Always point pot handles toward the rear of the stove. Using the back burners is preferable.
4. Keep matches in containers in high places that are impossible for even a determined three- or four-year-old to reach. At this age, many children go through a phase of being fascinated by fire. It's hard for them to resist the temptation to play with matches.
5. If you use space heaters, make sure that they aren't in contact with curtains, bedclothes, or towels.
6. Children's sleepwear for children nine months and older is required by law to be either flame-retardant or snug-fitting (clothing that fits snugly is less likely to catch fire, because oxygen cannot get under it). If sleepwear is washed repeatedly with nonphosphate detergent or soap with or without chlorine bleach, it may lose its flame-retardant property.

Finally, keep your children safe by teaching them what to do to prevent fires, and how to respond if one occurs.

1. Talk to toddlers about what is hot and warn them not to touch these things.
2. Discuss fire safety with young children. Include instructions to "Stop, drop, and roll" and "Crawl low under the smoke."
3. Teach your children that if they smell smoke and suspect a fire, they should immediately get out of the house. They can call the fire department from a neighbor's phone.
4. Make a fire evacuation plan with two escape routes from each bedroom, and choose a designated meeting place outdoors. Have the whole family practice evacuating.

POISONS

It is amazing and horrifying what young children will put in their mouths. Among the substances that most frequently cause dangerous poisoning in children are aspirin and other medicines, insect and rat poisons, kerosene, gasoline, benzene, cleaning fluids, liquid furniture polish, auto polish, lye, other alkalis used for cleaning drains, toilet bowls, and ovens, oil of wintergreen, and plant sprays. Potentially harmful substances in the bathroom include perfume, shampoo, hair tonic, home permanent and beauty preparations.

There are over two million calls each year to poison control centers about children who have ingested possible poisons. Every medicine, prescription item, vitamin, and household product should be considered poisonous to your child. Even medicines that your child may take regularly can be dangerous if they are taken in large quantities. Some substances are dangerous, though they may not seem so: tobacco (one ingested cigarette is dangerous for a one-year-old), aspirin, vitamin pills containing iron, nail-polish remover, perfume, and dishwasher detergent. It is always best to be certain by calling the poison control center or your doctor or nurse practitioner for advice.

From about twelve months to five years is when children are at greatest risk. Children under age six account for more than half of all poisonings. More poisonings happen in the home than anywhere else. A child who is active, bold, and persistent is more likely to get hold of a poison, but even quiet toddlers who seem to prefer to stay in one place can find opportunities—an open bottle of pills or an irresistible house plant—to swallow something they shouldn't.

Childproofing your home. The first step is to inspect your house with an eagle eye or rather a child's eye. Then follow these steps to childproof your home against poisoning.

1. Post the poison control center phone number, 800 222-1222, by your telephone, or write it on a piece of paper and tape it to the phone. If possible, program it as a one-touch number as well. If your child does swallow a poison or something that *might* be poisonous, call that number for instant expert advice.

2. Store potentially hazardous medications out of reach or in a cabinet with a childproof lock or latch. Simple hook-and-eye latches may be installed high up on bathroom doors to prevent a child from exposure to the hazards associated with the bathroom, which include poisoning, drowning and hot-water burns.

3. Find safe places in the kitchen bathroom and utility room to store cleaning fluids and powders; detergents; drain, toilet bowl, and oven cleaners; ammonia; bleach; wax remover; metal polish; borax; mothballs; lighter fluid; shoe polish; and other dangerous substances. A safe place is a cabinet that locks or one that is high up and has nothing

near it that a child can climb on. Get rid of rat poisons, and insect pastes, and poisons. They are just too dangerous.

4. In the basement or garage, find truly safe places for turpentine, paint thinners, kerosene, gasoline, benzene, insecticides, plant sprays, weed killers, antifreeze, and car cleaners and polishes. Before you discard the containers, empty them and rinse them out. Check with your city or county sanitation department for instructions on disposing of hazardous waste.

5. In the past, parents were advised to keep on hand a bottle of syrup of ipecac, a medicine that causes vomiting. The idea was to give the ipecac to a child who had swallowed poison, to make him throw it up. New research has shown that using ipecac doesn't actually help in the treatment of poisoning, and can sometimes make things worse. It's best to get rid of any ipecac you might have at home.

Helpful habits. Effective prevention of poisoning depends on what you do every day. Here are some things to think about:

- Put medicine safely out of reach immediately after each use. A cabinet or drawer with a childproof latch is best.
- Put bold, clear labels on medicines so that you won't give your child the wrong one. Flush medicine down the toilet after an illness is over. It's unlikely you'll use it again, and it may deteriorate. It's confusing to have old medicines in with others still in use.
- More than a third of medicine poisonings are from children taking their grandparents' prescription drugs. Check to be sure the grandparents' medicines are locked away or out of reach before visiting them.
- Federal and state laws require that all medicines dispensed by a pharmacist come in childproof containers. Don't put medicine in another container.

- Keep cleaning supplies and other chemicals in their original containers. Don't put plant spray in a soft drink bottle or oven cleaner in a cup; this is a frequent cause of serious injuries.

Poisonous plants. We think of plants and flowers as merely beautiful. Crawling babies and small children think of them as a tasty snack. This is a dangerous combination of attitudes, for many plants and flowers—over seven hundred of them—can cause illness or death. The best rule is to have no plants or flowers in the house until children are past the eat-everything stage and can accept prohibitions. At the least, place plants out of reach. Watch small children when they are around plants and flowers in the garden or away from home.

Here is a partial list of potentially fatal plants: caladium, diffenbachia, philodendron, elephant's ear, English ivy, hyacinth, daffodil, narcissus, mistletoe, oleander, poinsettia, rosary pea, castor bean, delphinium, larkspur, belladonna, foxglove, lily of the valley, azalea, laurel, rhododendron, daphne berries, golden chain, hydrangea, jessamine berries, privet (hedges), yew, jimsonweed (thorn apple), morning glory seeds, mushrooms, nightshade, holly berries.

Some plants are toxic but not fatal; they will cause skin irritation if touched or swelling of lips and tongue if ingested. Be able to identify poison ivy, poison oak, and poison sumac to avoid the painful irritation of an allergic reaction.

Your local poison control center or health department can tell you if a plant in your house or yard is poisonous or toxic.

LEAD AND MERCURY

The danger of lead poisoning. Lead is a metal that is everywhere in our industrial world, including—until recently—house paint, gasoline, and food cans. We've known for a long time that lead serves no purpose in the human body, in contrast to other metals, such as iron and copper, which are essential for life. But only in the last twenty or so years have we understood how really bad lead is, especially for children. At very high levels, lead causes obvious brain damage and other severe illness. Even at at very low levels, it's likely that lead has negative effects, on average, on children's learning.

I stress the words, *on average* because the effects of low-level lead are hard to see in any given child. Only when scientists study hundreds or thousands of children together does it become clear that lead lowers children's IQ's. In other words, if a child has a slightly elevated blood lead level—in the range of ten to twenty micrograms per deciliter—no one can say for sure whether the lead will affect that specific child. Plenty of very smart people had high lead levels in childhood. That doesn't mean we can forget about lead, only that you don't need to panic if your child's lead is slightly high.

Who gets it and how. Lead poisoning is mostly a problem for young children, age one through five, who crawl around the floor and often put things other than food into their mouths. Children who are hungry or low on iron absorb more lead. So good general nutrition is important to prevent lead poisoning.

The source of lead is often old paint around windows or on outside walls. As the paint crumbles, lead gets into dust, which children get on their hands. Other sources include pottery with lead glazes (modern machine-made pottery does not contain lead), lead in the water pipes leading to older buildings, and some traditional medicines.

What to do. If you live in housing built before 1980 or in a city where there is a lot of lead poisoning, your children should have their blood-lead levels checked regularly in their early years. For high levels, doctors prescribe medicine to remove the lead from the body; for lower levels, the main treatment is to remove the lead from the environment, make sure the child has plenty of iron, and allow the child's body to get rid of the lead on its own. Some tips for dealing with lead include:

- Check for peeling or cracking paint, especially around windows and doors. Remove whatever comes off easily, then cover with new paint.
- Don't try to remove lead paint by stripping, sanding, or using a heat gun; these methods dramatically *increase* lead exposure. If you have to remove lead-containing paint, have a professional do it while you and your child are out of the house.
- Mop floors regularly with a high-phosphate cleaning solution to pick up lead dust.
- Pay attention to all the places your child spends time: your home, outside, your porch, the sitter's or day-care center.
- If you have older plumbing (a home built before 1950), let the cold water run for a few minutes before using it for drinking or cooking. That way, you don't use water that has been sitting for a long time in the pipes collecting lead. (Boiling water doesn't remove lead; it only makes the problem worse.)
- Avoid glazed pottery unless you are sure it is lead-free.
- Be careful about using folk medicines made from old recipes (medicines your grandmother swears by, perhaps); some of them contain lead.

Learn more! If you have lead in your environment, you need to know much more than there is space for here. Talk to your child's doctor. Pick up brochures from your local health department. Visit the internet sites listed in the Resource Guide (page 917).

Mercury. Mercury is like lead in many ways: Both are metals, both are common in our industrial world, and both cause brain damage at high levels and abnormal brain development even at low levels. Mercury from factories and mines makes its way into lakes and oceans. From there it is picked up by microscopic organisms, little fish, bigger fish, and the ultimate consumers: us. For this reason, avoid eating a lot of fish in pregnancy and while breast-feeding. Fish caught in highly polluted waters and large predator fish (such as swordfish) whose long lives allow them to accumulate mercury are probably best avoided altogether.

Another source of mercury is the mercury thermometer. When thermometer break, the lovely beads of liquid mercury give off an odorless vapor that is poisonous. It's best to treat your glass thermometer like the toxic waste it is: Don't just throw it out; bring it to your doctor's office or a hospital for proper disposal. Then buy a cheap, accurate, safe digital thermometer (see page 704).

CHOKING

Choking is the fourth leading cause of death in young children. A baby or small child who puts things in her mouth should not have small objects (like buttons, beans, and beads) within reach. These are easily breathed (aspirated) into the windpipe, causing choking.

Dangerous toys. Children under age five are most at risk of choking on toys or their parts. Children of any age who put non-food items in their mouths can choke on them. A good test is to take a standard toilet paper tube. If a toy is small enough to fit inside the tube, it's small enough to be a choking hazard. The Consumer Products Safety Commission makes a similar device called a No Choke Test Tube that is a bit smaller than a toilet paper tube. Any item that fails the No Choke Tube test will also fail the toilet paper tube test.

Look, also, for any small parts that might break off a toy in rough play. Pull at the parts yourself. Small balls or dice (from children's toys and games) are also a common item that children under the age of three choke on. Keeping a child's toys away from a younger sibling or visitor to your home is always a challenge.

One of the items that most commonly cause choking are broken balloon pieces, which are easily inhaled. Children can also choke on the pieces of a balloon they blow up if it bursts. For this reason, it's best to keep balloons away from small children.

Choking on foods. By age four or five, most children are able to handle the same foods that adults can. Before that, you have to be very careful with certain foods. Round, hard slippery foods, such as nuts, hard candies, carrots, popcorn, grapes and raisins, are especially dangerous to young children. Hot dogs can plug up the windpipe like a stopper in a bottle. One of the most dangerous foods is peanut butter eaten from a spoon or knife. When it's aspirated, nothing can remove it from the lungs. It should always be spread thin on bread.

An excellent way to prevent choking on large pieces of food is to chew and chew well. Children can be taught to chew well; and if you set an example, they will most likely follow, especially if not rushed. Take away lollipops and popsicles if your child runs with them in his mouth. Don't let your child lie down while eating, and never leave a baby alone with a propped-up bottle.

See page 791 for first aid for choking.

SUFFOCATION AND STRANGULATION

In children under age one, suffocation is the leading cause of death from unintentional injury. An infant spends a majority of his time in the crib, so steps should be taken to make sure this is a safe environment. See pages 36 and 60 for guidelines on preventing suffocation in infants.

Toddlers can strangle themselves in cords hanging from curtains, blinds, or appliances. Tie cords up, wrap them around cleats mounted on the wall, hide them behind heavy furniture, or use cord shorteners (little plastic devices to wrap the cords tightly around).

For older children, it's important to be aware of the risk of plastic bags. For some reason, many children have the urge to play with plastic bags by putting them over their heads, occasionally with tragic results. Keep all plastic bags stored where you have your other hazardous household materials, in a locked or inaccessible cabinet or drawer.

If you have an unused refrigerator or freezer or are discarding one, be sure to take the door off.

GUNS IN THE HOME

Many families own handguns or rifles. Parents often feel they need a gun for protection, though every study shows that children (and adults) are much more likely to be killed by a gun already in their home than by a criminal who breaks in. Every day in this country, a child is unintentionally killed by a gun. The safest thing by far to do with a gun is not to own it in the first place.

Very young children can become victims of unintentional gun deaths if they play with loaded guns or are with other children who do. Children ages seven to ten who want to show off a gun to their friends may inadventently end up as either shooter or victim. You may be reluctant to ask the parents of your children's playmates if they have a gun, but tragic statistics tell us that you should do so.

Older children and adolescents, especially as they begin to experiment with drinking, may lack self-control and take stupid risks if a gun is accessible. In addition, teenagers who are depressed or using drugs are at higher risk for suicide if there is a gun in the home.

If there is a gun in your home. Rifles and handguns should be stored unloaded, preferably in a locked cabinet, with the ammunition locked away in a separate place. In addition to completing a gun safety program offered by local police or a gun club, gun owners should investigate newer safety technologies such as trigger locks or "smart" guns, which can be fired only by the gun owner.

FALLS

Falls are the sixth leading cause of injury death and are the leading cause of nonfatal injury. The highest death rate from falls is during the first year of life. Three million children are treated in emergency rooms for fall-related injuries every year, and for every child who is treated, at least ten fall but don't seek medical attention.

Falls occur in as many places as you can imagine: from beds, changing tables, windows and porches, trees, bicycles and play equipment, on ice, down stairs, and so on. Toddlers are especially at risk for falls from windows and down stairs; older children are at risk of falling from rooftops and playground or recreational equipment. The majority of falls in the home are of children age four and under. The peak hours for falls in the home are around mealtimes; 40 percent occur between 4 and 8 P.M.

Stairs. To prevent toddlers from falling down stairs, gates should be installed at the top and bottom of stairs, including porch steps, until the child can go up and down steadily. Teach children to use handrails when going up or down stairs, and let them see you taking the same precaution. To avoid falls in winter, keep walkways free of ice by using rock salt or sand.

Falls out of windows. Window falls occur most frequently in the spring and summer and in urban environments. Window falls are most common from the second and third story; the most serious falls occur above the third story. There are many ways to prevent children from falling out of windows. You can keep them locked, of course, but that's undesirable in good weather. You can move all toys and furniture away from windows. But once a child is big enough to push a chair over, this solution won't work. If possible, open windows from the top.

If you're good with tools or have a handy friend, metal stopper devices can be attached to the window frame to prevent the window from opening more than four inches (or use blocks of wood to do the same thing).

You can also install window guards. These are metal gates that have a maximum of four inches between the bars and can withstand one hundred fifty pounds of pressure. Place guards on all the windows in a room. But at least one window must have a guard that can be opened or removed without use of a special key or tool (which would probably be lost the one time you need it the most, such as during a fire). Child safety window guards

are not the same as burglar bars, which are meant to keep grown people from getting in. Some states and cities have laws requiring the use of window guards.

Baby walkers. Once considered a necessary piece of infant equipment, the walker is now seen as a menace. Walkers give a great deal of mobility to infants who have no perception of the risks. They can easily walk right off the stairs and have no way to break their fall. All it takes is for a parent to turn his back for an instant. Many thousands of babies are hurt this way each year.

Walkers don't teach babies to walk. In fact, babies who rely on walkers are often slow to develop the strength and coordination needed to walk on their own, because the walker does all the work for them. Walkers without wheels (standers, you might say) are becoming popular. They can give a child a sense of independence without the risk of falls. Make sure there are no exposed springs to pinch the baby's fingers.

TOY SAFETY

Every year, thousands of children are injured by their toys and hundreds of toys are recalled because they prove dangerous. Always observe age recommendations when purchasing toys for children. Manufacturers are now required by federal law to place warning labels on toys with small parts, but many unlabeled toys slip through the cracks. Such toys as marbles, balloons, and small blocks present a choking hazard for children age three and under or any child who tends to put objects in his mouth. Toys with sharp points or edges may cause a young child to stab or cut himself or another person. Propelled toys, such as toy darts and projectiles, can injure eyes. Electric toys should be used only by children eight or older. Toys made from soft plastic contain chemicals called phthalates that can cause kidney damage and other health problems. If you're unsure about whether a product contains phthalates, call the manufacturer.

Even your child's toy *chest* can be a hazard. Make sure yours has a lid support, so it won't come down hard on your child's head. And it should not have a lock, which could trap a child inside.

You can learn much more about toy safety on the Consumer Products Safety Commission website, www.cpsc.gov, and on another very helpful website, www.toysafety.net.

HOME SAFETY EQUIPMENT

What to buy? Gizmo makers love to sell safety equipment to nervous parents. My favorite is the rubber bathtub spout cover in the shape of an elephant's trunk. This item scores high for cuteness, even if it doesn't add much security. Only a few things are absolutely necessary for home safety. These include working smoke detectors with fresh batteries, a fire extinguisher in the kitchen, locked cabinets for medications and other dangerous chemicals, and if you own a gun or rifle a trigger lock and locked storage cabinet. For stairs in your home, gates at the top and bottom can prevent tumbles. If your home is on the second floor or above, you may need window guards.

The list below contains several other items that aren't costly that you might find useful. Most are mentioned in the sections above. Remember that nothing is a substitute for close adult supervision.

- Childproof cabinet and drawer latches in the kitchen and bathroom.
- Hook-and-eye door latches, mounted high on the door, to keep young children out of bathrooms, stair wells or areas where dangerous cleaners or tools are stored.
- Velcro latches to keep toddlers out of hard-to-lock objects such as refrigerators, toilets, or sliding cabinets.
- Cord shorteners to prevent children from putting long cords around their necks.

- A reusable water temperature gauge to ensure that your hot water is no hotter than 120.
- Spring-loaded outlet covers to prevent shocks. (Spring-loaded covers, which mount permanently to the wall, are better than the little plastic plugs; they don't get lost, can't be swallowed, and automatically block off the outlet when you take out the plug.)
- Corner cushions on coffee tables to soften a blow.

The U.S. Consumer Product Safety Commission can answer your questions or respond to your concerns about the safety of any product you own or are considering buying (www.cpsc.gov or 800 638-2772).

FIRST AID AND EMERGENCIES

⸎

CUTS AND SCRATCHES

The best treatment for scratches and small cuts is to wash them with soap and warm water. Careful washing is the key to preventing infection. After drying the cut with a clean towel, cover it with a bandage so it will remain clean until healed. Wash the cut once a day until it has completely healed.

For large cuts that spread open, consult your doctor. Some larger cuts will require stitches to close the wound and lessen the chance of a disfiguring scar. It is important to keep the stitches clean and dry until they are removed. Inspect the wound each day for signs of infection, such as increased pain, swelling, redness, or drainage from the wound. Many cuts now are closed using tissue adhesives that are faster than sutures, just as effective, and require no needles.

Wounds that may be contaminated by dirt or soil or caused by dirty objects, such as knives, should be reported to your doctor. The doctor may recommend a tetanus booster, especially for deep cuts or puncture wounds. If your child has completed the initial series of four DTaP immunizations and had a booster no more than five years ago, he may not need one. It is always best to check with your physician if you are uncertain.

Occasionally, a wound occurs from a fall on broken glass or

wood. A splinter or bit of glass, wood, or gravel may remain in the wound. Unless you can easily remove the fragments, it's best to have a physician evaluate these cuts. An X-ray may show foreign matter. Any cut that does not heal properly or becomes infected (with redness, pain, or drainage) may have foreign matter inside.

SPLINTERS

Next to small cuts and bruises, splinters are probably the most common minor injury of childhood. Try the soak-and-poke approach: Wash the area with soap and water, then soak it in fairly hot water for at least ten minutes. Use a hot compress if you can't cover the area with water. (You'll have to reheat the water or compress every couple of minutes.) If the splinter sticks out of the skin, grasp it with a good pair of tweezers and gently pull it out. If the splinter is entirely under the skin, you'll need a sewing needle that's been wiped with rubbing alcohol. The soaking softens the skin so that you can gently prick it open with the tip of the needle, opening enough skin so that you can grasp the splinter with the tweezers. After the splinter is out, wash the area with soap and water and cover the area with a clean bandage.

Don't poke at the skin too much. If you can't get the splinter out after the first soak, give it another ten minutes of hot soaking and then try again. If you still can't get it, have your doctor take over.

BITES

Animal or human bites. The mouths of all animals, including humans, contain many bacteria that can cause infection. A bite usually results in a deep puncture wound, which may be more difficult to clean than a simple cut. A physician should be notified of all bites that break the skin. Meanwhile, first aid is the same as for cuts. Wash the wound with running water and soap for several minutes.

The most common complication of an animal or human bite is infection by bacteria. To prevent an infection from developing, your doctor or nurse practitioner may prescribe an antibiotic at the time of the initial treatment. Even if your child has been given an antibiotic, notify the doctor if you see signs of infection, such as redness, swelling, tenderness, or drainage.

Rabies, a life-threatening infection, may result from animal bites. Bites by foxes, raccoons, and bats should be considered as potentially rabies-producing. If they have not been immunized, domestic animals, such as dogs and cats, can also transmit the rabies virus. You rarely need to worry about gerbils, hamsters, or guinea pigs carrying rabies. There is no treatment for rabies once the infection has developed, but it can be prevented by special vaccines given as soon as possible after the bite.

Your doctor can advise you on the best course of treatment for all types of animal bites and whether rabies vaccination is needed. Another resource for information on the risk of rabies infection is your local board of health or state department of public health. They may also assist you by observing the animal after the bite to be certain it does not have rabies symptoms.

Insect bites. Most don't need treatment, but watch for signs of infection (see page 781) that can follow as a result of scratching. After a bee sting, see if the stinger is still in the skin; if it is, gently scrape the area with a credit card or other piece of plastic. Don't use tweezers: You might squeeze more venom into the skin. Gently clean the area and apply ice to prevent or reduce swelling.

For an insect bite that itches, apply a paste made by mixing a few drops of water with a teaspoonful of baking soda (bicarbonate of soda). Oral antihistamine (diphenhydramine; trade name Benadryl, nonprescription) can reduce itching; antihistamines make some children tired, others become hyper, and others are unaffected. The best strategy is prevention (see page 752).

BLEEDING

Minor wounds. Most wounds bleed a little for a few minutes. This is helpful because the bleeding washes out some of the germs that were introduced. Only profuse or persistent bleeding requires special treatment. To stop the bleeding of most cuts, apply direct pressure while elevating the wound. Have the child lie down and put a pillow or two under the limb. If the wound continues to bleed freely, press on it with a sterile gauze square or clean cloth until the bleeding stops. Clean and bandage the wound while the limb is still elevated.

To bandage a cut that bled a lot or is still bleeding, place several gauze squares (or folded pieces of clean cloth) on top of each other so that you have a thick pad on the cut. After you snugly apply the adhesive or gauze roll bandage, it will exert more pressure on the cut, making it less likely to bleed again.

Severe bleeding. If a wound bleeds at an alarming rate, you must stop it immediately. Apply direct pressure to the wound and elevate the limb if possible. Make a pad of the cleanest material you have handy, a gauze square, clean handkerchief, or the cleanest piece of clothing on the child or yourself. Press the pad against the wound and keep pressing until help arrives or the bleeding stops. Don't remove your original pad. As it becomes soaked through, add new material on top. If the bleeding eases up and you have suitable material, apply a pressure bandage.

The pad over the wound should be thick enough to press on the wound when it is bandaged. If the pressure bandage fails to control the bleeding, continue hand pressure directly on the wound. If you have no cloth or material of any kind to press against a profusely bleeding wound, press your hands on the edges of the wound or even in it.

Most hemorrhages can be stopped by simple direct pressure. If you are dealing with one that doesn't stop, continue to apply direct pressure and have someone call an ambulance. While awaiting the ambulance, have the patient lie down, keep her warm, and elevate her legs and the injured body part.

Nosebleeds. There are a number of simple remedies for stopping a nosebleed. Having a child sit still for a few minutes is often sufficient. Keep him from blowing his nose or pressing and squeezing it with his handkerchief. You can sometimes stop a severe nosebleed by gently pinching the nostrils for five minutes. (Look at your watch; five minutes is an eternity in these circumstances.) Let go slowly and gently. If the nosebleed continues for ten minutes after these measures, get in touch with the doctor.

Nosebleeds are most frequently caused by trauma to the nose, repeated nose-picking, allergies, or colds or other infections. If a child has repeated nosebleeds from no apparent cause, he needs to be examined by the doctor or nurse practitioner. If a child has persistent nosebleeds it may be necessary to cauterize (seal) an exposed blood vessel that constantly breaks. Your doctor can easily do this in his office, usually just after the nose has stopped bleeding.

Nosebleeds in infants are not common. They should be reported to your doctor or nurse practitioner.

BURNS

Burn severity. Burns come in three categories. Burns of only the most superficial layer of the skin usually produce only redness in the area; these are often called first-degree burns. Partial thickness burns affect the deeper layers of the skin and usually result in the formation of blisters; these are also called second-degree burns. Full-thickness burns affect the deepest layers of the skin, often damaging nerves and blood vessels beneath the skin; these are third-degree burns. Full-thickness burns are serious injuries, that often require a skin graft. The size of the burn is also important. A superficial burn over much of the body (as with a sunburn) is often enough to make a child feel very ill.

Minor burns. Burns usually result from accidental contact with hot water; hot oil, grease, and other substances can also burn the skin. For minor burns, hold the burned area under cold running water for several minutes until the area feels numbed. Don't use ice; freezing can worsen the injury. Never apply ointment, grease, butter, cream, or petroleum product: they may hold in the heat. After rinsing the burn with water, cover the area with a bulky sterile dressing. This will reduce the pain from the burn.

If blisters form, leave them intact. As long as a blister is unbroken, the fluid inside is sterile. When you open one, you allow germs to enter the wound. If a blister does break, it is better to remove the loose skin with nail scissors or tweezers that have been boiled for five minutes to sterilize them. Then cover with a sterile bandage. A doctor or nurse practitioner should see any blister that has broken and may prescribe a special antibiotic ointment to prevent infection. If the blister remains intact but shows signs of infection—pus, for example, or redness around it—consult your doctor or nurse practitioner. Never put iodine or other antiseptic on a burn unless directed to do so by your doctor or nurse practitioner.

It's especially important that a physician or nurse practitioner see all burns on the face, hands, feet, and genital area. Delays in treatment can lead to scars or functional impairment. Mild sunburns are the exception.

Sunburn. The best treatment for sunburn is not to get it in the first place (see page 750). Severe sunburn is painful, dangerous, and unnecessary. A half hour of direct sunshine at a beach in summer is enough to cause a burn on a fair-skinned person who is unprepared for the sun.

To relieve sunburn, apply a cool compress and give a mild nonaspirin pain reliever, such as ibuprofen or acetaminophen. If blisters develop, treat them as described in the previous section. A person with a moderately severe burn may have chills and fever and feel ill. You should then consult a doctor or nurse practitioner, since sunburn can be just as serious as a heat burn. Keep sunburned areas completely protected from sunshine until the redness is gone.

Electrical injuries. Most electrical injuries in children occur in the home and are relatively minor. The degree of injury is directly proportional to the amount of current that passes through the child. Water or moisture of any kind increases the risk of significant injury. For this reason, no electrical device should ever be operated in the bathroom while a child is washing or bathing.

Most electrical injuries produce a shock that causes the child to pull his hand back before any damage is done. In a more significant injury, your child may develop a burn with a blister or area of redness. You may also see an area of charred tissue, which is dead skin. First aid for these injuries is the same as for burns caused by heat (see page 779).

An electrical current can travel through nerves and blood vessels. If your child has both an entrance and exit wound, the current may have damaged nerves and blood vessels along the way. If your child has neurologic symptoms, such as numbness, tingling, or pain, she should be examined by a doctor.

Occasionally children will get an electrical burn after they bite into an electrical cord, perhaps a small burn near the corner of the mouth. Children with this type of burn need to be evaluated by a physician. Since any burn may leave a scar, the child may need special care to avoid developing one that might interfere with his ability to smile or chew.

SKIN INFECTIONS

Minor skin infections. Look for redness, swelling, warmth, pain, or pus. If a child has a boil, an infection at the end of his finger, or an infected cut of any type, it should be examined by the doctor or nurse practitioner. If there is a delay in getting medical care, the best first aid treatment is to soak the infected area in warm water or apply warm, wet dressings. This softens the skin, hastening the time when it breaks to allow the pus to escape. The warm water will then keep the opening from closing too soon. Place a fairly thick bandage over the infection, pouring enough warm water onto it to make it thoroughly wet. Let it soak for twenty minutes, then replace the wet bandage with a clean, dry one. Repeat this wet soak three or four times a day while you try to reach the doctor or nurse practitioner. If you have an antibiotic ointment apply it over the affected area. This should not replace a visit to the doctor.

More serious skin infections. Signs that an infection is spreading seriously include fever, red streaks starting from the site of infection, or tender lymph glands in the armpit or groin. Get the child to a doctor, nurse practitioner, or hospital at once: Intravenous antibiotics are vitally important to combat serious infections.

OBJECTS IN NOSE AND EARS

Small children often stuff things—beads, small pieces from toys or games, or wads of paper—into their noses or ears. Using a pair of tweezers, you may be able to grasp a soft object that isn't too far in. Don't go after a smooth, hard object; you are almost certain to push it farther in. If your child won't sit still, be careful with sharp tweezers; they may cause more damage than the foreign object itself. Even if you can't see the object, it may still be there.

Sometimes an older child may be able to expel the object by blowing her nose, but don't try this if she's so young that she sniffs when told to blow. The child may sneeze the object out in a little while. If you have a decongestant nose spray, squirt a little in the child's nose before having her blow her nose. If the object stays in, take the child to your doctor or nurse practitioner or to a nose specialist. Foreign objects that remain in the nose for several days usually cause a bad-smelling discharge tinged with blood. A discharge of this kind from one nostril should always make you think of this possibility.

OBJECTS IN THE EYE

To remove specks of dirt or grit in the eye, try having the child hold his eye open in a pan or sink of water, and blink several times. Pulling the upper lid down and out can help. If you can see a grain of dirt, you may be able to use a moistened cotton swab to gently brush it out. If the feeling of grittiness persists for more than thirty minutes, seek medical care. If the eye was hit forcefully or by a sharp object, or if there is pain, cover both eyes with a damp cloth and go for help immediately.

SPRAINS AND STRAINS

Sprain and strain are the terms used to describe a stretched or torn ligament, tendon, or muscle. Muscles are attached to the bone by thick, cordlike fibers known as tendons. Ligaments are the strong tissues that provide support for joints. Falls, sports injuries, and unusual twists and turns can produce a sprain or a strain. A sprain may be serious, requiring as much treatment as a broken bone.

If your child sprains an ankle, knee, or wrist, have him lie down for a half hour and elevate the sprained limb on a pillow. Put an ice pack on the injury. Applying cold immediately helps to prevent swelling and reduce the pain. If the pain resolves and your child can resume normal movement of the injured area without discomfort, there is no need to see a doctor or nurse practitioner.

If swelling occurs or the area is very tender, consult your doctor or nurse practitioner. A bone may have been cracked or broken. Even if an X-ray is normal, your child may require a cast or splint to immobilize the injury and allow the ligaments and tendons to heal properly. For a few days after the injury, it's wise to limit weight-bearing exercise, but you should allow some movement of the injured joint. The doctor may prescribe specific exercises. It's important to follow these instructions; excessive movement of the sprained area may reinjure the ligaments, leading to more pain or further susceptibility to chronic injuries, and complete immobility may cause residual stiffness and a reduced range of motion.

Elbow injury in toddlers. A common complaint is when a toddler suddenly refuses to use his arm, letting it hang limply at his side. This often happens right after the arm has been pulled sharply, as when the parent catches the child by the hand to prevent a fall. One of the bones at the elbow has been dislocated. A physician who recognizes toddler's elbow can usually painlessly pop the joint into place.

FRACTURES

Children's bones are different. A fracture is a broken or splintered bone. Broken bones in children may differ from those in adults. Children may fracture or break the growth center of the bone, typically found at the end of long bones, thus interfering with future growth. Only one side of a bone may break (greenstick fractures), or children may have the typical adult pattern, a crack through both surfaces of a bone.

It may be hard to tell whether an injury is a sprain or a fracture. If there is an obvious deformity—an arm bent at an odd angle—there's little doubt that the bone is broken. Often, however, the only signs are mild swelling or tenderness. Bruising at the site of injury or pain that persists for days suggests a fracture. Often the only way to be sure is to take X-rays.

If you suspect a fracture, avoid further injury by preventing movement to that area. Acetaminophen, ibuprofen, or aspirin can reduce pain. If possible, apply a splint and ice and take your child to the doctor.

Broken wrists. A very common childhood injury is a broken wrist, which may occur when the child falls from a jungle gym or slips on the ice and lands with his arm outstretched. The wrist hurts right away, but because the pain may not be severe, several days often go by before the child is taken to the doctor.

An X-ray confirms the diagnosis, and a cast takes care of the problem.

Splinting. Splinting reduces pain and prevents further damage from movement of the broken bones until you get to a doctor. To be most effective, a splint needs to hold the limb motionless both above and below the injury. For an ankle injury, the splint should reach to the knee; for a break in the lower leg, it should go up to the hip; for a broken wrist, the splint should go from the fingertips to the elbow; for a broken lower or upper arm, it should go from the fingertips to the armpit.

You need a board to make a long splint. You can make a short splint for a small child by folding a piece of cardboard. Move the limb with extreme gentleness when you apply the splint and avoid movement near the area of the injury. Tie the limb to the splint snugly in four to six places, using handkerchiefs, strips of clothing, or bandages. Two of the ties should be close to the break, on either side of it, and there should be one at each end of the splint. After you apply the splint, place an ice bag on the area of the injury. Never apply ice (without a bag) directly to an injury, and as a general rule, apply ice for no more than twenty minutes at a time. For a broken collarbone (at the top of the chest in front), make a sling from a large triangle of cloth and tie it behind the child's neck so that it supports the lower arm across the chest.

NECK AND BACK INJURIES

The spinal cord is a thick bundle of nerves that connects the brain to the rest of the body. Damage to the cord can result in permanent paralysis and loss of control over bladder and bowel functions and either loss of sensation or ongoing pain. The spinal cord runs inside a protective column formed by the bones of the neck and back, the vertebral column.

If the vertebral column has been damaged in a fall or other impact, the nerves of the cord are also in danger, either from the original trauma or from attempts to move the child afterward.

Therefore, *never* try to move a person after an injury that *may* have damaged the neck or back. This includes any trauma in which the child has lost consciousness and any serious high-impact injury. Instead, make the child comfortable and keep her quiet until an ambulance arrives. Only a specially trained health-care professional should move a child suspected of having a neck or back injury.

If the child *must* be moved and professional help has not arrived, one person should hold the child's head and neck in a neutral position. When the child is being moved her head and neck should be kept in this exact position at all times. Never turn the body separately from the head. These maneuvers will reduce the chance of further injury to the spinal cord.

HEAD INJURIES

Even before a baby has begun to walk, she may suffer a head injury by rolling off a bed or changing counter. If she cries immediately but stops crying within fifteen minutes, keeps a good color, doesn't vomit, acts as if nothing has happened, and doesn't develop significant swelling on her head, there is little chance that she has suffered an injury to her brain. A swelling that puffs out quickly on a child's forehead after a fall isn't serious in itself as long as there are no other symptoms. It was caused by a broken blood vessel just under the skin. Swellings on other parts of the skull may be a sign of broken bones.

When a head injury is more severe, the child is likely to vomit, lose her appetite, be pale for several hours, show signs of headache and dizziness, alternate between agitation and lethargy, and seem sleepier than usual. If a child has *any* of these symptoms, get in touch with your doctor or nurse practitioner so she can examine the child. Any child who lost consciousness after a fall should certainly be examined by a doctor immediately, even if there are no other symptoms.

After any head injury, a child should be observed closely for the next twenty-four to forty-eight hours. Bleeding under the bones of the scalp can put pressure on the brain, causing symptoms that are not obvious at first but develop over a day or two. Any change in behavior, especially increased sleepiness, agitation, or dizziness, is a red flag.

Finally, keep an eye on your child's performance in school, after a head injury. Children who have a concussion—that is, a head injury with loss of consciousness or memory of the incident—may develop difficulty with concentration or learning.

For dental injury, see page 812.

SWALLOWED OBJECTS

Objects that aren't food often pass through a child's stomach and intestines without difficulty. They may not even be noticed. However, they may become stuck somewhere in the digestive tract, usually the esophagus (the tube between the throat and stomach). The objects that are most likely to cause problems are needles, straight pins, coins, and button batteries. These can cause coughing or choking, the sensation of having something caught in the throat, pain or difficulty with swallowing, refusal to eat, drooling, or persistent vomiting.

If your child has swallowed a smooth object, like a prune pit or a button, without discomfort, the object is likely to pass on its own (although you should still notify your physician or nurse practitioner). Obviously, if your child develops vomiting, pain or any of the symptoms listed above, consult your doctor right away. Button batteries are especially dangerous, because they can leak acid that damages the esophagus or intestines. They need to be removed.

Metal objects show up on X-rays; plastic or wooden objects may not. An MRI scan might be necessary; or a doctor may have to look directly, using an endoscope. A skilled ear-nose-throat surgeon or gastrointestinal (GI) doctor can often remove a swallowed object with the endoscope.

Finally, never give ipecac (a medicine to induce vomiting) or a cathartic to a child who has swallowed an object. Doing so will not help, and may possibly make the situation worse. For objects lodged in the windpipe or bronchial tubes, see Choking and Rescue Breathing (page 790).

POISONS

First aid for suspected poisoning is simple: If your child appears ill, call an ambulance (911), then the National Poison Control hotline, 800 222-1222. If your child appears well, call the poison hotline directly. Other tips:

1. Stay with your child and make sure she is breathing easily and is alert. If not, call 911 or your local emergency unit for immediate help.
2. To prevent her from ingesting any more, remove any remaining substances or solutions. If you can, bring the substance with you if you take your child to the doctor to aid in identifying it.
3. Do not delay seeking help even if your child seems well. The effects of many poisons—aspirin, for instance—may take hours to show but can be prevented by early treatment.
4. Call the National Poison Control hotline, 800 222-1222. Tell them the name of the medication or product and the amount of the substance your child swallowed, if known.

Poisons on the skin. Although we often think of the skin as a protective barrier, it is important to realize that medications and poisons can be absorbed through the skin and can reach toxic levels in the body. If your child's clothes or skin come in contact with a potential poison, remove the contaminated clothing and flush the skin with plenty of plain water for fifteen minutes (which will seem like a very long time). Then gently wash the area with soap and water and rinse well. Place the contaminated clothing in a plastic bag, keeping it away from other children. Call the National Poison Control hotline (800 222-1222) or your doctor. If they refer you to a hospital, take the contaminated clothes with you in case they wish to test the clothes to identify the poison.

Harmful fluids in the eye. If a child is accidentally squirted or splashed in the eye with a possibly harmful fluid, promptly flush the eye. Have the child lie on his back and blink as much as possible while you flood the eye with lukewarm (not hot) water poured from a large glass held two to three inches above his face, or hold the eye open under a stream of lukewarm water from the faucet. Keep this up for fifteen minutes, then call the poison hotline, your doctor, or nurse practitioner. Some liquids, especially caustics, can cause serious damage to the eye and require a medical evaluation by your doctor or an eye specialist. Try to keep the child from rubbing his eyes.

ALLERGIC REACTIONS

Children may have an allergic reaction to a food, a pet, a medication, an insect bite, or almost anything. The symptoms can be mild, moderate, or severe.

Mild: Children who have mild allergies may complain of watery, itchy eyes. There is often sneezing or a stuffy nose. On occasion they may develop hives, a very itchy localized swelling of the skin that looks like a large mosquito bite. Other rashes, with small, itchy bumps, can also be caused by allergies. Mild allergic symptoms are usually treated with medications known as antihistamines, such as diphenhydramine (Benadryl), which is available without prescription.

Moderate: Moderate allergic symptoms occur when in addition to hives, the child develops respiratory symptoms, such as wheezing and coughing. Children with these symptoms need to be promptly evaluated by a doctor.

Severe: Symptoms of severe allergic reactions, also called ana-phylaxis, include swelling in the mouth or throat, difficulty in breathing due to blockage of the airway, and low blood pressure. Most of the time anaphylaxis is merely uncomfortable and frightening; rarely, it has very serious consequences, including death. Emergency treatment for anaphylaxis is a shot of adrena-line (also called epinephrine) injected under the skin; the child must be immediately brought to a hospital emergency room. Any child who has had an anaphylactic reaction should be eval-uated by a physician, who may prescribe a preloaded syringe of epinephrine; Epi-Pen and AnaKit are common brand names. Parents and teachers carry the syringe with them so that the child can receive an injection without delay.

An allergist can help you decide if allergy desensitization makes sense for your child.

CONVULSIONS AND SEIZURES

A generalized seizure or convulsion is frightening to witness. It's important to remain calm, and to realize that the child is not usually in danger. Place the child in a position where she can't hurt herself—for example, on a rug some distance from the fur-niture. Lay her on her side so that any saliva will run out of her mouth and her tongue does not block off her airway. Don't reach down her throat. Call the doctor or 911. See page 879 for more on convulsions.

DROWNING

A child found unconscious by a lake, pool, or bucket of water needs immediate resuscitation, ideally by a person trained in CPR (see page 791). To give rescue breathing, follow the instruc-tions on page 792. Be prepared to roll the child to one side if he vomits, to protect his lungs. If the child could have been diving, assume that his neck might be broken. Move his head as little as possible to avoid damaging the spinal cord. A child who almost drowns, but then seems to recover, still needs to be seen by a doctor. Severe injury to the lungs can show up hours after the event, and it's important for the child to be near medical care.

CHOKING AND RESCUE BREATHING

A parent who knows how to unblock a blocked airway and how to give rescue breaths to a child who is not breathing is prepared to deal with most life-threatening emergencies. Most children have healthy hearts. If a child's heart stops beating, it is usually because the child has stopped breathing, cutting off the oxygen supply to the heart. Reasons children may suddenly stop breathing include suffocation and drowning and choking on objects or food. (Severe pneumonia, asthma, or other diseases can occasionally cause a child to stop breathing, but this doesn't happen suddenly, so it's unlikely to be the sort of thing a parent has to face alone.)

CPR. Every adult should be trained in life-saving techniques and cardiopulmonary resuscitation (CPR). Courses are offered by fire departments, the Red Cross and many hospitals and clinics. They will teach you how to assess a seriously ill child and get help, administer artificial respiration, and start the heart beating if it has stopped. The instructions below are not a substitute for taking the course; they are only to give you an idea of what to do. To learn CPR, you have to take a course.

Choking and coughing. When a child has swallowed something and is coughing hard, give her a chance to cough it out. Coughing is the best way to clear an object from the air passages. If the person is able to breathe, speak, or cry, stay close by and ask someone to call for help. Make no attempt to remove the object. Do not slap her on the back, turn her upside down, or reach into her mouth and try to pull the object out; those actions can drive the object farther into the airway, causing complete obstruction of breathing. These actions are only appropriate if the airway is already completely blocked.

Unable to cough or breathe. When a child is choking and unable to breathe, cry, or speak, the object is completely blocking the airway and air is not entering the breathing tubes. In this situation—but *only* if the airway is completely blocked—follow the emergency steps outlined below.

The Infant (Up to One Year Old) with a *Completely Blocked* Airway:

1. If the baby is conscious, slide one hand under her back to support her head and neck. With your other hand, hold her jaw between your thumb and fingers and let your forearm lie along her abdomen.

2. Turn the child over so she is lying face down with her head lower than her trunk. Support her abdomen with the forearm that is resting on your thigh.

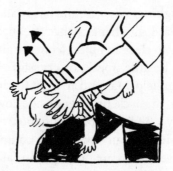

3. With the heel of one hand, give the baby up to five rapid blows in the middle of the back, high between the shoulder blades.

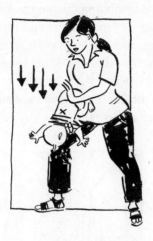

4. If the object was not dislodged by the blows, turn the infant face up while supporting her back with your forearm. Remember that the child's head should be lower than her feet. Place your middle and index fingers on her breastbone, in the center of her chest just below the nipple line. Give up to five quick downward chest thrusts, trying to create an artificial cough.

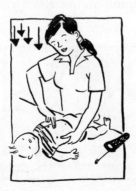

5. If the baby doesn't start to breathe or has become unconscious, have someone call for help while you begin rescue breathing. First, look for the object in the back of the baby's throat by grabbing the tongue and the lower jaw between your thumb and fingers and lifting upward. If you see something, slide your little finger down along the inside of her cheek to the base of her tongue and use a hooking motion to sweep the object out. (Don't poke your finger in her mouth if you don't see anything; this might make the blockage worse.)

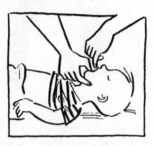

6. Next, reposition the baby to begin rescue breathing by opening her mouth by lifting the baby's chin as you press back on the forehead.

7. If the baby still hasn't started to breathe, tilt her head back, lift up her chin, and completely cover both her mouth and

nose with your lips. Breathe into her twice, each time for about one and a half seconds with just enough pressure to make her chest rise.

8. If the air does not enter the baby's lungs, making her chest rise, her air passage is still blocked. Start with the back blows again, and repeat steps 3 through 7. Continue repeating the sequence until the baby starts to cough, breathe, or cry or until help arrives.

The Child (Over One Year Old) with a Completely Blocked Airway

1. Remember, first check that the airway is completely blocked. If the child is coughing, speaking or crying, watch but don't intervene. If the child is conscious, start with the Heimlich maneuver. Kneel or stand behind the child and wrap your arms around his waist. Make a fist with one hand and put the thumb of your fist just above the child's navel, staying well below his breastbone.

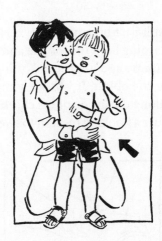

2. Cover your fist with your other hand and press your fist into the child's abdomen with up to five quick upward

thrusts. Be gentle with younger or smaller children. Repeat the maneuver until the object is expelled. This should get the child to breathe or cough. (Even if this treatment stops the choking and the child seems fully recovered call the doctor.)

3. If the child still isn't breathing after a Heimlich, open his mouth by grasping both the tongue and the lower jaw between your thumb and fingers and lifting the jaw. Look in his throat for the object. If you see something, slide your little finger along the inside of his cheek to the base of his tongue, and use a hooking motion to sweep the object out.

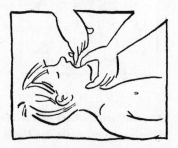

(Don't poke your finger around in his mouth if you don't see anything or can't hook the object; this might make the blockage worse.) Repeat the Heimlich maneuver until the foreign body is removed or the child becomes unconscious.

4. If the child becomes unconscious, use the Heimlich maneuver with the child lying on his back. Kneel at his feet (or straddle his legs if he's an older or bigger child). Put the heel of one hand above his navel, staying well below his breastbone. Put your other hand over the first hand with the fingers of both hands pointing toward his head. Press into his abdomen with a quick upward thrust. Be gentle with smaller or younger children. Repeat until the object is expelled.

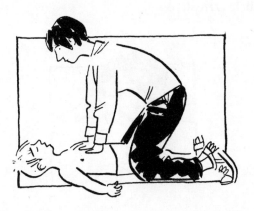

5. If the child remains unconscious or if you can't remove the object, have someone call for help immediately. With the child on his back, open his air passage by tilting his head back and lifting his chin with your fingers. Pinch his nose, cover his mouth completely with yours, and breathe into him twice. Each breath should last about three seconds. Use just enough breath to make his chest rise. If you can't

make his chest move, reposition the airway and give him two more breaths.

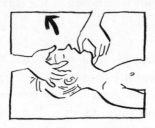

6. If the air does not enter the child's lungs, repeat steps 4 and 5. Continue to alternate mouth-to-mouth breathing and the Heimlich maneuver until the child resumes breathing or help arrives.

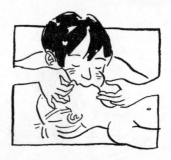

How to give rescue breathing. Each of your breaths goes into the victim. With an adult, breathe at your natural speed. With a child, use slightly quicker, shorter breaths. Never give rescue breathing to a person who is breathing.

First, open the air passages by properly positioning the child's head. Do this by tilting the forehead back while lifting up on the chin with your fingers. Maintain this position every time you provide a rescue breath.

With a child's small face, you can breathe into the nose and mouth together. (With an adult, breathe into the mouth while pinching the nose shut.)

Breathe into victim, using minimal force. (A small child's lungs cannot contain your entire exhalation.) Remove your lips, allowing the child's chest to contract while you take in your next breath. Breathe into the child again.

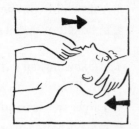

HOME FIRST-AID KIT

When an emergency situation develops, it is human nature to become upset and anxious. This is not the time to search for bandages, phone numbers, and other first aid equipment, which may have been placed in various closets throughout the house. It makes sense to keep a first aid kit for use in an emergency. A small box that you can purchase at your local hardware or houseware store will suffice. If you have young children, you'll need to store it in a place they cannot reach. The following should be included in the kit.

A list of emergency telephone numbers including:
1. How to reach an ambulance or emergency response team in your community (most communities use 911 for emergencies)
2. National Poison Control hotline, 800 222-1222 (this is a good number to tape to your telephone)

3. Your child's physician or nurse practitioner
4. A neighbor to call should you need an adult to assist you

The following first aid equipment:
- Small sterile bandages (Band-Aids)
- Larger sterile bandages or gauze pads
- An Ace bandage or a similar elastic wrap
- An eye patch
- Adhesive tape
- An ice pack (in the freezer)
- Any emergency medications your child may require
- A digital electronic thermometer
- Petroleum jelly
- A small pair of scissors
- Tweezers
- Antiseptic solution
- Antibiotic ointment
- Antifever medications (nonaspirin; acetaminophen or ibuprofen)
- A bulb syringe
- A tube of 1 percent hydrocortisone cream

DENTAL DEVELOPMENT
AND ORAL HEALTH

As a parent, you can follow that same advice for your children and ensure that their teeth are healthy and a joy to behold. Prevention is the key. What makes for healthy teeth? Can decay be prevented? What about teething? Fluoride? When should a child first visit the dentist? What about permanent teeth and braces? With the information here, supplemented by advice from your child's dentist and staff, you'll easily be able to sort it all out.

The dental topics of most concern to parents include—in a kind of chronological order—tooth development, teething, tooth decay, and avoiding traumatic injuries to the mouth. Most important of all is your ability to get your child's teeth off to a healthy start, an advantage that can last a lifetime.

TOOTH DEVELOPMENT

Baby teeth. How and when will your baby's teeth come through? The average baby gets his first tooth at around six months, but this is quite variable. One baby may get her first tooth at three months, another not until eighteen months. Both may be perfectly healthy, normal infants. It is true that certain diseases can influence the age of teething, but this is rare. For most children the age of teething is simply a matter of the pattern of development the child was born with.

Usually the first two teeth to appear are the lower central incisors. Incisor is the name given to the eight front teeth (four on the bottom, and four on the top) that have sharp cutting edges. After a few months come the four upper incisors, so the average baby has these six teeth, four above, two below, at about a year old. After this, there's usually a lull of several months before the next onslaught. Then six more teeth quickly appear: the two remaining lower incisors and all four first primary (baby) molars. The molars don't come in next to the incisor teeth but farther back, leaving space for the canine teeth.

After the first molars appear, there is a pause of several months before the canines (the pointed dog or eye teeth) erupt in the spaces between the incisors and the molars. The most common time for this to happen is in the second half of the second year. The last four teeth in the baby set are the second primary molars, which come in right behind the first primary molars, usually in the first half of the third year. Remember that these ages are all averages. Don't worry if your baby is ahead of or behind the schedule.

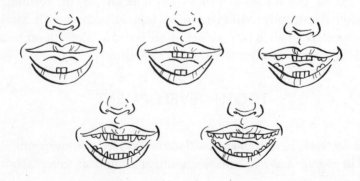

Permanent teeth. Permanent teeth begin to appear at about six years of age. The six-year (first permanent) molars come through behind the baby molars. The baby teeth lost first are usually the lower central incisors. The permanent incisors, pushing up underneath, come into position where the baby tooth roots have been dissolved away. Eventually, all the primary teeth become loose and fall out. The baby teeth are lost in about the same order in which they came in. Your toughest decision may be figuring out the monetary value of these baby teeth when the Tooth Fairy makes her appointed rounds.

The permanent teeth that take the place of the baby molars are called bicuspids or premolars. The twelve-year molars (second permanent molars) come in behind the six-year molars. The third molars (eighteen-year molars, or wisdom teeth) may be impacted in the jaw. Sometimes they need to be removed so they won't do any damage to neighboring teeth or the bone of the jaws. Permanent teeth often appear with jagged edges (called mammelons). They either wear down, or the dentist can trim them. Also, permanent teeth are more yellow than primary teeth.

Permanent teeth sometimes come through crooked or out of place. They may eventually straighten out by the muscular action of the tongue, lips, and cheeks. If they don't straighten out or are crowded or crooked or if the jaw alignment is abnormal, orthodontic treatment (braces) may be required for bite improvement.

TEETHING

Symptoms of teething. Teething has different effects on different babies. One chews things, frets, drools, has a hard time getting to sleep, and generally makes life miserable for the family for a month or two as each tooth comes through. In another baby, a tooth is discovered with no idea that he was teething. Most babies start to drool at around three to four months when their salivary glands become more active. Don't be fooled into thinking that drooling always indicates that teething has started.

Since babies get twenty teeth in their first three years, it's easy to understand why they seem to be teething for most of the infant and early childhood years. This also explains why it's so easy to blame every ailment on teething. It was once believed that teething caused colds, diarrhea, and fevers. Of course, these conditions are caused by germs (bacteria and viruses), not by teething. Teething mainly causes teeth and not much else. If your baby has a fever or appears ill, don't assume it's because of teething. Call her doctor or nurse practitioner.

Help for teething. Any teeth may distress a baby, but the first four molar teeth, at around twelve to eighteen months, are more likely to cause trouble than the others. What to do? First, let her chew! Provide chewable objects that are dull and soft enough so that if she falls with them in her mouth, they won't do any damage. Rubber teething rings of various shapes are good. You should avoid toys made from thin, brittle plastic, which can break and cause choking. You also need to be careful that your baby doesn't gnaw the paint off furniture and other objects if there is any danger that the paint is made with lead. (Anything painted before about 1980 may contain lead.) Fortunately, nowadays all baby furniture and painted toys sold in the U.S. are painted with lead-free paint.

Some babies prefer to chew on a certain kind of cloth. Try tying an ice cube or a piece of apple in a square of cloth. Some parents swear by frozen bagels. Frozen slices of banana can also work well. Many babies love to have their gums firmly rubbed at times. Be creative. Let your baby chew what she wants as long as it's not dangerous. And don't fret about germs on the teething ring or piece of cloth. Your baby is putting all sorts of things in her mouth anyway, none of them germ-free. Of course, it's a good idea to wash the teething ring after it has fallen on the floor or the dog has slobbered over it, and you should wash or boil the piece of cloth occasionally. There are lots of teething medicines on the market that may occasionally offer some relief, but you should talk to your doctor or nurse practitioner before using them.

WHAT MAKES GOOD TEETH?

Nutrition for strong teeth. The crowns (the parts that show) of a baby's first teeth are formed in the gums before birth. A few of the permanent (adult) teeth also begin forming before birth, and others begin within a few months after. Growing teeth need proper nutrition, including plenty of calcium and phosphorus, vitamin D, and vitamin C. Good sources of calcium and phosphorus include vegetables, cereals, calcium-supplemented juices, and milk (although nondairy diets may have some benefits; see page 337). Sources of vitamin D include fortified milk, vitamin drops, and sunshine (see page 336). If you are breastfeeding, it's wise to take a vitamin D supplement (200 units a day) just to be on the safe side. Sources of vitamin C include most fruits, especially citrus; vitamin drops; raw tomatoes; cabbage, and breast milk. Other vitamins are also helpful, including vitamin A (in yellow, orange, and red fruits) and some of the B vitamins (in grains).

Fluoride. One mineral known to be especially valuable in forming strong, decay-resistant teeth is fluoride. Fluoride is a naturally occurring mineral; we all have some in our teeth and bones. A small amount in the diet of the mother while she is pregnant and in the child's diet greatly reduces the risk of later tooth decay. When the enamel of a tooth is formed with fluoride, it resists the action of acid much better. In addition, fluoride in the mouth discourages the activity of the bacteria that cause tooth decay.

In regions with high levels of natural fluoride in the water, tooth decay is rare. The addition of fluoride to the water in most

American cities has had a similarly beneficial effect. Children can also get fluoride in the form of tablets or drops. It also helps to put fluoride directly onto the teeth, in the form of tooth-pastes, mouth rinses, or special preparations that dentists use.

Fluoride in the water. For decades, fluoride has been added in very small, safe amounts to the water of many communities as a public health measure. If you're not sure whether your water has enough fluoride, you can call the information number on your water bill and ask. Adequate fluoridation is 0.7 to 1.0 ppm (parts per million). If you have your own well, call your county health department for advice. If your water is low on fluoride, your family mostly drinks bottled water, or you use a home purifica-tion system that takes out all the fluoride and other minerals, it makes sense for you and your child to use a fluoride supplement (drops or pills).

Fluoride for babies. If you're breast-feeding and drinking fluor-idated water, you don't need to give your baby extra fluoride. If your water is not fluoridated, consider giving your baby an in-fant vitamin with fluoride. Baby formulas contain little fluoride, but if you mix the formula with fluoridated water, your child will get plenty of fluoride. If not, consider adding fluoride drops.

Enough, but not too much. Your child's doctor or nurse practi-tioner and dentist can help make sure your child gets the right amount of fluoride. If there is no fluoride in your water supply, your doctor or nurse practitioner may prescribe the appropriate daily dose for your infant, which will vary depending on your community and your child's age and weight. Too much fluoride can cause unattractive white and brown specks on the teeth, so it's important to give the correct amount. Your child may also re-ceive periodical topical applications of special fluoride solutions in the dentist's office. Fluoridated toothpastes are also beneficial for their surface effect on the enamel. But be careful: Children who eat toothpaste, as most young children will, are at risk of getting too much fluoride. So use very small amounts (pea size), and keep the toothpaste away from very young children so that it doesn't become a convenient bathroom snack.

DENTAL OFFICE VISITS

Getting to know the dentist and the dental office staff is very worthwhile. The best time to take your child to the dentist is shortly after the first tooth erupts, usually by twelve months of age. You can ask the dentist questions about your child's dental care and learn more about dental problems. In early preventive visits, the dentist is able to detect developing problems in the early stages, when they are solved more easily, painlessly, and inexpensively. More important, your child will have positive early experiences in the dentist's office. By the time she is three, she will be a dental-office veteran. Most future visits will be preventive in nature, rather than the traditional drill-and-fill sessions that haunt the childhood memories of so many adults.

TOOTH DECAY

Some children get a lot of cavities, others almost none. Why is this so? We still don't know all the factors that lead to tooth decay (dental caries), but we do know that heredity plays a role, as do the diet of the pregnant mother, the child, and access or lack of access to good dental care.

Bacteria and plaque. The principal cause of tooth decay is acid produced by bacteria living in the mouth. The bacteria combine with food debris to form a material called dental plaque that sticks to tooth surfaces. The more hours of the day this plaque remains on the teeth, the greater the number of bacteria and the more acid is produced. This acid dissolves the minerals that make up the enamel and dentin of the tooth, eventually destroying the tooth.

The bacteria live off sugars and starches in the child's diet. Anything that keeps sugars sitting in the mouth for a long time is likely to be good for the bacteria and bad for the teeth. That is why frequent between-meal snacking promotes tooth decay. Especially harmful are lollipops, sticky candy, dried fruit, soda pop, and sweets like cookies and crackers, which cling to the teeth.

Saliva contains substances that help teeth resist attack by bacteria. Since the body produces less saliva during sleep, nighttime is when cavities form the most. That is why brushing the teeth before bed is so important. Foods that promote saliva—such as sugarless gum—can help fight cavities. There are also substances in some sugarless chewing gums, xylitol and sorbitol, that kill cavity-forming bacteria and another substance, casein, that strengthens teeth.

Baby-bottle cavities. An especially severe type of tooth decay is nursing caries or baby-bottle tooth decay. When formula or breast milk sits on a baby's teeth for a long time, the sugars in the milk promote the growth of cavity-forming bacteria, which then destroy the teeth. The teeth most at risk are the upper front teeth, since the tongue covers the lower teeth during nursing and sucking. There is normally enough time between feedings for the flow of saliva to clean the teeth. But when babies keep a nipple in their mouths much of the time, this normal cleaning may not have a chance to occur. The worst baby-bottle tooth decay happens when babies fall asleep with the bottle in their mouths. While they sleep, the formula sits on their teeth and the bacteria multiply away.

Baby-bottle decay may start even before the first birthday. Sometimes nursing caries is so severe that the infected teeth have to be removed. For this reason, a baby should not be put to bed with a bottle of milk, juice, or other sweetened fluid. The only acceptable fluid for sleep time is water. Even diluted sweet fluids can promote decay.

TOOTHBRUSHING AND FLOSSING

Effective brushing. How can tooth decay be prevented? The secret is daily, consistent removal of dental plaque before it does its nasty work. First, a tip about cleaning babies' teeth: use a soft-bristled toothbrush. There is a myth that one should use a soft gauze or cloth to wipe a baby's teeth and gums so as not to damage the delicate gum tissue. Those "delicate" gum tissues chew on table legs, cribs, coffee tables, siblings, and anything else in their way. A baby's gums are no more delicate than alligator hide. Brush, don't wipe. Babies love it.

A child's teeth should be carefully brushed after breakfast and before bedtime, with daily flossing between adjoining teeth, usually before the evening brushing. If possible, an after-lunch

brushing is helpful too, to remove food residue. Starting at about two, your child may insist on doing everything herself, but most young children do not have the manual dexterity required for proper brushing and flossing until they are nine or ten years old. You can let your young child begin the brushing by herself from the earliest ages, but you will probably need to finish up to ensure that all dental plaque has been eliminated. You can gradually let your child take over completely when she proves capable, usually between six and ten years.

Flossing. Some parents question the need to floss a child's teeth. Most teeth in the back of a child's mouth are in close contact with those on either side. Even some front teeth may be in tight contact with their neighbors. Such teeth are so close together that food and dental plaque can get wedged in between. No matter how vigorously or carefully they are brushed, the bristles cannot penetrate to clear out the food and plaque. Dental floss disrupts and dislodges that debris so that the toothbrush can sweep it away.

It's worth getting your child used to gentle flossing as soon as you notice food wedged between her teeth. Your child's dentist

or dental hygienist can demonstrate all the methods used to hold a child for perfect brushing and flossing. Best of all, when your child is able to brush and floss effectively without your help, she will already be accustomed to the daily habit.

SEALANTS

Sealants are another important part of preventive dentistry. Many teeth have small grooves or pitted areas in the enamel where bits of food and dental plaque accumulate. Most of these tooth surface imperfections are too small for bristles to enter, so the food material and bacterial plaque cannot be brushed or flossed away. Tooth decay, called pit and fissure caries, usually results. However, the dentist or hygienist can often prevent such tooth decay. A sealant consists of a liquid resin that flows across the tooth surface and fills the grooves and pits. It then hardens, sealing off the enamel imperfections. Food debris and dental plaque cannot enter a groove or pit that has been sealed with bonded resin. Other materials are also used as sealants, as dentists continue to seek the ideal method of protecting enamel pits and fissures. Some primary molars may also be given the protection of sealants, but dentists are selective in sealing baby molars.

Clinical experience has shown that sealants don't stay bonded to primary teeth as well as they do to permanent teeth. Sealants last for many years; depending on a child's diet and oral habits, they eventually need to be repaired or replaced.

DENTAL INJURIES

Dental injuries can occur to all teeth, most commonly the teeth in the front of the mouth. Teeth can be cracked, displaced from their sockets, or completely knocked out. Dentists are concerned about trauma to primary teeth and even more so about damage to permanent teeth, which may have important lifelong consequences. Parents should always consult their child's dentist after tooth trauma. Some injuries are not easily observable. A dentist is trained to make a complete diagnosis and perform the proper treatment.

Cracked teeth. A tooth is composed of three layers: the outer protective enamel; the internal supportive structure, called dentin; and the soft tissue center of the tooth containing the nerves, called the dental pulp. A crack (fracture) in a tooth can affect any or all of these layers. A small fracture may require only smoothing by the dentist using a sandpaperlike instrument. A more extensive crack may require a dental restoration to reestablish the form, function, and appearance of the tooth. If a dental fracture affects the hollow portion in the center of the tooth and exposes the dental pulp (there is usually bleeding from the exposed region), a dentist should be seen as soon as possible so he can repair the damage and prevent loss of the pulp. If a part of the pulp does die, the tooth can still be saved with endodontic (root canal) therapy: removing the dead pulp tissue and filling the root canal space with a sterile filling material. The tooth can then be repaired in the usual manner.

Loosened teeth. Most times slightly loosened teeth will reattach themselves and become stable after a few days' rest. Sometimes, however, teeth are so loose that the dentist needs to splint them together to stabilize them while healing occurs. Antibiotics are sometimes beneficial, to prevent infection of the dental pulp and attachment tissues. Dentists will advise a soft diet for a time to help the healing process.

Avulsed teeth. Sometimes, a tooth may be completely knocked out of the mouth (an avulsed tooth). If a baby tooth is avulsed, dentists usually recommend not to reimplant it. Underlying permanent teeth may suffer developmental damage when a traumatized primary tooth is reimplanted. A permanent tooth should be reimplanted as quickly as possible, however, usually within thirty minutes, to maximize the chance of keeping the pulp alive. First, make sure that the tooth is indeed permanent and is intact. Gently hold it by the crown (the part that shows in the mouth), not by the pointed roots. Rinse it very gently under tap water. Do not scrub or rub the root in any way; that will damage the attached tissue, which is required for reattachment. Insert the tooth back into its normal position. If you cannot reimplant the tooth, place it in a glass of milk or a commercially available tooth rescue container. Then take the child to a dentist or seek dental emergency service at a hospital emergency room. Time is important with permanent tooth avulsions. After a tooth has been out of the mouth for thirty minutes, the chances for successful reimplantation drop fast.

PREVENTING MOUTH INJURIES

Young children stumble often, and their teeth are located at a perfect height for crashing into the edge of a coffee table. So crashproof your toddler's cruising area. Take extraordinary care to make sure he doesn't have the opportunity to bite any electrical wires. (And while you're at it, make sure you cover all electrical wall sockets, to prevent shocks.) Don't let your child parade around the house with a toothbrush in her mouth. It may do serious damage if she falls.

The risk of dental injuries rises when children play sports. A Little Leaguer can be kicked in the mouth, struck with a ball, or hit by a bat, or an opposing player running the bases. Similar catastrophes can happen to both girls and boys in soccer, field hockey, basketball—almost all sports. Children in organized sports generally need to wear a comfortable protective mouth guard, sort of a crash helmet for the teeth. Mouth guards are sold at sporting goods stores or pharmacies; or your child's dentist can make a custom-fitted mouth guard. Rough individual activities such as in-line skating, skateboarding, and martial arts also call for mouth guards.

COMMON CHILDHOOD ILLNESSES

Every parent has to deal with colds and coughs, and it's the rare child who escapes without at least one ear infection. Many illnesses that used to be common—measles, polio, and some brain infections—are now rare or gone altogether, thanks to the magic of vaccines. Still, troublesome conditions such as asthma and eczema continue to affect many children. Knowing something about the common illnesses of childhood and some of the uncommon ones can make you feel more confident to handle problems as they arise. The information that follows isn't meant to be a substitute for a doctor's judgment, however. If you don't find the condition you're interested in below, it may be discussed elsewhere in this book; check the index.

COLDS

Colds, viruses, and bacteria. Your child will probably be sick from colds (upper respiratory infections or URIs) ten times as often as from all other illnesses combined. We only partly understand colds at this time. Most are caused by viruses. These germs are so small that they cannot be seen through an ordinary microscope. It is believed that more than two hundred different viruses can cause the common cold. Usually, colds caused by viruses go away in three to ten days. Sometimes, cold viruses open the door to more serious infections.

Cold viruses can lower the resistance of the nose and throat to more troublesome bacteria, such as streptococcus and pneumococcus. These germs often live in healthy people's noses and throats in winter and spring but do no harm because they are held at bay by the body's resistance. It's only after the cold virus has lowered the resistance that these other germs get their chance to multiply and spread. They can then cause infections in the middle ears (otitis media), nasal sinuses (sinusitis) and lungs (pneumonia).

To prevent a cold, avoid close physical contact with anyone who has one and practice good hand-washing (see page 588). You can increase your child's ability to fight off colds by helping her to eat and sleep well and by keeping your home as stress-free as possible (for example, keeping yelling to a minimum).

Colds in the infant. If your baby has a cold in his first year, the chances are that it will be mild. He may sneeze in the beginning; his nose will be runny, bubbly, or stuffy. He may cough a little. He is not likely to have a fever. When his nose is bubbly, you may wish that you could blow it for him, but it won't seem to bother him. On the other hand, if his nose is obstructed by thick mucus, it may make him frantic. He keeps trying to close his mouth and is angry when he can't breathe. The stuffiness may bother him most when he tries to nurse at the breast or bottle, so much so that at times he refuses, altogether.

Bubbling and obstruction can often be relieved by sucking the mucus out with a nasal syringe. Compress the bulb, insert the tip into the nose, and release the bulb. The inside lining of the baby's nose is very sensitive, so don't push too hard, and limit suctioning to times when it's really needed, such as before eating or sleeping. A drop or two of salt water may be put into the nostril before suctioning; let it sit there for about five minutes to soften the mucus before sucking it out. Do one nostril at a time (babies hate this process but feel much better afterwards). You can buy salt water (saline) nose drops at a drug store without a prescription; they are inexpensive, and save you the trouble of mixing up salt water drops yourself (see page 820 for instructions).

Extra moisture in the room sometimes helps to prevent the mucus in a child's nose from drying out. If the obstruction is severe, the doctor may prescribe nose drops or an oral medication to use just before nursing. The baby may not lose much of her appetite. Usually the cold is gone in a week. Sometimes, though, a small baby's cold can last an unbelievably long time, even though it stays mild. When a cold lasts longer than two weeks, check with the doctor or nurse practitioner.

Of course, babies' colds can become severe. They may lead to ear infections, sinusitis, and other complications. A sign that this may have happened is that the baby develops a fever a few days into the illness. If she has a frequent, deep, or wheezy cough, she should be examined by a doctor or nurse practitioner, even if she has no fever. The same applies if she looks sick with a cold. Remember that a baby can be quite sick but not have a fever, especially in the first two to three months of life, when resistance to infection is low. A baby with a temperature of 100.5 or higher in that period should be checked by a doctor or nurse practitioner.

Colds and fever after infancy. Some children go on having the same mild colds, with no fever or complications, that they had during infancy. But it's more usual when children are over six months old for their colds and throat infections to act differently.

Here is a common story. A little girl of two is well during the morning. At lunchtime, she seems a little tired and has less appetite than usual. When she wakes up from her nap, she is cranky, and her parents notice that she is hot. They take her temperature. It's 102. By the time the doctor examines her, the temperature is 104. Her cheeks are flushed and her eyes are dull, but otherwise she doesn't seem particularly sick. She may want no supper at all, or she may want a fair amount. She has no cold symptoms, and the doctor has found nothing definite except that her throat is perhaps a little red. The next day she may have a little fever, and now her nose may begin to run. Perhaps she coughs occasionally. From this point on, it's just a regular mild cold that lasts anywhere from two days to two weeks.

There are several variations to this typical story. Sometimes the child vomits at the time her fever shoots up. This is particularly likely to happen if her parents have unwisely tried to get her to eat more of her lunch than she wanted. (Always take a child's word for it when she loses her appetite.) Sometimes the fever lasts several days before the cold symptoms appear. Sometimes the fever lasts for a day or two then goes away without a running nose or cough taking its place. The doctor may call it grippe or flu.

These terms are commonly used for infections that have no local symptoms (like running nose or diarrhea), only general ones (such as fever or a-sick-all-over feeling). You may suspect that this one-day fever is a cold that was stopped in its tracks: the child seems perfectly well for a day or two after her fever is gone then promptly develops a running nose or a cough.

The point is that children over the age of six months may start their colds with a sudden fever, so don't be alarmed if this happens. You should, of course, always consult the doctor or nurse practitioner when your child falls ill with a fever; occasionally it may mean a more serious infection. When children are five to six years old, they're more likely to start their colds with little fever.

Fever that begins after a cold is well under way has a different meaning entirely from the fever that comes on the first day. It usually indicates that the cold has spread or become worse. This isn't necessarily serious or alarming. Just have the doctor see the child again to make sure that her ears, lungs, and urinary system are still healthy.

Calling the doctor. You don't need to call the doctor when your child has only a running nose or a slight cough. But you should

call if new symptoms develop, such as ear pain, frequent coughing, or fever occurring several days after the cold began, which
suggests a complication. Rapid breathing, irritability, or excessive tiredness along with a cold should also prompt you to call
the doctor or nurse practitioner (see page 698).

Treatment. Most doctors and parents don't keep a child indoors
or prescribe special treatment for a simple cold. Remember that
colds are caused by viruses. Antibiotics are used only for a bacterial infection (which can follow the viral infection). The overuse
of antibiotics for simple colds is causing strains of bacteria to
become resistant to them. A result is that when the child is truly
ill with a bacterial infection, the usual antibiotics may not work.

Experiments have proved that chilling does not cause colds.
But chilling may make one worse by drying the lining of the
nose or generally putting strain on a body that is already busy
fighting off an infection. So if your child is particularly susceptible to frequent and prolonged colds or complications such as
bronchitis and ear infections, you may want to keep her indoors
for a day or two, unless the weather is warm.

Vaporizers and humidifiers. The doctor sometimes recommends humidifying the air of the child's room when she has a
cold. This counteracts dryness and soothes her inflamed nose
and throat. It is particularly valuable in the treatment of a tight,
dry cough or very thick mucus. Extra moisture is less necessary
in warm weather, when the heat is off. An ultrasonic humidifier,
which produces a cool mist, may cost as little as $40 or as much
as $400. A regular cool-mist humidifier costing $30 or less does
an adequate job. With either type of cool-mist humidifier, it's
important to clean the water reservoir at least once a week with a
cup of chlorine bleach in a gallon of water. This will prevent the
growth of molds and bacteria in the reservoir, which then would
be blown into the room.

An electric steam vaporizer gets moisture in the air by boiling
water with an electric heating element. But steam isn't any better

than cool mist for adding moisture to the air. With steam there is a danger of scalding if a child puts his hand or face in it or knocks the vaporizer over. If you buy one of these steam vaporizers, get a large size that holds a quart or more and turns itself off after the water has boiled away.

Nose drops. The doctor may prescribe nose drops. They generally fall into two groups. The first is saltwater (saline) nose drops. You can make these at home by dissolving a quarter teaspoon of table salt in four ounces of warm water, or you can buy them at a drugstore. These are good for loosening thick mucus so that a child can blow it out more easily. See page 821 for instructions.

The other group of nose drops includes solutions that shrink the tissues in the nose. This opens up more space for breathing and gives the mucus a better chance to drain. The drawback is that after the tissues have been shrunk for a time, they will expand again, sometimes more than before. This may leave the nose stuffier than ever and may be irritating to the delicate membranes if it's done too often.

There are two situations in which the shrinking kind of nose drops is useful. The first is when a baby is so stuffed up that she is frantic. She can't nurse without becoming irritable or gagging, and her sleep is interrupted. (This condition may be relieved by suction with a nasal syringe alone.) Older children with colds who cannot sleep comfortably may also benefit from these nose drops. The second situation is in the late stages of a bad cold or sinusitis, when the nose is filled with a thick secretion that does not discharge by itself.

Nose drops of the shrinking kind should be used only on a doctor's recommendation and no more often than every six hours. One disadvantage of nose drops is that many small children fight them. There are only a few conditions in which nose drops do enough good to be worth upsetting the child.

The doctor may prescribe an oral decongestant to shrink the

nose tissues. Many doctors use the oral medicine rather than nose drops because it reduces secretions in the sinuses and bronchial tubes (airways) as well as in the nose. Decongestants can sometimes cause disturbing behavior changes in young children or have other side effects, so it is best to use them only under a doctor's supervision, even though they are nonprescription drugs.

How to instill nose drops. Nose drops do a lot more good if they get back into the inner and upper passages of the nose. Suck out the mucus from the front of the child's nose with a nasal syringe. Then have her lie on her back across a bed with her head hanging well down over the side. Insert the drops and try to keep her in this position for half a minute while the drops work back and up.

Cough medicines. No cough medicine can cure a cold, in the sense of killing the cold-causing viruses. Cough medicine can only make the windpipe a little less ticklish or loosen up mucus. A person who has an infection in the windpipe or bronchial tubes needs to cough once in a while to bring up the mucus. The doctor prescribes a cough medicine to keep the cough from being so frequent that it tires the person out or interferes with sleep and eating. Any child or grown-up who has a cough that frequent should be under the care of a doctor. Your doctor may recommend a safe cough medicine (not all cough syrups are alike). Never give a child adult cough medicine.

Resistance to colds. Many people believe that they are more susceptible to colds when they're tired or chilled, but this has never been proved. Common sense tells us that adequate rest and appropriate outdoor clothing in cold climates is reasonable for children and adults.

Houses and apartments that are kept too hot and dry during the winter season parch the nose and throat, which may cause difficulty breathing when the nose is filled with mucus. Many people try to moisten the air by putting pans of water on the radiators. This is almost completely worthless (and dangerous for small children). It does help to keep the room temperature down to 70 or below (68 is a good figure to aim at); when you heat winter air much beyond that, it becomes extremely dry—dryer even than the Sahara Desert. You can also use a cool-mist humidifier to keep the air moist.

Diet and resistance to colds. Naturally, every child should be offered a well-balanced diet. But there is no proof that a child who is already eating a sensible variety of foods will have fewer colds if given more of one kind of food or less of another. Chicken soup is a favorite in many cultures, and there is even a little scientific evidence that chicken soup may help the body fight certain viruses, though it isn't something that's been studied a lot.

Vitamins, supplements, and herbs. There is no proof that larger than normal doses of vitamin C will prevent colds. Zinc, a mineral that is low in many people's diets, looked for a while like a possible cure, but more research showed that it didn't work in otherwise healthy children. People who have low zinc levels probably do benefit from taking zinc supplements, however. Echinacea—also known as cornflower—is an herb that may well help with colds. A fair amount of research, mostly in Europe, suggests that lozenges or tea made with echinacea may shorten colds a bit.

Age is a factor in resistance to colds. With more children in day care and preschool, children between four months and two years get more colds, have them longer, and experience more complications. (The average is seven colds a year in northern cities in the United States; more if there are older children in the family attending school.) After the age of two or three years, the frequency and severity lessen. Nine-year-olds are likely to be laid up only half as much as they were at six, and twelve-year-olds only half as much as at nine. This should comfort the parents of a small child who seems to be forever sick.

The psychological factor in colds. There is evidence that some children and grown-ups are more susceptible to colds when they are tense or unhappy. I think of a boy, six-years-old, who was nervous about school because he couldn't keep up with the class in reading. Every Monday morning for several months, he had a cough. You may think he was putting it on. It wasn't as simple as that. It wasn't a dry, forced cough; it was a real, thick one. The cough would improve as the week went by and by Friday would be all gone, only to reappear again on Sunday night or Monday morning. There's nothing mysterious about this. Scientists have learned that emotions and the immune system are closely linked. Stress appears to lower the body's immunity to infection by its effect on the white blood cells and other components of the immune system.

Exposure to other children. Another factor that influences the number of colds a child has is the number of children he plays with, especially indoors. The child living isolated on a farm has few colds because he is exposed to few cold viruses. The average child in preschool, day care, or elementary school has plenty. People can give their infection to others for at least twenty-four hours before they begin to show signs of it themselves. At times they can carry the virus and pass it on to others without ever showing symptoms themselves.

Can the spread of colds in a family be checked? Most colds that are brought into the home are caught by the younger children, at least in mild form, especially if the house is small and everyone has to use the same rooms. The viruses of colds and other infections are passed from one person to another in the spray of sneezes and coughs, so it's worthwhile for parents—especially those with a sore throat—to avoid sneezing, coughing, or breathing directly into their baby's or child's face. They should wash their hands with soap before handling things that will go into the baby's mouth to prevent the transfer of a large number of germs. If an outsider has a hint of a cold or any other illness, be firm about not letting the person in the same house as the baby or within a couple of yards of the carriage outside.

EAR INFECTIONS

Some children get ear infections with most of their colds; others never do. The ears are much more likely to be infected in the first three or four years of life. In fact, there is a slight inflammation of the middle ear in a majority of colds at this age, but it usually comes to nothing, and the child has no symptoms.

What is an ear infection? An ear infection (otitis media) is an infection of the middle ear, caused by a bacteria or a virus. The middle ear is a small chamber, behind the eardrum, that is connected to the back of the throat by a channel called the eustachian tube. When this tube is blocked for any reason— such as mucus from a cold or swelling from an allergy or en- larged adenoids—the fluid in the middle ear cannot drain into the back of the throat. Bacteria or viruses in the back of the throat then travel up the eustachian tube and infect the stagnant fluid in the middle ear. Pus forms, and the middle ear becomes inflamed and painful.

Usually the ear doesn't become inflamed enough to cause pain until a cold has been going for several days. The child over two can tell you what the matter is. A baby may keep rubbing his ear or just cry piercingly for several hours. He may have a fever.

If your child has an earache, get in touch with the doctor or nurse practitioner the same day, particularly if there is fever. The antibiotics that are used when necessary work much better in the early stages of ear infections.

Suppose it will be several hours before you can reach the doc- tor. What can you do to relieve the pain? Lying down aggravates

ear pain, so keep the child's head propped up. A hot-water bottle or an electric heating pad may help, but small children are often impatient with them. (Don't let a child fall asleep on a heating pad; he could be burned.) Acetaminophen or ibuprofen will relieve the pain somewhat. What will help even more is a dose of a cough medicine containing codeine that the doctor has prescribed for that child. (A medicine prescribed for an older child or adult might contain too much of the drug.) Codeine is an efficient painkiller as well as cough remedy. If the earache is severe, you can use all these remedies together, but never use more than one dose of the codeine cough medicine without talking to your doctor.

Once in a while, an eardrum breaks very early in an infection and discharges a thin pus. You may find the discharge on the pillow in the morning without the child ever having complained of pain or fever. Usually, however, the drum breaks only after an infection has been developing for several days, accompanied by fever and pain. Since the ear infection causes pressure on the eardrum, when it bursts, the pain is much improved. The pus now has a way to drain and sometimes this in itself cures the infection. So while a discharge of pus from the ear almost certainly indicates an ear infection, it can also indicate that the infection is on the road to recovery or will be easier to manage with antibiotics. The eardrum usually heals nicely in just a few days and will not cause further problems.

If your child's ear discharges, the most you should do is to tuck a loose plug of absorbent cotton into the opening to collect the pus, wash the pus off the outside of the ear with soap and water (don't put water in the ear canal), and get in touch with the doctor. If the discharge leaks out anyway and irritates the child's skin, gently wash the pus off the skin around the ear. Never insert a cotton swab into the ear canal.

Chronic ear infections. Some children have repeated ear infections in the first years of life; a thick fluid accumulates behind the eardrum. Your doctor or nurse practitioner may deal with this in one of three ways, especially if the ear infections are interfering with the child's hearing. First, she may prescribe an antibiotic to be taken daily, often for months. The purpose of the antibiotic is to prevent the fluid in the middle ear from becoming infected, even when it cannot drain through the Eustachian tube. This works well for some children, less well for others. (As we have become increasingly aware of the risk of antibiotic-resistant bacteria, the routine use of antibiotics has dropped.) Second, the doctor may look for allergies that cause fluid to remain in the ear and encourage infections. Finally, she may refer the child to an ear specialist, who will consider inserting tiny plastic tubes through the eardrums. This allows the air pressure to be the same in the middle ear as in the outer canal, which may reduce the chances of further infection or accumulation of fluid and return the child's hearing to normal. Secondhand exposure to cigarette smoke increases the risk of ear infections: another powerful reason to stop smoking or never start.

TONSILS AND ADENOIDS

Tonsils and adenoids were blamed for so many things in the twentieth century that many people still think of them as villains that have to be removed eventually, the sooner the better. This is the wrong way to look at them. They are there to help overcome infection and build the body's resistance to germs. The tonsils and adenoids are made of lymphoid tissue, like the glands (lymph nodes) that you can often feel along the sides of the neck or behind a child's ears. Lymphoid tissue swells up in the process of killing germs and builds immunity.

The tonsils. The tonsils normally grow until the age of eight, then shrink. Doctors used to think that all very enlarged tonsils were diseased and should be removed, but that isn't true. There is no need to remove the tonsils, even when they are large, from

a child who is otherwise healthy. Frequent colds, sore throats, and ear infections are not good reasons for a tonsillectomy. If tonsils are so large that they obstruct the airway, they may need to be removed. Tonsils that are chronically infected or that have pockets of infection in them may also need to go.

The adenoids. The adenoids are clusters of lymphoid tissue up behind the soft palate, where the nose passages join the throat. When they become greatly enlarged, they may block this passageway and cause mouth-breathing and snoring. They may also prevent the free discharge of mucus and pus from the nose, thus prolonging colds and sinus infections. Or they may block the Eustachian tubes that drain the middle ear, resulting in chronic ear infections. Sometimes these conditions can be treated with antibiotics; sometimes surgical removal of the adenoids is necessary.

There is also a condition, called obstructive sleep apnea, in which the adenoids are so large that they obstruct the breathing passages when the child sleeps. Not only does he snore loudly, which is not dangerous, but there are periods when he cannot breathe through the passages at all. The parents may hear a long pause (more than five seconds) in the child's snoring, during which he cannot move air at all and may act as if he is trying to catch his breath. This condition often requires removal of the adenoids to ensure open breathing passages at night. Milder forms of sleep apnea also exist: The child keeps breathing but the oxygen level in the blood drops low enough to interfere with sleep.

Occasionally an ear specialist will remove the adenoids in a child with chronic or recurrent ear infections as a way to drain the ear through the Eustachian tube. If the tonsils are removed, the adenoids are sometimes cut out, too, but there may be reason to take out the adenoids alone if they are a persistent obstruction and leave the tonsils.

The adenoids always grow back to some extent, and the body

always tries to grow new lumps of lymphoid tissue where the tonsils used to be. This isn't a sign that the operation was incompletely done or has to be done again. It shows only that the body means to have lymphoid tissue in that region and tries hard to replace it.

SORE THROAT AND SWOLLEN GLANDS

A sore throat without inflamed tonsils is called pharyngitis. Inflamed tonsils are tonsillitis. And a sore throat *with* inflamed tonsils is called pharyngo-tonsillitis. The main concern with sore throats is to detect those infections caused by the streptococcus bacteria (strep throats) so that they can be treated with antibiotics. Untreated strep throats often get better on their own, but sometimes they turn into more severe infections or cause rheumatic fever, a serious chronic condition.

Call the doctor in all cases of sore throat, especially if there is a fever of greater than 101. The doctor will do a throat culture or a rapid test for streptococcus if there is any suspicion. If the test is negative for strep, the cause is likely to be a virus, and the infection will most likely go away on its own without antibiotics. Rest, acetaminophen (Tylenol and other brands), and plenty of fluids help. Warm saltwater gargles and throat lonzenges for children old enough not to choke (after age four or five), are also good comfort measures.

Strep throat. This is the common name for a throat infection caused by the streptococcus bacteria. The child usually has high fever for several days and feels sick. The tonsils often become fiery red and swollen. The glands (lymph nodes) in the neck are swollen and sometimes tender. After a day or two, white spots or white patches may appear on the tonsils. Older children may complain of such a sore throat that they can hardly swallow; others complain of a stomachache or headache. Young children may be bothered surprisingly little by the sore throat, and strep throat is rare under age two. In strep throat there is usually no cough or runny nose. A child whose tonsils have been removed can still get strep throat.

The treatment for strep throats and scarlet fever (below) is an antibiotic of the penicillin family, either by mouth or injection, or another antibiotic if the child is allergic to penicillin.

Scarlet fever. This is an infection from a type of streptococcus that causes a rash. The rash typically appears a day or two after the child becomes sick. It begins on the warm, moist parts of the body, such as the sides of the chest, the groin, and the back. From a distance, it looks like a uniform red flush; if you look at it closely, you will see that it is made up of tiny red spots on a reddish background. It feels like fine sandpaper. It may spread over the whole body and the sides of the face, but the region around the mouth stays pale. The throat is red, sometimes fiery red, and after a while the tongue usually gets red, first around the edge. While it looks more dramatic than an ordinary strep throat, scarlet fever is no more dangerous. The treatment is the same as for any sore throat caused by streptococcus. In rare cases, a toxin that causes scarlet fever may produce a much more severe rash.

Other kinds of sore throat. There are all kinds and degrees of throat infections caused by a variety of germs, primarily viruses. Many people feel a slight sore throat at the beginning of every cold. The doctor, in examining a child with a fever, often finds a slightly red throat as the only sign of disease. The child may not notice any soreness.

Most of these sore throats are soon over. The child should stay indoors if he feels sick or has a fever. The doctor should be called if there is fever, the child looks sick, or the throat is more than slightly sore (even if there is no fever).

Some children wake on many winter mornings with a sore throat. They otherwise act well, and the sore throat goes away shortly. This kind of sore throat is due to dry winter air, not illness, and is of no significance. A humidifier can help prevent this.

Colds with runny, stuffy noses can also cause sore throats, especially in the early morning, because the mucus may run down the back of the throat during the night, causing irritation.

Swollen glands. The lymph glands or nodes that are scattered up and down the sides of the neck may become sore and swollen from any disease in the throat, mild or severe. The most common cause of swollen glands is infection of the tonsils, whether by strep or virus. Occasionally, the glands themselves become infected. They are then often very swollen, warm, or tender. A doctor needs to evaluate all such large neck swellings. Treatment is by antibiotics.

Neck glands may remain slightly enlarged for weeks or even months after some throat infections. Swollen glands have other causes, too, such as infected teeth, scalp infections, and general diseases, like rubella (German measles). You should consult your doctor about them, but if he finds that your child is generally healthy, don't worry about slightly swollen glands.

CROUP AND EPIGLOTTITIS

Croup. Croup is caused by swelling in and just below the vocal cords. There is usually a hoarse, ringing, barking or croupy cough, and some tightness of breathing, especially when the child inhales. The cause of croup is a viral infection. Croup is scary when you see it for the first time, but it's usually not as serious as it looks. It may recur several times in early childhood. Call the doctor promptly for any kind of croup.

Sometimes what looks like croup is really a child choking on a small object that has gotten stuck in the windpipe. So it's very important that any child who develops a sudden croupy cough be checked by a doctor.

Spasmodic croup is usually a mild form of croup that comes on suddenly during the evening. The child may have been perfectly healthy during the day or may have had the mildest of colds without a cough. Suddenly she wakes up with a violent fit of croupy coughing, is hoarse, and has difficulty breathing. The child struggles and heaves to get air in. She has no fever.

Croup that accompanies a viral cold and fever is usually more severe. The child has a croupy cough and tight breathing. As the child breathes in, the narrowed airway makes a loud gasping sound, called stridor. Croup may come on gradually or suddenly at any time of the day or night. The cough sounds like a dog or seal barking. When the swelling in the airway is severe, it can be very difficult for the child to breathe.

A child with a hoarse, croupy cough with fever, especially with tightness of breathing and rapid breathing, should be put under the close, continuous supervision of a doctor without delay. If you cannot reach your own doctor right away, find another one. If you can't reach any, take your child to a hospital. Medicines can open up the airway in an emergency but can be given only in a hospital.

The emergency treatment for croup until a doctor can be reached is moist air. Use a cold-mist humidifier if you have one. A small room is preferable because you can humidify it faster. You can also take the child into the bathroom and run very hot water into the tub to make steam, not to put the child in. If there is a shower, that works best of all. A twenty-minute steam in the bathroom with the child sitting upright in your lap and the door shut is the best first treatment.

Humidifier or vaporizer steam works much better if it's concentrated under a tent. You can make one by draping sheets over a crib or small table placed on the bed, or you can tack them to the wall. When the child breathes the moist air, the croup will usually begin to improve rapidly. Croup is made worse by an anxious child, so if the makeshift tent frightens the child, it's better not to use it. You or another adult should stay awake as long as there are any symptoms of croup. After the croup is over, wake up two to three hours later to check that the child is breathing comfortably.

Spasmodic croup and viral croup sometimes come back a night or two later. Having the child sleep in a room whose air has been moistened can help. You should take this precaution for three or four nights.

Epiglottitis. This infection is now rare, thanks to the Hib (Haemophilus influenza B) immunization. Epiglottitis looks like severe croup with a high fever. The epiglottis is a small bit of tissue that forms the trap door at the top of the windpipe that keeps food out. If it becomes infected and swollen, it can block off the windpipe completely.

A child with epiglottitis is likely to become ill very quickly. He leans forward, drools, refuses to take food or liquids, and usually makes no sounds at all for fear of provoking a typical croupy cough. He may be unwilling to turn his head because he's keeping his neck in the position that gives him the most room for air to pass between the swollen epiglottis and the windpipe. Epiglottitis is a true medical emergency. Get the child to a doctor or hospital as quickly as possible.

INFLUENZA, BRONCHITIS, AND PNEUMONIA

Influenza. The flu can be a miserable illness, with headache, sore throat, fever, muscle aches, cough, and running nose, and sometimes vomiting or diarrhea. Occasionally there is such severe pain in the calf muscles that the child is reluctant to walk. Fever can last a week or so, the cough even longer.

A person can come down with the flu just a few days after being exposed to it; usually symptoms start five to seven days after exposure. Even before the person begins to feel sick, she will be contagious and will remain so until the fever is gone. This is why the illness spreads so rapidly.

Flu vaccines are available, but because the virus changes, new vaccines must be made each year to keep up. Children with asthma and other chronic lung conditions, heart disease, diabetes, and some neurological disorders should have the flu vaccine each year. Otherwise healthy children, especially children under age two, also benefit from the vaccine.

The treatment for influenza is to keep the child comfortable: Have her rest at home until her temperature remains normal for twenty-four hours; offer fluids that appeal to the child every hour or even half hour, but do not force them; and give her acetaminophen or ibuprofen for the fever and aches. (Never give aspirin to children or teenagers with the flu; it increases their susceptibility to Reye's syndrome; see page 872.)

Early in the flu, treatment with a specific antiviral medication can help to shorten the illness. The doctor should be called at the onset of the flu and again if the child seems unusually ill, has an earache or trouble breathing, or after several days isn't getting better. Ear infections, sinusitis, or pneumonia can follow influenza as secondary infections and need treatment with antibiotics.

Bronchitis. Bronchitis is an infection of the bronchial tubes, which lead to the lungs; in children it's almost always caused by a virus. There is usually plenty of coughing. Sometimes a child seems short of breath. At times you can hear faraway squeaky noises as the child breathes. Parents worry when they think they hear mucus vibrating in the chest. Actually, the mucus is in the throat; the noise it makes is transmitted to the chest.

A mild case of bronchitis, with no fever or loss of appetite and only mild coughing, is only a little more serious than a cold in the nose. The treatment is the same as for a bad cold: rest, fluids in moderation, and tender loving care. If coughing interferes with sleep, a cough-suppressant may help. Antibiotics should not be prescribed because they do not kill the viruses that cause bronchitis.

However, if the child acts sick, becomes short of breath, or has a fever of more than 101, call the doctor. Bronchitis can be mistaken for other, more serious infections that may require treatment with antibiotics.

Pneumonia. Pneumonia is an infection of the lungs themselves caused by either a virus or bacteria. Bacterial pneumonia usually comes on after a child has had a cold for several days, or it may start without warning. Suspect it if the temperature climbs above 102, breathing becomes rapid, and the child coughs frequently. A child with pneumonia will sometimes make a grunting noise. Antibiotics usually promptly cure bacterial pneumonia if treatment is started early. Call the doctor if your child develops a fever and coughs frequently.

Pneumonias caused by viruses are more common and usually less severe, often getting better on their own in two to four weeks. Although viral infections cannot be cured by antibiotics, it's often hard to be sure whether pneumonia is caused by a virus or bacteria, so antibiotics are usually prescribed for all children with pneumonia.

Bronchiolitis. Bronchiolitis (not to be confused with bronchitis; see previous page) is an inflammation by a virus of the small respiratory passages in the lungs (bronchioles). It is a wheezing respiratory illness that affects infants and toddlers, usually two to twenty-four months of age. The child usually has a cold in addition to a cough and wheezing and breathes fast and has to work harder than normal to exhale. Several viruses cause bronchiolitis. One you may hear about is called RSV, which stands for respiratory syncytial virus. Many of the children admitted to hospitals with severe wheezing illness have RSV.

Bronchiolitis can be mild or severe. Some children become short of breath and have to work hard to breathe. They cannot comfortably eat or rest and become exhausted from the exertion of breathing. Most children with bronchiolitis do well and can be treated at home; about one in twenty require hospitalization to carefully monitor the breathing status. There is also a new medication that can prevent RSV infection in high-risk babies, such as those with underlying chronic lung disease; unfortunately, it has to be given by monthly injection during the flu season.

Because bronchiolitis can occasionally lead to significant respiratory problems, it is important to contact your doctor or nurse practitioner so she can help you monitor your child's symptoms. Most children are better in seven to ten days, but a few may wheeze with succeeding colds.

HEADACHES

Headaches are common in children and teenagers. Though a headache can be an early sign of a wide variety of illnesses, ranging from the common cold to more serious infections, the most frequent cause by far is stress. Think of the child who for days has been memorizing his part in the school play or the child who's been practicing extra hours after school on the gymnastics team. Fatigue, tension, and anticipation often combine to produce changes in the blood flow to the muscles of the head and neck, causing a headache.

When a young child complains of a headache, call the doctor promptly, because it's more likely at this age that the headache is an early symptom of an oncoming illness. An older child who has a headache can be given the appropriate dose of acetaminophen or ibuprofen, followed by a rest period—lying down, playing quietly, or engaging in another restful activity—until the medicine starts to work. Sometimes an ice pack helps. If a headache lasts as long as four hours after the child has taken a medication or other symptoms of illness (such as fever) appear, the doctor or nurse practitioner should be called.

A child who has frequent headaches should have a thorough physical examination, including a check of his vision, a dental exam, a neurological evaluation, and a careful review of the child's diet. It's also worth considering whether something in the child's home life, school, or social activities may be causing undue stress.

Children do get migraine headaches, although they are less likely to have characteristic migraine symptoms, such as an aura of flashing lights or other visual changes or weakness in one extremity. A pattern of severe headaches in a child should indicate the possibility of migraines, especially (though not only) if they run in the family.

If a headache comes on after a fall or a blow to the head, get in touch with the doctor promptly. Headaches on rising or in the morning or that wake a child at night are often signs of serious illness. Discuss with your child's doctor any recurrent early-morning headaches and any associated with dizziness, blurred or double vision, nausea and vomiting.

STOMACHACHES AND INTESTINAL INFECTIONS

Most stomach aches are brief and mild; simple reassurance often does the trick. Fifteen minutes later, you'll probably notice your child playing normally. For any stomachache that lasts an hour or more, it's reasonable to call the doctor for advice. For very severe stomachaches, don't wait even that long. There are dozens of causes of stomachaches and upsets. A few are serious; most are not. People are apt to jump to the conclusion that a stomachache is due either to appendicitis or something that the child ate. Actually, neither of these causes is common. Children can usually eat strange foods or an unusual amount of a regular food without any indigestion.

Before you call the doctor, take the child's temperature (page 704). Until you reach the doctor put the child to bed and give him nothing to eat. If the child is thirsty, small sips of water are fine.

Common causes of stomachache. Young infants often have colic, which can look like stomach or abdominal pain. If your baby has abdominal pain and is irritable or vomiting, it's wise to call the doctor immediately.

After the age of a year, one of the commonest causes of stomachache is the onset of a simple cold, sore throat, or flu, especially when there is fever. Stomachache is a sign that the infection is disturbing the intestines as well as other parts of the body. In a young child, almost any infection may cause stomachache or abdominal pain. A small child is likely to complain that her tummy hurts when she really means that she is nauseated. She often vomits soon after this complaint.

Constipation is the most common reason for children to have stomachaches that come back over and over again (see page 844). The pain may be dull and nagging, or it may be sudden and very painful (and it may go away just as suddenly). The pain is often worse after a meal. The source of the pain appears to be cramping of the intestines as they fight to squeeze out the hard, dry bowel movements.

Pain from constipation often occurs when a toddler withholds stool in potty training (see page 584). Constipation occurs in older children when fluid intake is reduced or when a very busy child forgets to go to the bathroom.

Stomachaches and stress. It's important to realize that even if the cause is psychological the pain is very real. Children with feeding problems often complain of stomachaches when they sit down to a meal or after they have eaten a little. The parents may think that the child has made up the stomachache as an excuse not to eat. I think that it's more likely that the stomach is tight because of the child's tension at mealtimes and that the stomachache is real. The treatment here is for the parents to handle mealtimes so that the child enjoys the food. (See page 353).

Children who have never had feeding problems but have other worries can have stomachaches, too, especially around mealtime. Think of the child who is nervous about starting school in the fall and has a stomachache instead of an appetite for breakfast or the child who feels guilty about something that hasn't been found out yet. All kinds of emotions, from fear to pleasant excitement, can affect the stomach and intestines. They can cause not only pains and lack of appetite but also vomiting and diarrhea or constipation. Pain in such cases tends to be in the center of the abdomen. Since there's no infection, the child won't have a fever.

This type of stomachache is common in children and teenagers and often follows a pattern of recurring two or three times a week or more. The pain is almost always in the midline, either around or just above the belly button. It is often hard for the child to describe.

The treatment is to identify the stresses at home, at school, in sports, and in the child's social life and do whatever is necessary to reduce them. Doctors have studied this condition, which they call recurrent abdominal pain syndrome. It's very important to realize that the pain experienced by these children is real pain, not all in the child's head or just to get attention.

Infections (diarrhea and vomiting). Many stomach and intestinal infections can cause stomachache, sometimes with vomiting, sometimes with diarrhea, sometimes with both. The medical term for these is acute gastroenteritis. They are often called stomach flu or intestinal flu, indicating contagious disease caused by an unknown virus or bacteria. These infections often pass through several members of a family, one after the other. There may or may not be fever.

Dehydration. Dehydration (excessive loss of body water) can be a result of either vomiting, diarrhea, or both. It is most often seen in babies or very young children since they don't have as much reserve body water as older children and adults and can't understand the need to drink extra fluids when they're sick.

The first sign of dehydration is that the baby produces less urine than usual; this can be hard to judge, however, if the diaper is filled with liquid stool. As dehydration worsens, the child is likely to become listless or lethargic; his eyes look dry, and there may be no tears when he cries; his eyes may also be sunken and shadowed; his lips and mouth are parched and dry; and, in a baby, the soft spot on the top of the head appears sunken. If your child shows any signs of dehydration, get him to a doctor or to a hospital as soon as possible.

Food poisoning is caused by eating food that contains toxins manufactured by certain bacteria. The food may or may not taste unusual. Food poisoning is seldom caused by food that has been recently and thoroughly cooked, because cooking kills these germs. It's caused most often by custard or whipped cream, creamy salads, poultry stuffing, and undercooked meat. Bacteria multiply readily in these substances if they remain out of the refrigerator for many hours. Another cause is improperly home-canned foods.

The symptoms of food poisoning are usually vomiting, diarrhea, and stomachache. Sometimes there are chills and fever. Everyone who eats the contaminated food is likely to be affected by it to some degree at about the same time, in contrast to an intestinal flu, which usually spreads through a family over a number of days. The doctor should always be called when you suspect food poisoning.

Appendicitis. Let me at the start contradict some common notions about appendicitis. There isn't necessarily fever. The pain isn't necessarily severe. The pain doesn't usually settle in the lower right side of the abdomen until the attack has gone on for some time. Vomiting doesn't always occur. A blood count doesn't show whether a stomachache is due to appendicitis.

The appendix is a little offshoot from the large intestine, about the size of a short earthworm. It usually lies in the central part of the right lower quarter of the abdomen but can be lower down, over toward the middle of the abdomen, or as far up as the ribs. When it becomes inflamed, it's a gradual process, like the formation of a boil. That's how you know that a sudden severe pain in the abdomen that lasts a few minutes then goes away for good isn't appendicitis. The worst danger is that an inflamed appendix will burst, very much as a boil does, and spread the infection through the abdomen. The condition that ensues is called peritonitis. Appendicitis that develops very rapidly can reach the point of bursting in less than twenty-four hours. That's why any stomachache that persists for as long as an hour should be discussed with the doctor, even though nine out of ten cases will prove to be something other than appendicitis.

In the most typical cases of appendicitis, there is pain around the navel for several hours. Only later does it shift to the lower right side. There is apt to be vomiting once or twice, but this doesn't always occur. The appetite is usually diminished but not always. The bowels may be normal or constipated, rarely loose. After this has gone on for a few hours, the child's temperature is likely to be mildly elevated, though it's possible to have appendicitis with no fever at all. The child may feel pain when he pulls his right knee up, when he stretches it way back, or when he walks around.

You can see that the symptoms of appendicitis vary a lot and that you need a doctor to make the diagnosis. When doctors find a tender spot in the right side of the abdomen, they suspect appendicitis but they sometimes need a blood count, X-ray, or ultrasound to help them decide.

It's sometimes impossible for even the most expert doctors to be absolutely certain that a child has appendicitis. When there is enough suspicion, an operation is usually performed. That is because if it is appendicitis, it is dangerous to delay surgery. The appendix might burst and cause an infection in the abdomen.

Intussusception. A typical case is an infant who suddenly looks ill, vomits, and has bouts of abdominal pain that cause her to

draw her legs up to her belly. Sometimes the vomiting is more prominent; sometimes the pain is. The vomiting is more copious and repetitious than the usual spitting-up of a baby. The cramps are sudden and usually severe. They come only a few minutes apart; between them the baby may be fairly comfortable or sleepy. After several hours (during which there may be normal or loose bowel movements) the baby may pass a movement containing mucus and blood, the classic currant jelly or prune juice stool; more often than not, this does not occur. The problem, which is common, is due to an obstruction of the intestines, which occurs when a small section of the intestine slides inside the one next to it, like a telescope folding up. Children as young as four months through about six years can develop this problem. If it's caught early, it can often be easily fixed; if the bowel has been injured, however, surgery may be necessary.

Also rare but serious are other types of intestinal obstructions. A part of the intestine becomes kinked and stuck in a pocket in the abdomen, most frequently in an inguinal hernia. There usually is vomiting and sharp cramps.

Persistent diarrhea. The most common type of persistent or chronic diarrhea occurs in a young child who is obviously thriving and does not complain of feeling sick. The diarrhea may come out of the blue or with a stomach flu. The child may have three to five soft or runny and smelly bowel movements a day, though he may begin the day with a normal one. There may be mucus or undigested food in the bowel movements. His appetite remains good, and he is playful and active.

The child continues to gain weight normally and laboratory tests of the bowel movement reveal nothing abnormal. The condition usually gets better by itself, over several weeks. Often the diarrhea can be much reduced by cutting down on juice in the child's diet. The most likely culprit is apple juice. That's why this condition is sometimes called apple juice diarrhea. Juice should generally be limited to eight to ten ounces a day.

There are several uncommon, more serious digestive diseases that cause chronic diarrhea in infants and young children. For this reason, it's a good idea to have the problem evaluated by the doctor.

Cystic fibrosis. The two most common symptoms of this disease are foul-smelling diarrhea and a cough. Many other symptoms also occur. The baby's rectum may protrude. The intestines may be obstructed right after birth by dry meconium and from time to time in later years by hard, dry bowel movements. After the baby starts eating solid foods, there may be frequent bowel movements that look normal but are mushy, greasy, and foul-smelling. Most infants have a good, even ravenous appetite while they have this disease. Nevertheless, because of the inability to digest food properly, malnutrition and poor growth sets in. Persistent bronchitis develops, though in a mild case this may not happen until later in childhood.

Cystic fibrosis is a progressive, hereditary disease of specific glands. The pancreas, which normally supplies digestive juices to the intestines, doesn't function well. The glands that normally make the mucus that coat the bronchial tubes secrete only abnormally dry, sticky mucus. As a result, serious lung infections are common.

The diagnosis is made by measuring the amount of salt in a child's sweat; there are also genetic tests. Antibiotics and other medications can reduce the lung infections. Use of digestive enzymes can help combat malnutrition and promote normal growth. A child with cystic fibrosis should be evaluated and have his treatment supervised at a center that specializes in the disease. For more information, see the Resource Guide (page 917).

Malabsorption. In this condition, the intestines are unable to absorb all the nutrients that are presented to them; the nutrients come out as diarrhea, and the child is apt to become deficient in them.

The most common cause of malabsorption is the inability to

digest certain types of sugar, fat, or protein. With this condition there is always diarrhea, sometimes foul-smelling, sometimes burning, often with cramps. Usually the child gains weight poorly and seems unwell. The condition resolves when the offending food is removed from the diet. It is important for parents and doctors to work together to make sure the child's diet is still nutritionally adequate.

Following prolonged diarrhea, a child may have difficulty digesting lactose, the sugar in milk. In the past these children were said to be allergic to milk, but this is not really an allergic reaction. Rather, the irritated lining of the intestines simply needs time to heal before normal digestion returns. Difficulty in digesting the lactose in cow's milk may be inherited. Cramps or diarrhea usually start in school-age children. Elimination of dairy products is the treatment.

Worms. It horrifies parents to find worms in their child's bowel movements, but there is no reason to be distressed or to decide that the child has not been properly cared for.

Pinworms, or threadworms, are the commonest variety. They look like white threads a third of an inch long. They live in the lower intestine, coming out from between the buttocks at night to lay their eggs. They can be found there at night or in the bowel movement. They cause itching around the anus, which may disturb the child's sleep. (In earlier times worms were thought to be the chief cause of children's grinding their teeth at night, but this is not so.) A clear description of the worm will help your doctor make the diagnosis.

Roundworms look very much like earthworms. The first suspicion comes when one is discovered in the bowel movement. They usually don't cause symptoms unless the child has a great number of them.

Hookworms are common in some parts of the southern United States. They may cause malnutrition and anemia. The disease is contracted by going barefoot in infested soil.

Children born in less-developed countries and children who have lived for a time in a group home or shelter for the homeless may carry intestinal parasites (that is, worms) without having symptoms. Discovering the problem is a matter of sending samples of bowel movement to a laboratory for microscopic examination. Intestinal worms are fairly easy to treat with prescription medications.

CONSTIPATION

Constipation refers to hard, dry stools, which are difficult to pass. It's not the number of bowel movements each day that determines whether a baby or child (or adult) has constipation.

Infants often go through periods of constipation that are related to changes in their diets or changes in their intestines that come with age. Adding four ounces a day of water or prune juice often loosens things up. This amount of nonmilk fluid is safe for babies. If this doesn't work or if constipation is severe, ask the doctor about it, since it can be a sign of more serious illness. (Some parents feel that the iron in infant formula causes constipation. Studies have not found this to be the case, however, and iron is very important for other reasons; see page 332.)

At any age, constipation is common in a mild illness. Any disease that can make a person feel sick all over is likely to affect the stomach and the intestines, slowing down the bowels, taking away the appetite, perhaps causing vomiting. With fever, the body loses more water through the skin and in the breath, so the intestines may absorb more water from the bowel movement, making it hard and dry.

Chronic constipation is uncommon in the older baby or child, especially those who eat a varied diet that includes whole-grain cereals, vegetables, and fruits. A diet rich in meats and processed grains may provide too little fiber for regular, soft bowel movements. The solution may be as simple as substituting whole wheat for white bread, and fresh orange or peach slices for cookies or cake after meals. Remember the "P fruits that make you poop": prunes, plums, peaches, and pears. Apricots, too. You can also add unprocessed millers bran (available in most supermarkets) or bran cereal to muffins, applesauce, or a peanut-butter sandwich. If you add bran or other dried fiber, be sure to give your child two or three extra glasses of water or fruit juice a day. A slurry of applesauce, bran, and prune juice is sweet and crunchy, and it often works well.

In some children, milk and other dairy products slow the intestines down, resulting in constipation. Cutting down on dairy products or cutting them out altogether is often an effective treatment for constipation. If you do this, be sure to add other sources of calcium and vitamin D (see page 331). It's also important to see that your child has plenty of exercise and time set aside to sit quietly on the toilet each day.

It's best to make as little fuss as possible about your child's bowel movements. At age two or three, children begin to see their bowel movements as their own concern, something they are rightly in charge of; later they develop modesty about their bottoms and what does—or doesn't—come out. It can be difficult to respect a child's privacy and avoid making a child too self-conscious while helping the child make the necessary changes in diet and behavior.

If you find that these simple remedies aren't working, consult your child's doctor. There are many over-the-counter medications available to treat constipation, but I recommend you use them under a doctor's guidance. Even something seemingly as harmless as mineral oil can interfere with vitamin absorption, or cause pneumonia in a child who inhales some into his lungs (for this reason, it's not recommended for children under age three). Children who use laxatives sometimes become dependent on them. The guidance of an experienced doctor should help you avoid such pitfalls.

Psychological constipation. There are two varieties of constipation that are largely psychological in origin. They start most frequently between age one and two. If children at this age have one or two painfully hard movements, they may hold back for weeks or even months afterward for fear of being hurt again. If they hold the movement in for a day or two, it's likely to be hard again, and this keeps the problem going. Occasionally, when a parent goes at toilet training in an overbearing manner, small children, being at an independent stage in their development, automatically resist and hold the movement back, which leads to constipation. (For a discussion of soiling due to constipation, see page 590.)

Painfully hard movements should be treated promptly in a child of one to three years to avoid the vicious circle of with-holding and further constipation. Your doctor can recommend one of several preparations that will keep the movements soft. Treatment usually lasts for at least a month, allowing the child to become confident that the painful hardness will not recur.

GENITAL AND URINARY DISTURBANCES

Frequent urination. Frequent urination has several possible causes. When it develops in a child whose urination was not pre-viously frequent, it may indicate disease, such as an infection of the urinary system or diabetes. The child and a urine specimen should be examined promptly by the doctor.

A few individuals, even calm ones, have bladders that hold less than average. This may be the way they were made. But some children (and adults, too) who have to urinate frequently are high-strung or worried. In one case it's a chronic tendency; in another, the need to urinate often is due to temporary strain. A healthy athlete may have to go to the toilet every fifteen minutes before a race.

The parents' job is to find out what, if anything, is making the child tense. In one case it's the handling at home; in another it's relations with other children; in yet another it's the child's school situation. Most often it's a combination of these.

A common story involves the timid child and a teacher who

seems severe. To begin with, the child's apprehensiveness keeps his bladder from relaxing sufficiently to hold much urine. Then he worries about asking permission to be excused. If the teacher makes a fuss about his leaving the room, it's worse still. It's wise to get a note from the doctor that not merely requests that the child be excused but also explains his nature and why his bladder works that way. If the teacher is approachable and the parent is tactful, a personal visit will help, too.

Painful urination. A fairly frequent cause of painful urination in girls is an inflammation of the area around the urinary opening, perhaps from some contamination by BM or irritation from bubble bath. This may frequently make her feel as if she has to urinate, though she may be unable or too scared to, or she passes only a few drops. The doctor should be consulted and a urine specimen examined to make sure the child has no bladder infection. Until then, she can get relief by sitting several times a day in a shallow warm bath to which you have added a half cup of bicarbonate of soda. After the bath, gently blot dry the urinary region. Get rid of bubble baths, fabric softeners (including dryer sheets), and perfumed toilet paper, and use only cotton, not nylon, panties.

Infrequent urination. Occasionally in hot weather, when a child is perspiring a great deal and not drinking enough, he may pass his urine infrequently, perhaps not for eight hours or more. What does come is scanty and dark. The same thing may happen during a fever. When water is in short supply, the kidneys hold on to every drop possible making a very concentrated urine. A child in hot weather or when feverish needs plenty of chances and occasional reminders to drink between meals, especially if he is too young to tell his parents what he wants.

Sore on the end of the penis. Sometimes a small raw area appears around the opening, of the penis. There may be enough swelling of the tissues to close up part of the opening and make it difficult for the boy to pass urine. This little sore is a localized diaper rash. The best treatment is to expose the sore to the air as much as is practical. Bathing daily with a mild soap will encourage healing. If the child is in pain from having been unable to urinate for many hours, have him sit in a warm bath for half an hour and encourage him to urinate while in the tub. If this doesn't make him urinate, the doctor should be called.

Infections of the urinary tract. Infections of the kidneys or bladder (cystitis) may cause a stormy illness with a high, irregular fever. Most urinary tract infections are mild without a high fever, however. An older child may complain of frequent, burning urination, but most often there are no signs pointing to the urinary tract. These infections are more common in girls and in the first two years of life. Prompt medical treatment is necessary.

If there is a lot of pus, the urine may be hazy or cloudy. A little pus may not be visible to the naked eye. Infected urine smells somewhat like a bowel movement. On the other hand, a normal child's urine may be cloudy, especially when it cools, from the ordinary minerals in it. So you can't definitely tell from looking at the urine if it is infected; your sense of smell is more reliable. Regardless of the color or odor of the urine, if your child complains of burning or pain when urinating, take her to the doctor. A urine culture is essential to make the diagnosis and select the antibiotic.

After a urinary infection, the child's whole urinary system should be investigated to make sure there are no abnormalities that could lead to future infections or kidney problems. Recurrent or chronic urinary infections are a common cause of kidney failure later in life. An ultrasound of the kidneys can detect a malformed kidney, or scarring from past infections which may have been silent. A test called a voiding cystourethrogram (VCUG) uses X-rays to detect urine flowing backward from the bladder up into the kidney, a common abnormality that causes recurrent kidney infections. A school-age or teenage girl who has had a single uncomplicated bladder infection may not need to undergo a VCUG, because the likelihood of there being an underlying abnormality is low. Other children with urinary infections—boys, children under age five, or any child with a kidney infection—ought to have the test. After taking antibiotics for a urinary infection, all children should have two or more urine cultures done over time, to look for chronic or recurrent urinary infections that may require special treatment.

It's very important to teach girls to wipe themselves from front to back after they urinate or have a bowel movement. This prevents the transfer of germs from the anal region into the opening of the urethra (the tube between the bladder and the outside world). Wiping from back to front (wiping up) is a frequent cause of repeated urinary tract infections in girls.

Pus in the urine. Pus in a girl's urine may not mean urinary infection. Pus can also come from a vaginal infection, even one so mild that there is no visible inflammation or discharge. For this reason, it should never be assumed without further investigation that pus in an ordinary specimen indicates an infection of her urinary system. The first step is to secure a clean urine specimen. Separate the labia, briefly and gently sponge the genital region with a piece of wet absorbent cotton, and blot dry with a soft towel or a piece of dry absorbent cotton before letting her pass urine for the specimen. The important test is the culture of the specimen for bacteria. With infants, the doctor may have to use a very fine plastic tube or catheter to remove some urine from the bladder for testing.

Vaginal discharge. It is fairly common for young girls to have a slight vaginal discharge. A majority are caused by unimportant germs and clear up in a short time. However, a thick, profuse discharge that is irritating may be caused by a more serious infection and needs prompt medical treatment. A mild discharge that persists for days should be examined, too. A discharge that is partly pus and partly blood is sometimes caused by a small girl having pushed some object into her vagina. If the object remains, it can cause irritation and infection. If this is found to be the case, it is natural and sensible for her parents to ask her not to do it again; but it's better not to make the girl feel really guilty or imply that she might have seriously hurt herself. The exploring and experimenting she did is not much different from what most children do at this age.

If there is a delay in reaching the doctor, the burning sensation from a slight discharge can often be relieved without fuss by sitting the child twice a day in a shallow bath to which half a cup of bicarbonate of soda has been added.

Wearing white cotton panties, using unperfumed white toilet paper, and wearing clothes that provide adequate air ventilation to the vaginal area may help in the prevention and treatment of vaginal irritation. Proper wiping (from front to back) and avoiding bubble baths may also help.

A recurrent chronic or severe vaginal discharge in a child may be a sign of sexual abuse (see page 507. Your doctor may ask you questions about your child's caretakers and the possibility of abuse. A careful examination of the vagina and a culture of the discharge will be performed. Most young girls with a vaginal discharge have not been sexually abused.

ALLERGIES

Milk allergy and special formulas. Milk allergy is a lot less common than most people think. Young babies have many stomach complaints, but most are due to their immaturity rather than allergy. Truly allergic babies often have symptoms such as severe eczema, chronic nasal congestion, and poor weight gain and come from allergic families. Breast-feeding is ideal for babies from allergic families, but for babies already on formula who have allergic troubles, you and your doctor or nurse practitioner may want to consider switching formulas. Your doctor is most likely to recommend a more specialized formula aimed at your baby's special problems. Laboratory tests can sometimes confirm milk allergy, or a trial of milk can be given at some later time. Most children outgrow milk allergies by one to two years. Parents may choose, however, to raise their children without milk or other dairy products for a variety of health reasons (see page 337).

Allergic nose troubles, including hay fever. You probably know people who have ragweed hay fever. When ragweed pollen (found in the eastern part of the United States) gets in the wind in mid-August, these people sneeze and their noses are stuffed up and itch and run. This is because the nose is allergic to the pollen, which doesn't bother other people. Some people have hay fever in spring because they are allergic to certain tree pollens. If your child has a running, itching nose that lasts for weeks at the same time every year, consult your doctor or nurse practitioner. Liquid medicines or tablets and nasal sprays can eliminate some of the sneezing and congestion. The most effective treatment is to minimize exposure to the offending allergens: Close the windows in the car and the house, or at least the bedroom (air conditioners remove much of the pollen), avoid parks and fields during pollen season, and limit time outdoors on the days when the pollen count is highest. In the most severe cases of hay fever, injections may be recommended.

Other nose allergies may be less dramatic but more troublesome than hay fever. Some noses are sensitive to the feathers in pillows, or dog hair, house dust, or any number of other substances. Such year-round allergies may keep a child's nose stuffy or running and require him to breathe through the mouth, month in and month out. The chronic obstruction may make an allergic child more susceptible to sinus infections. If your child is much bothered this way, your doctor or an allergy specialist may be able to find the cause.

The treatment is different in each case and depends on the causes. If the cause is goose feathers, change the pillow. If it's dog hair, you may have to give away the dog. If it's something hard to avoid, like grass, the doctor may give your child injections of the offending substance over a long period. Stripping the room—especially the bedroom—may be recommended to lessen exposure to dust mites (see page 854), especially if the symptoms occur mainly at night or first thing in the morning. Remove the rugs and curtains for good, and give the room a wet-mopping every day. Eliminate all wool and stuffed toys from the room.

You may buy dust-proof coverings for the mattress and pillow, use a mattress and pillows of foam rubber, or use a canvas cot with no pillow at all. Allergy symptoms usually can't be eliminated completely. You may have to be satisfied with partial improvement.

Hives. An allergic reaction can show up on the skin as raised red welts or blotches, often with a pale spot in the middle, that itch, sometimes unbearably. Hives are unlike most other rashes in that they often disappear in one spot then appear in another. Sometimes it's obvious that hives are in response to a specific food or medicine. Other triggers include heat, cold, plants, soaps or detergents, viral infections (including mild coldlike illnesses), even strong emotions. Often, though, it's impossible to tell what has set off the hives. A few individuals repeatedly get hives; many have them only once or twice in a lifetime. First aid is with an antihistamine (nonprescription diphenhydramine, trade name Benadryl, often works well). More powerful medicine is available by prescription.

On very rare occasions, hives are accompanied by swelling of the inside of the mouth and throat and difficulty breathing (anaphylaxis). If this happens, call an ambulance immediately. This is a medical emergency. Children who have had one episode of anaphylaxis should carry a rapidly acting life-saving injection called an Epi-Pen or AnaKit (see page 790).

Behavioral problems and allergies. In recent years all kinds of behavioral problems in children have been blamed on allergies, often to food additives and food colorings, or to common foods such as wheat. There is no question that having chronically itchy eyes and a runny nose can make a child irritable and interfere with learning. Ironically, the antihistamines used to treat the allergies can also cause learning problems. Diphenhydramine (Benadryl and other brands) is notorious for causing children to become either drowsy or hyper. Newer, more expensive antihistamines are better overall, but some children react negatively to them, too.

I'm not convinced that allergies are responsible for learning and behavior problems *in the absence of other obvious allergy symptoms.* Solid scientific evidence for these effects is lacking, and some nonmedical practitioners make extravagant claims for expensive tests and exotic treatments that don't end up helping. There is no harm, of course, in making a simple change such as cutting out processed foods or wheat products for while, to see if the problem gets better, as long as your child's overall nutrition doesn't suffer. Still, it's a good idea consult with your doctor or nurse practitioner if you think that your child has a behavior problem due to an allergy, before you embark on an unproven treatment.

ASTHMA

Asthma is responsible for a tremendous number of missed school days and hospitalizations of children. Instead of the sensitive organ being the nose, as in hay fever, it is the small bronchial tubes in the lungs. When the irritating substance reaches the small airways, they swell, thick mucus is secreted, and the passageways for air are narrowed. Breathing becomes difficult, labored, and noisy, especially exhalation. When air is forced through the narrowed breathing passages, it makes a whistling sound, known as wheezing. Coughing occurs, sometimes even in the absence of wheezing (most commonly as a nighttime cough or coughing with exertion).

Causes of asthma. The tendency to develop asthma is inherited. In those children whose airways are susceptible, an asthma attack is usually an overreaction to a variety of conditions or substances, which include cigarette smoke, colds and respiratory infections (mostly viruses), allergies, exercise, changes in the weather, stress, and specific foods. Some children have many triggers; others only one. Identify your child's triggers. Foods may also play a part, especially in very young children. The child who has chronic asthma of more than slight degree is usually tested in an attempt to discover the offending substances.

When an older child has chronic asthma, it's likely due to substances that float in the air, such as horse dander, dog hair, or molds. Allergists call these inhalants. Two of the most common offending inhalants come from cockroaches and dust mites, which are tiny insects that live in carpets, draperies, and upholstery. The shells and droppings of these insects get crushed into a fine dust that drifts into the air then into children's lungs.

Treatment. Children with asthma should be under the care of attentive doctors. Untreated, the condition often gets worse, resulting in missed school, disrupted sleep, and serious limitations on a child's activities. With proper treatment, however, children with asthma should be able to live symptom-free.

The treatment of asthma depends on the triggers and its severity. Foods to which the child is sensitive should be eliminated from his diet. When inhalants are the cause, the treatment is much the same as in year-round allergies of the nose (see page 850). No children should be exposed to secondhand smoke, but it is especially important that children with asthma not be exposed, because the smoke irritates their sensitive bronchi.

Children with very mild asthma may need treatments only once in a while for brief periods of time (rescue treatment). Children with more severe or persistent asthma will need treatment every day, even if they are not wheezing that day (preventive treatment).

There are two main types of medication for asthma. Bronchodilator medications open up (dilate) the bronchial tubes by causing the tiny muscles that surround the tubes to relax. Anti-inflammatory medications prevent or reverse the inflammation that causes the lining of the bronchial tubes to swell. Bronchodilators work well for mild asthma. Anti-inflammatories are required for persistent and severe asthma, often in combination with bronchodilators. Asthma medications are often given in the form of a mist, either from a nebulizer machine or a small spray can or "puffer," and there are also effective medications in pill form.

A child who has frequent recurring episodes of asthma should be on a continuous preventive medication program. The goal is for the child to have a completely normal life, with unrestricted activities and no serious attacks. Many children with asthma grow out of the condition; others carry it with them into adulthood. Prediction is difficult. Early, effective treatment may increase the chances that the illness will go away altogether.

Reactive airways disease. In the first two to three years of life, a child may have spells of wheezing and difficult breathing, not in response to an allergic or irritating trigger but only when he has a cold. This tendency may remain a factor as the child grows older or may turn into actual asthma.

The treatment for the wheezing episodes is the same as for asthma: medications to open up the bronchial tubes (bronchodilators). If a baby is having a great deal of difficulty breathing, admission to the hospital for more intensive monitoring and treatment makes sense.

ECZEMA

Eczema is a rough, red rash that comes in patches, associated with very dry skin. Eczema itches, and scratching makes it worse.

Like hay fever and asthma, eczema is caused by allergy. The allergic reaction may be to a food in the diet or a material, like wool or silk, that comes in direct contact with the skin. Eczema is more common in children who have a family member with either eczema or a related illness, such as asthma, hay fever, or hives.

Even when eczema is primarily due to a food allergy, irritation of the skin from the outside may play a role. In general, winter is worst for eczema, because it dries out skin that is already too dry. Other children develop worse eczema in hot weather, reacting to their own perspiration. If a baby has eczema only where wool comes in contact with his skin, he may be allergic to wool directly; or he may be allergic to a food, and the wool merely acts as an irritant. In older children, emotional stress may make the rash worse from time to time.

The most common place for eczema to begin in a young baby is on the cheeks or forehead. From there it may spread back to the ears and neck. The scaliness looks from a distance as if salt has dried there, especially on the ears. On a child who's near a year of age, eczema may start almost anywhere, on the shoulders, arms, or chest. In children between one and three years, the most typical spots are the creases in the elbows and behind the knees.

When eczema is mild or just starting, its color is usually light red or tannish pink; if the condition becomes severe, it turns a deeper red. Constant scratching and rubbing cause scratch marks and weeping (oozing). When the oozing serum dries, it forms crusts. Scratched areas often become infected with bacteria from the skin, making the weeping and oozing worse. When a patch of eczema is healing even after the redness has all faded away, you can still feel the roughness and thickness of the skin. In darker-skinned children, areas that have healed may look lighter than the rest of the skin. This tends to even out over time but may take weeks.

Treatment. The single most important thing the parent can do is to keep the skin well moisturized, using a plain moisturizing cream (one with no dye or fragrance) several times a day. Ask your child's doctor or a pharmacist to suggest one. Many cases are much improved by lotions and ointments alone. Use soap as infrequently as possible, since it robs the skin of oils. When you do use soap, use one with a lot of moisturizers (Dove is a favorite of many doctors), or use a nondetergent cleanser. Baths should be in warm, not hot, water and should last about ten minutes; if much shorter, the skin does not have time to soak up the water; if much longer, the skin can become overhydrated and itches more. When drying your child after a bath, pat the skin dry; don't rub with the towel. The best time to apply moisturizer is within three minutes after a bath.

Severe eczema in a baby can be a very trying disease to take care of. The itching drives the baby wild. The parents go wild trying to keep the child from scratching. The rash can last for months. It's important to keep the baby's fingernails short (filing works best, because it doesn't leave sharp edges). The less the baby can scratch her skin, the less chance there is of an infection getting started in the scratched areas. For babies who tolerate it, covering the hands with a pair of white cotton mittens at night is helpful, since a lot of scratching can go on while the baby is asleep. Medication to reduce itching can also help.

In more persistent cases, an effort must be made to find out what food or foods the child is allergic to. Cow's milk is occasionally found to be the cause. A few babies can be cured only by giving up dairy products altogether and shifting to artificial milk made from soy beans, rice, grains, or other special formulas. It's best to undertake the search for food allergies under the direction of an experienced doctor; trying to do it yourself often ends in confusion. In severe and persistent cases, blood tests or skin-testing can sometimes help pin down the offending substance. When an external irritant seems to play a part, that needs attention, too. Wool is very commonly irritating to eczema.

In addition to moisturizers, eczema is often treated with hydrocortisone. Hydrocortisone belongs to a family of medications called corticosteroids, steroids for short. (The wording here confuses many parents; the steroids used to treat eczema are different from the anabolic steroids that some bodybuilders or athletes use, illegally, to bulk up.) Steroids like hydrocortisone work by combating the allergic response in the skin. The allergic response is a form of inflammation; hydrocortisone and related steroids are among the most effective anti-inflammatory medications.

Hydrocortisone is available without prescription in 0.5 percent and 1 percent strength; more concentrated preparations and more potent steroids require a prescription. A doctor will often prescribe a potent steroid to start, then substitute a milder one when the eczema is under control. Newer, nonsteroid medications are showing promise as well.

Antihistamine medications such as diphenhydramine (Benadryl) can reduce itching. Antibiotics, either applied as ointments or given by mouth, may be necessary in some cases. It's fine to use a moisturizer, 1 percent hydrocortisone, and diphenhydramine on your own to treat mild eczema. For more severe eczema, work closely with your child's doctor or a dermatologist.

The thing to remember about eczema is that it's a tendency inside the child. It's not an infection that you can get rid of completely. Eczema that starts early in infancy usually clears up completely or at least becomes much milder in a year or two.

OTHER SKIN CONDITIONS

Distinguishing among rashes. If your child has a rash, you're likely to need your doctor's or nurse practitioner's help. Rashes vary so greatly among different individuals that even a skin specialist sometimes has difficulty diagnosing them. The purpose of this section is only to give you a few general pointers about some of the more common rashes of children, to relieve your mind until you can reach your doctor or nurse practitioner.

Common rashes in babies, including diaper rashes, are dealt with on page 122.

Insect bites and stings. There are many different kinds of insect bites, from big puffy swellings the size of a half-dollar down to a simple blood-crusted spot with no swelling. Most bites have two common characteristics: There is a tiny hole or bump in the center where the stinger went in, and they're usually located on the exposed parts of the skin. See page 777 for first aid.

Ticks can carry a number of diseases, such as Rocky Mountain spotted fever and Lyme disease, which have characteristic rashes. If you live in an area where ticks are present, check with your doctor about what precautions to take during tick season. You should remove a tick with a fine tweezer. Grasp the tick close to the skin and gently pull it straight out without twisting. If you do not have tweezers, use your fingers, protecting them with a tissue, and wash your hands thoroughly after you remove the tick.

Scabies. Caused by a burrowing mite, this condition itches like crazy. It looks like groups of pimples topped with scabs, with a lot of scratch marks prompted by the incessant itching. Scabies usually appears on parts of the body that are frequently touched: backs of hands, wrists, pubic area, and abdomen (but not on the back). Although scabies is not dangerous, it is very contagious and needs immediate treatment with a prescription medication.

Ringworm. This skin condition is caused not by a worm but by a fungus (related to athlete's foot) in the top layers of the skin. The typical rash is one or more circular patches with heaped up, rough, slightly reddened borders and clear centers, most commonly about the size of a nickel. The outer rim is made up of little bumps. Ringworm does not appear suddenly; it enlarges slowly over time. In ringworm of the scalp, there are round patches of scaly skin in which the hair is broken off short. The condition is mildly contagious. Treatment is usually the application of a cream to the rash for more than a month. Ringworm on the scalp has to be treated with oral medication.

Impetigo. Impetigo is an infection of the skin caused by bacteria, usually the streptococcus (strep for short). In a child past infancy, impetigo consists of scabs or crusts, partly brown, partly honey-colored. You should suspect that any scabs on the face are impetigo. The infection usually starts as a pimple with a yellowish or white blister on top, most often on the face. This blister soon gets rubbed off, and the scab takes its place. Other spots develop on the face or any part of the body to which the child's hands can carry the infection.

Have the doctor or nurse practitioner see your child promptly for diagnosis and treatment. Impetigo is usually not a serious medical problem, but it spreads easily if neglected and is contagious. When impetigo is not treated, the body's response to the strep infection can sometimes result in damage to the kidneys.

Poison ivy appears as clusters of small blisters of various sizes on shiny, reddened skin, usually on exposed parts of the body. Use 1 percent hydrocortisone cream and oral diphenhydramine (Benadryl) for mild cases. Consult your doctor or nurse practitioner about treatment if the outbreak is extensive.

Head lice. It's easier to find the eggs than the lice. The eggs are tiny, pearly white, and egg-shaped. Each is firmly cemented to a hair near the root. There may be itchy red pimples where the hair meets the back of the neck. Look especially in the part line and behind the child's ears. Many people believe incorrectly that head lice occur only under conditions of very poor hygiene. In fact, they can exist on any child in school or day care. Although they're disgusting, they're not really harmful. They are very contagious, however, and should be treated. There are nonprescription medications that often work; many come packaged with fine combs for removing the nits.

In recent years, some lice have developed resistance to these medications. If you've followed the directions carefully and the lice persist, talk to your child's doctor. There are various prescription medications that can help. Some traditional remedies, such as covering the child's head with mayonnaise, have not been found to be effective. One foolproof cure is to pick every last nit off the child's head, then examine the head every few days for any new ones. This takes a great deal of time and patience.

Warts. Warts are caused by viral infections in the skin. There are various types of ordinary warts that grow on the hands, the soles of the feet, the genitals, and the face. Warts can be flat, mounded, or tall and thin. One variety, known by the poetic name of molloscum cantagiosum, causes round, smooth, waxy bumps the size of a pinhead that are white or pink. They often multiply, enlarge, and develop a small dimple in the center. When present in large numbers, they may be treated to prevent them from spreading. For the usual hand and foot warts, over-the-counter medicines often work well. A recent report claims that duct tape (yes, duct tape) works. Hypnotherapy also speeds up the disappearance of warts, and often they go away on their own.

Herpes. Herpes is a virus found worldwide. There are two main types. Type I is found in or around the mouth and usually is not sexually transmitted. During the initial infection, it commonly causes an illness in toddlers characterized by high fever, swollen glands, and canker sores in the mouth: a miserable illness. Older children sometimes develop recurrent fever blisters along the edges of their lips, just as adults do. These, too, may be from the Type I herpesvirus. In some children they recur in times of increased stress, fatigue, or illness; in others they never recur. An adult or child with Type I herpes shouldn't kiss anyone until the sores are gone. Medicated cream (acyclovir) helps but does not cure the infection.

Type II herpes virus usually occurs on or around the genitals and is almost always a sexually transmitted disease. Small blisters develop that may break, forming painful ulcers. It's the genital type that has received so much publicity. The greatest danger is to babies infected with genital herpes during birth; they need immediate treatment to prevent a devastating infection in the brain.

Washing with soap and water kills the herpesvirus. So if parents and caregivers with either type of herpes wash their hands thoroughly with soap and water after touching the areas where they have sores or ulcers, they won't pass the virus to a child they're caring for.

CLASSIC CHILDHOOD INFECTIONS

Measles (rubeola). For the first three or four days, measles has no rash. It looks like a bad cold that is becoming worse. Your child's eyes are red and watery. If you pull the lower lid down, you see that it is fiery red. The child has a hard, dry cough that becomes frequent. The fever usually goes higher each day. The rash comes out about the fourth day, when the fever is high, as undefined pink spots behind the ears. They spread gradually over the face and body, becoming bigger and darker. The fever stays high, the cough remains frequent in spite of medicine, and the child feels sick while the rash fully comes out, which takes one to two days. After that, your child should improve rapidly.

You may suspect a complication if the fever stays high for more than two days from the time the rash begins or if the fever goes down for a day or more, then comes back. The most common complications are ear infections, bronchitis, and pneumonia. There is no treatment for measles, only prevention. The complications can be serious (see page 723); unlike measles itself, some can be successfully treated with modern drugs.

If your child has been fully immunized, measles is very unlikely though not impossible. You should contact the doctor or nurse practitioner, whether you suspect the disease or not, when your child has a cough and fever with a rash.

The first symptoms of measles begin anywhere from nine to sixteen days after exposure. The disease is contagious from the very beginning of the cold symptoms. It is unusual for a person to catch measles twice.

Measles can and should be prevented by immunization at twelve months of age. The child should get a booster shot at age four. If a child who has not been protected is exposed, the disease can still be prevented or made milder, so it is very important to seek medical care.

German measles (rubella). The rash of rubella looks much like the rash of real measles, but the two diseases are unrelated. In rubella there are no cold symptoms (running nose or cough), though the child's throat may be a little sore. His fever is usually low (under 102), and he may hardly feel sick. The rash consists of flat pink spots, which usually cover the body the first day. The second day they usually fade and run together, so that the body looks flushed instead of spotty. The most characteristic sign is swollen, tender glands on the back of the skull, behind the ears, and on the sides of the neck toward the back. These glands may swell before the rash comes out, and the swelling is apt to last some time after the disease is over. In some cases, the rash is so slight that it is not noticed. There may be joint pains, especially in older patients.

Rubella usually develops from twelve to twenty-one days after exposure. The child usually doesn't need to stay in bed. A doctor or nurse practitioner should make the diagnosis, since rubella is easily confused with rubeola, scarlet fever, and some virus infections. There is no specific treatment for rubella.

It can be bad for a woman to have rubella during the first three months of pregnancy since it may cause severe birth defects. If exposed at this time, she should promptly discuss the situation with her doctor. Rubella immunization (usually in the MMR combination vaccine; see page 722) should be given to all children at age twelve months and repeated at age four.

Roseola. Also called exanthem subitum by those who favor Latin, roseola is a less well known but common contagious disease. It usually occurs between the ages of one and three years, rarely afterward. The child has a steady, high fever for three or four days without cold symptoms and usually without seeming to be sick. (There is occasionally a convulsion on the first day from the fever; see page 702.) The temperature suddenly falls to normal, and a flat pinkish rash, something like the one in measles, comes out on the body. By this time the child no longer looks ill but may be cranky. The rash is gone in a day or two.

Roseola can be hard to diagnose until the rash erupts. By then, however, the child's fever is down and she feels well. Roseola is caused by a kind of herpesvirus, different from the one that causes cold sores (page 861). Children aren't immunized against roseola; it's not that serious a disease.

Chicken pox (varicella). The first sign of chicken pox is usually a few characteristic pimples on the body, face, and scalp that look like ordinary small pimples except that some have tiny yellow water blisters on top (like a dew drop on a rose petal). The base of the pimple and the skin around it are reddened. The delicate blister head breaks within a few hours, drying to a crust. New pox continue to appear for three or four days. The eruptions usually itch, sometimes a great deal. When trying to make the diagnosis, a doctor or nurse practitioner examines the crusted pimples to find a fresh one that still has the blister.

An older child or adult may feel sick and have a headache or fever the day before the pox appear. A small child won't notice these symptoms. The fever is usually slight at the beginning but may rise during the next day or two. Some children never feel sick and never have a temperature of more than 100. Others feel sick and have high fever.

A medication is sometimes used to shorten the duration or

severity of chicken pox. You can discuss with your doctor or nurse practitioner whether it is advisable for your child. Chicken pox can be confused with other diseases, such as impetigo, so you should call your doctor or nurse practitioner about any rash, especially if there is a fever or the child feels sick.

The doctor may prescribe a mild antihistamine to help relieve the itching. Acetaminophen may help the child feel better, especially if he has fever. (Don't give aspirin to children or teenagers with chicken pox; it increases their susceptibility to Reye's syndrome.) The itching may also be relieved by soaking in a lukewarm bath with cornstarch, baking soda, or oatmeal powder for ten minutes, two or three times a day. Use one cup for a small tub, two cups for a large one. The dry cornstarch should be placed in a two to four cup container. Add cold water slowly, stirring constantly, until the cornstarch is completely dissolved. (This prevents the formation of lumps.) Then add the cornstarch slurry to the bathwater.

Try to prevent your child from rubbing the scabs off, which can lead to a secondary bacterial infection or scarring. Wash the child's hands several times a day with soap. Cotton gloves worn while sleeping will help prevent damage by scratching.

Chicken pox usually develops between eleven and nineteen days after exposure. The usual rule is to let a child go out and back to school after every last bump has scabbed over, usually on the sixth day after the onset of the rash. In mild cases, a child may return sooner if the rash is crusted with scabs. The dried scabs are not contagious.

Immunization against chicken pox either reduces the severity of the disease or prevents it altogether (page 722). A child or adult who has a severely weakened immune system—one with AIDS or a child receiving chemotherapy for cancer—who is exposed to chicken pox needs medical treatment right away to prevent severe illness.

Other infectious diseases with rashes. Other common cold or intestinal viruses (with names like adenovirus, ECHO, and Coxsackie virus) can come with rashes. Often they are faint polka-dot rashes on the body, sometimes spreading to the face, arms, and legs. They fade in a couple of days.

Whooping cough (pertussis). There's nothing about whooping cough in the first week to make you suspect that disease. It's just like an ordinary cold with a little runny nose and a little dry cough. It is during the second week that the first suspicion may arise. Now you notice that the child has long spells of coughing at night. She coughs eight to ten times on one breath. One night, after several of these long spells, she gags and vomits. Or maybe she whoops. The whoop is the crowing noise she makes trying to get her breath back after a spell of coughing.

It's possible, though uncommon, for a child to get whooping cough even after being immunized with the vaccine. But such cases usually aren't bad enough to reach the whooping stage. The diagnosis is based on the character of the cough in the second week (a string of coughs in rapid succession with no breath in between) and the occurence of other cases in your neighborhood. Whooping cough takes five to fourteen days to develop after exposure. Anyone who is a close family contact of a child with whooping cough should receive antibiotics to prevent further spread of the disease.

You should never jump to the conclusion that your child has whooping cough simply because she has a bad cough in the first few days of a cold. In fact, a bad cough in the beginning of a cold argues against the diagnosis of whooping cough.

Whooping cough lasts for weeks and weeks. In an average case, the whooping stage lasts four weeks; in a severe one, up to three months. A doctor thinks of whooping cough in a child under a year of age whenever a dry cough lasts a month and in an older child if there's been an outbreak of the illness in the area.

When there is a doubtful case and it is important to make the diagnosis, laboratory tests sometimes help. Your doctor will prescribe treatment based on the age of the child and the severity of the case. Antibiotics are useful to prevent the disease from spreading. Cough medicines are often used but usually have only a small effect. Most do better in cold air, day and night, but the child must of course be protected from being chilled. Children are sometimes allowed to play outdoors through the entire course of the disease as long as they have no fever. They should not play with other children until after they have received treatment with erythromycin, an antibiotic. Some children have many fewer coughing spells when they are kept in bed. If vomiting is a problem, serve frequent small meals: They stay down better than the regular three full meals. The safest time to feed children is right after they have vomited, since they won't usually have another bad spell for some time.

Since whooping cough is sometimes a serious disease, especially in babies and young children, it is important to call a doctor promptly if there is a suspicion. There are two reasons for this: to make sure of the diagnosis and to get the right treatment. Special treatment is called for and is valuable in infants. It's a disease to avoid like the plague if you have a baby in your household. The main danger at this age is exhaustion and pneumonia. (See page 722 about pertussis immunization.)

Mumps. Mumps is principally a viral disease of the saliva glands, most commonly the parotid glands, which lie in the hollow just under the ear lobe. Thanks to immunization, it is now rare.

First the gland fills in the hollow; then it causes the whole side of the face to swell. It pushes the lobe of the ear upward. If you run your fingers up and down the back part of the jawbone, you can feel that the hard swelling runs forward, covering part of it. When a child has a swelling in the side of his neck, a question always comes up: Is it mumps, is it one of the other, rarer diseases of the parotid gland (which may recur repeatedly), or is it an ordinary swollen gland (one of the lymph glands in the side of the neck)? The ordinary lymph glands that sometimes swell after a sore throat are lower down on the neck, not tucked up under the earlobe. The hard swelling does not cross the jawbone.

When a small child develops mumps, the swelling under the ear is usually the first thing you notice. An older child may complain of pain around his ear or in the side of his throat, especially when swallowing or chewing, for a day before the swelling begins. He may feel generally sick. There is often little fever in the beginning, but it may go higher on the second or third day. The swelling most commonly begins on one side then spreads to the other side in a day or two. Sometimes it takes a week or more to spread to the other side; sometimes the second side never swells.

There are other salivary glands beside the parotids, and mumps sometimes spreads to these, too. The submaxillary glands are tucked up under the lower part of the jawbone. The sublinguals are just behind the point of the chin. Occasionally a person gets one of the complications of mumps without having had a swelling in any of these glands.

A very mild mumps swelling may go away in three or four days; the average swelling lasts seven to ten days. Mumps can spread to the testicles in men and boys who have reached puberty. This usually involves only one testicle. When both are inflamed sterility can result, although it is not common. Adolescent boys and men should avoid exposure. The ovaries in the female may also be affected, but that rarely affects childbearing ability in later life.

Sometimes a person who believes he previously had mumps will again get a swelling of a parotid gland. Most doctors believe that one attack or the other was caused either by some germ other than the mumps virus or by an obstruction of the salivary duct. All children should receive mumps vaccine at twelve months of age and again at four years. It is usually given in the MMR combination vaccine (see page 722).

Call the doctor about a suspected case of mumps. It is important to be certain of the diagnosis. If it turns out to be a swollen lymph gland, the treatment is different.

Diphtheria. Diphtheria is a serious but completely preventable disease. If your child is properly immunized (see page 722), there's almost no chance of his catching it. It begins with a sick feeling, sore throat, and fever. Dirty-white patches develop on the tonsils and may spread to the rest of the throat. The disease occasionally begins in the larynx with hoarseness and a barking cough; the breathing becomes tight and difficult. The disease develops within a week after exposure.

Call a doctor promptly anytime your child has sore throat and fever or croupy symptoms. The treatment of any case of suspected diptheria is the immediate use of special drugs.

Poliomyelitis (polio). This viral disease has been eliminated wherever polio vaccine is systematically used. Every child should be protected in early infancy (see page 722).

The disease begins, like so many other infections, with a generally sick feeling (malaise), fever, and headache. There may be vomiting, constipation, or a little diarrhea. Most cases do not go on to paralysis; of those that do, a fair number recover completely. If any paralysis remains after the acute stage of the infection is over, it is vitally important that the child continue to have regular, expert medical attention.

TUBERCULOSIS (TB)

Tuberculosis is an ancient and treatable disease that tragically still kills millions of children and many adults in poorer countries. International travel and the AIDS epidemic make TB an illness that cannot be ignored even in the United States.

Most people think of TB as it typically occurs in adults. A spot, or cavity, develops in the lung and produces such symptoms as fatigue, loss of appetite, weight loss, fever, cough, and sputum. However, TB in childhood usually takes other forms. In the first two years of life, resistance is not as strong as in later years, and there is more chance of the infection spreading to other parts of the body. That is why you should never take the slightest chance of exposing a baby to a known case of TB unless the doctor and the X-ray guarantee that the person is completely cured. This is also a reason for anyone in a household who has a chronic cough to be examined and given a tuberculin test. It's wise to have a new housekeeper, caregiver, or any other new member of the household tuberculin-tested. If the test results are positive, an X-ray of the chest should be done.

In later childhood, TB is more common and less likely to cause serious trouble. This is not a reason to treat it lightly or take any chances, however. Tuberculin tests show that in some cities, as many as 10 percent of children have had a slight infection with TB by the time they are ten years old. Most of these cases have been so mild that at the time no one suspected that anything was wrong. An X-ray may show at most a little scar where the infection healed in the lung or the lymph glands at the roots of the lungs.

Sometimes, however, childhood TB is active enough to cause symptoms, such as fever, poor appetite, poor color, irritability, fatigue, and perhaps a cough. There isn't much sputum; what there is is swallowed. The infection may be in other parts of the body, such as the bones, kidneys, the neck glands, or covering of the brain; most commonly it's in the lungs and in the lymph glands at the roots of the lungs.

In most active cases, healing gradually takes place over one to two years if the child is well cared for and only a scar is left. Proper treatment with special drugs will foster healing and prevent a serious spread of infection. Children with TB are usually not contagious and frequently do not need to be separated from their families for treatment.

As children reach adolescence, they become more susceptible to the serious, adult type of TB. This should be kept in mind whenever an adolescent or young adult is run down, tired, and loses appetite or weight, whether there is cough or not.

The tuberculin (PPD) test. A few weeks after tubercle bacilli (the germs that cause TB) have gotten into the body, a person becomes sensitized by actively making antibodies to the bacilli. After that, if tuberculin (material from dead TB germs) is injected into the skin, a raised spot develops. The presence of a raised area of a certain size indicates a positive result. Redness alone does not. A health-care professional should evaluate the test site to determine the significance of the response.

Generally speaking, if a person has ever had a TB infection, he will react with a positive test result for the rest of his life, even if the infection was healed long ago. Tuberculin skin tests are given periodically throughout childhood in routine examinations in communities where TB frequently occurs. The test is also done if a child isn't doing well or has a chronic cough or if TB is discovered in another member of the household. If a household member grew up or has lived for a time in a part of the world where TB is common—for example, Southeast Asia or Central America—it's wise to have that person and perhaps other family members tested for TB.

What if your child tests positive? There's no need to be alarmed, since a great majority of the cases discovered throughout middle childhood have either already healed or will in time.

The first step is an X-ray of the lungs to detect active infection or healed scars. All children with a positive tuberculin test, even those with no evidence of active disease, should receive specific anti-TB drugs for at least nine months. During that time, if the disease is inactive, they can live normal lives. The doctor may ask for further X-rays at intervals. Modern drug therapy is generally effective, and without serious side effects.

In addition to the affected child, all other members of the household (and any other adult the child regularly comes in contact with) should be tested to discover, if possible, where the TB bacteria came from and find out if other children in the household have been infected. In many cases, no disease is found in any adult in the household, and it has to be assumed that the child picked up the germs from a source outside the home. In other cases, an active case of TB is found in an adult in the house. It's lucky for the person to have the disease discovered at an early stage and lucky for the rest of the family to have the danger removed. No person with active TB should stay in a house with children. He should go elsewhere for drug therapy until the doctor says there is no chance of contagion.

REYE'S SYNDROME

This rare but serious condition can cause permanent damage to the brain and other organs. It can also be fatal. Its cause is not completely understood, but it usually occurs during a viral illness. It is now known that children and adolescents who take aspirin when they have a viral illness, especially influenza or chicken pox, are much more likely to get Reye's syndrome than those who are given acetaminophen or other nonaspirin medicines.

JOINTS AND BONES

Joint pains and growing pains. Children often complain of vague pains in their legs and arms for which no reason is found. A child between the ages of two and five may wake up crying complaining of pain in his thigh, knee, or calf. This happens only during the evening and may recur every night for weeks on end. Some people believe this pain is caused by muscle cramps or by the aching of the rapidly growing bones.

Generally, if the pains move from place to place, there is no swelling, redness, local tenderness, or limp, and the child is otherwise entirely well, it is unlikely that there is serious illness. If the pain is always in the same spot on the same limb or if other symptoms are present, the problem should be brought to medical attention.

Pain just below the kneecap, especially in a growing adolescents, is often caused by strain on the ligament where it connects to the top of the shinbone, a condition called Osgood-Schlatter's disease. Hip pain always needs to be checked, since the hip joint is vulnerable to injury. Any joint pain with fever needs to be evaluated immediately because of the risk of joint infection. Limping that cannot be explained by a recent fall or other injury also needs to be seen promptly, since it may be a sign of serious illness.

Fractures and disolocations are discussed on page 784.

Rheumatic fever. Following infection by the streptococcus bacteria (usually strep throat), the body produces antibodies to fight off the infection. Rheumatic fever develops when these antibodies also attack some of the person's internal organs. The disease can affect the joints, the heart, the skin, and other parts of the body.

When not treated promptly and adequately, an attack may last for weeks, even months. Moreover, this disease tends to recur repeatedly through childhood whenever the child has strep throat.

Sometimes rheumatic fever takes an acute form with high fever. Or it may smolder for weeks with only a little fever. If the person has severe arthritis, it travels from joint to joint, causing the affected areas to become swollen, red, and exquisitely tender. Where the arthritis is mild, there will be an ache now and then in one joint or other. If the heart is severely affected, the child will be visibly weak, pale, and breathless. It is sometimes discovered that the heart was damaged by a past attack so mild it was not noticed. Occasionally, there are even psychiatric symptoms or movement disorders associated with the strep infection.

In other words, rheumatic fever is an exceedingly variable disease. Naturally, you should consult your doctor or nurse practitioner if your child develops any of the symptoms in a severe form. It's just as important to examine a child with vague symptoms, like paleness, tiredness, slight fever, mild joint pains, or an unexplained rash.

Several drugs are effective in clearing up streptococcal infection in the throat and hastening the end of the rheumatic inflammation of the joints or the heart. Children who have had one attack of rheumatic fever can usually avoid further attacks and heart damage. To do so, they must take antibiotics by mouth or injection to prevent new streptococcal infections right into adulthood. Rheumatic fever can be prevented if strep throats are treated within seven days of onset.

Scoliosis. This is a curvature of the spine that appears usually between the ages of ten and fifteen. It is a problem of growth rather than posture. Schools in many states screen for this condition. Approximately one child in twenty-five has a detectable curvature of the spine. It's twice as common in girls as in boys and it runs in families. The cause is unknown. Any curvature warrants an evaluation by a physician. Many cases can simply be watched, never requiring intervention.

The treatments for scoliosis—bracing and surgery—are complex, expensive, and controversial. If treatment is recommended for your child, you or your child's doctor should get in touch with the Scoliosis Research Society of the American Academy of Orthopedic Surgeons for their current recommendations (at www.aaos.org or 747 823-7186).

HEART MURMURS

A heart murmur is simply a sound made by blood as it is pumped through the heart. Although the term heart murmur has an alarming sound to parents, it's important to realize that a great majority of heart murmurs don't point to anything serious. Generally speaking, there are three kinds: functional (or innocent), congenital, and acquired. Children with either congenital or acquired heart disease should receive antibiotic therapy before having dental work or before surgery to prevent germs from lodging in the heart.

A functional or innocent murmur is simply the sound made by a perfectly normal heart. These innocent murmurs are very common in early childhood, tending to fade out as the child reaches adolescence. Your child's doctor will tell you about an innocent murmur so that if it is discovered later by another doctor, you'll know that it has been there all along.

A murmur caused by congenital heart disease is usually discovered at birth or within a few months (though occasionally not till several years later). Such a murmur is usually not caused by inflammation but by the heart having been improperly formed in the first place. The important thing is not so much the murmur itself but whether the malformation interferes with the efficiency of the heart. If it does, the baby may have blue spells, breathe too hard, or grow too slowly. A baby or child with a congenital heart murmur needs careful examination by specialists. Many of these malformations can now be repaired by surgery.

If a child with a congenital murmur can exercise without turning blue and becoming abnormally out of breath, and if she grows at the normal rate, it is important for her emotional development that she not be thought of or treated as an invalid. She does need to avoid infections, especially influenza, for which she should be given a vaccine every year.

An acquired murmur in childhood may come from rheumatic fever (see page 873), which inflames the valves and may leave scars on them. This causes them either to leak or to obstruct the proper flow of blood. When a doctor hears a murmur in a child's heart that wasn't there before, it may indicate that active rheumatic inflammation is present. If so, there will be other signs of infection, such as fever, rapid pulse, and an elevated blood count. The doctor will treat such a child with drugs until all signs of inflammation are gone. It may take months. If there have been no signs of active infection for some time, the murmur may be due to scars from a previous attack.

HERNIAS AND TESTICLE PROBLEMS

Hernias. A hernia is the protrusion of an organ or tissue through an abnormal opening in the muscles or skin. The most common hernia, protruding navel, is discussed on page 87. The next most common is in the groin (inguinal hernia).

There is a small passage inside the abdomen that goes down along the groin (the groove between the abdomen and the thigh) into the scrotum (in a boy). It carries the blood vessels and nerves that go to the testicles. This passage goes through the layers of muscle that make up the wall of the abdomen. If the openings in the muscles are large, a section of intestine may be squeezed out of the abdomen into the passageway when the child strains or cries. If the intestine goes only partway down, it causes a bulge in the groin. If it goes all the way down into the scrotum, the scrotum becomes enlarged. Inguinal hernia does occur, though less commonly, in girls. It appears as a protrusion in the groin.

In most such hernias, the intestine slips back up into the abdomen when the baby or child lies down. It may push down every time he stands up or only once in a while, when he strains.

Occasionally, an inguinal hernia becomes strangulated, that is, the intestine becomes stuck in the passage, causing the blood vessels to become kinked and shut off. It is a form of intestinal obstruction. This causes abdominal pain and vomiting and calls for emergency surgery.

Strangulation of an inguinal hernia occurs most often in the first six months of life. Usually it is a hernia that has not previously been noticed. The parent changes the baby because he is crying so hard and notices the lump in his groin. The best response is to put the baby's hips on a pillow to elevate and apply an ice bag to the area. These actions may make the intestine slip back into the abdomen. Do not try to push the lump down with your fingers. You shouldn't feed the baby by breast or bottle until you have discussed the situation with the doctor. If surgery is needed, the stomach should be empty.

If you suspect a hernia in your child, report it to the doctor or nurse practitioner right away. Nowadays, inguinal hernias are usually promptly repaired by surgery. It is not a difficult operation; the child is often out of the hospital the same day.

Hydroceles. Hydroceles are often confused with hernias because both cause swelling in the scrotum. Each testicle in the scrotum is surrounded by a delicate sac that contains a few drops of fluid. This helps it slide around. In newborn babies there is often extra fluid in the sac that surrounds a testicle, making it appear to be several times its normal size. Sometimes this swelling begins later in infancy. A hydrocele is usually nothing to worry about. The fluid usually diminishes as the baby gets older, so nothing needs to be done. Occasionally an older boy has a chronic hydrocele, which should be operated on if it is uncomfortably large. You should not try to make the diagnosis yourself. Let the doctor decide whether it's a hernia or hydrocele.

Testicular torsion. The testes hang in the scrotum on a stalk of blood vessels, nerves, and tubes. Sometimes a testicle twists around, squeezing the structures in the stalk and cutting off the blood flow. This condition, called testicular torsion, is very painful. The skin of the scrotum may look red or purplish. This is an emergency; prompt medical attention is needed to save the testicle.

Testicular cancer. The risk of testicular cancer rises in the teen years; teenage boys should be taught to examine their testicles at least once a month, feeling each one carefully for unusual lumps or areas of tenderness. Any suspicious changes should be checked promptly. With early treatment, the prognosis is good.

EYE PROBLEMS

Reasons for seeing the eye doctor. Children need to go to an eye doctor if their eyes turn in (cross-eyes) or out (walleyes) at any age; they have trouble with schoolwork; they complain of aching, smarting, or tired eyes; their eyes are inflamed; they have headaches; they hold their books too close when they read; they cock the head to one side when carefully looking at something; or their vision is found to be defective by the chart test. Chart testing should be performed by your child's regular doctor between three and four years of age and at each well-child visit thereafter. However, the fact that your child reads a chart satisfactorily in school does not guarantee that her eyes are all right. If she has symptoms of eyestrain, she should be examined.

Nearsightedness (myopia) means that close objects appear sharp and distant objects are blurred. This is the most common eye trouble that interferes with schoolwork. Nearsightedness develops most often between six and ten years. It can come on rapidly, so don't ignore the signs of it (holding the book closer, trouble seeing the chalkboard at school) merely because the child's vision was fine a few months before.

Inflammation of the eye (conjunctivitis) is caused by many different viruses, bacteria, or allergens. Most mild cases—the eye is only slightly pink, and the discharge from the eye is scant and clear—are caused by ordinary viruses that cause colds in the nose. Inflammation that appears *without* an accompanying cold is more likely to signal a more serious infection. Get in touch with your doctor or nurse practitioner, especially if the white of the eye becomes reddened, there is pain, or the discharge is yellow and thick. Bacterial conjunctivitis can be treated with antibiotic ointments or drops prescribed by your doctor. Conjunctivitis is very contagious. Its spread can be significantly reduced by frequent hand-washing after contact with the infected eye or the discharge.

If the conjunctivitis does not clear up after a few days of medication, there may be a speck of dirt or other foreign material in the eye, visible only through an opthalmoscope.

Styes. A stye is an infection around the root of an eyelash, caused by ordinary bacteria that live on the skin. The stye usually comes to a head and breaks. Your doctor or nurse practitioner may prescribe an ointment to promote healing and prevent spreading. A stye feels more comfortable after the application of warm compresses; this also hastens healing. (Eyelids are temperature-sensitive, so use only warm, not hot, water.) One stye often leads to another, probably because when it breaks, the germs are spread to other hair roots. This is why you should try to keep a child from rubbing or touching her eyelid when a stye is coming to a head.

An adult with a stye should wash his hands and face thoroughly before caring for a baby or small child, because the germs are easily passed from person to person.

Things that don't harm children's eyes. Watching television, sitting close to the set, and reading a lot probably have no effect on the eyes. Habitually reading in poor light may make nearsightedness somewhat worse, however.

NEUROLOGICAL PROBLEMS

Seizures and convulsions. A seizure is caused by abnormal electrical discharges in the brain. The result depends on where in the brain these discharges occur. When most people think of a seizure they picture the generalized type involving the entire brain: The person loses consciousness and has convulsive twitches of the arms and legs. But seizures can also involve just a very small part of the brain. In these seizures, the person may remain awake and experience twitching in only part of his body or may briefly lose consciousness and stare blankly.

A full-blown convulsion is a frightening thing to see, especially in a child. The child's eyes roll up, his teeth clench, and his body or parts of it shake with twitching movements. He breathes heavily, and there may be some frothing at the mouth. Sometimes he will urinate and pass a bowel movement. Most seizures are not dangerous in themselves, and most stop in a short time, whether treatment is given or not.

Epilepsy. This is the name given to convulsions that occur repeatedly without fever or other disease. Nobody knows the real cause in the great majority of cases. The two most common forms of epilepsy are grand mal and petit mal. In generalized grand mal attacks, the person loses consciousness completely and has convulsions.

In partial, petit mal attacks, the seizure is so brief that the person doesn't fall or lose control of herself. She may stiffen momentarily or just stare.

Every case of epilepsy should be investigated by a neurologist. Though the condition is often chronic, several drugs are helpful in stopping the spells or reducing their frequency. For information, see the Resource Guide (page 930).

What to do during a generalized convulsion. Call the doctor right away. If you cannot reach one immediately, don't worry. The convulsion will usually be over and the child asleep by the time you talk to the doctor. There is very little you need to do for a child during a convulsion except keep her from hurting herself. Put her on the floor or some other place where she can't fall. Turn her on her side to allow saliva to run out of the corner of her mouth. Make sure that her flailing arms and legs will not strike something sharp. Time the seizure's duration. Keep cool, remembering that most seizures end in a few minutes (although it seems like hours) and do no harm. If the seizure lasts more than five minutes, it is advisable to call 911 or your local emergency response team. If it continues for more than ten minutes, it should be medically stopped. After a seizure, there is usually a period of sleepiness in which the child is minimally responsive and disoriented. If a fever accompanies the seizure, wait until the child is fully awake, then give acetaminophen by mouth; an alternative is to use a rectal suppository.

Seizures with fever. By far the most common cause of convulsions in young children is fever. Febrile seizures occur in 4 percent of children under age five. The seizure usually occurs at the beginning of an illness with fever, such as a cold, a sore throat, or the flu. (Seizures with fever are much less common after the first day or two of fever.) When the fever comes on quickly, it apparently makes the nervous system excitable. Some children at this age tremble at the start of a fever, even if they don't have convulsions. Others hallucinate (they may see tiny insects, animals, or bright colors) and are temporarily disoriented. If the nervous system's excitability leads to abnormal electrical discharges in the brain, a seizure ensues.

Therefore, if your young child has a convulsion at the onset of a fever, it doesn't necessarily indicate a serious disease, nor does it mean that the child will have convulsions in later life. The odds are that it is a simple seizure with fever. Most studies show that the vast majority of children who have seizures with fever outgrow them and do not suffer from problems because of them.

Of course, any child who has a seizure should see his doctor or be taken to an emergency room to make sure that it indeed was a simple seizure with fever, not another kind of disease.

There is no agreed-upon treatment of seizures with fever except to administer a fever medication at the beginning of any potential infectious illness. Unfortunately, it often happens that by the time the parent is aware of the possible illness, the fever has already shot up and the child has had a seizure. For children who have recurrent seizures with fever, the doctor may prescribe antiseizure medication to prevent future ones.

HORMONAL DISTURBANCES

Many diseases are caused by hormonal disturbances. Hypothyroidism is one of the more common. When the thyroid gland does not secrete sufficiently, a child's physical growth and mental development will be slowed down. She may be sluggish, have dry skin, coarse hair, and a low voice. Her face may be puffy. Insufficient thyroid secretion may also cause obesity. Her basal metabolism—the rate at which her body burns fuel when resting—will be below normal. The proper dose of thyroid medication brings remarkable improvement.

People who have read popular articles on hormonal glands assume that every short person, every slow pupil, every nervous girl, every overweight boy merely has a hormonal problem that can be cured by the proper tablet or injection. This assumption is not supported by scientific knowledge. It takes more than one symptom to make a hormonal disease.

When a boy is heavy in the years before puberty development, his penis appears smaller than it really is because his plump thighs are large in comparison and the layer of fat at the base of his penis may hide three-quarters of its length. Most of these boys have normal sexual development in puberty. Many of them lose their excess weight at that time.

Certainly every child who is not growing at the usual rate or in the usual shape or who is dull or extremely nervous should be examined by a competent physician. If the doctor finds that the child's stature results from her inborn constitutional pattern or that her mental state is due to unknown causes—a common situation (see page 932 in the Resource Guide and page 609, **Causes of MR**)—what she needs is assistance in her adjustment to life, not a search for a magic cure.

SUDDEN INFANT DEATH SYNDROME (SIDS)

About one in every thousand babies born in the United States dies of sudden infant death syndrome (crib death). Most commonly it is a baby between three weeks and seven months of age (three months is the most frequent) who is found dead in his crib. By definition no other explanation is found, such as infection or an unrecognized metabolic condition, even when a postmortem examination (autopsy) is done.

All infants should be put on their backs to sleep unless there is a medical reason not to do so. The simple change from sleeping on the front to sleeping on the back has reduced the number of SIDS deaths by 50 percent. Other measures to reduce the risk of SIDS are described on page 60. However, even with the best precautions, it is not possible to prevent all cases of SIDS.

Responses to SIDS. The parents are in shock: A sudden death is even more shattering than one that follows a worsening illness. They are overwhelmed by guilt, believing that they should have noticed something or that they should have checked on the child, even though there was no reason to do so. No sensible parent would call a doctor for the very slight cold that the child had. If the doctor had seen the baby, he or she would not have prescribed any treatment, because there was no reason to do so. No one could have anticipated the tragedy.

The parents will usually be depressed for many weeks or months and have many ups and downs. They may have difficulty concentrating and sleeping, poor appetite, or symptoms such as chest or stomach pain. They may have a strong urge to get away or a dread of being alone. If there are other children, the parents may fear to let them out of their sight, want to shun responsibility for caring for them, or treat them irritably. Some parents want to talk; others bottle up their feelings.

Other children in the family are sure to be upset, whether they show ordinary grief or not. Small children may either cling or behave badly to get their parents' attention. Older children may appear remarkably unconcerned, but experience tells us that they are protecting themselves from the full force of grief and guilt. It is hard for adults to see why a child should feel guilty, but all children resent their brothers and sisters at times. Their immature thinking may persuade them that their hostile feelings brought about the death.

If the parents avoid talking about the dead baby, their silence may add to the other children's guilt. So it is good for the parents to talk about the baby, to explain that a special sickness of babies caused the death, and that it was not anyone's fault. Euphemisms like "The baby went away" or "She never woke up" simply add new mysteries and anxieties. It's especially helpful if the parents respond in a gentle way to the children's questions and comments, so that they too will feel that it is all right to bring up their deeper worries.

The parents should seek counseling from a family social agency, a guidance clinic, a psychiatrist, a psychologist, or a member of the clergy so that they can express and come to understand their overwhelming feelings.

ACQUIRED IMMUNE DEFICIENCY SYNDROME (AIDS)

AIDS is caused by the human immunodeficiency virus (HIV). HIV impairs the body's ability to defend against other infections. So a person with AIDS can die of an infection which, in a normal person, would soon be cured by the body's protective mechanisms. It has been estimated that 20 million people in the world are infected by HIV.

HIV is transmitted through body fluids such as blood, semen, and vaginal secretions. It is not spread by hand or body touch, or by kissing, or living in the same home, or sitting in the same classroom, swimming in the same pool, eating or drinking from the same utensils, or by sitting on the same toilet as someone with AIDS. Blood products, once a source of HIV, are now thoroughly screened for the virus. AIDS began by affecting mainly homosexuals in developed countries; it has changed into a plague spread mainly by heterosexual contact, disproportionately affecting the poor and minorities, and devastating developing countries worldwide.

Young children typically contract HIV from their mothers, during pregnancy or at the time of birth. Antiviral treatment during pregnancy can greatly reduce the chance that the baby will become infected. For many children and adults, combinations of powerful anti-viral medications have changed AIDS into a manageable disease with a long life expectancy. For millions of poor people in developing countries, however, HIV remains a terrifying death sentence.

How (and why) to talk to children and teens about AIDS. By mentioning the subject even in a casual way, you make it possible for your child to ask questions and get your reassurance and support. Most likely, your child will have heard about AIDS from television, videos, movies, or at school.

⚭ **CLASSIC SPOCK**
The two greatest protections against contracting HIV, I feel, are education about safe sex techniques and a belief that the spiritual aspects of sexual love, including the desire of many adolescents raised with high ideals to postpone intercourse until there is a deep commitment, are as important and as worthy of respect as the purely physical. I've explained why I believe that the positive aspects of sex and love, including the spiritual side, should come first, over a considerable period of time. This is to prevent, if possible, a casual attitude that permits intercourse after brief acquaintance. The main reason for early education is that preteens are much more willing to listen to their parents. If preteens or teens have become anxious about AIDS, they need to know all the ways in which the disease is not transmitted, and they need to know how to keep their sexual contacts "safe."

Adolescents need to know that the greatest risk of becoming infected with HIV comes from shared needles and from unprotected sex with multiple partners. The greater the number of sexual partners, the greater the chance that one of them has AIDS or is carrying HIV without having developed the symptoms of AIDS. The surest way to avoid being infected is, of course, to delay intercourse until marriage, but simply telling a teen to do this hasn't been shown to be a reliable strategy (see page 452). Teens should also know that condoms—latex, not lambskin—offer much, though not total, protection during intercourse. The diaphragm and the pill do not protect against AIDS. Preteens and teenagers should also understand the risks drug addicts take when they share drug equipment with each other.

Children hear about intravenous drug use and anal intercourse in relation to AIDS on television and in the media. That makes open communication and information-sharing with parents all the more important. Talking with children about sex and drugs does not make them more likely to indulge in those dangerous activities—just the opposite.

WEST NILE VIRUS

West Nile Virus (WNV) frightens many people, but in fact it rarely causes severe illness in humans. The most serious form of WNV disease is an infection of the brain, signaled by muscle weakness, seizures, or other neurological symptoms. This occurs in only a very small fraction of the people who become infected with the virus. WNV is carried by mosquitoes, who give it to birds as well as to humans. The best protection against the disease is to avoid mosquito bites: Use an effective insect repellant (see page 752), when possible wear long-sleeved clothing and long pants, and stay indoors at dawn and dusk, when mosquitoes bite most. Make sure your home has effective screens on the windows. Participate in neighborhood clean-up activities to remove places where mosquitos breed, such as old tires and other things that collect water. The symptoms of WNV are usually mild (if any) and resemble the flu: fever, weakness, headache and muscle aches, nausea, loss of appetite. Blood tests can confirm the diagnosis, but there is no specific medicine to treat the virus; the body has to fight it off on its own.

GLOSSARY OF MEDICAL TERMS

Doctors and nurses try to avoid using medical jargon but don't often succeed. If your doctor's office or the hospital seems like a foreign country to you, learning its language is the first step toward feeling more at home.

Abrasion: A superficial scrape of the skin.

Abscess: A collection of pus due to a walled-off infection, causing pain, fever, swelling, and redness at the site. To be cured, an abscess usually needs to be cut open and allowed to drain.

Adenoiditis: An infection and inflammation of the adenoids, the lymph glands located at the back of the nose above the tonsils.

ADHD: Attention deficit hyperactivity disorder, also known as ADD (attention deficit disorder); hyperactivity.

AIDS: Acquired immunodeficiency syndrome, caused by HIV, which damages the body's ability to ward off infection.

Allergic rhinitis: An allergy that causes a runny, stuffy nose.

Allergy: A condition in which the body is especially sensitive to certain substances that trigger a response by the immune system, characterized by inflammation, sneezing, itching, and/or rash.

Alopecia: Baldness or bald spots.

Amblyopia: Poor, dim vision despite a normal eye; in children, often caused by a wandering eye ("lazy eye") that did not focus sharply in the early years of life.

Amenorrhea: The absence or abnormal cessation of menstrual periods.

Anemia: A reduction in the number of red blood cells in the circulatory system or a reduction in hemoglobin, the pigment in red cells that carries oxygen.

Anorexia nervosa: A psychological eating disorder marked by an abnormal fear of obesity, deliberate significant weight loss by reducing food intake, and a distorted body image; typically seen in adolescent girls and young women.

Antibiotic: A chemical substance (such as penicillin) that inhibits the growth of or kills bacteria. (Antibiotics have no effect on viruses. There are other medicines that, when given internally, will kill some viruses.)

Apgar score: A score from 0 to 10 that rates the newborn infant's well-being at one, five, and ten minutes after delivery. A perfect score is 10; less than 6 is considered low, but the one-and five-minute scores don't mean anything in the long term. A low score at ten minutes is cause for concern.

Apnea: Temporary cessation of breathing efforts for at least ten seconds.

Arteriosclerosis: A condition marked by the hardening and thickening of the arteries.

Artery: A blood vessel that carries blood away from the heart to the tissues.

Arthritis: Inflammation of the joints resulting in pain and swelling.

Artificial respiration: A part of cardiopulmonary resuscitation (CPR) in which air is forced into the victim's breathing passages by another person or by a bag-and-mask apparatus.

Asphyxia: Suffocation; a state in which there is insufficient oxygen and too much carbon dioxide in the blood.

Aspiration: Breathing liquid or solid substances into the windpipe.

Asthma: A chronic respiratory disease marked by recurrent wheezing due to spasm, inflammation, and mucus buildup in the small breathing passages; may be caused by allergies or by nonallergic agents, such as smoke.

Athlete's foot: A fungus infection of the feet marked by redness and scaling between the toes.

Autism: A neurological condition marked by disordered communication, play, and social relationships.

Autoimmune disease: An illness (like lupus or rheumatic fever) in which the body's immune system turns against tissues in the person's body, causing damage to them.

Bacteremia: The presence of bacteria in the blood.

Bacteria: Very small round or rod-shaped organisms that can cause infections when introduced into the body.

Benign: Not harmful. When talking about a tumor, not cancerous.

Bilirubin: A yellowish pigment created when red blood cells break down. High levels of bilirubin cause jaundice, often a sign of blood or liver disease; mild jaundice is normal in newborns.

Birthmark: A mole or blemish that is present from birth.

Blood poisoning: An illness caused by bacteria or toxins from bacteria in the blood.

Boil: A painful, pus-filled nodule under the skin, often starting in a hair follicle or skin pore, caused by bacterial infection, usually staphylococcus.

Bronchiolitis: An inflammation of the small bronchial tubes from a viral infection that causes wheezing and difficulty breathing.

Bronchitis: Inflammation of the larger bronchial tubes. Usually from a viral infection.

Bronchopulmonary dysplasia (BPD): A condition in some premature infants in which there is scarring, chronic swelling, and inflammation of the lungs; typically improves as the infant grows and new lung tissue is formed.

Bulimia: A psychological eating disorder marked by periods of binge eating followed by self-induced vomiting or purging.

Cancer: Abnormal growth of cells that are malignant; they invade surrounding tissues and can travel to and take root (metastasize) in other sites.

Candida: A yeastlike fungus that commonly causes diaper rash and mouth infections in infants.

Canker sore: Recurrent ulcerations of the mouth or lips; the cause is usually unknown, probably viral.

Cardiopulmonary resuscitation (CPR): An emergency measure using artificial respiration and chest compressions, in order to maintain blood flow to the brain following cardiac arrest or the absence of breathing.

Cellulitis: Infection and inflammation of the tissue just below the skin.

Cerebral palsy: A neurological condition, due to brain damage often without known cause happening usually before birth, that causes impairment of the use of muscles, movement, and posture.

Chicken pox: A contagious disease caused by the varicella virus and marked by fever and an itchy, vesicular rash.

Chlamydia: An unusual bacterium that lives only inside the cells of the body's tissues; probably the most common sexually transmitted disease; also can cause pneumonia and conjunctivitis in the first year of life.

Circumcision: The surgical removal of the foreskin of the penis.

Cleft lip, cleft palate: A congenital opening in the lip and the roof of the mouth, respectively.

Clubfoot: A congenital deformity of the foot marked by twisting in of the ankle, heel, and toes.

Cold: A viral infection of the upper breathing passages, nose, and throat; does not respond to antibiotics.

Cold sore: A small blister on the lips or next to them; caused by the type 1 herpes simplex virus (not the type that generally causes genital herpes); also called a fever blister.

Colitis: Inflammation of the colon; cause may be infectious, autoimmune, or unknown.

Colostrum: Thin, milky, yellowish fluid, full of protein, antibodies, and minerals, low in carbohydrates and fat, secreted by the glands in the breast before the true milk arrives.

Coma: A prolonged state of unconsciousness from which the person cannot be aroused; often caused by trauma, poisoning, infection, shock, or heart and lung disorders.

Concussion: A temporary impairment of consciousness with reduced responsiveness and awareness lasting for seconds, minutes, or hours after a head injury; may be accompanied by loss of memory of the traumatic event.

Congenital: Existing at or before birth and caused by hereditary, genetic, or environmental influences.

Congestive heart failure: Inability of the heart to pump sufficient blood to meet the body's demands; causes a backing-up of the blood leading to swelling of the body, weakness, and shortness of breath.

Conjunctivitis: An inflammation of the membrane over the white of the eye, with redness and with or without discharge; typically caused by a viral or bacterial infection or an allergy.

Constipation: Infrequency of or difficulty in passing bowel movements, often because of dry, hardened feces.

Convulsions: Violent involuntary twitching of the muscles due to an abnormal electrical discharge in the brain.

Cradle cap: Greasy yellowish crust on the skin due to excess production of oils; can cause rash and irritation of the scalp, face, or groin; also called seborrhea.

Craniosynostosis: Premature joining of the different sections of the skull, leading to an abnormal skull shape.

Cyanosis: Reduced oxygen in the blood, leading to a bluish skin color.

Cyst: A small closed sac below the skin, usually containing fluid.

Cystic fibrosis: A hereditary condition in which various glands have a reduced function, leading to pulmonary and digestive problems.

Cystitis: Inflammation of the bladder, usually due to a viral or bacterial infection or chemical irritation.

Dehydration: A condition in which an excessive amount of water has been lost from the body, resulting in less fluids in the tissues and circulation; usually due to vomiting or diarrhea without adequate liquid intake to compensate for the loss of fluids. It may occur in hot weather from sweat losses.

Dermatitis: Inflammation of the skin caused by allergies, infection, or irritation.

Diabetes mellitus: A disease in which the pancreas secretes insufficient insulin or the tissues fail to respond. As a result, blood sugar (glucose) rises abnormally, causing excessive urination, extreme thirst and hunger, weight loss, and weakness if untreated. Treatment is typically with injections of insulin and careful dietary control.

Diarrhea: Watery and frequent bowel movements, usually caused by a viral infection; also may be due to a bacterial infection or other intestinal disease.

Diphtheria: A severe bacterial disease, rarely seen now, marked by a severe sore throat, high fever, and weakness.

Doula: A woman who provides continuous emotional and physical support for a couple (or a woman) during labor and delivery.

Dysentery: Inflammation of the intestines, especially the colon, with frequent, painful, bloody, mucusy bowel movements. Usually infectious in origin and caused by bacteria, parasites, or protozoans.

Dysphagia: Difficulty in swallowing; often due to cerebral palsy or some anatomical abnormality of the throat.

Eczema: Inflammation of the skin marked by blistery red bumps, itching, scaling, and crusting; usually due to allergies or direct irritation of the skin.

Edema: An excess of fluids accumulating in the tissues.

Encephalitis: Inflammation of the brain; typically caused by a virus infection.

Encephalopathy: A generalized disturbance of the brain causing changes in behavior, consciousness, and seizures; usually noninfectious. Lead poisoning (at very high levels) is one cause.

Encopresis: Soiling of the underpants with feces, usually due to severe constipation.

Endocarditis: An inflammation of the lining of the heart; usually due to a bacterial infection or rheumatic fever.

Endocrine system: The system of hormone-secreting glands, such as the thyroid and adrenal glands.

Enuresis: Involuntary discharge of urine after the age of five.

Epilepsy: A disease with episodic, recurrent seizures caused by an underlying disorder that affects the electrical activity of the brain.

Epistaxis: A nosebleed.

Erythema: Redness of the skin caused by increased blood flow, usually due to inflammation or infection; seen also in sunburn.

Esophagus: The muscular tube through which food passes from the mouth to the stomach.

Failure to thrive: A syndrome in young children whose rate of weight gain and, possibly, growth are chronically and significantly below the average; may be due to illness or psychosocial disturbances.

Febrile: Feverish.

Febrile convulsions: Seizures that occur only with an elevated temperature; usually not dangerous and usually don't lead to epilepsy.

Fetal alcohol syndrome: A congenital syndrome of birth defects caused by exposure to excessive amounts of alcohol during pregnancy; can lead to poor growth, learning problems, and a characteristic facial appearance.

Food poisoning: Vomiting and diarrhea caused by eating food contaminated by bacteria.

Foreign body: An object that becomes lodged in a body cavity, such as the nose, ear, or vagina.

Fracture: A break or crack in a bone, usually diagnosed by X-ray study.

Fragile X syndrome: A genetic syndrome seen mainly though not exclusively in males, marked by a spectrum of developmental, learning, and behavioral problems and characteristic physical features. Caused by a mutation in the X chromosome; probably the most common inherited form of mental retardation.

Frostbite: Damage to tissues, usually fingers, toes, nose and ears, due to exposure to very cold temperatures.

Fungus: A class of low-level vegetable organisms that include yeast, molds, and mushrooms. Can cause mild or serious infections requiring treatment with antifungal medications.

Gamma globulin: A blood product containing antibodies to various bacterial and viral diseases; used for prevention of certain diseases, such as hepatitis and measles, and for treatment of certain diseases, such as Kawasaki's syndrome and immune deficiency states.

Gangrene: An infection, usually bacterial, that causes the death and decomposition of tissues, leading to poor blood supply to the area and further invasive infection.

Gastroenteritis: Inflammation of the lining of the stomach and intestines, usually leading to vomiting or diarrhea. Typically caused by a viral infection but also can be due to a bacterial or parasitic infection or other causes.

Gastroesophageal reflux: Regurgitation of stomach contents into the esophagus; can lead to heartburn, vomiting, and aspiration.

Giardia: A protozoan organism that can infect the intestines and cause diarrhea and abdominal pain; usually comes from drinking contaminated water.

Glaucoma: Abnormally increased pressure of the fluids in the eyeball, leading to blindness if untreated.

Gynecomastia: Excessive development of the male breasts, often seen in twelve- to fifteen-year-old boys.

Haemophilus influenzae: A bacteria that can cause significant infections in young children; now very rare because of early immunization against it; also called H flu.

Hay fever: An allergy with congestion, runny nose, sneezing, and watery eyes that recurs the same time every year; often from a sensitivity to pollen.

Health maintenance organization (HMO): A managed-care health system where a primary care doctor (or nurse practitioner) coordinates medical care, including prevention, diagnosis and treatment.

Heart murmur: A whooshing sound made by blood as it is pumped by the heart; can signify an abnormality of the structure of the heart, although most murmurs occur in normal, healthy hearts.

Heat stroke: Delirium, convulsions, or coma due to a rectal temperature above 106 degrees Fahrenheit; usually due to excessive exercise in hot weather, almost never due to infection.

Hemangioma: A benign tumor made up of blood vessels, usually found in the skin.

Hematocrit: The percentage of the blood occupied by red blood cells. A low hematocrit, often caused by iron deficiency in young children, is the same as anemia.

Hematuria: Blood in the urine; the blood can come from anywhere in the urinary tract, including the kidneys or bladder.

Hemoglobin: An iron-containing substance within the red blood cell that carries oxygen from the lungs to the tissues.

Hemophilia: A hereditary disease seen almost always in boys marked by the inability to clot the blood following trauma, leading to bleeding into joints and other deep tissues.

Hemoptysis: Coughing up blood from the respiratory tract; in adults, a common cause is tuberculosis (TB); in children other causes are more common.

Hemorrhage: Profuse bleeding.

Hemorrhoids: Swollen enlarged veins in the rectum causing pain, itching, and occasional bleeding.

Hepatitis: Inflammation of the liver causing jaundice and discomfort, usually due to a viral infection or a chemical or drug that is toxic to the liver.

Hepatomegaly: An enlarged liver.

Hernia: The protrusion of tissue or an organ through an abnormal opening in the muscles below the skin; typically seen in the navel area (umbilical hernia) or in the groin (inguinal hernia).

Hip dislocation: Usually a congenital disorder, in which the thigh bone (femur) does not sit properly and securely in the hip joint; can lead to an abnormally formed hip joint if left untreated.

Hirsute: Excessively hairy.

HIV: Human immunodeficiency virus, the causative agent of AIDS.

Hives: An allergic reaction, causing itchy red welts of the skin with a pale area in the middle.

Hydrocele: A collection of fluid around the testicles, causing swelling of the scrotum; usually resolves spontaneously.

Hydrocephalus: An abnormal accumulation of fluid in the brain. If left untreated, it may exert pressure leading to the destruction of brain tissue; often managed with a piece of tubing (a shunt) that drains the fluid from the brain to the abdomen or chest.

Hypertension: Abnormally high blood pressure.

Hyperthyroidism: Excessive secretion of thyroid hormone by the thyroid gland. Severe hyperthyroidism causes a very fast heart and respiratory rate, weight loss, bulging of the eyeballs, irritability, and hyperactivity; usually treated with medications.

Hypospadias: A congenital abnormality of the penis in which the opening of the urinary tract (urethra) is found on the underside of the penis or even below it; may require surgical repair.

Hypothyroidism: Abnormally low secretion of thyroid hormone by the thyroid gland, causing low muscle tone and activity, constipation, lethargy, and a weak, hoarse cry; can easily be treated with oral thyroid hormone. Screening at birth allows this condition to be identified before damage occurs.

Hypotonia: Abnormally low muscle tension or activity when at rest; sometimes described as a floppy baby.

Hypoxia: Reduced amount of oxygen in the blood, usually due to a respiratory problem.

Impetigo: A bacterial (usually strep or staph) infection of the skin, very contagious, with a thick yellow crust.

Inflammation: The body's response to injury, irritation, or infection; a complicated process marked by pain, heat, redness, and swelling caused by a flood of blood elements, such as white blood cells and various chemicals, to the site.

Influenza: An illness marked by fever, chills, lethargy, muscle aches, and respiratory symptoms, lasting three to fourteen days (flu).

Ischemia: Insufficient blood flow to tissues.

Jaundice: A yellow tinge to the skin, mucous membranes, and whites of the eyes caused by excess bilirubin in the blood, usually due to temporary immaturity of the liver in a newborn or by bile duct obstruction or inflammation of the liver in older children.

Knock-knees: A deformity of the legs in which the knees are abnormally close together and the ankles are spread too far apart.

Laceration: A cut in the skin; may require stitches depending on location, depth, and severity.

Laryngitis: Inflammation of the voice box causing hoarseness or loss of voice, usually caused by a self-limited viral infection.

Lazy eye: When one of the eyes does not focus on the object but turns either inward or outward (strabismus); often requires patching of the unaffected eye to promote focusing of the lazy one.

Leukemia: Cancer of the white blood cells, marked by anemia, bleeding, infections, and swollen lymph glands. Some forms of leukemia are now curable.

Lice: Small, flat-bodied parasites that usually make their home in hairy areas of the body, where they lay small white eggs (nits) that stick to the bottom of the hair shafts. Lice are a common childhood nuisance, contagious but essentially harmless.

Lockjaw: An early sign of tetanus in which the jaws are clenched shut; caused by the tetanus toxin. Tetanus is now rare because of immunization.

Lupus (systemic lupus erythematosus): An autoimmune disorder in which the body's immune system attacks its own tissues, especially in the skin, joints, and kidneys.

Lyme disease: A disease caused by a bacteria (spirochete) carried by the deer tick. Symptoms include a distinctive skin rash, followed by fever, fatigue, headaches, joint aches, and, later on, sometimes various neurological symptoms.

Lymphadenopathy: Enlarged lymph glands; may be due to a variety of disease states and infections that stimulate the lymphoid tissue to fight the disease.

Lymph glands (or lymph nodes): Round organs that contain high numbers of immune cells (lymphocytes). Lymph nodes usually enlarge when fighting an infection.

Lymphocytes: White blood cells that fight viral and bacterial infections.

Malaria: An infectious disease caused by a protozoan parasite that lives in red blood cells; marked by recurring cycles of fever, chills, and sweating; spread by a mosquito.

Measles (rubeola): A viral infection marked by fever, chills, rash, conjunctivitis, and upper respiratory symptoms.

Melanoma: Cancer of the pigment-secreting cells of the skin; may occur in moles. Melanomas in adults are in part triggered by sunburns in early childhood.

Meningitis: Inflammation of the membranes that line the brain and spinal cord, usually due to a bacterial or viral infection; marked by headache, stiff neck, and vomiting. Bacterial meningitis is a medical emergency; viral meningitis is largely self-limited and usually does not cause serious problems.

Microcephaly: An abnormally small head, often associated with mental deficiency but sometimes merely a family trait with no mental problems at all.

Migraine: A specific kind of periodic headache, usually one-sided and accompanied by nausea, vomiting, and visual disturbances. Migraines often run in families.

Mittelschmerz: Abdominal pain occurring in the middle of the menstrual cycle, presumably due to ovulation.

Mole: A pigmented, slightly raised, sometimes hairy blemish in the skin. Most moles are benign, but some kinds are prone to turning into cancer in later life and should be removed.

Molluscum contagiosum: A contagious viral infection of skin that causes pearly white bumps with a central depression. These are benign but may last months to years without treatment.

Mongolian spots: Bluish-black superficial coloring of the skin, usually in dark-skinned infants. These typically occur on the buttocks and back but can be found anywhere. They fade in time and are not associated with any problems.

Mongolism: An old-fashioned, no longer acceptable term for Down syndrome (trisomy 21).

Mononucleosis: A viral infection (the Epstein-Barr virus, or EBV) marked by swelling of the lymph glands (especially those in the neck), sore throat, fatigue, fever, and rash.

Mucus: A slippery, slimy, thick substance secreted by glands to protect the lining of the breathing and other passages (mucous membranes). These cells are stimulated by infectious agents to produce more mucus.

Mumps: A viral illness that attacks and inflames the saliva-secreting glands of the face and neck and occasionally the pancreas, testicles, ovaries, and brain. There is no specific treatment.

Muscular dystrophy: A group of inherited conditions marked by gradual and progressive muscle wasting. There are various forms of muscular dystrophy, some severe, some mild.

Nephritis: Inflammation of the tissues of the kidney, usually causing blood in the urine; may be caused by an autoimmune disorder (as in nephritis following a streptococcal infection) or an infectious disorder.

Nephrotic syndrome: A kidney disorder in which the kidney excretes excessive amounts of protein into the urine, causing low protein levels in the blood and swelling (edema) of the body. Medications, such as steroids, are sometimes helpful.

Nevus: A mole.

Obstructive sleep apnea: A condition occurring when the child sleeps. The breathing passages in the back of the throat become obstructed and the child cannot breathe despite active efforts to do so; sometimes caused by very large adenoids. Can cause significant problems if not treated promptly, usually by removing the adenoids and the tonsils.

Osteomyelitis: An infection, usually bacterial, of the bone; often takes many weeks or months to cure.

Otitis externa: Swimmer's ear; a bacterial infection of the ear canal.

Otitis media: A middle-ear infection caused by a bacteria, or virus, or both.

Pediculosis: See Lice.

Pelvic inflammatory disease (PID): Infection of the uterus, Fallopian tubes, and genital tract; usually occurs in adolescents fifteen to nineteen years of age; caused by bacteria (typically chlamydia, gonorrhea, or a variety of other organisms) ascending from the vagina into the genital tract; can cause infertility if not treated promptly with antibiotics.

Peptic ulcer: An area of the stomach whose lining is raw, inflamed, and irritated by stomach acids; now known to often be caused by infection by a bacteria, Heliobacter pylori.

Peritonitis: Inflammation of the membrane lining the abdomen and pelvis, usually a bacterial infection from a rupture of the intestines (as in a ruptured appendix).

Pertussis: Whooping cough; a contagious respiratory disease caused by a bacterial infection, marked by paroxysms of forceful coughing. Treatment includes antibiotics and supportive care.

Petechiae: Small, pinpoint, nonraised, round, dark red spots just below the skin caused by a hemorrhage in the small blood vessels; can be from a viral or serious bacterial infection.

Pharyngitis: Inflammation of the throat caused by a virus or bacteria, sometimes streptococcus.

Phimosis: On the penis, a very tight foreskin that cannot be retracted over the shaft; normal in the first year of life when not accompanied by symptoms; may require circumcision if it persists.

Pinkeye: See Conjunctivitis.

Pinworms: A common intestinal infection of small, thin white worms. Typically the only symptom is itching around the anus. Effectively treated by oral medications.

Platelet: A component of blood that promotes coagulation of the blood and stops bleeding when a small blood vessel ruptures.

Pneumococcus: A bacteria causing infections in the lungs, ears, or nervous system, marked by rapid onset and high fever. Usually responds well to antibiotics; also called Streptococcus pneumoniae.

Pneumonia: A bacterial or viral infection of the lung causing cough, fast breathing, and sometimes fever.

Polio: A contagious virus that attacks the nerves of the spinal cord responsible for voluntary movement; completely preventable by childhood immunizations.

Proteinuria: Protein in the urine, caused by "leaky kidney"; seen in nephrotic syndrome, chronic kidney infections, and other kidney disorders.

Psoriasis: A chronic skin disorder marked by recurrent red itchy patches covered with silvery scales and plaques. Cause is unknown; there is no cure. Symptomatic treatment is with lubricating lotions, steroid cream, and sunlight.

Purpura: Purplish spots in the skin from hemorrhage. Can be due to a low platelet count, a viral infection, trauma, or, less commonly, an autoimmune disorder.

Pyelonephritis: A bacterial infection of the kidney, causing fever, fatigue, and flank pain; treated with large doses of antibiotics.

Pyloric stenosis: An obstruction of the stomach in infants (typical age is three to four weeks) due to an enlarged circular muscle (pylorus) at the stomach outlet to the intestines; often requires surgical repair.

Quadriplegia: Paralysis of the body from the neck down.

Reactive airway disease: Inflammation and destruction of small passages in the lungs caused by some infections, pollutants, toxins, cold air, and tobacco smoke, producing wheezing and cough. This condition can be treated with medications.

Respiratory syncytial virus (RSV): A virus that is the primary cause of bronchiolitis in infants. May be prevented in high-risk infants with injected medication.

Rheumatic fever: An autoimmune disorder following an upper respiratory infection with the streptococcus bacteria, marked by inflammation of the heart, blood vessels, joints, nervous system, and skin. Treatment is primarily the prevention of further streptococcal infections by taking penicillin daily.

Rhinitis: Inflammation of the mucous membranes of the nose, causing nasal discharge and stuffiness. Usually caused by a viral upper respiratory infection.

Rickets: A weakening of the bones usually due to a lack of vitamin D intake and limited exposure to sunlight.

Ringworm: A fungal infection (not a worm at all) of the skin with ring-shaped, reddish, itchy patches; mildly contagious.

Roseola: A viral infection of infants marked by very high fever for three to four days, followed by the eruption of a generalized rose-colored rash after the fever subsides and the child is well. No treatment is needed.

Rotavirus: A virus that is a major cause of vomiting and watery diarrhea throughout the world, usually occurring in the winter months.

Rubella (German measles): A viral infection marked by upper respiratory symptoms and a rash that looks very much like measles; can cause birth defects if contracted early in pregnancy; preventable by childhood immunizations.

Salmonella: A bacteria that can cause severe diarrhea, fever, or bacteremia. The person may be a carrier with no symptoms. Spread by undercooked chicken, raw eggs, pet turtles.

Scarlet fever: A streptococcal throat infection accompanied by a generalized salmon-colored rash. Scarlet fever is no longer considered more dangerous than any other strep infection.

Scoliosis: An abnormal curvature of the spine, usually of unknown origin. Early detection is the key to treatment.

Seizure: A sudden attack of twitching of the arms or legs or change in consciousness due to abnormal electrical activity in the brain. Recurrent seizures are known as epilepsy.

Septicemia: See Blood poisoning.

Sexually transmitted disease (STD): Any infectious disease that is transmitted through sexual intercourse or other intimate sexual contact. May be caused by chlamydia, gonorrhea, syphilis, HIV, herpes, or other agents.

Shigella: A bacteria that causes dysentery and high fever; treated with antibiotics.

Shingles: Painful skin lesions caused by the varicella (chicken pox) virus, which lives dormant in the nerves of the skin then travels down the nerve, causing intense pain. The pain of shingles is usually mild in children; it may be severe in adults.

Shock: Inadequate circulation due to loss of blood volume, with inadequate oxygen delivered to the tissues; marked by pale and clammy skin, low blood pressure, rapid heart rate; can lead to unconsciousness and death.

Sickle-cell anemia: A genetic disease, primarily of people of African or Mediterranean origin, causing deformation of the red blood cells so that through the microscope they look like sickles. The abnormal cells become wedged in the small blood vessels, causing pain and tissue damage.

Sinusitis: Inflammation of the sinuses, of bacterial or viral origin.

Smegma: A normal thick, cheeselike secretion that collects around the head of the penis and clitoris.

Spasticity: Increased muscle tone due to brain damage, causing stiff and awkward movements.

Spina bifida: A congenital defect marked by incomplete closure of the bones that encase the spinal cord, often associated with hydrocephalus and neurological problems of the lower body.

Splenomegaly: An enlarged spleen, often due to an acute infection or a blood disorder in which the red blood cells are broken down at a rapid rate (hemolytic anemia).

Sprain: An injury to a joint caused by excessive stretching though not tearing of the ligaments, marked by pain and swelling.

Staph: Short for staphylococcus, a type of bacteria that commonly causes moderate to severe infections (similar in some ways to strep).

Strain: An injury to a joint through over-use, not as severe as a sprain.

Strep: Short for streptococcus, a type of bacteria that commonly causes moderate to severe infections.

Strep throat: An infection of the pharynx with the streptococcal bacteria. Treatment is with penicillin or another antibiotic.

Stridor: A harsh sound made when the child breathes in; often heard in croup, allergic reactions, foreign-body aspiration, and other infections of the throat.

Sudden infant death syndrome (SIDS): The unexpected death of an infant, typically three to four months of age, from unknown causes.

Syphilis: A contagious, sexually transmitted bacterial (spirochete) disease that can infect all organ systems.

Swollen glands: See Lymphadenopathy.

Syncope: A fainting episode, usually caused by temporarily diminished blood flow and oxygen to the brain.

Tendinitis: Inflammation of the tendons, the fibrous cords that attach muscles to bones.

Tetanus: A severe bacterial infection. The bacteria produce a toxin that causes spasm of the muscles of the mouth (lockjaw) then other muscles of the body; prevented by routine childhood immunizations and a booster shot every ten years.

Thalessemia: A hereditary blood disorder in which the body produces abnormal hemoglobin, causing significant anemia.

Thrush: See Candida.

Tonsillitis: Inflammation of the tonsils, the lymphoid tissues in the back of the throat, from a bacterial or viral infection.

Tourette's syndrome: A disorder marked by chronic physical tics (eye-blinking, facial grimacing, head jerking) and vocal tics (repetitive throat clearing, grunting, or words).

Tuberculosis (TB): A contagious infectious disease, caused by Mycobacterium tuberculosis, of the lungs, lymph nodes, and other organs. Treatment is the taking of anti-TB drugs for at least nine months.

Ulcer: A painful disintegration of the surface of the lining of an organ, such as the stomach, usually due to inflammation or inadequate blood flow to the area.

Urinary tract infection (UTI): A bacterial (rarely viral) infection of the bladder or kidneys.

Urticaria: See Hives.

Vaginitis: Inflammation of the vagina, with pain or itching and a discharge, usually due to bacterial infection or a foreign body.

Varicella: See Chicken pox.

Virus: A minute infectious agent that can live only in the cells of a living host, causing infection. The usual antibiotics have no effect on viruses.

Wart: A viral infection of the skin causing a round, heaped-up lump on the skin; most will disappear on their own within two years.

Wheezing: The high-pitched whistling sound made by air passing through a narrowed airway; occurs in asthma, bronchiolitis, foreign-body aspiration, and other conditions in which the small respiratory tubes are narrowed.

Whooping cough: See Pertussis.

Yeast infection: A mild fungal infection, usually of the mouth, diaper area, or vagina.

COMMON MEDICATIONS
FOR CHILDREN

At some point, almost every child runs a fever, gets a rash, has a cough, or develops some other symptom that calls for medication. A basic knowledge of just a few frequently used drugs can help you treat these common complaints with confidence. But giving medication to a child can be a confusing business. Drug companies complicate things by giving medications multiple names. There's the trade name you probably know (Tylenol, for instance), and the generic name—often unpronounceable—that identifies the active ingredient (acetaminophen, in this case). Many over-the-counter drugs contain several active ingredients. Robitussin Allergy & Cough Syrup, for example, contains brompheniramine, dextromethorphan, and pseudoephedirine; each does something different. When you give your child a spoonful of medicine, it's not always easy to know just what you're giving.

To clear things up a bit, the guide that follows lists the generic names for some of the most common medications, tells what the medication is supposed to do, and gives its most frequent side effects. Most prescriptions include the generic names, and all over-the-counter drugs list the generic ingredients on the box under active ingredients. Many commonly used medications fall into a few categories—antibiotics, antihistamines, and anti-inflammatory medications, for example. Information about those drugs is grouped under the applicable categories.

The purpose of this guide is not to replace the advice of doctors or pharmacists. It is to help you better communicate with them. So when the doctor says, "Let's give her some ibuprofen for that sore shoulder," you can be thinking, "Oh, Motrin; we already tried that."

A special word of caution about side effects is in order: This guide includes only *some* of the most common side effects. The package inserts that come with prescription drugs list many more. In fact, it is not possible to list every possible side effect for any medication, because individuals can have unusual reactions. Any unexpected, unpleasant symptom that pops up after taking a medication is a side effect until proven otherwise.

MEDICATION SAFETY

All medications should be treated with respect. Powerful prescription drugs can have powerful side effects. But over-the-counter medications can also be dangerous, especially if a child takes an overdose. Some commonsense principles can lower the risk:

- Keep medications in a locked cabinet or drawer. Even timid children have been known to climb up to high cabinets or shelves when curiosity drives them.

- Don't put your trust in childproof caps. They will slow a persistent child down, but they might not stop her.

- Pay special attention when you have visitors who might be carrying medications with them or when you and your child visit others' homes. A handbag left sitting on a low table is a tempting target for a toddler.

- Tell your child that the medication is medicine, not candy.

- At times of stress or when your daily routine undergoes a change, think about medications, cleaning supplies and other poisonous chemicals, and household hazards in general. Times of change are times of danger.

A WORD ON TERMINOLOGY

When doctors write prescriptions, they use a shorthand that can be confusing. When they say take one pill twice daily (BID in doctorese), they mean one pill every twelve hours. Three times a day (TID) means every eight hours; four times a day (QID), every six hours. PRN means as needed. PO means simply by mouth. A prescription that reads, "take one tab PRN PO QID" means you may—but aren't required to—take one tablet as often as every six hours.

Measurements may also need translating. The instructions that come with over-the-counter medicines speak of teaspoons, table-spoons, ounces, or, occasionally, capfuls. But prescriptions are likely to be written in milliliters (ml) and milligrams (mg). A standard tea-spoon equals five milliliters, a tablespoon equals fifteen milliliters and an ounce equals thirty milliliters. A doctor who instructs you to give "one teaspoon three times a day" wants you to give five milliliters every eight hours. Of course, the teaspoons in your home may not hold ex-actly 5 ml; it's safer to use a medicine cup or an oral syringe to get the dose right.

The reason it's good to be familiar with these terms is so you can ask questions. If the doctor tells you to take one tablet three times a day then writes BID on the prescription, you should ask. If the doctor writes QID and you're not sure whether you should give the medicine every six hours on the button, even if it means waking your baby, you should ask. Be sure you understand the instructions before you leave the office. Ask the pharmacist, too. You can't be overcareful.

GLOSSARY OF COMMON MEDICATIONS

The following guide includes only a fraction of the drugs used today. For a more complete listing, look online at www.nlm.nih.gov/medlineplus, and click on Drug Information. Many medications are sold under different trade names; only examples are listed.

Acetaminophen
(over the counter) *Trade names:* Tylenol, Tempra.
Effects: See under Nonsteroidal anti-inflammatories. Acetaminophen reduces fever and pain.
Side effects: In large overdoses, causes serious liver disease. Ask the doctor if you are giving it for more than a couple of days.

Acetylsalicylic Acid (Aspirin)
(over the counter) *Trade names:* Bayer, Ecotrin, many others.
Effects: See Nonsteroidal anti-inflammatories.
Side effects: Use only under doctor's guidance. In children, aspirin can cause life-threatening liver disease (Reye's syndrome).

Advil
(over the counter) See ibuprofen.

Albuterol
(prescription only in the U.S.) *Trade names:* Proventil, Ventolin.
Effects: See Bronchodilators.

Amoxicillin

(prescription only in the U.S.) *Trade names:* Amoxil, Trimox.

Effects: See under Antibiotics. Amoxicillin is the first-line treatment for ear infections.

Amoxicillin clavulanate

(prescription only in the U.S.) *Trade name:* Augmentin.

Effects: Often the second choice, if amoxicillin fails because of drug resistance (see above).

Side effects: More likely than amoxicillin to cause stomach upset, diarrhea.

Amoxil

(over the counter) See Amoxicillin.

Antibiotics

(prescription only in the U.S.).

Effects: Antibiotics kill bacteria (see page 711); not helpful in common viral infections, however.

Side effects: In infants especially, look for signs of thrush or candidal diaper rash (page 122); stomach upset, rashes are common.

Antihistamines

(mainly over the counter)

Effects: These drugs block the action of histamine, a major component of allergic reactions. Used commonly to treat hay fever, hives, itching, etc.

Side effects: In young children, often cause hyper or overexcited response; in older children, sedation or drowsiness. Newer, more expensive drugs (Claritin or Zyrtec, for example) may have fewer such side effects.

Augmentin

(prescription only in the U.S.) See Amoxicillin clavulanate.

Azithromycin

(prescription only in the U.S.) *Trade name:* Zithromax.

Effects: See under Antibiotics; this drug is very similar to erythromycin but is given less frequently (and costs much more).

Side effects: stomach upset, mainly.

Bacitracin ointment

(over the counter) *Trade names:* Neosporin, Polysporin.

> *Effects:* A mild antibiotic that can be applied to the skin (topical).
>
> *Side effects:* rare.

Beclomethasone nasal inhalation

(prescription only in the U.S.) *Trade names:* Vancenase, Beconase.

> *Effects:* See under Corticosteroids, inhaled. Nasal corticosteroids, like Vancenase and Beconase, reduce symptoms of hay fever.
>
> *Side effects:* rare when used as directed.

Benzocaine

(over the counter) *Trade name:* Anbesol.

> *Effects:* Dulls pain sensation (anesthetic). However, effects wear off with repeated use.
>
> *Side effects:* Stinging or burning feeling. Overdose can cause heart rhythm disturbances.

Bisacodyl

(over the counter) *Trade name:* Dulcolax.

> *Effects:* Stimulates the intestines to contract and propel feces forward.
>
> *Side effects:* Cramping; diarrhea.

Brompheniramine

(over the counter) *Trade names:* Dimetapp, Robitussin.

> *Effects:* See Antistamines.

Bronchodilators

(prescription only in the U.S.).

> *Effects:* Combat tightness of the bronchial tubes caused by asthma.
>
> *Side effects:* Increase in heart rate and blood pressure; nervousness, jitters, anxiety, nightmares, and other behavior changes.

Chlorpheniramine

(over the counter) *Trade names:* Actified, Sudafed, Triaminic.

> *Effects:* See Antistamines.

Clemastine
(over the counter).
> *Effects:* See Antihistamines.

Clotrimazole cream or ointment
(over the counter) *Trade name:* Lotrimin.
> *Effects:* Kills the fungi that cause ringworm and some diaper rashes.
> *Side effects:* rare.

Corticosteroids, inhaled
(prescription only in the U.S.).
> *Effects:* Inhaled corticosteroids are the best medications for reducing inflammation in the lungs caused by asthma.
> *Side effects:* With overuse or misuse, enough corticosteroid is absorbed into the body to produce serious side effects; talk with the doctor about how to avoid them.

Corticosteroids, topical
(over the counter or prescription).
> *Effects:* Corticosteroid creams, ointments, and lotions reduce itching and inflammation of the skin; especially useful for eczema and some allergic reactions. There is a range of strengths.
> *Side effects:* Thinning of the skin, lightening of pigment, absorption of medicine into the body; all worse with stronger corticosteroids used over larger areas for longer periods of time. Use of weaker types for short periods is usually safe.

Co-trimoxazole
(prescription only in the U.S.) *Trade name:* Bactrim.
> *Effects:* An antibiotic, often used for bladder infections; no longer used for ear infections (see Antibiotics).
> *Side effects:* Stomach upset; call if paleness, rash, itching, or other new symptoms appear.

Cromolyn
(prescription only in the U.S.) *Trade name:* Intal.
> *Effects:* Reduces inflammation in the lungs in asthma; not as powerful as inhaled corticosteroids
> *Side effects:* rare.

Decongestants

(over the counter).

Effects: These medications cause blood vessels in the nose to contract so that the nose makes less mucus.

Side effects: Increase in heart rate and blood pressure; nervousness, jitters, anxiety, nightmares, and other behavior changes; after a couple of days, the body often adjusts so the medications no longer work. Be especially careful when taking with other medications that may have similar side effects, such as stimulants.

Dextromethorphan

(over the counter) *Trade names:* Robitussin Pediatric Cough, and many others.

Effects: Suppresses the cough reflex.

Side effects: rare.

Diphenhydramine

(over the counter or prescription) *Trade names:* Benadryl.

Effects: See Antistamines.

Docusate

(over the counter) *Trade names:* Dulcolax, Colace.

Effects: A stool softener; not absorbed by the body.

Side effects: diarrhea.

Electrolyte Solutions

Trade name: Pedialyte, Oralyte, Infalyte, and others

Effects: Used to prevent dehydration in children who are losing water through vomiting and diarrhea, these solutions consist mainly of water, salt, potassium, and different kinds of sugar in just the right proportions, so that as much water as possible is absorbed from the intestines into the bloodstream. Flavored varieties and freeze-pops work well, too.

Side effects: None. However, a child who is having a lot of vomiting and diarrhea should be under a doctor's supervision. It's possible to become dehydrated, even taking one of these rehydration solutions.

Erythromycin
(prescription only in the U.S.) *Trade name:* EryPed.
  Effects: An antibiotic, often used when penicillin allergy is present.
  Side effects: upset stomach, mainly.

Ferrous Fumarate, Ferrous Gluconate, Ferrous Sulfate
(over the counter or prescription) *Trade names:* many.
  Effects: Iron preparations; combat anemia caused by iron deficiency.
  Side effects: In overdose, iron is extremely dangerous, causing ulcers
  and other problems. Be careful with these medicines.

Flunisolide oral inhalation
(prescription only in the U.S.) *Trade name:* Aerobid Inhaler.
  Effects: See Corticosteroids, inhaled.

Fluticasone nasal inhalation
(prescription only in the U.S.) *Trade name:* Flonase.
  Effects: See Corticosteroids, inhaled.

Fluticasone oral inhalation
(prescription only in the U.S.) *Trade name:* Flovent.
  Effects: See Corticosteroids, inhaled.

Guaifenisin
(over the counter) *Trade name:* Robitussin, Sudafed.
  Effects: An expectorant, supposed to loosen mucus to make it easier
  to cough up.
  Side effects: rare.

Hydrocortisone cream or ointment
(over the counter) *Trade name:* Cortizone.
  Effects: See Corticosteroids, topical. Hydrocortisone 0.5 percent and
  1 percent are fairly weak; good for minor itching rashes, with few
  side effects.
  Side effects: Like all corticosteroids, side effects increase with higher
  dose and longer use; check with the doctor.

Ibuprofen

(over the counter) *Trade names:* Advil, Motrin, Pediaprofen.

Effects: See under Nonsteroidal anti-inflammatories. Ibuprofen is good for aches and pains.

Side effects: Causes stomach upset, especially in high doses. Overdose is dangerous.

Ketoconazole lotion or cream

(over the counter) *Trade name:* Nizoral.

Effects: Kills the fungi that cause ringworm and some diaper rashes.

Side effects: rare.

Loperamide

Prescription only in the U.S.; not for children under six.

(over the counter or prescription) *Trade name:* Imodium.

Effects: Reduces diarhea by reducing contractions in the intestines.

Side effects: bloating, stomach pains.

Loratidine

(over the counter) *Trade name:* Claritin.

Effects: See Antistamines. Loratidine may cause less drowsiness than older (far cheaper) antihistamines.

Side effects: rare headache, dry mouth, drowsiness, or hyper behavior.

Metaclopramide

(prescription only in the U.S.) *Trade name:* Reglan.

Effects: Reduces acid reflux from the stomach by strengthening the sphincter muscle that closes off the top of the stomach.

Side effects: Drowsiness, restlessness, nausea, constipation, diarrhea.

Miconazole

(over the counter) *Trade name:* Desenex.

Effects: Kills the fungi that cause athlete's foot and other rashes.

Side effects: rare.

Montelukast

(prescription only in the U.S.) *Trade name:* Singulair.

Effects: Reduces inflammation in the lungs in asthma.

Side effects: headache, dizziness, upset stomach.

Motrin

(over the counter) See Ibuprofen.

Mupirocin

(prescription only in the U.S.) *Trade name:* Bactroban.

Effects: Kills bacteria that commonly cause skin infections.

Side effects: rare.

Naproxen

(over the counter or prescription) *Trade name:* Aleve.

Effects: See Non-steroidal anti-inflammatories. Naproxen is good for aches and pains.

Side effects: Causes stomach upset, especially at high doses. Dangerous in overdose. Take with food; talk to the doctor if taking for more than a day or two.

Nonsteroidal anti-inflammatories (NSAIDS)

(over the counter or prescription).

Effects: These medications reduce inflammation in muscles and joints, lower fever, reduce pain.

Side effects: All can cause stomach upset, especially at higher doses; overdose can be very dangerous. Talk with your doctor if using at high doses or for long periods of time.

Penicillin (Pcn)

(prescription only in the U.S.) *Trade name:* PenVK.

Effects: See Antibiotics. PenVK by mouth or penicillin by injection is the treatment of choice for strep throat.

Side effects: Allergic reactions, usually a rash with little itchy bumps, are common; more serious allergic reactions are rare but do happen. Notify your doctor if you are allergic.

Phenylephrine

(over the counter) *Trade names:* Neo-Synephrine, Alka-Seltzer Plus.

Effects: See Decongestants.

Polymyxin

(over the counter) *Trade names:* Neosporin.

Effects: A mild antibiotic that can be applied to the skin (topical).

Side effects: rare.

Pseudoephedrine

(over the counter) *Trade names:* Pediacare.

   Effects: See under Decongestants.

Pyrethrum, or pyrethrins

(over the counter) *Trade names:* RID, NIX, others.

   Effects: These medications kill head lice.

   Side effects: rare.

Ranitidine

(prescription only in the U.S.) *Trade name:* Zantac.

   Effects: Reduces stomach acid, reducing heartburn (a symptom of acid reflux).

   Side effects: Headache, dizzines, constipation, stomach pain.

Triamcinolone oral inhalation

(prescription only in the U.S.) *Trade name:* Azmacort.

   Effects: See Corticosteroids, inhaled.

Tylenol

(over the counter) see Acetaminophen.

RESOURCE GUIDE

For almost any concern, challenge, problem, or diagnosis, there is at least one organization devoted to providing help. Often there are several. In addition to information, these organizations offer connections to other parents dealing with the same issues and to dedicated professionals. Many provide services in Spanish.

The listings below include websites and phone numbers (many toll-free) as well as addresses. Probably the best way to access these groups is through the internet. Most public libraries have high-speed internet connections that are free. Librarians are trained in finding information, both in books and online, and they are always glad to help.

Those listed below are mainly nonprofit organizations. You also might want to explore www.DrSpock.com, a website that offers a large collection of articles written by the authors of this book and other experts at the Dr. Spock Company. With this and, indeed, *all* expert information, you need to use your own judgment to decide what makes sense for you and your child.

LARGE WEBSITES WITH INFORMATION ON MANY TOPICS

American Academy of Pediatrics (AAP)
141 Northwest Point Boulevard
Elk Grove Village IL 60007-1098
847 434-4000
www.aap.org

Pediatricians rely on the AAP for authoritative information. The information for parents is also very solid. On the home page, click on You and Your Family.

Centers for Disease Control and Prevention
1600 Clifton Road
Atlanta GA 30333
800 311-3435
www.cdc.gov
The Centers for Disease Control (CDC) is the single most respected authority on everything to do with infections. Click on Health Topics A-Z.

Child and Family Web Guide
105 College Avenue
Medford MA 02155
617 627-3642
www.cfw.tufts.edu
A collection of well-reviewed websites and web-based information sheets covering a wide range of topics: family, education, child development, health, and recreation. A good bet for helpful information.

KidsHealth Website
www.kidshealth.org
A large collection of articles on a wide range of issues for parents, kids, and teens: clear, nontechnical, and reviewed by doctors.

Medline Plus
www.medlineplus.gov
A large site, sponsored by the National Library of Medicine and National Institutes of Health, that includes drug information, an encyclopedia and dictionary of health, and directories for finding doctors in various specialties.

PROFESSIONAL ORGANIZATIONS

Developmental and Behavioral Pediatricians
The Society for Developmental and Behavioral Pediatrics
17000 Commerce Parkway, Suite C
Mt. Laurel, NJ 08054
856 439-0500
www.sdbp.org

Family Therapists
The American Association for Marriage and Family Therapy
112 South Alfred Street
Alexandria, VA 22314-3061
703 838-9808
www.aamft.org

Licensed Professional Counselors
The American Counseling Association
5999 Stevenson Avenue
Alexandria, VA 22304
800 347-6647
www.counseling.org

Psychiatrists
The American Academy of Child and Adolescent Psychiatry
3615 Wisconsin Avenue, NW
Washington, DC 20016-3007
202 966-7300
www.aacap.org

Psychoanalysts
The American Psychoanalytic Association
309 East 49th Street
New York, NY 10017
212 752-0450
www.apsa.org

Psychologists

American Psychological Association
750 First Street NE
Washington, DC 20002-4242
800 374-2721
www.apa.org
On the website, click "Consumer Help Center." There is a toll-free helpline: (800) 964-2000.

ORGANIZATIONS FOCUSED ON FAMILY AND SOCIAL POLICY, CHILD DEVELOPMENT, AND PARENTING

Adoption

National Adoption Information Clearinghouse
330 C Street, SW
Washington DC 20447
888 251-0075
http://naic.acf.hhs.gov

Advocacy

The Children's Defense Fund
25 E Street, NW
Washington DC 20001
202 628-8787
www.childrensdefense.org
Many opportunities to help improve children's lives; includes a large list of like-minded organizations.

Auto Safety

NHTSA—Car Safety Information
800 327-4236
www.nhtsa.gov
NHTSA is the federal agency that sets safety standards and is the most reliable source of information on car seats and related topics. Click on Child Passenger Safety.

Breast-Feeding
La Leche League
1400 North Meacham Road
Schaumburg IL 60173-4808
847 519-7730
www.lalecheleague.org
A reliable source of information. For local groups, follow links at the bottom of the home page to Local Contacts (groups).

Bullying
Bullying
www.bullying.co.uk
A very helpful site (based in Britain, so some legal terms don't apply) with a good collection of links.

Child Abuse
Parents Anonymous
675 West Foothill Boulevard, Suite 220
Claremont CA 91711-3475
909 621-6184
www.parentsanonymous.org
There are local chapters in many communities for personal support.

Child Care
Child Care Aware
1319 F Street, NW, Suite 500
Washington DC 20004
800 424-2246
www.childcareaware.org
A fast way to find high-quality child care in your community: On the home page, enter your zip code into the Child Care Connector box. Also good for reliable information on quality child care, guides for choosing quality care, child development, etc.

College

U.S. Department of Education
400 Maryland Avenue, SW
Washington DC 20202
800 USA-LEARN
www.ed.gov/offices/OSFAP/Students
Information from the U.S. Department of Education on how to plan for, choose, and pay for a college education; a good place to start. Another very helpful site is www.finaid.org.

Cooperative Games

Cooperative Games
888 51-EARTH (888 513-2784)
www.abundantearth.com/store/games1.html
A catalog of cooperative games for children and adults.

Death and Dying

Children's Hospice International
901 North Pitt Street, Suite 230
Alexandria VA 22314
800 2-4-CHILD
www.chionline.org

Domestic Violence

National Coalition Against Domestive Violence
PO Box 18749
Denver, CO 80218
303 839-1882
www.ncadv.org
If you need help coping with domestic violence, or you need to find a shelter, click on Getting Help on the website or call the National Domestic Violence Hotline at 800 799-7233.

Education

Schools and Learning (Ask ERIC)
www.eduref.org

The Educational Resources Information Center (ERIC), a project of the U.S. Department of Education, is a huge collection of articles and reports. At the bottom of the Ask ERIC page, click on Topics A–Z.

Foster Parents
National Foster Parent Association
7512 Stanich Avenue, #6
Gig Harbor WA 98335
800 557-5238
www.nfpainc.org
Provides links to state and local organizations, information, and advocacy.

Gay and Lesbian
National Gay and Lesbian Task Force
1325 Massachusetts Avenue, NW, Suite 600
Washington DC 20005
202 393-5177
www.ngltf.org

Parents, Families and Friends of Lesbians, and Gays, Inc.
PFLAG
1726 M Street, NW, Suite 400
Washington DC 20036
202 467-8180
www.pflag.org

Gifted Children
National Association for Gifted Children
1707 L Street, NW, Suite 550
Washington DC 20036
202 785-4268
www.nagc.org

Council for Exceptional Children
1110 North Glebe Road, Suite 300
Arlington VA 22201-5704

703 620-3660
888 CEC-SPED
www.cec.sped.org
Targeting children with special education needs, including emotional problems. The information for teachers can be very helpful for parents who want to take an active role in their children's education.

Grandparenting

American Association of Retired Persons (AARP)
Grandparent Information Center
601 E Street, NW
Washington DC 20049
800 424-3410
www.aarp.org/grandparents
Information, links to related websites, and a very helpful directory of support groups for grandparents raising children.

Infant Development, Child Care, Parenting

Zero to Three National Center for Infants, Toddlers, and Families
2000 M Street, NW, Suite 200
Washington DC 20036
202 638-1144
www.zerotothree.org
A wonderful organization, with great information on babies' and families' development (I've been a member for years). Some of the best educational materials anywhere are available on this site.

Learning Disabilities

Learning Disabilities of America
4156 Library Road
Pittsburgh PA 15234-1349
412 341-1515
www.ldanatl.org
A good source for information on learning disabilities and special education, including links to related sites and resources.

Schwab Learning
1650 South Amphlett Boulevard, Suite 300
San Mateo CA 94402
650 655-2410
www.schwablearning.org
A private, nonprofit organization with very good, practical information.

Racism and Intolerance
The Southern Poverty Law Center
400 Washington Avenue
Montgomery AL 36104
334 956-8200
www.tolerance.org
Teaching Tolerance is a project of the Southern Poverty Law Center (SPLC), a fine organization that combats racism, intolerance, and bias. Separate sections for parents, teens, and kids makes this site especially useful.

Safety, First Aid
The American Red Cross National Headquarters
2025 E Street, NW
Washington DC 20006
202 303-4498
www.redcross.org
An easy way to locate your local Red Cross chapter for training, information on safety and first aid, giving blood, etc.

Single Parents
Parents Without Partners
1650 South Dixie Highway, Suite 510
Boca Raton FL 33432
561 391-8833
www.parentswithoutpartners.org

Stepparenting

Stepfamily Association of America
650 J Street, Suite 205
Lincoln NE 68508
800 735-0329
www.saafamilies.org

INFORMATION ABOUT MEDICAL CONDITIONS, AND SUPPORT GROUPS FOR SPECIFIC CONDITIONS

ADHD

Children With ADD (CHADD)
8181 Professional Place, Suite 150
Landover MD 20785
800 233-4050
www.chadd.org
A large national organization, CHADD provides information, advocacy, and parent support groups (click Support Groups on the home page).

See also American Academy of Pediatrics, Child and Family Web Guide, Learning Disabilities of America

AIDS

CDC National HIV AIDS Hotline
800 342-AIDS
www.cdc.gov/hiv/hivinfo/nah.htm

Alcohol and Drugs

Alcoholics Anonymous and Alateen
1600 Corporate Landing Parkway
Virginia Beach VA 23454-5617
888 4AL-ANON (meeting information)
www.al-anon.alateen.org
Access to local groups. Al-Anon and Alateen are very helpful for people affected by alcoholism, either themselves or a family member. See also the Alcoholics Anonymous site: www.aa.org

National Clearinghouse for Alcohol and Drug Information
POB 2345
Rockville MD 20857-2345
800 729-6686
www.health.org

Allergy
American Academy of Allergy, Asthma, and Immunology
611 East Wells Street
Milwaukee WI 53202
800 822-2762
www.aaaai.org

Anorexia Nervosa and Bulimia
Anorexia Nervosa and Related Eating Disorders (ANRED)
www.anred.com
A large, well-written collection of articles.

Asthma and Allergy
Asthma and Allergy Foundation of America
1233 Twentieth Street NW, Suite 402
Washington DC 20036
800 7-ASTHMA
www.aafa.org

Autism
Autism Society of America
7910 Woodmont Avenue, Suite 300
Bethesda MD 20814-3067
www.autism-society.org
A very large organization, with local chapters all over. On the home page, click on Autism Society Chapters under Other Links.

Bed-Wetting
Ideas for Living, Inc.
1285 North Cedarbrook Road
Boulder CO 80304
800 497-6573
www.pottypager.com

Palco Labs
800 346-4488
www.wetstop.com
The Potty Pager and the Wetstop are both effective bed-wetting alarms. The Potty Pager, which clips to the pocket of a boy's brief, vibrates. The Wetstop, which attaches to the shoulder of the pajamas, buzzes.

Cerebral Palsy
United Cerebral Palsy
1660 L Street, NW, Suite 700
Washington DC 20036
800 872-5827
www.ucp.org

Cystic Fibrosis
The Cystic Fibrosis Foundation
6931 Arlington Road
Bethesda Maryland 20814
800 FIGHT CF (344-4823)
www.cff.org
The national organization for cystic fibrosis.

Deaf-Blind
National Information Clearinghouse on Children who are Deaf-Blind
800 438-9376
www.tr.wou.edu/dblink

Depression
See Mental Health, page 932.

Diabetes
American Diabetes Association
ATTN: National Call Center
1701 North Beauregard Street
Alexandria VA 22311
800 DIABETES (342-2383)
www.diabetes.org

Disabilities
National Easter Seals Society
230 West Monroe Street, Suite 1800
Chicago IL 60606
800 221-6827
www.easter-seals.org
Many services for children and families affected by disabilities.

**National Information Center for Children and
Youth with Disabilities**
POB 1492
Washington DC 20013
800 695-0285
www.nichcy.org

Down Syndrome
National Down Syndrome Society (NDSS)
666 Broadway
New York NY 10012
800 221-4602
www.ndss.org
The largest national organization, with a solid board, excellent educational materials, and links to local chapters.

Dyslexia

International Dyslexia Association
Chester Building, Suite 382
8600 LaSalle Road
Baltimore MD 21286-2044
800 ABCD123; Office: 410 296-0232
www.interdys.org
Most useful: Click on Parents then IDA Branches/Affiliates to find a
local support group or Dyslexia FAQ for information on dyslexia.

Epilepsy

Epilepsy Foundation of America
4351 Garden City Drive
Landover MD 20785-7223
800 332-1000
www.epilepsyfoundation.org

Fetal Alcohol Syndrome

National Organization on Fetal Alcohol Syndrome
900 Seventeenth Street, NW, Suite 910
Washington DC 20006
202 785 4585
800 66 NOFAS (666-6327)
www.nofas.org
Click on Information and Resources for local chapters and links to
relevant organizations and information.

Fragile X

The National Fragile X Foundation
POB 190488
San Francisco CA 94119
800 688-8765
www.fragilex.org
Click on For the Newly Diagnosed for links to local support groups
and helpful information.

Head Injuries

Brain Injury Association of America
8201 Greensboro Drive, Suite 611
McLean VA 22102
800 444-6443
www.biausa.org

Hearing Impairments
**Alexander Graham Bell Association for the Deaf and
Hard of Hearing**
3417 Volta Place, NW
Washington DC 20007
202 337-5220
www.agbell.org
This national organization promotes spoken-language communication for the deaf and hard of hearing.

**National Institute on Deafness and
Other Communication Disorders**
NIDCD Office of Health Communication and Public Liaison
31 Center Drive, MSC 2320
Bethesda MD 20892-2320
800 241-1044
www.nidcd.nih.gov
Click on Health Information for reliable information on deafness, auditory processing, ear infections, etc. (NIDCD is a branch of the National Institutes of Health.)

Lead
Lead Poisoning
800 424 5323
www.epa.gov/lead
The U.S. Environmental Protection Agency (EPA) provides much solid information about lead poisoning, including how to protect your children and clean up safely. The hotline 800 424-LEAD is very helpful.

Mental Health

The National Institute of Mental Health
Office of Communications
6001 Executive Boulevard, Room 8184, MSC 9663
Bethesda MD 20892-9663
866 615-NIMH (6464), toll-free
www.nimh.nih.gov
On the home page, click on For the Public for a wealth of information on depression, ADHD, anxiety, and many other mental health issues.

Mental Retardation

The ARC of the United States
1010 Wayne Avenue, Suite 650
Silver Spring MD 20910
301 565-3842
www.thearc.org
Advocacy and networking for children with mental retardation and other disabilities.

Muscular Dystrophy

Muscular Dystrophy Association—USA
National Headquarters
3300 East Sunrise Drive
Tucson AZ 85718
800 572-1717

Nutrition and Preventive Medicine

Physicians Committee for Responsible Medicine
5100 Wisconsin Avenue, NW, Suite 400
Washington DC 20016
202 686-2210
www.pcrm.org
This organization advocates vegetarian diets for children and adults that are based on scientific research; it's also an excellent source for recipes and tips.

Prematurity and Birth Defects
March of Dimes Birth Defects Foundation
1275 Mamaroneck Avenue
White Plains NY 10605
718 981-3000
www.modimes.org
This organization, which was co-founded by President Franklin Delano Roosevelt to combat polio, is now dedicated to fighting prematurity, birth defects, and low birth weight. There is much information for parents on the site, but you have to look around.

Rare Medical Conditions
National Organization for Rare Disorders (NORD)
55 Kenosia Avenue
POB 1968
Danbury CT 06813-1968
800 999-6673 or 203 744-0100
www.rarediseases.org
Information on more than a thousand rare and genetic disorders from a reliable nonprofit organization; also conferences, networking, publications, etc.

Sickle Cell Disease
Sickle Cell Disease Association of America
200 Corporate Pointe, Suite 495
Culver City, CA 90230-8727
800 421-8453
www.sicklecelldisease.org

Speech and Language
American Speech-Language-Hearing Association (ASHA)
10801 Rockville Pike
Rockville MD 20852
800 638-8255
www.asha.org

Click on Find a Professional for a national directory of professionals; click on For the Public for well-written information pages on speech, language, and hearing, and a listing of related organizations.

Spina Bifida

Spina Bifida Association of America
4590 MacArthur Boulevard, NW, Suite 250
Washington DC 20007-4226
800 621-3141
www.sbaa.org

Spinal Cord Injuries

National Spinal Cord Injury Association
6701 Democracy Boulevard, Suite 300-9
Bethesda MD 20817
800 962-9629
www.spinalcord.org

Spinal Cord Injury Hotline
2200 North Forest Park Avenue
Baltimore MD 21207
800 526-3456
Referrals and information for patients with spinal cord injury.

Stuttering

Stuttering Foundation of America
3100 Walnut Grove Road, Suite 603
POB 11749
Memphis TN 38111-0749
800 992-9392
www.stutteringhelp.org
Information about stuttering evaluation and treatment and what parents can do at home; also books, newsletters, and more.

Sudden Infant Death Syndrome (SIDS)
Sudden Infant Death Syndrome Alliance
1314 Bedford Avenue, Suite 210
Baltimore Maryland 21208
800 221-7437
www.sidsalliance.org

Tourette's Syndrome
Tourette Syndrome Association
42-40 Bell Boulevard
Bayside NY 11361
718 224-2999
www.ts-usa.org

Twins
National Organization of Mothers of Twins Clubs, Inc.
POB 438
Thompsons Station TN 37179-0438
877-540-2200
www.nomotc.org

Vaccines
Centers for Disease Control and Prevention
1600 Clifton Road
Atlanta GA 30333
800 311-3435
www.cdc.gov
The Centers for Disease Control (CDC) is the authority on anything to do with infections and vaccines. From the home page, click on Health Topics A-Z then "V" for vaccines.

Visual Impairments (Blindness)

American Council of the Blind
1155 Fifteenth Street, NW, Suite 1004
Washington DC 20005
800 424-8666
www.acb.org

American Foundation for the Blind
11 Penn Plaza, Suite 300
New York NY 10001
800 AFB-LINE (800 232-5463)
www.afb.org

National Federation of the Blind
National Organization of Parents of Blind Children
1800 Johnson Street
Baltimore MD 21230
410 659-9314
www.nfb.org

INDEX